SEVENTH EDITION

Community-Based Corrections

Leanne Fiftal Alarid
University of Texas, San Antonio

Paul Cromwell
Wichita State University

Rolando V. del Carmen
Sam Houston State University

THOMSON
───✦───
WADSWORTH

Australia • Canada • Mexico • Singapore • Spain • United Kingdom • United States

THOMSON
WADSWORTH

Acquisitions Editor: Carolyn Henderson Meier
Assistant Editor: Meaghan Banks
Editorial Assistant: Beth McMurray
Technology Project Manager: Amanda Kaufmann
Marketing Manager: Terra Schultz
Marketing Assistant: Emily Elrod
Marketing Communications Manager: Tami Strang
Project Manager, Editorial Production: Matt Ballantyne
Creative Director: Rob Hugel
Art Director: Vernon Boes

Print Buyer: Nora Massuda
Permissions Editor: Bob Kauser
Production Service: International Typesetting and Composition
Text Designer: Lisa Langhoff
Photo Researcher: Terri Wright
Copy Editor: Kate Bresnahan
Cover Designer: Yvo Riezebos
Cover Image: Don B. Stevenson/Alamy
Compositor: International Typesetting and Composition
Text and Cover Printer: West Group

Printed in the United States of America
1 2 3 4 5 6 7 11 10 09 08 07

For more information about our products, contact us at:
Thomson Learning Academic Resource Center
1-800-423-0563

For permission to use material from this text or product, submit a request online at **http://www.thomsonrights.com.** Any additional questions about permissions can be submitted by e-mail to **thomsonrights@thomson.com.**

Library of Congress Control Number: 2004108375

ISBN-13: 978-0-495-09482-1
ISBN-10: 0-495-09482-X

Thomson Higher Education
10 Davis Drive
Belmont, CA 94002-3098
USA

Asia
Thomson Learning
5 Shenton Way #01-01
UIC Building
Singapore 068808

Australia/New Zealand
Thomson Learning
102 Dodds Street
Southbank, Victoria 3006
Australia

Canada
Nelson
1120 Birchmount Road
Toronto, Ontario M1K 5G4
Canada

Europe/Middle East/Africa
Thomson Learning
High Holborn House
50/51 Bedford Row
London WC1R 4LR
United Kingdom

Latin America
Thomson Learning
Seneca, 53
Colonia Polanco
11560 Mexico D.F.
Mexico

Spain/Portugal
Paraninfo
Calle Magallanes, 25
28015 Madrid, Spain

DEDICATION

*To my best friend Crazyhorse, to my wonderful
family on both sides, and to all the Mojo Riders.*
Leanne Fiftal Alarid

*To Jimmie Cromwell, my wife and best friend;
to our children, Christopher Cromwell,
Rebecca Pettis, and Karen Van der Kroon;
and our four wonderful grandchildren,
Katy, Paul, Erin, and Tori.*
Paul Cromwell

To my wife, Josie, and daughter, Jocelyn.
Rolando V. del Carmen

Brief Contents

Contents   vii

Preface   xvii

About the Authors   xxi

PART I: OVERVIEW OF COMMUNITY CORRECTIONS   1

Chapter 1 • The State of Corrections Today: Why Community
Corrections Is Important   2

Chapter 2 • Pretrial Release and Diversion   21

Chapter 3 • Sentencing and the Presentence Investigation Report   39

PART II: PROBATION   75

Chapter 4 • History of Probation   76

Chapter 5 • Probation Officer Issues   89

Chapter 6 • Classification and Supervision in Probation and Parole   109

Chapter 7 • Probation Modification and Termination   138

PART III: INTERMEDIATE SANCTIONS   159

Chapter 8 • Residential Intermediate Sanctions   160

Chapter 9 • Nonresidential Intermediate Sanctions   187

Chapter 10 • Economic and Restorative Justice Reparations   210

PART IV: PRISONER REENTRY   231

Chapter 11 • The History of Parole: From Its Origin
to the Present   232

Chapter 12 • Preparing for Prisoner Reentry:
Discretionary Parole and Mandatory Release   258

Chapter 13 • Parole Conditions and Revocation   281

PART V: SPECIAL ISSUES IN COMMUNITY CORRECTIONS   **307**

Chapter 14 • Juvenile Justice, Probation, and Parole   308

Chapter 15 • Collateral Consequences of Conviction, Pardon,
and Restoration of Rights   336

Glossary   367

References   373

Table of Cases   389

Name Index   391

Subject Index   395

Contents

Preface   xvii

About the Authors   xxi

PART I: OVERVIEW OF COMMUNITY CORRECTIONS   1

Chapter 1 • The State of Corrections Today: Why Community Corrections Is Important   2

The Correctional Dilemma   3
     Change in Sentencing Laws   3   •   The Toughening of Juvenile Justice   6

The Paradox   6
     Public Perceptions of Community Corrections   7   • Correctional Budgets   8

The Role of Corrections at Three Major Decision Points   9
     Pretrial and the Bail Decision   12   •   Sentencing Decision   12   Reentry Decision   13

How Community Corrections Fits Correctional Goals   13
     Protection of the Public   13   •   Rehabilitation   14   Community Reintegration   15   •   Restorative or Community Justice   15   •   Public Shaming as Punishment   16

What You Should Know about Evaluations of Community-Based Corrections   17
     What Works?   17   •   How Is Effectiveness Measured?   18   Other Outcome Measures for Evaluation   19

Top Things You Should Know   19

Discussion Questions   20

Websites   20

Chapter 2 • Pretrial Release and Diversion   21

Introduction   22

Pretrial Services   22
     The Pretrial Release Decision   22   •   History of Pretrial Release   22   •   The Least Restrictive Option   23   •   Types of Bonds   24   •   Characteristics of Pretrial Releasees   25   • Pretrial Supervision   26   •   Failure to Appear   26   • Reducing Failure to Appear Rates   26

Diversion   28

    Candidates for Diversion 28 • Drug Courts 29
    Assumptions of Drug Courts 29 • Gender and Drug Court
    Treatment Strategies 31 • Evaluating Drug Courts 32
    Mental Health Courts 34 • Criticisms of Diversion
    Programs 35

Top Things You Should Know   35

Discussion Questions   35

Websites   36

Case Study Exercise   37

**Chapter 3 • Sentencing and the Presentence
Investigation Report**   **39**

Introduction   40

    Factors That Affect Granting a Community Sentence 40 •
    Eligibility for Community Corrections 40 • Conditions of
    Probation Fixed by Statute 40 • Availability and Quality
    of Intermediate Sanctions and Other Community-based
    Services 41 • Other Factors 41 • Sentencing
    Guidelines 41 • Voluntary Sentencing
    Guidelines 42 • Punishment Units 42 • Sentencing
    Commissions 44

Conditions of Community Corrections   44

    Standard Conditions 44 • Special Conditions 44
    Limitations of Special Conditions 45 • Supervision
    Conditions Must Be Constitutional 45 • First Amendment
    Rights 45 • Searches and Seizures 46 • The Privilege
    Against Self-Incrimination 47

The Presentence Investigation Report   48

    Purposes of the PSI Report 48 • Contents of the PSI
    Report 49 • Offender-Based PSI Reports 49 •
    Offense-Based PSI Reports 50 • Preparing the PSI
    Report 52 • The Initial Interview 53 • Investigation and
    Verification 54 • The Evaluative Summary 54 • The
    Sentence Recommendation 55

Legal Issues Concerning the Presentence Report   56

    Disclosure of the PSI Report 56 • Inaccuracies in the PSI
    Report 57 • Hearsay in the PSI Report 57 • Does the
    Exclusionary Rule Apply? 58 • *Miranda* Warnings and the
    PSI Interview 58 • Right to a Lawyer during the PSI
    Interview 58

Top Things You Should Know   59

Discussion Questions   59

Websites   60

Probation Conditions   60

Case Study Exercise 1   62

Case Study Exercise 2   64

PART II: PROBATION   **75**

Chapter 4 • History of Probation   **76**

Introduction   77

Precursors to American Probation   77

Recognizance and Suspended Sentence   78
    Two Kinds of Suspended Sentence   78   •   The Power to
    Suspend Sentence   78

Early Probation   79
    The Role of Volunteers and the Settlement Movement   82   •
    Development of Federal Probation   82   •   History of Juvenile
    Probation and Female Probation Officers   83   •   Early
    Probation Legislation in Other States   84

Changing Concepts of Supervision   85
    The Casework Era: 1900–1970   85   •   Brokerage of Services
    Era: 1970–1980   85   •   Community Resource Management
    Team   86   •   Justice Model of Supervision:
    1980–1995   86

Top Things You Should Know   87

Discussion Questions   88

Websites   88

Chapter 5 • Probation Officer Issues   **89**

Introduction   90

Organization of Probation Services   90
    Arguments for and Against State or Executive
    Branch Administration   92   •   Community
    Corrections Acts   93

A Typology of Probation Officer Work Styles   94

Selection and Appointment of Probation Officers   95
    Appointment System   96   •   Merit System   97   •   Combined
    System   97

Officer Qualifications, Training, and Salary   98
    Education and Experience   98   •   Adult Preservice
    Training   98   •   Juvenile Preservice and Orientation
    Training   98   •   In-Service Training   100   •   Officer
    Salary   100

Firearms Policies for Probation and Parole Officers   101

Probation Officer Job Stress   102
    Sources of Stress   103   •   Decreasing Stress: Types of
    Immunity   104   •   Absolute Immunity   105   •   Qualified
    Immunity   105

Private Probation   106

Top Things You Should Know   107

Discussion Questions   107

Websites   107

Chapter 6 • Classification and Supervision in Probation and Parole 109

Introduction 110

Neighborhood-Based Probation Supervision 110
The Surveillance Function in Supervision 116 • Developing
Prosocial Behaviors 117 • Building on Assets and
Strengths 117 • Employment Services 117 • Using
Informal Social Controls 118

Classification: The First Step in Supervision 118
Actuarial Risk Assessment 121 • Identifying Treatment
Needs 121 • Developing the Case Plan 124 • Levels of
Supervision 124 • Caseload and Workload Standards 126

Specialized Caseloads 126
Supervising Offenders Who Are Mentally Ill 127 •
Supervising Offenders Who Have Abused Drugs and
Alcohol 128 • Gender-Responsive Strategies 129
Supervising Sex Offenders 130 • Polygraph Tests 130 •
Global Positioning Systems 130

Interstate Compacts on Probation 131
New Interstate Compact for Adult Offender Supervision 132 •
Revocation and the Interstate Compact 132

Top Things You Should Know 132

Discussion Questions 133

Websites 133

Case Study Exercise 135

Chapter 7 • Probation Modification and Termination 138

Introduction 139

Modifying Probation Conditions 140
Early Termination of Probation 140 • Modifying Conditions
before the Revocation Decision 141

The Decision to Revoke 141

Types of Probation Violations 143
Law Violations 143 • Technical Violations 144 •
Probation Absconders 145

Revocation Procedure 145
The Power to Arrest Probationers 146 • Time on
Probation or Parole Is Usually Not Credited if Revoked 146

Revocation Rights of Probationers and Parolees 147
Gagnon v. Scarpelli—The Facts 148 • The Right to a
Hearing 148 • The Right to a Lawyer 149 • Level of Proof
and Evidence Required 149 • Other Revocation
Situations 150 • Revocation for an Inability to
Pay? 150 • Juvenile Probation Revocation 150 •
Revocation After Probation Term Expires 150

Probation Effectiveness 151
Probation Recidivism Rates 151 • Who Is More Likely to
Succeed or Fail on Probation? 152 • Probationers Compared
with Parolees 153

Top Things You Should Know   154

Discussion Questions   154

Websites   154

Case Study Exercise   156

PART III: INTERMEDIATE SANCTIONS   159

Chapter 8 • Residential Intermediate Sanctions   160

Introduction   161

Residential Community Corrections Facilities   162

Halfway Houses   162
History of Halfway Houses in the United States 164 •
Program Components 166 • Levels System: A Form of
Behavior Modification 166 • Worker Perspectives and Role
Orientation 167 • Punishment and Treatment Role
Orientations 168 • Evaluations of RCCFs 168

Shock Incarceration   169
Correctional Boot Camps 170 • Prison Boot Camps: The Case
of New York State 171 • Probation Boot Camps 172 •
Offender Perspectives 173 • Criticisms of Boot
Camps 176 • Evaluations of Boot Camp Programs 176 •
Eight Site Study 176 • Attitude and Behavoral
Change 177 • Reduction of Crowding and Costs 177 •
The Future of Shock Incarceration Programs 177

Other Types of Residential Community Corrections Facilities   177
Restitution Centers 178 • Minnesota Restitution 178 •
Georgia Community Diversion Center 178 • Therapeutic
Communities 178 • The Therapeutic Community
Environment 178 • Challenges of the TC 180 • Types and
Uses of Therapeutic Communities 180 • Evaluations of
Therapeutic Communities 181 • Work Release and Work
Ethic Camps 181 • Work Ethic Camp 182 • Combined
Work Release and Therapeutic Community 182 • Women
Offenders Living with Their Children 182 • John P. Craine
House 183

Top Things You Should Know   184

Discussion Questions   184

Websites   185

Case Study Exercise   186

Chapter 9 • Nonresidential Intermediate Sanctions   187

Introduction   188

Intensive Supervision Probation   188
ISP Caseloads 189 • Attitudes toward ISP 189 •
Evaluations of ISP 189 • Reduction of Prison
Beds 190 • Cost-Benefit Analyses 190 •
Treatment Participation 190 • Summary of ISP
Evaluations 190

House Arrest   191

    Purposes of Home Detention   191 • Criticisms of House
    Arrest   191 • Effectiveness of House Arrest   192 • House
    Arrest Versus Residential Community Corrections
    Facilities   192 • Pretrial Detainees   193

Electronic Monitoring and Global Positioning Systems   193

    History of Electronic Monitoring   194 • Problems of Early
    EM Programs   194 • Remote Location Monitoring   195
    Officer Carries a Portable Receiver   196 • Global Positioning
    Systems   196 • Frequency of Use   197 • Attitudes toward
    EM   198 • Attitudes of EM Participants   198 • Citizen
    Attitudes   199 • Empirical Evaluations of Home-Based
    Electronic Monitoring   200 • Long-Term Effects   200
    Completion Rates   200 • Gender Differences   200

Day Reporting Centers   201

    Purposes of DRCs   202 • Treatment-Oriented versus
    Supervision-Oriented DRCs   202 • Evaluations of
    DRCs   205 • Completion Rates   205 • Rate of
    Rearrest   205 • Predictors of DRC Failure   206

Top Things You Should Know   206

Discussion Questions   207

Websites   207

Case Study Exercise   209

Chapter 10 • Economic and Restorative Justice Reparations   210

Introduction   211

Restorative Justice Principles   211

    Forms of Restorative Justice   212 • Victim–Offender
    Mediation   213 • Reparation Boards   213 • Family Group
    Conferencing   214 • Circle Sentencing   214 • Effectiveness
    of Restorative Justice Methods   214

Restitution   216

    Restitution in History   216 • Losses Eligible for
    Compensation   218 • Problems Associated with
    Restitution   218 • Indigent Offenders   219 • Determining
    the Restitution Amount   219 • Collecting Restitution   219
    Increasing Restitution Collection Rates   220 • Effectiveness
    of Restitution   220 • Victim and Public Views Toward
    Restitution   220

Community Service   221

    History of Community Service   221 • The English
    Model   221 • Purpose of Community Service   221 •
    Prevalence of Community Service   222 • Effectiveness of
    Community Service   222

Fines   224

    Prevalence of Fines   224 • Revoking Probation for Fine
    Nonpayment   225 • Forfeitures   225 • Day Fines   226
    Evaluation of Day Fines   226

Fees and Costs   227

Top Things You Should Know   228

Discussion Questions   229

Websites   229

Case Study Exercise   230

PART IV: PRISONER REENTRY   231

Chapter 11 • The History of Parole: From Its Origin to the Present   232

Introduction   233

The Origins of Parole   233
Manuel Montesinos   234   •   Georg Michael
Obermaier   235   •   Alexander Maconochie   235   •
Transportation of English Prisoners to America   235   •
Transportation of English Prisoners to Australia   236   •   Marks
System   236   •   Norfolk Island   236   •   Sir Walter Crofton and
the Irish System   237

Development of Parole in the United States   237
Reward for Good Conduct   237   •   Postrelease
Supervision   238   •   Zebulon R. Brockway and the
Indeterminate Sentence   238   •   Reducing the Cost of
Incarceration   238

The Medical Model: 1930–1960   239
Changing Public Opinion   239

A Philosophical Change   240
Origins of Modern Determinate Sentencing   240   •   The Justice
Model   241

Changing of the Guard: From Discretionary Parole
to Mandatory Release   242

Parole Today   244
Characteristics of Parolees   246   •   Functions
of Parole   248   •   Prison Population Control   249   •
Medical Parole   250

Top Things You Should Know   251

Discussion Questions   252

Websites   252

Case Study Exercise   254

Chapter 12 • Preparing for Prisoner Reentry: Discretionary
Parole and Mandatory Release   258

Introduction   259

Issues in Reentry   259
The Prisoner's Family   260   •   The Victim's Role in
Reentry   261   •   Reentry and the Community   261   •
Community-Based Reentry Initiatives   262   •   Reentry
Courts   262   •   Types of Reentry   263

Eligibility for Parole   263
    Time Sheets and Eligibility Dates   264   •   Prerelease
    Preparation within the Institution   265

The Parole Board   266

Term and Qualifications of the Parole Board   268

The Parole Hearing   268
    Number of Parole Board Members   268   •   Recommendations
    and Attendees   269   •   Victim Participation in Parole
    Hearings   270

Models of Parole Release Decisions   271
    The Surveillance Model   271   •   The Procedural Justice
    Model   271   •   The Risk Prediction Model   271

Due Process During Discretionary Parole Hearings   274
    Menechino v. Oswald   274   •   *Greenholtz v. Inmates of the*
    Nebraska Penal and Correctional Complex   274   •   State-Created
    Liberty Interest   275   •   Extending the Time Intervals between
    Parole Hearings   275

Prisoners' Perceptions of Parole Selection   276

Top Things You Should Know   276

Discussion Questions   277

Websites   277

Case Study Exercise   279

Chapter 13 • Parole Conditions and Revocation   **281**

Introduction   282

Prisoner Perspectives on Getting Out   282
    California Study   283   •   Iowa Study   284

The Field Parole Officer   285

The Officer's Perspective   285

Conditions of Parole   286
    Legal Issues in Parole Conditions   286   •   Limited Parolee
    Rights   288   •   First Amendment Rights   288   •   Fourth
    Amendment Rights   288

Violating Parole   289
    Warrants and Citations   289   •   Due Process Rights under
    "Preparole"   291

Characteristics of Parole Violators   291
    Parole Revocation Rate   291   •   Reasons for
    Revocation   292   •   Why Have Revocation Rates
    Increased?   293   •   Attitudes on Revocation   294

Parole Absconders   295
    Why Do Parolees Leave?   295   •   Type I Absconders:
    Benign   295   •   Type II Absconders: Menace to Society   295   •
    Locating and Apprehending Fugitives   296   •   Predicting
    Absconding Behavior   297

Parole Effectiveness   298
    Recidivism Studies   299   •   Predicting Parole
    Outcomes   300   •   Gender Differences   300   •

Number of Prior Arrests   300   •   Supervision Versus
No Supervision   300

Top Things You Should Know   302

Discussion Questions   303

Websites   303

Case Study Exercise   304

PART V: SPECIAL ISSUES IN COMMUNITY CORRECTIONS   307

Chapter 14 • Juvenile Justice, Probation, and Parole   308

Introduction   309

Background and History   309
   Mens Rea and Juveniles   309   •   *Parens Patriae* and Its
   Decline   310

Juvenile Justice and Adult Justice Systems Compared   310
   Differences   310   •   Reality   311

Juvenile Courts   311
   Created in the U.S.A.   311   •   Jurisdiction of Juvenile
   Courts   312   •   Based on Age   312   •   Based on Acts
   Committed   314   •   Differences from Adult Courts   314   •
   Transfer from Juvenile Courts to Adult Courts   315

An Overview of the Juvenile Justice Process   316
   Procedure before Adjudication   317   •   The Intake
   Stage   318   •   The Adjudication Stage   318   •   The Disposition
   Stage   319   •   Blended Sentences   320   •   Release from an
   Institution   320

In Re Gault: The Most Important Juvenile Justice Case   320

Juvenile Probation   322
   Origin   322   •   Conditions of Probation   323   •   Judges Have
   Much Discretion   323   •   Types of Conditions   323   •
   Supervision   323   •   Juvenile Probation Officers   323   •
   Intensive Supervision Probation   325   •   School-Based
   Probation   325   •   *Fare v. Michael C.:* An Important Case in
   Juvenile Probation Supervision   326   •   The Probation Record
   of Juveniles   327

Juvenile Parole (Or Aftercare)   328
   Background   328   •   Similarities with Probation   328   •
   Differences from Probation   329   •   Parole Boards   329   •
   Responsibilities of Juvenile Parole Officers   329   •   Evaluating
   Juvenile Parole Programs   330

Revocation of Juvenile Probation or Parole   330
   No Standards for Revocation   331   •   Result of
   Revocation   331

Top Things You Should Know   331

Discussion Questions   332

Websites   332

Case Study Exercise   334

Chapter 15 • Collateral Consequences of Conviction, Pardon, and Restoration of Rights   **336**

Introduction   337
   Civil and Political Rights Defined   338   •   Background of Civil
   Disabilities   338

Civil Disabilities Today   339
   Differences by State   339   •   Other Differences   340

Civil and Political Rights Affected By Conviction   340
   Loss of Right to Vote   341   •   Loss of Right to Serve on a
   Jury   342   •   Loss of Credibility As a Witness   343   •   Loss of
   the Right to Hold Public Office   343   •   Employment-Related
   Rights   343   •   Public Employment   343   •   Private
   Employment   344   •   Right to an Occupational
   License   344   •   Loss of Capacity to be Bonded   345   •   Loss
   of Good Moral Character   346   •   Loss of Right to Own or
   Possess a Firearm   346   •   Loss of Welfare Benefits   347   •
   Loss of Parental Rights   347   •   Problems with Civil Disability
   Laws   347

Other Effects of Conviction   348
   Sex Offender Registration Laws   348   •   Sex Offender
   Notification Laws   349   •   Involuntary Commitment
   of Sexual Predators   351   •   Social Stigmatization   353

Pardon   353
   Definition and Purpose   353   •   The Power to Pardon   354   •
   Kinds of Pardon   354   •   Procedure for Obtaining a
   Pardon   355   •   Legal Effects of a Pardon   355   •   Effects of a
   Pardon on Occupational Licensing   355

Restoration of Rights   356
   Restoration upon Application   356   •   Automatic
   Restoration   356   •   Restoring the Right to Vote   357

Restoring Good Moral Character   357

Expungement of Criminal Records   359

Sealing of Criminal Records   360

Top Things You Should Know   361

Discussion Questions   362

Websites   362

Case Study   364

Glossary   **367**

References   **373**

Table of Cases   **389**

Name Index   **391**

Subject Index   **395**

Preface

More than 4 million offenders were being supervised by probation, parole, and other community-based correctional programs in 2007. Most people who are convicted of a crime serve their sentences in the community, and even those who are incarcerated eventually return to the community, often on a form of supervised release. This book examines various community-based methods of corrections.

The goal of the seventh edition of *Community-Based Corrections* is to provide students with comprehensive, up-to-date, objective knowledge of the procedures, practices, and personnel that constitute probation, release from prison, and other community-based alternatives. We have sought to present community-based correctional programs in their historical, philosophical, social, and legal contexts and to integrate real-life practice to the greatest extent possible.

Because we want this book to be of practical use, we have provided many examples of community-based programs, laws, and procedures from state and federal jurisdictions. In this edition, as in previous ones, we wrestled with the problem of using examples and laws from as many states as possible to make the materials relevant to a broad audience. However, the states' systems vary widely in their programs, laws, and sophistication. We decided we would not do students justice if we included laws and examples from only the large, populous states, and we could not possibly incorporate examples and laws from every jurisdiction. We therefore decided to use the federal system as our primary point of reference. We have cited state laws and programs throughout the book nonetheless.

NEW UPDATES AND ORGANIZATION OF THE SEVENTH EDITION

All sections of *Community-Based Corrections*, Seventh Edition, have been updated, and we wish to highlight some exciting changes from the previous edition.

We moved the section on "Sentencing" from Chapter 2 to Chapter 3 so that the link between sentencing and the presentence investigation report is clearer. We also moved the sentencing case study (formerly in Chapter 2 of the sixth edition) to Chapter 3, so that Chapter 3 now has two different case study exercises. Chapter 2 incorporates additional material on the bail decision, pretrial release, and diversion. A new case study has been added to the end of this chapter.

Chapter 4 includes a new section on how probation supervision styles have changed over time. This section was previously in Chapter 6 of the sixth edition, and we thought the section was more fitting in the "history" chapter, in order to make room for more contemporary supervision material in Chapter 6.

Chapter 5 includes more discussion on officer stress and job burnout. The section at the end of Chapter 5 titled "Interstate Compacts on Probation" has been moved to Chapter 6.

Chapter 6 presents contemporary supervision issues, and is updated to include supervising specialized caseloads, such as clients who have issues related to alcohol and substance abuse, domestic violence, HIV/AIDS, and gang membership.

We added one more case study example in Chapters 7 and 13 to the existing case study listed so there are two cases to choose from in each of those chapters. Chapter 8 has updated sections on boot camps and therapeutic communities. Chapter 9 has a brand new case study exercise directing students to conduct a site visit of a community-based corrections program.

Chapter 10 has updated information on fines and forfeitures, whereas Chapter 12 has expanded information on reentry programs.

Material on parole revocations in Chapter 13 was moved earlier in the book and incorporated into the Chapter 7 section on probation revocation. This was because the revocation information applied in the same way, and this avoided later duplication. Chapter 14 includes new information on juvenile intermediate sanctions.

Chapters 15 and 16 have been combined into one chapter, to include the collateral consequences of conviction and the means by which the offender may regain some of these lost rights, such as pardons, expungement, and sealing. We believe that the information presented in this final chapter can be of enormous benefit to students and practitioners in corrections.

We have updated all of our websites at the end of each chapter and have a few new case studies. As in the previous edition, the case studies were prepared for in-class discussion or for out-of-class written exercises to initiate critical thinking.

PEDAGOGICAL FEATURES AND LEARNING TOOLS

Each chapter begins with "What You Will Learn"—a bulleted outline of key concepts and learning objectives. Key terms are boldfaced in the text, with their accompanying definitions in the margins, and are defined in the glossary at the end of the book. Some of the chapters have boxed material. One box theme is titled: "Technology in Corrections" and illustrates how advancements in equipment and knowledge about data have impacted aspects of corrections programs. Another theme is "Corrections Up Close." This theme investigates a particular topic in more detail as it pertains to the chapter material.

The "Top Things You Should Know" is a bulleted list that summarizes the chapter. Each chapter is followed by discussion questions that will encourage students to think critically about the materials presented in the chapter. The discussion questions could also serve as written exercises in many cases or as topics for essays or research papers. Each chapter has updated Internet sites for more information on topics found within that chapter. The book contains many photographs, tables, and figures that will help students to visualize the phenomena and processes under discussion. Twelve chapters contain one case study each, to allow for in-class discussion or written assignments. An *Instructor's Manual with Test Bank* and a computerized Test Bank are also available. The following supplements are available for bundling to aid student comprehension:

- Crime Scenes: An Interactive Criminal Justice CD-ROM—The first introductory criminal justice CD-ROM available. This interactive CD-ROM places students in various roles as they explore all aspects of the criminal justice system: policing and investigations, courts, sentencing, and corrections.

- InfoTrac® College Edition—Gives students access to full-length articles from more than 600 scholarly and popular periodicals. Students can print complete articles or use the cut-and-paste and e-mail techniques. Includes readings from *U.S. News and World Report, Corrections Today, Prison Journal, American Criminal Law Review,* and much more.
- Internet Investigator IV—Includes new criminal justice–related websites categorized by course for ease of use: policing, investigations, courts, corrections, research, juvenile delinquency, and much more. Save students money by bundling with the book.

ACKNOWLEDGMENTS

This book could not have been written without the generous assistance of many colleagues and corrections professionals. We wish to express our appreciation to Kent Sisson, Parole Director, Southern Parole Region, Kansas Department of Corrections, and Terri Sisson, Deputy Chief U.S. parole officer, District of Kansas, for preparing many of the case studies that follow the chapters and for their advice and consultation in preparing previous editions. Our thanks to Richard Russell, supervising U.S. probation officer (retired), Western District of Texas, for his contribution, "A Day in the Life of a Federal Probation Officer."

We would like to acknowledge the following colleagues who so kindly provided us with information and referrals to use in our text: William Barton, Indiana University; Dan Beto, now retired from the Correctional Management Institute of Texas; John Byrd, University of Texas-San Antonio; and Trey Williams, University of Houston-Downtown.

Thanks are also due to colleagues in the probation and parole field who have given Rolando del Carmen the necessary background in field training that has been invaluable in writing chapters in the book. Among those are Rick Faulkner, program specialist, National Institute of Corrections; Ron Corbett, deputy commissioner, Massachusetts Department of Probation; and Todd Jermstad, assistant legal counsel, Texas Department of Criminal Justice.

Chris Caldeira of Wadsworth Publishing Company was extremely supportive and helpful throughout the entire process—thanks very much, Chris; you are awesome! Our project development editor Gina Ruggeri and our copy editor Kate Bresnahan significantly improved our book by a keen eye and attention to every detail.

We express our special appreciation to our colleagues who reviewed drafts of earlier editions of the book. Their insightful comments and suggestions proved invaluable. In particular, we appreciate the work of Joseph Apiahene, University of Texas-Pan American; Lincoln Chandler, Florida Memorial College; Dana DeWitt, Chadron State University; Teresa Hall, Sandhills Community College; Charles Hinman, Kirtland Community College; G. G. Hunt, Wharton County Junior College; David Jaso, Austin Community College; J. H. Koonce, Edgecombe Community College; Sheri Short, Navarro College; David Stumpf, Central Lakes College; and Ron Walker, Trinity Valley Community College. For the seventh edition we would like to thank Rodney Henningsen, Sam Houston State University; Patrice Morris, Rutgers University-Newark; Gaylene Armstrong, Southern Illinois University; Denny Langston, Central Missouri State University; and Thomas Allen, University of South Dakota.

Finally, Leanne Alarid would like to personally thank the following individuals for their pictorial contributions to the text: Ray Alarid, Bob Goodson, Mike "Twinkie" Hicks, Alex Holsinger, Kristi Holsinger, LaShaun Lars, Wayne Lucas, Eric Myers, Dolly Owen, Donnie Turner, "Chopper" Dave Vargo, Jennifer "Pinky" Vargo, and Jim Wuster. This text is more interesting because of you.

Leanne Fiftal Alarid

Paul F. Cromwell

Rolando V. del Carmen

About the Authors

Leanne Fiftal Alarid is associate professor in the Department of Criminal Justice at the University of Texas-San Antonio. From 1996 to 2006, she taught at the University of Missouri-Kansas City. While at UMKC, she received a faculty scholar award for excellence in research. She earned her M.A. in criminal justice/criminology and her Ph.D. in criminal justice, both from Sam Houston State University in Huntsville, Texas. She double majored with a B.A. in psychology and sociology from the University of Northern Colorado.

Dr. Alarid's areas of expertise are institutional and community corrections, women and crime, and criminal justice policy. She is the author of more than twenty journal articles and book chapters. She most recently co-authored Corrections: A Contemporary Introduction 1e (Allyn and Bacon, 2008). She co-edited four books, including *In Her Own Words: Women's Offenders' Views on Crime and Victimization* (Roxbury, 2006); *Behind a Convict's Eyes: Doing Time in a Modern Day Prison* (Wadsworth, 2004); *Correctional Perspectives: Views from Academics, Practitioners, and Prisoners* (Roxbury, 2002); and *Controversies in Criminal Justice* (Roxbury, 2003).

Alarid worked as a counselor for a girls' group home and as a correctional case manager at an adult halfway house, both in Denver, Colorado.

Paul Cromwell is a professor of criminal justice at Wichita State University. He received his Ph.D. in Criminology from Florida State University. He is the author and/or editor of sixteen books, *including Breaking and Entering: Burglars on Burglary, In Their Own Words: Criminals on Crime, Correctional Perspectives, In Her Own Words: Women Offenders Perspectives on Crime and Victimization, and Crime and Justice in America*. He has extensive experience in the criminal justice system, including service as Parole Commissioner and Chairman of the Texas Board or Pardons and Paroles, Chief Juvenile Probation Officer and Director of Juvenile Services, and as a United States Probation Officer.

Rolando V. del Carmen is distinguished professor of criminal justice at the Criminal Justice Center, Sam Houston State University, in Huntsville, Texas. He holds a B.A. and a bachelor of laws degree from the Philippines; a master of comparative law from Southern Methodist University; a master of laws from the University of California at Berkeley; and a doctor of the science of law from the University of Illinois.

Del Carmen was assistant dean and associate professor of a school of law in the Philippines and has held various administrative and academic positions in the United States. He has taught at various universities and has written extensively. His publications include more than ten books and numerous articles in several journals on law-related topics in criminal justice. His books include *Criminal Procedure: Law and Practice,*

Fourth Edition, Civil Liabilities of Law Enforcement Personnel, Texas Probation Law and Practice, and *Potential Liabilities of Probation and Parole Officers.*

Del Carmen travels and lectures extensively and has served as a consultant to criminal justice agencies in a number of states. He was appointed for a six-year term to the Texas Commission on Jail Standards. In 1986, he won the Faculty Excellence in Research Award at Sam Houston State University, the first such award ever to be given by the university. The Academy of Criminal Justice Sciences, the national organization of criminal justice professors, has named del Carmen as the recipient of the following awards during its yearly national convention: 1990 Academy Fellow Award; in 1996, the Bruce Smith Award; and in 2005, the Academy Founder's Award. He therefore holds the rare distinction of being the recipient of all three major awards given by the Academy of Criminal Justice Sciences.

I

Overview of Community Corrections

The idea behind community corrections programs is that most offenders can be effectively punished within their community of origin if they are held accountable for their crimes at the same time that they fulfill legitimate living standards. Most offenders do not pose a danger to themselves or to others in the community and therefore can remain in the community to maintain relationships. Punishing offenders in the community confers several benefits.

First, the offender remains in the community where he or she has responsibilities. With legitimate employment, offenders can continue supporting themselves and their family of origin, and they will pay taxes. Second, offenders in the community are more likely than prison-bound offenders to compensate their victims through restitution or to pay back the community through community service. Finally, community corrections programs do not expose offenders to the subculture of violence that exists in many jails and prisons.

Chapter 1 introduces the basic goals and programs of community corrections and explains why the study of community corrections is important. Chapter 2 examines the bail decision as the first major decision point and includes information on diversionary programs and specialty courts such as drug and mental health courts. Chapter 3 focuses on sentencing as the second major decision point and explains the presentence investigation report to aid judges.

The Correctional Dilemma
Change in Sentencing Laws
The Toughening of Juvenile Justice

The Paradox
Public Perceptions of Community
  Corrections
Correctional Budgets

**The Role of Corrections at Three
Major Decision Points**
Pretrial and the Bail Decision
Sentencing Decision
Reentry Decision

**How Community Corrections
Fits Correctional Goals**
Protection of the Public
Rehabilitation
Community Reintegration
Restorative or Community Justice
Public Shaming as Punishment

**What You Should Know About
Evaluations of Community-
Based Corrections**
What Works?
How Is Effectiveness Measured?
Other Outcome Measures for
  Evaluation

Top Things You Should Know

1

The State of Corrections Today: Why Community Corrections Is Important

What You Will Learn in This Chapter

- *Correctional agencies and programs perform the function of carrying out the sentence imposed by a judge.*
- *Corrections is a social control mechanism for convicted offenders, and it also serves to keep others law abiding.*
- *Sentencing policies have contributed to correctional growth in institutional and community-based corrections.*
- *Community corrections consists of two basic types of programs: sanctions that serve as alternatives to incarceration and programs that assist prisoners in community reentry after prison.*

THE CORRECTIONAL DILEMMA

"Let's get tough on crime"
The "war on drugs"
"Lock 'em up and throw away the key"
"Juvenile offenders should be treated as adults"

These ideas related to crime control reflect public sentiment and echo political rhetoric that have existed since the mid-1970s. The political climate has resulted in a greater percentage of convicted misdemeanants and felons in the correctional system today, more so than ever before in the nation's history. In addition, the budget allocations for corrections have grown to support this expansion. In the United States nearly 7 million people, equivalent to about 3 percent of the total adult population, are currently under correctional supervision. Table 1.1 tracks the number of adults under supervision since 1980; you can see that the numbers have been steadily increasing every year. Table 1.1 shows that in 2004 there were 4.1 million offenders on probation and over 765,000 on parole, which is considerably more than offenders incarcerated in jail and prison. In the last decade, there was an average increase of 2.7 percent *each year* in the corrections system (Glaze and Palla 2005). The number of female offenders has grown as well, although women have always been underrepresented in the criminal justice system in comparison to their numbers in the general population. Sources say that in the last 15 years, the number of women on probation and parole has doubled. While this sounds like a lot, women comprise only 13 percent of all parolees and 23 percent of probationers today. Most women are eligible for a community corrections sentence because they tend to have shorter criminal records and are not violent as men.

The steady rise of convicted offenders is directly related to a number of factors, including: (1) a change in sentencing laws and longer sentences for violent offenders, (2) differential police responses to drug offenses, (3) a decreased rate of release on discretionary parole, and (4) an increase of probation and parole violators returning to prison (Beck 2000).

Change in Sentencing Laws

From the 1930s to the mid-1970s, **indeterminate sentencing** was the primary sentencing philosophy in the United States. Under the indeterminate sentencing model, judges decided who went to prison, and parole boards decided when offenders were rehabilitated and ready for release on parole (Forst 1995). The release date was

INDETERMINATE SENTENCING

A sentencing philosophy that focuses on treatment and incorporates a broad sentencing range or undetermined amount of time served in prison or in the community where release is reliant on offender rehabilitation or readiness to function prosocially.

TABLE 1.1   *Adults on Probation, on Parole, in Jail, and in Prison: 1980–2004*

Year	Total estimated correctional population[a]	COMMUNITY SUPERVISION		INCARCERATION	
		Probation	Parole	Jail	Prison
1980	1,840,400	1,118,097	220,438	182,288[b]	319,598
1981	2,006,600	1,225,934	225,539	195,085[b]	360,029
1982	2,192,600	1,357,264	224,604	207,853	402,914
1983	2,475,100	1,582,947	246,440	221,815	423,898
1984	2,689,200	1,740,948	266,992	233,018	448,264
1985	3,011,500	1,968,712	300,203	254,986	487,593
1986	3,239,400	2,114,621	325,638	272,735	526,436
1987	3,459,600	2,247,158	355,505	294,092	562,814
1988	3,714,100	2,356,483	407,977	341,893	607,766
1989	4,055,600	2,522,125	456,803	393,303	683,367
1990	4,348,000	2,670,234	531,407	403,019[c]	743,382
1991	4,535,600	2,728,472	590,442	424,129[c]	792,535
1992	4,762,600	2,811,611	658,601	441,781[c]	850,566
1993	4,944,000	2,903,061	676,100	455,500[c]	909,381
1994	5,141,300	2,981,022	690,371	479,800	990,147
1995	5,342,900	3,077,861	679,421	507,044	1,078,542
1996	5,490,700	3,164,996	679,733	518,492	1,127,528
1997	5,734,900	3,296,513	694,787	567,079	1,176,564
1998	6,134,200	3,670,441	696,385	592,462	1,224,469
1999	6,340,800	3,779,922	714,457	605,943	1,287,172
2000	6,445,100	3,826,209	723,898	621,149	1,316,333
2001	6,581,700	3,931,731	732,333	631,240	1,330,007
2002	6,758,800	4,024,067	750,934	665,475	1,367,547
2003	6,936,600	4,144,782	745,125	691,301	1,392,796
2004	6,996,500	4,151,125	765,355	713,990	1,421,911
Average annual percent change 1995 to 2004	2.7%	2.8%	1.3%	3.9%	3.1%

Note: Counts for probation, prison, and parole populations are for December 31 of each year; jail population counts are for June 30 of each year. Counts of adults held in facilities for 1993–1996 were estimated and rounded to the nearest 100. Totals in 1998 through 2002 exclude probationers held in jail or prison. Data for jail and prison are for inmates under custody in the public and private facilities. These data have been revised based on the most recently reported counts and may differ from previous editions of Sourcebook.

[a] Because a small number of individuals have multiple correctional statuses, totals were rounded to the nearest 100.

[b] Estimated.

[c] The estimated jail population for 1990–1993 includes an unknown number of people supervised outside jail facilities.

Source: U.S. Department of Justice, Bureau of Justice Statistics. *Correctional Populations in the United States* 1994, NCJ-160091, Table 1.1; 1995, NCJ-163916, Table 1.1 (Washington, DC: U.S. Department of Justice). Lauren E. Glaze and Seri Palla. 2005. *Probation and Parole in the United States*. NCJ 210676 (Washington, DC: U.S. Department of Justice).

unknown by the offender and subject to the decision of the parole board, which, by majority decision, decided if the offender was making progress toward rehabilitation and was ready to rejoin the larger society. While incarcerated, offenders were able to enroll in a variety of programs aimed at self-improvement and skill building to demonstrate readiness for the parole board.

Parole was also used as a backdoor strategy for controlling the prison population. When prisons became too crowded, the parole rate increased to make room for incoming prisoners. Under indeterminate sentencing, offenders who did not go to prison were, for the most part, placed on probation. Few intermediate sentencing options existed other than prison or probation, and those that did, such as halfway houses and intensive probation, were used infrequently (Tonry 1997).

Support for indeterminate sentencing declined in the 1970s as people questioned whether prison rehabilitation worked and whether parole boards could accurately determine when offenders were ready for release. Questions were also raised as to whether indeterminate sentencing was administered fairly. Because the release date was ambiguous, some offenders spent many more years behind bars than their crimes warranted, whereas others—who may have convinced the parole board that they were "cured"—were released after only a few years.

In 1975 Maine became the first state to return to a sentencing philosophy of **determinate sentencing.** In determinate sentencing, the sentence range is narrow and release is determined either by legislative statute or by a sentencing guideline matrix that lists the sentence the offender should receive based on the offender's prior criminal record and the current conviction (Forst 1995). The sentence length is therefore determined by the crime severity rather than by how long it takes for the offender to become rehabilitated behind bars. The slogan "you do the crime, you do the time" became more popular, and funding for prison treatment programs diminished. In determinate sentencing, judges lost most of their sentencing power and discretion, and prosecutors gained some discretionary power by being able to decide with what crime to initially charge the offender. Judges are sometimes able to deviate slightly (higher or lower) from the prescribed sentencing guidelines, but must provide justification for doing so. Parole board decision making has also been limited in many states to only certain types of offenders.

Examples of determinate sentencing include mandatory minimums, truth in sentencing, three strikes laws, and sentencing guidelines. All states have adopted mandatory minimum sentencing laws for certain types of offenses, such as violent crimes, carrying of firearms, narcotics, and repeat felonies. Mandatory minimum prison terms must be served before release can be considered. "Truth in sentencing" laws require that offenders serve at least 85 percent of the sentence length before becoming eligible for release (Petersilia 2003). About half of all states and the federal system have "three strikes and you're out" laws for the third felony conviction. This habitual offender law mandates long prison terms, and in a small number of states the third-time felon might be incarcerated for the rest of his or her natural life. To add to the problem of prison crowding, not only are offenders serving longer prison terms up front, but 16 states have also abolished parole as a backdoor release strategy (Petersilia 2003).

The most controversial set of sentencing guidelines is at the federal level. Proponents contend that the guidelines decrease judicial disparity and the potential for discrimination and make judges accountable for sentencing decisions. Opponents say that the federal guidelines were developed with little thought as to how sentence length would affect burgeoning prison populations. Federal guidelines also decreased the use of probation and other community corrections sanctions. Federal parole was abolished as an option to control federal prison crowding, and prisoners were allowed one year of mandatory release.

State sentencing guidelines seem to provide for more judicial discretion and more alternatives to incarceration (Lutjen 1996). Evaluations of state sentencing guidelines have found that dispositional polices (whether offenders will or will not be incarcerated—the "in/out decision") have had a greater impact on prison population growth than the sentence length (Parent et al. 1997). However, in the federal system for drug crimes, long sentence length has been the primary reason for prison expansion (Parent et al. 1997).

DETERMINATE SENTENCING

A sentencing philosophy that focuses on certainty and severity for the crime committed and incorporates an exact amount of time or narrow sentencing range of time to be served in prison or in the community. Amount of time served depends on the legislative statutes or the sentencing guidelines, which mandate how much time is to be served before the offender is eligible (if at all) for early release.

Whereas discretionary parole rates have decreased, a short period of mandatory release from prison has increased (both of these types of community supervision are discussed in Chapters 11 and 12). With a focus on public safety under the watchful eye of officers, tolerance for offenders who violate conditions of community supervision has contributed to high failure rates of probationers and parolees who are ultimately incarcerated.

Some believe that the pendulum may be beginning to swing away from conservative sentencing policies. In his August 2003 address to the American Bar Association, Supreme Court Justice Anthony Kennedy called for an end to our policy of mandatory minimum sentences, saying that we should revisit the federal sentencing guidelines because our prison sentences are too severe. Justice Kennedy felt that, in striving to reduce sentencing disparity by eliminating indeterminate sentencing and parole, our criminal justice system has removed too much authority from judges and the parole board (Israel 2003). Only time will tell if Kennedy's plea will be an impetus to change.

The Toughening of Juvenile Justice

"Getting tough" with crime and changing sentencing laws have not been limited to adults. Nearly every state has somehow changed juvenile statutory laws to either more closely resemble the adult criminal justice system or create options for prosecutors to treat juveniles as adults for violent crimes. Some juveniles are now tried and punished as adults automatically by the type of crime committed (such as murder) or by discretion of the prosecutor or the judge. Other key issues involved in juvenile justice changes vary by state. These issues include allowing juveniles to be fingerprinted, opening juvenile records, opening juvenile court proceedings to the public, allowing victims to attend juvenile court, making offenders pay victim restitution, and obligating parents to take responsibility for their children's actions (Altschuler 1999).

The juvenile justice system still exists as a separate entity from the adult criminal justice system. Since the juvenile justice system began more than 100 years ago, rehabilitation and diversion have been its core missions. Because the vast majority of juvenile offenders are nonviolent, they are tried in juvenile courts under a private and more informal process than adult offenders. As discussed in Chapter 14, the juvenile justice system provides a wider variety of intermediate sanctions for nonviolent juveniles and also pays more attention to crime prevention factors outside of the system, such as the family, peers, education, and the neighborhood (Altschuler 1999).

THE PARADOX

We are used to thinking of community safety as contingent upon who is allowed to live in the community. Justice seems separationist because formal justice processes remove offenders from everyday life for accusation and conviction ceremonies, and they often result in penal removal, as well. The idea that communities are made safe by eliminating unsafe residents is equally an ingrained idea in American traditions (Clear and Corbett 1997, p. 2).

Paradoxically, correctional policy shifts according to legislators' perceptions of what the public wants. Many times, public opinion polls ask crime policy questions in too simplistic a manner to be valid indicators of the true public sentiment. In addition, the media tend to report a biased, sensationalist view of the criminal justice system, so the average American citizen may not be well informed about the true nature of punishment and corrections.

Public Perceptions of Community Corrections

We discuss a sampling of survey research that has queried the public on their perceptions of community corrections and of rehabilitation of offenders. It appears that the public is most interested in strategies that create safer communities and realizes that harsh punishment without treatment is an ineffective strategy, particularly for offenders who remain in the community after sentencing or who will one day return to the community. Eight out of 10 adults surveyed in 2001 (sample size of 2,000 nationally) favored prison alternative programs for nonviolent offenders such as community service, mandatory education, and job training (Eagleton Institute of Politics Center for Public Interest 2002).

A survey of 400 citizens representing six areas within Pennsylvania determined similar results to the nationwide sample. The Pennsylvania public supported the use of community corrections sentences for drug or property offenders, preferably those sanctions that obligated the offender to pay the victim back or work to repair the harm to the community (Farkas 1993).

To measure the extent to which the public believes that community corrections programs are severe punishments, researchers used psychophysical scaling techniques to obtain severity judgments of six kinds of sentences: imprisonment, fines, intensive supervision probation (ISP), weekend sentencing, home detention, and regular probation. After having been given in-depth descriptions of each of the six sentencing types, the public ranked 32 different types of penalties according to length of sentence or amount of fine. The researchers found that regular probation was viewed as lenient and prison was viewed as the most severe, but that intermediate sanctions were perceived as intermediate in severity, with home detention, ISP, and weekend sentences ranked from most to least severe of the three intermediate punishments (Harlow, Darley, and Robinson 1995).

Another group of researchers conducted a mail survey of a random sample of 400 Cincinnati residents using four different factorial design vignettes (robbery with injury, robbery without injury, burglary of $250, and burglary of $1,000) and included demographic information about the offender in each scenario (Turner et al. 1997). The 237 respondents were asked to read a vignette and select one type of sentence (prison, shock incarceration, halfway house, house arrest, intensive supervision probation, and regular probation) for each vignette. The survey findings indicated that the majority of the Cincinnati public is open to house arrest, halfway house, or intensive supervision probation.

> [The public] also favored general equivalency diploma classes, drug and alcohol treatment, and psychiatric treatment for mentally ill offenders. In short, they endorsed community-based alternatives that would achieve multiple goals: that would punish, restrain, and change offenders. (Turner et al. 1997, p. 22)

While the public is supportive of prison alternatives for nonviolent offenders, there is a low tolerance for failure of people who have been to prison. Two-thirds of the public believe that parolees who fail drug tests should be sent back to prison. In sum, these studies indicate that public opinion research on sentencing preferences demonstrate higher validity if the public is given diverse sentencing options and adequate information, such as program descriptions and detailed information about an offense or an offender. Armed with sufficient information, members of the general public support the use of community-based corrections and intermediate sanctions for a variety of offenses, particularly if treatment will create safer communities.

FIGURE 1.1 *A Continuum of Sanctions*

ESCALATING PUNISHMENTS TO FIT THE CRIME

This list includes generalized descriptions of many of the sentencing options that are in use in jurisdictions across the country.

PROBATION
Offender reports to probation officer periodically, sometimes as frequently as several times a month or as infrequently as once a year, depending on the offense.

INTENSIVE SUPERVISION PROBATION
Offender sees probation officer three to five times a week. Probation officer also makes unscheduled visits to offender's home or workplace.

RESTITUTION AND FINES
Used alone or in conjunction with probation or intensive supervision and requires regular payments to crime victims or to the courts.

COMMUNITY SERVICE
Used alone or in conjunction with probation or intensive supervision and requires completion of set number of hours of work in and for the community.

SUBSTANCE ABUSE TREATMENT
Evaluation and referral services provided by private outside agencies and used alone or in conjunction with either simple probation or intensive probation.

Correctional Budgets

Billions of dollars are spent annually to support correctional agencies in the United States. Within corrections, budgets for jails and prisons have significantly increased, while some probation and parole budgets have actually decreased despite having to support more people on supervision. In one year, for example, a total of $36.1 billion was spent nationwide on adult state and federal prison institutions, with a median of $368 million per state (Camp, Camp, and May 2003). This amount was an increase of 12 percent from four years previous and does not include the budgets for city and county jails.

An additional $3.9 billion was spent on probation and parole programs across the nation (down from $4.6 billion in 1999). Probation and parole agencies, whether combined or separate, had an average annual budget of $82.9 million for the entire state (Camp, Camp, and May 2003). Traditional incarceration is much more expensive than most community sanctions, including probation and parole. At the same time, resources and funding have not kept pace with community corrections growth. Less than 11 cents of every correctional dollar is directed to probation and parole, although more than 70 percent of all people under correctional supervision are probationers and parolees. To pay the price tag for this supervision, state legislators must

DAY REPORTING
Clients report to a central location every day where they file a daily schedule with their supervising officer showing how each hour will be spent—at work, in class, at support group meetings, etc.

HOUSE ARREST AND ELECTRONIC MONITORING
Used in conjunction with intensive supervision and restricts offender to home except when at work, school, or treatment.

HALFWAY HOUSE
Residential settings for selected inmates as a supplement to probation for those completing prison programs and for some probation or parole violators. Usually coupled with community service work and/or substance abuse treatment.

BOOT CAMP
Rigorous military-style regimen for younger offenders, designed to accelerate punishment while instilling discipline, often with an educational component.

PRISONS AND JAILS
More serious offenders serve their terms at state or federal prisons, whereas county jails are usually designed to hold inmates for shorter periods.

Source: William M. DiMascio. 1997. *Seeking Justice: Crime and Punishment in America*. New York: Edna McConnell Clark Foundation. Used with permission.

appropriate tax dollars annually because the corrections system (except for private agencies) is dependent entirely on tax dollars and government appropriations.

THE ROLE OF CORRECTIONS AT THREE MAJOR DECISION POINTS

The criminal justice system is guided by formal written laws, codes, and statutes, and by informal discretion. Discretion is a form of subjective decision making that begins when a victim or witness decides whether to report a crime to the police. Another decision point early in the process is the arresting decision made by a law enforcement officer. Some would argue that discretion plays as important, if not more important, a role than formal law.

This text focuses exclusively on community-based corrections. **Community corrections** is a sanction in which offenders serve some or all of their sentence in the community. A community sentence seeks to repair the harm the offender may have caused the victim or the community, and to reduce the risk of re-offending in the future. Figure 1.1 shows the wide variety of community-based sanctions available,

COMMUNITY CORRECTIONS

A nonincarcerative sanction in which offenders serve all or a portion of their sentence in the community.

BOX 1.1   COMMUNITY CORRECTIONS UP CLOSE   •

WHAT IS THE PURPOSE OF PROBATION?

The purpose of probation is to assist in reducing the incidence and impact of crime by probationers in the community. The core services of probation are to provide investigation and reports to the court, to help develop appropriate court dispositions for adult offenders and juvenile delinquents, and to supervise those people placed on probation. Probation departments in fulfilling their purpose may also provide a broad range of services including, but not limited to, crime and delinquency prevention, victim restitution programs, and intern/volunteer programs.

POSITION

The mission of probation is to protect the public interest and safety by reducing the incidence and impact of crime by probationers. This role is accomplished by:

- assisting the courts in decision making through the probation report and in the enforcement of court orders
- providing services and programs that afford opportunities for offenders to become more law abiding
- providing and cooperating in programs and activities for the prevention of crime and delinquency
- furthering the administration of fair and individualized justice

Probation is premised upon the following beliefs:

- *Society has a right to be protected from persons who cause its members harm, regardless of the reasons for such harm.* It is the right of every citizen to be free from fear of harm to person and property. Belief in the necessity of law to an orderly society demands commitment to support it. Probation accepts this responsibility and views itself as an instrument for both control and treatment appropriate to some, but not all, offenders. The wise use of authority derived from law adds strength and stability to its efforts.
- *Offenders have rights deserving of protection.* Freedom and democracy require fair and individualized due process of law in adjudicating and sentencing the offender.
- *Victims of crime have rights deserving of protection.* In its humanitarian tradition, probation recognizes that prosecution of the offender is but a part of the responsibility of the criminal justice system. The victim of criminal activity may suffer loss of property, emotional problems, or physical disability. Probation thus commits itself to advocacy for the needs and interests of crime victims.
- *Human beings are capable of change.* Belief in the individual's capability for behavioral change leads probation practitioners to a commitment to the reintegration of the offender into the community. The possibility for constructive change of behavior is based on the recognition and acceptance of the principle of individual responsibility. Much of probation practice focuses on identifying and

---

PROBATION

The community supervision of a convicted offender in lieu of incarceration under conditions imposed by the court for a specified period during which the court retains authority to modify the conditions or to resentence the offender if he or she violates the conditions.

including residential programs such as halfway houses and therapeutic communities; economic sanctions such as restitution, fines, and forfeitures; and nonresidential options such as probation, parole, and electronic monitoring.

The most common form of community supervision is **probation.** Probation is defined as the release of a convicted offender under conditions imposed by the court for a specified period during which the court retains authority to modify the conditions or to resentence the offender if he or she violates the conditions. Probation forms the base of the community supervision, and most of the other sanctions introduced in Figure 1.1 are programs or conditions of probation or reentry from prison on parole.

making available those services and programs that will best afford offenders an opportunity to become responsible, law-abiding citizens.

- *Not all offenders have the same capacity or willingness to benefit from measures designed to produce law-abiding citizens.* Probation practitioners recognize the variations among individuals. The present offense, the degree of risk to the community, and the potential for change can be assessed only in the context of the offender's individual history and experience.
- *Intervention in an offender's life should be the minimal amount needed to protect society and promote law-abiding behavior.* Probation subscribes to the principle of intervening in an offender's life only to the extent necessary. Where further intervention appears unwarranted, criminal justice system involvement should be terminated. Where needed intervention can best be provided by an agency outside the system, the offender should be diverted from the system to that agency.
- *Punishment.* Probation philosophy does not accept the concept of retributive punishment. Punishment as a corrective measure is supported and used in those instances in which it is felt that aversive measures may positively alter the offender's behavior when other measures may not. Even corrective punishment, however, should be used cautiously and judiciously in view of its highly unpredictable impact. It can be recognized that a conditional sentence in the community is, in and of itself, a punishment. It is less harsh and drastic than a prison term but more controlling and punitive than release without supervision.
- *Incarceration may be destructive and should be imposed only when necessary.* Probation practitioners acknowledge society's right to protect itself and support the incarceration of offenders whose behavior constitutes a danger to the public through rejection of social or court mandates. Incarceration can also be an appropriate element of a probation program to emphasize the consequences of criminal behavior and thus effect constructive behavioral change. However, institutions should be humane and required to adhere to the highest standards.
- *Where public safety is not compromised, society and most offenders are best served through community correctional programs.* Most offenders should be provided services within the community in which they are expected to demonstrate acceptable behavior. Community correctional programs generally are cost-effective, and they allow offenders to remain with their families while paying taxes and, where applicable, restitution to victims.

Source: American Probation and Parole Association. 1987. "APPA Position Statement: Probation." Accessed: http://www.appa-net.org/about%20appa/probatio.htm. Reprinted with permission.

Due to the combination of many of these sanctions, it is helpful to understand community corrections as having many alternatives from which sanctions can be applied to different offenders to achieve individualized results. The American Probation and Parole Association (APPA) was created to bridge these alternatives. The APPA is an international policy and educational organization for practitioners who work with adults and juveniles in the field of community corrections. The APPA serves to educate and train members and develop standards for the discipline. The APPA's policy statement explains the purpose of probation in Box 1.1. This policy statement is broadly applicable to the function of all programs and agencies in community corrections. No matter what combination of sanctions is used, think of community corrections as playing a pivotal role at three major decision points that follow the arrest: bail, sentencing, and reentry.

Pretrial and the Bail Decision

After a police officer makes an arrest, the suspect is booked into jail and the prosecutor's office decides whether to charge the suspect with a crime. If the prosecutor chooses not to charge, the suspect is automatically released. If the prosecutor opts to charge, the suspect officially becomes a defendant and goes before a judge, magistrate, or other official authorized to inform the defendant of the charges, determine whether the defendant is requesting appointed counsel, and ascertain whether the defendant is eligible for release from jail. Although most defendants are released on their own recognizance with the promise to appear at their next court date, some defendants must secure their next appearance with **bail,** or monetary payment deposited with the court to ensure their return. When the conditions of the bond have been satisfied, the defendant is released on a bond. Many times, particularly in the federal system, the defendant is released on **pretrial supervision,** which is a form of correctional supervision of a defendant who has not yet been convicted. Forms of pretrial supervision may include client reporting, house arrest, and electronic monitoring. Pretrial supervision accounts for the defendant's whereabouts to keep the community safe, it allows the defendant to prepare for upcoming court appearances, it allows the defendant to continue working and supporting dependents, and it keeps bed space in the jail available for another defendant who may not be eligible for release. We discuss bail and pretrial decision points in Chapter 2.

Sentencing Decision

Community corrections agencies and programs perform the important function of implementing the sentence imposed by a judge. At a basic level, corrections is a social control mechanism for convicted offenders, and it also keeps others law abiding through general deterrence. We recognize the importance of incarcerating offenders who are dangerous to the public or who have committed violent crimes so heinous that incarceration is a deserved punishment. However, the vast majority of people who commit a crime can be punished in ways that do not warrant imprisonment. Judges and prosecutors need a variety of "front-end" punishments from which to choose, and community corrections offers a diversity of sentencing options.

The community-based punishments shown earlier in Figure 1.1 are known as **intermediate sanctions** because they offer graduated levels of supervision. They provide rewards for positive behavior with gradually less supervision when offenders achieve and maintain desired program outcomes. Intermediate sanctions can also impose greater levels of surveillance, supervision, and monitoring than probation alone but less supervision than that provided in jail or prison. A full range of sentencing options gives judges greater latitude to select punishments that closely fit the circumstances of the crime and the offender (DiMascio 1997). We discuss the sentencing decision in Chapter 3, and then devote seven chapters to the forms community corrections takes, beginning with probation and the various graduated residential, monetary, and nonresidential sanctions.

BAIL

Monetary payment deposited with the court to ensure the defendant's return for the next court date in exchange for the defendant's release.

PRETRIAL SUPERVISION

Court-ordered correctional supervision of a defendant who has not yet been convicted whereby the defendant participates in activities such as reporting, house arrest, and electronic monitoring.

INTERMEDIATE SANCTIONS

A spectrum of community supervision strategies that vary greatly in terms of their supervision level and treatment capacity, ranging from probation to partial custody.

Reentry Decision

Approximately 95 percent of prisoners incarcerated today will one day leave prison and rejoin the larger society. Community corrections serves an important purpose to assist prisoners in community reentry after they have spent time in prison. **Prisoner reentry** is any activity or program "conducted to prepare ex-convicts to return safely to the community and to live as law-abiding citizens" (Petersilia 2003, p. 3). Prisoner reentry applies to prisoners who are released automatically based on mandatory statutes as well as prisoners released early at the parole board's discretion.

A **prerelease program** is a minimum-security institutional setting for imprisoned offenders who have already done some time and are nearing release. Prerelease offenders are chosen by corrections officials and transferred to a different type of residential program that the offenders can complete in a shorter duration than if they served their full prison sentence. Prerelease programs are considered to be more treatment oriented than prison. Examples of these programs are halfway houses, boot camps, and therapeutic communities that are located inside a prison, separate from the general prisoner population. The purpose of back-end programs is to save money and prison space while also providing program participants with a specialized treatment regimen. Examples of prerelease programs are fully discussed in Chapters 8 and 9.

Parole is the discretionary release of an offender before the expiration of his or her sentence under conditions established by the paroling authority. Parole is in many ways similar to probation. Both involve supervised release in the community and the possibility of revocation should the parolee or probationer violate the conditions of release. Although some technical differences do exist, the primary difference is that probation is supervision in the community instead of incarceration and parole is supervised release after a portion of the prison sentence has been served. Chapter 11 covers the history of parole as well as the conditions that led to the current decreasing rate of release on discretionary parole. Chapter 12 explains the process of preparation for prisoner reentry, and Chapter 13 reviews conditions of discretionary parole and discusses the increase of parole violators returning to prison.

HOW COMMUNITY CORRECTIONS FITS CORRECTIONAL GOALS

The goals of community corrections complement the overall goals of **institutional corrections.** Community corrections attempts to punish offenders while at the same time protecting the public, addressing victims' needs, and preventing future criminal behavior through one or more of the following objectives: rehabilitation, community reintegration, restorative justice, and shaming.

Protection of the Public

Most offenders have shown by their offenses that they cannot easily conform to the norms of society. One of the goals of community-based corrections, therefore, is to help offenders conform to behavioral expectations and to monitor their progress toward that goal. Perhaps the major criticism of traditional probation and parole has been their failure to protect the public from further criminal acts by individuals under supervision in the community. Crime control is currently a primary concern of

PRISONER REENTRY

Any activity or program conducted to prepare ex-convicts to return safely to the community and to live as law-abiding citizens.

PRERELEASE PROGRAM

A minimum-security community-based or institutional setting for offenders who have spent time in prison and are nearing release. The focus of these programs includes transitioning, securing a job, and reestablishing family connections.

PAROLE

Conditional privileged release of a convicted offender from a correctional institution to serve the remainder of the sentence under community supervision.

INSTITUTIONAL CORRECTIONS

An incarcerative sanction in which offenders serve their sentence away from the community in a jail or prison institution.

community corrections administrators (Byrne and Taxman 1994). For probation or any other community-based program to be effective and accepted by policy makers and the public, it must first demonstrate that the offenders under supervision are adequately monitored and that the public has nothing to fear from their actions.

Control may be accomplished in a variety of ways. First, as is discussed in Chapter 6, offenders should be assessed to determine the degree of risk posed by their participation in community programs. Community-based programs are not generally appropriate for violent offenders or those with extensive criminal records. Second, those who supervise offenders in community-based programs must accept responsibility to protect the public by monitoring compliance with court orders and conditions of release. Finally, violations of supervised conditions must be taken seriously. If the programs are to become credible sanctions, courts and paroling authorities must be willing to revoke probation or parole for those who cannot or will not comply with the conditions of release (Morris and Tonry 1990). The procedures and reasons for violating probation and parole are covered in Chapters 7 and 13.

Rehabilitation

A second goal of community corrections programs is to correct some of the inadequacies of offenders that may be linked to their criminal behavior and their continued involvement in the criminal justice system. Some of these problems include, but are not limited to, drug or alcohol addiction, lack of emotional control, inadequate education or vocational training, lack of parenting skills, and mental illness or developmental disability.

Correctional treatment or "programming" is the means by which offenders can receive assistance for their problems to reduce further criminal behavior. The basis of effective rehabilitation is that the offender has to have the genuine desire to change and has to want to complete the mental, emotional, and sometimes spiritual work to promote this transformation (Samenow 1984). This is an important point, because some offenders refuse to adequately respond to treatment. Offenders who pose a serious danger to society or to themselves should not be in a community corrections program. Instead, these offenders should remain incarcerated in prison (or sometimes in a mental health facility) until they have completed their sentence or until they are judged to be not dangerous to themselves or others.

Another point is that oftentimes offenders receive more treatment outside of prison than they do in prison. This results in part because programs in prison have been trimmed as correctional budgets have tightened. Also, taxpayers bear less of the cost for offender treatment in the community because employed offenders usually pay for either a portion or all of their treatment. DiMascio (1997) wrote that community-based sanctions

> provide a means for offenders who are not dangerous to repay their victim and their communities. Intermediate sanctions also promote rehabilitation—which most citizens want, but most prisons are no longer able to provide—and the reintegration of the offender into the community. And, once the programs are in place, they do this at a comparatively low cost. (p. 41)

Most offenders can reduce their likelihood of future criminal behavior by changing other behaviors, such as abstaining from drugs or alcohol or controlling their emotions. Proponents of rehabilitation believe that for certain types of offenders, if the issues that are related to recidivism are addressed, the likelihood of future criminal behavior may be reduced by between 10 and 60 percent. The Corrections Program Assessment Inventory (CPAI), designed by Andrews and Gendreau (Gendreau 1998), indicates that currently only 10 to 20 percent of all correctional rehabilitation programs are of "high quality." A high-quality treatment program contains elements indicating that an effective correctional service is being provided. Offenders are all different, and different treatment approaches must be used to address unique problems. Some advances have been made, and more is now known about what works (and what does not) with different types of offenders. The key is to replace ineffective programs with those that work and to fill the treatment programs with appropriate offenders who will respond to the type of treatment offered (Palmer 1992).

Community Reintegration

Over 40 years ago the President's Commission on Law Enforcement and Administration of Justice (1967) introduced the term *reintegration*. Its report stated,

> Institutions tend to isolate offenders from society, both physically and psychologically, cutting them off from schools, jobs, families, and other supportive influences and increasing the probability that the label of criminal will be indelibly impressed upon them. The goal of reintegration is likely to be furthered much more readily by working with offenders in the community than by incarceration. (p. 165)

This statement still holds true today. The vast majority of prisoners behind bars will be released, and programs should be available to ease their reentry into society. Instead of clamoring for longer sentences, U.S. citizens should ask how best to aid in the reentry of large numbers of long-term offenders. Longer prison terms are not the answer.

Reintegration stresses adaptation to the community by requiring the offender to participate in programs that develop legitimate accomplishments and opportunities and allow the offender to use and refine those skills in a community setting. The role of the community in providing needed services and opportunities is also emphasized. The commission called for mobilization and change of the community and its institutions including development of employment, recreational, and educational opportunities for all its citizens. To achieve reintegration objectives, it is important that community-based correctional programs allow the offender to assume some daily responsibilities and satisfy various normal social roles (such as being a parent, a spouse, or an employee) with a minimal level of supervision while at the same time being involved in supportive programs that fulfill the needs of the offender. Community correctional workers act as advocates and resource brokers, linking offenders to programs and monitoring their progress once the contact has been established.

Restorative or Community Justice

Along with "get tough" retributive-style correctional policies, a different philosophy of justice has emerged in recent years. This alternative is known as **restorative justice** or community justice. Restorative justice is centered on the victim throughout the whole process and emphasizes offender responsibility to repair the injustice that offenders have caused their victims (Karp 1998; Van Ness and Strong 1997; Wright 1996).

When a crime is committed, the offender harms both the individual victim and the community at large. Through shaming, mediation, and face-to-face meetings with the individual victim, restorative justice attempts to strengthen community life by drawing on the strengths of the offenders and the victim instead of focusing on their deficits (Umbreit 1999). Local volunteers and the faith community agree to mentor or assist in the supervision of the offender's reparation. The offender must repair the damage by

RESTORATIVE JUSTICE

The philosophy and sanction of allowing the offender to remain in the community with the responsibility of restoring the victim's losses.

remaining in the community and performing community service, providing victim restitution, and participating in victim impact panels and other educational programs.

Restorative justice is most effective for property crimes, particularly those committed by juveniles or first-time adult felony offenders, because the victim is compensated for property losses. What many victims may not realize is that incarcerating offenders for property crime will provide a loss of temporary freedom, but the victim will rarely, if ever, be compensated. When given a choice between compensation and incarceration, 75 percent of respondents to a study conducted in Minnesota indicated that they would rather be compensated for a property crime than demand the offender be incarcerated (Umbreit 1999). Thus, community-based corrections programs are necessary and important to guide the restorative justice process. At this time, however, restorative justice is less likely to be endorsed for violent crimes. Reparations based on the restorative justice model are discussed in Chapter 10.

Public Shaming as Punishment

Another way that is thought to deter offenders is by using shaming penalties, or scarlet-letter sanctions, to shame offenders publicly. The idea behind shaming is to integrate a punishment that is consistent with affecting an offender's dignity. Examples of shaming sentences include forcing offenders to issue public apologies, obligating offenders to place a bumper sticker on their car or a sign in their front yard acknowledging their crime, or forcing a slumlord to live in one of his rat-infested apartments (Reske 1996). According to Kelly (1999), for shaming to be effective, five conditions must be present:

> First, the offender must belong to an identifiable group, like a religious or an ethnic community. Second, the form of the shaming penalty must be sufficient to compromise the offender's social standing in this group. Third, the punishment must be communicated to the offender's community, and the community must in fact withdraw or shun him. Fourth, the offender must actually fear being shunned. Finally, there must be some method for regaining social status by bringing the offender back into her community, unless the offense is so grave that the offender must be permanently shunned. (pp. 806–807)

One researcher uncovered anecdotal evidence that organizations like the American Civil Liberties Union believe that the government has no business degrading citizens who have broken the law. However, very little empirical evidence exists on the effectiveness of shaming punishments (Reske 1996).

Although used only rarely by a small number of judges, shaming is quite controversial because commentators question whether it violates the Eighth Amendment of the Constitution. In an analysis of the constitutionality of scarlet-letter sanctions, one researcher recommends that the condition not be extremely long in duration and that it not endanger the offender's safety in any way. Kelly (1999) suggests that we need "to create a more objective test that asks whether a reasonable person would consider the particular scarlet-letter probation condition severely humiliating and shameful" (p. 860).

In sum, community corrections is important because the sanctions can provide many options for individuals who have committed a crime but do not pose a serious threat to community safety. Community-based corrections seeks to sanction offenders through punishment while also attempting to improve individual life circumstances. Reintegration, rehabilitation, and restorative justice are important components in changing offenders' attitudes and behaviors, leading to the prevention of future criminal behavior. Community corrections also serves to ease institutional crowding in jails and prisons by drawing from the population of convicted offenders those who are predicted to be less risky to the outside community.

WHAT YOU SHOULD KNOW ABOUT EVALUATIONS OF COMMUNITY-BASED CORRECTIONS

How effective are community-based sanctions? For citizens to view community corrections as the preferred punishment option, agencies should constantly evaluate themselves. "Evidence-based corrections" attempts to measure both the process of a program and the impact a program had after the participants depart in order to report results that make sense to the average citizen (MacKenzie 2000). Evaluations of each type of community corrections can be found throughout the book—probation can be found in Chapter 7; intermediate sanctions in Chapters 8, 9, and 10; and parole in Chapter 13. This section introduces an abbreviated history of the "what works?" debate and discusses how to interpret and understand the evaluations that you will come across in the later chapters.

What Works?

Community-based sanctions came under attack for failing to provide any assurance that released offenders will not continue their criminal activity while under supervision. This lack of confidence in correctional programming peaked in 1974 with Robert Martinson's study of 231 correctional treatment programs across the nation. His study has been referred to as the "nothing works" research. Martinson concluded that, "with few and isolated exceptions, the rehabilitative efforts that have been reported so far had no appreciable effect on recidivism" (p. 25). In the complete report published the next year, Douglas Lipton, Robert Martinson, and Judith Wilks (1975) concluded,

> While some treatment programs have had modest successes, it still must be concluded that the field of corrections has not as yet found satisfactory ways to reduce recidivism by significant amounts. (p. 627)

These studies set off a national debate about the efficacy of corrections—both institutional and community based—resulting in what one commentator called "a mixed and unsettled atmosphere regarding effectiveness" (Palmer 1994, p. xxi). Martinson's findings were poorly stated, and many criticisms were lodged against the methodology used in many of the earlier program evaluations. Martinson and his research team later restated his findings to accommodate the possibility that some treatment programs did work and that much of the research may be invalid (Lipton, Martinson, and Wilks 1975). Despite his recanted statements, the damage had already been done. People believed that no program would work to change offenders. Hubert G. Locke (1998) commented,

> Martinson's study was a prelude to one of the most conservative eras in American politics, one in which policy makers in many political jurisdictions were looking for reasons to repudiate the putative liberal policies of previous decades. The study confirmed what a cadre of reactionary policy makers wanted to hear, at a time in which the sentiments within the professional corrections community still ran toward a philosophy of rehabilitation rather than retribution. Currently, it is reactionary politics that still holds sway over the public policy process, at least in this nation and certainly regarding issues of crime and corrections. (p. 257)

At issue was the question of methodology, or whether research was sophisticated and rigorous enough to determine what does and does not work. If the treatment does work, the research must be able to identify which type of offender and under what conditions the treatment works the best. Although more is now known about what works, continuing to evaluate community-based programs and other offender treatment efforts is important (Latessa and Holsinger 1998; Locke 1998).

When evaluating the effectiveness of a program, it would be ideal to compare offenders who are randomly selected to receive the "treatment" (for example, the community corrections program) with matched "control" groups (those on regular probation, in prison, or both). Then the groups can be compared on a number of outcome measures. This ideal situation is hard to come by in reality because sentencing guidelines prevent it and many judges cannot be persuaded to randomly assign offenders to programs.

Furthermore, many offenders are sentenced to multiple types of programs. Thus, it is difficult to isolate one treatment effect from another and to evaluate which program had the intended effect. It is also difficult to assess which of the program elements were responsible for positive or negative effects.

A final difficulty with evaluating the effectiveness of intermediate sanctions, in particular, is determining whether the sanction has participants that were diverted from probation (a front-end strategy) or prison (a back-end strategy). In other words, suppose that the only two sentencing choices were probation or prison (control group). The intermediate sanction (the program to be measured) that targets criminals who would have gone to prison anyway but are being given one last chance is getting more serious offenders than if the intermediate sanction recruited offenders who were not prison bound. Intermediate sanctions would be an increased penalty for offenders who would have been sentenced to probation had that intermediate sanction not existed. This is called **net widening** or "widening the net," and it usually results in a cost increase instead of a cost savings. Tonry (1997) demonstrates how this works with the following example:

> [With] evaluations of community service, intensive supervision, and boot camps comes the consistent finding that offenders given intermediate sanctions have similar recidivism rates for new crimes as comparable offenders receiving other sentences. [These] findings may be interpreted as good or bad—good if the offenders involved have been diverted from prison and the new crimes are not very serious [and not so good for offenders recruited from standard probation]. Sentences to prison are much more expensive than [most intermediate sanctions] and if they are no less effective at reducing subsequent criminality, they can provide nearly comparable public safety at greatly reduced cost. (p. 6)

However, most intermediate sanctions programs cost more than traditional probation, so all evaluation results must be interpreted with the following question in mind.

How Is Effectiveness Measured?

The most commonly used measure of program or treatment effectiveness is the rate of **recidivism.** Recidivism is defined as the repetition of or return to criminal behavior, measured in one of three ways: rearrest, reconviction, or reincarceration (Latessa and Holsinger 1998). Determining success or failure is difficult because recidivism is defined differently by different researchers, and no universally accepted means by which to measure it exists:

> Different studies have identified it variously as a new arrest, a new conviction, or a new sentence of imprisonment, depending on the kinds of data they had available or their project goals. As a result it is exceedingly difficult and complex to make comparisons about their results. (Petersilia et al. 1985, p. 20)

NET WIDENING

Using an intermediate sanction as a stiffer punishment for offenders who would have ordinarily been sentenced to probation or other lesser sanctions.

RECIDIVISM

The repetition of or return to criminal behavior, variously defined in one of three ways: rearrest, reconviction, or reincarceration.

Thus, the effectiveness of probation, parole, and other community-based corrections programs depends on the following factors:

- How recidivism is defined
- Whether recidivism is measured only during periods of supervision
- Whether recidivism rates are compared with rates of offenders of similar age and criminal history or simply reported with no comparison group
- Whether group assignment is random or quasi-experimental
- If offenders in the treatment group would have received probation (a lesser sanction) or prison (an increased sanction)

Strict reliance on arrests, convictions, or reimprisonment may not provide a valid measure of success or failure.

Other Outcome Measures for Evaluation

Recidivism as the primary or only measure of success has caused concern among criminal justice professionals, who suggest that one should look at other factors, including the contributions of those on probation to the overall crime problem. Petersilia (2003) found that of all people arrested and charged with felonies, 17 percent of them were on probation and 8 percent were on parole supervision at the time of their arrest. This suggests that probationers represent a small percent of those arrested in a community.

Other data such as the amount of restitution collected, the number of offenders employed, the amount of fines and fees collected, the number of community service hours performed, the number of probationers enrolled in school, and the number of drug-free days are all variables to be considered along with recidivism. Effectiveness could also be measured based on the impact that community corrections programs have in reducing the institutional crowding problem or on the total cost savings they incur. Community corrections has been encouraged to develop evidence-based practices that incorporate sound diagnostic and classification testing of risks and needs, as well as cognitive-behavioral treatment paired with community supervision techniques, all of which we discuss later in the text.

TOP THINGS YOU SHOULD KNOW

- Community corrections can provide many options for individuals who have committed a crime but do not pose a serious threat to community safety.
- Community-based corrections seeks to sanction offenders through punishment while also attempting to improve individual life circumstances. Reintegration, rehabilitation, and restorative justice are important components in changing offenders' attitudes and behaviors, leading to the prevention of future criminal behavior.
- Community corrections also serves to ease institutional crowding in jails and prisons by drawing from the population of convicted offenders those who are predicted to be less risky to the outside community.
- The public demands correctional programs that satisfy both punishment and public safety objectives. Although we recognize that prisons and jails are expensive to build and maintain, we often forget the human cost of incarceration in terms of the loss of human potential and stable families.
- Providing a range of community-based sanctions allows the rewarding of positive behavior by increasing freedom or the sanctioning of negative behavior by increasing the sanction.

DISCUSSION QUESTIONS

1 What is the purpose of corrections?

2 What factors have contributed to correctional growth?

3 How does community corrections fit the general correctional goals?

4 Why does public opinion poll research indicate a "punitive public," which is different from social science research that found a public that would tolerate community corrections?

5 What does a "continuum of sanctions" mean in the sentencing process? If you were a judge, how would you apply this continuum?

6 How is effectiveness of community corrections measured? What other outcome measures could be used?

 ## WEBSITES

National Center on Institutions and Alternatives
A nonprofit policy and research organization founded in 1977 that provides information on a wide range of community-based alternative initiatives

http://www.ncianet.org/

RAND Bibliography of various areas in community corrections

http://www.rand.org/psj/cjc.index.html

Community-Based Corrections: Detailed Service Overview

http://www.co.clark.wa.us/corrections/index.html

U.S. Department of Justice, Bureau of Justice Corrections Statistics

http://www.ojp.usdoj.gov/bjs/correct.htm

The Official Home of Corrections

http://www.corrections.com

Fortune Society
Nonprofit community-based organization dedicated to educating the public about criminal justice issues and the causes of crime

http://www.fortunesociety.org/

2

Pretrial Release and Diversion

Introduction

Pretrial Services
The Pretrial Release Decision
Pretrial Supervision
Failure to Appear (FTA)

Diversion
Candidates for Diversion
Drug Courts
Assumptions of Drug Courts
Gender and Drug Court Treatment
Strategies
Evaluating Drug Courts
Mental Health Courts
Criticisms of Diversion Programs

Top Things You Should Know

© James L. Schaffer/PhotoEdit

KEY TERMS

Pretrial release

Delegated release authority

Pretrial supervision

Failure to appear

Diversion

Drug courts

Completion rates

Retention rates

Mental health courts

What You Will Learn in This Chapter

- *The difference between pretrial release and diversion*
- *The factors involved in the decision to release from detention*
- *The challenges that pretrial programs face in offenders appearing for their next court date*
- *Drug courts and mental health courts as a form of diversion*

INTRODUCTION

When a felony offender is arrested by police, he or she is typically booked into a local jail. Within a 24-hour period (maximum of 72 hours if the arrest takes place on a weekend), defendants are interviewed by a pretrial officer to assist the court in making decisions about the bond or the way the defendant will be released from jail, if at all. Most people who are accused of a crime do not need to be held in jail while waiting for their next court date, and holding them there is expensive and inefficient. Although some defendants are detained in jail, most people are released on some kind of bond, which is a general term for a method of release from detention.

This chapter discusses the release and community supervision of individuals who have been *accused* of a crime but not convicted. We begin first with pretrial services.

PRETRIAL SERVICES

Pretrial services is a department that has two overlapping functions. First, it assists the court in deciding who to release and who to detain (the release decision). Second, pretrial services attempts to improve the efficiency of the courts through helping to supervise released defendants so they appear at their next court date (pretrial supervision). Ultimately, the pretrial defendant's case will likely result in one of four options: dismissal, diversion, a conviction as a result of a plea agreement, or the defendant requesting to go to trial.

We discuss the two pretrial services functions separately.

The Pretrial Release Decision

PRETRIAL RELEASE

A defendant's release in the community following arrest as an alternative to detention while the defendant prepares for the next scheduled court appearance.

Pretrial release is defined as the defendant's release from jail while awaiting his next court appearance. The pretrial release decision is one of the first decisions judges make following an arrest so that defendants who qualify can be effectively released, whereas other defendants are released pending supervision in the community prior to their next court date. Pretrial release allows defendants who have not yet been convicted the opportunity to live and work as productive citizens until their next scheduled court date.

HISTORY OF PRETRIAL RELEASE. The first pretrial release program began in 1960 as the Manhattan Bail Project to assist judges in identifying defendants who could be released on their own recognizance (ROR) before their next scheduled court date. Pretrial programs became so successful that within two decades more than 200 cities had developed pretrial programs. The Federal Bail Reform Act of 1984 included the safety of the public as an important criterion in the decision to release a pretrial defendant, but at the same time this act made certain that releases are considered on a case-by-case basis (Wolf 1997).

Bail bond offices help provide the means of release for many pretrial detainees who do not have the money to pay the court-ordered bail amount.

Only three nationwide studies on pretrial release programs have been conducted since their inception in 1960. The most recent one comprehensively reviewed more than 200 programs in terms of services offered, how they were administered and budgeted, staff training issues, and how each program measured up against national standards set by the American Bar Association and the National Association of Pretrial Services (Clark and Henry 2003). The researchers found that most programs were funded by the county level of government, and increasingly there were significantly more pretrial release programs managed by probation (34 percent) than administered by jails (27 percent) or the courts (24 percent). Newer pretrial release programs tend to be smaller in size, with an average staff size of 18. Only 2 percent of pretrial programs in the sample had a staff with more than 200 people, and 10 percent of pretrial programs (usually in rural areas) had a staff size of one person.

THE LEAST RESTRICTIVE OPTION.   The pretrial release decision at the state level typically consists of a quantitative point system (using factors of risk and need similar to one we present later in Chapter 6), whereas the federal system relies more on professionally guided subjective assessment. In both cases, pretrial services recommends the least restrictive option available to the court, taking into consideration the safety of the community and the defendant's likelihood of reappearance in court. This requires judges to consider all possible alternatives and detain only if none are appropriate. In this way, jails won't likely become overcrowded, defendants can better prepare for their defense, and defendants can also return to work or school while their case is pending. However, not every defendant placed on pretrial release is supervised by a pretrial program. Defendants on supervised pretrial release in the federal system may remain in this condition for one to two years (Wolf 1997). One federal district in Maryland reportedly detained about 35 percent of defendants and released the remaining 65 percent on pretrial supervision (Quinn 2002).

When recommending the least restrictive measure and possible release of a suspect from custody, pretrial services officers examine the chances of the defendant appearing for his or her next court date and whether the defendant poses a danger to the community or to him- or herself (Newville 2001). The pretrial officers collect information on the defendant's character, mental condition, local address, time spent in the area, employment, prior convictions, prior incidents of failure to appear for court, and financial resources, as well as comments from the arresting officer and victims. The defendant is not required to answer any questions about the pending crime, nor does the pretrial services officer consider the weight of the evidence against the defendant (Wolf 1997).

To ascertain whether the defendant should be released, the National Association of Pretrial Services recommends that all defendants be interviewed by a pretrial services officer before the initial court appearance. In practice, not every individual supervised by pretrial services obtains a bond interview before program placement. In one Illinois county, for example, just over half of defendants on pretrial supervision were evaluated by a bond officer (Cooprider, Gray, and Dunne 2003). One-fourth of all programs nationwide waited to conduct the bond interview until after the first court appearance (Clark and Henry 2003). Programs that interviewed the defendant before the initial court appearance and that used objective risk assessment instruments in their release decision were less likely to have an overcrowded jail than programs that subjectively assessed defendants and interviewed them following the first court appearance. Most pretrial services officers made a release/detain recommendation to the court (88 percent), but 21 percent of these programs had **delegated release authority,** which allowed the pretrial services officer to release the defendant before the initial court appearance (Clark and Henry 2003).

**DELEGATED RELEASE
AUTHORITY**

Statutory authority that allows pretrial services officers to release the defendant before the initial court appearance in front of the judge.

TYPES OF BONDS.   The judge ultimately both makes the release (in/out) decision and sets the type of bond or bail. Table 2.1 identifies and defines the various types of bonds. Four types of bonds require cash or property assets, and three are based on other assurances. The percentages in Table 2.1 provide the breakdown of bond type for released defendants and do not include defendants who were denied bail or who could not afford their set bail amount. Bail amounts are set according to the severity of the offense, and about 6 percent of felony defendants are detained without the opportunity to make bail.

Figure 2.1 shows that bail amounts for felony offenders vary from under $5,000 to well above $50,000. Considering the overall socioeconomic status of

FIGURE 2.1   *Bail Amounts Set for Felony Defendants*

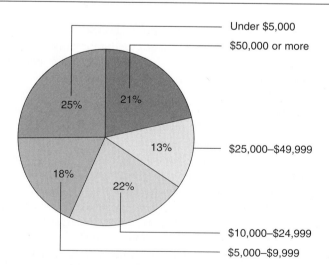

Source: Thomas H. Cohen and Brian A. Reaves. 2006. *Felony Defendants in Large Urban Counties, 2002.* Washington, DC: U.S. Department of Justice, p. 18.

Percentages may not add up to 100% because of rounding.

TABLE 2.1 *Types of Federal Pretrial Releases from Jail*

Release Type	Percent of Released Defendants*	Definition
Unsecured bond	5%	Defendant pays no money to the court but is liable for the full bail amount if fails to appear (FTA).
Release on recognizance	23%	Defendant signs an agreement to appear; no money is paid or owed to the court for FTA.
Conditional release	19%	Defendant is under pretrial supervision but pays no money to the court.
Surety bond	41%	Use of a bail bond company where the bail company is liable if the defendant FTA; bail company charges a 10–15% fee for taking the risk.
Deposit bond	10%	Defendant deposits 10–15% of bail amount with court; court charges a fee for this service; defendant is liable for entire amount if FTA.
Full cash bond	2%	Defendant posts the full bail amount in cash with the court; money is returned after all court dates; bond is forfeited for FTA.
Property/collateral bond	1%	Defendant posts property valued at full bail amount; property is forfeited if defendant FTA.

* Percentages may not add up to 100% because of rounding; the percentages include released defendants only and do not include defendants who were denied bail or who could not afford their set bail amount.

Source: Thomas H. Cohen and Brian A. Reaves. 2006. *Felony Defendants in Large Urban Counties, 2002.* Washington, DC: U.S. Department of Justice, p. 38.

most defendants and their families, a significant proportion of defendants remains in detention if they cannot meet the financial conditions of their bail amount. Following the bail decision, nearly half (45.7 percent) of all federal defendants were released; 54.3 percent of defendants were detained for part or all of the time prior to case disposition (Clark and Henry 2003). In the 75 largest counties, 62 percent of state defendants were released and 38 percent were detained until case disposition (Cohen and Reaves 2006).

CHARACTERISTICS OF PRETRIAL RELEASEES.   Pretrial release decisions are based on whether the defendant is a potential danger to the public and the likelihood that the defendant will appear for his or her next court date. Individuals more likely to be released pretrial tended to have no prior convictions or had only one misdemeanor conviction, were employed at arrest, had some college education, were more than 40 years of age, or were female (Cohen and Reaves 2006). In addition, assessments were made to measure whether juveniles charged as adults should be released from custody. In Clark and Henry's (2003) study, clients with mental illnesses were considered for pretrial release because they could obtain the necessary services in the community more often than in a jail environment.

Pretrial Supervision

Once a decision has been made to release a defendant, a certain percent of defendants are supervised on what is known as **pretrial supervision.** Most felons in the federal system and some state felons have some form of pretrial supervision. In the state system, the number of those evaluated for pretrial supervision is significantly less than those who receive it. For example, for every 10 defendants evaluated, only two are recommended for supervision. This is primarily because many clients on pretrial supervision are directly referred by judges without an evaluation. Direct referrals are primarily misdemeanor and traffic defendants, 60 percent of whom are accused of DUI and misdemeanor domestic battery (Cooprider, Gray, and Dunne 2003).

One-third were mandated to attend substance abuse treatment, and 7.6 percent mental health treatment. Less than 10 percent of all pretrial detainees were also on some form of electronic monitoring or home detention. Clients on pretrial supervision were required to call in weekly until their scheduled court date, comply with curfew, submit to drug testing, maintain employment, and avoid contact with victims and any complaining witnesses. In the federal system, pretrial officers supervised a caseload of 35 defendants and assisted the probation officer in preparing presentence reports on clients who are ultimately convicted—a topic we will discuss in Chapter 3 (Quinn 2002).

When a defendant is not in compliance with the pretrial supervision conditions set by the court (for example, the client has not called or has not attended treatment programs), 89 percent of programs will give the defendant a warning the first time. Eight-six percent of programs will report the second act of noncompliance to the court with a recommendation for specific action. Officers may recommend to the court either that either no action be taken or that more restrictive action be taken, such as increasing telephone contact with the defendant (Clark and Henry 2003). More serious acts of noncompliance, such as absconding or a rearrest, may result in the court's issuance of a bench warrant, the detention of a suspect, or bail revocation. Defendants who were on bond for murder, burglary, or motor vehicle theft were more likely than other types of felony offenders to commit new felony crimes while on pretrial release, but were more likely to appear for court dates (Cohen and Reaves 2006).

Failure to Appear

The whole purpose of pretrial supervision is to ensure the defendant appears for court and the public is safe while the defendant is out on bond. Defendants who **failed to appear** (FTA) did not attend their scheduled court date. Clark and Henry (2003) found that the number of jurisdictions nationwide that issue warrants and conduct other forms of follow-up for failure to appear has actually decreased in recent years. Still, local jurisdictions reported that one out of every four defendants was unsuccessfully terminated from pretrial supervision, mostly for repeated nonappearance (Cooprider, Gray, and Dunne 2003). Most pretrial programs (52 percent) called the defendant to follow up, 25 percent sent a letter, and 12 percent conducted a home visit (see Table 2.2). A surprisingly high number of programs (21 percent) provided no follow-up whatsoever after an FTA. An additional problem is the fact that almost half of all pretrial programs do not even calculate FTA rates, and most (71 percent) do not figure the pretrial rearrest rates for their jurisdiction.

REDUCING FAILURE TO APPEAR RATES.   Clark and Henry (2003) found that 87 percent of pretrial programs reminded defendants of their upcoming court date, but that may not be enough to reduce the high FTA rates. Goldkamp and White (1998) conducted an experiment in Philadelphia that included random assignment to one of four

TABLE 2.2 *Failure-to-Appear (FTA) Followup by Pretrial Programs*

FTA Follow-Up Action	PERCENTAGE OF PRETRIAL PROGRAMS		
	2001 (*N* = 191)	1989 (*N* = 155)	1979 (*N* = 117)
Send letter to defendant urging return	25	43	55
Call defendant urging return	52	64	80
Make home visit to defendant urging return	12	17	45
Have arrest authority with FTA warrant	19	13	14
Assist police in locating defendant	35	52	57
Attempt to locate defendant who left jurisdiction	24	33	32
Seek to have warrant quashed when defendant returns	20	22	N/A
Place defendant's case back on court calendar	19	27	N/A
No FTA follow-up action taken	21	N/A	14

Source: John Clark and D. Alan Henry. 2003. *Pretrial Services Programming at the Start of the 21st Century: A Survey of Pretrial Services Programs.* Washington, DC: Bureau of Justice Assistance.

experimental groups. The researchers measured the degree to which various pretrial notification and deterrence services made a difference in the rate of participation in orientation sessions, failure to appear rates, and rearrest rates of pretrial releasees. The treatment or experimental groups were compared with a baseline group that received none of these services.

- Group 1 received an orientation session and was required to call in once per week.
- Group 2 received the same services as Group 1, plus they received a personal phone call to remind them the night before the court date.
- Group 3 received the same services as Group 1, except that this higher risk group had to make phone contact twice per week and had to meet in person three days before the court date.
- Group 4 (also a higher risk group) received the same services as Groups 1 and 3, except that a warrant officer visited the residence for any noncompliance during the pretrial period.

Groups 1 and 2 showed no significant differences; phone contact the night before the court date had no significant effect on FTA and rearrest rates, largely because few defendants could actually be reached by phone (not home, wrong numbers, answering machine, and so forth). The small number of defendants who were successfully contacted had high rates of attendance/compliance (Goldkamp and White 1998).

No significant differences were found for Groups 3 and 4, showing that the threat of a warrant officer had no significant deterrent impact on FTA and rearrest rates. Issuing a warrant or threat letter did not seem to increase compliance. When all four experimental groups were compared simultaneously with the baseline group that received none of the pretrial services, there were no significant differences on rate of orientation session attendance (56 percent experimental and 51 percent baseline), failure to appear (18 percent experimental and 19 percent baseline), fugitive status

(20 percent experimental and 21 percent baseline), and rearrest rates (6 percent experimental and 8 percent baseline). This experiment raised serious questions about the impact of notification and deterrence, since the "do nothing" approach was no better or worse than any service provided by a pretrial program (Goldkamp and White 1998).

Pretrial program officers prepare and submit reports to the court at the time of the plea and/or sentencing to detail the defendant's compliance during the period on prerelease supervision. If the defendant is not formally on pretrial supervision but has been granted release, lack of rearrest for a new crime is considered to be in compliance with the prerelease conditions.

DIVERSION

Following the pretrial release decision, and with the assistance of counsel, the defendant enters a plea of guilty or not guilty and may qualify for a diversion program. **Diversion** is an alternative to traditional criminal sentencing or juvenile justice adjudication that gives first-time offenders a chance or addresses the unique needs of the offender. The successful completion of diversion results in the dismissal of the current charges. For this reason, many jurisdictions consider diversion a type of pretrial program (Ulrich 2002).

The idea of diversion began in the mid-1960s with programs such as Treatment Alternatives to Street Crime (TASC) for drug abusers and the Manhattan Court Employment project for vocationally disadvantaged offenders. Diversion attempts to keep offenders from the negative effects of incarceration, while at the same time providing rehabilitation programs in the community that address challenges the offender may face. For juveniles, diversion serves to eliminate the stigmatization effect of the criminal process; labeling theory posits that processing youths further into the system may contribute to future delinquency (Shelden 1999). Box 2.1 discusses how risk assessment instruments have been developed to predict candidates for diversion.

Candidates for Diversion

Diversion programs attempt to provide services for three types of individuals. First, diversion helps youthful offenders in an attempt to avoid the criminal label or deviant stigma that results from having a conviction. Diversion can help first-time adult offenders who do not pose a risk to public safety and who, upon completion of the program, are unlikely to return to criminal behavior. Women are generally good candidates for diversion because they pose a low risk to public safety, commit primarily nonviolent offenses, and are more responsive than men to completing and abiding by the conditions of probation (Acoca and Austin 1996). In the federal system, white-collar criminals such as those accused of fraud, larceny theft, and embezzlement are eligible for pretrial diversion. Offenders who are ineligible include those with two or more prior felony convictions, addicts, public officials, or those accused of a crime violating national security (Ulrich 2002)

A second candidate for diversion is a person with special needs such as a mental illness that is related to the individual's criminal behavior. We address the issue of mental health courts later in the chapter. A third candidate for diversion is a person who requires treatment for a problem, such as drug or alcohol abuse, that is also related to his or her reason for arrest. These types of programs are called drug courts, and we now turn our attention to describing the drug court approach.

BOX 2.1   COMMUNITY CORRECTIONS UP CLOSE   •

CAN RISK ASSESSMENT INSTRUMENTS DETERMINE DIVERSION ELIGIBILITY?

Objective risk assessment instruments are able to identify nonviolent property and drug offenders who may qualify for diversion programs. Using history of prior juvenile contact with authorities, adult criminal history, current offense, and offender characteristics, one instrument in Virginia was designed to complement the state's sentencing guidelines. The instrument was tested in six pilot sites and saved $1.2 million in these sites during the study, with an estimated net savings of between $2.9 million and $3.6 million annually (Ostrom el al. 2002).

When examining diverted youths with higher risk scores against a comparison group, Shelden (1999) cautioned that risk scores may not always accurately predict recidivism. In other words, youths with the higher risk scores actually had lower recidivism rates than a comparison group. More long-term studies need to follow diverted and nondiverted youths into adulthood.

Drug Courts

Drug courts are a common way to use a suspended sentence for people with a substance abuse problem, but who have not yet been convicted (see Figure 2.2). The drug court concept integrates outpatient substance abuse treatment with criminal justice case processing. Upon successful completion of the drug court program, charges are dismissed. If offenders withdraw or are terminated from the program without successfully completing it, they are charged and tried for the original offense, and sentenced accordingly. Figure 2.2 also shows that drug courts are used as a "postadjudication proceeding," which means that following a plea of guilty, the sentence is deferred. Provided individuals remain crime free for a certain amount of time, they can get their offense reduced or dismissed by the court. There are approximately 1,600 drug courts operating, with another 400 in the planning stages (Galloway and Drapela 2006).

DRUG COURTS

A diversion program for drug addicts in which the judge, prosecutor, and probation officer play a proactive role and monitor the progress of clients through weekly visits to the courtroom, using a process of graduated sanctions.

Assumptions of Drug Courts

The idea of drug courts began in 1989 in Dade County, Florida, under the assumption that punishing first-time drug offenders or low-level drug users with a criminal record would be less likely to curb future drug use than treatment interventions. A second assumption is that the sooner the treatment intervention begins after arrest, the better (Brown 1997). This reduces the number of days spent in jail without treatment and in a negative environment where drug use continues.

Another assumption of drug courts is that the courts, including the judge, the prosecutor, and the probation officer, play a proactive and nonadversarial role. A nonadversarial role allows more informal and direct interaction between the client and the judge to occur. It allows the team to work for the client and not in a game to see "who wins." Judges monitor the progress of clients through weekly visits (or status hearings) to the courtroom and use a process of graduated sanctions as

FIGURE 2.2 *Flowchart of Two Drug Court Approaches*

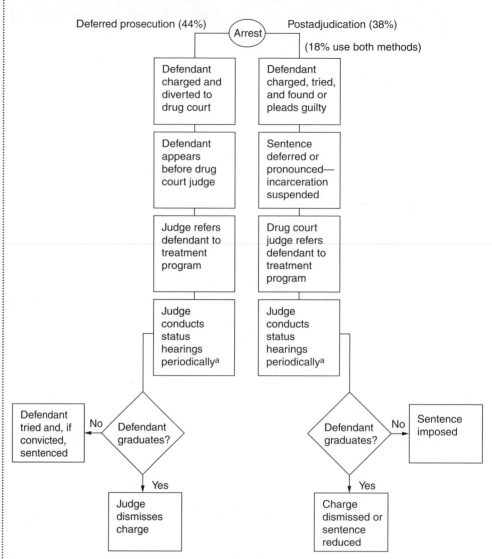

a Judges may reward progress and impose sanctions for noncompliance with program requirements.

Source: Daniel C. Harris et al. 1997. *Drug Courts: Overview of Growth, Characteristics, and Results* [GAO-GGD-97-106]. Washington, DC: United States General Accounting Office, p. 92.

behavior improves or worsens. For example, if a client relapses, she may have to repeat certain segments of the program. Repeated relapses may mean short-term incarceration. Thus, judges intervene before the pattern of technical violations occurs as in regular probation, and the court collaborates with the drug treatment specialists. A final assumption about drug courts is that with any addiction, relapse is to be expected, but participants are also expected to prevent relapse from becoming a pattern.

A drug court participant accepts her graduation certificate from a judge.

Drug courts are specifically for nonviolent drug offenders with at least "moderate substance usage." The offenders may be misdemeanants or felons, and they must voluntarily agree to participate. An initial substance abuse assessment determines eligibility for program participation (Listwan et al. 2003). This assessment examines history of drug use and/or results of drug screening. A system of levels varies the intensity of the program balanced against freedoms and privileges. Treatment is one year in length and typically begins with an intensive two weeks of inpatient treatment. Treatment involves detoxification through acupuncture, drug testing through urine screenings, and group and individual counseling. Clients are referred to Narcotics Anonymous and Alcoholics Anonymous when in the community (Brown 1997). As the client progresses through the program, the levels gradually taper to day treatment and then to outpatient, which is the most common status. Most clients relapse at least once during their treatment phase, but a pattern of a return to drug use is not acceptable and results in program failure. Drug court completion rates for those who successfully finish the one-year program vary from 29 percent to 43 percent (Taxman and Bouffard 2003).

Gender and Drug Court Treatment Strategies

One of the issues in drug court research is that drug courts might not effectively address populations such as women or minorities because of the failure to address gender and cultural differences. Women accounted for one-fourth of all drug treatment participants, so they are no longer a population to be ignored. Part of effective treatment is uncovering potential causes and patterns of use so that these may be overcome.

Women and men have different reasons for abusing drugs, different drugs of choice, and different drug use patterns. Women are more likely to be primary caretakers of dependent children, have lower education levels, and be impoverished, all of which may affect their ability to complete treatment programs. Research shows that women use drugs to cope with traumatic situations such as domestic violence, mental illness, sexual abuse, and physical abuse. In this manner, women are likely to self-medicate alone and need to be drawn out of the despair they feel. Women also use to maintain a relationship with a significant other who also uses (Dannerbeck, Sundet, and Lloyd 2002).

Men who participate in drug court tend to abuse alcohol or marijuana. Men use in a more social and public context that involves establishing or maintaining a reputation, or gaining (a false sense of) control. Men have better completion rates, perhaps because drug courts were modeled to better address their needs, patterns, and reasons that they drink (Dannerbeck, Sundet, and Lloyd 2002).

Although drug courts address other problems in conjunction with substance abuse treatment, such as housing, employment, food, transportation/bus passes, and health screenings, gender-specific and cultural issues need to be addressed. States such as Michigan, California, and New York have developed separate drug court programs for men and women. Programs for women can be directed more specifically at reasons why women use in the context of trauma and significant relationships. Furthermore, the programs may be able to spend more time on parenting, abuse, and domestic violence. This allows women to establish closer relationships with other drug court participants and the judge, and should increase completion rates. Another benefit of a single-sex environment is that women (and men) are less distracted by the opposite sex and thus take the program more seriously (D'Angelo 2002).

Federal grant money to fund drug courts was initially approved under the Violent Crime Control and Law Enforcement Act of 1994 to expand the use of drug courts. Between 1989 and 1997, over $200 million dollars were used to open, operate, and evaluate drug courts (General Accounting Office 1997). Since 1997, increased funding has been available for drug courts, to the tune of $45 million to $64 million each year. Presently, there are about 1,200 drug courts in operation across the United States (von Zielbauer 2003).

Evaluating Drug Courts

Drug courts reportedly saved money over traditional court processing in Multnomah County, Oregon, when the costs for arrest, booking, court time, treatment, jail time, and probation were summed for 120 people, some of whom went through drug court and some of whom did not. When the 120 people were tracked to determine recidivism, the drug court participants were less likely to be rearrested than those in the control group. The cost of obtaining drug court treatment was $5,928 per year per offender, whereas it cost $7,369 for traditional processing of one drug offender for one year (Carey and Figgin 2004). Other researchers disagree that drug courts save money. Although drug court clients did indeed spend less time behind bars prior to court disposition, they spent twice as long in jail for noncompliance of drug court sanctions than a randomized control group who were eligible but did not go through drug court (Gottfredson, Najaka, and Kearley 2003).

Related to the concern of overuse of incarceration for noncompliance, a General Accounting Office (GAO) study found that completion and retention rates varied by program, and they were lower than expected. **Completion rates** represent individuals who are favorably discharged as a percentage of the total number admitted and not still enrolled. According to Figure 2.3, only 31.2 percent of those enrolled had graduated, whereas 30.2 percent were still actively enrolled. Nearly 21 percent had been terminated for violations, and an additional 3.5 percent voluntarily withdrew.

FIGURE 2.3 *Status of Drug Court Program Participants*

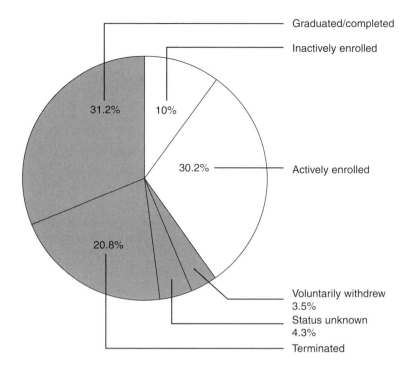

Source: Daniel C. Harris et al. 1997. *Drug Courts: Overview of Growth, Characteristics, and Results* [GAO-GGD-97-106]. Washington, DC: United States General Accounting Office, p. 55.

Retention rates are a combined total of the successful completers and those actively enrolled compared to the total number admitted (GAO 1997, p. 50). Later retention rates have remained between 40 to 60 percent. It is a disappointment that half of those who are eligible cannot or do not wish to complete the full phase of treatment (Fischer 2003).

Although relapse may be expected, rearrests for new crimes are not tolerated while in the program. According to Taxman and Bouffard (2003), 42 percent of unsuccessful terminations in one program were due to a new offense, compared to a 14 percent rearrest rate for participants who successfully completed the drug court program. Program graduates were also compared one year later with program failures. Recidivism (measured through rearrest) was 9 percent for graduates, compared to 41 percent for noncompleters. This method of comparing groups is improper and leads to self-selection bias, given that treatable drug offenders are being compared with those who were noncompliant (Fischer 2003).

The best method would be random assignment to drug court and to regular supervision (either probation or prison). Sites where this has been done found that drug courts had a positive effect on reducing recidivism. The control group was rearrested at nearly three times the rate of the drug court participants (Gottfredson and Exum 2002), and the difference between the two groups remained apparent two years later (Gottfredson, Najaka, and Kearley 2003).

A study of six jurisdictions compared drug court graduates with drug offenders who went to prison without treatment to determine rearrest rate over a three-year period. Although the groups were not randomly assigned, this quasi-experimental

RETENTION RATES

The combined total of the successful completers and those actively enrolled compared to the total number admitted to drug court.

group is a more valid comparison. Drug court graduates had a rearrest rate that was significantly lower than a comparison group in multiple studies (Galloway and Drapela 2006; von Zielbauer 2003).

A nationwide study of 95 drug courts (a total of 2,020 participants in one year) over a two-year period revealed an average rearrest rate (where a charge was filed) of 16 percent after the first 12 months following graduation, and 27 percent after 24 months (Roman, Townsend, and Bhati 2003). Recidivism rates varied widely among the different programs, making comparison across programs difficult. Programs serving felony offenders and offenders who had a more severe drug problem had higher recidivism rates than programs that treated only misdemeanor clients. Access to other community services, program size, police practices, prosecutor decisions, program duration, and violation policies affected the recidivism rate as well. Researchers caution against the use of recidivism as the sole determiner of program success, and also against making too many program comparisons across programs that should not be compared. Two consistent conclusions were drawn when comparing program participants. First, women had lower recidivism (rearrest) rates than men. Also, Caucasian individuals had lower recidivism rates than minority drug court participants (Roman, Townsend, and Bhati 2003). These findings may be due to drug court participant behavior, the justice system response, or a combination of both factors. The drug court model may not be applicable to all substance abusers within the offender population, and researchers encourage flexibility and different treatment strategies within the general drug court framework (Listwan et al. 2003).

Mental Health Courts

People who have mental illnesses may not always follow societal expectations or rules, and may appear more deviant than criminal. An indigent person who is mentally ill but poses no danger to public safety may benefit more from mental health and social services than from the criminal justice system (Ulrich 2002). However, some mental health providers fear not getting reimbursed for a client who does not have health insurance. Thus, indigent people are turned away and come to police attention (Slate et al. 2003). Some mentally ill individuals commit crimes and must be supervised. The vast majority of mentally ill individuals are best served in the community rather than in jails or prisons. While incarcerated, mentally ill people are more likely than others to commit suicide, harm themselves, or be victimized by other inmates. Mental health courts began in 1997 as a more favorable option for people who need to be helped more than they need to be punished.

MENTAL HEALTH COURTS

A diversion program for mentally ill defendants in which the judge, prosecutor, and probation officer play a proactive role and monitor the progress of clients through weekly visits to the courtroom.

Like the drug courts, **mental health courts** use a team approach, made up of a judge, a treatment provider, and a pretrial services officer with specialized training in mental health (Slate 2003). Diagnostic tools are put in place to ensure that defendants are receiving treatment on a voluntary (rather than coercive) basis. There are approximately 30 mental health courts nationwide, with their success contingent upon the availability of community services for homelessness, lack of family and community support, and medication stability (Ruddell, Roy, and Diehl 2004).

Many mental health courts use specially trained probation officers who have what are called "specialized caseloads," which are smaller caseloads that use a more unique case management style specific to the needs and challenges that people with mental illnesses face. We discuss specific strategies and types of specialized caseloads in more detail in Chapter 6. So far, one evaluation of a mental health court found that about 85 percent of mental health court clients complete the required conditions, and a site in Tennessee boasted only a 6 percent recidivism rate (Slate 2003).

Criticisms of Diversion Programs

One criticism of diversion programs overall, whether they are youth programs, drug courts, or mental health courts, is that it is unclear what to do if a participant fails to complete the necessary requirements of a diversion program. Some diversion programs use the threat of a criminal record if a participant does not successfully complete the diversion program. In theory, this defeats the purpose of diversion—to keep the offender out of the system—and it is possible that other programs may gain control over individuals who otherwise would not have been in the system in the first place, a situation known as net widening.

A second critique of diversion programs is that evidence that may have been inadmissible in court, which would have led to a dismissal of the case, instead results in a diversion proceeding—yet another example of net widening. In summary, average citizens may not support diversion programs because they are unfamiliar with the positive effects of many of these programs.

TOP THINGS YOU SHOULD KNOW

- Pretrial services consists of the pretrial release decision from jail and pretrial supervision of defendants as a condition of their release.
- Pretrial release can consist of either a quantitative point system (as in state and local cases) or professional subjective assessment (for the federal system) to determine risk of flight.
- The purpose of pretrial supervision is to ensure that the defendant appears for court and the public is safe while the defendant is out on bond.
- Diversion focuses on offenders who voluntarily agree to enter a contractual agreement with the courts, jail, or probation office whereby the offender is supervised in the community.
- Upon completion of the period of diversion supervision, the offender will not have a formal record of conviction. If the offender on diversion supervision does not comply with the conditions, a formal execution of the sentence ensues.
- Drug court is a type of diversion program that integrates substance abuse treatment in a coordinated and ongoing interactive team approach of judges, prosecutors, and probation officers.
- Mental health courts are organizationally structured similar to drug courts, except that they deal with offenders who are mentally ill and link with a variety of community service providers.

DISCUSSION QUESTIONS

1 What kinds of individuals do you think are best suited for pretrial release?

2 How would you know which individuals are not good candidates for pretrial release?

3 How does diversion differ from pretrial release?

4 What kinds of individuals are best suited for diversion programs?

5 Are drug courts a good idea for drug abusers?

6 Should mental health courts be expanded for mentally ill people? Why or why not?

7 Are there any other individuals who would benefit from a specialized diversionary-style court?

 **WEBSITES**

Factors Considered in the Diversion Decision
Vancouver, Washington, City Attorney's Office

> *http://www.ci.vancouver.wa.us/cityattorney.asp?*
> *menuid=10462&submenuid=10483&itemID=16898*

American Bar Association: Steps in a Trial

> *http://www.abanet.org/publiced/courts/pretrial_appearances.html*

San Francisco Pretrial Diversion Project, Inc.

> *http://www.sfpretrial.com/community.html*

Minnesota (Clay County) Pretrial Diversion Programs for Juveniles

> *http://www.co.clay.mn.us/Depts/Attorney/PJDivPro.htm*

Louisiana (Baton Rouge) Parish Attorney Pretrial Diversion Division

> *http://brgov.com/dept/parishattorney/pretrial.htm*

Adult Drug Court Programs

> *http://www.judiciary.state.nj.us/criminal/crdrgct.htm*

National Estimates of Recidivism Rates for Drug Court Graduates

> *http://www.ncjrs.org/pdffiles1/201229.pdf*

University of Cincinnati Research Reports: Evaluations of Various Drug Courts

> *http://www2.uc.edu/criminaljustice/ResearchReports.html*

Florida Drug Courts

> *http://www.flcourts.org/gen_public/family/drug_court/index.shtml*

Policy on Mental Health Courts

> *http://www.nmha.org/position/mentalhealthcourts.cfm*

Anchorage, Alaska, Mental Health Court

> *http://www.state.ak.us/courts/mhct.htm*

King County District Court, Mental Health Court

> *http://www.metrokc.gov/kcdc/mhhome.htm*

The Diversion Decision

This chapter discussed factors that affect the decision to grant a diversionary sentence. The following case examples are before the court, and you are tasked with deciding if the case should or should not be diverted. You must justify your decision in writing.

CASE A

Defendant Smith has been arrested for possession of ecstasy—enough for two hits. Smith has no criminal history, and has been employed as a laborer with a construction company for two years, other than during a brief layoff period. He has a good work record with the company. He admits that he uses alcohol and had been drinking and using ecstasy the night of the offense. Smith has used marijuana and cocaine, but indicates all of the usage has been in the past and not recent. Smith lives by himself; he has never been married and has one child from a previous relationship. Smith is two months behind on his child support payments and does not see the child very often. Smith's defense attorney argues that his client has never been in any form of mental health counseling or substance abuse treatment/ counseling, and would agree to go to drug court as a diversionary measure. The state's attorney is opposed to drug court for Defendant Smith because of the type of drug—ecstasy. The police have recently been trying to rid the streets of the supply of ecstasy and believe that Smith may be tied somehow to a major ecstasy drug ring in the area, but they need more time to prove the allegations, which right now, are "shaky" at best.

CASE B

Defendant Thompson has been arrested for a felony crime, "throwing objects from an overpass," which resulted in injury to a passenger of a vehicle. Thompson is a 19-year-old college freshman. He and another college friend had prepared shredded paper in their school colors for the homecoming football game. While walking across an overpass over the interstate highway, he and another student decided to throw some of the shredded paper, which was in black plastic trash bags. They proceeded to cut open a bag and pour the paper down on the vehicles. When they cut into a second bag and poured the contents onto the passing vehicles, they were unaware that a brick had been put into the bag for weight. The brick struck the windshield of a vehicle, causing the windshield to break and chip; a piece of the glass flew into the eye of the victim, causing permanent loss of vision.

Defendant Thompson has a prior misdemeanor for theft when he was 17, for which he received a one-year diversionary sentence, which he completed just six months ago. Thompson is not employed and is a full-time college student. He makes passing grades and has not had any student violations at the university. Thompson denies any illegal drug usage and admitted to drinking in the past, but denies drinking at all since his prior misdemeanor arrest. Thompson's attorney proposes diversion once again to the court; he will continue to attend school, and he will participate in community service by helping the victim and her family at their farm without pay. The state's attorney is adamantly opposed to diversion, as this is Thompson's second arrest in less than two years. Due to the seriousness of the victim's injuries, the state's attorney feels that this offense should become part of the court record. The district attorney feels that diversion would trivialize the victim's injuries and appeals to you not to grant diversion.

3

Sentencing and the Presentence Investigation Report

Introduction
Factors That Affect Granting a
    Community Sentence
Sentencing Guidelines
Sentencing Commissions

**Conditions of Community
Corrections**
Standard Conditions
Special Conditions
Supervision Conditions Must Be
    Constitutional

**The Presentence Investigation
Report**
Purposes of the PSI Report
Contents of the PSI Report
Preparing the PSI Report
The Initial Interview
Investigation and Verification
The Evaluative Summary
The Sentence Recommendation

**Legal Issues Concerning the
Presentence Report**
Disclosure of the PSI Report
Inaccuracies in the PSI Report
Hearsay in the PSI Report
Does the Exclusionary Rule Apply?
Miranda Warnings and the PSI
    Interview
Right to a Lawyer during the PSI
    Interview

Top Things You Should Know

KEY TERMS

Sentencing

Presumptive sentencing grids

Voluntary sentencing guidelines

Sentencing commission

Standard conditions

Special conditions

Clear conditions

Reasonable conditions

Presentence investigation (PSI) report

Postsentence report

Offender-based presentence report

Presentence investigation

Indeterminate sentence

Determinate sentence

Offense-based presentence report

Victim impact statement

Disclosure

Hearsay evidence

Exclusionary rule

SENTENCING

The postconviction stage, in which the defendant is brought before the court for formal judgment pronounced by a judge.

What You Will Learn in This Chapter

- *Legal factors in granting community sentences*
- *The purpose and contents of the presentence investigation report*
- *How the presentence investigation report is prepared by way of an investigation interview, verification, and evaluative summary*
- *Legal issues and criticisms regarding the presentence investigation report*

INTRODUCTION

Sentencing has long been considered the most difficult decision in the criminal justice process. **Sentencing** can be defined as the postconviction stage in which the defendant is brought before the court for formal judgment pronounced by a judge. The judge is influenced by the presentence investigator's report prior to the sentencing hearing, as well as the wishes of the prosecutor and the defense attorney. Sentencing demands choosing from among a number of alternatives and involves an examination of public safety, rehabilitation, deterrence, and retribution.

The philosophy behind community sentences is that an offender can best learn how to live productively in a community by remaining in free society under supervision, as opposed to being transferred to a warehouse-like setting of a jail or prison.

Factors That Affect Granting a Community Sentence

The judge's decision to allow a defendant to serve a community corrections sentence depends on four factors, each of which we discuss briefly:

- Offender's eligibility
- Sentencing conditions fixed by statute
- Availability and quality of community-based services
- Other factors

ELIGIBILITY FOR COMMUNITY CORRECTIONS. A community corrections sentence is discretionary and a privilege, not a right. All eligible defendants must at least be considered for probation or some other intermediate sanction. States sometimes legislate restrictions against the use of probation for crimes of violence or for those defendants with too many prior felony convictions. However, more serious felony offenders are being punished in the community due to plea bargaining and institutional crowding.

CONDITIONS OF PROBATION FIXED BY STATUTE. The ability of the defendant to meet the statutory conditions of probation and other types of intermediate sanctions must be considered in the decision. If the presentence information about the defendant shows that he or she cannot meet the statutory conditions that must be imposed, then services will not be sought and probation conditions not met. For example, if restitution is required by statute, and a defendant is ordered to pay restitution in the amount of $700 per month but has a job that pays minimum wage, the defendant is barely able to meet his or her own bills, let alone be expected to make payments of an additional $700 per month. To avoid confronting the defendant and the court with dilemmas of this sort, many authorities recommend that statutes refrain from describing specific conditions, leaving the matter open for the judge to decide based on the most up-to-date information that can be obtained by competent presentence investigations about the defendant and the available treatment facilities and programs.

AVAILABILITY AND QUALITY OF INTERMEDIATE SANCTIONS AND OTHER COMMUNITY-BASED SERVICES. Granting a sentence in the community also depends on the availability and quality of other sentencing dispositions for that defendant. A range of sentencing alternatives, including drug and alcohol counseling, day reporting centers, electronic monitoring, restitution, community service, home confinement, and intensive supervision programs, is widely utilized. The court may also be influenced by knowledge of institutional crowding or deplorable conditions in the adult prison system or of lack of treatment in youth institutions.

OTHER FACTORS. Wicharaya (1995) found that when determining whether to grant probation, judges consider the social stability of the defendant, defined by family ties, marital status, employment length, and drug abuse history. In addition, judges take into account whether the case was plea bargained or a trial, the political nature of the offense, and how their decision may affect public opinion. Not all offenders can benefit from community-based punishment. Some offenders must be incarcerated for the safety of the public.

Because judges can take so many factors into account, there was fear that individual judges would inconsistently apply their own philosophy, resulting in disparate or even discriminatory sentencing. Many states opted to control judicial discretion through sentencing guidelines, which we discuss next.

Sentencing Guidelines

Among the goals of sentencing guidelines and the determinate sentencing movement are to reduce or eliminate perceived sentencing disparity, increase judicial accountability for sentences, increase punishments for violent offenders, and provide

© MAI/HO /Landov

Mel Gibson pleaded no contest to a misdemeanor drunken-driving charge and was sentenced to three years' probation

a basis for population projections and resource allocation (Lubitz and Ross 2001). About half of all states have adopted some form of sentencing guidelines. Although these guidelines vary greatly from jurisdiction to jurisdiction, they generally establish a sentence based on the severity of the offense and the offender's prior criminal history.

With **presumptive sentencing grids,** judges are obligated to use the guidelines, and they must provide written reasons for any deviation from the guidelines. These departures may also be subject to appellate court review. North Carolina and Pennsylvania have "structured presumptive sentencing zones"; that is, these states have integrated intermediate sanctions directly into both their felony and misdemeanor sentencing guidelines. Violent offenders in these states receive lengthier prison sentences, whereas nonviolent offenders can receive intermediate sanctions or other forms of community-based or even restorative justice sanctions (Lubitz and Ross 2001). North Carolina has three categories of sentences: confinement, residential intermediate sanctions/intensive supervision, and nonresidential community punishments (see Figure 3.1). Judges may impose any combination of sentence categories according to the offense as they see fit but may not exceed the maximum sentence length. Judges do not need to give a reason for their sentencing choice, and there is no appeal available. North Carolina has also abolished parole and good time, so the sentence is the actual time to be served without early release. Research shows that North Carolina has been fairly effective in differentiating the type of offenders sent to prison versus those who serve time in the community (Tonry 1997, 1999b).

Federal sentencing guidelines are an example of a presumptive sentencing mandate that does not provide much judicial discretion or integration of intermediate sanctions. According to the U.S. Sentencing Commission (2002), 64 percent of all federal sentences were within the guideline range, while 35 percent of all cases were a "downward" departure, especially in immigration, antitrust, and bribery cases. In less than 1 percent of all federal cases, judges decided to sentence more than the guidelines recommended, especially in cases of manslaughter (8 percent of manslaughter cases). Even though judges were allowed to depart from the guidelines, only 14 percent of federal offenders received probation without institutional confinement, and another 8 percent had a combination confinement/probation sentence (Tonry 1997). Critics of presumptive sentencing argue that this type of "rule-of-law" sentencing is the outcome of the government's failure to create or sustain conditions of public safety (Smith and Dickey 1999).

VOLUNTARY SENTENCING GUIDELINES.   A small number of states (Arkansas, Delaware, Missouri, and Virginia) have voluntary guidelines that are suggestions that the judge may or may not accept. Because **voluntary sentencing guidelines** have not changed judicial sentencing patterns, many states have replaced voluntary guidelines with presumptive sentencing.

PUNISHMENT UNITS.   Oregon tried a system of converting various types of sentences into a currency called "punishment units." For example, 1 year in prison = 100 units; 1 year probation = 20 units; 25 days community service = 50 units; 30 days of intensive supervision probation = 5 units; and so on. The guidelines specify the number of total punishment units to be imposed for each crime (say, 200 units for felony theft), and the judge merely selects any combination of sanctions that totals the predefined unit number. Although this system was abandoned because it was too complicated, it illustrates a way that sentencing has been conceptualized.

PRESUMPTIVE SENTENCING GRIDS

A narrow range of sentencing guidelines that judges are obligated to use. Any deviations must be provided in writing and may also be subject to appellate court review.

VOLUNTARY SENTENCING GUIDELINES

A narrow range of strategies or suggested determinate sentences based on offense seriousness and prior criminal history that the judge may or may not choose to accept.

FIGURE 3.1 *North Carolina Felony Sentencing Grid (Numbers Represent Months)*

PRIOR RECORD LEVEL

CURRENT FELONY CRIME CLASS		I 0 Pts	II 1–4 Pts	III 5–8 Pts	IV 9–14 Pts	V 15–18 Pts	VI 19+ Points
Class A: Murder		Death or Life Without Parole ONLY					
Class B1:	Sentence Type	Prison	Prison	Prison	Prison	Prison	Prison
Agg Sexual Battery	Aggravating	240–300	288–360	336–420	384–480	Life Without Parole	Life without Parole
Agg Child Molestation	Presumptive	192–240	230–288	269–336	307–384	346–433	384–480
Rape, Agg Sodomy	Mitigating	144–192	173–230	202–269	230–307	260–346	288–384
Class B2:	Sentence Type	Prison	Prison	Prison	Prison	Prison	Prison
Second Deg. Murder	Aggravating	135–169	163–204	193–238	216–270	243–304	270–338
	Presumptive	108–135	130–163	152–190	173–216	194–243	216–270
	Mitigating	81–108	98–130	114–152	130–173	146–194	162–216
Class C:	Sentence Type	Prison	Prison	Prison	Prison	Prison	Prison
Kidnapping	Aggravating	63–79	86–108	100–125	115–144	130–162	145–181
Second Deg. Rape	Presumptive	50–63	69–86	80–100	92–115	104–130	116–145
Agg Assault	Mitigating	38–50	52–69	60–80	69–92	78–104	87–116
Class D:	Sentence Type	Prison	Prison	Prison	Prison	Prison	Prison
Armed Robbery	Aggravating	55–69	66–82	89–111	101–126	115–144	126–158
Burglary	Presumptive	44–55	53–66	71–89	81–101	92–115	101–126
First Deg. Arson	Mitigating	33–44	40–53	53–71	61–81	69–92	76–101
Class E:	Sentence Type	Res CC or Prison	Res CC or Prison	Prison	Prison	Prison	Prison
Child Molestation	Aggravating	25–31	29–36	34–42	46–58	53–66	59–74
Drug Trafficking	Presumptive	20–25	23–29	27–34	37–46	42–53	47–59
Drug Manuf/Selling	Mitigating	15–20	17–23	20–27	28–37	32–42	35–47
Class F:	Sentence Type	Res CC or Prison	Res CC or Prison	Res CC or Prison	Prison	Prison	Prison
Involun. Manslaughter	Aggravating	16–20	19–24	21–26	25–31	34–42	39–49
Att Rape, Incest,	Presumptive	13–16	15–19	17–21	20–25	27–34	31–39
Cocaine 200–400 g	Mitigating	10–13	11–15	13–17	15–20	20–27	23–31
Class G:	Sentence Type	Res CC or Prison	Res CC or Prison	Res CC or Prison	Res CC or Prison	Prison	Prison
Vehicular Homicide	Aggravating	13–16	15–19	16–20	20–25	21–26	29–36
Sec Degree Arson	Presumptive	10–13	12–15	13–16	16–20	17–21	23–29
Robbery	Mitigating	8–10	9–12	10–13	12–16	13–17	17–23
Class H:	Sentence Type	Probation or Res	Res CC	Res CC or Prison	Res CC or Prison	Res CC or Prison	Prison
Forgery, Theft	Aggravating	6–8	8–10	10–12	11–14	15–19	20–25
Sale/Distribution LSD	Presumptive	5–6	6–8	8–10	9–11	12–15	16–20
or Cocaine	Mitigating	4–6	4–6	6–8	7–9	9–12	12–16
Class I:	Sentence Type	Probation	Probation or CC	Res CC	Res CC or Prison	Res CC or Prison	Res CC or Prison
Poss Control. Sub	Aggravating	6–8	6–8	6–8	8–10	9–11	10–12
Bad Checks	Presumptive	4–6	4–6	5–6	6–8	7–9	8–10
Agg Stalking	Mitigating	3–4	3–4	4–5	4–6	5–7	6–8

OFFENSE CLASS

Source: North Carolina Sentencing and Policy Advisory Commission, Structured Sentencing for Felonies—Training and Reference Manual. (Raleigh: North Carolina Sentencing and Policy Advisory Commission, 1994).

Note: For each class of crimes, there is a disposition that directs the judge where the offender is to go (prison, residential community corrections, or probation), and then the judge selects the presumptive row, unless aggravating or mitigating circumstances warrant a deviation.

Sentencing Commissions

SENTENCING COMMISSION

A governing body that monitors the use of the sentencing guidelines and departures from the recommended sentences.

The federal government and about half of all states each have their own **sentencing commission** that monitors the use of the guidelines and judicial departures from the recommended sentences. This is to keep judges accountable for their decisions. Voting members of most commissions number between 7 and 27, and a small number of commissions have both voting and nonvoting members. Commission members are typically appointed and are individuals with experience as prosecutors, defense attorneys, judges, academics, and probation or parole officers. The commission is responsible for evaluating the effect of the sentencing guidelines and making revisions when and where appropriate.

The Minnesota Sentencing Commission rules state that although the sentencing guidelines are advisory to the sentencing judge, departures from their established presumptive sentences should occur only when substantial, compelling circumstances exist. Pennsylvania sentencing guidelines stipulate that the court's failure to explain sentences deviating from the recommendations are grounds for vacating the sentence and resentencing the defendant. Furthermore, if the court does not consider the guidelines or if it inaccurately or inappropriately applies them, an imposed sentence may be vacated upon appeal to a higher court by either the defense or the prosecution.

CONDITIONS OF COMMUNITY CORRECTIONS

The authority to impose conditions of a community corrections sentence is vested with the courts. Although conditions may be recommended by the presentence investigator, the judge has the final say regarding the conditions imposed on an offender.

Standard Conditions

STANDARD CONDITIONS

Conditions imposed on all offenders in all jurisdictions.

Standard conditions are imposed on all probationers and people with community sentences in a jurisdiction, regardless of the nature of the offense committed. Standard conditions are either prescribed by law or set by court or agency practice and require any offender sentenced to a community corrections sanction to:

- Obey all federal and state laws and municipal ordinances
- Follow all directives of the supervising officer
- Work and/or attend school regularly
- Submit to drug testing
- Obtain permission from the probation officer before changing residence or employment, or leaving the jurisdiction
- Report regularly to the probation officer
- Report police contact or arrests to probation officer
- Refrain from associating with people who have criminal records unless permission is granted by the supervising officer

Special Conditions

SPECIAL CONDITIONS

Conditions tailored to fit the needs of an offender.

Special conditions are additional stipulations tailored to fit the problems and needs of the offender. As such, the judge imposes them consistent with the crime committed. For example, the defendant may be required to:

- Attend counseling sessions
- Attend literacy classes if the offender does not know how to read or write
- Obtain a GED

- Serve time in jail first if the offender needs exposure to the realities of incarceration
- Participate in drug or alcohol treatment if the offender is addicted
- Refrain from entering designated areas if the offense involves crimes against children
- Pay restitution if damage was caused
- Seek mental health treatment if the offender suffers from mental dysfunction

LIMITATIONS OF SPECIAL CONDITIONS.   Special conditions must be **clear** and specific (not vague). Unclear conditions are invalid because they are unfair to the offender and therefore violate the offender's right to due process.

Second, the condition must be reasonable. **Reasonable conditions** result in compliance; conversely, unreasonable conditions lead to failure because the probationer cannot possibly comply with them. The definition of reasonable depends on an offender's circumstances and is decided on a case-by-case basis. For example, requiring a well-paid offender to pay $500 each week in restitution may be reasonable, but the same condition would be unreasonable if it were imposed on an indigent probationer.

Third, the supervision condition must either protect society or rehabilitate the offender, and it must be related in some way to the offense of conviction. For example, a state court invalidated a condition that a probationer be ordered to attend sex offender treatment because the treatment was not related to the offender's nonsexual offense (*State v. Bourrie* 2003).

Even a probationer who has never had a drinking problem and whose crime is unrelated to use of alcohol can be ordered to refrain from the use of alcoholic beverages. The Federal Court of Appeals held that the trial court could require that a defendant totally abstain from using alcohol during probation because in this case the defendant's *family* at the same residence had an active history of alcohol abuse and the defendant had a serious problem with illegal drugs (*United States v. Thurlow* 1995).

On the other hand, a defendant was placed on probation for tax-related offenses. One of the conditions imposed prohibited the defendant from leaving the judicial district without the permission of the court or the probation officer. The defendant thrice sought permission to travel to Russia, but permission was denied. The Federal Court of Appeals concluded that the denial of the travel request was not reasonably related to the defendant's rehabilitation or the protection of the public; thus the probationer was allowed to go to Russia (*United States v. Porotsky* 1997).

There is controversy over whether conditions known as "scarlet letter" conditions, known for their public shaming qualities, do or do not serve a rehabilitative purpose (see Box 3.1). If a condition of probation is found to be unclear, unreasonable, or unrelated to rehabilitation or public safety, that particular condition is voided, but the community sentence as a whole remains valid.

Supervision Conditions Must Be Constitutional

By virtue of a criminal conviction, offenders have diminished constitutional rights, but they nonetheless retain rights that are considered basic and fundamental. When fundamental constitutional rights are limited or infringed upon by a condition of probation, the government must establish a "compelling state interest" that would justify keeping the condition.

FIRST AMENDMENT RIGHTS.   First Amendment rights of religion, speech, assembly, press, and petitioning the government for redress of grievances are considered

CLEAR CONDITIONS

Conditions that are sufficiently explicit so as to inform a reasonable person of the conduct that is required or prohibited.

REASONABLE CONDITIONS

Probation conditions that the offender can reasonably comply with.

BOX 3.1   COMMUNITY CORRECTIONS UP CLOSE   •

ARE SCARLET LETTER PROBATION CONDITIONS REHABILITATIVE OR UNNECESSARY?

Scarlet letter conditions of community supervision involve publicly shaming an offender by notifying the community of the nature of the offender's conviction. For example, notification laws inform the public of the identity and residence of sex offenders. These laws vary from state to state, with some laws requiring information regarding the residence of a sex offender to be published in a local newspaper and others requiring residents living near a convicted sex offender to be individually notified of the offender's residence. Although the legislative purpose was to protect the community by informing people of potentially dangerous offenders living in their midst, these laws also make it extremely difficult for a sex offender to become rehabilitated. Oftentimes the identity of these offenders, including their

photograph, and a description of the crime committed are made public on the Internet (Zevitz and Farkas 2000). We discuss these laws in more detail in Chapter 15.

A more controversial condition of probation is one that requires an offender to personally proclaim guilt to the public. Appellate courts in the country are sharply divided on the validity of such a condition. For example, in *Goldschmitt v. State* (1986) a trial court ordered a probationer, convicted of drunken driving, to place a bumper sticker on his car reading "Convicted D.U.I.—Restricted Licensee" as a condition of probation. The appellate court upheld the imposition of this condition, stating that it served a sufficient rehabilitative purpose and that it did not constitute cruel and unusual punishment. In *Ballenger v. State* (1993), a Georgia appellate court upheld the imposition of a

condition requiring a probationer to wear a fluorescent pink plastic bracelet imprinted with the words "D.U.I. CONVICT."

Critics of shaming sentences say that it is inappropriate for the government to become involved in degradation practices; others believe that some offenders will use this opportunity as a "publicity stunt" (Reske 1996). A number of jurisdictions, however, have disallowed the imposition of scarlet letter conditions. In *People v. Heckler* (1993), the trial court imposed a condition on a probationer, convicted of shoplifting, that he wear a T-shirt bearing a bold, printed statement of his status as a felony theft probationer whenever he was outside his living quarters. The appellate court, relying on state constitutional grounds, found that this condition impinged on his inalienable right to privacy. The

basic, fundamental rights that deserve protection by the courts. For example, much of the literature of Alcoholics Anonymous (A.A.) refers to God and encourages prayer, leading the court to conclude that the meetings tended to establish a form of religion. Therefore, requiring A.A. meeting attendance as a condition of probation was ruled unconstitutional (*Warner v. Orange County Department of Probation* 1994). Not all courts agree. Another court concluded that A.A., although bearing a religious flavor, is basically a secular treatment program that does not violate a probationer's freedom of religion. This issue has not been decided authoritatively by the U.S. Supreme Court, and disagreement among lower courts continues.

SEARCHES AND SEIZURES.   The Fourth Amendment right against unreasonable searches and seizures is not as highly protected for probationers as other constitutional rights. In *Griffin v. Wisconsin* (1987), the U.S. Supreme Court ruled that a warrantless search of a probationer's home is valid as long as reasonable grounds exist to believe contraband is present in violation of the conditions of probation. The Court

court further noted that this condition, which required him to wear this T-shirt whenever he was outside his home, would undermine certain other aims of his probation, such as procuring gainful employment and staying employed.

In *People v. Meyer* (1997), a trial court ordered a defendant to erect at his home a 4-foot by 8-foot sign with 8-inch high lettering that read "Warning! A Violent Felon Lives Here. Enter at Your Own Risk!" The Illinois Supreme Court found that the purpose of this sign was to inflict humiliation on the probationer. The court further noted that the statutory provisions for probation in Illinois did not include humiliation as a punishment. Thus, the court disallowed this condition.

A California court, however, has disallowed the imposition of a scarlet letter condition on state,

not federal, constitutional grounds. Challenging the constitutionality of scarlet letter or shaming conditions based on a violation of federal constitutional rights is more difficult, but it may raise First Amendment violations of free speech if the condition requires probationers to "speak their own shame" (P. Kelly 1999, p. 863).

Finally, in *People v. Letterlough* (1995), the New York Court of Appeals rejected the imposition of a condition that the defendant affix to the license plate of any vehicle he drove a fluorescent sign stating "convicted DWI" on the grounds that this condition was not reasonably related to the defendant's rehabilitation.

These cases indicate a split in court decisions. Courts that have disallowed the imposition of scar-

let letter or shame conditions usually do so on the grounds that the trial court exceeded its statutory authority. They thus leave open the question to the U.S. Supreme Court of whether a state legislature can amend its laws and authorize a trial court to impose a scarlet letter condition.

Jurisdictions that have upheld scarlet letter or shaming conditions have done so on the grounds that the condition furthers the rehabilitation aims of probation by deterring the offender from committing similar crimes in the future. These courts have also held that shaming conditions do not violate the Eighth Amendment prohibition against cruel and unusual punishment. The U.S. Supreme Court has yet to rule on this matter, so the issue has not been conclusively resolved.

also found that the departmental policy regulation permitting the search, on which the probation officer had relied, was consistent with the Fourth Amendment's "reasonableness" requirement and was therefore valid.

When a police officer or a probation officer has reasonable suspicion to believe a probationer has violated one or more probation conditions, or if a search may yield evidence that a probationer has been engaged in criminal activity, the Supreme Court ruled that the police officer can conduct a warrantless search of a probationer's home (*United States v. Knights* 2001).

THE PRIVILEGE AGAINST SELF-INCRIMINATION.   The Fifth Amendment guarantees the privilege against self-incrimination. Does a probation condition that compromises this right violate the Constitution? The answer is probably "no." In *McKune Warden v. Lile* (2002), the U.S. Supreme Court held that a sex offender treatment program inside a Kansas prison that required an acknowledgement of all prior sex offenses does not violate the Fifth Amendment's privilege against self-incrimination. The Court justified its decision by stating that acknowledging past crimes in the treatment program was the beginning of rehabilitation because doing so meant that the prisoner accepted responsibility for his or her actions. According to the Supreme Court, acknowledging past crimes for rehabilitation purposes (even if the state offered no immunity and made no promises not to prosecute) for convicted offenders is different from the Fifth Amendment protection used when the state gathers information for investigatory purposes for criminal prosecution. It is likely that this case would extend to convicted probationers who are ordered to attend treatment, but the future for probationers is uncertain at this point.

THE PRESENTENCE INVESTIGATION REPORT

Prior to the judicial sentencing decision, many probation departments provide the judge a **presentence investigation (PSI) report.** The PSI is a document prepared by a probation officer to aid judges in the felony sentencing decision, or for offenders who have violated probation and are facing a potential incarceration sentence. The PSI is also used by prosecutors, defense attorneys, parole boards, and probation or parole officers in carrying out their tasks and making decisions. Although U.S. probation officers are involved in both case supervision and conducting five or six presentence investigations per month (Quinn 2002), most state and local probation agencies separate the investigation and supervision duties—designating some probation officers to only conduct presentence investigations and write PSI reports, whereas other officers supervise cases.

The probation officer submits the presentence investigation report to the court before sentencing. The PSI report describes the nature of the offense, offender characteristics, criminal history, loss to the victim, and sentencing recommendations. In juvenile court, the judge is furnished with a social history, or predispositional report, prior to the disposition hearing. Presentence reports are seldom required in sentencing for misdemeanor crimes. In practice, the judge who sentences for a misdemeanor relies on the police officer for information about the defendant's criminal history and the circumstances of the offense.

Although the PSI has been used since the reformatory movement of the early 1900s, the U.S. Supreme Court declared the PSI report to be a valid instrument in 1949 (*Williams v. New York*). The original function of presentence investigation reports was to assist the court in resolving the issue of whether to grant probation. Over the years, however, the PSI report has been used for the entire range of correctional punishments and programs. The PSI report's content and prevalence of use have changed with the philosophical shift from rehabilitation to punishment, and the statutory shift from indeterminate to determinate sentencing.

Purposes of the PSI Report

The primary purpose of the presentence investigation report is to provide the judge with timely, relevant, and accurate data on which to base a rational sentencing decision. The PSI report also assists jail and prison institutions in their classification of inmates, and in suggesting types of institutional programming that would fit the offender's needs while incarcerated. Paroling authorities use the PSI report to obtain information that is pertinent to resources upon release, such as family support, employment opportunities, and the like. Probation and parole supervisors use the PSI report when assigning offenders to caseloads. Field officers use the PSI report when writing a treatment or program plan (Petersilia 2002; Norman and Wadman 2000). Another purpose of the PSI report is to enable probation officers to establish and maintain credibility with judges, prosecutors, and probation supervisors. Probation officers are not seeking to change a judge's mind—they are merely attempting to justify their recommendation with sufficient and reasonable evidence (Kittrie, Zenoff, and Eng 2002).

About 64 percent of all felony cases nationwide included a PSI prior to sentencing. About half of all states require a presentence investigation in all felony cases, whereas a PSI is discretionary in 16 states, and nonexistent in about 10 states (Petersilia 2002). In the federal system, PSIs have increased in significance because federal probation officers are considered to be experts on federal sentencing guidelines. This expertise has been bestowed on probation officers out of convenience, and some scholars believe that this new responsibility conflicts with the original philosophical intent of probation (Kittrie, Zenoff, and Eng 2002).

A **postsentence report** may be written after the defendant has pled guilty and waived the presentence report, and the court proceeds directly to sentencing in accordance with the plea agreement. In such cases, the postsentence report serves to aid the probation or parole officer in supervision efforts during probation or parole or supervised release and to assist the prison system in classification, programming, and release planning (Stinchcomb and Hippensteel 2001). It is estimated that half of all PSI reports written at the state level are postsentence reports. In the federal system, PSI reports are commonly written and used for multiple purposes. In one year in the federal system alone, federal probation officers wrote 65,156 presentence and postsentence reports and completed an additional 52,047 collateral presentence investigations for another district and 27,117 prerelease investigations for military defendants (U.S. Department of Justice 2005a).

With the introduction of sentencing guidelines, sentencing has become less discretionary, and the importance of the PSI has declined in some states. For example, in some jurisdictions where sentencing guidelines are used, probation officers no longer write presentence reports. Instead they complete a "guidelines worksheet" and calculate the presumptive sentence. This short form deprives other agencies in the criminal justice system of valuable information about the offender.

Contents of the PSI Report

What are the essentials of a presentence report? The philosophy guiding the preparation of presentence reports may be characterized as either offender-based or offense-based.

OFFENDER-BASED PSI REPORTS: 1920s–1980s. During the era of indeterminate sentencing, presentence investigation reports were **offender-based** and focused on rehabilitation. That is, probation officers were guided in their **presentence investigation** by a philosophy that attempts to understand the causes of an offender's antisocial behavior and to clinically evaluate the offender's potential for change. By learning about the character of the person under consideration, and the external influences that surrounded him or her, an offender-based PSI suggested alternatives for sentencing beyond incarceration that were specific to that offender. An **indeterminate sentencing** structure formed the foundation of the "rehabilitative ideal." Under an indeterminate system, judges were authorized to impose a sentence within a wide range, with a set maximum. Release from probation or prison was determined by whether the defendant had been rehabilitated.

POSTSENTENCE REPORT

A report written by a probation officer after the defendant has pled guilty and been sentenced in order to aid probation and parole officers in supervision, classification, and program plans.

OFFENDER-BASED PRESENTENCE REPORT

A presentence investigation report that seeks to understand the offender and the circumstances of the offense and to evaluate the offender's potential as a law-abiding, productive citizen.

PRESENTENCE INVESTIGATION

An investigation undertaken by a probation officer for the purpose of gathering and analyzing information to complete a report for the court.

INDETERMINATE SENTENCE

A model of sentencing that encourages rehabilitation through the use of broad sentences with release to be determined by a parole board based on its evaluation of the offender's readiness to return to society.

By the mid-1980s the philosophy of rehabilitation and the indeterminate sentence were under heavy attack from conservative advocates of "get tough" approaches to crime control as well as liberal groups that pushed for decreasing disparate and discriminatory sentences that ranged widely for each individual. Rehabilitation and the indeterminate sentence were chief among the targets selected for abolition. To decrease sentencing disparity, **determinate sentences** were defined by legislative bodies, giving judges less discretion in sentencing options. Furthermore, personal and social variables, previously considered important in the sentencing decision, were no longer considered or played a very minor role in sentencing. The content of the presentence investigation reports changed to reflect the change in sentencing philosophy.

OFFENSE-BASED PSI REPORTS: 1980s– PRESENT. An **offense-based presentence report** focuses primarily on the crime committed. The sentencing court is concerned with the offender's culpability in the offense, whether anyone was injured, whether a firearm was used, the extent of loss to the victim(s), and other aspects of the offense. Secondary information about the offender is considered relevant, such as prior criminal record, employment history, family ties, health, and drug use. Box 3.2 describes a typical format of an offense-based presentence report. A sample federal PSI report is included in the Case Study section at the end of this chapter.

In jurisdictions where the court uses sentencing guidelines to determine appropriate sentences, the emphasis of the PSI report is on applying the particular guidelines to the facts of the case. This means that all presentence reports should be factually

DETERMINATE SENTENCE

A sentencing model that establishes a narrow range of punishment for a specific crime, taking previous criminal convictions into consideration.

OFFENSE-BASED PRESENTENCE REPORT

A presentence investigation report that focuses primarily on the offense committed, the offender's culpability, and prior criminal history.

BOX 3.2   CONTENTS OF PRESENTENCE REPORTS   •

1. Defendant's Personal Characteristics

   - Name and aliases
   - Case number
   - Gender and age
   - Education level
   - Employment history and skills
   - Vocational skills
   - Military
   - Mental health
   - Physical health
   - Drug history, dependency, and/or current addiction
   - History of violent behavior
   - Known gang affiliation

2. Current Offense
   - Facts of the crime from the police report
   - Initial charge(s) and final plea agreement or conviction(s)
   - Accomplices and/or role in current offense
   - Defendant's acceptance of responsibility for crime
   - Level of cooperation or terms of the agreement upon which a plea of guilty was based

3. Defendant's Prior Criminal History

   - Juvenile adjudications (Case numbers, offense type, dates, and dispositions)
   - Adult diversions or convictions (Case numbers, offense type, dates, and dispositions)
   - Previous time spent in custody
   - Pending charges or outstanding warrants

4. Family History and Background
   - Family of origin (parents, upbringing, siblings)

accurate, objective, nonjudgmental, and ideally verified by the presentence officer. The report's length and content should be appropriate to the seriousness of the offense. The greater the consequences of a judgment, the more likely it is that the court or a subsequent decision-making body will need more information.

Probation officers have often noted that judges frequently only skimmed their lengthy reports and skipped to the end of the report where the officer recommends a sentence. In response to this reality, some jurisdictions have moved to a shortened version that focuses only on certain relevant variables. In some cases these brief versions of the PSI report are presented to the court in a "fill-in-the blanks" format. This practice places a duty on the probation officer to present the most critical information in a concise, yet complete, manner.

Congress decided that federal PSIs should include a defendant's financial status and ability to pay fines and restitution (28 U.S.C. 235, 1984). Federal and some state presence reports also require a **victim impact statement.** The use of victim impact statements stems from renewed interest in victims' rights and mitigating the harm the offender caused. The victim impact statement identifies the name of the victim and his or her relationship to the offender. This statement informs the judge about the physical injury the victim may have suffered, whether the victim sought medical attention, whether he or she endured physical rehabilitation, and the permanency of the injuries. A victim impact statement includes the emotional and psychological toll the offense had on the victim and the victim's family. A breakdown of the victim's financial costs that were not covered by the victim compensation fund are also provided. An example of a victim impact statement is shown in Box 3.3.

VICTIM IMPACT STATEMENT

Information in a presentence investigation report about the impact of the offense on identifiable victims or the community.

- Criminal history of family members
- Marital status
- Dependent children
- Current family ties and responsibilities

5. Victim Impact Statement
   - Any statements made by the victim to police or the probation officer
   - The type of harm done to the victim
   - The monetary amount of the victim's loss

6. Collateral Information from People Who Knew the Defendant:
   - Former employers
   - Former educators and teachers
   - Former probation or parole officers
   - Former neighbors
   - Interviews with family members
   - Written recommendation letters if applicable

7. Sentencing Options and the Defendant's Suitability for Each Option

- Custody
- Intermediate sanctions
- Probation

8. Fines and Restitution
   - Mandatory and recommended restitution and/or fines to be assessed against the defendant
   - Defendant's ability to pay restitution and fines

9. Factors Warranting Departure from Sentencing Guidelines

10. Summary Sentencing Recommendation to the Court

BOX 3.3   A SAMPLE VICTIM IMPACT STATEMENT

A male defendant, age 34, charged with Assault First Degree, two counts Assault Second Degree, Armed Criminal Action, Kidnapping, two counts of Burglary and Felonious Restraint.

The male defendant followed the female victim when she moved from South Carolina to Missouri. They had two young boys together, ages 8 and 10. Based on the defendant's previous arrests for domestic violence in South Carolina, the victim obtained a full order of protection upon arriving in Missouri, with the court giving her full custody of their children and prohibiting him from having any contact with her. She chose not to list her residence since she was attempting to keep that information confidential. She did allow for him to call their sons on weekends; however, she indicated that he never called to speak to their children.

On Valentine's Day, he broke into her apartment, ripped out the lining of her couch, and hid inside of it. Upon her arrival home with their sons, he woke up (he had fallen asleep waiting for her). She sat on the couch, and he popped out of it and began to assault her. She was beaten severely around her face, arms, and stomach area. The entire assault was in front of their two sons. Finally, she was able to get to a gun, which she kept loaded in her bedroom closet. He managed to rip the gun from her hands, and he shot her point blank in the forehead.

The victim survived the attack and attempted murder. She chose to give the following victim impact statement at the sentencing hearing:

"In front of our boys, you tried to kill their mother. It has always been about you. I had to move six states away from you, to another time zone, and it wasn't far enough. You have cost me two jobs and a lifetime of self-esteem. The bullet is lodged in my forehead. Would you like to feel it? You put it there. I know that it wasn't smart of me to have a loaded gun in my house with two young children. Does everyone see now what choice I had? I didn't have any choices. You made all of my decisions for me. I told you that I wanted to live near my family again someday. I did not take the children away from you, and I did not move for any man. Although, that is what you want to believe.

The funny thing is, I forgive you. Even though I have two hundred thousand dollars in medical expenses to pay, the state was only able to cover the first $15,000, I would rather be stuck with that debt, than stuck with you. Tell me again that you will pay for my hospital bills as long as I don't testify against you. Well, you always said that you wanted to live in Missouri, congratulations, now you have your chance."

Source: *State of Missouri v. Anthony Williams* CR2000-00704.

Preparing the PSI Report

Preparing the PSI report requires many important skills, including interviewing, investigating, and writing. The probation officer's responsibility is to gather the facts about the offense and the offender, verify the information received, and present it in an organized and objective format.

The preferred practice is to conduct the presentence investigation and prepare the presentence report after adjudication of guilt but before the sentencing hearing (Storm 1997). The presentence investigation should not be undertaken until after a finding of guilt because none of the material in the presentence report is admissible at the trial or during plea negotiation, and the investigation represents an invasion of privacy.

A probation officer interviews an offender to prepare a presentence investigation report before the sentencing hearing.

Exceptions to this rule are allowed when the defendant's attorney consents to the preparation of the report before conviction and plea. When the presentence investigation report is prepared before the defendant pleads or is found guilty by the court, the report may be more accurately referred to as the pretrial/plea investigation report. Judges may require a pretrial investigation before agreeing to the plea and sentence negotiated by the parties. In some areas, a shorter pretrial investigation report is more common than the traditional PSI report.

The Initial Interview

The first task in preparing any type of PSI report is to interview the newly convicted offender. This meeting usually occurs in the probation officer's office or, if the defendant has not been released on bail, in jail. In some cases, the initial interview takes place at the defendant's home, which provides the officer the opportunity to observe the offender's home environment and thus offers an additional dimension to the officer's understanding of the defendant. The home visit may also allow the probation officer to verify information gained from the offender with family members. The officer may also assess the offender's standard of living and relationships with family members.

The initial interview is devoted to completing a worksheet that elicits information about the offender: his or her criminal history, education, employment, physical and emotional health, family, and other relevant data. The officer also uses this time to develop some initial sense of the offender's character, personality, needs, and problems. It is important that the presentence investigator understand a wide variety of crimes so that each PSI report is tailored to the particular crime committed (for example, see Box 3.4 for factors that a presentence probation officer must consider when writing a PSI for a cybercriminal).

BOX 3.4   TECHNOLOGY IN CORRECTIONS

THE PSI REPORT FOR THE CYBERCRIMINAL

A "cybercriminal" uses the computer to commit a wide array of crimes, from sex crimes such as child solicitation and child pornography to identity theft, fraud, and computer hacking. When writing a presentence investigation report for a cybercriminal, it is recommended that the probation officer "determine the offender's computer knowledge and motive for participation in the offense [whether it be greed, anger, or mental illness]" (p. 8).

The PSI officer should conduct a home visit to determine what type of computer equipment and access are present. In addition, the officer should recommend special conditions such as anger management, mental health counseling, restitution, and limiting the offender's usage of a computer. Such conditions include disallowing access to a computer or a connected device, Internet or intranet access, bulletin boards, and the use of encryption (p. 8).

Source: Brian J. Kelly. 2001. Supervising the Cyber-Criminal. *Federal Probation* 65(2): 8–10.

Investigation and Verification

Following the initial interview, the probation officer begins the task of investigating and verifying information supplied by the offender and obtaining employment, military, education, and criminal history records from local, state, and federal agencies. Many of these records are protected by state and federal privacy laws, and obtaining them may require the defendant's written permission. A presentence officer may need to review "court dockets, plea agreements, investigative reports from numerous agencies, previous probation or parole records, pretrial services records, criminal history transcripts, vital statistics records, medical records, counseling and substance abuse treatment records, scholastic records, employment records, financial records, and others" (Storm 1997, p. 13).

If time permits, the officer should also interview the defendant's family and friends, the prosecutor of the case, the defense counsel, the arresting police officer, the victim and/or victim's family, and the defendant's present employer or school officials. The probation officer is interested in information that might influence the sentencing decision but which is omitted during the trial, particularly any aggravating or mitigating circumstances. When obtaining information from any source—particularly from relatives, friends, acquaintances, and employers—the probation officer must be careful to distinguish facts from conclusions. As a general rule, the report should contain only information the probation officer knows to be accurate. In some cases, information may be presented that the officer has been unable to verify. When that is necessary, the officer should clearly denote the information as "unconfirmed" or "unverified."

The Evaluative Summary

In writing the evaluative summary, probation officers call into play their analytical ability, diagnostic skills, and understanding of human behavior. They must bring into focus the kind of person that is before the court, the basic factors that brought the person into trouble, and the special assistance the defendant needs for resolving those difficulties. Part of the evaluative summary should include the offender's probability

BOX 3.5 TECHNOLOGY IN CORRECTIONS •

TELECOMMUTING FOR PRESENTENCE OFFICERS

Probation office budgets have not kept pace with the increased numbers of probationers being supervised in the community. Many probation officers across the country must share office space, which makes officer rapport and confidentiality difficult to maintain. As a result, many federal probation offices have experimented with telecommuting. Telecommuting allows presentence officers to complete the presentence investigation report from home using laptops, telephone calling cards, electronic computer access, and remote system linkages. Telecommuters are home two or three days out of every workweek and reportedly are more satisfied with their jobs than when they were working strictly out of the office. In addition, presentence officers who telecommuted were more productive from home than they had been before the telecommuting program began. One federal probation office in Florida found that telecommuting was more successful for officers who wrote presentence investigation reports than for officers who supervised a caseload full of clients. Telecommuting was so successful that the Middle District of Florida now allows officers with at least two years of presentence experience and "above average performance evaluations" to apply.

Source: Christopher Hansen. 2001. The Cutting Edge: A Survey of Technological Innovation: Where Have All the Probation Officers Gone? *Federal Probation* 65(1): 51–53.

of risk to the community, the amount of harm the offender caused the victim and/or the community, the defendant's ability to pay restitution and court fines, and the defendant's need for treatment (Storm 1997).

In this era of determinate sentencing, the decision-making process in PSIs is seen as "routine and predictable," and presentence officers actually require little if any supervision from probation administrators (Kittrie, Zenoff, and Eng 2002, p. 124). Indeed, writing the presentence report can actually be conducted while telecommuting from home (see Box 3.5).

The Sentence Recommendation

The probation officer's recommended sentence to the judge largely depends on the sentencing guideline system or statutory equivalent. Sentencing guidelines calculate a narrow sentencing range based on the seriousness of the current offense and the defendant's prior criminal record. The severity of the sentence can also be adjusted for aggravating and mitigating circumstances (Norman and Wadman 2000).

One study in Ohio demonstrated that the probation officer's recommendation was adopted by the sentencing judge in 66 percent of the cases when prison was recommended and in 85 percent of the cases when probation was recommended. Another study in Utah found that the court agreed with the probation officer's recommendation about 91 percent of the time in felony and misdemeanor cases. Of the 9 percent of cases that resulted in a departure, half resulted in a more severe sentence and the other half in a less severe sentence than originally recommended (Norman and Wadman 2000).

When judges, prosecutors, and public defenders were surveyed on their attitudes about the PSI, judges and prosecutors were in higher agreement than were public defenders that the sentencing recommendation should be retained as a part of the PSI report, and that the recommendations made by probation officers were appropriate. The majority of judges, prosecutors, and public defenders surveyed believed that the appropriate use of sentencing guidelines facilitated the reduction of sentencing disparity (Norman and Wadman 2000). It seems, then, that sentencing guidelines affect the sentencing recommendation more than does any direct influence of the probation officer. Some states such as Idaho allow presentence officers to recommend a sentence type but not a sentence length. "Probation officers can play in the ball park but they don't make the rules" (Kittrie, Zenoff, and Eng 2002, p. 125).

LEGAL ISSUES CONCERNING THE PRESENTENCE REPORT

Several legal issues have been addressed by various courts concerning the PSI report. The most important questions raised are these: Does the defendant have a constitutional right to disclosure of the PSI report? Are inaccuracies in the PSI report legal grounds for resentencing? Is hearsay information in the PSI report allowable? Does the exclusionary rule apply to the PSI report? Must the *Miranda* warnings be given when a defendant is asked questions by the probation officer for the PSI report? Does the defendant have a right to counsel during the PSI report interview?

Disclosure of the PSI Report

DISCLOSURE

The right of a defendant to read and refute information in the presentence investigation report prior to sentencing.

Disclosure is the opportunity for the defendant (and/or the defendant's attorney) to view a draft of the presentence report. In the federal system, the defendant can view the PSI draft at least 35 days prior to sentencing, and then has 14 days to refute any statements prior to the final report's submission to federal court. The U.S. Supreme Court held that there is no denial of due process of law when a court considers a presentence investigation report without disclosing its contents to the defendant or giving the defendant an opportunity to rebut it (*Williams v. Oklahoma* 1959; *Williams v. New York* 1949). A defendant may have such right, however, if disclosure is required by state law or court decisions in that jurisdiction. The PSI is not, however, a public document, so disclosure is limited to the defendant, the defendant's attorney, and the prosecutor.

After the final report has been submitted to the court, "The probation officer must be prepared to discuss the case with the sentencing judge in chambers or in court, to answer questions about the report that arise during the sentencing hearing, and, ultimately, to testify in court as to the basis for the factual findings and guideline applications recommended in the report" (Storm 1997, p. 15).

Compulsory disclosure has generally been opposed by judges and probation officers because third parties having knowledge about the offender may refuse to give information if they know that they can be called into court and subjected to cross-examination and that the defendant will have access to their statements (Kittrie, Zenoff, and Eng 2002). In the words of one court, the fear is that disclosure of the report "would have a chilling effect on the willingness of various individuals to contribute information that would be incorporated into the report" (*United States v. Trevino* 1996).

A second concern is that permitting the defendant to challenge the presentence report could unduly delay the proceedings. The defendant may challenge everything in the report and transform the sentencing procedure virtually into a new trial.

A third concern is protecting the confidential nature of the information in the report. To safeguard these concerns, the federal system requires withholding various parts of the PSI from the defendant when:

- Disclosure might disrupt rehabilitation of the defendant (such as psychiatric reports addressing future dangerousness).
- Information was obtained on a promise of confidentiality.
- Harm may result to the defendant or to any other person from such disclosure.

The opposite view—advocating disclosure of the presentence report—is rooted in due process, meaning fundamental fairness. Because the PSI report might have a significant influence on the type and length of sentence to be imposed, due process demands that convicted people should have access to the information on which their sentence is to be based so that they can correct inaccuracies and challenge falsehoods. Furthermore, in jurisdictions where the accused has access to the reports, the sentencing hearings have not been unduly delayed.

In sum, federal rules represent an intermediate position between complete disclosure and complete secrecy. In jurisdictions that practice disclosure, the release of the presentence report has not resulted in the problems that have been anticipated by the opponents of the practice. Instead, it seems to have led the probation services to develop skills for analyzing the offense and the offender more objectively. With greater objectivity has come greater reliance on the reports by the courts and a resultant increase in the number of reports requested and people granted probation.

Inaccuracies in the PSI Report

Disclosure policies attempt to minimize errors in the final PSI report submitted to the court. Two federal circuit courts ruled that detected inaccuracies in the PSI report are not grounds for automatic revocation of the sentence imposed (*United States v. Lockhart* 1995; *United States v. Riviera* 1996). Both courts based their decisions on a determination of whether the inaccuracies were harmless or harmful. If the error is harmless (meaning that the error would *not* have affected the sentencing outcome), then reversal is not justified. If the inaccuracies would have changed the sentencing outcome, the defendant has the burden of establishing that the error was harmful. If a defendant is sentenced on the basis of a report that is materially false or unreliable, that person's due process rights are violated (*Moore v. United States* 1978; *United States v. Lasky* 1979). The remedy in these cases is vacating the original sentence and remanding the case to the trial court to prepare a new PSI report prior to resentencing.

Hearsay in the PSI Report

Hearsay evidence is information that does not come from direct knowledge of the person giving the information but from knowledge that person received from a third party. Although hearsay is not admissible in trial, hearsay is not in and of itself constitutionally objectionable in a PSI report. The reason for this is that the purpose of the report is to help the judge determine an appropriate sentence for the defendant. It is important that the judge be given every opportunity to obtain relevant information during sentencing without rigid adherence to rules of evidence. Because the report is usually

HEARSAY EVIDENCE

Information offered as a truthful assertion that does not come from the personal knowledge of the person giving the information but from knowledge that person received from a third party.

not compiled and written by a person with legal training, the judge must exercise proper and wise discretion as to the sources and types of information he or she might want to use.

Does the Exclusionary Rule Apply?

The **exclusionary rule** provides that evidence seized in violation of the Fourth Amendment prohibition against unreasonable searches and seizures is not admissible in a court of law. The exclusionary rule does not apply to PSI reports. Courts have consistently resisted efforts to extend the exclusionary rule to proceedings other than the trial itself and only in instances in which the misconduct was by the police. Some might argue that sentencing is so closely related to the trial that the use of illegally obtained evidence should not be allowed to influence the sentencing proceedings. Courts, however, have rejected this argument.

Another issue that has arisen is whether the exclusionary rule applies in cases in which the illegally obtained evidence is acquired by the probation officer or the police solely for use in a PSI report and not in connection with an investigation for a criminal act. Local courts likely will decide based on state rules rather than on a possible violation of a constitutional right. Evidence illegally seized cannot be used in the PSI report if its use is prohibited by state or case law.

Miranda Warnings and the PSI Interview

Miranda v. Arizona (1966) held that warnings must be given whenever a suspect is under "custodial interrogation." These warnings are as follows:

1. You have a right to remain silent.
2. Anything you say can be used against you in a court of law.
3. You have the right to an attorney.
4. If you cannot afford an attorney, one will be appointed for you prior to questioning.

Appellate courts held that *Miranda* warnings do not need to be given by the probation officer when interviewing a defendant in connection with the PSI report. The presentence investigation does not trigger the defendant's right to be free from self-incrimination even if the defendant is in custody and facing serious punishment (*United States v. Allen* 1993; *United States v. Washington* 1993).

Right to a Lawyer during the PSI Interview

The Tenth Circuit court held that a defendant does not have a Sixth Amendment right to have an attorney present during the PSI report interview (*United States v. Gordon* 1993; *United States v. Washington* 1993). During the interview the probation officer acts as an agent of the court charged with assisting the court in arriving at a fair sentence, not as an agent of the prosecution. In most cases, guilt has already been determined; hence, the adversarial situation that requires the assistance of a lawyer is absent.

However, a Massachusetts court disagreed, saying the defendant has a right to counsel at the PSI interview because this interview plays a crucial role in the officer's sentencing recommendation to the judge and therefore has "due process implications with respect to a defendant's interest in a fair and even-handed sentence proceeding" (*Commonwealth of Massachusetts v. Talbot* 2005). Defense counsel can, in fact, be helpful in clarifying legal terms for the defendant and assist in articulating the defendant's views for the probation officer so that revisions of the initial draft will be minimal. The legal issues of the PSI continue to be clarified over time.

TOP THINGS YOU SHOULD KNOW

- Granting a community sentence to an individual offender depends primarily on the severity of the current offense and prior criminal history.
- Community values and the individual judge's philosophy of sentencing contribute to the decision. Sentencing philosophy can be based on one or more of the following: retribution, incapacitation, deterrence, rehabilitation, and "just deserts."
- The needs of the offender, the risk the offender poses in the protection of society, and the maintenance of social order must all be carefully weighed. The balancing of the best interests of both the offender and society is the crux of sentencing.
- The use of sentencing guidelines has reduced some sentencing inequalities at the expense of reducing judicial discretion to sentence on a case-by-case basis.
- Supervision conditions are both standard conditions (imposed on all probationers in a jurisdiction) and special conditions (tailored to fit the offender and offense).
- Each community condition must be clear, reasonable, related to the protection of society and the rehabilitation of the offender, and constitutional.
- The presentence investigation report is a confidential document written by a person with a social science background rather than a strictly legal background.
- The primary purpose of a presentence report is to examine and expose the factors that will mitigate for or against successful community supervision.
- Even though the offender has the opportunity to refute information contained in the PSI, hearsay evidence is allowed, and the presentence interview does not require Miranda warnings, nor the presence of an attorney.

DISCUSSION QUESTIONS

1 What should be the purpose of sentencing for first-time felony offenders—rehabilitation, deterrence, incapacitation, or retribution? What about for repeat offenders?

2 Is it more important that sentences be consistent to all offenders of a similar class of crimes or that sentences be individualized to the characteristics and needs of each offender?

3 How might sentencing guidelines affect the sentencing decision?

4 How might the availability and quality of other sentencing dispositions affect the decision to grant a sentence in the community?

5 What are the ways a judge obtains sentencing information? Which do you believe is the most useful way to establish just and fair sentences? Why?

6 Argue for or against the proposition that probation conditions should be left solely to the discretion of judges and should not be prescribed by law.

7 What are the limitations on the power of courts to impose conditions? Why are these limitations important?

8 Argue for or against scarlet letter conditions for a person convicted of Driving While Intoxicated for the first time.

9 Does a condition that dictates participation in a treatment program that requires admission of guilt as a prerequisite violate a probationer's right against self-incrimination? Justify your answer.

10 Given the time and effort it takes to complete a PSI interview and report, is the effort worth it? Why or why not?

11 How have sentencing guidelines affected the content of the PSI report?

12 What is the purpose of the victim impact statement in a PSI report? What factors brought about the use of this statement?

13 What is the federal rule regarding disclosure of the PSI report? What are the arguments for and against disclosure? What is the middle-ground approach to disclosure?

14 What factor(s) might explain why probation officers' recommendations are so highly correlated with actual sentences imposed by judges?

15 What suggestions do you have for improving the content of the PSI report?

 # WEBSITES

Families against Mandatory Minimums
Nonprofit group against the sentencing laws that require offenders to serve a mandatory number of years in prison before becoming eligible for release

> *http://www.famm.org*

Executive Summary of the Risk Assessment Used in Virginia Sentencing

> *http://www.ncsconline.org/WC/Publications/*
> *Res_Senten_RiskAssessExecSumPub.pdf*

U.S. Sentencing Commission
Information on federal sentencing laws

> *http://www.ussc.gov*

History of the Presentence Investigation Report

> *http://www.cjcj.org/pubs/psi/psireport.html*

California Court Guidelines for the Presentence Investigation Report

> *http://www.courtinfo.ca.gov/rules/titlefour/title4-43.htm*

Kansas Guidelines for the Presentence Investigation Report

> *http://www.accesskansas.org/ksc/2005%20PSI%20Instructions.doc*

Colorado Attorney Advice for Offenders Regarding the PSI

> *http://www.hmichaelsteinberg.com/thepresentencereport.htm*

Probation Conditions

Conditions of probation in Alaska

> *http://touchngo.com/lglcntr/akstats/Statutes/Title12/*
> *Chapter55/Section100.htm*

Intensive probation conditions in Arizona

> *http://www.azleg.state.az.us/legtext/42leg/1r/bills/hb2015s.htm*

Terms and conditions of probation in Benton County, Indiana

> *http://www.in-map.net/counties/BENTON/probation/terms.html*

Conditions of probation in Maine

> *http://janus.state.me.us/legis/statutes/17-A/title17-Asec1204.html*

Conditions of probation in Mississippi

> *http://www.mscode.com/free/statutes/47/007/0035.htm*

Conditions of probation in Missouri

> *http://www.doc.mo.gov/division/prob/pdf/*
> *White%20book.pdf*

Conditions of probation in Washington, DC

> *http://prop1.org/legal/840385/850124a.htm*

CASE STUDY EXERCISE 1

The Sentencing Decision

The following two cases assume that probation has been granted by the judge. Discuss what probation conditions would be appropriate and an appropriate length for the term of probation supervision.

CASE A

Defendant Green devised a scheme to pass fictitious payroll checks. He recruited other individuals to pass the fictitious checks in exchange for money. Mr. Green would open a bank account using a fictitious check he had produced. Green would then produce additional fictitious payroll checks using the bank's logo, routing number, and account number. Mr. Green would recruit individuals who had valid identification from homeless shelters. Upon receiving checks from Green, the individuals would go to area stores to pass the fictitious payroll checks. Green gave a portion of the money to the individuals passing the checks and kept the remainder. When Green's residence was searched subsequent to his arrest for the offense, an electronic typewriter, 29 payroll checks matching those previously passed, a computer, marijuana, and drug paraphernalia were confiscated. Upon further examination of the computer, evidence of payroll check counterfeiting was discovered on it. Nine retail stores were victimized in the offense as the stores had cashed the payroll checks. A total loss of $14,503 was determined through documentation and investigation.

Mr. Green's prior criminal history includes a conviction for misdemeanor possession of marijuana and disorderly conduct. He was raised in a two-parent home. Neither of his parents has a criminal record, and it appears they provided Green with appropriate structure and discipline. Green revealed he has used marijuana for the past 12 years. He is currently 28 years of age. He has a high school diploma and a sporadic work history. His personal finances reveal his only asset to be an automobile valued at $4,500. He has four credit card accounts. Two of the accounts are current with combined balances of $670. The other two accounts are in collection status and their balances total $6,210. The defendant is eligible for not less than one nor more than five years probation by statute.

CASE B

Police officers stopped Defendant Tuff after they observed his vehicle stopping and starting at an accelerated speed. They subsequently arrested him on several charges.

Police observed Mr. Tuff's vehicle accelerate at an unsafe speed after stopping at a yield sign. Tuff's vehicle had come to a stop at the yield sign, although there was no traffic requiring the stop. Police stopped Tuff. They smelled the odor of alcohol on Mr. Tuff, and a breath test showed Tuff had a blood alcohol content of .162. Tuff was arrested. Found on his person were a .38 caliber handgun and a small amount of marijuana. An open container of beer was inside the vehicle. Police reports reveal Tuff became angry and violent during the arrest. He had to be placed in restraints.

Tuff was convicted of Driving Under the Influence, Transporting an Open Container, and Carrying a Concealed Weapon. All were misdemeanor charges. Mr. Tuff has a prior arrest for Disorderly Conduct. The prior offense involved police responding to a disturbance where shots had been fired. Upon arrival, officers saw the defendant throw a pistol up onto a roof. He was chased and appeared to be intoxicated when apprehended. Tuff told officers he had called police because someone had shot at his home. Tuff was irate, shouting profanities and screaming he was going to kill someone. When attempts to calm him were unsuccessful, Tuff was taken into custody and charged with Disorderly Conduct.

Defendant Tuff is 21 years of age. His parents were divorced when he was born. At the age of 6, he began living with his maternal grandparents because his mother worked nights at a tavern. Tuff reports going to the Job Corp when he was 16 years old. He was terminated early from the two-year program with the Job Corp after assaulting a security guard for not being allowed a pass into town. Tuff has been employed as a laborer for three different firms. The longest term of employment in any of the positions was eight months. He was terminated from two of the positions due to absenteeism. He states he resigned from the third job due to personal problems with his spouse and a dispute with his employer over pay. Mr. Tuff completed one year of high school before the Job Corp. Tuff completed his GED as a condition of a previous term of probation.

Mr. Tuff states he was referred for anger management classes when in junior high school. He acknowledged he has had prior thoughts of suicide and, on one occasion, played Russian roulette. On another occasion he tried to shoot himself in the head and pulled the trigger; however, a friend pulled the gun away causing the bullet to miss him. He states he was "depressed with life" at the time. Tuff explains he does not currently feel a desire to commit suicide and does not desire counseling. Mr. Tuff began using marijuana when he was in high school. He has also reported use of crack cocaine and methamphetamine. A urine specimen submitted by Tuff during the presentence phase revealed the use of marijuana.

The defendant was married two years ago. He has a daughter. The marriage lasted only a short period of time, and Tuff states the couple has been separated for more than a year. He does not have contact with his wife or child and is court ordered to pay $250 monthly in child support. His personal finances reveal his only reported asset to be a pickup he estimates to be valued at $8,000. His only outstanding debt is $3,600 in child support owed to the county in which his daughter resides. The defendant is eligible for not more than five years probation by statute.

A Presentence Investigation Report

Below, you will find an example of a federal presentence investigation report (all the names and places are fictitious). After reading the report, you may wish to discuss the case in class, or you may wish to use the sample PSI to construct your own.

IN UNITED STATES DISTRICT COURT FOR THE WESTERN DISTRICT OF ATLANTIS
UNITED STATES OF AMERICA *VS.* MICHAEL MALI
PRESENTENCE INVESTIGATION REPORT
DOCKET NO. CR 03-010-OL-KGG

The Honorable Kelly G. Green U.S. District Judge

Craig T. Doe, U.S. Probation Officer, Breaker Bay, Atlantis (123) 111-1111

Asst. U.S. Attorney, Mr. Robert Prosecutor, United States Courthouse, Breaker Bay, Atlantis (123) 111-1122

Defense Counsel, Mr. Arthur Goodfellow, 737 North 7th Street, Breaker Bay, Atlantis, (123) 111-2345

Sentence Date:	August 5, 2004
Offense:	Count one: Conspiracy to Violate Federal Narcotics Laws
	(21 U.S.C. § 846)—20 years to Life/$4,000,000 fine
Release Status:	Detained without bail since 9/19/03
Detainers:	None

Codefendants:		
	Sammy Maples—	Authur Kent—
	CR 03-011-02	CR 03-011-04
	John Smith—	Leon Williams—
	CR 03-011-03	CR 03-011-05

Related Cases:	None

Date Report Prepared: June 15, 2004

Identifying Data

Date of Birth:	3/19/70
Race:	White
Sex:	Male
S. S. #:	222-22-2222
FBI #:	222-22-22B
USM #:	22222-222
Education:	11th grade
Dependents:	two
Citizenship:	U.S.

Legal Address:	1430 Bird Avenue, Breaker Bay, AT 10101
Aliases:	Matthew Mali; Michael Mahi; M. Maui
Tattoos:	Right forearm—Virgin Mary
	Upper left shoulder—Sword with dripping blood
Gang Affiliation:	None known

PART A. THE OFFENSE

Charge and Conviction(s)

1. Michael Mali, Sammy Maples, Arthur Kent, John Smith, and Leon Williams were named in a two-count indictment returned by a Western District of Atlantis grand jury on December 1, 2003. Count one charges that from June 2003 until September 19, 2003, the defendants conspired to violate the federal narcotics laws, in violation of 21 U.S.C. § 846. Count two charges that on September 19, 2003, the defendants possessed with intent to distribute 500 grams or more of heroin, in violation of 21 U.S.C. §§ 812, 841(a)(1).

2. On January 10, 2004, Michael Mali and Sammy Maples both pled guilty to count one and are scheduled to be sentenced on August 5, 2004. On January 12, 2004, Leon Williams pled guilty to count one and he is scheduled to be sentenced on August 6, 2004. On January 16, 2004 Arthur Kent and John Smith pled guilty to count one and are scheduled to be sentenced on August 25, 2004. All of the above defendants have pled guilty in accordance with the terms of written plea agreements which require a plea of guilty to count one in return for the dismissal of count two in the original indictment.

3. The assistant U.S. attorney has filed a motion pursuant to 18 U.S.C. § 3553(e) and U.S.S.G. § SKl.l, advising that the defendant has provided substantial assistance to the Government. Accordingly, the Government will recommend a sentence below the mandatory minimum sentence and applicable guideline range.

The Offense Conduct

4. This case was initiated by the Drug Enforcement Administration in June 2003, upon the receipt of information from a confidential informant that Michael Mali and Sammy Maples were involved in the distribution of multiple-ounce quantities of heroin from an apartment located in the Breaker Bay housing project. Subsequent investigation revealed that Mali and Maples were regularly distributing heroin to Arthur Kent. After several months of investigation and surveillance, drug enforcement agents learned that Kent regularly purchased heroin from Mali and Maples, and sold the heroin to Leon Williams, who would travel to the Breaker Bay area each month from Bodega Bay, Atlantis, a small community approximately 200 miles south of Breaker Bay. Williams gave Kent the money to purchase the heroin but generally waited in a parked car near the housing project while Kent conducted the heroin transaction inside apartment 4J in the housing project. Mali and Maples relied on a number of heroin sources, including two unidentified Asian males, and on at least two occasions, John Smith.

5. According to information provided by a confidential informant, Mali told Smith that he sold small quantities of heroin in Breaker Bay and relied on various suppliers. Mali complained that his suppliers were unreliable and frequently provided him with heroin of poor quality. Smith, although cautious and somewhat suspicious of Mali, revealed that he might be aware of

other suppliers whom Mali might use for future drug distribution operations.

6. On June 14, 2003, Smith was observed by Federal agents outside the housing project near Mali's apartment, accompanied by an unidentified Hispanic male. Prior to entering the apartment building, Smith was observed handing a package (which investigators later learned contained 500 grams of heroin) to the Hispanic male. A short time later, Smith and his companion were observed leaving Mali's apartment.

7. Later that afternoon, Federal agents observed Arthur Kent and Leon Williams driving a red Porsche (believed to be a 2003 or 2004 model) in the vicinity of the housing project. Williams parked the vehicle nearby and Kent was observed carrying a brown duffle bag as he entered the housing project, where he proceeded to Mali's apartment. According to the confidential informant, once inside the apartment, Kent briefly spoke to Mali and the two proceeded to a back bedroom where Mali was known by police to weigh and package drugs. A few moments later, Kent and Mali returned to the living room of the apartment and Mali was carrying the brown duffle bag that Kent brought to the apartment. Mali then emptied the duffle bag that contained a large sum of U.S. currency. Mali assured Kent that he would find the heroin to be of high quality and agreed to provide additional quantities of heroin to Kent whenever his out-of-town buyer needed them. A short time later, Kent left the apartment and returned to the vehicle in which Williams was waiting.

8. For several months, agents maintained surveillance on Mali's apartment, and on several occasions the agents monitored Smith's arrival at Mali's apartment, followed by the arrival of Kent and Williams. On each occasion, Williams would remain outside, sitting in the Porsche, while Kent entered Mali's apartment. Kent would deliver a large duffle bag to the apartment and return a short time later carrying a small package under his arm. On September 14, 2003, an undercover agent of the Drug Enforcement Administration, posing as a drug purchaser, met with Mali in the vicinity of the housing project to negotiate the purchase of 20 grams of heroin. Mali told the undercover agent that he expected to receive a shipment of heroin the following day and that, although he anticipated transacting a large heroin deal with another out-of-town customer, he would be able to sell the undercover agent 20 grams of heroin from the shipment for $6,000.

9. For the next five days, Federal agents maintained 24-hour surveillance of the housing project, and on September 19, 2003, the agents observed Smith when he arrived at Mali's residence carrying a shopping bag. Smith arrived at the apartment with the shopping bag and had a gun that was visible in his waistband. Smith remained in Mali's apartment, and a short time later Williams and Kent arrived. As on previous occasions, Williams remained in the car parked nearby while Kent went to Mali's apartment, carrying a blue gym bag. Shortly thereafter, the agents entered the apartment and the defendants scattered. The agents observed Maples, Kent, and Smith seated in the back bedroom of the apartment, and they were all placed under arrest without incident. Other Federal agents, who were positioned outside of the apartment building, observed Mali as he jumped out of the apartment's kitchen window and landed in a patch of bushes on the ground below, where he was placed under arrest. At the time of his arrest,

a loaded 50 caliber Browning machine gun was found in the bushes near the spot where Mali landed. In addition, other agents proceeded to the parked Porsche where Williams was waiting. At the time of Williams' arrest, agents recovered a .357 Magnum from his waistband. Williams told the agents that he had driven to Breaker Bay from Bodega Bay and had driven Kent to the vicinity to visit some friends.

10. The agents searched Mali's apartment and from the toilet recovered a large quantity of suspected heroin that the defendants had attempted to destroy. The agents safeguarded the seized narcotics using plastic bags. The following day, the bags were reopened and the water/heroin solution was drained into plastic bottles for laboratory submission. According to the results of a later laboratory report, the agents recovered a total of 725.12 grams of 20 percent pure heroin. In addition, the agents recovered an additional 55.4 grams of 20 percent heroin from the top of the refrigerator in the kitchen, as well as heroin residue from a table in the bedroom, along with an Ohaus triple beam scale, a strainer, and other drug-related paraphernalia. Moreover, the agents seized $103,160 in cash bundles of U.S. currency from the blue gym bag that the agents had previously observed being carried by Kent, and $16,870 from Kent's jacket pocket.

11. The agents then proceeded to apartment 6J, where, according to confidential informant information, Mali was believed to store narcotics proceeds and other property. The apartment was occupied by Michael Mali's mother, Carol Mali, who consented to a search of the apartment. Agents recovered an additional $13,000 in cash and jewelry later appraised to be valued at $50,000.

12. All of the participants in this offense shared equally important functions in this loosely organized heroin distribution operation. Defendant John Smith was the heroin supplier. Michael Mali and Sammy Maples were the brokers, and Arthur Kent was Williams' courier. Williams was a buyer, who authorities believe operated a street-level heroin distribution operation in Bodega Bay, Atlantis, and he frequently traveled to Breaker Bay to purchase heroin. During the course of this offense, a total of 1090.52 grams (or slightly more than one kilogram) of heroin was distributed, which has an estimated wholesale value of $350,000.

Victim Impact

13. There are no known victims in this offense.

Adjustment for Obstruction of Justice

14. Although the defendant attempted to flee prior to his arrest, he was apprehended almost immediately. The probation officer has no other information to suggest that the defendant impeded or obstructed justice.

Adjustment for Acceptance of Responsibility

15. During an interview with drug enforcement officials shortly after his arrest, and later during an interview with the probation officer, Mali readily admitted his involvement in this offense. In substance, Mali acknowledged that he participated in this conspiracy to distribute heroin and takes full responsibility for his conduct.

Offense Level Computation

16. The latest edition of the Federal *Guidelines Manual* has been used in this case.

17. **Base Offense Level:** The guideline for a 21 U.S.C. § 846 offense is found in U.S.S.G. § 2D1.4. That section provides that the base offense level for a narcotics conspiracy shall be the same as if the object of the conspiracy or attempt had been completed. In this case, the defendant conspired to distribute 1090.52 grams of heroin. In accordance with the provisions found in U.S.S.G. § 2D1.1(a)(3)(c)(6), the base offense level is 32.

18. **Specific Offense Characteristic:** Pursuant to the provision found in U.S.S.G. § 2D1.1(b)(1), because the agents retrieved a loaded 50 caliber machine gun in the bushes where the defendant was arrested, the offense level is increased by two levels. +2

19. **Victim Related Adjustments:** None 0

20. **Adjustment for Role in the Offense:** None 0

21. **Adjustment for Obstruction of Justice:** None 0

22. **Adjustment for Acceptance of Responsibility:** The defendant has shown recognition of responsibility for the offense, and a reduction of two levels for Acceptance of Responsibility is applicable under U.S.S.G. § 3E1.1. −2

23. **Total Offense Level:** 32

Chapter Four Enhancements

24. **Career Criminal Provision:** In accordance with the provisions found in U.S.S.G. § 4B1.1, because the defendant was at least 18 years old at the time of the instant offense, the instant offense is a felony controlled substance offense, and the defendant has at least two prior felony controlled substance convictions as detailed below, Mali is a career criminal and the adjusted offense level is 37. 37

25. **Adjustment for Acceptance of Responsibility:** The defendant has shown recognition of responsibility for the offense and a reduction of two levels for Acceptance of Responsibility is applicable under U.S.S.G. § 3E1.1. −2

26. **Total Offense Level:** 35

PART B. THE DEFENDANT'S CRIMINAL HISTORY

Juvenile Adjudication(s)

27. None

28. **Adult Criminal Conviction(s)**

Date of Arrest	Conviction/ Court	Date Sentence Imposed/Disposition	Guideline/ Points
March 2, 2001	Criminal Sale of Controlled Substance, Class D Felony, Breaker Bay Superior Court, Breaker Bay, AT Dkt. #86541	9/23/01, 4 years probation	4A1.1(c) 1 —

The defendant was represented by counsel. Mali was arrested, along with Sidney Reynolds, after Breaker Bay police officers observed them selling a quantity of heroin to a third individual not arrested. At the time of arrest, the police recovered 20 glassine envelopes of heroin, which, according to a later laboratory report, had a combined total net weight of 3 grams. Mali was represented by counsel and subsequently pled guilty as noted above, although during his interview with the Breaker Bay county probation officer, he denied his guilt in the offense, stating that he pled guilty in return for the assurance that he would be placed on probation supervision. According to local county probation records, Mali successfully completed probation supervision and was given an early discharge on June 10, 2003.

29. April 4, 1997

Criminal Sale	10/24/97	4A1.1(a)
of Controlled.	2 to 4 years	<u>3</u>
Substance, Class C	imprisonment,	
Felony, Breaker Bay	paroled 8/4/99,	
Superior Court,	parole revoked	
Breaker Bay, AT	2/27/00, returned	
Dkt. # 86926	to custody, released 12/27/00	

The defendant was represented by counsel. Police officers observed the defendant passing glassine envelopes to others in exchange for money. At the time of his arrest, police officers recovered 55 glassine envelopes containing 2.5 grams of heroin and 16 glassine envelopes containing 26 grains of cocaine, marked "Freeze," wrapped to Mali's arm. Mali failed to return to court as scheduled, and a bench warrant was issued for his arrest. The defendant was subsequently returned to court when he was arrested on a new unrelated charge. During his interview with the probation officer, Mali acknowledged possession of the narcotics, although he explained that the drugs were for his own personal use. Mali was arrested on the below-listed charges shortly after his release on parole. According to State parole officials, the defendant's parole was violated and he was returned to state custody until December 27, 2000.

30. April 14, 1996

Criminal	4/19/96,	4A1.1(c)
Possession of	7 days	<u>1</u>
Marijuana, 5th	imprisonment	
degree, Class B		
Misd., Breaker		
Bay Criminal		
Court. Dckt # 89541		

The defendant was represented by counsel. Mali was arrested and originally charged with assault, resisting arrest, and criminal possession of marijuana, while at liberty on bail in connection with the above-mentioned offense.

Criminal History Computation

31. The criminal convictions above result in a subtotal criminal history score of 10.
32. According to the sentencing table, 10 to 12 criminal history points establish a criminal history category of V; however, the defendant's criminal history category is enhanced to VI because he is considered a career criminal.
33. As detailed above, the defendant has two prior felony convictions involving controlled substances and a crime of violence, and as such, pursuant to the

provisions found in U.S.S.G. § 4131.1, Mali is a career criminal and his criminal history category must be VI.

PART C. OFFENDER CHARACTERISTICS

Personal and Family Data

34. Michael Mali was born on March 19, 1970, in Breaker Bay, Atlantis, to the union of Carlos Mali and Carol Hewson. His parents were never married and seldom lived together, making it necessary for his mother to obtain public assistance for financial support. According to the defendant, his father died in 1995 following a massive heart attack. Prior to his death, the father collected public assistance for financial support and had difficulty maintaining employment.

35. The defendant was reared by his paternal grandmother, Claudia Mali, now age 75, who has resided at the Breaker Bay housing project at 1430 Bird Avenue, for the past 40 years. According to the defendant, he has a good relationship with his mother and brother David, although he acknowledged that he has not seen them in several months primarily because his mother abuses alcohol and is difficult to talk to when she is intoxicated.

36. According to the defendant's grandmother, she assumed responsibility for Michael when he was approximately 12 years old because of the frequent fights and discord in the mother's residence, which is located in a nearby building within the same housing project. Michael was a quiet child and was frequently neglected by his mother, who never provided a positive living environment for Michael and frequently allowed him to miss school. The defendant's mother has a reported history of narcotics abuse and was frequently hospitalized and treated for alcohol and narcotics abuse. The grandmother explained that she was employed as a laundry worker prior to her retirement eight years ago and now collects Social Security insurance and retirement benefits for financial support. She explained that she has always felt that Michael had the potential for positive contributions to the community but was frequently "sidetracked" by his friends.

37. The defendant has never been married, but from 1990 until 1997 maintained a long-term relationship with his former girlfriend, Jackie Smith. This union produced one child, Chanel Mali, now age 10, who currently resides with Smith's mother in an apartment at the Breaker Bay housing project. Several attempts to contact Ms. Smith have been unsuccessful.

38. Simultaneously, from 1996 until the present, Defendant Mali has maintained an ongoing relationship with Sandra Dee. This union has produced one child, Tabitha Mali, who was born on October 1, 2000. Mali states that for approximately four months prior to his arrest, he was residing in a third-floor apartment in a three-family house in Bodega Bay, Atlantis, which he shared with Ms. Dee, that rented for $700 per month. Mali states that after his arrest, Ms. Dee lost the apartment because she was unable to pay the rent and she now resides with her mother in an apartment on the lower west side of Breaker Bay. Attempts to contact Ms. Dee have proven negative in that she has failed to appear at the probation office for several scheduled interviews. Although the defendant describes his relationship with Ms. Dee in positive terms, he has elected to reside with his grandmother upon his release from custody.

Physical Condition

39. Michael Mali is 5'7" tall and weighs 170 pounds. He has brown eyes and brown hair and, at the time of our interview, he wore a mustache and goatee. The defendant states that he is in good general health but noted that he was hospitalized in October 1999 and treated for a gunshot wound to the arm, which he states he received from a stray 9mm hollow-point round. Although medical records have been requested and are awaited, the defendant states that the bullet broke his arm and he still has bullet fragments in his arm.

Mental and Emotional Health

40. The defendant states that he has never been seen by a psychiatrist and describes his overall mental and emotional health as good. We have no documented evidence to suggest otherwise. During our interview, the defendant communicated effectively, but his demeanor is streetwise and tough.

Substance Abuse

41. The defendant states that prior to his arrest he drank alcohol almost every day; however, he does not believe that he is in need of alcohol treatment. The defendant revealed that he has smoked marijuana regularly since 1989, and from 1991 until 1992 he snorted powder cocaine and smoked crack cocaine, although he never used heroin. According to Mali, prior to his state incarceration, he spent approximately $200 a day to support his cocaine habit, but has been drug free since his release from state custody. While in state custody, Mali completed the Network Substance Abuse Program. He attended an outpatient drug treatment program for a brief period after he tested positive for cocaine in October 2001 while under probation supervision. At the time of his arrest in this offense, a urine specimen collected from the defendant by a pretrial services officer tested positive for marijuana.

Educational and Vocational Skills

42. Mali attended Breaker Bay High School from September 1985 until October 6, 1987, when he was discharged in the first semester of the 12th grade. According to school officials, the defendant had a poor scholastic record but had an average attendance record and attitude. According to State corrections records, the defendant was administered the BETA IQ test and scored 93. The defendant was enrolled in adult education programming and a pre-GED while in custody, but was removed from the program due to disciplinary action. While in the program, he was characterized as an average student, according to available academic reports. Prior to his removal, Mali was characterized as an average student. While incarcerated, the defendant participated in a vocational training building maintenance program and took office machine repair courses. Mali received average to excellent evaluations and was awarded a certificate in plumbing.

Employment Record

43. Mali states that he was briefly employed by messenger services prior to his state prison sentences. While under parole supervision, Mali was gainfully

employed for a messenger service, was a waiter, and later was a cook until approximately February 1997. Mali was also employed as a porter and dishwasher, earning $6.00 per hour, with Caroline's at the Breaker Bay Sea Port from October 2, 1996, until he resigned in February 1997. According to a representative from Caroline's, Mali was reliable and a good worker, and would be considered for rehire.

Financial Condition: Ability to Pay

44. The defendant prepared a signed financial statement, wherein he reported no assets or liabilities. His counsel has been appointed by the court, and a recent credit bureau inquiry reveals that the defendant has never established credit. Mali has no known sources of income and upon his release he will be financially dependent upon others.

PART D. SENTENCING OPTIONS

Custody

45. **Statutory Provisions:** The minimum term of imprisonment for this offense, a Class A felony, is 20 years and the maximum term of imprisonment is life, pursuant to 21 U.S.C. § 846 and 841(b)(1)(A).
46. **Guideline Provisions:** Based on an offense level of 35 and a criminal history category of VI, the guideline range of imprisonment is 360–480 months.

Impact of Plea Agreement

47. Under the plea agreement, Mali has entered a guilty plea to count one, the conspiracy count, in return for the dismissal of all other counts. Pursuant to U.S.S.G. § 3D1.2(d), counts involving the same transaction are grouped together into a single group. Accordingly, a conviction on the additional counts would not affect the offense level or any other guideline calculation.

Supervised Release

48. **Statutory Provisions:** If a term of imprisonment is imposed, a term of supervised release of one year must also be imposed, pursuant to 21 U.S.C. § 846 and 841(b)(1)(A).

Probation

49. **Statutory Provisions:** The defendant is ineligible for probation pursuant to 21 U.S.C. § 846 and 841(b)(1)(A).

Fines

50. **Statutory Provisions:** The maximum fine for this offense is $4,000,000, pursuant to 21 U.S.C. § 846.
51. A special assessment of $100 is mandatory, pursuant to 18 U.S.C. § 3013.
52. **Guideline Provisions:** Pursuant to U.S.S.G. § SE1.2(c)(3) the minimum fine in this offense is $20,000 and the maximum fine is $4,000,000.
53. Subject to the defendant's ability to pay, the court shall impose an additional fine amount that is at least sufficient to pay the costs to the Government of any imprisonment, probation, or supervised release, pursuant to U.S.S.G. § SE1.2(i). The most recent advisory from the Administrative Office of the U.S. Court suggests that a monthly cost of $1,800 be used for imprisonment, and a monthly cost of $200 for community supervision.

Restitution

54. Restitution is not an issue in this case.

Denial of Federal Benefits

55. **Statutory Provisions:** Pursuant to 21 U.S.C. § 862, upon a second conviction for possession of a controlled substance, a defendant may be declared ineligible for any or all Federal benefits for up to five years as determined by the court.

56. **Guideline Provisions:** Pursuant to U.S.S.G. § 5171.6, the court may deny eligibility for certain Federal benefits of any individual convicted of distribution or possession of a controlled substance.

PART E. FACTORS THAT MAY WARRANT DEPARTURE

57. The assistant U.S. attorney has filed a motion pursuant to 18 U.S.C. § 3553(e) and U.S.S.G. § SK1.1, advising that the defendant has provided substantial assistance to the Government. Accordingly, the Government will recommend a sentence below the mandatory minimum sentence and guideline range.

   Respectfully submitted,

   Craig T. Doe
   U.S. Probation Officer
   Approved:

   Mark T. Clark   Date
   Supervising U.S. Probation Officer

SENTENCING RECOMMENDATION
UNITED STATES DISTRICT COURT FOR THE WESTERN DISTRICT OF ATLANTIS
UNITED STATES *V.* MICHAEL MALI, DKT. # CR 03-010-OL-KGG

Total Offense Level: 35
Criminal History Category: VI

	Statutory Provisions	Guideline Provisions	Recommended Sentence
Custody:	20 years to life	360 to 480 months	360 months
Probation:	Ineligible	Ineligible	Not Applicable
Supervised Release:	1 year	1 year	1 year
Fine:	$4,000,000	$20,000 to $4,000,000	$0
Restitution:	Not Applicable	Not Applicable	Not Applicable
Special Assessment:	$100	$100	$100

Justification

We have been advised by the assistant U.S. attorney, who has filed a motion for downward departure in this case, that Mali entered into a cooperation agreement shortly after his arrest. In addition to his testimony at the trial of his codefendant

John Smith, Mali has reportedly provided substantial and extraordinary cooperation relative to organized crime figures, over and beyond the scope of this offense. Although the Government has filed a motion for downward departure, the conduct in this offense, coupled with the defendant's prior criminal record, would have otherwise supported a sentence near the higher end of the guideline range. Mali has an extensive criminal record, which includes two prior drug-related convictions. Mali has a limited employment record and, by his own admission, has primarily supported himself through narcotics trafficking. As such, his overall prognosis for rehabilitation is poor, he poses a risk for recidivism, and a sentence of 30 years imprisonment appears appropriate for the protection of the community, given his age.

The mandatory one-year statutory term of supervised release is recommended in this case with a special condition requiring drug testing and treatment in view of the defendant's history of drug and alcohol abuse. Although the defendant is subject to the provision of Federal benefit denial, in view of his expected jail sentence, these provisions will expire prior to his release from custody. The defendant does not have the ability to pay a fine at this time. No fine is recommended and, therefore, the fine payment should be waived by the court. Although the court may deny Federal benefits to the defendant for up to five years, denial of such benefits is not recommended. Unless the defendant were to receive less than a five-year sentence in this case, the period of ineligibility would expire while he is incarcerated.

Recommendation

It is respectfully recommended that sentence in this case be imposed as follows:

It is the judgment of the court that the defendant, Michael Mali, is hereby committed to the custody of the Bureau of Prisons to be imprisoned for a term of 360 months.

Upon release from imprisonment, the defendant shall be placed on supervised release for a term of one year. Within 72 hours of release from the custody of the Bureau of Prisons, the defendant shall report in person to the probation office in the district to which the defendant is released.

While on supervised release, the defendant shall not commit another Federal, state, or local crime. The defendant shall be prohibited from possessing a firearm or other dangerous device, and he shall not possess a controlled substance or any alcoholic beverage. In addition, the defendant shall comply with the standard conditions of supervised release as recommended by the United States Sentencing Commission. The defendant shall also comply with the following special conditions of supervised release: The defendant shall participate in a program of testing and treatment for drug and alcohol abuse, as directed by the probation officer, until such time as the defendant is released from the program by the probation officer.

THE COURT FINDS that the defendant does not have the ability to pay a fine. IT IS ORDERED that the defendant pay a special assessment in the amount of $100 for count one, which shall be due immediately.

Respectfully submitted,

Craig T. Doe
U.S. Probation Officer

Approved:

Mark T. Clark   Date
Supervising U.S. Probation Officer

II

Probation

Probation is the most frequently used and possibly the most misunderstood sentence in corrections. Two out of every three convicted offenders are on probation, yet probation budgets account for only 10 percent of the entire correctional budget. As a result of a severe shortage of probation personnel over the years, the quality of supervision seems to have diminished or been replaced altogether by technological devices.

Chapter 4 provides the history of probation from the early 1800s to the present, including a section on how supervision philosophies have changed over time. Chapter 5 pays particular attention to recent trends in the field of probation and how officers are selected and trained. Chapter 6 examines issues involved in the contemporary supervision of probationers, including classification of risk and needs and probation officer supervision styles. Chapter 7 discusses probation condition modification and both successful and unsuccessful termination. Revocation is an unsuccessful termination that occurs when conditions of probation are not followed.

Introduction

Precursors to American Probation

Recognizance and Suspended Sentence
Two Kinds of Suspended Sentence
The Power to Suspend Sentence

Early Probation
The Role of Volunteers and the Settlement Movement
Development of Federal Probation
History of Juvenile Probation and Female Probation Officers
Early Probation Legislation in Other States

Changing Concepts of Supervision
The Casework Era: 1900–1970
Brokerage of Services Era: 1970–1980
Community Resource Management Team
Justice Model of Supervision: 1980–1995

Top Things You Should Know

4

History of Probation

What You Will Learn in This Chapter

- *The social and legal history of probation in England and the United States*
- *How probation grew in popularity due to John Augustus, the father of probation*
- *How supervision philosophies have changed in the United States over time from an emphasis on casework (rehabilitation) to one of surveillance and monitoring court orders*
- *The way probation services are organized within the courts and how this organization affects delivery of services*

INTRODUCTION

Probation, as it is known and practiced today, evolved out of ancient precedents in England and the United States that were devised to avoid the mechanical application of the harsh penal codes of the day (Rotman 1995). Early British criminal law, which was dominated by the objectives of retribution and punishment, imposed rigid and severe penalties on offenders. The usual punishments were corporal: branding, flogging, mutilation, and execution. Capital punishment was commonly inflicted on children and animals as well as men and women. At the time of Henry VIII, for instance, more than 200 crimes were punishable by death, many of them relatively minor offenses against property.

Methods used to determine guilt—what today is called *criminal procedure*—also put the accused in danger. Trial might be by combat between the accused and the accuser, or a person's innocence might be determined by whether he or she sank when bound and thrown into a deep pond—the theory being that the pure water would reject wrongdoers. Thus the choice was to drown as an innocent person or to survive the drowning only to be otherwise executed. Sometimes the offender could elect to be tried "by God," which involved undergoing some painful and frequently life-threatening ordeal, or "by country," a form of trial by jury for which the accused first had to pay an **amercement** to the king. The accepted premise was that the purpose of criminal law was not to deter or rehabilitate but to bring about justice for a past act deemed harmful to the society.

PRECURSORS TO AMERICAN PROBATION

Early legal practices in the United States were distinct from British common law in a number of ways. First, **security for good behavior,** also known as *good abearance,* was a fee paid to the state as collateral for a promise of good behavior. Much like the modern practice of bail, security for good behavior allowed the accused to go free in certain cases either before or after conviction. Under **filing,** the indictment was "laid on file" in cases in which justice did not require an immediate sentence. However, the court could impose certain conditions on the defendant. The effect was that the case was laid at rest without either dismissal or final judgment and without the necessity of asking for final continuances.

Massachusetts judges also often granted a **motion to quash** after judgment, using any minor technicality or the slightest error in the proceedings to free the defendant in cases in which they thought the statutory penalties inhumane. Some early forms of bail had the effect of suspending final action on a case, although the

KEY TERMS

Amercement

Security for good behavior

Filing

Motion to quash

Surety

Recognizance

Suspended sentence

Conviction

John Augustus

Parens patriae

Casework

Brokerage of services

Community resource management team (CRMT) model

Justice model

AMERCEMENT

A monetary penalty imposed arbitrarily at the discretion of the court for an offense.

SECURITY FOR GOOD BEHAVIOR

A recognizance or bond given the court by a defendant before or after conviction conditioned on his or her being "on good behavior" or keeping the peace for a prescribed period.

FILING

A procedure under which an indictment was "laid on file," or held in abeyance, without either dismissal or final judgment in cases in which justice did not require an immediate sentence.

MOTION TO QUASH

An oral or written request that the court repeal, nullify, or overturn a decision, usually made during or after the trial.

chief use of bail then (as now) was for the purpose of ensuring appearance for trial, such as using the assistance of **sureties.**

All of these methods had the common objective of mitigating punishment by relieving selected offenders from the full effects of the legally prescribed penalties that substantial segments of the community, including many judges, viewed as excessive and inappropriate to their offenses. They were precursors to probation as it is known today. The procedures most closely related to modern probation, however, are recognizance and the suspended sentence.

RECOGNIZANCE AND SUSPENDED SENTENCE

As early as 1830, Massachusetts courts had begun to release some offenders through the use of innovative and possibly extralegal procedures instead of imposing the prescribed punishments. In the 1830 case of *Commonwealth v. Chase,* often cited as an example of the early use of release on **recognizance,** Judge Peter Oxenbridge Thacher found the defendant (Jerusha Chase) guilty on her plea, suspended the imposition of sentence, and ruled that the defendant was permitted to be released upon her word that she would reappear at a later date for her next court appearance. Recognizance came to be used in Massachusetts as a means of avoiding a final conviction of young and minor offenders in the hope that they would avoid further criminal behavior. The main thrust of recognizance was to humanize criminal law and to mitigate its harshness. Recognizance is used today to ensure a defendant's presence at court and is not a disposition in itself.

A **suspended sentence** is a court order, entered after a verdict, finding, or plea of guilty that suspends or postpones the filing, imposition, or execution of sentence contingent on the good behavior of the offender. Suspended sentences grew out of efforts to mitigate the harsh punishments demanded by early English law.

Two Kinds of Suspended Sentences

There are two kinds of suspended sentences—suspension of *imposition* of sentence and suspension of *execution* of sentence. In the case of suspension of imposition of sentence, a verdict or plea may be reached, but no sentence is pronounced and there is no conviction. This means that there is no criminal record and no loss of civil rights provided law-abiding behavior continues for a specified period of time (for example, for three years). The withholding or postponement of sentence is revoked or terminated if the offender commits a new crime.

In the case of suspension of execution of sentence, the defendant is placed on probation and the **conviction** remains on record. A conviction is followed by the execution of criminal sanctions and loss of civil rights and privileges. The suspended sentence can thus be either a separate disposition or a sentencing alternative connected with probation.

The Power to Suspend Sentence

English common law courts had the power to suspend sentence for a limited period or for a specified purpose. Handing down suspended sentences and calling it "probation" was a common practice in the federal courts. In a case known as the "Killits" case, Judge Killits refused to vacate the suspended sentence even when the victim did not wish to prosecute. This case went all the way to the U.S. Supreme Court, and in

---

SURETY

An individual who agrees to become responsible for the debt of a defendant or who answers for the performance of the defendant should the defendant fail to attend the next court appearance.

RECOGNIZANCE

Originally a device of preventive justice that obliged people suspected of future misbehavior to stipulate with and give full assurance to the court and the public that the apprehended offense would not occur. Recognizance was later used with convicted or arraigned offenders with conditions of release set.

SUSPENDED SENTENCE

An order of the court after a verdict, finding, or plea of guilty that suspends or postpones the imposition or execution of sentence during a period of good behavior.

CONVICTION

A judgment of the court, based on a defendant's plea of guilty or *nolo contendere,* or on the verdict of a judge or jury, that the defendant is guilty of the offense(s) with which he or she has been charged.

1916 the Court held that federal courts had no power to suspend indefinitely the imposition or execution of a sentence (*Ex parte United States* 242 U.S. 27, 1916). This aspect—the recognition of legislative authority to grant the power of indefinite suspension to the courts—made probation as now defined and practiced in the United States largely statutory. As a result of the Killits case, approximately 2,000 people were pardoned by the president. Probation legislation was suggested by the Court as a remedy to an indefinite suspension.

The early controversy about the court's authority to suspend sentence has also resulted in differing ideas about the relationship between probation and suspended sentence. In some jurisdictions, probation was not a sentence in itself but was a form of a suspended execution of sentence. In 1984 the Federal Sentencing Reform Act recognized probation as a bona fide sentence (18 U.S.C.A. 3561).

EARLY PROBATION

Although the first probation law was enacted in Massachusetts in 1878, the credit for founding probation in the United States is reserved for **John Augustus,** a Boston boot maker. Augustus (1939) was the first person to apply the term *probation* to his new method; therefore, probation is said to be of U.S. origin, and Augustus is regarded as the "father of probation." (See Box 4.1.)

As is true today, probation was not universally accepted. Augustus repeated over and over that "the object of the law is to reform criminals and to prevent crime, and not to punish maliciously or from a spirit of revenge" (1939, p. 23), and he did not hesitate to castigate the police, the judges, and others who did not share his views.

JOHN AUGUSTUS

A Boston boot maker who was the founder of probation in the United States.

© Ted Streshinsky/CORBIS

Early juvenile courts focused on rehabilitation rather than punishment.

BOX 4.1   COMMUNITY CORRECTIONS UP CLOSE   •

JOHN AUGUSTUS—BONDSMAN AND PROBATION OFFICER (1785–1859)

Although the first official probation law was passed in Massachusetts in 1878, defendants had been placed on probation in Boston as early as 1830. The probation movement came into being by using volunteer probation officers. In the Act of 1878, the general court reflected public opinion that for nearly 50 years had favored placing defendants on probation. The probation movement as it developed before formal legislation is the story of devoted men and women of Massachusetts, many of them volunteers, who saw in probation an opportunity for rehabilitation. Of all volunteer officers, John Augustus made the most significant contribution.

Probation was not discovered by John Augustus; the idea was apparent in the enlightened legal thought of Boston judges in the decade before him. But there could be no real development of probation until a demonstration showed its possibilities and value as a treatment process. Then, probation needed the interest, understanding, and respect of the courts and of the public. John Augustus, the boot maker of Boston, made such a demonstration from 1841 until his death in 1859. It was Augustus's practice to bail, after conviction, an offender in whom there was hope of reformation. The man would

be ordered to appear before the court at a stated time, at which Augustus would accompany him to the courtroom. If the judge was satisfied with Augustus's account of his stewardship, the offender, instead of being committed to the House of Correction, would be fined one cent and costs (amounting to three to four dollars) and Augustus paid the fine.

John Augustus was born in Burlington, Massachusetts (then part of Woburn), in 1785. About 1806 he moved to Lexington and operated a shoe manufactory in part of his home. His first wife and child died when his daughter was an infant. Augustus married again and had four children, one of whom died at age 10. He apparently prospered, as he owned a large tract of land on both sides of Bedford Street. Augustus had four or five employees working for him. His old home, now renovated and restored at One Harrington Road and known as the Jonathan Harrington House, faces the Lexington Common.

It was in his shop at 5 Franklin Avenue near the police court, now only an alley, that Augustus received frequent calls from those who sought his help. His business there suffered owing to the time he spent away from it bailing people in the

courts. All of Augustus's residences are of particular interest because as soon as he began his work in the courts, his home became a refuge for people he had bailed until more permanent plans could be made for them. From 1845 until his death in 1859, Augustus lived at 65 Chambers Street, in the West End of Boston. Nothing remains today of this old house.

Augustus was influenced by the formation of the Washington Total Abstinence Society in Boston on April 25, 1841, of which he was also a member. Its members pledged not only to abstain from intoxicating liquors themselves but to assist alcoholics in the belief that they could be saved through understanding and kindness, rather than through commitment to prison.

Augustus (1852) describes in his own words the moving story of his first probationer:

"In the month of August 1841, I was in court one morning, when the door communicating with the lock-room was opened and an officer entered, followed by a ragged and wretched looking man, who took his seat upon the bench allotted to prisoners. I imagined from the man's appearance that his offence was that of yielding to his appetite for intoxicating drinks, and in a few moments I found that my suspicions were correct, for the clerk read the complaint, in which the man was charged with being a common drunkard. The case was clearly made out, but before sentence had been passed, I conversed with him a few moments, and found that he was not yet past all hope and reformation, although his appearance and his looks precluded a belief in the minds of others that he would ever become a man again. He told me that if he could be saved from the House of Correction, he never again would taste intoxicating liquors; there was such an earnestness in that tone, and a look expressive of firm resolve, that I determined to aid him; I bailed him, by permission of the Court. He was ordered to appear for sentence in three weeks from that time. He signed the pledge and became a sober man; at the expiration of this period of probation, I accompanied him into the court room; his whole appearance was changed and no one, not even the scrutinizing officers, could have believed that he was the same person who less than a month before, had stood trembling on the prisoner's stand. The Judge expressed himself much pleased with the account we gave of the man, and instead of the usual penalty—imprisonment in the House of Correction—he fined him one cent and costs, amounting in all to $3.76, which was immediately paid. The man continued industrious and sober, and without doubt has been, by this treatment, saved from a drunkard's grave." (pp. 4–5)

With this encouragement, Augustus continued to appear in court to assist alcoholics who appeared likely prospects for reformation, to rehabilitate them and then to return with them to court for a report on their progress. By January 1842, he began accepting donations from private philanthropists to carry on his work. From this time on, Augustus's record is one of dedication to a cause to which he devoted the remainder of his life, much of his own financial resources, as well as the money contributed by Boston people.

By 1858, John Augustus had assisted a total of 1,946 people (1,152 males and 794 females). He had acted as a bondsman for them to the amount of $19,464, and he paid $2,417.65 for fines and costs.

John Augustus faced opposition, misunderstanding, and even physical abuse, especially from court officers. For every person bailed by Augustus, the jailer lost a fee of between 62 and 75 cents; the clerk lost 25 cents, and the turnkey was out 40 cents.

Although the opposition of the court officers was discouraging, the judges and the press were friendly, and influential people in the community continued to give him both moral and financial support of between $750 and $1,700 annually.

Augustus varied his answers to his critics. To some he said that for each person bailed to him, a commitment to a house of correction was prevented. To those who understood social progress and justice only in terms of a dollar saved, he pointed out that the public was saved the greater expense of caring for the person in jail. When he was charged with cheating the jails of their rightful tenants, he replied that his form of treatment was more effective, that it saved the offender for his family and for society and did not disgrace him forever as a commitment would.

Augustus dedicated his life to being both a bondsman and a probation officer in charge of reforming the lives of the wayward, until his death on June 21, 1859.

Sources: John Moreland, an unpublished paper presented at the 35th Annual Conference of the National Probation Association, Boston, Massachusetts, May 29, 1941; Augustus, John. 1972. *A report of the labors of John Augustus, for the last ten years, in aid of the unfortunate.* Montclair, NJ: Patterson Smith. (Originally published 1852)

John Augustus and his volunteer successors were not officials of the court and hence lacked official status, although Massachusetts had passed a law in 1689 that authorized an agent of the State Board of Charities to investigate cases of children tried before the criminal courts. In 1878, almost 20 years after the death of John Augustus, adult probation in Massachusetts was sanctified by statute. A law was passed authorizing the mayor of Boston to appoint a paid probation officer to serve in the Boston criminal courts as a member of the police force. Three years later this law was changed so the probation officer reported to the prison commissioner. Due to corruption, the law was revised again to disallow police officers from becoming probation officers (Panzarella 2002). Statewide probation did not begin until 1891, when a statute transferred the power of appointment from the municipalities to the courts and made such appointment mandatory instead of permissive. For the first time, the probation officer was recognized as an official salaried agent of the court.

The Role of Volunteers and the Settlement Movement

Volunteers and philanthropists were thus instrumental in the development and acceptance of probation in practice long before probation became law. Followers of John Augustus included John Murray Spear, who served as a "voluntary public defender, lecturer, and traveler, a tract distributor, and a worker with discharged prisoners" (Lindner and Savarese 1984b, p. 5).

The settlement movement, a group of university students and professors, was prominent in the establishment of probation in New York. In protest of materialism, industrialization, and widening gaps between social classes, settlement residents lived and worked in the poorest sections of the city and resolved to teach and learn from the local residents. The University Settlement was a grassroots social reform organization that used politics and influence to advocate for the poor people of the community, including those on probation (Lindner and Savarese 1984c, 1984d).

Development of Federal Probation

Historical accounts of federal probation suggest that federal judges were extremely resistant to enacting probation legislation. Between 1909 and 1925, 34 unsuccessful attempts were made to pass a law authorizing federal judges to grant probation. The Volstead Act (the Prohibition Amendment) and the intense lobbying that the prohibitionists conducted convinced judges not to support probation because prohibitionists were afraid that judges would place violators of the Volstead Act on probation (Evjen 1975). The bill was finally passed in 1925 and sent to President Coolidge, who was formerly governor of Massachusetts and understood how probation worked. Since probation in Massachusetts had been successful for nearly five decades, Coolidge had no problem signing the National Probation Act. The act authorized each federal district court to appoint one salaried probation officer with an annual income of $2,600.

Between 1927 and 1930, eight probation officers were required to pass the civil service examination. In 1930, the original law was amended to empower judges to appoint without reference to the civil service list, and the limitation of one officer to each district was removed. At the same time, the Parole Act was amended to give probation officers field supervision responsibility for federal parolees and probationers. Thus, the average caseload was 400 probationers per probation officer. Officers relied heavily on as many as 700 volunteers (Evjen 1975).

Between 1930 and 1940, the federal probation system was administered by the Federal Bureau of Prisons (FBP), and Colonel Joel R. Moore became the first federal probation supervisor. The number of officers increased from 8 to 233, but the appointments remained largely political.

In 1940 the U.S. probation system had increased so dramatically that the administration of probation was moved from the FBP to the Administrative Office of the U.S. Courts. The era from 1940 to 1950 concentrated on initial qualifications, standardized manuals, and in-service training. Initial qualifications for federal probation officers were that they be at least 25 years old, but preferably 30–45 years of age; have a baccalaureate degree; possess two years of experience in social work; and be mature, intelligent, of good moral character, patient, and energetic (Evjen 1975).

In 1984, the Comprehensive Crime Control Act abolished federal parole and brought all supervised prison releases under the auspices of federal probation. Federal probation is administered as an appendage of the federal courts.

History of Juvenile Probation and Female Probation Officers

From the 1700s to the early 1800s, children were disciplined and punished for crimes informally by parents and other adults in the community. Although formal laws were developed to punish children who disobeyed their parents, and to punish parents who could not control their children, most children were thought of as miniature adults but had no constitutional rights. Most children contributed to the family income, but there were no formal mechanisms to care for children whose parents died or were left homeless.

Between 1817 and the mid-1840s, middle-class female reformers or "child savers" institutionalized runaway or neglected children in houses of refuge to provide them a family environment, but the good intentions of the child savers did not occur. Although some institutions were humane, most children were further exploited for labor, abused, and victimized.

To protect children from this exploitation, the New York Children's Aid Society shipped children to farmers in the West to keep them from being committed to the House of Refuge. In 1890, the Children's Aid Society of Pennsylvania offered to place in foster homes delinquents who would otherwise be sent to reform school. Known as *placing out,* this practice was an early form of juvenile probation (Binder, Geis, and Bruce 1997).

The Illinois Juvenile Court Act of 1899 legally established a juvenile system different from the adult system to stop the exploitation of children. The principles and characteristics of the new juvenile system were based on reformation and treatment. The prevailing societal beliefs about women as maternal nurturers of wayward children, a concept that originated with the child savers, contributed to women as the first juvenile probation officers.

John Augustus also had volunteer successors who were influential in the development of juvenile probation in the United States. These volunteers included Rufus R. Cook, Miss L. P. Burnham, and Lucy L. Flower, among others. Rufus "Uncle" Cook provided supervision to juveniles while he also served as chaplain of the Suffolk County Jail in Boston. Miss L. P. Burnham was credited with being "the first career woman in the probation field" (Lindner and Savarese 1984b, p. 5). Lucy Flower, wife of a prominent Chicago attorney, was responsible for the establishment of the first juvenile court in 1899 and for the creation of juvenile probation services in Illinois. She obtained support from the Chicago Bar Association to draft and pass the necessary legislation to provide a separate court and detention system that was different from the adult system (Lindner and Savarese 1984b).

Given that juvenile probation was formed under English common law and the doctrine of **parens patriae,** juvenile court proceedings were informal. The state intervened as a substitute parent in an attempt to act in the best interest of the child by using four principles. First, the court appointed a guardian to care for the child. The second principle was that parents of offenders must be held responsible for their children's wrongdoing. Third, no matter what offense children have committed, placing them in jail was an unsuitable penalty. The fourth principle stated that removing children from their parents and sending them even to an industrial school should be avoided, and

> that when it [a child] is allowed to return home it should be under probation, subject to the guidance and friendly interest of the probation officer, the representative of the court. To raise the age of criminal responsibility from seven or ten to sixteen or eighteen without providing for an efficient system of probation, would indeed be disastrous. Probation is, in fact, the keynote of juvenile court legislation. (Mack 1909, p.162)

Mack further related,

> Whenever juvenile courts have been established, a system of probation has been provided for, and even where as yet the juvenile court system has not been fully developed, some steps have been taken to substitute probation for imprisonment of the juvenile offender. What they need, more than anything else, is kindly assistance; and the aim of the court, appointing a probation officer for the child, is to have the child and the parents feel, not so much the power, as the friendly interest of the state; to show them that the object of the court is to help them to train the child right, and therefore the probation officers must be men and women fitted for these tasks. (p. 163)

Since this time, the juvenile system has become more formalized, youths have become more accountable for their own behavior, and for some youths, the juvenile system more closely resembles the adult system. The juvenile system is focused on community safety, emphasizing performance measures and quantitative outcomes. A detailed discussion of the contemporary juvenile court and other types of community corrections for juveniles can be found in Chapter 14. For now, we return to a discussion of early probation laws in the adult system at the time when probation first began in the northeastern region of the United States.

Early Probation Legislation in Other States

New York's probation law allowed for police officers to be probation officers, but one of the two positions was occupied by three different University Settlement members (Lindner and Savarese 1984d). Later probation legislation in other states had a provision that the probation officer should not be an active member of the regular police force. Although this early legislation provided for the appointment of probation officers, most legislation did not provide money for salaried positions. According to Lindner and Savarese (1984a), this omission was deliberate because there was a feeling that the probation legislation would not have passed at all if there were appropriations and costs attached. Thus, probation workers in many areas were volunteers, paid from private donations, or they were municipal workers and other court officers who supervised probationers in addition to their regular jobs.

As various states enacted probation legislation, they did not do so uniformly. Probation legislation followed either Vermont's local organizational pattern or Rhode Island's state organizational pattern. Some states combined adult and juvenile probation services, and some combined probation with parole services. States developed joint or separate agencies for felony and misdemeanor probation services. And they placed probation services in the executive branch or the judicial branch of the state government. Thus, various organizational combinations were adopted as a patchwork quilt.

After Massachusetts, Vermont was the second state to pass a probation statute, adopting a *county* plan of organization in 1898. Each county judge was given the power to appoint a probation officer to serve all of the courts in the county. California enacted a probation statute in 1903 following the Vermont pattern of county-based probation administration. The California law provided for adult as well as juvenile probation (U.S. Department of Justice 1974).

On the other hand, Rhode Island in 1899 adopted a *statewide* and state-controlled probation system. A state agency, the Board of Charities and Correction, was given the power to appoint a probation officer and assistants. States such as New York ultimately followed a state-controlled system (U.S. Department of Justice 1974).

CHANGING CONCEPTS OF SUPERVISION

As probation departments were established, they created a consistent philosophy of supervision for all officers. In this section, we review how probation supervision styles have changed over the last 100 years.

The Casework Era: 1900–1970

When probation began, the supervision process was oriented toward **casework,** providing therapeutic services to probationers or parolees (often referred to as clients) to assist them in living productively in the community. Probation and parole officers frequently viewed themselves as "caseworkers" or social workers, and the term "agent of change" was a popular description of their role. The literature of probation and parole supervision during this period was replete with medical and psychiatric terminology, such as *treatment* and *diagnosis*. Casework stressed creating therapeutic relationships with clients through counseling and directly assisting in behavior modification (National Advisory Commission on Criminal Justice Standards and Goals 1973). The probation officer was thus viewed as a social worker engaged in a therapeutic relationship with the probationer "client."

> **CASEWORK**
>
> A community supervision philosophy that allowed the officer to create therapeutic relationships with clients through counseling and directly assisting in behavior modification to assist them in living productively in the community.

Brokerage of Services Era: 1970–1980

In the early 1970s the casework approach began to break down. Many services needed by probationers and parolees could be more readily and effectively provided by specialized community agencies that provide mental health, employment, housing, education, private welfare, and other services. The National Advisory Commission on Criminal Justice Standards and Goals (1973) reported: "Probation also has attempted to deal directly with such problems as alcoholism, drug addiction, and mental illness, which ought to be handled through community mental health and other specialized programs" (pp. 107–108). This alternative strategy for delivering probation and parole services is referred to as the **brokerage of services** approach. The "service broker" type of probation or parole officer does not consider him- or herself the primary agent of change as in the casework approach. Instead, the officer attempts to determine the needs of the probationer or parolee and locates and refers the client to the appropriate community agency. Thus, an unemployed parolee might

> **BROKERAGE OF SERVICES**
>
> Supervision that involves identifying the needs of probationers or parolees and referring them to an appropriate community agency.

be referred to vocational rehabilitation services, employment counseling, or the state employment office. Instead of attempting to counsel a probationer with emotional problems, the service broker officer would locate and refer the probationer to agencies whose staff are skilled in working with problems such as those faced by the probationer. In this supervision strategy, developing linkages between clients and appropriate agencies is considered one of the probation or parole officer's most important tasks. Probation and parole officers were encouraged to differentiate between services that could be provided internally—by the probation officer—and those that needed to be obtained from other social institutions. Under the brokerage model, the kinds of services provided directly to probationers through the probation system:

- Relate to the reasons the offender was brought into the probation system
- Help him or her adjust to the status of probationer
- Provide information and facilitate referral to needed community resources
- Help create conditions permitting readjustment and reintegration into the community as an independent individual through full utilization of all available resources

The thinking during this era was that probationers' needs related to employment, training, housing, and health were the responsibility of other social agencies and should be provided by them.

COMMUNITY RESOURCE MANAGEMENT TEAM   Another approach to supervision, closely allied to the brokerage approach, was the **community resource management team (CRMT) model.** Using the CRMT strategy, individual probation and parole officers became specialists by developing skills and linkages with community agencies in one or two areas. One officer might be designated the drug abuse specialist and another the employment specialist, whereas another developed expertise in family counseling. The CRMT concept recognized that the diverse needs of the probation or parole caseload cannot be adequately satisfied by one individual. Thus the caseload is "pooled," and the probationer might be assisted not by one officer but by several. For example, Officer Smith might assess all probationers' needs for drug treatment, while Officer Jones might work with probationers in obtaining job training and employment from other community social agencies. Each officer applies his or her particular skills and linkages in the community to serve the needs of the offender.

Justice Model of Supervision: 1980–1995

By the mid-1980s, the **justice model** dominated probation and parole supervision. The justice model advocates an escalated system of sanctions corresponding to the social harm resulting from the offense and the offender's culpability. The justice model repudiates the idea that probation is a sanction designed to rehabilitate offenders in the community and, instead, regards a sentence of probation as a proportionate punishment that is to be lawfully administered for certain prescribed crimes (Gemignani 1983).

In the justice model of probation, the probationary term is not viewed as an alternative to imprisonment but as a valid sanction in itself. The popular view that probation is an alternative to incarceration has led the public to regard probation as an expression of leniency, and the public often feels that the offender is "getting off." Justice and the community's welfare are best served when some offenders are imprisoned. But for the majority, who can safely remain in the community, the public must

COMMUNITY RESOURCE MANAGEMENT TEAM (CRMT) MODEL

A supervision model in which probation or parole officers develop skills and linkages with community agencies in one or two areas only. Supervision under this model is a team effort, with each officer utilizing his or her skills and linkages to assist the offender.

JUSTICE MODEL

A supervision model that focuses on fairness and due process while assisting offenders in complying with conditions of probation or parole.

feel that appropriate penalties are imposed. Therefore, the justice philosophy regards probation as a separate, distinct sanction requiring penalties that are graduated in severity and duration corresponding to the seriousness of the crime (Gemignani 1983).

A justice model probation penalty has two major components: (1) some degree of deprivation of personal liberty and (2) reparation to the victim or to the community (Gemignani 1983). Advocates of the justice model hold that practices of counseling, surveillance, and reporting accomplish very little and have minimal impact on recidivism. They favor probation that consists of monitoring court orders for victim restitution or community service and that ensures that the imposed deprivation of liberty is carried out (Gemignani 1983).

Justice model probation specifically gears offender assistance to helping probationers comply with the conditions of their probation. Other services such as mental health counseling, alcohol and drug treatment, and so on should be available for probationers who express a need or desire for them. These services should be brokered through social agencies in the community. The primary responsibility of the probationer is to satisfactorily complete the conditions imposed by the court. Likewise, the primary task of the probation officer is to assist the probationer in satisfactorily completing the conditions. The probation agency, however, should be prepared to assist those individuals who voluntarily request rehabilitative assistance (Gemignani 1983).

In sum, the shift in philosophy in probation and parole systems throughout the country was traced to the philosophical and political movements of the late 1970s and early 1980s, which inaccurately perceived rehabilitation to be a failure and placed greater emphasis on public safety. Unfortunately, the justice model approach was no more successful in reducing recidivism than the approach it replaced. Chapter 6 discusses more contemporary probation supervision philosophies.

TOP THINGS YOU SHOULD KNOW

- In the American colonies, where English law prevailed, distinct American practices developed. Filing, security for good behavior, recognizance, and suspension of imposition of sentence were procedures by which American judges exercised discretion to reduce the severity of punishment in cases in which the circumstances of the crime or characteristics of the offender warranted leniency.
- The increasing awareness that prisons were not accomplishing their stated purpose of reforming the offender and that suspension of sentence without supervision was not a satisfactory alternative brought about the development of probation as it is known today.
- With the foundation laid by judges, volunteers, and the University Settlement movement, John Augustus brought about the practice of probation as it is known today.
- The concept that crimes committed by children should be dealt with differently, with special courts and special facilities for juveniles, was formalized by the creation of the first juvenile court in Illinois in 1899.
- There are two kinds of suspended sentences—suspension of *imposition* of sentence and suspension of *execution* of sentence. Imposition of sentence means that there is no conviction, and it will be dropped if the defendant completes probation successfully. Execution of sentence means the defendant is placed on probation and the conviction remains on record.

- Probation organizational patterns have little uniformity in the United States.
- Probation services may be combined with parole or kept separate.
- Adult and juvenile probation may be combined or entirely separate.
- Probation may be administered by the executive branch of government or by the judiciary.
- Probation services may be organized at the state level or at the local level. There are arguments for and against each of these organizational schemes. Generally, however, the evidence seems to support state executive branch control of probation services as the most effective and efficient approach.
- Community corrections acts provide state funding to local probation agencies for development of a wider range of sanction alternatives to prison and probation.

DISCUSSION QUESTIONS

1 What is the importance for probation of the ruling in *Commonwealth v. Chase?*

2 What are the two kinds of suspended sentences? Why is the distinction critical to an understanding of modern probation?

3 What is the Killits case? What was its impact on modern probation?

4 Who was John Augustus, and how did he assist in creating probation legislation?

5 How has the concept of supervision changed over the past century? What factors have brought about these changes?

6 How do the "casework" and "brokerage of service" supervision models differ?

7 What are the probation or parole officer's major functions under the justice model?

 WEBSITES

Colorado Association of Probation Offices

> *http://www.capo.net*

History of New York Corrections, N.Y. Corrections Society

> *http://www.correctionhistory.org/*

History of U.S. Probation Office

> *http://www.nmcourt.fed.us/web/PBDOCS/FIles/history.html*

Hampshire Probation Service, United Kingdom

> *http://www.hampshire-probation.gov.uk*

American Probation and Parole Association

> *http://www.appa-net.org/*

Federal Probation

> *http://www.uscourts.gov/library/fpcontents.html*

5

Probation Officer Issues

Introduction

Organization of Probation Services
Arguments for and against State or Executive Branch Administration Community Corrections Acts

A Typology of Probation Officer Work Styles

Selection and Appointment of Probation Officers
Appointment System
Merit System
Combined System

Officer Qualifications, Training, and Salary
Education and Experience
Adult Preservice Training
Juvenile Preservice and Orientation Training
In-Service Training
Officer Salary

Firearms Policies for Probation and Parole Officers

Probation Officer Job Stress
Sources of Stress
Decreasing Stress: Types of Immunity

Private Probation

Top Things You Should Know

© Spencer Grant/Stock, Boston Inc.

KEY TERMS

Community Corrections Acts

Preservice training

Peace Officer State Training

In-service training

Role ambiguity

Role conflict

Negligence

Absolute immunity

Qualified immunity

Private Probation

What You Will Learn in This Chapter

- *Probation is organized either locally or through the state government, and operates through the judicial or executive branch.*

- *As the role of probation officers has changed from a rehabilitative approach to a law enforcement orientation, officer working styles encompass elements of both orientations.*

- *Particular educational and character qualifications are needed to manage a caseload of offenders.*

- *Issues important to probation officers include continual training, salary, firearms policies, and job stress.*

- *Private probation agencies are growing in number, and the standards by which they operate vary widely.*

INTRODUCTION

There are about 93,000 probation officers and correctional treatment specialists nationwide. Female probation and parole officers make up 54 percent of line staff and 13 percent of supervisors (Camp, Camp, and May 2003). People are attracted to probation and parole careers because of simultaneous emphases on helping people and protecting the community. This chapter will discuss the selection process, desired qualifications, and training involved in working in probation and parole, or any community corrections position involving the supervision of offenders.

As you learned in Chapter 4, probation began as a practice of supervision involving rehabilitation and assistance in solving problems related to housing, employment, and alcoholism. As probation work developed into a paid position, probation officers were challenged by their dual roles as therapeutic change agents and as officers invested in ensuring that their clients obeyed the law and did not threaten public safety. Legislative statutes define probation departments to have a twofold mission of law enforcement and rehabilitation/reintegration.

The two goals are not emphasized equally, however. Law enforcement and public safety are accentuated more than other tasks probation officers are expected to accomplish. For example, out of all 50 states,

> the six tasks most prescribed by states are . . . supervision–46, investigate cases–32, keep records–27, surveillance–26, develop/discuss probation conditions–24, and arrest–24. (Purkiss et al. 2003, p. 13)

Over the last decade, probation officers have increasingly become licensed peace officers (in 15 states in 2002), which allows them to carry firearms and make arrests. More probation officers also serve warrants. Rehabilitation tasks were of secondary importance.

ORGANIZATION OF PROBATION SERVICES

As we've already seen, most probation services are separated into those for juveniles and those for adults. However, juvenile and adult probation services are fully integrated in at least ten states and partially integrated in select jurisdictions in another six states (Krauth and Linke 1999). Probation departments are also administered from either the executive (department of corrections) branch or the judicial (courts) branch. Some probation services are combined with parole at the state level, whereas others are stand-alone departments administered locally. Table 5.1 indicates the branch of government administering juvenile and adult probation services in each state and whether probation is under state or local control. The most common organizational structure for adult and juvenile probation is a state agency administered through the executive branch of government. The states with one or more asterisks (about half of all states) are ones in which the adult and juvenile systems are each administered differently. In most of the differences, the juvenile system is more fragmented and local, or a combination of both judicial and executive, depending on the county (Krauth and Linke 1999).

TABLE 5.1   *Organizational Structure of Adult and Juvenile Probation Services*

State	State Level	Local Level	Adult Probation Stand-Alone	Adult Parole & Probation Combined	Juvenile & Adult Probation Combined
Alabama*	Executive			All	
Alaska	Executive			All	
Arizona		Judicial	Some		Some
Arkansas*	Executive			All	
California		Exec, Judicial			All
Colorado*	Judicial				All
Connecticut	Judicial		All		
Delaware	Executive			All	
Florida	Executive			All	
Georgia***	Executive		All		
Hawaii	Judicial		All		
Idaho*	Executive			All	
Illinois		Judicial			All
Indiana		Judicial			All
Iowa**		Executive		All	
Kansas	Judicial				All
Kentucky	Executive			All	
Louisiana***	Executive			All	
Maine	Executive		All		
Maryland	Executive			All	
Massachusetts	Judicial		All		
Michigan*	Executive			All	
Minnesota	Executive	Exec, Judicial		Some	Some
Mississippi***	Executive			All	
Missouri***	Executive			All	
Montana**	Executive			All	
Nebraska	Judicial				All
Nevada***	Executive			All	
New Hampshire	Executive			All	
New Jersey	Judicial				All
New Mexico	Executive			All	
New York		Executive			All
North Carolina	Executive			All	
North Dakota***	Executive			All	
Ohio***	Executive	Judicial	Some	Some	Some
Oklahoma***	Executive			All	

(continued)

TABLE 5.1   *(Contd.)*

State	State Level	Local Level	Adult Probation Stand-Alone	Adult Parole & Probation Combined	Juvenile & Adult Probation Combined
Oregon		Executive		All	Some
Pennsylvania*	Executive	Judicial	Some	Some	Some
Rhode Island	Executive			All	
South Carolina	Executive			All	
South Dakota	Judicial				All
Tennessee***	Executive		All		
Texas		Judicial		All	Some
Utah**	Executive			All	
Vermont	Executive			All	
Virginia***	Executive			All	
Washington***	Executive			All	
West Virginia**		Judicial			All
Wisconsin***	Executive			All	
Wyoming***	Executive			All	
Total	41	12	9	33	16

Executive = Administered under the executive branch of government

Judicial = Administered under the courts/judicial branch

All = Exists statewide

Some = Exists in some, but not all jurisdictions

* = Juvenile probation services differ from adult in that juvenile is local level and judicial

** = Juvenile probation services differ from adult in that juvenile is state level and judicial

*** = Juvenile probation services differ from adult in that juvenile is local and a combination of both judicial and executive, depending on the county

States without asterisks: Both the adult and juvenile systems are administered in the same way as defined by each state

Source: Barbara Krauth and Larry Linke. 1999. *State Organizational Structures for Delivering Adult Probation Services.* Longmont, CO: LIS, Inc. for the National Institute of Corrections, U.S. Department of Justice.

Arguments for and Against State or Executive Branch Administration

There are good arguments on both sides of the issue for having different levels of government administer probation departments. The top six points that favor state-level or executive branch administration are

- Program budgeting is better coordinated because of the state's ability to negotiate in the resource allocation process.
- There is greater assurance that goals and objectives can be met by uniform policies and procedures.
- More funding is available to provide staff training and services to probationers.
- The executive branch facilitates a more efficient and coordinated continuum of services to offenders.
- Executive branch administrators are trained in business and administration, whereas judges are trained in law and may not be as equipped to administer probation services.
- If probation officers view themselves as working for judges, the officers may attempt to satisfy judges before attending to the needs of their caseload or the community.

On the other hand, arguments favoring local-level or judicial branch administration include

- Local administrators are more familiar with local community values and resources where probationers are being supervised
- The judicial branch is more attuned to human services than the executive branch. The courts, it is contended, are more aware of the resource needs of probation than is the executive branch, and the relationship of the probation staff to the courts provides automatic feedback on the effectiveness of probation services.
- The judicial branch and/or local levels tend to have a less rigid chain of command.
- Keeping probation under the judicial branch means probation will have more autonomy and won't get lost like it might when combined with prison and jail budgets (Krauth and Linke 1999).

When probation is centralized at the state level under the department of corrections, the budgetary emphasis tends to be on prisons, to the detriment of community corrections. The president of the Texas Probation Association argued that community corrections in Texas should be separated from the state institutional division:

> In my opinion, this relationship has not been in the best interest of community corrections. . . . Under the direction of the prior agency, the Texas Adult Probation Commission, the State of Texas was at least sensitive to the needs of the local level, where the roots of our criminal justice system should be focused. Communication with our state agency was open and productive. The ideas we had were heard with open ears, and the frustrations we felt were shared. The current system, whose priority is justifiably centered about the Institutional Division of the Department of Criminal Justice, has not proven beneficial to our community corrections system, nor to our constituency. (Scott 1997, p. 1)

The best organizational structure for probation departments is still open for debate.

Community Corrections Acts

To address concerns about local community differences and the lesser ability of local government to render political pull, community corrections acts were developed to capitalize on a partnership between state and local agencies. **Community Corrections Acts** (CCAs) are statewide laws through which funds are granted to local governments to develop and deliver community correctional sanctions and services. CCAs decentralize correctional sanctions so that they reflect community values and attitudes, as well as allow private citizen groups and agencies to participate. The first community corrections act was enacted in Minnesota in 1973 (Harris 1996). Their overall purpose is to expand local sentencing options in lieu of imprisonment (McManus and Barclay 1994). In other words, state-run programs do not qualify as CCAs; only those that are operated locally or through private agencies qualify. In this way, local governments benefit from the greater revenue-generating capacity of state government. We discuss the implications of this later in the chapter when we discuss the growth of private probation agencies.

Harris (1996) conducted an analysis of all CCAs and found that three primary CCA models exist, all of which share the following characteristics. They all

- *Are legislatively authorized statewide:* Statutes provide the framework and the authority for the other defining features of CCAs.

COMMUNITY CORRECTIONS ACT

A statewide mechanism through which funds are granted to local units of government to plan, develop, and deliver correctional sanctions and services. The overall purpose of this mechanism is to provide local sentencing options in lieu of imprisonment in state institutions.

- *Require local planning:* CCAs provide that local planning will precede and serve as the basis for the development, implementation, and modification of local correctional sanctions and services.
- *Provide for state funding:* CCAs provide for state subsidies to support local correctional programs and services.
- *Provide for citizen participation:* CCAs provide for citizen involvement and specify roles that citizens may play.
- *Call for decentralized program design and delivery:* CCAs provide for local control of the processes employed to assess local needs, to establish local priorities, and to deliver programs services. (p. 202)

Most states have passed CCA legislation to reflect individual community needs. CCAs are constantly undergoing revision and modification, but very few CCAs have been evaluated. A statewide evaluation of Ohio's Community Corrections Act revealed that the act was successful in diverting appropriate offenders from prison at no increased risk to public safety (Latessa, Travis, and Holsinger 1997). The focus of these CCAs, along with general statutory mandates, defines what probation officers do and how officers see themselves.

A TYPOLOGY OF PROBATION OFFICER WORK STYLES

How individual officers perceive themselves is important to carrying out legislative mandates. Klockars (1972) developed a typology of probation officers that defined four basic work styles: the law enforcer, the time-server, the therapeutic agent, and the synthetic officer.

Law Enforcers stress the legal authority and enforcement aspects of their job, dictating firmness and obeying the laws as essentials. Of prime importance to such officers are the court order, authority, and decision-making power.

Time-Servers have similar philosophies as law enforcers, but time-servers have little aspiration to improve their skills or change their ways. Their conduct on the job is to abide by the rules and meet minimal job responsibilities, but they do not strive to excel. Rules and regulations are upheld but unexamined. They do not make the rules; they just work there.

Therapeutic Agents see their role as administering a form of treatment, introducing the probationer or parolee to a better way of life and motivating constructive patterns of behavior. They give guidance and support to those who are unable to solve their problems by themselves and provide their clients with an opportunity to work through their ambivalent feelings. The philosophy of the therapeutic agent includes respecting clients, demonstrating concern, and helping individuals perceive the degree to which their old ways of behaving have been problematic.

Synthetic Officers are distinguished by their recognition of the balance between both the treatment and law enforcement components of probation officers' roles. Thus, they frequently encounter role conflict while combining the paternal, authoritarian, and judgmental with the therapeutic roles. Duffee (1984) talks about this role conflict when he states: "It is this officer who wraps his client in a warm hello hug, bruising him with his gun butt as he does so" (p. 191).

Many probation officers initially adopt a particular work style according to their personality and their ideological beliefs about crime causation. As time passes and officers become more experienced, these work orientations are strong predictors for how probation officers deal with offenders (Stowe 1994). We now turn to a discussion of what departments look for in hiring officers and how they select them.

SELECTION AND APPOINTMENT OF PROBATION OFFICERS

The initial selection of probation officers is similar to the system used to select other public employees; for instance, California requires that its officers be American citizens. See Box 5.1 for a discussion of whether requiring probation officers to be U.S. citizens is unconstitutional. Probation and parole officers are also prohibited from having any felony convictions and must undergo a criminal background check. Officers are either appointed, selected on merit, or some combination of the two.

BOX 5.1 COMMUNITY CORRECTIONS UP CLOSE

IS THE U.S. CITIZENSHIP REQUIREMENT TO BECOME A PROBATION OFFICER UNCONSTITUTIONAL?

The issue of employment rights for immigrants remains a central concern today, with state laws protecting people who have a legal right to work in the United States from being refused a job. However, there are some jobs or functions that require that the employee be a citizen of the United States, such as positions with political or peace-keeping functions. This requirement excludes permanent residents who are legally able to be in the United States, but who are not citizens or who have not sought "naturalization."

The state of California mandated that its probation officers be American citizens. A lawsuit was filed by a group of permanent resident aliens saying that the citizenship requirement was unconstitutional in that it violated the equal protection clause of the Fourteenth Amendment. The lower court of California

agreed that this was unconstitutional. The state appealed the decision, and the case went to the U.S. Supreme Court.

The state of California argued that all of its probation officers were by law, "peace officers." In other words, by definition, probation officers were authorized to carry and use a firearm, and exercise broad discretion in the potential use of coercive force and removal of freedom of probationers on community supervision. Second, all peace officers in California were required to be U.S. citizens, including local and state police. The state argued that they were merely extending to probation officers the requirement already in place for the police. The U.S. Supreme Court reversed the lower court decision and sided with the state of California. In upholding the citizenship requirement, the Supreme Court recognized that

". . . the probation officer acts as an extension of the judiciary's authority to set the conditions under which particular individuals will lead their lives and of the executive's authority to coerce obedience to those conditions. From the perspective of the probationer, his probation officer may personify the State's sovereign powers; from the perspective of the larger community, the probation officer may symbolize the political community's control over, and thus responsibility for, those who have been found to have violated the norms of social order. From both of these perspectives, a citizenship requirement may seem an appropriate limitation on those who would exercise and, therefore, symbolize this power of the political community over those who fall within its jurisdiction." (*Cabell v. Chavez-Salido* [1982] 454 U.S. 432).

Appointment System

Jurisdictions that appoint probation officers have a judge or selection committee that appoints a chief probation officer, who in turn selects assistants subject to the approval of the advisory body. Salary scales are fixed, and broad policy matters are determined by the judicial body that holds the power to select the chief probation officer.

BOX 5.2   COMMUNITY CORRECTIONS UP CLOSE

DUTIES OF A FEDERAL PROBATION OFFICER

A probation officer shall—

1. Instruct a probationer or a person on a supervised release, who is under his supervision, as to the conditions specified by the sentencing court, and provide him with a written statement clearly setting forth all such conditions;

2. Keep informed, to the degree required by the conditions specified by the sentencing court, as to the conduct and condition of a probationer or a person on supervised release, who is under his supervision, and report his conduct and condition to the sentencing court;

3. Use all suitable methods, not inconsistent with the conditions specified by the court, to aid a probationer or a person on supervised release who is under his supervision, and to bring about improvements in his conduct and condition;

4. Be responsible for the supervision of a probationer or a person on a supervised release who is known to be within the judicial district;

5. Keep a record of his work, and make such reports to the Director of the Administrative Office of the United States Courts as the Director may require;

6. Upon request of the Attorney General or his designee, assist in the supervision of, and furnish information about, a person within the custody of the Attorney General while on work release, furlough, or other authorized release from his regular place of confinement, or while in the prerelease custody pursuant to the provisions of section 3624c;

7. Keep informed concerning the conduct, condition, and compliance with any condition of probation, including the payment of a fine or restitution of each probationer under his supervision and report thereon to the court placing such person on probation and report to the court any failure of a probationer under his supervision to pay a fine in default so that the court may determine whether probation should be revoked;

8. (A) when directed by the court, and to the degree required by the regimen of care of treatment ordered by the court as a condition of release, keep informed as to the conduct and provide supervision of a person conditionally released under the provisions of section 4243 or 4246 of this title, and report such person's conduct and condition to the court ordering release and to the Attorney General or his designee; and

9. (B) immediately report any violation of the conditions of release to the court and the Attorney General or his designee;

10. If approved by the district court, be authorized to carry firearms under such rules and regulations as the Director of the Administrative Office of the United States Courts may prescribe; and

11. Perform any other duty that the court may designate.

Source: United States Sentencing Commission. 2002. *Federal Sentencing Guidelines* Chapter 3603, 1–10:1001–1002. Accessed: http://www.ussc.gov/2002guid/TABCON02.htm

As the probation officer's role focuses increasingly on public safety, more officers now carry firearms and handcuffs.

© Sgt David Hopkins, Columbus, GA, Police Department

In the federal system, for example, the judges of each federal district court appoint a chief probation officer. The chief probation officer selects the subordinate probation officers, who are all classified as law enforcement personnel. There are more than 4,000 U.S. probation officers in 94 judicial districts. supervising offenders under mandatory supervised release and those on military parole. See Box 5.2 for the responsibilities of a federal probation officer.

Where juvenile and adult probation services are administered locally and separately, the chief probation officer for adult probationers may be chosen by the judge or judges of the criminal courts, and the chief probation officer for juveniles by the juvenile judge or a juvenile board. Sometimes the juvenile board has the additional authority to designate which court is to be the juvenile court for the particular geographic area.

Merit System

Merit or civil service systems were developed to remove public employees from political patronage. In a merit system, applicants who meet minimum employment standards are required to pass a competitive exam. People who score above a specified minimum grade are placed on a ranked list. Candidates are selected from the list according to their order of rank. In some systems, applicants are also graded on the basis of their education and employment history. The merit system is used in some states to determine promotions and is required in four states (Delaware, Indiana, Rhode Island, and Wisconsin).

Combined System

Elements of both the appointment and merit systems may also be used. Applicants are initially screened through a merit exam, and candidates are selected by the agency in a process similar to the appointment system.

OFFICER QUALIFICATIONS, TRAINING, AND SALARY

Probation and parole officers should possess good oral and written communication skills to be able to interview offenders, provide testimony to judges, empathize with victims, and correspond with offenders' employers and family members. It is desirable for officers to know how to treat people fairly, consistently, firmly, and with respect. It is helpful for officers to be knowledgeable about different cultures and to be good time managers. These skills are gained by education, experience, and training.

Education and Experience

Most adult probation and parole officers must have a minimum of a baccalaureate degree, and at least 86 percent of states hiring juvenile probation officers require that they possess a degree (Reddington and Kreisel 2003). Traditionally, probation officers were recruited out of the social work and psychology fields. As the emphasis of probation changed from treatment to public safety and control, a preference has emerged to recruit individuals with degrees in criminal justice, criminology, and sociology. This is because knowledge of crime causation, criminal law, and systematic issues are important. It is an advantage for applicants who work with juveniles to have knowledge of development and adolescent psychology and juvenile justice. In addition to educational requirements, some jurisdictions may also require psychological evaluations, physical fitness tests, and drug screening.

Adult Preservice Training

Once an officer has been selected and hired, he or she begins training. **Preservice training** is training newly hired officers before they begin working independently. Combined probation and parole departments require an average of 208 hours of preservice training before officers assume their duties. However, probation and parole offices that are separate require significantly less training for probation officers (84 hours on average), and 182 hours for parole officers. Preservice training requirements range from 0 hours for probation officers in West Virginia to 600 hours for parole and probation officers in North Dakota. Preservice training requirements have become more standardized throughout most states (Camp, Camp, and May 2003). Table 5.2 lists selection and training requirements for adult probation officers by state. A variety of topics are covered, from interviewing skills to avoiding manipulation techniques, to HIV/AIDS education and training so that probation officers can prevent on-the-job exposure and also so that officers can provide prevention education to probationers (Logan 1992).

In many states where probation and parole officers carry firearms, they must complete **Peace Officer State Training** (POST). POST topics include strategies of case supervision, record keeping, legal liability, professional ethics, arrest and detention procedures, firearms handling, defensive tactics, and stress reduction. During the training process, POST instructors use metaphors and stories from their own field experiences that greatly influence how new recruits perceive the organizational culture. POST trainers thus shape the attitudes and values of the probation and parole officer subculture, which affect their work role orientation (Crank 1996).

Juvenile Preservice and Orientation Training

For the supervision of juveniles, the American Correctional Association recommends that juvenile probation officers receive 40 hours of preservice training, whereas the

TABLE 5.2 *Probation and Parole Staff Introductory and In-Service Training*

	Introductory Hours	Annual In-Service		Introductory Hours	Annual In-Service
Probation			**Probation and Parole**		
Arizona	40	16	Alaska	186	40
Colorado	120	40	Arkansas	280	40
Connecticut	160	40	Delaware	358	40
District of Columbia	80	80	Florida	438	40
Georgia	160	20	Idaho	120	40
Illinois	40	20	Kentucky	40	40
Massachusetts	80	3	Louisiana	40	40
Nebraska	120	40	Maryland	240	18
Texas	40	40	Michigan	80	40
West Virginia	0	35	Minnesota	40	40
			Missouri	220	40
Average	84	33	Mississippi	40	40
			Montana	160	40
			North Dakota	600	40
Parole			Ohio	240	40
Arizona	64	40	Oklahoma	480	40
California	400	92	Oregon	160	40
Colorado	152	40	Rhode Island	50	10
Connecticut	107	41	South Carolina	440	24
Georgia	320	40	Tennessee	40	40
Illinois	40	40	Utah	360	40
Indiana	150	40	Virginia	145	40
Kansas	200	40	Washington	80	80
Massachusetts	37.5	40	Wyoming	128	24
Nebraska	280	40			
New York	280	40	Average	208	38
Pennsylvania	160	40	**Summary**		
South Dakota	120	40	Probation	84	33
Texas	220	20	Parole	182	42
West Virginia	200	40	Probation and Parole	208	38
Average	182	42	Overall Average	128	38

CT: Introductory hours are 320 hours over a three-year period. Annual in-service is 123 hours over a three-year period. KY: Actually do 75 hours of in-service training. LA: Postacademy is 9.5 weeks. MA: Eight hours every three years. PA: Plus, introductory training includes three weeks of Basic Officer Training, one week of New Employee Orientation, and six months of on-the-job training prior to promotion to Parole Agent 2. RI: Training hours are estimated. TX: Probation: 40 introductory hours within the first year; 80 in-service hours per biennium. Parole: Introductory Institutional Parole Officers require 89 hours of training. WV: The annual in-service training required for officers/agents ranges from 30 to 40 hours.

Source: Camille Graham Camp, George M. Camp, and Bob May . 2003. *The 2002 Corrections Yearbook*. Middletown, CT: Criminal Justice Institute, p. 224. Reprinted with permission.

American Bar Association suggests 80 hours of preservice training with an additional 48 hours within the first six months. Reddington and Kreisel conducted a nationwide survey to determine trends in juvenile probation officer training. They found that 36 states mandated some sort of orientation training, whereas 20 states certified juvenile probation officer positions with an average of just over 100 hours of preservice training. The difference between preservice training and orientation (or fundamental skills) training is that preservice training is completed before the job begins, whereas orientation training is a "learn as you go" model. Tennessee provided the highest amount of preservice training at 120 hours, and other states required between 8 and 200 hours within the first year of employment (Reddington and Kreisel 2000, 2003). Compared to adult probation officers, who average 125 training hours, juvenile probation officers averaged just over 77 hours.

Though over 87 percent of survey respondents agreed that national training standards are needed in the juvenile probation area, there are no standards currently in existence. The vast majority of training (69 percent) was mandated by state statute, law, agency policy, or administrative order, and 30 percent of states had either voluntary or recommended training (Reddington and Kreisel 2003).

In-Service Training

In-service training is continuing education training that occurs annually for seasoned officers following the first year of employment. All states and the federal system require probation and parole officers to undergo a certain number of hours to keep current with new developments in the field, or to repeat important topics from the initial training. Forty hours annually appears to be the most common requirement for adult probation and parole departments, with the average ranging between 33 and 42 hours (Camp, Camp, and May 2003).

Probation officer training topics may include rational behavior training, which focuses on the officer using the principles of rationality to persuade the probationer to change old beliefs and attitudes. This training is particularly useful in influencing a hostile offender to develop new beliefs, which are reinforced by the probation officer (Ruby 1984). In at least one jurisdiction, probation officers are exposed to empathy training, which aims to sensitize probation officers to what juvenile probationers endure during arrest and detention (Rainey 2002).

While the American Correctional Association recommended that seasoned juvenile probation officers receive 40 hours of annual training, only 30 states require in-service training, ranging from 8 hours to 40 hours, with the median number of hours being 30 per year (see Reddington and Kreisel [2000] for a state-by-state breakdown of preservice and in-service hour requirements).

Officer Salary

The U.S. Department of Labor reported that "the median annual earnings of probation officers and correctional treatment specialists in May 2004 were $39,600. The middle 50 percent earned between $31,500 and $52,100. The lowest 10 percent earned less than $26,310 and the highest 10 percent earned more than $66,660." (U.S. Department of Labor 2006, p. 4). Probation officers in urban areas working for local government agencies tended to earn higher salaries than if the department was situated in a state government.

Another general trend is that parole officers in stand-alone departments had a higher starting salary. They also had higher salaries over their career than did parole or probation officers in combined departments. The differences in salary could be due to there being less turnover of probation officers in stand-alone departments, or their earning better raises over time than those provided by combined departments or by stand-alone parole departments.

Probation and parole administrators earned considerably more than field officers. The average salary for parole administrators was $161,435, and for probation administrators, $101,109. For combined departments, probation and parole administrators earned an average of $84,442 (Camp, Camp, and May 2003). As officers' job expectations have risen, so have the amount of training and their salaries. One example of increased responsibility is the authorization to carry weapons.

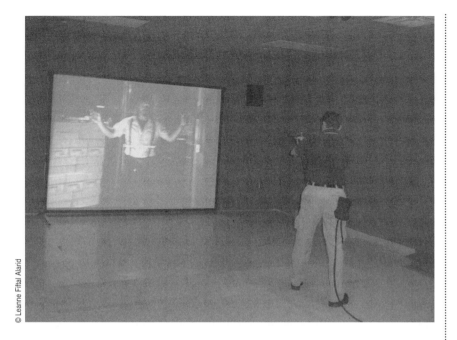

A probation officer participates in Firearms Training System (FATS), a more realistic decision-making test in potential uses of deadly force.

© Leanne Fiftal Alarid

FIREARMS POLICIES FOR PROBATION AND PAROLE OFFICERS

One of the strongest indicators of individual work styles or whether law enforcement is emphasized over rehabilitation is in the area of firearm policy. Officers favoring the carrying of firearms while on duty tended to be younger and more likely to practice law-and-order case management strategies rather than casework or treatment-oriented approaches (Sluder, Shearer, and Potts 1991). The real question is whether officers can effectively perform traditional casework strategies while armed (Small and Torres 2001).

A clear difference exists between juvenile and adult community supervision in that the vast majority of states do not allow officers supervising juveniles to carry firearms. Increasingly, probation and parole officers in the adult system are trained to carry firearms while on duty. As of April 2006, the American Probation and Parole Association reported that officers in 35 adult probation jurisdictions and 40 adult parole jurisdictions carry firearms (see Table 5.3). About half of all firearm-carrying jurisdictions in the adult system are mandatory, whereas other jurisdictions depend on the type of supervision, or allow officers to choose. In the juvenile system, only three states mandate firearms for officers, two give officers the option, and seven states narrow firearms to only certain counties or to officers who supervise serious juvenile offenders.

In the federal system, 85 out of 94 judicial districts allow federal probation officers to carry firearms of .40 caliber and above. The firearms policy for the Eastern District of Missouri states that "officers should avoid the use of a firearm except in self-defense or in defense of a fellow probation officer. The officer may not use a firearm unless the officer believes he/she, or a fellow officer, is in imminent danger of death or serious bodily injury and there is no means of a safe retreat" (Scharr 2001, p. 47). This firearm policy, as written, does not allow a probation officer to use a firearm to come to the aid of any other third party. Federal officers receive two weeks of training that includes qualifying with at least 80 percent accuracy and passing a written exam.

TABLE 5.3 *Number of States with Firearms Policies for Probation and Parole Officers*

Firearms Policy	PROBATION		PAROLE	
	Adult	Juvenile	Adult	Juvenile
Officers Not Armed Statewide	17	40	12	43
Mandatory Arming Statewide	17	4	25	3
County Specific	6	5	2	2
Optional Choice	9	2	9	2
Job Specific (Intensive)	3	2	4	1

Source: American Probation and Parole Association. 2006. *APPA Adult and Juvenile Probation and Parole National Firearm Survey 2005–2006*. Lexington, KY: APPA. Accessed: http://www.appanet.org/information%20clearing% 20house/survey.htm.

Some states allow probation officers to carry firearms on the job if authorized by the Chief Probation Officer of that county. For example, 60 percent of counties in California authorized the use of firearms, but wide variation existed on who was authorized. Some counties allowed only officers who supervised a specialized caseload, such as violent or other high-risk offenders, to carry a firearm, whereas other counties allowed any officer the option (Nieto 1996).

Those opposed to officers carrying a firearm argue that not every probation officer may need to carry a deadly weapon, especially if that officer supervises misdemeanants or juveniles. Furthermore, an officer's safety or life may be at greater risk if a probationer or parolee is carrying a weapon because a greater chance exists that the offender may use a gun against an armed officer than an unarmed officer (Scharr 2001). An early study found that probation officers who carried a firearm experienced more confrontation incidents than officers who did not carry a firearm. In addition, male probation officers were significantly more likely to be confronted and/or physically assaulted than female probation officers (Parsonage and Bushey 1989). Since that study, officer confrontations have greatly decreased as officers pay more attention to safety issues by conducting home visits in pairs, wearing body armor, and training in self-defense techniques. Of the serious incidents that have occurred, over half occurred in the field, and only 28 percent occurred in the probation office. The three most common incidents were threats, animal attacks, and other situations defined as "dangerous" (Small and Torres 2001).

Researchers agree that other options should be provided if an officer is philosophically opposed to carrying a firearm. These options include chemical agents, stun guns, pressure points training, and field visits with two officers. The APPA (1994) neither supports nor opposes the carrying of weapons by probation and parole officers. The association argues that, should officers be authorized to carry weapons, decisions should be made according to actual need, proper training, liability issues, and selection procedures that minimally include a physical and psychological examination. All probation officers who choose to carry a firearm receive training, such as the interactive video Firearms Training System, or FATS (see Box 5.3).

PROBATION OFFICER JOB STRESS

Probation and parole supervision is a job centered around people rather than around information and data. Dealing with people can result in a great deal of satisfaction and reward when officers can impact the lives of their clients. One federal probation

BOX 5.3   **TECHNOLOGY IN CORRECTIONS**

INTERACTIVE FIREARMS VIDEO TRAINING

The Firearms Training System (or FATS) is the use of interactive video technology to enhance firearms training for any peace officer, including probation, parole and pretrial services officers. FATS training is different from shooting at traditional fixed targets. In FATS training, a video image is projected onto a screen, and this image is connected to a computer, speakers, and firearm replicas that spray a harmless liquid peppermint when the trigger is pulled. Each different scenario requires the trainees to choose what action to take. After a variety of scenarios, the trainees discuss and justify their actions to the instructor.

An evaluation of FATS training found that 32 percent of probation officers reported that the training had altered their perceptions "to a great extent" of the value of a firearm for self-defense, and another 34 percent said that their perceptions changed "to some extent." The training helped clarify the meaning of the firearms policy, as well as the moral issues and liability that accompany the use of potentially deadly force. Scharr concluded: "After the training, officers clearly indi-cated they were surprised at how quickly a critical incident could occur, how likely it is that they will be perceived as law enforcement officers during a critical incident, how difficult it can be to work in teams and communicate during a critical incident. . . . This suggests that the training was effective in heightening officer awareness of danger and the necessity for continued training in mental preparedness and self-defense proficiency" (p. 49).

Source: Timothy M. Scharr. 2001. Interactive Video Training for Firearms Safety. *Federal Probation* 65(2): 45–51.

officer said: "It's a person's life you are dealing with. . . . If you can help someone lead a stable and productive life, then it is worth all the effort. You can't explain the rewards of helping someone else. To see someone make it through that system and lead a productive life is a reward" (Quinn 2002, p. 265).

Jobs that are people centered also tend to have higher levels of risk and burnout than jobs that are data centered. Although most jobs are stressful to some degree, being a probation and parole officer can be stressful because of its unpredictability. One of the purposes of this section is to inform readers of the realistic concerns of community corrections supervision so that people interested in this profession are aware of the potential concerns this line of work may hold. Studies of probation officer stress can certainly apply to any position in the area of community corrections supervision.

Most studies of probation officer stress do not compare the job with other types of employment, so it is difficult to say whether being a probation officer is a "high-stress" or "low-stress" job overall. One study found adult and juvenile probation officers had higher stress levels than members of the general public who had other noncriminal justice occupations. However, probation officers seem to have less stress than police officers or correctional officers working in prisons.

Sources of Stress

Researchers have uncovered the following sources of stress for line probation officers (Holgate and Clegg 1991; Slate, Johnson, and Wells 2000; Whitehead 1985; Wells, Colbert and Slate 2006):

- Excessive paperwork
- Lack of time to accomplish the job

- Role ambiguity
- Role conflict
- Lack of participation in decision making
- Court leniency
- Failure to recognize accomplishments

Sometimes feeling overly stressed may simply mean that the job is not a good fit for the person. In criminal justice, written documentation is an important part of taking legal responsibility for the supervision of another person. Officers spend a lot of time documenting everything on every client they supervise, and that is what some officers may refer to as "excessive paperwork." Time spent on paperwork and the large number of people under the supervision of one officer lead to the feeling that there is not enough time for the actual supervision part.

ROLE AMBIGUITY

The discretion that exists in the role of the probation and parole officer to treat clients fairly and consistently and according to individual circumstances.

ROLE CONFLICT

The two functions of a probation and parole officer, that of enforcing the rules and laws, and providing support and reintegration, that are sometimes contradictory and difficult to reconcile.

Role ambiguity refers to the idea that community supervision officers have discretion and can choose whether or not to exercise it. This is why common sense, ethics, and consistency are so important. Officers also have to manage their time because they may be out in the field. People who are accustomed only to following the lead of others and who cannot manage their time well may experience a sense of uneasiness because they may not feel comfortable acting on their own.

Role conflict, a common source of stress, refers to the idea that officers must be empathetic, understanding, and objective enough to help offenders who have broken the law. At the same time, they must also be able to revoke or terminate clients who are not following the conditions of their supervision (as we will discuss in the next chapter).

Lack of participation in decision making is related to line officers who make recommmendations to their supervisors, judges, and parole boards, but who do not actually get to make the final decision. The decision is therefore made by a third party who does not have daily interactions with the offender, and the officer may at times feel a sense of betrayal by the court that does not agree with the officer's recommendations.

Finally, supervising offenders all too often ignore the basic principles of behavior modification: reward positive behavior and discourage negative behavior. Community corrections supervision all too often takes action on negative behavior and ignores or downplays positive or prosocial behavior. This would make a behavioral psychologist shudder and might explain in part at least why so many offenders "fail" on supervision.

Many people find this line of work very rewarding and have spent their entire career in community corrections. Work-related stress can be decreased by changing some aspect of the organization or the job or by improving how a person responds to these stressful factors. Parsonage and Bushey (1989) recommend that employers inform employees of the potential risks of the job and provide training to minimize this risk.

Decreasing Stress: Types of Immunity

One of the ways to decrease probation and parole officer stress is for officers to know general limits of the law regarding actions or inactions on the job. One of the general principles is that it is important for officers to minimize risk by keeping track of the people they are supervising, and responding appropriately to inappropriate behaviors. No matter how accomplished and organized the officer, the probationer or parolee may at times injure or victimize the general public. What happens if the victim feels the injury could have been prevented if only the officer had "properly supervised" the client?

Given that it is impossible for officers to control the actions of their clients at all times, the best officers can do is to follow department policy, follow the orders of the court or the parole board, and justify their actions with accurate paperwork. **Negligence** is the failure to do that which a reasonably prudent person would have done in like or similar circumstances. For example, if an officer finds out through credible sources that one of her probationers is planning to commit a crime, and the officer could have prevented it but failed to do so, the officer is likely negligent. A person may be held liable (or responsible) if the negligence was gross or willful. All of these terms are subjective according to the meaning assigned by a judge or jury, but gross or willful negligence generally means that a person must have intentionally or maliciously failed to act (del Carmen et al. 2001).

Since probation and parole officers are government officials (as are police, judges, and prosecutors), probation and parole officers are entitled to different types of legal protection so that they may feel comfortable exercising discretion without fear of being personally sued over actions of clients under their supervision. The type of immunity officers have depends on what *function* they are performing (del Carmen et al. 2001).

ABSOLUTE IMMUNITY. **Absolute immunity** protects government officials from any legal action unless they engage in actions that are intentionally and maliciously wrong. Absolute immunity provides the highest level of protection. In *King v. Simpson* (1999), the court ruled that parole board officials have absolute immunity in adjudicatory decisions to grant, deny, or revoke parole. Probation and parole officers have absolute immunity only when acting in a quasi-judicial or prosecutorial function, such as when probation officers are preparing and submitting a presentence investigation report (*Spaulding v. Nielsen* 1979), and only if those actions are specifically defined as a quasi-judicial function under state statute—otherwise that function is eligible for qualified immunity.

QUALIFIED IMMUNITY. Qualified immunity is much more narrow and limited to those in the executive branch or when workers are performing administrative functions. In **qualified immunity,** workers are not liable for wrongdoing when their actions are found to be "objectively reasonable" and within the scope of employment. This standard is also subjective. Given that most functions of probation and parole officers are administrative rather than quasi-judicial/adjudicatory, probation and parole officers have qualified immunity (del Carmen et al. 2001).

Parole officer functions are defined differently from jurisdiction to jurisdiction. In New York, parole officers have only qualified immunity when recommending the issuance of a revocation warrant. This is because under New York law, issuing a revocation warrant is considered an investigatory, not a prosecutorial, function (*Best v. State* 1999). In another state, the same activity—initiating a parole revocation proceeding and presenting the case during parole revocation hearings—was identified as a quasi-judicial function and therefore subject to absolute immunity.

As probation and parole officers are increasingly carrying firearms on the job, they are also a type of law enforcement officer, particularly if they have completed peace officer training. With this training also comes more liability and responsibility, making the decision to carry very much a personal and individual choice that should be carefully considered. We recommend that applicants find out in advance what kind of firearms policy exists (mandatory, optional, none, and so forth) and determine what situation is most suitable.

NEGLIGENCE

The failure of an officer to do what a reasonably prudent person would have done in like or similar circumstances.

ABSOLUTE IMMUNITY

Protection from legal action or liability unless workers engage in discretion that is intentionally and maliciously wrong.

QUALIFIED IMMUNITY

Protection from liability in decisions or actions that are "objectively reasonable."

PRIVATE PROBATION

Private, nonprofit entities have been involved in community supervision of offenders since the 1800s. The Salvation Army has a long history of providing such services. Over time, state codes and statutes were formulated to permit the use of private agencies for ancillary treatment services (mental health, driving while intoxicated classes, drug treatment, anger management, and so on) to be provided for state and local probationers or for private agencies to provide direct probation supervision. Because of the growing number of probationers for the number of staff available to supervise them, states are increasingly contracting with **private probation** agencies to assist with supervision.

At least 18 states use private agencies for some form of supervision, 10 of which rely on private agencies for the sole responsibility of supervising misdemeanor and low-risk clients, while the state agency focuses on felony probationers (Schloss and Alarid 2007). For example, the adult probation office in Connecticut contracted with a private probation service to take on cases that required a lower level of supervision. The private contractor had no face-to-face contact with any low-level probationers but assisted the state in monitoring compliance of community service via phone calls and the mail and by completing paperwork for each case. The state probation office was able to concentrate its efforts on the supervision of high-risk cases (Bosco 1998).

Statutes examined by Schloss and Alarid (2007) in seven states that authorized private probation (Alabama, Arkansas, Florida, Georgia, Missouri, Utah, and Tennessee) found that most states required agencies to sign a formal contract with the government that outlined the scope of services to be provided, the responsibilities of the contractor, and the obligations of the court. For example, private agencies in Missouri wishing to provide services must make application to provide services with the Circuit Judge, and must be able to prove financial ability and liability insurance to operate a probation office. However, Missouri has few standardized guidelines for private agency approval other than that the agency cannot be related in any way to the judge. Once agencies are approved for a three-year term, there are no requirements to provide verification of fees collected.

Critics of privatization say that the need to provide effective correctional services seems to be at odds with the prerequisite of making a profit for the business. Private sector probation is seen as intruding and competing with the government's traditional and ultimate responsibility to carry out punishment in a fair manner (Bosco 1998). Furthermore, the private sector is usually not equipped to be a full-service organization, and thus it might only be able to take low-risk offenders who require little if any monitoring. Private sector services have no uniform method of monitoring probation conditions or ensuring that victim restitution is collected (Leznoff 1998).

State statutes also uncovered broad requirements for hiring officers as employees. Some states, such as Georgia, provided specific requirements for ongoing training and education of private probation officers. Georgia required officers to have completed two years of college, not be convicted of a felony, and be a minimum age of 21. Other states have no educational or training requirements for hiring individuals who wish to become probation officers (Schloss and Alarid 2007).

Another concern relates to the lack of standardization for agencies that wish to become program providers for probation agencies. Some states have no requirement that providers demonstrate qualifications such as licensing and experience. Ethical questions arise if private probation agencies are also treatment providers and require their ancillary services as a part of probation supervision. Schloss and Alarid (2007) argue for more stringent and standardized requirements for the supervision of offenders by private probation agencies and believe that Georgia, Utah, Colorado, and Tennessee provide good examples in this endeavor.

PRIVATE PROBATION

An agency that is owned and operated by a private business or nonprofit organization, and contracts with the state, local, or federal government to supervise clients.

TOP THINGS YOU SHOULD KNOW

- Probation or parole officers are selected by appointment, merit, or a combination of the two. In most states necessary qualifications include being a U.S. citizen, being at least 21 years of age, possessing a baccalaureate degree, passing a drug test, and not having a felony record.
- Issues continually evolving are the provisions for preservice and in-service training, and the effect of firearms policies in probation and parole.
- Applicants should find out about the firearms policy of the department they are applying to and also determine whether carrying a firearm is suitable to them, as this is very much an individual decision.
- The future of probation aims to give line-level officers more decision-making opportunities and responsibility, which, in turn, will likely decrease job stress and burnout.
- Corrections workers have absolute immunity when acting in a quasi-judicial or prosecutorial function, but have only qualified immunity when performing administrative or other discretionary functions.
- Some private community corrections organizations have the potential to effectively supervise low-risk clients, but requirements range widely by jurisdiction.

DISCUSSION QUESTIONS

1. How are probation officers selected in your jurisdiction? What are the advantages and disadvantages of administering probation services in this way?
2. Why are community corrections acts advantageous to local-level supervision?
3. Why are college degrees required for probation and parole officers, but not necessarily for entry-level police officers?
4. What are the advantages and disadvantages of having a college education in the field of community correctional supervision?
5. Do probation officers receive enough training for the responsibilities they have? Why or why not?
6. What are the advantages and disadvantages regarding probation and parole officers carrying weapons?
7. Would you carry a weapon on the job? Why or why not? Would you carry a firearm only under certain conditions (such as supervising a certain type of individual)?
8. How can probation and parole officers minimize the chances that they will lose a civil lawsuit if they are ever sued?
9. Agree or disagree with the following statement: Private probation supervision and treatment services should be expanded.
10. What limitations or controls would you place on private probation agencies? Why?

 ## WEBSITES

Career Planning Resources for Probation, Parole, and Correctional Treatment Workers

http://www.career-planning-education.com/law-criminal-justice/probation-officers.htm#outlook

U.S. Probation Office, Southern District of Ohio, Job Description

http://www.ohsp.uscourts.gov/aboutus.html

Occupational Guide to Probation and Parole Officers in California

http://www.calmis.ca.gov/file/occguide/PROBOFF.HTM

Job Description for Probation and Parole Officer in Australia

http://www.jobguide.thegoodguides.com.au/text/jobdetails.cfm?jobid=615

Oregon Juvenile Probation Officer Job Description

http://www.hr.das.state.or.us/Hrsd/class/6634.htm

Arizona Probation Officer Firearms Policy

http://www.azleg.state.az.us/DocumentsForBill.asp?Bill_Number=HB2350

California Penal Code 830.5: Carrying a Firearm

http://law.onecle.com/california/penal/830.5.html

Pennsylvania (Carbon County) Adult Probation and Parole Officer Firearms Policy

http://www.courts.state.pa.us/judicial-council/local-rules/carbon/carbon_ chg_ 121399.pdf

6

Classification and Supervision in Probation and Parole

Introduction

Neighborhood-Based Probation Supervision
The Surveillance Function in Supervision
Developing Prosocial Behaviors

Classification: The First Step in Supervision
Actuarial Risk Assessment
Identifying Treatment Needs
Developing the Case Plan
Levels of Supervision
Caseload and Workload Standards

Specialized Caseloads
Supervising Offenders Who Are Mentally Ill
Supervising Offenders Who Have Abused Drugs and Alcohol
Supervising Sex Offenders

Interstate Compacts on Probation
New Interstate Compact for Adult Offender Supervision
Revocation and the Interstate Compact

Top Things You Should Know

KEY TERMS

Supervision

Neighborhood-based supervision

Classification

Risk assessment

Static factors

Dynamic factors

Collateral contact

Field contact

Caseload

Penile plethysmograph

Sending state

Receiving state

Interstate Compact for Adult
  Offender Supervision

SUPERVISION

The oversight that a probation or parole officer exercises over those in his or her custody.

What You Will Learn in This Chapter

- *How neighborhood-based supervision probation officers are involved with the community*
- *The importance of caseload classification in identifying risk and needs in order to match the level of supervision to client characteristics and develop a treatment plan*
- *How workload allocation is important to keep caseloads down*
- *The various supervision strategies for offenders with special needs*
- *How offenders are supervised if they want to move to another state*

INTRODUCTION

Probation departments provide both an investigatory and a supervisory function in the criminal justice system. In Chapter 3, you learned about the investigatory function of probation as illustrated by the officer's preparation of presentence investigation reports. In this chapter, we discuss the supervisory function of probation and parole officers as it pertains to managing offenders in the community. In its simplest terms, **supervision** may be defined as an officer's oversight of clients committed to his or her custody. Much of this chapter applies to both probation and parole supervision because the mechanics of the supervision process and the condition terms are similar. In many states and in the federal system, the same officers supervise a mix of both probationers and parolees on the same caseload. Recall that in Chapter 3 we introduced the idea that supervision includes both standard conditions, which are mandatory and apply to all offenders in a jurisdiction, and special conditions, which are discretionary and unique to an offender's special circumstances. Special conditions are defined by judges or the parole board, but conditions are enforced by probation and parole officers. Box 6.1 lists standard/mandatory conditions for federal probationers, and then displays a list of special or discretionary conditions that may or may not be a part of the sentence.

What are the types of sentences that people on probation must complete? About 60 percent of probationers nationwide have a direct sentence to probation, 30 percent have some type of suspended sentence (such as diversion), and 9 percent have a split sentence (a short time in jail, followed by a longer period of probation). The vast majority of probationers have been sentenced for a drug or alcohol violation, followed by property offenses, with less than 20 percent of probationers sentenced for a violent offense. About 77 percent of all adult probationers are men, and 23 percent are women. The race/ethnic group composition for probationers varies by region of the country, but on a nationwide scale more than half (56 percent) of probationers are white, 30 percent are African American, 12 percent are of Hispanic origin, and 2 percent are either Native American or Asian/Pacific Islander (see Table 6.1).

NEIGHBORHOOD-BASED PROBATION SUPERVISION

Recall from Chapter 4 that probation supervision began with the casework approach, in which probation officers were like social workers. In the 1980s, probation officers became more concerned with public safety and monitoring. Offenders were referred to specialized services where they could participate and pay for treatment.

BOX 6.1   CONDITIONS OF FEDERAL PROBATION   •

Mandatory Conditions

The court shall provide, as an *explicit condition* of a sentence of probation

1. for a felony, a misdemeanor, or an infraction, that the defendant not commit another Federal, State, or local crime during the term of probation;

2. for a felony, that the defendant also abide by at least one condition set forth in subsection (b) (2), (b) (3), or (b) (13), unless the court finds on the record that extraordinary circumstances exist that would make such a condition plainly unreasonable, in which event the court shall impose one or more of the other conditions set forth under subsection (b);

3. for a felony, a misdemeanor, or an infraction, that the defendant not unlawfully possess a controlled substance;

4. for a domestic violence crime as defined in section 3561(b) by a defendant convicted of such an offense for the first time that the defendant attend a public, private, or private nonprofit offender rehabilitation program that has been approved by the court, in consultation with a State Coalition Against Domestic Violence or other appropriate expert, if an approved program is readily available within a 50-mile radius of the legal residence of the defendant;

5. for a felony, a misdemeanor, or an infraction, that the defendant refrain from any unlawful use of a controlled substance and submit to one drug test within 15 days of release on probation and at least two periodic drug tests thereafter (as determined by the court) for use of a controlled substance, but the condition stated in this paragraph may be ameliorated or suspended by the court for any individual defendant if the defendant's presentence report or other reliable sentencing information indicates a low risk of future substance abuse by the defendant;

6. that the defendant: (A) make restitution in accordance with sections 2248, 2259, 2264, 2327, 3663, 3663A, and 3664; and (B) pay the assessment imposed in accordance with section 3013;

7. that the defendant will notify the court of any material change in the defendant's economic circumstances that might affect the defendant's ability to pay restitution, fines, or special assessments;

8. for a person described in section 4042(c) (4), that the person report the address where the person will reside and any subsequent change of residence to the probation officer responsible for supervision, and that the person register in any State where the person resides, is employed, carries on a vocation, or is a student (as such terms are defined under section 170101(a) (3) of the Violent Crime Control and Law Enforcement Act of 1994).

9. If the court has imposed and ordered execution of a fine and placed the defendant on probation, payment of the fine or adherence to the court-established installment schedule shall be a condition of the probation.

Discretionary Probation Conditions

The court may provide, as further conditions of a sentence of probation, to the extent that such conditions are reasonably related to the factors set forth in section 3553(a) (1) and (a) (2) and to the extent that such conditions involve only such deprivations of liberty or property as are reasonably necessary for the purposes indicated in section 3553(a) (2), that the defendant

1. support his dependents and meet other family responsibilities;

2. make restitution to a victim of the offense under section 3556 (but not subject to the limitation of section 3663(a) or 3663A(c) (1) (A));

(continued)

BOX 6.1   CONDITIONS OF FEDERAL PROBATION (contd)

3. give to the victims of the offense the notice ordered pursuant to the provisions of section 3555;

4. work conscientiously at suitable employment or pursue conscientiously a course of study or vocational training that will equip him for suitable employment;

5. refrain, in the case of an individual, from engaging in a specified occupation, business, or profession bearing a reasonably direct relationship to the conduct constituting the offense, or engage in such a specified occupation, business, or profession only to a stated degree or under stated circumstances;

6. refrain from frequenting specified kinds of places or from associating unnecessarily with specified persons;

7. refrain from excessive use of alcohol, or any use of a narcotic drug or other controlled substance, as defined in section 102 of the Controlled Substances Act (21 D.S.C. 802), without a prescription by a licensed medical practitioner;

8. refrain from possessing a firearm, destructive device, or other dangerous weapon;

9. undergo available medical, psychiatric, or psychological treatment, including treatment for drug or alcohol dependency, as specified by the court, and remain in a specified institution if required for that purpose;

10. remain in the custody of the Bureau of Prisons during nights, weekends, or other intervals of time, totaling no more than the lesser of one year or the term of imprisonment authorized for the offense, during the first year of the term of probation;

11. reside at, or participate in the program of, a corrections facility (including a facility maintained contract to the Bureau of Prisons) for all or part of probation;

12. work in community service as directed by the court;

13. reside in a specified place or area, or refrain from residing in a specified place or area;

14. remain within the jurisdiction of the court, unless granted

---

Monitoring increasingly occurred in probation offices, where offenders were required to make a special trip to see their officer. This monitoring style is called a "fortress style" of supervision because it separated the officer from the offender and the community; officers were confined to the office, and supervision occurred between 8:00 and 5:00 during the week.

In the last decade, a philosophical change has unfolded yet again to rethink the way that probation supervision is implemented to encompass both the offenders and the communities in which they reside. This supervision strategy is more visible in the community and is known by a variety of terms such as **"neighborhood-based supervision"** (the term we will use in this text), "community justice," or "broken windows probation" (Beto 2000).

In neighborhood-based supervision (NBS), the probation officers are in the community more than the office and engage community groups as partners and collaborators in offender supervision. By making probation more visible and establishing leverage with community groups, NBS aims to make probation a more respected

NEIGHBORHOOD-BASED SUPERVISION

A supervision strategy that emphasizes public safety, accountability, partnerships with other community agencies, and beat supervision.

permission to leave by the court or a probation officer;

15. report to a probation officer as directed by the court or the probation officer;

16. permit a probation officer to visit him at his home or elsewhere as specified by the court;

17. answer inquiries by a probation officer and notify the probation officer promptly of any change in address or employment;

18. notify the probation officer promptly if arrested or if questioned by a law enforcement officer;

19. remain at his place of residence during nonworking hours and, if the court finds it appropriate, that compliance with this condition be monitored by telephonic or electronic signaling devices, except that a condition under this paragraph may be imposed only as an alternative to incarceration;

20. comply with the terms of any court order or order of an administrative process pursuant to the law of a State, the District of Columbia, or any other possession or territory of the United States, requiring payments by the defendant for the support and maintenance of a child or of a child and the parent with whom the child is living;

21. be ordered deported by a United States district court, or United States magistrate judge, pursuant to a stipulation entered into by the defendant and the United States under section 238(d)(5) of the Immigration and Nationality Act, except that, in the absence of a stipulation, the United States district court or a United States magistrate judge, may order deportation as a condition of probation, if, after notice and hearing pursuant to such section, the Attorney General demonstrates by clear and convincing evidence that the alien is deportable;

22. satisfy such other conditions as the court may impose.

U.S. Code, Title 18, Part II, Chapter 227, Subchapter B, Sec. 3563. *Conditions of Federal Probation.*

punishment in the community. The strategies of NBS would in turn help improve the overall quality of life in the community and contribute to decreasing crime. The elements of NBS include holding probation administrators and line officers accountable for achieving specific outcomes, such as (Beto 2000, p. 12)

- Emphasis on public safety
- Partnerships with police, treatment providers, and faith-based initiatives
- Supervision in field beats
- Strong and consistent enforcement of probation conditions
- Use of satellite tracking and geographic information systems technology
- Rational allocation of resources using offender assessments
- Measuring program effectiveness by establishing performance-based initiatives

This philosophy has required a paradigm shift in how probation officers and supervisors currently think and operate. Probation officers are community organizers,

TABLE 6.1 *Characteristics of Adults on Probation, 1995, 2000, and 2004*

	1995	2000	2004
Gender			
Male	79%	78%	77%
Female	21	22	23
Race			
White	53	54	56
Black	31	31	30
Hispanic	14	13	12
American Indian/Alaska Native	1	1	1
Asian/Pacific Islander[a]	**	1	1
Status of Probation			
Direct imposition	48	56	56
Split sentence	15	11	8
Sentence suspended	26	25	24
Imposition suspended	6	7	10
Other	4	1	1
Status of Supervision			
Active	79	76	75
Inactive	8	9	9
Absconded	9	9	9
Supervised out of state	2	3	2
Warrant status	2	3	5
Type of Offense			
Felony	54	52	49
Misdemeanor	44	46	50
Other infractions	2	2	1
Most Serious Offense			
Sexual assault	*	*	3
Domestic violence	*	*	6
Other assault	*	*	10
Burglary	*	*	5
Larceny/theft	*	*	12
Fraud	*	*	5
Drug law violation	*	24	26
Driving while intoxicated	16	18	15
Minor traffic offenses	*	6	7
Other	84	52	10
Adults Entering Probation			
Without incarceration	72	79	76
With incarceration	13	16	14
Other types	15	5	10
Adults Leaving Probation			
Successful completions	62	60	60
Returned to incarceration	21	15	15
With new sentence	5	3	8
With the same sentence	13	8	6
Unknown	3	4	1
Absconder[b]	*	3	4
Other unsuccessful[b]	*	11	10
Death	1	1	1
Other	16	11	9

Notes: For every characteristic there were people of unknown status or type.

*Not available. **Less than 0.5 percent. [a]Includes Native Hawaiians. [b]In 1995 absconder and other unsuccessful were reported among "other."

Source: Lauren E. Glaze and Seri Palla. 2005. *Probation and Parole in the United States, 2004.* Washington, DC: U.S. Department of Justice, Bureau of Justice Statistics.

working with both community organizations and criminals. Cases are assigned to officers according to geographic beat areas in a community (Reinventing Probation Council 1999), which is ideal for using geographic information systems (GIS) technology (see Box 6.2).

NBS sites started in Boston; Phoenix; Tucson; Dallas/Ft. Worth; Waco, Texas; and Spokane, Washington. Preliminary evaluations of these sites compared probationers supervised in the NBS program, which had smaller caseloads, with probationers supervised using traditional probation. An evaluation of one site indicated that probationers supervised in the NBS program perceived more support and help from their probation officer in finding employment and in making connections to treatment providers than did probationers supervised on traditional caseloads (Lutze, Smith, and Lovrich 2004). NBS officers had more autonomy and a closer connection with police and the community than traditional probation officers, but relationships with treatment service providers were similar for both groups. NBS probationers were more likely to be violated for technical violations than traditional probationers, yet both groups committed a similar number of new crimes while on supervision. Overall recidivism rates between the two groups were not significantly different (Lutze, Smith, and Lovrich 2004). Evaluations of the other sites need to be completed to

BOX 6.2   TECHNOLOGY IN CORRECTIONS

USING GEOGRAPHIC INFORMATION SYSTEM TECHNOLOGY IN PROBATION AND PAROLE SUPERVISION

Geographic information system (GIS) mapping uses special computer software to visually diagram locations in a neighborhood, or the entire city, of individuals and/or events. GIS mapping enables a probation or parole agency to obtain a full picture of who is on probation and where probationers live. By "parsing" and "geocoding" the data, probation supervisors have detailed information to use when assigning new cases to their officers. Available data includes number of police calls for service, the number and location of orders of protection, and access to treatment venues from probationers' residence. An officer who supervises an entire caseload of offenders in the same area can achieve a higher level of field surveillance than an officer who

must drive all over the city. GIS technology can also overlay information on bus routes, employer locations, locations of alcohol establishments, and schools to determine feasibility of probationer success and how travel time can be minimized when probationers move from one location to another. This technology gives probation officers more details about their jurisdiction or the "beat" in which their clients live, and information can be shared with police departments, which already use GIS to locate suspects and investigate new crimes.

GIS technology is also helpful to supervisors when assigning new clients to a caseload. The supervisor can examine where the offender lives and assign offenders in the same

neighborhood to the same officer, such as in neighborhood-based supervision. In this way, officers can supervise their caseload in a small area of town where they can be more likely to visit them in the neighborhood, rather than driving haphazardly all over town. Using GIS mapping, routes from one house to the next can be planned for a series of home visits. The possibilities of GIS applications for corrections are still being discovered and linked to other agencies within the broader criminal justice system.

Sources: Keith Harries. 2003. Using Geographic Analysis in Probation and Parole. *National Institute of Justice Journal* 249: 32–33; Jaishankar Karuppannan. 2005. Mapping and Corrections: Management of Offenders with Geographic Information Systems. *Corrections Compendium* 30(1): 7–9, 31–33.

obtain a more comprehensive picture of NBS. NBS and traditional probation supervision are similar in that they are both involved in surveillance and the development of prosocial behaviors.

The Surveillance Function in Supervision

We discussed how the current probation supervision philosophy aims to make probation a more visible and respected supervision tool in the community. In practice, broken windows probation has elements of surveillance, accountability, and managing risk. An offender must first be notified of his or her supervision conditions, and the officer in turn has the responsibility to clarify how each condition is to be fulfilled, as well as the consequences for not fulfilling each condition. Compliance with probation conditions assists offenders in learning how to structure their daily lives in a crime-free way. Surveillance is an important element of supervision that provides a means of ascertaining whether probationers and parolees are continuing to meet the conditions imposed by the court or the parole board.

Surveillance is also a tool for reducing an offender's access to crime opportunities (Cullen, Eck, and Lowenkamp 2002). Formal methods of surveillance include unannounced and announced field visits, curfew, electronic monitoring, phone verifications, graduated sanctions, and collection of urine samples for drug testing (Taxman 2002). In addition to surveillance by probation officers, probationers and parolees are watched by police. Warrantless searches of probationers' homes can be conducted by

Claude Allen, a former aide to President Bush, pleaded guilty to theft for making false returns at discount department stores while working for the White House. Allen pleaded guilty in Montgomery County Circuit Court to one misdemeanor count of theft under $500 and was sentenced to two years of supervised probation with a $500 fine.

police if the search was based on the police's "reasonable suspicion" that the person the police verified was on probation was also thought to be engaged in criminal activity (*United States v. Knights* 2001). Reasonable suspicion is a lower standard of proof than "probable cause," which is needed for most residence searches. However, the U.S. Supreme Court said that the probationer has a diminished expectation of privacy while on probation and the probationer is more likely to violate the law than a citizen not on probation. Public support and cooperation are difficult to obtain for any probation or parole system that does not assure the community of at least minimum protection against potential criminal activities by those under supervision.

Developing Prosocial Behaviors

Along with reducing opportunities for crime, supervision must also be directed toward removing or reducing barriers that may result in recidivism, as well as assisting the offender in positive behavioral change, which may involve placing offenders into treatment programs (Cullen, Eck, and Lowenkamp 2002). Officers do this by building on an offender's strengths, assisting with employment, and integrating family as informal social controls.

BUILDING ON ASSETS AND STRENGTHS.   Think of community supervision as a two-way relationship between the officer and the offender that is affected by the motivation that the offender has to change, coupled with the way the officer responds to and encourages that change. One study revealed that few probation officers used effective techniques of building rapport and eliciting information that would help lead to offender change (Taxman 2002). Most styles of supervision use a "deficit-focused" approach in which the officer responds to negative rule-breaking behavior with punitiveness and graduated sanctions. Probation and parole conditions are worded as "shall nots" (Maloney, Bazemore, and Hudson 2001).

A different way of looking at supervision could be a "strength-based" or "asset-building" approach that rewards offenders with oral or written praise, certificates of completion, vouchers with small monetary rewards, or special privileges to encourage certain positive behaviors. At the same time, removing privileges would be expected for negative behavior, but simultaneously incorporating a reward system is more of a motivating factor for the probationer to change (Maloney, Bazemore, and Hudson 2001).

This style of supervision has also been called "motivational interviewing" in that the community supervision officer learns how to create a climate that will assist the offender in changing (Clark 2005). An honest, direct relationship, along with good communication skills, is another effective means of promoting change and ensuring successful completion of the term of probation. Effective techniques include asking open-ended questions of the offender, demonstrating empathy, using motivational interviewing techniques, and taking a genuine interest by follow-up statements and positive recognition (Taxman 2002). Statements such as

"How can we come together on this?"

"It's your choice, but is there anything we can do to help you avoid those consequences?" (Clark 2005, p. 26) are less confrontational than mandates and threats.

EMPLOYMENT SERVICES.   Petersilia (2003) suggests that employment is the single most important element in preventing recidivism for probationers and parolees. Not only does employment provide financial support for the offender and his or her family, but it is also crucial for establishing and maintaining self-esteem and personal dignity—qualities that are seen by most authorities as essential to successful reintegration into the community. Experienced probation and parole officers know this to be true, and most probation and parole conditions require the offender to maintain employment during the period of supervision. However, finding and maintaining employment are not simple. Offenders are often the last to be hired and the first to be terminated. Many of them are unskilled, and many have poor work habits. Some are barred from employment in their chosen fields as a result of regulatory and licensing laws that preclude people with a criminal conviction (we discuss these issues in Chapter 15).

Because of the critical relationship between success on parole or probation supervision and meaningful employment, probation and parole officers must assess the employment status of each person under their supervision and work with him or her to locate a job. In many cases the probationer or parolee will require a vocational assessment to determine his or her employability, interests, and capabilities, as well as any barriers to employment. Many will require vocational or job-readiness training before they can seek a job. Ideally, these services are obtained from external agencies and organizations such as state employment offices or vocational rehabilitation services. The probation or parole officer's job is to locate the existing service, assist the probationer in obtaining the service, and monitor progress and participation. This requires networking and connections with community agencies.

USING INFORMAL SOCIAL CONTROLS.   Informal social controls such as family members and community agencies are also significant resources that officers can access to help probationers develop prosocial behaviors. Probationers were significantly more likely to succeed on probation if they had the support of family or friends than if they did not have such support (Taxman 2002). Neighborhood-based supervision uses these techniques to aid in supervision.

Read one federal probation officer's view (see Box 6.3) about a typical day on the job, and see if you are able to determine which activities are surveillance functions and which are oriented toward treatment.

CLASSIFICATION: THE FIRST STEP IN SUPERVISION

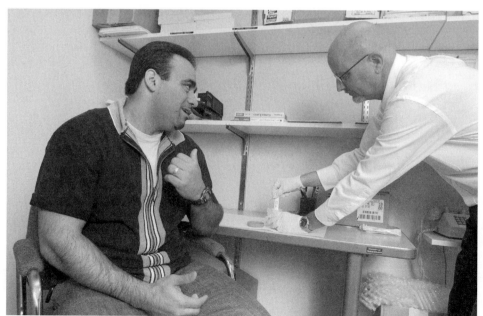

Drug and alcohol testing is common while on probation supervision.

© Bob Daemmrich / The Image Works

BOX 6.3   COMMUNITY CORRECTIONS UP CLOSE   •

A DAY IN THE LIFE OF A FEDERAL PROBATION OFFICER

It's Tuesday, and I've got my work cut out for me on this cold January day in West Texas. On the way in to work I mentally review the upcoming scheduled events for the day: 8:30 a.m. meet with assistant U.S. attorney regarding a probation revocation hearing on John D.; 9:00 a.m. revocation hearing in Judge B's court—contested; thereafter, head for the counties to do field supervision and collateral work. This will be an overnighter, so I'll be back in the office on Thursday—another court day.

I'm almost at the office, but I need to make a quick stop at Joe R. to collect a random urinalysis (UA). He's been out a month now and seems to be doing all right. He's working, home is stable, and the UA will address the primary supervision issue in this case—history of drug abuse. I'm almost ready to complete an initial supervision plan in this case. Although he participated in drug treatment in the institution, he may need treatment in the community. Time will tell; but for right now random UAs will do.

Well, I caught him before he left for work, and things seem solid. The wife seemed happy, the job is stable, and there was no problem with the UA. It's going to be a great day! I love this job! On to the office.

Oops, I spoke too soon. Telephone voice mail—David S. got arrested for DWI [driving while intoxicated]—he's still locked up at County. I'll swing by the county jail on the way out of town. Other than that, no other emergencies.

The assistant U.S. attorney is ready for a contested hearing. That's fine; five dirty UAs and failure to participate in drug treatment will get you every time. The supervision file is well documented, and I'm prepared to testify as to chain of custody on the dirty UAs. Our contract provider was subpoenaed and will testify on the failure to participate violation. We're in Judge B's court, and the AUSA [assistant U.S. attorney] tells me the defendant has decided to plead true and throw himself on the mercy of the court—good luck. Sure enough, the judge revokes John D.'s probation and sentences him to 24 months' custody. John takes it all right, but his mother doesn't. If he had taken the judge's advice and "lived at the foot of the cross," he'd still be on probation—instead, he's locked up, and his mother is crying in court. It's always harder on the family. I'll talk to her—maybe it will help. John couldn't do it on the street, so maybe he will get the help he needs inside. [The federal correctional institution in] Fort Worth has an excellent treatment program—I'll tell her that and maybe she will feel better. I hate this job!

Well, it's midmorning and time to hit the road. Fort Stockton is 100 miles down the road, but I've got to stop at the county jail on the way out of town. I'll check out the government vehicle with the four-wheel drive in case the roads get bad; cellular phone 1; pepper spray; sidearm; and laptop in case I have time to do chronos. Gosh times have changed; in the good old days I'd be leaving town in my personal vehicle with a smile on my face.

At the county lockup David S. advises he was arrested by the P.D. [police department] for DWI—but he really only "had a couple." Of course, he forgot he was supposed to abstain completely from alcohol. When I get back in town I'll get the offense report, staff the case with the boss, and decide what type of action to take. David has been on supervision for over a year and has done exceptionally well. Graduated sanctions may be in order, and if so, I'll ask the court to place him in the halfway house with a required treatment condition.

On the road again. This is what I've got to do in Fort Stockton: check in with the sheriff—he knows everything that is going on in his county; go by our drug contractor's office and visit with the therapist regarding Mary J.; go by the county clerk's office and finish this collateral request out of the Northern District; and conduct home inspections on Bob S. and Joe R. Talk about time management—the boss will love this! Sheriff B. is in a great mood, and he says all my people have been behaving themselves. Over coffee I advise him John D. will be getting out on parole—for the second time—

(continued)

BOX 6.3 COMMUNITY CORRECTIONS UP CLOSE (contd.)

A DAY IN THE LIFE OF A FEDERAL PROBATION OFFICER

and will be coming back home to Fort Stockton. That didn't make his day. At the drug treatment facility the contractor gives me a good report on Mary J. She's keeping all her appointments and has not submitted any dirty UAs. Her participation in treatment is good, and her mother has also attended a couple of counseling sessions. Great report!

The county clerk was busy, but she did have the judgments I had called ahead about—that was a quick and easy collateral, not like the last one that took two hours to find an old judgment. These people in Fort Stockton are great to work with; they really know how to help you. Man I love this job!

Well, there's Bob S.'s house. I think I'll drive past and around the block—just in case. Everything looks cool, and his car is in front, so he should be home.

Bob was surprised to see me, advising it was his day off since the day before he had pulled a double on the rig he works. Oil field work is steady, but the cold weather is hard, and it shows on Bob's face. The wife seems to be doing well, and the house is neat and clean. Things look solid, but I know better than to start bragging. This offender has a history of drug violations, which presents certain risk control issues. Risk control issues never go away!

At Joe R.'s no one comes to the door, but I thought I heard someone inside. I leave my card, drive around the block, and call Joe on the cellular phone. It amazes me how sneaky I can get

when I have to. Sure enough, Joe's girlfriend answers the phone and advises Joe is still at work. Work is 15 miles out of town at a ranch, so I'll try to catch him first thing in the morning.

I'm running a little ahead of schedule, so I'll stop by and see Mary J. She should be home from work; if she's not, her mother will be, and she'll let me know how her daughter is really doing. The supervision issues here are enforcing court-ordered sanctions and drug treatment. Sure enough, Mary J. is there and seems to be doing really well. She gives me her community service hours documentation and discusses her progress in the drug treatment program. Her mother is obviously very satisfied with her daughter's progress and is a good supervision resource to me.

Before I check into the motel, I call the office on the cellular to check my voice mail. David S. called to advise he bonded out of jail. I call him back and set up an appointment for him to come in on Thursday. We'll staff him at that time. I'm glad now that I brought the laptop—I can catch up on some chronos. Since I lucked out and saw all the people I needed to, I won't need to go out tonight—it's getting too cold out here in West Texas anyway. What a day—win a few, lose a few. Gosh I love this job!

The next morning comes early, and I catch breakfast before I hit the road. I figure I'll work my way back to the office and try to catch Joe R. at the ranch before he gets

busy. I'm positive his girlfriend told him I was by the house, so he should be expecting me. I'm not quite comfortable with this offender because he does have some violence in his background. Therefore, officer safety and risk control are the primary supervision issues I am addressing. Wouldn't you know it, he locked the main gate on me—but what he doesn't know is the rancher previously gave me a key to the gate. As I drive up to the ranch headquarters, I can see my man out by the horse corral. He seems surprised to see me. We visit, and he convinces me he is making a "good hand." I try not to be too obvious, but I'm looking for any signs of contraband or a weapon. Ranch hands and rifles seem to go hand in hand—no pun intended. Nothing is obvious, although Joe just seems to be nervous. As I drive back down the road to the main gate, I call the Border Patrol sector headquarters and check in with the duty agent. Joe is clean as far as they know, but they agree to drive by in the next few days. They'll let me know. The agent advised they have received recent intelligence of illegal aliens working in the area where Joe works.

Well, I'm almost home, and it's a beautiful day. In fact, it looks like it will warm up. The only pressing issue I know of is the staffing on David S. You know what, I really do love this job!

Source: The author, Richard V. Russell, was supervising U.S. probation officer for the Western District of Texas. He is now retired and resides in Midland, Texas. Reprinted with permission.

Each new client on community supervision must first be classified. **Classification** consists of the supervising officer using an objective assessment scale to compute the risks posed by the offender, identifying offender needs requiring intervention, and selecting the appropriate supervision strategies. Researchers indicate that objective actuarial prediction models, if used by a trained officer, are more reliable and efficient than subjective methods. Highest priority is placed on identifying risks that would likely jeopardize public safety if not addressed. Risk variables also determine the level of supervision required by the offender. At the same time, a priority is placed on identifying needs that, if not addressed, will likely lead to a return to criminal behavior (Lowenkamp, Latessa, and Holsinger 2006).

Actuarial Risk Assessment

Risk assessment provides a measure of the probationer or parolee's degree of dangerousness to the public and also measures the offender's propensity to engage in future criminal activity. Probation and parole jurisdictions have developed some form of risk prediction scale to assist them in developing supervision plans and in caseload classification. These instruments differ in some respects, but all of them place offenders in groups with a known statistical probability of committing new crimes or violating the conditions of supervision. Risk assessments have been known to predict erroneously in some cases, as assessments use previous behavior to forecast likelihood of recidivism. "Statistical risk assessment devices rarely explain more than 20 percent of the variance" (Holsinger, Lurigio, and Latessa 2001, p. 47). Recent empirical evidence in 97 residential and nonresidential programs in Ohio showed that risk assessment tools and the existence of cognitive–behavioral therapy were beneficial to target high-risk clients and reduce recidivism in this population (Lowenkamp, Latessa, and Holsinger 2006). However, no matter whether the programs were treatment oriented or supervision oriented, mixing low-risk offenders with high-risk offenders in the same program actually led to an *increase* in recidivism.

Many types of assessment tools are available, including the Level of Service Inventory-Revised (LSI-R), Client Management Classification (CMC), and the Correctional Offender Management Profiles for Alternative Sentences (COMPAS). The LSI-R is a 54-item scale that assigns a numerical value to many of the same factors identified in the presentence report. The officer completes the LSI-R by interviewing the offender and scoring his or her answers. The LSI-R has been validated on male and female offender populations (as opposed to the general population), and it includes both **static** and **dynamic factors** (Lowenkamp, Holsinger, and Latessa 2001). One study of the LSI-R scores predicted that men exhibited a significantly higher risk of recidivism than women, and that Native Americans had higher risk scores than people of other ethnic groups, though recidivism data were not available to determine the validity of these predictions (Holsinger, Lowenkamp, and Latessa 2003).

Figure 6.1 shows the risk and needs assessment instrument used by one or more probation departments in New York state. The probationer is assigned to one of several levels of supervision (designated by color) on the basis of an individual classification score, taking age and special needs into consideration. The Salient Factor Score (SFS-81) is the assessment version for federal parolees.

Identifying Treatment Needs

The officer must also identify those characteristics, conditions, or behavioral problems that limit the offender's motivation or may lead to a return to criminal behavior. Such treatment needs include drug or alcohol abuse, mental illness, anger management issues, or deficiencies in education or vocational skills. Treatment activities are

CLASSIFICATION

A procedure consisting of assessing the risks posed by the offender, identifying the supervision issues, and selecting the appropriate supervision strategy.

RISK ASSESSMENT

A procedure that provides a measure of the offender's propensity to further criminal activity and indicates the level of officer intervention that will be required.

STATIC FACTORS

Correlates of the likelihood of recidivism that (once they occur) cannot be changed (age at first arrest, number of convictions, and so forth).

DYNAMIC FACTORS

Correlates of the likelihood of recidivism that can be changed through treatment and rehabilitation (drug and alcohol abuse, anger management, quality of family relationships, and so forth).

FIGURE 6.1   *Example of a Case Classification Instrument*

CASE NAME: _____

CASE NUMBER:_____

NYSID NUMBER:_____

I. CASE CLASSIFICATION INSTRUMENT

SCORING

1. Defendant is eligible for a Probation sentence.

<u>32</u>

2. How many victims were physically injured in the instant offense?   _ × 6 =   _

3. How many prior misdemeanor arrests does the offender have for offenses against persons?   _ × 7 =   _

4. Does the offender have any juvenile arrests?   No = 0 Yes = 11   _

5. Is the current or any prior arrest for a violent offense?   No = 0 Yes = 19   _

6. Is the offender a Youthful Offender?   No = 0 Yes = 11   _

7. What is the offender's age?   Subtotal of Items 1–6   _
(Subtract from Subtotal)

Classification Score   ____

II. TRACK/UNIT ASSIGNMENT CRITERIA

Classification Score is 23 or above, and;

1. Offender is male, 20 years of age or less, speaks English, and is not developmentally or psychiatrically disabled.

Assign to Enforcement Blue

2. Offender does not meet Blue Criteria

Assign to Enforcement Amber

Classification Score is 22 or below and;

1. There is a Court-ordered special condition of Probation, such as a fine, restitution, community service, or participation in a treatment program.

Assign to Special Conditions

2. Offender has no special conditions.

Assign to Reporting

3. There are exceptional circumstances:
(a) Current or prior history of child abuse, sexual abuse, domestic violence:

Assign to Amber

(b) Probationer has completed STAR

Assign to Green

(c) "High-Profile" case:

Assign to Green with BC Approval

III. CASE ASSIGNMENT

Case Assigned to _____ Track/Unit P.O. _____

Date Completed: _____ Completed by: _____
(P. O. Name and I.D. No.)

CASE CLASSIFICATION AND ASSIGNMENT INSTRUMENT GUIDELINES

Score each of the items in Section I as they apply to the offender using the definitions included below. Add items 1 through 6. Subtract the offender's age to obtain the Classification Score. Refer to Section II, Track/Unit Assignment, to determine the correct assignment. Record the assignment in Section III.

I. CASE CLASSIFICATION INSTRUMENT

Item 1.   Include the Score of 32 points for every case legally eligible (at PSI stage) or received on Probation (supervision stage).

Item 2.   Multiply the number of individuals who are reported to have suffered a physical injury in the instant offense by 6 and enter the **result** on the appropriate line.

Item 3.   Misdemeanor crimes against persons are defined as: Assault 3, Menacing 2, Hazing 1, Reckless Endangerment 2, Sexual Misconduct, Sex Abuse 2 or 3, Unlawful Imprisonment 2, Coercion 2, Criminal Possession of a Weapon 4.

Item 4.   Include any juvenile arrest regardless of the disposition of the case.

Item 5.   The following are defined as violent offenses: assault, homicide, sex offenses, kidnapping, burglary 1st and 2nd, arson, robbery, endangering the welfare of a child, and firearms and other dangerous weapons.

Item 6.   Has the Court made a Youthful Offender adjudication at sentencing?

Item 7.   Enter the Offender's age at time of sentence and subtract from total value of Items 1 through 6. **The result is the classification score.**

II. TRACK/UNIT ASSIGNMENT CRITERIA

Cases with a Classification Score of 23 or above will be assigned to the Enforcement Track.

Cases with a Classification Score of 22 or below will be assigned to either Special Conditions or Reporting Tracks unless there are exceptional circumstances as described in Item 3 in this section.

III. ASSIGNMENT

Use the criteria in Section II to assign the case to the appropriate Track or Unit. P.O. assignment is to be made by consulting the appropriate **Unit Supervisor.**

The instrument assigns clients into one of two risk categories:

- Persons scoring 23 points or above are placed in the high-risk Enforcement Track, which consists of Blue, Amber, and Green units. The Blue unit consists of cognitive–behavioral groups for male adolescents between the ages of 16 and 20 years. Amber applies cognitive–behavioral techniques primarily to the individual supervision and case management of offenders. Green focuses on relapse prevention and is a step down from Blue or Amber.
- Probationers scoring 22 points or below are funneled to either a low-risk Special Conditions Track, if the judge appended specific conditions of probation to the person's sentence, or to an automated kiosk Reporting Track.

Source: F. Domurad. 1999. So You Want to Develop Your Own Risk Assessment Instrument. *Topics in Community Corrections: NIC Annual Report 1999: Classification and Risk Assessment.* Longmont, CO: National Institute of Corrections.

defined as actions taken by the supervising officer intended to bring about a change in the offender's conduct or condition for the purpose of rehabilitation and reintegration into the law-abiding community. Together, both risk and needs assessments can (and should) define the types of correctional services that are made available to offenders (Andrews, Bonta, and Wormith 2006).

Sources of information that may be used to identify treatment needs include the presentence report, prison disciplinary records and the prerelease plan, physical or medical health evaluations, records of drug or alcohol abuse and other related criminal conduct, financial history, and residential history. Because the federal PSIs are so detailed, they capture most of the information in the risk and needs assessment of the LSI-R. In these cases, case managers use the LSI-R to gauge client honesty (or consistency) by comparing their responses to the PSI and the LSI-R. The importance of carefully gathering and evaluating the offender's history cannot be overstated, for past behavior is, at the moment, the best predictor we have of future behavior.

Developing the Case Plan

After reviewing the conditions of probation, assessing the offender's risk, and determining treatment concerns, the officer will identify specific supervision issues and select the appropriate strategies for addressing them (Storm 1997). Supervision issues may involve any or all of these areas: conditions, risk control, and treatment.

A supervision issue is a condition or offender characteristic or pattern of conduct that requires intervention by the officer to correct or control. When an issue is identified, the officer should then develop a strategy to deal with or monitor that issue. In Box 6.3, the probation officer has identified "history of drug abuse" as a supervision issue in the case of Joe R. Recognizing that Joe R. may need drug treatment in the community at some point, the supervising officer has elected to monitor drug use through random urinalyses for the time being.

Levels of Supervision

Although various names are used to differentiate the levels of supervision, most are essentially restatements of the traditional *maximum, medium,* and *minimum* supervision classes. Practically all classification systems specify the smallest amount of contact requirements for each level in terms of these factors:

- Type of contact (face-to-face visit, **collateral,** field visit, phone verification, mail-in)
- Location of contact (offender's home, offender's employment, probation office)
- Frequency of contacts per month

The type, location, and frequency of contacts exist in various combinations and vary among different agencies. At the minimal level, there may be no requirement that the probationer personally visit or contact a probation officer. Rather, the probationer may be required to call in and leave a message on a voice-recorded line, or when paged to do so. This level of supervision in California is called "banked probation," and it has received its share of criticism because it provides little information on whether probationers are committing more crimes (Nieto 1996). Petersilia (1995) reported that 60 percent of all Los Angeles probationers were tracked solely by computer and had no contact with an officer.

Regular probation supervision includes an endless variety of contact types that can be made for higher supervision levels. For example, Offender A on medium supervision

COLLATERAL CONTACT

Verification of the probationer or parolee's situation and whereabouts by means of the officer speaking with a third party who knows the offender personally (such as a family member, friend, or employer).

may expect two face-to-face contacts per month and verification of residence and employment once every 12 months. Offender B on medium supervision may only have one quarterly face-to-face contact but weekly mail-in and quarterly home visits. The frequency and intensity of contacts increases with the supervision level, such that an offender on intensive (maximum) supervision can expect one or two weekly face-to-face or field contacts, one monthly collateral contact, verification of residence and employment every 3 months, and a criminal history check every 12 months.

About 5.3 percent of all probationers require intensive supervision because of public safety concerns, and another 5 percent of probationers have a special need requirement (for example, mental illness or a development disability). Less than 1 percent (.08 percent) of the total probationer population is on electronic monitoring (Camp, Camp, and May 2003). Camp and Camp (1999) reported that the overall average number of face-to-face contacts per year for probationers and parolees was 18 contacts on regular supervision, 79 contacts on intensive supervision, and 63 contacts on electronic monitoring.

Few offices, however, specify the quality of the contact. Generally, if the officer needs to verify information or compliance, the officer may make contact by phone, e-mail, or regular mail, or require the offender to come in for an office visit. A **field contact** is considered to be the most time consuming but is also the most valuable type of contact. In a field contact, the officer visits the offender's home or place of employment to monitor progress and to meet family members or other individuals who influence the probationer's life on a daily basis. Other ways that probationers have to contact their probation officer include kiosk machines in the community (see Box 6.4).

BOX 6.4 TECHNOLOGY IN CORRECTIONS

USING PAGERS AND KIOSK MACHINES IN COMMUNITY SUPERVISION

Technology has assisted officers in spending less time in their offices responding to calls from their probationers and more time out in the field seeing their clients in person. Probation officers increasingly have cell phones, pagers, and laptop computers. These portable offices enable officers to complete their reports from the field.

For federal probationers in rural areas or probationers who cannot afford telephones, special pagers are provided that allow a pretrial officer or a probation officer to beep the client with a directive, such as to call the officer immediately or to submit a urine sample within a designated period of time. Clients do not

know the number to their personal pagers, so no one else can beep them with personal calls (Ogden and Horrocks 2001).

A kiosk machine has also been used in certain jurisdictions to aid probation officers in their duties. A kiosk machine is an interactive computerized touch screen machine that allows only the offender to receive and send personal messages back and forth to the probation officer at any time of day. A kiosk machine can be set up anywhere that is monitored, such as in a lobby of a police station or in a grocery store that is open 24 hours a day. Each probationer who uses it is iden-

tified via his or her fingerprints, which also become the password to each screen. Offenders can use kiosk machines to notify the probation officer of a change of address or employment, and the probation officer can use them to ask the individual client questions, to which the client could type a response. Like GIS technology, a kiosk can also store information on bus routes, job postings, and schedules for services such as treatment programs, employment offices, and driver's license bureaus.

Thomas G. Ogden and Cary Horrocks. 2001. Pagers, Digital, Audio, and Kiosk: Officer Assistants. *Federal Probation* 65(2): 35–37.

The overall supervision plan optimistically looks toward gradual reduction of the level of supervision if the offender manages to avoid further transgressions of rules or laws. In many instances, the final level is that of no supervision or level of assistance other than that specifically requested by the client or necessitated by a new arrest.

Caseload and Workload Standards

A probation or parole officer's **caseload** is defined as the number of individuals or cases one officer can supervise effectively. In practice, caseloads vary widely because not every offender requires the same amount of supervision. The more intensive the supervision, the lower the caseload. U.S. probation officers supervise 50–60 cases and conduct five or six presentence investigations per month, so they are involved in both supervision and investigation (Quinn 2002). For stand-alone local probation departments, the average caseload of adult probationers on regular supervision is 127, ranging from 15 in Pennsylvania to 314 in Rhode Island. In contrast, a single caseload of parolees on regular supervision is 70 per officer. Intensive supervision probation and parole caseloads average 18 to 29 offenders, and offenders requiring special needs average 35 to 55 offenders per officer nationwide (Camp, Camp, and May 2003).

The American Probation and Parole Association recommends that a "workload standard" of about 120 hours per month is more reasonable than caseload size. The workload standard is calculated by totaling the number of hours required to supervise each client based on that client's level of supervision (maximum, medium, or minimum). A maximum supervision case may require, for example, four hours of the probation or parole officer's time per month. A medium supervision case may require two hours per month, whereas a minimum supervision case may only require one hour or less per month of the officer's time. This allows the total workload to be divided more evenly and fairly, especially for officers who supervise clients of various supervision levels. Given these calculations, one officer could effectively supervise 30 maximum supervision cases, 60 medium cases, and as many as 120 minimum cases. Development of a workload standard would allow for comparison between jurisdictions, guide research in probation and parole effectiveness, and assist probation administrators in interpreting their work to legislators and other policy makers.

SPECIALIZED CASELOADS

Standard probation provides sufficient monitoring for most sentenced offenders, but there are some offenders who need a more intensive form of monitoring, and they may require a particular kind of treatment. The use of specialized caseloads is effective in improving supervision quality and effectiveness for offenders who are addicted to drugs, gang members, sex offenders, and offenders with mental illness (see Box 6.5 for a discussion of strategies for gang members on probation). About 5 percent of probationers and parolees are classified under a "special" caseload, which may include probationers in a boot camp or a substance abuse residential treatment program, or those who require special treatment services (Camp, Camp, and May 2003). But McKay (2002) reports that as many as 30 percent of probation agencies nationwide operate with specialized caseloads. The difference in numbers is likely due to how each source defines "specialized caseloads." We will briefly discuss supervision of three types of offenders: mentally ill offenders, drug-abusing offenders, and sex offenders.

BOX 6.5 STRATEGIES FOR SUPERVISING GANG MEMBERS

Gang members on supervision are significantly more likely than non-gang members on supervision to be rearrested for drug and violent crimes (Olson, Dooley, and Kane 2004). Gang members have more extensive criminal histories and associate with other people who were themselves involved in criminal activity. This situation creates a high propensity for recidivism, making it necessary to assign active gang members to intensive supervision caseloads. A number of different strategies are used in the intensive supervision of probationers and parolees in the federal system.

Strategy #1: Prepared Profiles for Officers

An information clearinghouse called the Sacramento Intelligence Unit (SIU) has detailed information on gang history, activity, and interpretation of tattoos and gestures. SIU staff prepare profiles of gang members for community supervision officers just before a prisoner is released. Nearly 4,000 profiles are compiled annually for this purpose (Administrative Office of the U.S. Courts 2006).

Strategy #2: Information Exchange with Law Enforcement

In addition to using the SIU databases, federal probation officers can interact with local law enforcement as a second source of information and education. Some officers attend workshops and are members of gang task forces to further specialize.

Strategy #3: Drug Education and Mentoring for Youths Who Are At Risk of Joining Gangs

Officers in one federal district in Massachusetts visit local high schools and juvenile detention centers to present a drug education program to educate at-risk youth on legal consequences of getting convicted of crimes. Young offenders are also provided with mentors, some of whom are former offenders who have succeeded in the reentry process (Administrative Office of the U.S. Courts 2006).

Administrative Office of the U.S. Courts. 2006. Gang Member Supervision Growing Part of Job for Probation Officers. *The Third Branch* 38(2): 1–3, retrieved on June 2, 2006, from: http://www.uscourts.gov/ttb/02-06/gangsupervision/index.html; David E. Olson, Brendan Dooley, and Candice M. Kane. 2004. The Relationship between Gang Membership and Inmate Recidivism. *Illinois Criminal Justice Information Authority Research Bulletin* 2(12): 1–12.

Supervising Offenders Who Are Mentally Ill

People with mental illnesses who lack adequate insurance coverage and have a substance abuse problem may eventually find themselves in jail and on probation because the police eventually will remove them from the streets; these are the same people who have been turned away from a resource-depleted mental health system. Severely mentally ill people who are not stabilized on medications may act out in deviant ways and be less apt to follow the law, but not necessarily be criminal. As police focus on quality-of-life issues, ordinance violations, and small-time drug offenses, people who are homeless and who have a substance abuse problem get caught up in the corrections system (Slate et al. 2003).

As a result, about 16 percent of all probationers have general mental health needs, and between 5 and 10 percent of parolees have serious mental illnesses that require medication and therapy (Slate et al. 2003).

A study compared traditional probation caseloads with probation caseloads specializing in mental health issues using a sample of 90 probation supervisors drawn from a nationwide sample of 25 different departments (Skeem, Emke-Francis, and

Louden 2006). The elements that distinguished officers who supervised specialized mental health caseloads from traditional ones were ongoing training on mental health issues and a reduced caseload number. The caseload size was less than half (an average of 48 probationers) on the specialized caseloads compared with 130 on traditional probation, allowing officers on specialized caseloads the opportunity for a different style of case management that includes a greater focus on both treatment and supervision (Skeem, Emke-Francis, and Louden 2006).

The supervisors of specialized caseloads said that their two greatest challenges when working with mentally ill probationers were coordinating treatment and ensuring compliance with medication and counseling sessions. Mentally ill individuals tend to behave in a noncompliant manner more often than probationers on traditional caseloads. Problem-solving strategies and court appearances were used much more often than revocation to address noncompliance, in part because 15 percent of agencies with specialized caseloads were partnered with a mental health court (Skeem, Emke-Francis, and Louden 2006). As we learned in Chapter 2, mental health courts emphasize keeping mentally ill offenders out of jail and prison unless they are a clear threat to themselves or to others. To accomplish these goals, it was important for probation officers to maintain a positive working relationship with treatment providers. However, only about 15 percent of probation and 25 percent of parole departments have staff who are specially trained to deal with specialized caseloads of mentally ill clients (Slate et al. 2003). Two recommendations are made: first, structural changes need to be made so that mental health services can work in collaboration and partnership with criminal justice agencies. Examples of programs with criminal justice collaborates in the community are those in Milwaukee, Wisconsin, and Multnomah County, Oregon. Second, a standardized training curriculum for probation and parole officers is necessary to continually educate workers in criminal justice about mental health issues. A model program exists in New York state that incorporates elements of crisis intervention and recognizing signs of mental disorder (Slate et al. 2004).

Supervising Offenders Who Have Abused Drugs and Alcohol

The majority of offenders serving community correction sentences have problems with drugs or alcohol, or their crime was drug related. A nationwide survey of a stratified random sample of more than 2,000 probationers on active supervision found nearly half of them admitted to being under the influence of drugs or alcohol during the commission of their crime. For a number of others, substance abuse contributed directly or indirectly to the crime(s) that led to their conviction. While under probation supervision, half of probationers surveyed were randomly tested for drug use, and 38 percent were treated for drug and/or alcohol abuse (Mumola and Bonczar 1998). Ways of drug and alcohol testing include urine screenings, hair analysis, saliva analysis, skin patches that measure blood alcohol levels, and pupillometry, or measuring how a pupil responds to light.

Ways of treating drug offenders include drug court and residential placements like therapeutic communities. Recall that in Chapter 2, drug courts were discussed as a way to treat offenders who were convicted of drug possession and who admitted having problems with drugs. Drug courts allowed these offenders a chance at avoiding a prison term, and upon successful completion of drug court many of them were able to avoid a conviction altogether. Therapeutic communities will be discussed in Chapter 8 as a way to allow offenders to focus solely on sobriety and relapse prevention.

In this section, we will discuss general supervision strategies that probation and parole officers use for clients who have a problem with drugs or alcohol. According to Steiner (2004), obstacles that probation and parole officers face in the supervision of offenders with substance abuse problems include

- Identifying quality drug treatment programs with trained staff
- Being able to refer clients to a community-based program (due to space availability)
- Limited ability to keep offenders in mandatory treatment
- Relapse prevention after the intensive treatment ends (events, thought patterns, or stressful situations may trigger substance use)

Because of these challenges, a supervision style called the "treatment retention" model was proposed for parole officers. The model recommends that treatment begin for offenders while they are incarcerated and that, when they are released from prison, a cognitive–behavioral relapse prevention program retain offenders in treatment throughout the reentry and parole period (Steiner 2004). When offenders with substance abuse problems begin to have problems following conditions or relapse back into drug use while on supervision, Steiner argues for graduated sanctions that are tailored to a treatment plan rather than merely just revocation to prison.

Another supervision tool is the monitored use of Antabuse, a prescription medication that negatively reacts with a person's system if he or she ingests alcohol. Clients on Antabuse must take this medication every two to three days under the watchful eyes of staff who administer the medication in community clinics or in day reporting centers. Another medication, Methadone, is administered to clients with addictions to heroin or other opiate-based drugs. Naltrexone is an opiate antagonist that blocks opiate access from receptors in the brain (Petersilia 1998a). These substances are used over a long period of time to decrease dependency on opiate-based drugs.

GENDER-RESPONSIVE STRATEGIES. Treatment approaches for substance abuse should vary depending on why clients abuse substances in the first place. Female drug abusers have significantly higher levels of physical and sexual abuse histories than do men who enter treatment. Females are more likely to have been convicted of drug offenses, and they report using drugs and alcohol to self-medicate or escape childhood violence and sexual abuse (Festervan 2003). Women tend to have less serious criminal histories of offending behavior than men, and women enter treatment being more communicative about problems related to economic marginalization, homelessness, caring for dependent children, battling depression, and overcoming previous victimizations or abusive relationships that become "pathways to crime" (Alarid and Cromwell 2006). Female probationers are also more likely than male probationers to be open to change using motivational drug therapy activities, but it is unclear whether increased motivation leads to decreased relapse behavior following treatment completion (Czuchry, Sia, and Dansereau 2006).

Bloom and McDiarmid (2000) note another important gender difference: "Men in recovery tend to emphasize the problems caused by the consequences of drug use, and women more often report the 'stressors' leading to drug use" (p. 15). Female offenders respond to strategies that incorporate their problems, and supervision of female probationers should therefore be "relational" in that they should engage the children and the spouse in the recovery process. Family group conferencing (discussed in Chapter 10) may be one tool to accomplish treatment and healing goals. Programs that use an "empowerment model of skill building to develop competencies that enable women to achieve independence" are ideal strategies for female offenders (Bloom and McDiarmid 2000, p. 13).

Supervising Sex Offenders

The term *sex offender* refers to a wide range of offenders, some of whom are aggressive and violent, and others who are quite the opposite and, in fact, are quite passive. About 60 percent of convicted sex offenders are under conditional supervision in the community (Jenuwine, Simmons, and Swies 2003). We will discuss public notification laws and civil commitment of sex offenders in Chapter 15. In this section, we discuss supervision techniques for sex offenders on probation. To ensure public safety, intensive forms of supervision coupled with intensive treatment specific to the type of sex offender is necessary. Aggressive rapists have an entirely different treatment approach than do more passive pedophiles.

Probation departments are modeled based on the containment approach, which has the following characteristics (English et al. 1996):

- Two to four face-to-face contacts between officer and probationer per month
- Two probationer home and computer searches per month
- Weekly cognitive–behavioral group therapy and individual counseling
- Sharing of information on a regular basis between probation officers and treatment providers

Probation and parole officers in sex offender units are specially trained in the area of sex offenses and in recognizing secrecy and deceit, which frequently characterize crimes against children. Special conditions required of sex offenders may also include electronic monitoring, submission of a blood sample for DNA recording, prohibition of any pornography, banning of Internet access to chat rooms involving minors, prohibition of patronizing sex-oriented businesses, **penile plethysmographs,** and child safety zones (McKay 2002). A child safety zone condition means that the offender is not allowed within a certain range of places where children typically congregate. These places include schools, day care centers, and playgrounds (McKay 2002). We discuss two ways of supervising sex offenders below: using polygraph tests and using global positioning systems.

POLYGRAPH TESTS.   Some jurisdictions require that sex offenders, when initially placed on probation, submit to a baseline polygraph examination that explores previous sexual behaviors and current deviant thoughts. This is because polygraphed sex offenders "reported many more victims [especially male victims], far less history of being sexually abused themselves, and a much higher incidence of having offended as juveniles" than did the nonpolygraphed sex offender group (Hindman and Peters 2001, p. 10). Polygraph tests have been recognized as a way to reduce the secrecy and deceit that sex offenders typically use with their victims and supervising probation officers. If used properly, a baseline measure can then be compared against any later polygraph tests given throughout the period of probation.

GLOBAL POSITIONING SYSTEMS.   Sex offenders are increasingly being monitored using global positioning systems (GPS). Each offender on a GPS system records "track points" throughout the day—this is where the device makes a connection with the satellite to record the exact location of the offender. One Virginia-based company called Veridian Corporation developed a system called "VeriTracks." Another company founded Pro Tech Monitoring Inc. to create a SMART® System Technology. A third supplier of equipment is called iSecureTrac. With these systems, an offender either has a portable tracking receiver attached to an ankle bracelet that the offender wears at all times, or carries the tracking device in a purse or waist pack. The portable device must be charged at home every night. The GPS is integrated with a

---

PENILE PLETHYSMOGRAPH

A device that measures erectile responses in male sex offenders to determine level of sexual arousal to various types of stimuli. This device is used for assessment and treatment purposes.

computerized geographic information mapping system. A map can show where the offender lives and works, along with all the potential risk areas (bars, schools, day care centers, and so forth) as well as the proximity of service providers where the offender must go for treatment. A typical parolee records about 1,400 track points in a 24-hour period, which is approximately once per minute. GPS signals can be lost when people enter buildings. If the signal is temporarily disconnected, the disconnection time is recorded and the device attempts to reestablish a connection with the satellite. These systems cost $37 per day for one person to be monitored, which includes $17 for the technology and $20 for the monitoring. We discuss GPS technology in more depth in Chapter 9.

INTERSTATE COMPACTS ON PROBATION

Prior to 1937, a probationer or parolee could not be supervised outside the state where he or she was convicted, even though many transient offenders were arrested and convicted far away from home. As a result, the offender often could not be provided with supervision in the very place that would offer the best chance for success on probation or parole. A group of states entered into a statutory agreement by which they would supervise probationers and parolees for each other. Known as the **interstate compact,** the agreement was originally signed by 25 states in 1937. By 1951, the interstate compact had been ratified by all the states, as well as Puerto Rico and the Virgin Islands.

The Interstate Compact on Juveniles was established in 1955 to provide for return of juvenile runaways, escapees, and absconders as well as for cooperative supervision of juvenile probationers and parolees. A survey of field staff and interstate compact administrators found that 15,000 youths in the United States were being supervised via interstate compact but that one-third of all requests submitted by the sending state were denied by the receiving state (Linke and Krauth 2000).

The compacts identify the **sending state** (the state of conviction) and the **receiving state** (the state that undertakes the supervision). The receiving state informs the sending state on a quarterly basis of the probationer's progress, but the sending state retains ultimate authority to modify the conditions of probation, revoke probation, or terminate probation. It is also generally held that the sending state alone has authority to determine upon what basis a violator may be returned. The reasons for return cannot be challenged by the receiving state.

The offender must meet certain residence requirements of the receiving state. Ordinarily, the probationer or parolee must be a resident of the receiving state, have relatives there, or have employment there. The receiving state agrees to provide "courtesy supervision" at the same level that it gives to its own cases.

The three main problems with interstate compacts were liability, monitoring compliance, and slow processing speed. Since probation supervision styles varied from state to state, each state had different thresholds and policies for when a probationer was considered to be in violation. For example, one state might consider a probationer to be in violation even though the other state wished to continue supervision (Cushman and Sechrest 1992). In addition, some states were asked to accept far more interstate compact supervision cases than they sent out. At times, some states sent their most noncompliant cases elsewhere, and this form of supervision became a "dumping ground." Finally, the process of obtaining approval was slow, and some offenders relocated prior to being approved for supervision. Interstate compacts were largely unorganized and inconsistent in their approaches (Linke and Krauth 2000).

INTERSTATE COMPACT

An agreement signed by all states and U.S. territories that allows for the supervision of parolees and probationers across state lines.

SENDING STATE

Under the interstate compact, the state of conviction.

RECEIVING STATE

Under the interstate compact, the state that undertakes the supervision.

Because of these problems, the National Institute of Corrections (NIC) Advisory Board spent two years, from 1997 to 1999, studying the problem and determining the best resolution. The NIC joined with the Council of State Governments to provide a new way to administer interstate compacts (National Institute of Corrections and the Council of State Governments 2002).

New Interstate Compact for Adult Offender Supervision

The **Interstate Compact for Adult Offender Supervision** program began in 2000. This revised compact developed an interstate commission that is composed of one commissioner representative from each participating state. The commission is a national organization empowered to create and enforce the same rules for all states, collect national statistics, coordinate training and education, and notify victims for public safety. The commission has annual meetings to modify rules and to deal with conflicts among states as needed.

In addition to the commission, each state has its own council, composed of a compact administrator and at least one person from each branch of government (legislative, judicial, and executive). The compact administrator is charged with administering and managing all interstate compacts for his or her own state (National Institute of Corrections and the Council of State Governments 2002). With this new structure and oversight commission, correctional administrators are hopeful that the problems with interstate compacts will be a thing of the past. As of 2004, all states except Virginia and Mississippi were members. There are reportedly as many as 250,000 offenders nationwide on interstate compact supervision.

Revocation and the Interstate Compact

The sending state may enter the receiving state to take custody of the probationer or parolee who has violated the terms of release without going through extradition proceedings. The probationer waives extradition prior to leaving the sending state, so the sending state may retake a person being supervised in another state simply by having its officer present appropriate credentials and proving the identity of the person to be retaken. The probation violator is usually incarcerated in the receiving state at the expense of the sending state.

The receiving state is obligated to surrender the probationer unless a criminal charge is pending against the individual in the receiving state. In such a case the probationer cannot be retaken without the receiving state's consent until he or she is discharged from prosecution or from any imprisonment for such offense. The effect is that the sending state cannot retake the probationer into custody until all local charges are disposed of.

A national organization called the Parole and Probation Compact Administrators' Association (PPCAA) was formed so that interstate compact officers could exchange information and solve challenges that arise. PPCAA meets twice per year to address issues as they occur so that all state policies are consistently enforced.

TOP THINGS YOU SHOULD KNOW

- The most vital aspect of the probation and parole process in the criminal justice system is supervision. Few offenders can be expected to transform themselves into law-abiding citizens without a combination of monitoring and treatment.
- Merely observing conditions of release or managing not to be arrested for a new offense does not indicate that an offender has been rehabilitated. The

personality, training, and experience of the supervisory officer determine the outcome just as much as the offender's motivation.

- Adequate supervision must deal with all phases of offenders' lives, including family and the community in which they live and work. Neighborhood-based probation supervision (NBS) seeks to change the operation and accountability to make probation a more respected and more visible part of the corrections system.
- The effectiveness of NBS rests in part on the officer being able to secure the assistance and cooperation of community agencies and individuals within his or her beat.
- Use of a valid classification is important to assess risk and identify treatment needs, which in turn lead to developing the case plan and appropriate level of supervision.
- Specialized caseloads are important for certain offenders, such as those who have abused drugs or alcohol, offenders who have mental health issues, and offenders who are on community supervision for a sex crime.
- Interstate compacts are written agreements between two agencies that allow probationers and parolees to be supervised in another state.

DISCUSSION QUESTIONS

1 Argue for the use of neighborhood-based probation supervision over traditional methods. In what situations might NBS be most useful?

2 How does assessing client needs in education, employment, treatment, and so on help develop the program plan? How much should a client be expected to do while on supervision?

3 Discuss the use of risk prediction scales. How might risk assessment be used in community supervision?

4 Discuss the concept of caseload and workload computation. Why might workload be a better method of allocating probation or parole officer resources?

5 How does a specialized caseload differ from a traditional caseload?

6 What is at issue in the surveillance and treatment of sex offenders on probation or parole?

7 What other types of offenders should be on specialized caseloads other than the ones mentioned in this text?

8 How might interstate compact supervision (supervision in a state other than where an offender was arrested) be more *helpful* for the offender than local supervision? How might interstate supervision be more *difficult* for the offender than local supervision?

 ## WEBSITES

General Information about Risk and Needs Assessments, Inc.

   http://www.riskandneeds.com

Empirical Validation of the Arizona Risk/Needs Assessment

   http://www.nicic.org/library/018821

Using Risk/Needs to Improve Decision Making in the Maryland Juvenile Justice System

   http://www.bgr.umd.edu/pdf/Risk_Needs_Assessment.pdf

A Study of the Efficiency and Effectiveness of Juvenile Risk/Needs Assessment in Texas

http://www.la.utexas.edu/research/cccjr/research/intakerib.htm

A Research Study of Assessments and Conditional Releases in Canada

http://www.csc-scc.gc.ca/text/copyright_e.shtml

Information on Case Management and Risk Assessment

http://www.justiceconcepts.com/

Association for the Treatment of Sexual Abusers

http://www.atsa.com

Center for Sex Offender Management

http://www.csom.org

Department of Community Justice: Adult Sex Offender Supervision

http://www.co.multnomah.or.us/dcj/acjsoffendersup.shtml

Sex Offender Risk and Needs Assessment (Canada)

http://www.csc-scc.gc.ca/text/rsrch/reports/r48/r48e_e.shtml

Interstate Parole and Probation Policy in Oklahoma

http://www.doc.state.ok.us/Offtech/op160108.htm

Classification and Supervision in Probation and Parole

There are two new clients on your caseload. Below is the information that you have received on each person. Use the risk classification instrument on p. 122–123 of the text to assess the risks posed by the offender and select the appropriate supervision assignment.

Then consider the factors that have placed the client at risk and which of these factors are related to the offense.

Third, consider the treatment needs of the client. What are the client's strengths? Prioritize the top two problems and write a program plan that includes a reachable goal, along with what the client will do to reach each goal (objective).

PROGRAM PLAN

Client:

Offense:

Needs Assessment	Offense-related? Y = Yes	Priority 1 = high 2 = Medium 3 = low n/a = not applicable
Life skills		
Emotional adjustment problems	_____	_____
Financial management	_____	_____
Associates	_____	_____
Employment	_____	_____
Vocational or educational	_____	_____
Marital/family relations	_____	_____
Medical/dietary	_____	_____
Mental health	_____	_____
Substance abuse	_____	_____
Other: _____	_____	_____

Problem #1:

Goal 1:
    Objective 1A:
    Objective 1B:

Problem #2:

Goal 2:
    Objective 2A:
    Objective 2B:

CASE A

Thomas User, age 18, has been placed on probation for possession of methamphetamine and ecstasy. There were no known victims in the current offense. Police reports indicate that Mr. User was stopped by a police cruiser because he had been standing on the same corner for hours. An outer pat search revealed that he had eight tablets that were confirmed by drug testing to be ecstasy, and he had enough methamphetamine for upto 12 hits.

Mr. User has two previous misdemeanor convictions as a juvenile, one for disorderly conduct and one for minor in possession of alcoholic beverages. He has one misdemeanor conviction as an adult for Menacing in the second degree.

Mr. User has a spotty employment record, having only been employed at one fast-food restaurant for four months out of the last two years. The rest of the time Mr. User says he sold and used drugs. He has a drug habit that is related to his arrest but has not yet been assessed for drug treatment. It is unclear how motivated Mr. User is to attend treatment.

Mr. User has an IQ of 68, which defines him as developmentally disabled. Although there are no apparent signs, it is unclear whether Mr. User is also mentally ill. He is a high school dropout, having only completed the 10th grade. He does not have his GED. He reports himself to be in good physical health. You notice he seems underweight and he has two teeth missing.

Mr. User reports that he has fathered one child, but he does not know the whereabouts of the child or the mother. The child is approximately 2 years of age, and there is no claim by the mother for child support.

CASE B

Sue Steel was convicted of two charges—criminal possession of a weapon and passing bad checks. Steel stole a box of checks from the mailbox belonging to Janine Smith. Posing as Ms. Smith, Client Steel wrote a total of four checks to retail stores that totaled $975 over a period of three days. A JC Penney clerk notified mall security when Steel became agitated and irate because the clerk refused to accept a check without proper identification. As Steel tried to leave the mall, she was approached for questioning by private security. One of the private security officers happened to notice a "shiny metal object" in her waistband that appeared to be a weapon of some sort. Private security detained Steel at the mall until police arrived to conduct a frisk. She was carrying a .38 caliber weapon and a book of checks for "Janine Smith" when she was arrested.

She is 25 years of age and has a history of criminal conduct; her prior convictions began at age 15, with one juvenile conviction for simple robbery and two adult convictions involving forms of fraud. Her simple robbery conviction involved one victim who was injured, reportedly by Steel's codefendant. Records indicate she successfully completed juvenile probation by age 17.

Her first conviction as an adult was at age 19 for felony fraud. She completed probation and was released from supervision after 14 months. Her current conviction, passing bad checks, resulted in a confinement sentence of 6 months. The jail uncovered a pending misdemeanor case for "theft by deception." As she had been in detention prior to sentencing, she was given "time served" for the misdemeanor conviction, which ran concurrently with her other two current charges. She was incarcerated for 3 months and 22 days, and the sentencing court ordered her to serve the remaining 2 months and 8 days on home confinement with electronic monitoring, and then transfer out to probation supervision for another 2 years.

Ms. Steel has a high school diploma, and she has a "transient" job history—moving from job to job. She has employment at a janitorial service cleaning office buildings. Ms. Steel worked at this firm prior to detention in this case and her employer was willing to rehire her upon her release from custody. Her employer is aware of her conviction and supervision. Ms. Steel was ordered to pay $975 in restitution for her current offense. She has not yet made any payments toward her restitution. She is living with her sister and her sister's child, and has one dependent child who is currently in the temporary custody of her mother.

Client Steel reports a prior history of child abuse at the hands of her father, who died of cirrhosis of the liver when Steel was 15 years old. Steel says her father abused her and her mother, but this cannot be confirmed through any police records. She reports to be in good medical health and there is no evidence indicating otherwise. There is no evidence of drug use in any previous offenses or the current offense, and Steel has never attended drug treatment.

Introduction

Modifying Probation Conditions
Early Termination of Probation
Modifying Conditions before the
   Revocation Decision

The Decision to Revoke

Types of Probation Violations
Law Violations
Technical Violations
Probation Absconders

Revocation Procedure
The Power to Arrest Probationers
Time on Probation or Parole Is
   Usually Not Credited if Revoked

**Revocation Rights of
Probationers and Parolees**
Gagnon v. Scarpelli—The Facts
The Right to a Hearing
The Right to a Lawyer
Level of Proof and Evidence
   Required
Other Revocation Situations

Probation Effectiveness
Probation Recidivism Rates
Who Is More Likely to Succeed or
   Fail on Probation?
Probationers Compared with
   Parolees

Top Things You Should Know

7

Probation Modification and Termination

© AP/Wide World Photos

What You Will Learn in This Chapter

- *How probation conditions are modified and under what circumstances*
- *How many people successfully complete probation*
- *The reasons for revoking probation as a type of unsuccessful termination*
- *The rights probationers have during the revocation process*
- *Whether probation is or is not an effective sanction*

KEY TERMS

Revocation
Early termination
Law violations
Technical violations
Due process
Preliminary hearing
Final revocation hearing
Standard of proof
Preponderance of evidence

INTRODUCTION

Placing an offender on probation implies that, in the best judgment of the court, the offender is able to abide by the law and observe the conditions of release while remaining in the community under supervision. Probation is conditional, meaning that the probationer's liberty is subject to compliance with specified rules. The good news is that if the probationer is compliant with the rules, probation can be successfully terminated early.

A resistant probationer has either not sufficiently met probation conditions or may be involved in a pattern of deviant or criminal behavior violations. Although not every probation violation leads to revocation, a pattern of violations or serious misbehavior can cause an extension of probation, imposition of additional conditions, or revocation of probation. When considering modifying or revoking probation, the courts assess the risk the offender poses to the community, whether the change will increase compliance, and whether the change will better serve the needs of the offender at the present time. **Revocation** is a serious matter to the probationer because most of the time, it denotes a sentence to a more intensive punishment such as a residential facility, electronic monitoring (to be discussed in Chapter 9), or even jail. Probation revocation (via incarcerating the offender) increases the cost to the community because probation supervision costs much less than providing care and treatment in a correctional institution. Table 7.1 shows the daily costs in various jurisdictions to keep an offender on probation versus in prison. Note that the cost of

REVOCATION

The process of hearings that result when the probationer is noncompliant with the current level of probation. Results of a revocation are either modifying probation conditions to a more intensive supervision level, or the complete elimination of probation and sentence to a residential community facility, jail, or prison.

TABLE 7.1 *Daily Cost per Person of Probation Compared to Other Sanctions*

Jurisdiction	Probation	Community Correction Residential Centers	Jail or Prison
Federal (U.S. Courts/BOP)	$9.46	$55.07	$63.57 (prison)
Suffolk Co, New York	$4.00	—	$125.00 (jail)
Texas Dept. of CJ-ID	$2.00	$36.50	$44.00 (prison)
Georgia Dept. Corrections	$1.27	$39.05	$46.62 (prison)

References: Retrieved on May 2, 2006, from: Administrative Office of the U.S. Courts (May 2005). *The Third Branch: Newsletter of the Federal Courts* 37(5). http://www.uscourts.gov/ttb/may05ttb/costs/index.html

(for Suffolk County) http://www.co.suffolk.ny.us/probation/

(for Texas) Texas Probation Association: http://www.tdcj.state.tx.us/publications/cjad/fact-sheets/TPA_Presentation_4-02-03_FFF.pdf

(for Georgia) http://www.dcor.state.ga.us/CORRINFO/ResearchReports/ ResearchReports.html

probation is offset to taxpayers by monthly fees that the probationer pays to the probation office or court. These fees average between $35 and $40 per month, thus making probation self-sustaining and avoiding most charges to the taxpayer.

When we imprison an offender, judges have decided that the public safety risk outweighs our desire for that person to be a contributing member of society. When offenders are imprisoned, their dependents may be forced to rely on government assistance, and the offender also becomes dependent on taxpayers. Revocation, however, is one way to protect the community from offenders who may become a danger to public safety or who continue to commit criminal acts. Incarceration is not, however, the *only* viable alternative for probationers who continually fail to abide by supervision conditions. Sometimes, modifying probation is a practical option.

MODIFYING PROBATION CONDITIONS

The length and conditions of probation may be modified by the court in two ways in response to changing circumstances. For offenders who are abiding by conditions, shortening the term or easing restrictions is used as a reward. Probationers who are not abiding by conditions may have their term extended or additional restrictions imposed.

Early Termination of Probation

In many states the court is given authority to reward a probationer for good behavior by terminating probation after a portion of time has been served. Some states, such as Texas, allow felony probationers to apply for **early termination** after having satisfactorily served one-third of the probation term or two years, whichever is less. Article 3564 of the *Federal Rules of Criminal Procedure* states that the court may "terminate a term of probation previously ordered and discharge the defendant at any time in the case of a misdemeanor or an infraction or at any time after the expiration of one year of probation in the case of a felony, if it is satisfied that such action is warranted by the conduct of the defendant and the interest of justice." The authority to terminate probation early is vested in the judge, who acts on the initial recommendation of the probation officer.

Other rewards for good behavior may include the reduction of supervision level (thus reducing the number of contacts), waiving fines, or modifying conditions such as curfew time, intensive home detention time, or community service hours. Positive recognition may include giving the probationer completion certificates, affirmation letters, or reference letters from his or her employer or school, or from the court (Carter and Ley 2001). All of these incentives are discretionary, and the probation supervisor or judge reviews the behavioral record of the probationer before granting or rejecting the request.

In cases of deferred adjudication probation or suspended sentences, where the finding of guilt is deferred but the person still must complete conditions, if the deferred adjudication period is successful, charges are dismissed and the finding of guilt is never made. Recall that radio host Rush Limbaugh received a deferred adjudication in May 2006 for his admitted addiction to painkillers, if he agreed to complete 18 months of treatment and to be randomly tested for drugs. Note that in some states the prior deferred adjudication probation can be used as a "prior" to increase the sentence if the offender commits another crime in the future.

The rate of successful termination on local and state level probation varies by jurisdiction due to the lack of uniform law on when a probation revocation must be filed. Approximately 80 percent of federal probationers terminate probation successfully with no violations. About 20 percent will not complete probation or will fail and be resentenced (see Table 7.2).

Modifying Conditions before the Revocation Decision

Although setting the initial conditions and length of probation is a judicial function, jurisdictions have increasingly developed policies to allow probation officers in limited and well-defined circumstances to modify probation conditions in response to specific violations without having to go back to court. One example is to have the probationer sign a waiver that he or she is agreeing to the new sanctions in lieu of going to court, and thus is waiving the right to a court hearing. This waiver is kept on file to show the court if need be what additional sanctions were tried before the probation officer requested a formal revocation proceeding.

An example of guidelines that determine the response options from probation officials can be found in Table 7.3. Note that the response depends on the severity of the probation violation, the offender's predefined risk level defined by the risk/needs assessment (see Chapter 6), and assaultive history. Once the response range has been determined, with or without a second opinion from a supervisor, probation officers can choose from a variety of responses depending on what they feel would be most appropriate in each particular case. In the most serious of violations, the probation officer can then recommend a revocation hearing before the court.

THE DECISION TO REVOKE

When probation conditions have been modified and are still not being followed, the case must ultimately come before the court so the court can make the decision whether or not to revoke. Various issues are involved in probation revocation, including revocation authority, types of probation violations, revocation procedures, and rights during revocation.

Although the probation officer or the supervising department may recommend revocation, only the court judge has the discretionary authority to revoke probation. This authority remains with the court that granted probation unless the case has been transferred to another court that is given the same powers as the sentencing court (18 U.S.C. sec. 3561, sec. 3563). Discretionary revocation allows the court to (1) continue probation with or without extending the term, (2) modify the conditions of probation, or (3) revoke the sentence of probation and resentence the defendant. Probation officers are encouraged beforehand to motivate their clients by threatening to recommend revocation if the probationer doesn't modify his or her behavior immediately. These warnings from the probation officer are often sufficient to gain compliance.

While most revocation decisions are discretionary, some jurisdictions explicitly mandate automatic revocation and resentencing for some behaviors. In the federal system, instances of mandatory revocation include: (1) committing any crime of violence or facilitating sexual contact against a child under the age of 16 (Carlie's law); (2) possession of a firearm; (3) possession of a controlled substance or positive drug test; or (4) refusal to comply with drug testing. Revocation may not always result in imprisonment, but additional conditions or stricter supervision will be imposed.

An example of a state that has mandatory probation revocation rules is Michigan. In Michigan, mandatory revocation is imposed on juveniles who have been "waived" to adult probation supervision and who subsequently commit a new misdemeanor or

TABLE 7.2   Federal Probation Terminations

Most Serious Conviction	Number of Probation Terminations	Successful Completion	PERCENT TERMINATING SUPERVISION WITH:				
			Committed New Crime (a)	Drug use Detected by Test	Escape/ Fugitive	Other (b)	Admin. Closure
All offenses	15,237	80%	6%	4%	2%	6%	2%
Felonies	8,013	82%	6%	4%	2%	5%	2%
Violent	235	69%	10%	2%	4%	13%	3%
Property	4,230	82%	5%	4%	2%	5%	2%
Drug	1,361	80%	6%	6%	2%	5%	1%
Public-order	1,830	90%	3%	2%	1%	3%	2%
Immigration	357	73%	11%	6%	3%	5%	2%
Misdemeanors & petty crimes	7,224	78%	7%	4%	3%	6%	2%

Note: All percentages have been rounded to the closest whole number. Each termination was counted separately. Technical violations and terminations for new crimes are shown only if supervision terminated with incarceration or removal from active supervision for reason of a violation. The data exclude corporate offenders. Total includes 80 felony offenders whose offense category could not be determined.

(a) Supervision terminated with incarceration or removal to inactive status after arrest for a felony or misdemeanor.

(b) Other technical violations range widely from repeated acts of not following probation conditions, such as quitting a job without permission, not reporting, associating with other felons, etc.

Sources: U.S. Department of Justice. 2005. *Compendium of Federal Justice Statistics, 2003.* Washington, DC: U.S. Department of Justice.

TABLE 7.3   *Probation Violation Decision Guidelines*

Decision-Making Level	Probation Violation Type*	Possible Responses to Probationer
Probation Officer	Failure to report Making false statements Violating curfew Changing residence/jobs w/o permission Failure to pay restitution Failure to perform community service Drug use/positive drug test	Verbal warning/reprimand Case Staffing Home visit + 7-day curfew Loss of travel Community service: 1–8 hrs. Increase reporting Increase drug testing Probationer sign waiver
Supervisor Staffing	Failure to test for drugs/take Antabuse Failure to participate in drug treatment Possession of contraband Failing to register as a sex offender Repeated curfew violations Second positive drug test Repeated failure to report	Drug treatment Increase supervision level Community service: 20–40 hrs. Curfew (up to 30 days) Curfew (up to 30 days) Drug treatment Increase supervision level
Court Hearing	Third positive drug test Possession of weapons Absconding after 60 days Denying access to searches Committing new offense Threatening victim Deliberate pattern of noncompliance	Residential treatment Boot camp Electronic monitoring Intensive probation Jail or prison Day reporting center Extension of probation

* Response also depends on level of risk probationer poses

Source: Madeline M. Carter (Ed.). 2001. *Responding to Parole and Probation Violations: A Handbook to Guide Local Policy Development.* Prepared for the National Institute of Corrections, U.S, Department of Justice (Washington, DC), pp. 54, 75.

felony crime while on supervision. In this case, the new crime runs concurrent with the original offense—that is, the length of supervision for the new charge cannot exceed the term left on the original charge, but probation must be revoked (Michigan Judicial Institute 2003).

TYPES OF PROBATION VIOLATIONS

Revocation of probation is generally triggered in two ways: law violations and technical violations. A **law violation** occurs if a probationer commits another misdemeanor or felony crime. By contrast, **technical violations** are a pattern of infractions that breach a condition of probation. Examples of technical violations include testing positive for drugs, failure to report, failure to maintain employment, failure to attend treatment, and association with known felons.

Law Violations

Revocation for violating the law occurs in about 16 percent of all revocations (12 percent of revocations filed involve a felony and 4 percent involve a misdemeanor). In misdemeanors and drug use/possessions, most jurisdictions simply revoke probation instead of prosecuting the offender for the new crime. Revocation for a new crime is

LAW VIOLATIONS

Violations of probation or parole conditions that involve the commission of a crime.

TECHNICAL VIOLATIONS

Multiple violations that breach one or more noncriminal conditions of probation.

a more convenient option that achieves the same result, which is a modification of conditions or incarceration and removal from society. Even if the offender is guilty of a new crime, however, revocation is not automatic. Instead, it is left to the discretion of the court.

On the other hand, acquittal for a new offense may lead to revocation because of the differences in standards of proof. Although conviction for an offense requires guilt beyond reasonable doubt, the standard of proof for revocation is only a "preponderance of the evidence." What may not suffice for conviction may be adequate for revocation. There is no double jeopardy because revocation is merely an administrative and not a criminal proceeding, even if it results in incarceration. As you can see in Table 7.2, only 6 percent of all federal probationers were terminated unsuccessfully for a new crime. Violent felony offenders (10 percent) and people convicted of immigration offenses (11 percent) are the most likely to commit a new crime, whereas felons who are on probation for a "public-order" offense are the least likely (3 percent). As we discussed previously, jurisdictions vary on whether probation revocation is mandatory or automatic for new crimes.

Technical Violations

Most violations (85–90 percent) come under the category of technical violations, meaning they do not constitute criminal acts, but rather, a pattern of rule violations. Research in two studies on revocation motions filed provides the following findings: Because filing and/or granting a revocation is so subjective, the revocation rate varies

	BURKE (1997)	GRAY, FIELDS, AND MAXWELL (2001)
Positive urinalysis for drug use	27%	22.4%
Failure to participate in treatment	20%	9.0%
Abscond	18.5%	2.5%
Failure to report to probation or parole officer	10%	33.6%
All other technical violations	8.5%	22.9%
New crimes	16%	9.6%

greatly by jurisdiction. For example, one study found that about half of all probationers did not abide by their probation conditions. Of those violators, about half went to jail or prison for their noncompliance (Langan 1994).

Gray and his colleagues (2001) found that 30 percent of all "failures" on probation were terminated within the first three months of supervision, mostly with technical violations. They also found that people of color, individuals with low education, those with a history of prior drug use, and those on probation for assaultive offenses tended to be terminated more often for technical violations. This finding does not necessarily indicate discrimination. A study in Alaska found no evidence to support that Native Alaskan groups were unfairly treated during the revocation petition or resentencing process (Alaska Judicial Council 1998). Probationers who committed a "new crime" seemed to violate later in the probationary period, but they were also more likely to be unemployed, to have a prior criminal history, to be on probation for an assaultive offense, and to have a pattern of technical violations.

As a general rule, probation is not revoked for occasional violations of technical conditions. Probation officers are instead urged to address these violations promptly and with the least restrictive means necessary to ensure compliance. Because incarceration results in high costs, revocation is the last resort for dealing with a pattern of continual technical violations.

Probation Absconders

Absconding from probation supervision is a significant problem in many jurisdictions. Burke (1997) found that 18.5 percent of all county- and state-level probation terminations were because the probationer left the jurisdiction. The problem seems less extensive at the federal level. Table 7.2 shows that about 2 percent of all federal probationers are terminated from probation because they are "fugitives." What differentiates a probationer who absconds from a probationer who succeeds? One study in Michigan (Gray, Fields, and Maxwell 2001) found that after a 30-month follow-up, 2.5 percent of all probationers absconded on active supervision. Probation absconders had more extensive felony criminal histories, longer terms of probation, and more stringent conditions than probationers who terminated successfully (Mayzer and Gray 2000).

REVOCATION PROCEDURE

Revocation procedures are governed by a combination of constitutional rules, state law, and agency policies. Constitutional rights, such as the right to a hearing and basic due process, are required in all jurisdictions and must be afforded the probationer. Revocation statutes vary greatly from state to state or even within a state.

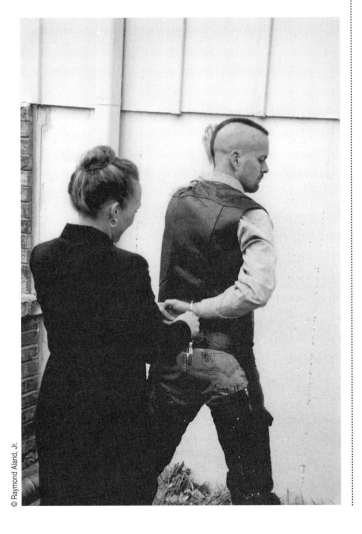

© Raymond Alarid, Jr.

A probation officer arrests one of her clients for violating his probation.

Revocation proceedings begin with a violation report prepared by a probation officer. The report is passed directly to the court that originally granted probation or to the prosecutor to file a motion with the court. Should the court decide to pick up the probationer for a revocation hearing, the court will issue a warrant for arrest (in 82 percent of cases) or a summons (in 18 percent of cases) (Burke 1997).

Peggy Burke (1997) studied what happened in probation and parole revocation proceedings. She found that 60 percent of all revocations resulted in some form of incarceration, whereas 40 percent remained on probation with additional conditions. Of the incarcerative sanctions, the most frequent type was prison (36 percent) or some time in jail followed by release back out to probation (21 percent).

The state of Georgia has "probation detention centers," which are minimum-security units specifically for people who have violated probation and are either waiting for their revocation hearing or are serving time away from the community following their revocation hearing. There are 16 men's units and three women's units with approximately 3,500 probationers. Georgia officials have used these probation detention centers as an alternative to ease jail crowding.

The Power to Arrest Probationers

Arresting a probationer for a technical violation or arrest for a new crime does not automatically mean that probation will be revoked—it just means that the officer can incarcerate the offender and request that the court conduct a revocation hearing. Federal law has the following provision for federal probationers:

> If there is reason to believe that a probationer or a person on supervised release has violated a condition of his probation or release, he may be arrested, and upon arrest, shall be taken without unnecessary delay before the court having jurisdiction over him. A probation officer may make such an arrest wherever the probationer or releasee is found, and may make the arrest without a warrant (Federal Criminal Code and Rules 2004).

In states where probation officers are peace officers, they are usually authorized to make an arrest of a probationer with or without a warrant as long as the arrest is justified (see Box 7.1). In states where probation officers are expressly prohibited from making an arrest, the probation officer must rely on the police.

These differences in the arrest powers of probation officers reflect the orientation of probation departments in the various states. Agencies with a treatment orientation, such as juvenile probation departments, do not want their officers to be viewed as law enforcement agents because it lessens their effectiveness as treatment agents, so the power to arrest is denied. By contrast, agencies with a surveillance orientation believe that law enforcement is a necessary function of probation, and thus it is not unusual for probation officers to be armed and certified as law enforcement officers.

Time on Probation or Parole Is Usually Not Credited if Revoked

If probation is revoked and the offender goes to prison, most courts have ruled that time served on probation or parole is not credited toward the sentence in the same way that incarceration time in jail or prison would be (*Bruggeman v. State* 1996). However, a federal court and now a Florida statute permit the court the option to credit none, some, or all time spent on supervised release toward the sentence (*United States v. Pettus* 2002; *Summers v. State* 2002). Generally a parolee whose parole has been revoked may be paroled again, but the revoked parolee must remain in prison for a specified time before becoming eligible for another parole.

As long as the offender is abiding by the terms of their parole (or probation), he or she will minimally receive credit on the sentence as straight time, that is, without

Title 17-A, § 1205 of Maine Criminal Code. Commencement of probation revocation proceedings by arrest

1. If a probation officer has probable cause to believe that a person on probation has violated a condition of that person's probation, that officer may arrest the person or cause the person to be arrested for the alleged violation. If the probation officer cannot, with due diligence, locate the person, the officer shall file a written notice of this fact with the court that placed the person on probation. Upon the filing of that written notice, the court shall issue a warrant for the arrest of that person.

2. [1999, c. 246, §1 (rp).]

3. [1999, c. 246, §1 (rp).]

4. A person arrested pursuant to subsection 1, with or without a warrant, must be afforded a preliminary hearing as soon as reasonably possible, but not later than on the 3rd day after arrest, excluding Saturdays, Sundays, and holidays, in accordance with the procedures set forth in section 1205-A. A preliminary hearing may not be afforded if, within the 3-day period, the person is released on bail or is afforded an opportunity for a court hearing on the alleged violation. A preliminary hearing is not required if the person is charged with or convicted of a new offense and is incarcerated as a result of the pending charge or conviction. . . .

5. Whenever a person is entitled to a preliminary hearing, the failure to hold the hearing within the time period specified in subsection 4 is grounds for the person's release on personal recognizance pending further proceedings.

---

the benefit of good-time credits. In other states the parolee may receive reductions for good behavior while on parole.

REVOCATION RIGHTS OF PROBATIONERS AND PAROLEES

A probation or parole revocation is an "administrative hearing" that is closer to a civil proceeding because it is seen as an extension of the existing sentence (*Hampton v. State* 2001). As such, neither is governed by the same rules as are formal criminal trials. Given that the legal rights at time of revocation are virtually identical, the rights afforded in probation revocation proceedings are extended to parole revocations, and vice versa. For example, the result of a probation revocation hearing is not a conviction but a finding of either revoking or continuing probation (*Soliz v. State* 1961). If probation is revoked, the judge will modify the probation conditions or resentence the offender altogether. The judicial role may change in the future (see Box 7.2). On the other hand, if parole is revoked by the parole board, the parolee returns to jail or prison.

In revocation proceedings, the defendant is constitutionally entitled neither to a jury (*People v. Price* 1960) nor to a speedy trial. In some states, however, the law provides for a jury hearing in juvenile cases. The probationer or parolee is not entitled to the Fifth Amendment privilege against self-incrimination (*Perry v. State* 2001). Remaining silent at a revocation hearing may prejudice the outcome against the defendant, but testifying at a revocation hearing can be used as evidence at a later criminal trial unless the probationer (or parolee) has been given "immunity" on what he or she says at the revocation.

BOX 7.2   THE JUDGE'S ROLE IN PROBATION REVOCATION: WILL IT CHANGE?   •

In all states, if probation supervision is revoked after a hearing, the *judge* disposes of the case as if there had been no community supervision. This may mean modifying the original sentence or resentencing. In 2005, the U.S. Supreme Court held that the right to a trial by jury requires that *juries* (rather than judges) find facts relevant to sentencing (*United States v. Booker* 2005). So although the probation revocation is an administrative hearing, the question remains whether the revocation outcome is closer to a "sentencing" proceeding or just part of the administrative

process. This has not yet been answered by the Supreme Court.

Section 23 of the Texas Code of Criminal Procedure states: "If the judge determines that the best interests of society and the defendant would be served by a shorter term of confinement, the judge may reduce the term of confinement originally assessed to a term of confinement not less than the minimum prescribed for the offense of which the defendant was convicted. The judge shall enter the amount of restitution or reparation owed by the defendant on the date of revocation in the judgment in the case."

The way this clause is worded suggests that the judge may continue to choose outcomes following the revocation hearing. However, in *United States v. Booker,* when the sentence was enhanced or more severe, the jury was deemed to be the fact finder over the judge. It is yet to be determined whether the *Booker* decision is extended to revocation proceedings.

Sources: Texas Code of Criminal Procedure, Article 41.12, sec. 23 (a) & (b);

United States v. Booker, 125 S. Ct. 738, 160 LED 2d 621 (U.S. 2005).

During a revocation proceeding, offenders are entitled to certain rights prior to probation being revoked. These rights were granted by the U.S. Supreme Court in the cases of *Morrissey v. Brewer* (1972) and *Gagnon v. Scarpelli* (1973), arguably the two most important parole and probation cases ever to be decided by the Court. We discuss *Gagnon v. Scarpelli* here.

Gagnon v. Scarpelli—The Facts

Gerald Scarpelli was on probation for a felony when he was arrested for burglary. He admitted involvement in the burglary but later claimed that his admission was coerced and therefore invalid. His probation was revoked without a hearing and without a lawyer present. After serving three years of his sentence, Scarpelli sought release through a writ of habeas corpus. He claimed violations of two constitutional rights: the **due process** right to a hearing and the right to a lawyer during the hearing.

The Right to a Hearing

The Court said that probationers were entitled to a two-stage hearing consisting of a **preliminary hearing** and a **final revocation** hearing. The preliminary or "show cause" hearing is a recorded hearing to determine whether probable cause exists to believe that a probation violation has occurred. If the magistrate finds probable cause, a revocation hearing is held. If probable cause is not found, the judge must dismiss the proceeding. The total time that passes from the point the probation officer detects the violation until the court renders a decision regarding the revocation hearing is 44 to 64 days (Burke 1997). The vast majority of probation violators spend this time in the county jail waiting for the revocation proceeding decision.

DUE PROCESS

Laws must be applied in a fair and equal manner. Fundamental fairness.

PRELIMINARY HEARING

An inquiry conducted to determine if there is probable cause to believe that the offender committed a probation or parole violation.

FINAL REVOCATION HEARING

A due process hearing that must be conducted before probation or parole can be revoked.

Extending the same due process rights that parolees had afforded to them one year earlier in *Morrissey v. Brewer*, both probationers and parolees were now entitled to the following due process rights before and during revocation hearings:

1. Written notice of the alleged probation violation
2. Disclosure of the evidence of violation
3. The opportunity to be heard in person and to present evidence and witnesses
4. The right to confront and cross-examine adverse witnesses
5. The right to judgment by a detached and neutral hearing body
6. A written statement of the reasons for revoking probation, including evidence used in arriving at that decision

The Right to a Lawyer

A probationer is generally not entitled to a court-appointed lawyer during revocation proceedings, but there are exceptions. The first case that addressed this issue was *Mempa v. Rhay* (1967). In that case, the Court said that a defendant has a constitutional right to a lawyer during probation revocation *that is followed by sentencing.* This is because sentencing is an important phase that has always required the presence of a lawyer for the defendant. In *Gagnon v. Scarpelli* (1973), the Court said entitlement to a lawyer during revocation proceedings should be case-by-case on the basis of a "colorable claim" in which the defendant claims innocence of the allegations, or when defendants appear incapable of speaking for themselves. Given the fact that inarticulate people must articulate their need for counsel in order to get legal assistance, indigence is used as a proxy, with some states routinely providing counsel to indigent probationers in revocation proceedings.

Level of Proof and Evidence Required

The **standard of proof** varies widely among the states because this issue has not been decided by the U.S. Supreme Court. Most courts require **preponderance of the evidence** as the standard for revocation (*United States v. McCormick* 1995), which is the evidence that convinces the judge that a probationer violated the terms of his or her probation. If the state presents proof of a condition violation, the probationer has the burden of presenting evidence to meet and/or overcome prima facie proof (*State v. Graham* 2001). Preponderance of the evidence is approximately the same amount of evidence as that required to make an arrest (probable cause). However, one court case (*Benton v. State* 2003) said that arrest for a crime by itself is not enough to revoke probation, but probation may be revoked for an "indictment" by a grand jury (*Newsom v. State* 2004) or a conviction by a judge or jury. Interestingly, parole revocation is permissible even if charges are later dismissed (*Reyes v. Tate* 2001). So it seems that whether a lower burden of proof than preponderance of the evidence (such as reasonable grounds or reasonable suspicion) would suffice for revocation is being addressed by lower courts, but has yet to be addressed by the U.S. Supreme Court.

The testimony of the probation officer is often crucial at a revocation proceeding. Whether such testimony—unsupported by any other evidence—is sufficient to revoke varies by state and is related to the burden of proof. Illinois courts held that once a defendant has admitted violating probation, the admission eliminates the need on the part of the government to present proof of the violation (del Carmen 2003). Louisiana requires more evidence than a defendant's mere admission of guilt (*State v. Varnado* 1980).

STANDARD OF PROOF

The level of proof, measured by the strength of the evidence, needed to render a decision in a court proceeding.

PREPONDERANCE OF THE EVIDENCE

A level of proof used in a probation revocation administrative hearing, in which the judge decides based on which side presents more convincing evidence and its probable truth or accuracy, and not necessarily on the amount of evidence.

In Texas (*Herrington v. State* 1976) and Oklahoma (*Meyer v. State* 1979), revocation cannot be based merely on the statement of a probation officer that the probationer failed to uphold probation conditions. Other courts reached the opposite conclusion, holding that uncontradicted testimony of a probation officer and/or admissions made to a probation officer by the probationer were sufficient to support a revocation (*Fields v. State 2002*). Most states admit hearsay evidence during revocation, but some do not.

Reliable hearsay evidence (statements offered by a witness that are based upon what someone else has told the witness and not upon personal knowledge or observation) may be admitted in a parole (or probation) revocation hearing *(Belk v. Purkett* 1994). The court suggested using these questions to establish reliability:

1. Is the information corroborated by the parolee's own statements or other live testimony at the hearing?
2. Does the information fit within one of the many exceptions to the hearsay rule?
3. Does the information have other substantial indicia of reliability?

A "yes" answer to any of these questions signifies that the hearsay is reliable and therefore may be admitted as evidence in the revocation proceeding.

Other Revocation Situations

Three other situations may include revocation, such as probationers who are revoked for not fulfilling financial commitments, juvenile probation revocations in the federal system, and the policy on revocation when the probation term has expired.

REVOCATION FOR AN INABILITY TO PAY. Violating a probationer largely depends on whether the behavior was willful and intentional. For example, a probationer can be revoked for refusal to pay monthly fees, restitution, or fines. An indigent probationer cannot be revoked if he or she is unable to pay a fine or restitution provided the probationer was not somehow responsible for the failure to pay (*Bearden v. Georgia* 1983). The probationer, however, has the burden of showing that the inability to pay was not willful. In other words, the defendant has to show effort and desire to fulfill financial obligations (*State v. Gropper* 1995).

On the other hand, the courts will allow revocation, even in cases where the probationer is not at fault (there is no willful violation), if it can be shown that not revoking is a risk to public safety. For example, probationers on community supervision for predatory sex offenses were not able to complete mandatory sex offender treatment programs because none were available in their community. After finding no better alternatives, the court supported incarceration over allowing these offenders to remain in the community without treatment (*People v. Colabello* 1997).

JUVENILE PROBATION REVOCATION. In the federal system, the United States Code differentiates between juveniles age 17 and younger (18 U.S.C., sec. 5037(c)(1)) and juveniles between the ages of 18 and 21 (18 U.S.C., sec. 5037(c)(2)). In either case, a juvenile may not be sentenced to a prison term longer than an adult would be for the same offense (*United States v. RLC* 1992). The revocation options depend on the age of the juvenile at the time of sentencing for the original offense, not the age of the juvenile at time of revocation.

REVOCATION AFTER PROBATION TERM EXPIRES. Probation may still be revoked after the probation period has expired when the defendant is arrested for violation of probation, or when a warrant is issued for the probationer's arrest before the period of probation expires (*Jones v. State* 1996).

Federal law also authorizes delayed revocation, saying that "the power of the court to revoke a sentence of probation for violation of a condition of probation, and to impose another sentence, extends beyond the expiration of the term of probation for any period reasonably necessary for the adjudication of matters arising before its expiration if, prior to its expiration, a warrant or summons has been issued on the basis of an allegation of such a violation" (Federal Criminal Code and Rules 2004). Probation may also be revoked after the term of probation has expired if the probationer evades supervision before completing the sentence. Probation statutes usually provide that the term of probation is "tolled" if the defendant is either charged with a violation of probation or flees the jurisdiction (or cannot be found) and a warrant is issued. To toll the running of a sentence or a period of time limitation is to interrupt it, to "stop the clock." The Illinois statute, for example, provides that when a petition is filed charging a violation of a probation condition, the court may order a warrant for the offender's arrest. Meanwhile, the warrant "tolls" the probation sentence indefinitely, or until the offender "answers" a court summons or is arrested on the warrant.

PROBATION EFFECTIVENESS

How does probation measure up? Studies of the effectiveness of probation outcomes can be divided into three main groups: research measuring recidivism rates, studies that measure characteristics of probation recidivists, and those that compare probationers with another group of offenders, such as prisoners or offenders in a different community-based program.

Probation Recidivism Rates

As we discussed in Chapter 1, the rate of success on probation largely depends on the definition of "success" and "failure" used by researchers. A definition of failure used in one study was "non-compliance with probation conditions which results in (a) revocation; (b) absconding from supervision without notifying the probation department; or (c) being sentenced for another offense in another jurisdiction" (Morgan 1995, p. 143). Other researchers conceptualize "failure" as equivalent to recidivism, which could be the arrest, conviction, or incarceration for a new crime while on supervision. This second albeit narrower definition would not necessarily include technical violations.

The probation "success" rate, in contrast, includes individuals who have completed the term productively as well as those who may have been referred to court for a number of technical violations but were not revoked (Morgan 1995). One other factor to consider in effectiveness studies is the length of the follow-up period. Although the vast majority of violators have their sentences revoked within the first year, the total revocation rate is higher when the follow-up period extends, for example, for four years instead of only two.

About 35 studies have been published that measured probationer recidivism rates in the United States (see Geerken and Hayes 1993 for a review). While on probation, the rearrest rate varied from 12 percent to 65 percent, and the conviction rate fluctuated between 16 and 35 percent. The revocation rate, which for most studies included both technical violations and new crimes, varied from 14 percent to 60 percent

(Morgan 1994). The various recidivism rates are likely more indicative of diverse decision-making styles and behaviors of probation officers, judges, and police officers than actual differences in a probationer's return to criminal behavior.

For example, one study of 79,000 felons placed on probation in 17 states found that 43 percent were rearrested for a felony within three years while on probation. Within the rearrested group, 46 percent of the probationers that had been sent to prison or jail had absconded within the three years. Furthermore, 71 percent had either completed their probation or were still on probation (Langan and Cuniff 1992). This is similar to a Midwestern state where 73 percent completed successfully and the others were rearrested, of which 19 percent of all probationers were incarcerated as a result of the revocation (Stageberg and Wilson 2005).

Probationers who were revoked seemed to more commonly "fail" for technical violations rather than for major offenses (Gray, Fields, and Maxwell 2001; Minor, Wells, and Sims 2003; Sims and Jones 1997). The problem with revocation for technical violations is that this is an extremely costly option for taxpayers when probationers don't follow the rules. Many states recognize this and are responding with other options for probation violators. For example, Delaware's Probation Reform Law not only shortened the term of probation to no longer than two years, but technical violators could be placed on work release or in probation violation centers for up to five days per violation, not to exceed 10 days per calendar year (Sentencing Accountability Commission and the Statistical Analysis Center 2005). It remains to be seen how this policy change in how violations are handled ultimately affects probation violation rates, as well as jail and prison admissions.

The results of these studies are not necessarily conclusive as to success or failure of probation because of methodological design flaws, such as an overreliance on official data, lack of comparison groups, deficiencies of longitudinal designs, and conditions too inconsistent to allow comparison. Other problems include seeing success or failure as an either/or concept rather than as a matter of degree (Farrall 2003). Probation is most successful with people who are eligible for diversion, misdemeanor, and first-time felony offender status.

Who Is More Likely to Succeed or Fail on Probation?

Success on probation (or parole) seems to be predicted in part by the personal characteristics of the offender. Generally, women, offenders over the age of 30, and those with no prior adult or juvenile convictions were more likely to succeed. Also, offenders who had skills that allowed them to maintain employment, those who were high school graduates, and those who lived with their spouse or children were less likely to become recidivists. Offenders who were on probation for a misdemeanor are more likely to succeed than felony offenders (Morgan 1994, 1995; Petersilia et al. 1985; Sims and Jones 1997). It seems then that conventional ties and positive social support of friends and family significantly contribute to reintegration success. On the other hand, being young; being unmarried; having previous convictions; and lacking knowledge, skills, and abilities seem to be attributes that contribute to higher failure rates on probation.

An analysis of the effectiveness of treatment for drug offenders on probation was conducted. The study compared one group of probationers who were being drug tested with a second group that was being subjected to both drug testing and drug treatment. Researchers found that the group that received both testing and treatment had a higher failure rate on probation, likely due to more surveillance increasing the chance of revocation for technical violations (Albonetti and Hepburn 1997).

TABLE 7.4 *Offenders Convicted of Violent Offenses Were More Likely Than Others to Terminate Supervision with a Violation*

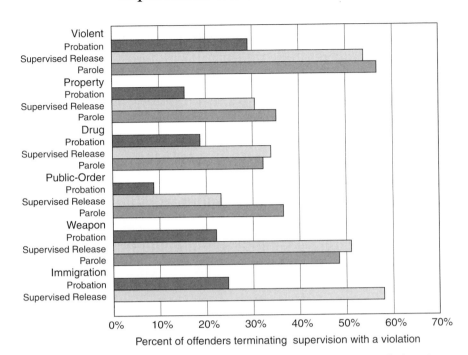

Percent of offenders terminating supervision with a violation

Violation rates of offenders completing probation, supervised release, or parole, by category of offense, October 1, 2002–September 30, 2003.

U.S. Department of Justice. 2005. Compendium of Federal Justice Statistics, 2003. Washington, DC: U.S. Department of Justice.

Probationers Compared with Parolees

Researchers comparing probationers with parolees discovered that probationers committed fewer technical violations and fewer new crimes than parolees. Of offenders on probation, about 6 percent committed a new crime (versus 15 percent of parolees). Probationers committed technical violations at a rate of 13 percent, about half that of parolees, at nearly 28 percent (U.S. Department of Justice 2005a).

As you can see in Table 7.4, there are three types of supervision compared for each type of offender: probation is the first type and the other two are both types of parole supervision that we discuss more in Chapter 13. This table shows that probationers were more likely to complete supervision successfully than parolees (both on discretionary parole and mandatory parole supervision), no matter what type of crime they had been convicted of.

Overall, the benefits of community supervision far outweigh the costs of public safety; probationers and parolees are not responsible for as many crimes as the public thinks. One study found that more than 90 percent of all burglaries and robberies were committed by people who were *not* on community supervision. Even if parole and probation were completely eliminated, there would be very little difference in overall burglary and armed robbery rates (Geerken and Hayes 1993).

TOP THINGS YOU SHOULD KNOW

- Probation costs significantly less than other forms of correctional supervision.
- Courts are empowered to terminate probation early for good behavior and to extend probation or issue more intensive conditions for noncompliance.
- The decision to revoke is initially recommended by the probation officer but left up to the judge's discretion.
- Probation violations include law violation and technical violations of conditions.
- The motion to revoke is filed by the prosecutor, and the court issues the warrant to revoke.
- For high-risk cases, the probationer is kept in detention pending an administrative hearing.
- Time served on probation is not credited as jail or prison time if the probation is revoked.
- Probationers and parolees must be given due process rights, including notice of charges and right to confront witnesses and present evidence in their favor.
- Probationers have lower recidivism rates than parolees.

DISCUSSION QUESTIONS

1 Should early termination of probation be given as an incentive for good behavior? Why or why not?

2 In the decision to revoke probation, what are implications for the probationer, the probation officer, and the community?

3 What are the two types of probation violations? Which type is worse, and why?

4 Discuss the revocation procedure. How does it start, and what are the steps?

5 Do probation officers have the power to arrest probationers? Under what circumstances?

6 What is the leading case on probation revocation? Discuss the significance of this case.

7 What are the six due process rights given to probationers during the revocation hearing?

8 Is the "preponderance of the evidence" standard of proof too low, or should a different standard be used? If so, should the new standard require more or less evidence?

9 How does revocation contribute to jail crowding? What alternatives could be tried to remedy this problem?

10 Does probation continue to be a viable punishment? Why or why not?

 WEBSITES

National Public Radio show titled: "Justice Talking: Probation and Parole: In Need of a Big Fix?"

http://www.justicetalking.org/viewprogram.asp?progID=536

Colorado Probation Services and Revocation

http://www.17thjudicialdistrict.com/probation_services.htm

Alaska Study on Probation Revocation by Ethnicity

http://www.uaa.alaska.edu/just/forum/f153fa98/c_prob.html

Maine Probation Revocation Policy

http://janus.state.me.us/legis/statutes/17-A/title17-Asec1206.html

Michigan Juvenile Probation Revocation Policy

http://courts.michigan.gov/mji/resources/jjbook/13ProbViolationsDelinquency. pdf

Missouri Probation Revocation Policy

http://www.moga.state.mo.us/statutes/c500-599/5590000036.htm

Policy in Oklahoma Probation and Parole Cases under Supervision: Opening and Closing Cases

http://www.doc.state.ok.us/offtech/op160201.htm

Ft. Worth, Texas, Court of Appeals Decision Regarding Juvenile Probation Revocation

http://www.tjpc.state.tx.us/publications/reviews/03/03-1-21.htm

Probation Modification and Termination

Chapter 7 explains the probation revocation process and the types of violations that can result in revocation. In the following two cases, list the violations of probation known to the probation officer. Would you concur with the probation officer's recommendation for revocation of probation? If not, at what point would you consider recommending revocation in this case? Are there other alternatives you might recommend?

CASE A

Probationer Conner was under supervision for possessing a destructive device. He has a history of some violent behavior (domestic violence, battery of a law enforcement officer). Special conditions of Conner's supervision require that he participate in mental health treatment and substance abuse treatment.

Shortly after Mr. Conner's supervision term begins, he tests positive for marijuana use. When confronted by his probation officer, he admits to using marijuana. However, Conner states he uses the marijuana to self-medicate and he will commit violent acts if he ceases its usage. Mr. Conner concludes his probation officer will be responsible for his violent acts toward others and himself, as the officer is instructing him to cease the marijuana usage. The probation officer reminds Conner of the condition of supervision that states he is not to use or possess illegal drugs and advises him his use of illegal substances cannot be allowed and that the sentencing court will be advised of the violation.

Mr. Conner entered treatment at the beginning of his supervision term. As a result of his response to the instruction to cease marijuana usage, the probation officer recommends to the court that Conner be referred for a psychiatric evaluation to see if he would benefit from psychotropic medications. The court concurs with the officer's recommendation and Conner is referred for the evaluation. The psychiatrist diagnoses Bipolar Affective Disorder, Type II, and prescribes Depakote. This medication requires regular lab work to evaluate its effectiveness. Mr. Conner fails to attend his next appointment with the psychiatrist. Results of a urine specimen taken from Conner a week after his evaluation with the psychiatrist are received. The specimen reveals Conner has used both marijuana and amphetamines. The probation officer petitions the court for a warrant to have Mr. Conner arrested and brought before the court for violations of his supervision.

CASE B

Probationer York is under probation supervision for simple assault. She has a history of violent behavior and anger management issues. She has no known drug or alcohol problems. She has been under probation supervision with you for the last five months and had been reporting regularly. Special conditions of York's supervision require that she complete anger management classes by the end of her term, which is supposed to end in four months if all goes well. Anger management treatment takes three months, and the program has a waiting list of clients who are court-ordered to attend treatment. Probationer York keeps saying she will go down for an anger management assessment but just never does. When you call to verify employment at the restaurant, her employer says that she quit coming three weeks ago and she was replaced.

Two weeks have gone by since you called her former employer and still no sign of York. York won't return your phone calls. She misses her regular appointment with you this afternoon. What should you do?

III

Intermediate Sanctions

Burgeoning prison populations and high recidivism rates among felony probationers have prompted alternative sanctions for certain offenders for whom a sentence of imprisonment is excessive but for whom regular probation may be too lenient. As we discussed in the first chapter, a wide array of intermediate sanctions lie on the continuum between probation and prison for this purpose.

Chapter 8 considers residential sanctions, in which offenders must live away from home and inside a facility within the community while completing their sentences. Residential programs include boot camps, halfway houses, and other specialized treatment facilities.

Chapter 9 explores nonresidential community corrections programs in which the offender resides at home while participating in the program under a strict set of rules and curfews. Nonresidential programs include intensive supervision probation, house arrest, electronic monitoring, and day reporting centers.

Finally, Chapter 10 discusses sanctions tied to restorative justice and economic sources. Restorative justice is a philosophy that underscores the need for offenders to repair the harm done to their victims and to the surrounding community. Community service, restitution, and fines are types of restorative justice sanctions that can be used as tools to accomplish punishment objectives for certain offenders.

Introduction

Residential Community Corrections Facilities

Halfway Houses
History of Halfway Houses in the United States
Program Components
Worker Perspectives and Role Orientation
Evaluations of RCCFs

Shock Incarceration
Correctional Boot Camps
Prison Boot Camps: The Case of New York State
Probation Boot Camps
Offender Perspectives
Criticisms of Boot Camps
Evaluations of Boot Camp Programs
The Future of Shock Incarceration Programs

Other Types of Residential Community Corrections Facilities
Restitution Centers
Therapeutic Communities
Work Release and Work Ethic Camps
Women Offenders Living with Their Children

Top Things You Should Know

8

Residential Intermediate Sanctions

© Mary Kate Denny/PhotoEdit

What You Will Learn in This Chapter

- *Offenders assigned to residential community corrections facilities live at the facility and are able to leave for work, for treatment intervention, or on special visitation passes.*

- *Residential community corrections programs are effective with high-risk offenders, as a less costly alternative to incarceration.*

- *The most common types of residential facilities in the community are halfway houses and prerelease centers.*

- *Other types of residential community corrections facilities include boot camps, restitution centers, drug and alcohol treatment centers, work release, and specialized residential programs for women offenders to live with their children.*

KEY TERMS

Intermediate sanctions

Widening the net

Residential community corrections facilities

Halfway house

Shock incarceration

Boot camp

Restitution center

Therapeutic community

Relapse

Work release

Work ethic camp

INTRODUCTION

Regular probation supervision is adequate for misdemeanor offenders and for many felony offenders. However, there are people who need closer supervision than traditional probation but who may not require the custodial nature of prison. **Intermediate sanctions** are sentencing options between prison and probation that provide punishment that fits the circumstances of the crime and the offender (DiMascio 1997). These sanctions are attempts to provide increased control over offenders within the community. Until the advent of these intermediate punishments, the courts were faced with the polarized choice of either probation or prison. Morris and Tonry (1990) contended that the United States has at times been too lenient with probationers who need tighter controls and too severe with prisoners who would present no serious threat to public safety if under supervision in the community. In the continuum of sanctions presented in Chapter 1, intermediate sanction programs are situated in the middle between probation and prison.

The positioning over where a particular sanction lies in the continuum of sanctions often depends on who selects program participants. For example, if prosecutors and judges are the key decision makers in program selection, they tend to choose offenders who should have received probation. This process is called **widening the net,** and it has received criticism because individuals who should have received probation are instead given a harsher sentence only because that sanction is available, and not because the offender requires more supervision. Widening the net increases costs because individuals eligible for probation receive more supervision and must abide by more conditions, increasing their chances of violating conditions. In addition, prison and jail populations are not reduced. Intensifying a punishment for probationers thus removes all the positive cost-saving benefits that intermediate sanctions are supposed to attain.

On the other hand, correctional administrators select participants who are bound for jail or prison and allow a chosen few the opportunity for a reduced sentence upon completion of a less costly program, thus reducing the institutional population and costs of confinement. Some of the evaluation components to bear in mind include whether the intermediate sanction reduced prison beds, whether it produced a cost savings, and whether it reduced recidivism—or a return to criminal behavior (Tonry 1997). This chapter addresses residential community corrections programs in which offenders reside while serving time.

INTERMEDIATE SANCTIONS

A range of punishments that fall between probation and prison.

WIDENING THE NET

When an individual who should have received probation is sentenced to a harsher intermediate sanction only because that sanction is available, not because the offender requires more intensive supervision.

RESIDENTIAL COMMUNITY CORRECTIONS FACILITIES

Residential community corrections facilities (RCCFs) are a popular intermediate sanction because they provide more intensive supervision than probation and parole but allow offenders to remain in the community where they have access to more treatment services than they otherwise would in prison. RCCFs cost less than jail or prison, in part, because offenders subsidize a portion of the cost through working full time. Offenders can continue to contribute to their own families as well as pay back victims for harm done.

RCCFs are the most diverse type of community corrections sanction. Thus, it is difficult to describe an "average" residential facility. Residential community corrections facilities do have the following commonalities:

- Residents live in the facility (not at home).
- Residents must be employed (or be working part time and going to school).
- Residents can leave the facility at any time for work at a verified job.
- Residents must be preapproved to leave the facility for any other reason, and they are limited to a certain pass duration, purpose, and curfew (Latessa and Travis 1992, p. 170).

Outside of those similarities, many differences exist, such as facility size, whether the facility is public or private, the types of treatment programs offered, and the types of clients selected. Halfway houses are the oldest type of RCCFs, having been around since the 1830s. But there are other newer adaptations of residential facilities including community corrections centers, prerelease centers, restitution centers, work ethic camps, work release centers, and residential drug treatment facilities. Some of these newer RCCFs are quite savvy about the newest technology. Box 8.1 discusses how states such as Utah and Alaska have used a database management system called O-Track to share information and link RCCFs with other criminal justice agencies.

Because of the diversity of RCCFs, it is difficult to estimate their numbers. At the last known nationwide count, in 1999, there were 628 RCCFs and halfway house facilities housing nearly 19,500 offenders. Of this number, 55 (8.7 percent) facilities are operated by the department of corrections, whereas the rest are privately owned and operated. The number of inmates in RCCFs at that time represented 4.4 percent of the total inmate population, at an average cost per day of around $43 per offender. Alaska, Iowa, Montana, and Wyoming were the most avid users of residential community corrections facilities, housing about 14 percent of their total inmate population in these facilities (Camp and Camp 1999).

HALFWAY HOUSES

Halfway houses are residential facilities for probationers, parolees, or those under intensive supervision probation (ISP) who require a more structured setting than would be available from living independently. Halfway houses are staffed 24 hours a day, seven days a week for various types of offenders and are also known as "community corrections centers."

"Halfway out":

- a) State-level prerelease offenders who are transferred from the department of corrections (DOC or prison) to the community and anticipate receiving parole within the next one to two years
- b) Paroled offenders who pose a greater community risk and need assistance in making the transition from prison to the community.

BOX 8.1   TECHNOLOGY IN CORRECTIONS

OFFENDER MANAGEMENT SYSTEMS LINKING RCCFS TO OTHER CRIMINAL JUSTICE AGENCIES

Historically, each major agency in criminal justice (law enforcement, courts, institutional corrections, and community corrections) has maintained its own database and can share information with other agencies of the same type but cannot readily share information with agencies in a different part of the criminal justice system. Each of these agency databases contains much of the same information (current offense, criminal history, age, gender, and so on) so an offender is reinterviewed each time the information must be entered. This includes residential community corrections facilities (RCCFs), which many times receive incomplete or missing information about the offender who is newly transferred from prison, parole, or probation. An offender tracking system known as "O-Track" solves the redundancy issue by automating data from six criminal justice agencies into one database. The six agencies are courts, county jails, probation, parole, community corrections centers, and state departments of corrections. The O-track system stores eight main categories for each individual. Each category has subcategories or fields called modules. Below each of the eight categories are examples of information that O-Track stores:

Category 1: Offender Case File is the shell of the offender's file. Basic fact sheets, vital statistics, photographs, fingerprints, locations, and movements are available in this section to form summary information collected from throughout the system's database. Caseload assignments, due date reports, overdue report lists, case file audits, and workload formula statistics are performed and managed.

Category 2: Case Management is the core of the system. This section collects data about the offender and tracks his or her progress through the corrections system from presentence investigation, diagnostics, and classification, through the prison system (if applicable) and conditional release on parole. Offender data are handled as a case file to develop case reports and to support decision-making in the case management process. Included here are offender education and training, employment, treatment programs, visits, and prerelease preparation.

Category 3: Parole Board has information about previous and upcoming parole board hearings for applicable offenders.

Category 4: Offender Management focuses on security and supervision functions that manage the offender as a member of a population, such as cell assignments, gang membership, security incidents, protective custody, intelligence information, escapes, and disciplinary reports.

Category 5: Offender Administrative Systems provides accounting for inmate funds while incarcerated, commissary purchases, clothing issues, and inmate property. This system also tracks offender grievances filed against the prison system.

Category 6: Interagency Linkages provides an electronic interface to allow information to be sent and received from external databases, such as local police, Federal Bureau of Investigations (FBI), Dept. of Motor Vehicles, Human Services, Social Services, medical hospitals, interstate compacts, and the Bureau of Prisons.

Category 7 is for Warrants and Category 8 is for Reports and Statistics.

Alaska, New Mexico, and Utah are currently using O-Track, whereas Colorado and Idaho are using some of its parts. It is expected that more states will automate their systems like this in the future.

Source: Utah Department of Corrections. 2004. *About O-TRACK.* Accessed May 23, 2006: http://www.cr.ex.state.ut.us/community/IT/otrackintroduction.html.

Halfway houses are a type of residential community correctional facility for probationers, parolees, or clients under SIPP supervision. Some halfway houses are privately owned and operated, and are located in the middle of residential neighborhoods.

"Halfway in":

a) As an intermediate sanction sentence for offenders requiring more structure and control than that provided by probation, ISP, or even house arrest, but for whom prison is too severe a sanction

b) As an increased sanction for probation and parole violators

c) As a diversion program, where, upon completion, charges are dismissed

d) For individuals who are awaiting trial but are unable to make bail or meet release on recognizance requirements, and are not a threat to the community (Wells 1997, pp. 10–12)

History of Halfway Houses in the United States

The halfway house concept has been traced back to the early 1800s in England and Ireland. In the United States, the halfway house idea originated in 1816, at the time when most penitentiaries still practiced the Pennsylvania-style system of solitude and complete silence. Prisoners were locked in their cells all day and were not allowed to interact with each other for fear that they would "contaminate" each other. Interaction would take away from the penance that prisoners must seek for full reformation (Keller and Alper 1970).

Following a tumultuous riot in a Pennsylvania prison, a commission was appointed to examine the problems with the prison system. One commission recommendation was to create temporary shelters for prisoners to get back on their feet as they were transitioning back to the community. This proposal was not adopted by the legislature because of strong feelings that prisoners, even after release from prison, should not be allowed to interact.

As penitentiaries transitioned from the solitude of the Pennsylvania system to the silent interaction of the Auburn or "congregate" system, prisoners were allowed to work outside of their cells but were not allowed to talk to each other. Because state support for halfway houses was still lacking, private, nonprofit organizations with the goal of prison reform opened halfway houses for the first time to provide a place for prisoners to go after their release from prison.

For example, in 1845, the Isaac T. Hopper Home opened for male prisoners in New York City. In 1864, the Temporary Asylum for Discharged Female Prisoners opened in the Boston area. The Boston halfway house for women received less opposition than facilities for men. The reason for this difference was an underlying belief that, unlike male prisoners, female prisoners did not associate for the purpose of talking about criminal activity. Female prisoners were believed to contribute to their own rehabilitation (Wells 1997). At that time, halfway houses merely provided food and shelter to ex-prisoners. They did not provide treatment and services.

By the end of the nineteenth century, private halfway houses opened in eight other states. Criminal justice officials, such as law enforcement officers and corrections administrators, remained opposed to this idea. Funds for halfway houses dwindled, and with the Great Depression of the 1930s, many were forced to close. Only one halfway house, The Parting of the Ways in Pittsburgh, remained open (Keller and Alper 1970).

In the 1950s, private halfway houses were viewed in a brand-new light. Concern about crime and high parole revocation rates prompted halfway houses to assume a role beyond offering food and shelter. Halfway houses were now providing transition services to prisoners and became involved in both treatment and correctional supervision. In addition to being less expensive than prison, halfway houses protect the community because residents are more heavily monitored than traditional parolees. Those who misbehave can be returned to prison (Glaser 1995).

In the 1960s, halfway houses became a more visible part of corrections when they received government assistance for the first time. At the urging of then Attorney General Robert F. Kennedy, Congress appropriated funds to open federal-level halfway houses for young offenders. Financial support increased as a direct result of emphasis placed on reintegration by the President's Commission on Crime and Administration of Justice (Latessa and Travis 1992). The Safe Streets Act of 1968 established the source of funding for halfway house expansion throughout the 1970s. In 1964, the first meeting of the International Halfway House Association was held in Chicago. The organization changed its name in 1989 to the International Association of Residential and Community Alternatives. This organization currently represents 250 private agencies operating approximately 1,500 programs throughout the world (International Community Corrections Association 2001).

Although government funding and support decreased substantially in the early 1980s, private halfway houses in the twenty-first century have increasingly found a niche in the corrections market to provide alternatives to imprisonment and to create an outlet for prison crowding control (Latessa and Travis 1992). For example, California Governor Schwarzenegger proposed in his most recent budget to move 40 percent of female prisoners (4,500 adults) out of prison and into privately operated community corrections facilities that would contract with the state (Warren 2006).

Currently, no one set model exists for the programs provided at halfway houses. Each halfway house is unique in structure, treatment programs offered, and type of clients it accepts (Walsh and Beck 1990). Private halfway houses can choose which clients they wish to accept on a contractual basis. Offenders who are eligible for placement are referred by their prison case manager or probation officer. The state or county government pays the facility a specified amount per day per offender, and the offender also assists in the per diem payment. For example, if it costs $43 per day per offender to operate a residential halfway house (Camp and Camp 1999), the government pays the halfway house about $32 per day per offender, and each client is charged about 25 percent of the cost, or $11 per day.

The halfway house can offer certain benefits. The following were listed in a survey of 37 halfway house residents:

- Assist in readjustment to living in the free world
- Help them find a better job
- Allow closer family relations than when in prison
- Assist in abstaining from drugs and alcohol
- Allow them to financially assist their families (Twill et al. 1998, pp. 77–92)

The researchers also found that compared with their arrival at the halfway house, residents who completed the program successfully also experienced an increased internal locus of control and decreased levels of loneliness (Twill et al. 1998, p. 87–88).

Program Components

Offenders live in the facility, leaving to go to work, attend church, and attend school or participate in rehabilitation activities such as drug treatment. Residents are required to maintain a full-time job or be going to school full time. When not at work, residents maintain the facility through assigned chores, perform court-ordered community service, and attend classes or counseling sessions that their case manager mandates. Most halfway houses require residents to submit to regular drug testing and breathalyzers. Prison systems make extensive use of halfway houses to allow inmates a graduated release—something to fill the gap between total incarceration and absolute freedom. A six-month stay in a halfway house allows the inmate to decompress and adjust to freedom more readily.

LEVELS SYSTEM: A FORM OF BEHAVIOR MODIFICATION. Increased freedom must be earned and is based on good behavior, the amount of time spent in the program, and the client's financial situation. Most halfway house programs have some kind of a behavior modification program called a "levels system," which we illustrate as a hypothetical example. In a levels system, the bottom level is the most restricted and the top level has more freedom away from the halfway house and more privileges. For example, in a five-level system, new clients start on Level 5, where there is a "hold" placed on them (they cannot leave the facility) until their case manager has completed the intake process. Once intake is complete, clients move to Level 4, where they remain until they obtain a job and get caught up on their rent. Level 4 clients are allowed passes to attend treatment (Alcoholics Anonymous and Narcotics Anonymous) and one four-hour pass per week to attend church (outside of leaving for work). Each level has its own curfew, which is not applicable to clients who work evenings or nights. In addition to treatment and church passes, Level 3 clients can take one daytime pass of no longer than eight hours, with a curfew of 10:00 P.M. Level 2 clients have Level 3 privileges, with a later curfew of 11:59 P.M. At Level 1, clients must be caught up on all restitution, community service, and rent. They must have $100 in savings. Level 1 clients have a weekday curfew of 11:59 P.M. but can take weekend passes, from Friday to Sunday, to visit preapproved friends and family. Level 1 clients can own an insured car and have driving privileges, whereas all other clients must depend on someone else for a ride or must take the bus. All clients, regardless of their level, must produce receipts and verification that the approved destination was visited. Passes are allowed to a verified address of a family member or for four hours at a time to see a movie or to go shopping. Some programs require clients to spend 14 days on each level before advancing to the next level.

Upon program completion of the residential phase, paroled clients are assigned a parole officer in the appropriate jurisdiction. Most successful probation clients are transferred to the "nonresidential" phase of the halfway house program. During the nonresidential phase, clients live at home but come to the halfway house to be tested for drugs, to attend group treatment, or to visit their nonresidential case manager.

Worker Perspectives and Role Orientation

Two different types of staff work at a halfway house. One group is primarily involved in activities that are custody oriented; the other staff (case managers and counselors) take care of treatment and rehabilitation. The job of the halfway house case manager has been described as similar to that of a probation and parole officer, in the sense that the counselor must be "capable of possessing conflicting goals of rehabilitation and punishment" (Wells 1997, p. 27).

Leanne Alarid, one of this book's coauthors, worked at a halfway house in Denver, Colorado. Alarid describes her job responsibilities working both types of positions:

> I began working as a member of the client management staff, involved in security and physical accountability for over 80 males and females. In this capacity, I conducted population counts, searched people and belongings for contraband, signed clients in and out of the facility, dispensed medications and Antabuse, and conducted breathalyzers and urine screenings. When an opportunity to work as a case manager became available, I transferred within the facility from the security-oriented job to one oriented around treatment. In this position, I became occupied with treatment, programming, and revocation issues for 20–24 individuals. A case manager is very similar to a parole or probation officer in that I assessed my client's needs and risks and I devised individual program plans to meet each of their needs. I assisted my clients with adjustment problems they experienced while in the program, and I supervised their progress. I also taught drug and alcohol treatment classes for new clients, and I prepared prerelease plans and attended monthly parole board hearings.

Another perspective on working in a halfway house comes from Melodye Lehnerer (1992), who describes the different roles she played during her two-year experience conducting ethnographic research from one halfway house. Lehnerer began as a volunteer, moved to being a "peripheral member," and then became an "active member" as an assistant caseworker. As membership involvement increased, role conflict arose between staff affinity and identification as a researcher. Lehnerer did not particularly like being a caseworker because it required that she be too much of a "social control agent" for her self-identity, and it also made collecting data more difficult (p. 180). Thus, Lehnerer decided to quit being case manager and take on more of a "helping agent" role and started teaching general equivalency diploma (GED) classes and life skills to clients. As a teacher and staff member, Lehnerer explains how the clients still viewed her differently as "staff" from when she was a volunteer:

> Quite often residents would approach me after class and apologize for their or someone else's behavior. It was their way of teaching me how the game was played. Given the context, staff members and residents were protagonists. That was just the way it had to be. . . . [I]n the classroom setting there existed a preexisting relationship based upon power differences. (p. 156)

Lehnerer discusses how residents maintained a code of secrecy from staff. She also stressed how residents and staff did not trust each other, and how information control was a valuable resource used by both parties: "Lack of trust was directly linked to staff beliefs that residents were concealing information and resident beliefs that staff were using information to further discredit them" (p. 228).

PUNISHMENT AND TREATMENT ROLE ORIENTATIONS. Halfway houses provide reintegration assistance, but they are primarily geared toward minimizing risk, which is a custody concern. Therefore, workers may experience role conflict, which is a clash between punishment and treatment goals. Ely (1996) stated that some staff members reduced their role conflict by detaching from their clients and suspending empathy, whereas other staff would convert, mentally retreat (do nothing), or resign. Alarid explains:

> When I moved from client manager (being involved in security issues and running facility operations) to case manager, I experienced more role conflict. The case manager role had two opposing sides of treatment and reprimand. The most effective case managers were the ones who could balance the two sides and who believed in both. However, some counselors were lopsided in that they invested heavily in treatment issues but could not bring themselves to put someone in jail who posed a liability risk to the community. No one ever likes sending someone back to prison, but you have to be willing to switch hats pretty readily from helping someone out one day and having to revoke them the next. Because of this difficulty, the burnout rate among staff is fairly high. The most valuable thing I learned through all this was, above all, to treat people with fairness and consistency.

Evaluations of RCCFs

As with other community-based programs, effectiveness of halfway house programs is subjective because wide variation exists in the quality of programs and in the types of offenders admitted. Effectiveness has typically been measured by examining the program success or failure rates or by comparing recidivism rates of halfway house residents with a matched sample of probationers or parolees.

Latessa and Travis (1992) found that RCCF residents had more treatment needs than regular probationers or parolees, and RCCF clients who completed the program performed better with more structured supervision than under regular probation supervision. Whereas 65 percent of halfway house residents successfully completed the program (Donnelly and Forschner 1984), halfway house residents generally received more treatment intervention than did those on regular probation or parole. The authors concluded that treatment participation might have been the critical difference.

Later studies attempting to pinpoint variables that predicted success and lower recidivism identified clients who did not use illegal drugs (Latessa and Travis 1991) or had skill sets and community ties (Donnelly and Forschner 1987). The researchers found that clients who were younger, used drugs and alcohol, had more extensive prior criminal histories, and had fewer community ties were more likely to fail in residential community corrections facilities. Similar predictors were found by Walsh and Beck (1990), who also found that individuals convicted of a violent crime were more likely to recidivate than were property offenders. The strongest predictor of program success is criminal history—clients with a more extensive criminal history are significantly more likely to fail (English and Mande 1991; Hartmann, Friday, and Minor 1994; Latessa and Travis 1991; Moczydlowski 1980). The continued use of drugs and alcohol, lack of employment and educational skills, and younger age of the offender are also strong predictors of failure (Donnelly and Forschner 1984, 1987; Hartmann, Friday, and Minor 1994, Latessa and Travis 1991).

While variables that predict a greater likelihood of success or failure can be identified, the more important question to be asked is how beneficial is it to have high-risk offenders in residential community corrections programs? Data of 53 Ohio RCCFs were used (comprising 7,306 clients) and compared with that of 5,801 parolees to analyze success rates and recidivism rates of low-risk versus high-risk clients. A risk score was calculated based on criminal history and demographic data, and scores separated low-risk and high-risk individuals in both the treatment and control groups (Lowenkamp and Latessa 2005). The researchers found that low-risk parolees outperformed low-risk RCCF clients—in other words, low-risk RCCF clients had higher recidivism rates than parolees. The exact opposite results occurred for high-risk individuals—high-risk RCCF clients were more successful than high-risk parolees, suggesting that RCCFs are effective with high-risk offenders, and not as effective with low-risk offenders (Lowenkamp and Latessa 2005).

SHOCK INCARCERATION

Shock incarceration refers to a brief period of imprisonment that precedes a term of supervised probation in hopes that the harsh reality of prison will deter future criminal activity. A variety of shock incarceration formats are used, and they go by a number of names—shock probation, shock parole, intermittent incarceration, split sentence, and boot camp. The programs vary somewhat in design and organization, but all feature a short jail or prison term followed by supervised release. The target population is young offenders with no previous incarcerations in adult prisons. An estimated 10 percent of all adults on probation received a split sentence consisting of some combination of incarceration and probation (Bonczar and Glaze 1999).

In shock probation, an offender is sentenced to imprisonment for a short time (the shock) and then released and resentenced to probation. The prison experience is thought to be so distasteful that the offender will fear returning and thereafter avoid criminal behavior. The original shock probation program was established in Ohio in 1965. It was praised for limiting prison time, assisting in reintegration into the community, helping the offender to maintain family ties, and reducing prison populations and the costs of corrections (Vito and Allen 1981). The program's stated purposes were as follows:

- To impress offenders with the seriousness of their actions without a long prison sentence
- To release offenders found by the institutions to be more amenable to community-based treatment than was realized by the courts at the time of sentencing
- To serve as a just compromise between punishment and leniency in appropriate cases
- To provide community-based treatment for offenders while still imposing deterrent sentences where public policy demands it
- To protect the briefly incarcerated offender against absorption into the inmate culture (p. 71)

Shock probation programs have been evaluated by a number of researchers. Early studies reported success rates between 78 and 91 percent. Programs were praised for limiting prison time, providing a chance for offenders to be reintegrated back into the community quickly, and making offenders more receptive to probation supervision by illustrating the problems they will encounter if they violate the terms of their probation.

SHOCK INCARCERATION

A brief period of incarceration followed by a term of supervised probation. Also called shock probation, shock parole, intermittent imprisonment, or split sentence.

However, shock incarceration was not always imposed on those for whom it was intended—young first offenders. Parisi (1981) found that a third of federal probationers who received split sentences had previously been incarcerated on other charges, which negated the value of the "shock." Furthermore, Parisi was unable to find evidence that probationers who had first served a short period of incarceration were more successful than those who went straight to probation. Another type of shock incarceration is correctional boot camp programs.

Correctional Boot Camps

The idea of **boot camp** programs for offenders first began in 1983 in Georgia, whereby correctional programs borrowed the military concept of breaking existing habits and thought patterns and rebuilding offenders to be more disciplined through intensive physical training, hard labor, drill and ceremony, and rigid structure. This concept multiplied as the most common form of shock incarceration from 1983 to the late 1990s. Boot camp programs exist inside state prisons or local jails, within the community, and even as a small part of the Federal Bureau of Prisons (MacKenzie and Hebert 1996). However, most correctional boot camps also provided therapeutic and educational activities, such as drug and alcohol education, individual or group counseling, vocational training, anger management, and academic education later in the day. Ronald Moscicki (1996), superintendent of a boot camp program in New York, stated the importance of having both military and treatment components:

> Boot camps often seem to begin with the assumption, "If it ain't rough, it ain't right." Most people think that "rough" is sweaty drills, "in your face," and bulging muscles. They never associate "rough" with inmates sitting in a circle in white shirts and ties, with counselors and drill instructors leading a treatment group or academic classes, teaching inmates how to read and write. . . . In truth, the military part is the easiest because it is constant repetition. . . . If all we expect from our inmates is that they follow orders, we will have good inmates. Inmates, even good ones, belong in jail. (pp. 287–288)

Correctional boot camp participants live in "barracks," wear military-style fatigues, use military titles, and address their drill instructors by "sir" or "ma'am."

Boot camp attempts first to break down offenders and then to rebuild them to respect authority, increase their self-control, and improve personal responsibility.

© Leanne Fiftal Alarid

Each "platoon" is responsible for the actions of every individual, and many boot camps use group rewards and punishments to encourage people to work together. A small number of programs even use "brigs" or punishment cells for temporary solitary confinement.

In general, eligible candidates are first-time felony offenders convicted of a nonviolent offense, they fall within a certain age group, and because of the physical demands, they must meet minimum physical requirements. Many eligible offenders have been involved with drugs or alcohol in the past, and most program participants volunteer to participate. Programs typically last 90 to 180 days before graduation to probation or parole supervision (depending on whether the boot camp is located in the community or in the prison). The two main types of boot camp programs are:

- Prison Boot Camps. Offenders are chosen by correctional administrators to participate, and ultimately the offender volunteers for the program. The boot camp is usually within a prison correctional facility, but boot camp participants remain separate from the general population for the program duration. Offenders are paroled upon graduation from boot camp. Time served is significantly less than with a regular prison sentence.
- Probation/Jail Boot Camps. Offenders are chosen to participate at the time of sentencing by judges or by jail authorities. Although the judges are directed to choose offenders who otherwise would have gone to prison, probation boot camps are criticized for widening the net—choosing offenders who otherwise would have been sentenced to probation. These boot camps are located in the community and are supervised by county sheriff departments, probation departments, or a combination of both. Offenders in probation boot camps do not go to prison but remain in a residential community facility. Following boot camp, offenders graduate to intensive supervision probation or regular probation.

Prison Boot Camps: The Case of New York State

In New York, those who are accepted into the program are assigned to one of four minimum-security facilities. Male participants work in platoons of 54 to 60 men and proceed through the 180-day program as a unit. Table 8.1 shows a schedule of the daily activities of participants. About 41 percent of their time is devoted to treatment and education. Physical training and drill constitute 26 percent of the time, and hard labor on facility and community projects constitutes the remaining 33 percent. For most a schedule this rigid is new, and many cannot conform to the program and drop out at a rate of 37 percent (Clark, Aziz, and MacKenzie 1994).

Those who successfully complete the six-month regimen are paroled and enter a six-month postrelease phase of the program known as AfterShock. The goal of AfterShock is to continue the close supervision that began in the institutional phase and to provide opportunities and programs in the community designed to improve the parolee's chances for successful integration. Each participant has two parole officers to allow increased contacts between the officers and parolees for home visits, curfew checks, and drug testing. AfterShock parolees have priority access to community services such as educational and vocational training. After completion of AfterShock, parolees are transferred to regular parole supervision (Bourque, Han, and Hill 1996).

Shock incarceration programs save money by reducing costs in regular prison programs and by avoiding capital costs for new prison construction. The New York

TABLE 8.1 *Daily Schedule for Offenders in New York Shock Incarceration Facilities*

Time	Schedule
A.M.	
5:30	Wake up and standing count
5:45–6:30	Calisthenics and drill
6:30–7:00	Run
7:00–8:00	Mandatory breakfast and cleanup
8:15	Standing count and company formation
8:30–11:55	Work and school schedules
P.M.	
12:00–12:30	Mandatory lunch and standing count
12:30–3:30	Afternoon work and school schedule
3:30–4:00	Shower
4:00–4:45	Network community meeting
4:45–5:45	Mandatory dinner, prepare for evening
6:00–9:00	School, group counseling, drug counseling, prerelease counseling, decision-making classes
8:00	Count while in programs
9:15–9:30	Squad bay, prepare for bed
9:30	Standing count, lights out

Source: National Institute of Justice. 1994. *Program Focus Shock Incarceration in New York.* Washington, DC: U.S. Department of Justice, National Institute of Justice (August).

State Department of Corrections estimates that it saves $2 million in prison costs for every 100 shock incarceration graduates. Recidivism rates for graduates 12 months after completion of the program were 10 percent compared with 15 percent for those who were screened but rejected and 17 percent for those who withdrew or were removed from shock incarceration before completion. After 24 months, 30 percent of graduates had returned to prison, compared with 36 percent of the considered inmates and 41 percent of those who failed to complete the program. At 36 months, shock incarceration graduates still returned to prison at lower rates, but the difference was significant only between program graduates and the considered group (Clark, Aziz, and MacKenzie 1994).

Probation Boot Camps

Like prison boot camps, boot camps operated by the probation department also intend to reduce institutional crowding, provide rehabilitation, punish offenders, and reduce recidivism. There are only a small number of probation boot camps left in the United States, such as one operated in Houston, Texas.

This co-ed program is for 48 young women and 336 men, each grouped together in cohorts of 48 members who stay together for the full 90 to 120 days of the program. Participants are engaged in activities for about 15 to 17 hours every day, with a few hours of free time every Saturday. Participants are provided with AIDS (acquired immune deficiency syndrome) counseling, voluntary HIV (human immunodeficiency virus) testing, computer literacy skills, and drug and alcohol counseling by counselors from the county health department and by probation staff (Burton et al. 1993, pp. 46–52).

Unlike most other boot camp programs, offender participation is not voluntary, and judges select the offenders for the program without any input from the boot camp staff. Furthermore, once an offender is in the program, he or she cannot voluntarily decide to quit the program (this may explain the 97 percent completion rate). Offenders who could not complete the program must appear in court before the same judge for resentencing.

Upon release, participants are transferred to a 90-day superintensive probation program (SIPP). Probationers have daily contact with probation officers for the first 30 days after release, semiweekly contact for the next 30 days, and one contact weekly for the following 30 days. The life skills classes that were started in boot camp are continued during SIPP two nights per week. In addition, a licensed counselor runs a boot camp support group one night per week.

An evaluation study measured attitudinal change in the areas of coping and self-control, perceptions of boot camp staff, benefits of participating in counseling, attitudes toward program staff, perceptions of future opportunities, and the quality of relationships with family and friends. The researchers found that the program produced significant positive measures of attitudinal change in probationers (Burton et al. 1993; Kilgour and Meade 2004), and seemed to affect staff as well. Box 8.2 tells the story of a probationer named Mr. John from the perspective of one of the boot camp teachers at this program.

A recidivism study on program graduates measured them at two years and then again at four years after release to see if the attitudinal changes transferred into behavioral changes. Two years after release, 22 percent of boot camp graduates had been sentenced to prison. Four years following boot camp, 61.7 percent of graduates had been sentenced to prison (including some recidivists from two years after release) (Anderson, Dyson, and Burns 1999). Generally, no significant differences have been found at either adult or juvenile boot camp programs when boot camp participants are compared with a matched group that is sentenced to prison (MacKenzie et al. 2001).

Offender Perspectives

Many participants of prison boot camps feel fortunate to have been chosen for the program because they obtain release upon boot camp program completion much faster than from a traditional prison sentence. Hank, age 23, was sentenced to prison for 18 months and provides his perspective on getting out early after participating in a Massachusetts boot camp:

> I came here to get out of jail in 4 months that is all. I've been in and out of jail for a lot of years. So I know about jail environments. This place is a positive community environment. You don't see anything like this in regular jail. My family tells me how much I've changed. I lost 25 pounds, learned to control my impulses, and learned to not drink. The program and classes are all supportive. I never expected to learn about wellness and parenting. I have a 2-year-old son and another one just 3 months old. I want to go home and do the right thing. I wanted to quit many times; for a while, every day I thought, "This is the day I quit and get out of here." The staff made me realize that I need to stick it out "one day at a time." I learned how to talk to other people, staff, and other inmates. . . . I was always a follower who got into trouble easily. I learned how to say "no" to my impulses. The first week I hated the DIs [drill instructors] . . . [but] they taught me respect. When I think of it, that was missing in my life. Today, when I leave here, I can hold my head high and be proud of my completion of the program. I also know I need a support system to keep myself from getting into negative situations. (as quoted in Ransom and Mastorilli 1993, pp. 307–318)

BOX 8.2 COMMUNITY CORRECTIONS UP CLOSE •

A BOOT CAMP TEACHER'S UNFORGETTABLE EXPERIENCE: THE STORY OF MR. JOHN

Despite the troubled and violent lives students at the Harris County Boot Camp have led, the story of Derrick John still seems to catch them off guard. I drag it out and use it to get their attention just once during the few weeks that I will be their teacher. I wait for the precise moment when I feel it will be most effective—sometimes at the beginning of our time together, sometimes at the end. Most of the time, however, I tell the story when I am feeling overwhelmed by the task in front of me.

He was a nice guy with a great smile, I always start. An attractive, lean young man, 6-foot-3 or taller, I often told him he should go to Hollywood when he got out of Boot Camp. I actually looked forward to seeing him in class. This is not always true of the students I teach. While it's easy to like the students, almost all are tough and drain on any teacher caring enough to look into their eyes. Even the smart, easy learners have needs for attention that are so deep they draw energy from you. They have holes in their young lives that have made them hard and violent or else depressed and despairing.

Simple autobiographies the students write their first class take days for me to read because of the harsh existence most have had. And that's just the parts of their lives they are willing to

write down. Even joking, these students have affectations that show they are covering up, trying for a resilience to bounce back from family cycles that have led them to crime.

For a while, Mr. John was one of those same draining students who spent the first half of his tenure at Boot Camp with a chip on his shoulder. "Why do we have to do this? I don't understand that," he'd say, without really ever listening or trying to understand in the first place.

When his mood was even darker, he'd just lay low and try not to call attention to himself. Those quiet students who try hard to go unnoticed are often the most troubled, I have found. On those quiet days, I worried the most about Mr. John, feeling like he was still fuming, boiling deep inside his youthful outward appearance.

Then, for whatever reason, a light went on inside Mr. John when he was about halfway through the program. I see this reaction to Boot Camp often. The program teaches discipline and respect, and the students seem to catch on at some point. Either that happens, or they realize they are here for the long haul and should take advantage of the county's services. Whichever is the case, an education immediately reduces their chances of returning to the criminal justice system.

Mr. John started caring, and then he started learning. He finished assignments quickly and made scores higher than I even expected of him. But halfway is often too late for some probationers, especially those who quit school as early as Mr. John. Time and his Boot Camp days were running out.

Every day his schoolwork improved. He became an ideal student, working hard and offering me a respect he had never shown before. I began to joke about having him stay in the program long enough to get his G.E.D. We call it "recycling," and it means more time at Boot Camp for probationers. It's the thing they dread the most. "If I could just keep you another three months, Mr. John," I'd say, "I could help you finish this G.E.D." "I think I'll just have to talk someone into getting you recycled."

It would make him crazy when I would say this. No one wanted to be recycled. Everyone wanted to go home, even those whose home life had led them to Boot Camp.

DODGING RECYCLING

No one ever jokes about recycling, either. It's much too serious a subject to the probationers. I was only half joking, though. I would have loved to have kept Mr. John in

Boot Camp and still think about the difference it would have made had he stayed there for another three months.

His beaming smile would fade for a moment at my attempt at humor. "You wouldn't do that to me," he'd start. "Would you?" Something in my returned look would tell him I wasn't serious, and his smile would reappear before I even needed to reassure him.

Of course, I could never have him recycled at that point. He was now the picture of a perfect student. I knew, however, he had started working too late to finish his G.E.D. in Boot Camp. I emphasized the importance of continuing his education now that he was on the right track. He could still get his G.E.D. in a few more months with the help of the continuing education program at the Harris County Adult Probation Department. He just had to take more of the responsibility on himself.

Finally, one Wednesday, as is always the case with graduations at Boot Camp, he left the program along with the other 45 members of his barracks. He marched for the crowd of parents and visitors and listened to the graduation speech of hope for the future—now with cleaned slates and new, healthier habits and minds. He was so nervous, like all the probationers are on

this day, that he shook my hand quickly with little notice as to whose hand it was. He never let his eyes meet mine, although I tried to impress him with one last remark. "Keep at it, Mr. John. You've come too far to stop," I said.

Nine days later, his last essay still in my briefcase, Mr. John was shot and killed by a police officer after a robbery. He had fallen back in with a peer group that had waited for him back home and outside the secure barbed wire fence of the Boot Camp. At 17 years old, Mr. John never even had a life. With little or no parenting and an unsuccessful school experience, he never had a chance. When he entered Boot Camp, he may have looked like a hardened street thug, but when he left, he looked like the boy he still was.

STORY'S IMPACT

I don't know what part of Mr. John's story reaches my other students first. Maybe they see their own vulnerability to death. Maybe they were shocked by his youth. Maybe they are just frustrated that I use him as an example of my desire to keep them out of trouble and into education.

I can't keep them alive just by keeping them locked up, which is what I wish I had done with Mr. John. I know that wouldn't be a

life. I know also that if they return to their former habits and former friends, things are going to happen to them anyway. Sooner or later. Prison or death.

I run across Mr. John's math workbook when I'm searching other files. Occasionally, I see an essay he wrote tucked in with other students' school papers. Maybe I run into the newspaper article about his death. I keep all these remembrances intentionally. It always surprises me for that minute; stuns me with reality.

I see his smile and picture his long legs stretching from his desk at the back of the classroom. And his eyes; I can still see the boy that would never live long enough to be a man. I want to be reminded of Mr. John. That's why I keep his schoolwork. I also want my other students to be reminded. I want them to realize that this same probationer could be any one of them. I tell them that I can't have it happen again. The story of Mr. John has broken my heart, and it will never harden to such blows. With this, I'm telling them that I care. I want them to try. I want them out of trouble and into a happy life that does not include violence and death.

Source: Denise Bray Hensley. 1995. One Boy's Life. *Houston Chronicle* (September 17) Reprinted with permission.

Another male prisoner named Wayne, an 18-year-old Native American convicted of assault and battery, was a perfect candidate for the Massachusetts boot camp. Not only does Wayne have a problem controlling his temper, but he also has a drinking problem. He talks about the changes he has experienced because of boot camp:

> This was a heck of an experience. I've been in several programs and halfway houses, and this is the best program I've ever seen. . . . The 12-step classes are outstanding. They teach you how to stay sober. In addition, they teach you how to be responsible for yourself. This is, mentally, a tough program. When I first got here, I thought this place was crazy, a bunch of cops yelling. I did not know what to expect. I thought about quitting often. I've been impulsive and did what I wanted to do. One day, I was tired and when a DI was yelling at me, I told him I would not give him the pleasure of seeing me quit. I've learned to respect the DI. I can talk to the DI. They're not cops, the enemy. They made me responsible for myself. They taught me to care. . . . When I leave here Friday, I've already got plans to go to A.A. [Alcoholics Anonymous] meetings. . . . There is no negativity here like regular jail. I've tried to think about something negative . . . nope, nothing. Now don't get me wrong. I hate this place. . . . However, I love what the program has done for me. I never had plans or goals in my life. I've learned to suck it up and drive on. Open my ears and shut my mouth, otherwise, you are in the front leaning push-up position a lot. I have not found myself in that position in about a month; that's progress. (Ransom and Mastorilli 1993, pp. 313–314)

Criticisms of Boot Camps

One of the primary concerns is that boot camps widen the net, especially probation and juvenile boot camps. In net widening, the costs increase because offenders who should be on probation are going through a more expensive program.

Another concern is that the confrontational style of the military-style boot camp can have potentially negative outcomes because many boot camp environments are characterized by coercion, stress, and leadership styles that are likely to reduce self-esteem, increase the potential for violence, and encourage the abuse of power. Lutze and Brody (1999) suggest that the harsh environment in many boot camps may violate the Eighth Amendment prohibition on cruel and unusual punishment, which may make boot camps targets for offender lawsuits. One boot camp closed in Tampa after a 14-year-old boy died as a result of a videotaped beating by boot camp staff (Associated Press 2006). Other camps in Maryland and Arizona have closed, citing possible abuses and high recidivism rates (Milligan 2001).

Finally, some boot camps have trouble retaining good staff and have high staff turnover. This results in inconsistent standards and behavioral problems for participants, which in turn is likely to affect later behavioral change.

Evaluations of Boot Camp Programs

Boot camp effectiveness has been determined by attitude or behavioral change, decrease in institutional crowding, and reduction in budget costs.

EIGHT SITE STUDY. A study of eight different state-level boot camps demonstrated that treatment mixed with discipline can reduce recidivism. In five of the states evaluated (Florida, Georgia, Oklahoma, South Carolina, and Texas), the boot camp programs did not reduce recidivism. In the other three states (New York, Illinois, and Louisiana), graduates had lower rates on one measure of recidivism. In the states in which recidivism was reduced, the researchers found a strong focus on postrelease supervision and an emphasis on rehabilitation, voluntary participation, selection from prison-bound offenders, and longer program duration (MacKenzie et al. 1995). The findings suggest that the physical side of the boot camp experience (drills, labor, and discipline), by itself, is not enough to reduce recidivism. Recidivism reduction was seen in programs that offered three or more hours of treatment per day mixed with physical drills and training.

ATTITUDE AND BEHAVORAL CHANGES.   Boot camps may have a lasting effect on some offenders. An early study found that boot camp graduates who were supervised more intensively following boot camp completion had higher positive adjustment scores than offenders in other programs who had less aftercare (Brame and MacKenzie 1996). When attitudes of boot camp graduates were compared with a matched group of regular prisoners, boot camp had a more positive attitudinal impact than did the deteriorating effects of prison (MacKenzie and Souryal 1995).

Most evaluations of boot camp programs found no significant difference between boot camp participants and matched comparison groups of jail or prison offenders (Bottcher and Ezell 2005; MacKenzie, Wilson, and Armstrong 2001). Thus, short-term positive attitude changes did not directly translate into long-term reduced recidivism.

REDUCTION OF CROWDING AND COSTS.   Whether boot camps reduce prison crowding depends on whether the program targets prison-bound offenders. Not surprisingly, programs that allowed departments of corrections' administrators to select participants were more likely than programs involving judicial selection to alleviate prison crowding because corrections' administrators were more likely to select offenders who were eligible for prison (MacKenzie et al. 1995). Of course, there are always exceptions in which judges were able to select prison-bound offenders rather than using boot camp as a probation enhancement. Parent (1996) explains why many boot camps have failed to reduce costs and institutional crowding:

> Many limit eligibility to nonviolent first offenders, select offenders who otherwise would receive probation, and intensively supervise graduates, thus increasing rates of return to prison for technical violations. In most jurisdictions, boot camps appear more likely to increase correctional populations and costs rather than reduce them. (p. 263)

The Future of Shock Incarceration Programs

The mid-1990s were the high point for boot camps; there were nearly 100 adult boot camps and 30 juvenile boot camps in operation. But by 2000, sparked by years of criticism, one-third of these boot camps had closed, and 51 programs remained in operation at a cost per day of $58 per offender (Parent 2003). Of those offenders, 553 (8.7 percent) were female and 5,836 (91.3 percent) were male. Today, fewer than 40 programs remain open in the United States, and the future of these programs remains uncertain.

OTHER TYPES OF RESIDENTIAL COMMUNITY CORRECTIONS FACILITIES

Most evaluation research has focused on halfway houses and boot camps. However, there are other types of residential community corrections facilities, such as restitution centers, therapeutic communities, work release, and specialized residential programs for women offenders to live with their children.

Restitution Centers

Restitution centers are a type of residential community facility specifically targeted for property or first-time offenders who owe victim restitution or community service. Restitution centers may provide some outside treatment, but the focus is on stable employment and paying back the victim. Some programs will release the offender when the restitution is paid in full.

MINNESOTA RESTITUTION CENTER   Minnesota provided the prototype for contemporary restitution centers. Established in 1972, the Minnesota Restitution Center (MRC) accepted adult males who had been sentenced to the Minnesota State Prison for two years or less and had served at least four months of their sentences. Recidivists, violent offenders, and professional criminals were not eligible for the program, nor were middle-class people who could make restitution without the assistance of the center. While in prison, the inmate, with the assistance of an MRC staff member, met with the victim face to face to establish a restitution plan. After the parole board approved the restitution plan, the offender was released on parole to the center, where he lived, secured employment, and fulfilled the terms of the agreement. The offender could also receive additional services there, including group therapy, supervision in the community corrections center, and assistance in obtaining employment. Although the MRC was considered a success, it was closed in 1976 because the number of property offenders being sent to prison was reduced by the implementation of the state's Community Corrections Act.

GEORGIA COMMUNITY DIVERSION CENTER   Georgia based its restitution program on the Minnesota model. Unlike the Minnesota model, however, Georgia residential programs—known as community diversion centers—serve both probationers and parolees. Residential centers located throughout the state house 20 to 40 offenders each for up to five months. During their stay, center residents develop restitution plans, receive individual and group counseling, and are referred for a variety of other services as needed. They may also be required to work at community service projects on weekends and during evening hours. The offenders normally remain at the center until their restitution is completed.

Therapeutic Communities

Whereas restitution centers focus on repayment to victims for harm done and maintaining public safety, **therapeutic communities** (TCs) focus on the treatment of alcoholism and drug addiction and abstinence from substances for criminal offenders. Helping an individual recover from addiction in an environment that is as least restrictive as possible is quite different from an environment that is centered on surveillance. Helping an individual through change takes much longer and entails more stumbling blocks than paying back restitution. Thus, a typical TC has a period of six to nine months of residential drug and alcohol treatment, with a period of aftercare as the offender transitions from the therapeutic environment to dealing with stressors of daily life.

THE THERAPEUTIC COMMUNITY ENVIRONMENT.   Both TCs and drug courts (discussed in Chapter 2) treat addiction problems (see Table 8.2 for a comparison of therapeutic communities and drug courts). TCs are better suited for long-term polydrug addictions (addiction to more than one kind of drug for an extensive period of time), whereas drug courts are geared toward moderate forms of addiction. TC candidates are thoroughly screened for suitability and readiness for treatment. If

Residents of Delancey Street, a private organization in San Francisco, walk across the gallery on the grounds of the facility. For 35 years, Delancey Street has helped turn around the lives of former convicts, drug addicts, and the homeless.

TABLE 8.2 *Comparing Therapeutic Communities and Drug Courts*

Characteristic	Drug Courts	Therapeutic Communities
Initial point of intervention	After arrest and before conviction	After conviction
Type of program	Nonresidential/outpatient	Residential/inpatient
Where located	Community only	Community, jail, or prison
Program length	12–18 months	12–18 months
Voluntary	Yes	Yes
Estimated percent of waking hours devoted to treatment and self-improvement	25–50%	100%
People involved in defendant's progress	Judge, prosecutor, public defender, probation officer/case manager, treatment provider	TC counselor, TC former addicts, TC peers in program
Who imposes rewards and sanctions Treatment and monitoring forms	Judge (nonadversarial collaborative)	TC participants/peers (confrontational)
	Group counseling, individual counseling, drug testing, acupuncture, community service, sitting in the jury box, case management visits	Group, confrontation, individual counseling, community meetings, drug testing, shaming, extra chores
Average annual cost per client	$1600–$6000	$3200–$9000

accepted, offenders with a substance abuse problem must be motivated to adhere to all rules and participate in all activities required by the TC program. A TC environment is considered to be like a supportive surrogate family, except that physical fighting and sexual relations are not allowed. Each day in a TC is highly structured and disciplined. Clients have daily cleaning chores within the facility and hours of peer group sessions that focus on confronting the attitudes and behavior of each resident. The goal of these sessions is for other clients in the group to tear down the defense mechanisms and excuses that addicts use to continue (or start) using drugs as a response to a desire or stressor. The sessions attempt to resocialize new thoughts, attitudes, and behavioral choices in all areas of one's life (family, friends, work, leisure time, spirituality, and so forth). Other types of counseling focus on self-worth, self-discipline, and respect for authority. There is little idle time, as even personal free time is used for some type of intellectual or creative self-improvement. Visits by friends and family are not allowed, and TC clients never mix or interact with non-TC prisoners. The TC is also the only type of program that is largely peer-operated and peer-enforced. Though there may be a free-world staff contact person, the TC rules are enforced by the residents, and the group is run by the residents, who earn various leadership roles based on a levels hierarchy. Clients who graduate from the program are transferred to probation or parole, depending on their initial status. Clients who refuse to participate in sessions or who use drugs and alcohol while in the TC program are removed and incarcerated for the remainder of their sentence.

CHALLENGES OF THE TC. One of largest challenges for TCs to overcome is the low program completion rate. Treatment programs should expect failures and relapses, but during the first 30 days, between 25 and 85 percent of new residents drop out of the program (Goldapple and Montgomery 1993). Efforts are needed to either improve retention rates (perhaps by redefining "success" and "failure") or better screen applicants' motivation to participate. For the first 30 days, new residents need to be more thoroughly educated about the process, and they may need confidence building before being confronted in group therapy (Goldapple and Montgomery 1993).

A second challenge is the use of shaming and humiliation that occurs for clients who misbehave or fail to participate. Examples include "PT" (extra chores or duties), wearing a dunce cap or a sign (stating what was done wrong) around the facility for a specified period of time, or shaving one's head. Some of the methods of punishment for disobedience have been criticized for their ineffectiveness toward changing behavior.

TYPES AND USES OF THERAPEUTIC COMMUNITIES. TCs can be prison-based or community-based. A prison-based TC accepts prisoners without disciplinary reports who are within one or two years of release; acceptance is based on a rigorous application interview. Many prison-based TC participants graduate to a community-based TC for aftercare upon release.

A community-based TC is designed for clients who may have failed in various other community programs (for example, a halfway house, probation, or parole) because of either alcohol abuse or illegal substance addiction. Residential drug and alcohol treatment programs are also used as diversion from prison. For example, Florida has an 18-month Drug Punishment Program, which includes six months in a secure facility, then three months in a community facility, followed by nine months of intensive supervision probation. Like the Colorado program, candidates are screened for suitability and readiness for treatment. This program targets males and females age 21 and younger. During the early phases, they are diagnosed, an individual treatment plan is developed, and clients receive group counseling (Bureau of Justice Assistance 1998).

Another similar program for nonviolent probationers exists in Dallas, Texas. This 300-bed facility provides 200 beds for clients in the first six-month residential phase of the program. Then, clients with adequate support systems enter a six-month aftercare program where they live at home and report to a probation officer. The remaining 100 beds are reserved for clients who do not have strong support systems and need an additional three months to make a successful transition through the "live-in, work-out" program. This is unique because transition from residential living to community living is seen as a prime opportunity for relapse. Probation officers work with the treatment facility staff to review clients' progress (Barthwell et al. 1995, pp. 39–47).

Sometimes community TC programs are used as a transition step for clients who graduate from prison-based therapeutic communities or other types of drug treatment programs while behind bars. For example, women in California with drug problems could attend a drug treatment program and then, upon their release, could be transferred to a residential program in the community to deal with issues of relapse and opportunity.

EVALUATIONS OF THERAPEUTIC COMMUNITIES. An evaluation of the California women's programs indicates that women who completed both the institutional treatment phase and the community residential treatment phase had lower incidences of drug use and higher levels of parole completion. Female drug offenders who participated in the institutional phase but did not enter the community phase did not fare so well. The researchers concluded that there was a shortage of facilities for female drug abusers. Many women applied but were unable to enter the community residential phase of the program because of space shortages. These women did not complete treatment, which left them vulnerable to **relapse** (Prendergast, Wellisch, and Wong 1996).

Another evaluation of a prison-based TC (Eisenberg and Fabelo 1996) found that recidivism was significantly reduced over a 12-month period for clients who completed the TC compared to TC dropouts, even when controlling for age and education. However, for TC dropouts, recidivism rates were the same as for a comparison group of people who had never entered the TC program.

Work Release and Work Ethic Camps

Work release could be considered a type of institutional corrections program, given that offenders reside in a facility (a community facility, jail, or prison) but are released into the community to work or attend education classes or both. Work release is much more restrictive than the halfway house environment because offenders are not allowed to leave the facility for any other reason except work and school. This type of release is for a specified purpose and for a specific duration. We discuss work release here because it is a form of prerelease program in the offender's preparation for release into the community.

Although work release was used in Vermont in the early 1900s, work release legislation was first introduced in the state of Washington in 1913. The federal system and all the states authorized work release programs by the mid-1970s primarily for minimum-security inmates.

Work release is useful for minimum-security inmates in jail or prison who are within six to nine months of being released. In these cases, work release provides the offender with an early start in finding and retaining employment, and retaining employment is the most important factor in reintegration success and reducing recidivism. Work release is an option for physically disabled or mentally disabled

RELAPSE

When an offender with a substance abuse problem returns to using alcohol or drugs.

WORK RELEASE

A program in which offenders who reside in a facility (a community facility, jail, or prison) are released into the community only to work or attend education classes or both.

offenders if program staff work with clients to help them seek gainful employment, a goal that is significantly more difficult than for the average offender (Mawhorr 1997).

Work release can also be a useful sentence for first-time offenders, particularly if the offender already has a job or is already going to school at the time the crime is committed, and if the offender has a high victim restitution payment but poses minimal public safety risk. In these specific cases, the judge orders that offenders must reside in jail and be allowed to continue working to pay restitution or to continue working or attending school (for example, high school or college classes). This option is sometimes used when restitution centers or halfway houses are not available in the area.

The frequency of placing offenders on work release has declined over the last decade. The available evidence shows that placing offenders on work release does not increase the risk to the community any more than any other community sentence. Two studies of prison work release programs in Washington show that few inmates committed crimes while on work release, and recidivism rates were similar for work release groups and a matched control group (Turner and Petersilia 1996b). Two other variations of work release deserve mention: work ethic camps and work release combined with drug therapy.

WORK ETHIC CAMP.   A different type of residential program is called a **work ethic camp,** which is a 120-day prison-alternative program based on a cognitive-behavioral treatment approach. One program in Nebraska allows inmates to be eligible once they have completed the 90-day intake and assessment period (Siedschlaw and Wiersma 2005). Once the participants have completed the 120-day program, they are released on intensive supervision probation. The work ethic camp is considered to be a minimum-custody facility but costs nearly $44 per day per person, but the duration of the work ethic camp stay is about half that of the cost to incarcerate, which translates into a cost savings. The higher program cost is due to the assistance the program offers in developing job readiness skills, decision-making skills, and life skills such as money management.

COMBINED WORK RELEASE AND THERAPEUTIC COMMUNITY.   A program called CREST combines the therapeutic community concept (discussed previously) with work release. Clients entering the program from prison must first progress through a significant amount of drug and alcohol education, counseling, and confrontation before they are eligible for the work release phase in the community. Preliminary evaluation data indicate that CREST participants have significantly lower relapse and lower recidivism rates than a comparison group (Nielsen, Scarpitti, and Inciardi 1996).

Women Offenders Living with Their Children

Given that most women offenders commit nonviolent offenses, have problems with drugs or alcohol, and are mothers of at least one child under the age of 18, residential community corrections facilities that address these issues have grown for women offenders with young children. There are more than 65 residential treatment programs and another 70 programs resembling halfway houses for women to live with their children while they are serving a residential community sentence. Studies indicate that the children of offenders suffer emotionally, developmentally, and economically when their parents go to prison. Children of incarcerated parents stand a greater chance of following in the footsteps of their parents by becoming involved in the juvenile justice system at an early age. Because the mother is still the primary

WORK ETHIC CAMP

A 120-day alternative to prison that teaches job skills and decision making using a cognitive-behavioral approach, followed by intensive supervision probation.

caregiver in the majority of families, the effect of incarcerating mothers with dependent children is pronounced (Mumola 2000). The question then becomes: How can women offenders be punished or sanctioned without punishing their children?

Statistics on convicted women offenders indicate that most women are nonviolent property or drug offenders, and they do not pose a threat to the community (Pollock 1999). Therefore, most women felons do not require prison sentences and would be ideal candidates for community placement. Most of these RCCFs are funded by the U.S. Department of Health and Human Services but are operated under the guidelines of the Center for Substance Abuse Treatment. One example of this kind of RCCF is the John Craine house.

JOHN P. CRAINE HOUSE. The John P. Craine House, opened in 1993 in Indianapolis, Indiana, is designed specifically for women offenders with preschool-aged children who have been convicted of misdemeanors or nonviolent felony offenses (Barton and Justice 2000). Craine House holds a maximum of six adults and eight children at one time and serves 10 to 17 women and about 20 children each year.

William H. Barton of the Indiana University School of Social Work conducted research in cooperation with the John Craine House staff (Barton and Justice 2000). The Craine House serves a dual role, "both as an alternative to incarceration for the women and as a preventive intervention for their children" (p. 7).

Craine House resembles a halfway house in the sense that women pay for part of the program cost through the expectation of employment. Staff assess the needs of each woman, and formulate an individualized treatment plan. However, unlike the halfway house, this facility seems to provide much more individualized and specialized attention, not only for the offender's needs, but also for her children. Specific interventions focus on the following:

> parenting skills, substance abuse treatment, job seeking skills, educational and/or job placement in the community, personal budgeting, nutrition information, and advocacy as indicated by individualized assessments. The program arranges for day care for the children at nearby locations to enable the women to work in the community. The program is staffed around the clock by counselors and family living specialists. . . . Basic goals for the Craine House program are to provide a safe, structured environment; promote the preservation of mother–child relationships; enhance the offenders' abilities to maintain economic and emotional independence while leading responsible, law-abiding lives; and prevent the neglect, abuse and potential delinquency of the offenders' children. (Barton and Justice 2000, pp. 7–8)

Because of the high level of services offered, it costs Craine House $80 per person per day. The disadvantage to this is that it costs more than incarceration. However, considering that the program is also providing prevention programs for the children, the cost may be money well spent in the long run. The long-term effects of this program remain to be seen.

The average length of stay in the program is five months (6.5 months for those who complete the program and two months for noncompleters). Just over 70 percent (53) of the women have successfully completed the program, whereas 22 women did not because of a technical violation or the commission of a new crime. The other five women still resided at Craine House.

Recidivism after successfully completing the program was measured by whether the women had appeared in court on a new charge or crime. Out of the 53 women who successfully completed the program, 11 committed a new crime. Most graduates were out for an average of two years before recidivating. Women who recidivated committed either a property or drug crime, but no one committed a violent crime.

The recidivism data for the first cohort of women extends six years. As the researchers note, it would be worthwhile to determine the long-term effects of Craine House as a prevention mechanism for the children who have participated.

TOP THINGS YOU SHOULD KNOW

- Offenders in intermediate sanction programs had more severe criminal records and more treatment needs than probationers but less severe criminal records than people incarcerated in prison.
- Offenders with intermediate community sentences were more likely than probationers and prisoners to acquire technical violations that later led to sentence revocation.
- Halfway houses remain the most common type of residential community program for offenders who have needs greater than offenders on regular probation or parole. Halfway houses are a more intensive form of supervision than probation and parole, but they are also valuable as a reentry tool for prisoners coming out of prison. Overall evaluations of halfway houses show that the benefits outweigh the costs, particularly for high-risk offenders.
- Boot camps are a type of shock incarceration program that varies in the degree of treatment programs offered. Voluntary participation, selection from the prison population, and intensive aftercare provisions are important elements of the boot camp experience. The recidivism rates for most boot camps are no different from recidivism for prisoners, so the popularity of boot camps has declined in recent years.
- Restitution centers assist in motivating offenders to pay back victims, whereas work release and work ethic programs teach offenders job skills and allow them the ability to maintain gainful employment.
- Therapeutic communities use peer support and cognitive behavioral interventions to help individuals overcome addiction to drugs and to prevent relapse episodes so a person can maintain a life of sobriety.
- Residential programs for women offenders allow their children to live with them so that the women can learn better parenting skills and can maintain close relationships, which in turn aids in preventing recidivism.

DISCUSSION QUESTIONS

1. What factor(s) brought about the development of intermediate sanctions?
2. What are some examples of residential community corrections facilities?
3. What would working in a halfway house be like? What might be some of the problems you would face?
4. What are some of the program components inherent in halfway houses?
5. Do halfway houses work?
6. Discuss the evolution and use of boot camps. What are the purposes of shock incarceration?
7. What are some of the positive and negative aspects associated with boot camps?
8. Compare a therapeutic community environment with a boot camp.
9. What goals does a therapeutic community attempt to achieve?
10. How are work release programs different from work ethic programs?
11. Should programs like the John Craine House be expanded?

 **WEBSITES**

International Association of Residential and Community Alternatives

http://www.iccaweb.org

Ohio Community Corrections Association

http://www.occaonline.org/links.asp

Community Corrections Association of Pennsylvania
Exchanges ideas and information regarding work release programs

http://www.cor.state.pa.us/stats/lib/stats/ccc.pdf

National Institute of Justice (NIJ) Research Review, Boot Camps

http://www.ojp.usdoj.gov/nij/rr/vol4_1/pro.html

NIJ Publication: Lessons Learned from a Decade of Boot Camp Research

http://www.ncjrs.org/pdffiles1/nij/197018.pdf

Evaluation of Two Boot Camps in the United Kingdom

http://www.crimereduction.gov.uk/workingoffenders36.htm

Are Juvenile Boot Camps Effective?

http://www.nmha.org/children/justjuv/bootcamp.cfm

Residential Facilities in Michigan

http://www.kpep.com/website/pages/_mainframes/frameset1.html

Idaho Residential Substance Abuse Treatment (RSAT) Program for Parole Violators

http://www.ncjrs.org/txtfiles1/nij/199948.txt

University of Cincinnati Research Studies: Halfway Houses

http://www2.uc.edu/criminaljustice/ResearchReports.html

CHAPTER 8

CASE STUDY EXERCISE
Residential Intermediate Sanctions

In the following cases, you are the judge, and you must decide which residential intermediate sanction program to send the offender to by considering the circumstances provided. After you have made your decision, defend your answer.

CASE A

John is a 29-year-old male who has been twice convicted of fraud by forging checks. His first conviction resulted in a sentence of five years; probation with an order to make restitution in the amount of $720. John made three payments of $30 each before absconding supervision. He turned up again after six months and was reinstated on probation by the Court after he promised to faithfully fulfill the terms of his supervision and to complete his restitution obligation. During his supervised release he was in violation of probation conditions regularly and never completed his restitution payments. However, due to the fact that the state prison was seriously overcrowded, the Court did not revoke his probation and he was finally released from supervision.

The current case involves passing a forged check at a local grocery store in the amount of $224. Due to his previous failure on probation, the Court is concerned that he is not capable of following court-ordered probation conditions, yet does not want to commit him to the state prison or to a jail term. John has a wife and two small children and is their only source of support. He is currently employed as a house painter.

CASE B

Ricardo is a 19-year-old male with a history of minor criminal offenses including car burglary, shoplifting, and several DUIs. He is not assaultive and has not been convicted of a felony. His current offense is larceny, involving theft from a customer of his employer, a local carpet laying company. The probation report concludes that Ricardo needs more structure than can be gained from probation or intensive supervision but does not recommend a prison sentence. The probation officer reports that Ricardo needs to learn discipline, good work habits, and respect for the rights of others.

9

Nonresidential Intermediate Sanctions

© Joel Gordon

Introduction

Intensive Supervision Probation
ISP Caseloads
Attitudes toward ISP
Evaluations of ISP

House Arrest
Purposes of Home Detention
Criticisms of House Arrest
Effectiveness of House Arrest

Electronic Monitoring and Global Positioning Systems
History of Electronic Monitoring
Problems of Early EM Programs
Remote Location Monitoring
Global Positioning Systems
Frequency of Use
Attitudes toward EM
Empirical Evaluations
of Home-Based Electronic
Monitoring

Day Reporting Centers
Purposes of DRCs
Treatment-Oriented versus
Supervision-Oriented DRCs
Evaluations of DRCs

Top Things You Should Know

KEY TERMS

Intensive supervision probation

House arrest

Electronic monitoring

Home-based electronic monitoring

Remote location monitoring

Real-time access

Global positioning system

Exclusion zones

Inclusion zones

Day reporting centers

What You Will Learn in This Chapter

- *Most offenders in the community live at the home of a family member and complete the conditions of their sentence using court-mandated services on an outpatient basis.*
- *Many of the following sanctions are used in some combination with each other: intensive supervision probation, house arrest, electronic monitoring, and day reporting centers.*
- *Offenders pay for services by making monthly payments to help keep the program cost down.*

INTRODUCTION

Programs that require offenders to live at a facility during their community-based sentence were discussed in Chapter 8. Each residential program provided some form of nonresidential aftercare, usually in the form of probation or parole, which further aided the transition process. This chapter examines sanctions and programs that offenders participate in while living at home. These programs can be sentences by themselves, or they can be combined with other sanctions such as probation, as a phase of aftercare or following a period of time spent in a residential facility, or following confinement in jail or prison. Types of nonresidential programs we will discuss independently in this chapter include intensive supervision probation, house arrest, electronic monitoring, and day reporting centers.

INTENSIVE SUPERVISION PROBATION

INTENSIVE SUPERVISION PROBATION

A form of probation that stresses intensive monitoring, close supervision, and offender control.

Intensive supervision probation (ISP) is an enhanced form of probation because offenders are subjected to closer surveillance, have more conditions to follow, and have more exposure to treatment than do regular probationers.

Through smaller caseloads, ISP was originally designed to enhance rehabilitation and public safety by affording greater contact between the probation officer and the probationer. ISP attempts to meet the following goals:

- Use prison diversion to relieve prison overcrowding and the costs of incarceration.
- Increase public safety by keeping offenders from committing crimes in the community while they are under supervision.
- Impose punishment that is less severe than imprisonment but more severe than regular probation.

ISP was originally designed for high-risk, high-need offenders who were eligible for prison. Most ISP programs today are considered "probation or parole enhancements," however, because participants are drawn from the pool of probationers rather than from those in prison. ISPs as alternatives to incarceration are viewed as socially effective because they are less likely than incarceration to contribute to the breakup of offenders' families, they allow offenders to remain employed, and they are less stigmatizing than prison.

The programs vary by jurisdiction, but most of them require contact three times per week with probation officers, community service, curfew, random night and weekend visits, weekly drug or alcohol testing, and strict enforcement of probation conditions (Deschenes, Turner, and Petersilia 1995). Many ISP programs also include one or more of the following: payment of probation fees, house arrest, restitution, and some form of electronic surveillance (DiMascio 1997).

ISP Caseloads

Probation officers who supervise ISP clients generally have smaller caseloads than officers with regular probation caseloads. Although smaller caseloads were found to provide greater protection to the community through increased surveillance and control, they did not necessarily decrease recidivism (Steiner 2004). The reduced caseload size allowed probation officers to conduct curfew checks and more frequent visits to the client's home or place of employment. Stand-alone parole officers averaged 63 cases on regular caseloads and 18 on intensive supervision caseloads (Camp, Camp, and May 2003). For probation officers, the data show a significant difference between regular probation caseloads (127) and intensive probation caseloads, at 29 probationers (Camp, Camp, and May 2003). Because of the vast differences in caseload sizes, probation officers averaged 14 face-to-face contacts per year with probationers on regular supervision and 74 contacts per year with offenders on intensive supervision probation (Camp and Camp 1999).

Attitudes toward ISP

Today, ISP programs continue to flourish. The surveillance orientation and punitive properties of ISP appeal to the public's preference that community penalties be demanding. An early study on how criminal justice practitioners in Chicago perceived ISP at first found that public defenders initially favored the approach, whereas prosecutors did not (Lurigio 1987). A later study adapted Lurigio's survey instrument to practitioner perceptions of ISP in Kansas City, Kansas. Criminal justice practitioners thought that ISP offenders had been appropriately placed according to risk and needs and that ISP was useful in reducing the number of offenders who would have gone to prison. However, when asked about what the purposes of ISP are and how the public might perceive ISP, practitioner responses were broad and, in some cases, contradictory (Bayens, Manske, and Smylka 1998). The researchers raised the issue that the success of ISP stems, in part, from effectively communicating the central goals and the importance of assessing risk and needs so that all participants are working toward similar goals.

Critics of ISP programs point to evidence of a net widening effect. Studies have found that ISP participants are not necessarily chosen from a high-risk, high-need offender pool as originally purported but may only be medium risk or have medium-level needs (Reichel and Sudbrack 1994). Critics also maintain that ISP is not designed for the restorative justice philosophy. Victim restitution is mandatory in many ISP programs, but victim needs and wants are peripheral to offender needs (Bayens, Manske, and Smylka 1998; Jones 1995).

Evaluations of ISP

Because of the demanding conditions of ISP coupled with closer contact with probationers, ISP officers discovered more rule violations than did regular probation officers. Therefore, many intensive supervision programs had higher failure rates for technical violations than those for regular probationers.

REDUCTION OF PRISON BEDS. Some observers doubt that ISP reduces prison populations, however. Morris and Tonry (1990) suggest that research evidence and experience show that intermediate punishments free up fewer prison beds and save less money than their proponents claim. Just as with boot camps, judges who impose ISP on probation-bound offenders widen the net, resulting in higher costs.

COST-BENEFIT ANALYSES. The costs of ISP programs are definitely greater than regular probation, but the key to cost savings lies in whether ISP can produce a cost savings over those destined for prison. Earlier evaluation studies produced mixed results. Cost savings were reported in Illinois and New Jersey, but no cost savings were achieved in Massachusetts or Wisconsin. Technical violations that sent ISP offenders to prison doubled the actual cost of ISP (Petersilia and Turner 1993a).

In one study of a Minnesota ISP program designed to divert prison-bound offenders, ISP was used in lieu of prison and regular parole. A group of minimum-security prisoners who were supervised on parole was compared with offenders who were sentenced to ISP. ISP offenders were rearrested at about the same rate and posed no greater or less risk to public safety than did prisoners on work release. The annual savings of $5,000 per offender was offset by the increased cost of intensive supervision for ISP offenders, which is more expensive than regular parole supervision. No overall cost savings resulted because the money saved in the beginning (diversion from prison) was made up for by the increased cost during the period of parole (Deschenes, Turner, and Petersilia 1995).

If we assume that ISP "saved" a state corrections department from using 250 beds in a prison facility that holds 1,250 offenders, the saved costs would be meals, medical care, and other minor supplies that would have been provided for those 250 offenders. However, the prison would have to remain open for the other 1,000 offenders. A true cost savings can only be realized if an entire prison unit closes.

TREATMENT PARTICIPATION. When ISP combined intensive supervision with intensive forms of treatment, there was a significantly lower recidivism rate for ISP offenders compared with high-risk offenders who were supervised in the community on traditional parole (Bonta, Wallace-Capretta, and Rooney 2000; Paparozzi and Gendreau 2005). Partial victim restitution rates were paid by more ISP participants (12 percent) than by routine probationers (3 percent) (Petersilia and Turner 1993a). The drug treatment literature demonstrates that ISP participation can reduce both drug use and crime by drug-using offenders (Steiner 2004).

Domestic violence offenders on ISP as a probation enhancement show some satisfying results. Compared to regular probationers, ISP offenders were less likely to be arrested for any new crime over a two-year period of supervision. Sanctions for probation violators were stricter in the ISP program than on regular probation (R. Johnson 2001). The size of the experimental group was small (25 in the ISP and 32 in the comparison group), so the results are not conclusive.

A matched sample of 240 ISP parolees was compared with 240 high-risk, high-needs parolees on traditional supervision. The ISP group had more technical violations but fewer new convictions than the traditional parolees who received fewer treatment services. This study and the previous one on domestic violence offenders suggest that cognitive–behavioral treatment interventions can reduce recidivism in high-risk, high-need populations in the community (Paparozzi and Gendreau 2005).

SUMMARY OF ISP EVALUATIONS. The weight of the evidence illustrates that ISP programs, if they currently operate as a form of close supervision with little treatment intervention, do not produce cost savings and they do not significantly decrease the number of prison beds. Technical violation rates are high, and as a result, probation and parole enhancement ISP programs may increase the number of jail and prison commitments. There seems to be potential in lowering recidivism through offering treatment intervention strategies in concert with intensive supervision to decrease the number of revocations and the number of new crimes committed while on supervision (Paparozzi and Gendreau 2005; Steiner 2004). We discuss house arrest next.

HOUSE ARREST

House arrest is an intermediate sanction designed to confine pretrial detainees or convicted offenders to their homes during the hours when they are not at work, attending a treatment program, or visiting their probation officer. For convicted offenders, house arrest is typically either a condition of ISP or is coupled with electronic monitoring. Florida uses house arrest extensively and has more than 14,000 offenders under house arrest, many of whom are also electronically monitored (DiMascio 1997).

HOUSE ARREST

A community-based sanction in which offenders serve their sentence at home. Offenders have curfews and may not leave their home except for employment and correctional treatment purposes. Also called home detention or home confinement.

Purposes of Home Detention

House arrest is otherwise known as home detention or home confinement; it is neither a new concept nor a U.S. innovation. Galileo (1564–1642) was placed under house arrest by church authorities for his heretical assertion that the earth revolved around the sun. House arrest programs proliferated in the United States in the 1980s. House arrest serves as an alternative to incarceration for pretrial detainees and a means of easing jail overcrowding while ensuring appearance in court. The purpose of house arrest is not, however, to deter or to reduce recidivism (Jones and Ross 1997).

Programs vary, but most require that offenders remain within the confines of their home during specified hours ranging from 24-hour-per-day confinement to imposition of late-night curfews. Most states and the federal system now operate some form of house arrest program. California, Florida, Georgia, Kentucky, Oklahoma, and Oregon all make extensive use of this option. Florida's "community controllees" (those under house arrest) are required to maintain employment and to participate in self-improvement programs, such as a general equivalency diploma (GED) program to obtain a high school diploma, drug and alcohol counseling, or other "life skills" programs. Many are required to perform community service as well. When they are not participating in work, self-help programs, or community service, they must be at home.

Florida's community control officer caseloads are limited by statute to 20 offenders, and the officers work weekends and holidays. They are required to make a minimum of 28 contacts per month with each offender for a period not to exceed 24 months. Officers' schedules vary from day to day, resulting in regular but random visits with the offenders. If an offender is not where he or she should be at any particular time, a violation of community control is reported to the court. Some house arrest programs randomly call offenders, and a computer verifies the offender's unique voice electronically. If the voice is that of another person or a tape-recorded voice of the offender, the computer will register an unauthorized absence. Too many unauthorized absences may result in a technical violation of probation and time in jail.

Criticisms of House Arrest

The first criticism directed at house arrest is that it does not seem to be a punishment. Staying at home for most people is considered a luxury and not a negative experience.

The courts recognize that home confinement is not the same as jail or prison confinement, and therefore time spent on home confinement awaiting trial as a pretrial detainee cannot be counted as time served toward the conviction as jail time is for other pretrial detainees (*People v. Ramos* 1990). In some jurisdictions home detention is considered a part of probation, and time spent is counted. However, house arrest programs for convicted offenders usually do not apply time served on home confinement if probation must be revoked. Thus, if an offender with a one-year sentence to home confinement fails to complete the program, and his home arrest is revoked, he must begin his one-year sentence in jail and serve the full term.

Another argument is that the intrusiveness of house arrest violates a pretrial detainee's constitutional right to privacy in the home (which is usually occupied by other family members). Although this may hold true for someone not yet convicted, most pretrial programs are voluntary, so if the offender does not agree to the conditions, he or she will be resentenced to another sanctioning option. A convicted offender's privacy rights, however, are not violated by the use of house arrest and/or electronic monitoring.

Potential risks with house arrest are that offenders can still commit crimes from their house. For example, pretrial detainees and probationers have been arrested for selling drugs out of their homes. Since customers came to the house and the detainee never left home, no violations were recorded. If it were not for suspicious neighbors calling the police, these probationers might have been able to continue selling drugs without getting caught for some time.

Another challenge of house arrest is that domestic violence incidents may erupt. Because the offender is home all the time and cannot leave the house to "cool off," some offenders take out their frustrations on family members in the wrong way. Several community control officers in Florida report that it is not unusual for the spouse of an individual on house arrest to complain that he or she cannot stand another day with the husband or wife at home all day. And according to the officers, several house arrestees have requested that they be sent to prison instead of continuing on house arrest. One told his supervising officer, "If I have to spend any more time with my old lady, I'll probably kill her. Send me on down to Raiford [the state prison]."

Petersilia (1987) warned that house arrest programs are often inaugurated with unrealistic goals and expectations of success. Considerable self-discipline is required to comply with house arrest, and many offenders are impulsive by nature and may be unable to sustain the required behavior for long periods.

Effectiveness of House Arrest

Given that house arrest is an enhancement for probation or parole and has more conditions than routine supervision, house arrest suffers from many of the same problems as ISP. Offenders on house arrest are twice as likely as regular parolees to have their parole revoked for a technical violation (Palumbo, Clifford, and Snyder-Joy 1992).

HOUSE ARREST VERSUS RESIDENTIAL COMMUNITY CORRECTIONS FACILITIES. Harjit S. Sandhu and his colleagues conducted a unique program comparison between offenders sentenced to house arrest and another group of offenders sentenced to a residential community treatment center (CTC) (Sandhu, Dodder, and Mathur 1993). The CTC residents had done time in prison and were within six to nine months of being released on parole. The CTC residents lived at the facility and paid room and board, whereas the house arrestees lived at home but did not wear electronic monitoring devices. A significantly higher percent of the CTC residents (51 percent) were unemployed compared with the people on house arrest (17 percent), who most likely never lost their present jobs. A follow-up one year later indicated that despite a significantly more serious criminal history, offenders on house arrest had lower recidivism rates than offenders sentenced to the residential community treatment center. The authors attribute the differences in success rates to house arrestees having stable employment and living with their family, which may have given them greater motivation to succeed in order to avoid going to prison (Sandhu, Dodder, and Mathur 1993). Although the high rate of current employment of offenders on house arrest appeared to contribute to their success, many offenders who fail residential community corrections facilities–type programs seem to have unemployment status in common. Offenders who do not remain employed or who have a difficult time finding a job after prison have a greater likelihood of program failure, especially in programs that charge for subsistence.

PRETRIAL DETAINEES.   House arrest could be used for defendants awaiting preliminary hearings, sentencing, or trial who would otherwise be held in jail. Defendants who cannot afford bail and who do not qualify for release on personal recognizance may be considered for house arrest. In Marion, Indiana, house arrest for defendants awaiting trial was paired with electronic monitoring to relieve jail overcrowding. The program accepted only 24 percent of those referred for screening, excluding people without telephones, parole violators, absconders, people with pending warrants, and those with a history of violence. Of the 256 people who were accepted, 73 percent successfully completed the program. Of those who failed to complete the house arrest program, 13 percent were technical violators and 14 percent absconded (Maxfield and Baumer 1990).

When house arrest was first used, offenders were monitored through telephone and in-person home visits, which were time-consuming and less reliable. Today, most house arrest programs use electronic monitoring, so we now turn to this type of technology.

ELECTRONIC MONITORING AND GLOBAL POSITIONING SYSTEMS

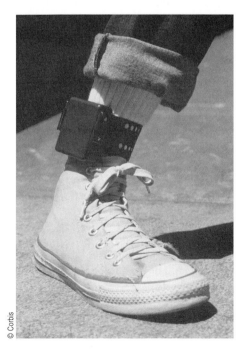

© Corbis

Electronic monitoring can be used in addition to probation or as an intermediate sanction.

Imagine this scenario: Samson has been in prison for the last three years, convicted of reckless endangerment. Samson was paroled from prison on the condition that for the first year he wear an electronic device that fits snugly around his ankle. The ankle device is waterproof and shock-proof, and Samson must wear the device even while showering and sleeping. A transmitter in Samson's ankle bracelet emits a continuous signal to his personal receiver, which is attached to the phone lines at his residence. This receiver only transmits to Samson's ankle device and to no other. If the signal is lost for any reason—say if Samson moves beyond 500 feet from his device—the transmitter is unable to communicate with the receiver, and the receiver automatically calls in to a centralized computer. The computer checks to see if the absence of the signal is authorized or unauthorized. The absence is authorized if Samson has received prior permission from his parole officer (for example) to go out looking for a job or is at work during his scheduled hours. If the absence is unauthorized, his parole officer is automatically notified. Samson has a curfew, and he still must visit his parole officer, who checks the device to make sure Samson has not tried to tamper with it or remove it in any way. Samson must get permission prior to going anywhere, so he has to plan everything in advance.

Samson's sanction is called **electronic monitoring** (EM). EM is a form of correctional technology used in intensive supervision probation, specialized parole caseloads, day reporting centers, and house arrest. EM can also be used for pretrial detainees; that is, for suspects who have not yet been convicted but require an elevated level of supervision while out on bail (discussed in Chapter 2). EM is a technological means of assuring that certain conditions of probation, such as curfew, are met. Like house arrest, EM has the potential to satisfy the goals of imprisonment without the social and financial costs associated with incarceration.

History of Electronic Monitoring

Electronic monitoring technology was developed in the 1960s by Robert Schwitzgebel at the University of California during the deinstitutionalization movement of the mentally ill. When thousands of mentally ill patients were released from mental hospitals, some mental patients were monitored in the community as an alternative to institutionalization (Roy 1997). The idea for use of EM devices in the criminal justice system was inspired by New Mexico judge Jack Love, who saw how the comic book character Spiderman was tracked by a wrist transmitter. The judge persuaded a computer salesman to develop the device. The wrist device was first tried in 1983 for offenders convicted of driving under the influence (DUI) and white-collar crimes (Vollum and Hale 2002). These wrist devices could not be removed very easily and had to be worn at all times. When the probation office called, offenders verified their whereabouts by turning their palm up and inserting the wrist device into a receiver that sat next to the telephone. After a positive evaluation by the National Institute of Justice, EM programs were expanded nationwide.

Problems of Early EM Programs

Early electronic monitoring programs required that offenders have a land line telephone and were able to afford a monthly fee to help subsidize the cost of electronic surveillance. Critics asserted that EM discriminated against those who could not pay the monthly fee or afford telephone service (Petersilia 1987).

A second drawback was that electronic monitoring using a land line phone was only able to track whether an offender was or was not within a certain number of feet of the receiver (which was hooked up next to the offender's telephone). Home-bound

A correctional technology used as a tool in intensive supervision probation, parole, day reporting, or home confinement, using a radio frequency or satellite technology to track offender whereabouts using a transmitter and receiver.

EM systems were not able to track where offenders went once they left their home (Greek 2002).

Third, some of the early wrist systems that required the offender to insert the device into the phone could be used by another offender on the same monitoring system. Thus, there was no guarantee that the probation office was actually communicating with the "correct" person over the telephone (Greek 2002).

Finally, technical and electric problems such as bad wiring, living close to radio stations, power outages, and call-waiting and call-forwarding features caused problems with the transmitter being able to send and receive the required information to central control. Friel and Vaughn (1986) reported that mobile homes or other large metal objects interrupted transmissions, and false alarms occurred when offenders positioned their bodies in a certain way (for instance, sleeping in the fetal position).

Technology has come a long way since then. The continuous-signal ankle device worn by Samson in the earlier example is called a **home-based electronic monitoring** system, as it operates from radio frequencies through phone lines. Although the use of the wrist EM systems has faded, the home-based ankle devices are still in use today and have become sturdier and virtually tamper-proof. Given the drawbacks with the early EM systems and the increased need to track offenders away from home, a variety of other means of offender tracking have become available, including remote monitoring and global positioning satellite devices (see Table 9.1).

Remote Location Monitoring

Remote location monitoring systems monitor an offender either periodically or continuously throughout the day and/or night by means of a special pager. When the pager beeps, the offender must immediately call the probation or parole office. Through voice verification, the computer ensures a positive match between the voice template (the official voice version made at the probation office) and the voice on the phone. The computer records whether or not the voice matched and the phone number from which the call originated (Gowen 2001). The offender doesn't know the number of the pager, so no one else but the computer and the officer can page the offender.

HOME-BASED ELECTRONIC MONITORING

An intermittent or continuous radio frequency signal transmitted through a land line telephone into a receiver that determines whether the offender is or is not at home.

REMOTE LOCATION MONITORING

Verifying an offender's physical location by phone caller identification, use of a pager, and voice pattern verification.

TABLE 9.1   *TECHNOLOGY IN CORRECTIONS: Electronic Monitoring Techniques for Various Offender Risk Levels*

Risk Level	Type of System	Contact Frequency	Verification
Low	Remote pager	Random/infrequent	Phone call/pager
Low/Medium	Home-based system	Programmed or random	Phone call/pager
			Plus voice verification
Medium/High	Hybrid (pager and home-based system)	Frequent/random	Phone call/pager plus voice verification
High	GPS/satellite	Continuous	GPS signals Emitted exclusion/ inclusion zones Video camera at home

Source: Adapted from Darren Gowen. 2001. Remote Location Monitoring—A Supervision Strategy to Enhance Risk Control. *Federal Probation* 65(2): 39.

OFFICER CARRIES A PORTABLE RECEIVER. In addition, some remote location monitors emit signals that may be intercepted by parole or probation officers who have handheld portable receiving units. This enables officers to drive by an offender's house (or work) randomly to verify where the offender is without stopping to see him or her in person. Remote monitoring reportedly "increases officer efficiency by reducing data entry time, increasing accuracy, and providing **real-time access** to monitoring data" (Gowen 2001, p. 40).

Global Positioning Systems

Global positioning systems (GPS) use military satellites that orbit the earth to pinpoint locations anywhere in the world using data coordinates. GPS technology has been used to monitor offenders in the community by means of the Satellite Monitoring and Remote Tracking, or SMART®, program. In the SMART program, offenders wear a permanent ankle or wrist transmitter device (similar to the home-based EM systems), but they also must carry a GPS receiver that contains a microprocessor and antennae. The external equipment is small enough to fit in a waist pack or purse, but the offender must always be within 100 feet of the portable receiver (Greek 2002). The transmitter and receiver that the offender have serve as the medium between the satellite and the central control unit that monitors many offenders. The receiver records data and transmits it via a cell phone or land line phone. A phone line continually calls a reporting station to update the offender's location, which is tracked by a computer.

The microprocessor inside the receiver also allows the probation officer to program in **exclusion zones** and/or **inclusion zones** (Gowen 2001). Thus, an offender on probation for an offense related to his compulsive gambling habit would not be allowed to enter any casino without the device sounding an unauthorized area alarm. Another exclusion zone would be the residence and workplace of an identified victim. In contrast, an inclusion zone allows the officer to program in the offender's work schedule, special appointments, and other events so that the computer can verify the location as it occurs. If necessary, the computer can page or e-mail the victim or police if the offender is near an unauthorized location. Authorities can potentially know an offender's whereabouts at all times (Gowen 2001; Greek 2002).

A system called VeriTracks uses a combination of data integration, geo-mapping, and GPS technology to continuously track the location of people and then to link offender location to location and time of crime incidents reported to the police. Although the match may be pure coincidence and not enough to gain a conviction, the correlation, if it occurs, allows police to begin their investigation with known offenders under supervision (Lilly 2006).

The drawbacks to GPS technology include loss of GPS signal, short battery lives, and cost. Despite the advances in technology, in some locations the receiver has trouble picking up the signal from the satellite (for example, in a basement of a high-rise office building). In addition, in cell phone "dead spots" the offender's receiver is unable to make the repeated cell phone calls to the central station with updates. Sometimes the Department of Defense has imposed restrictions on GPS technology (Vollum and Hale 2002). This system is not completely foolproof (for instance, a motivated offender could cut through the ankle device with specialized tools); the primary drawback, though, is cost. Greek (2002) suggests cutting costs by recording GPS data only once every 10 to 15 minutes rather than continuously or downloading the daily location information at night while the receiver is recharging. Perhaps we should reserve this technology for only the most high-risk offenders who must be out in the community.

REAL-TIME ACCESS

The ability to track locations of the offender as they occur (as opposed to obtaining the data up to 24 hours later).

GLOBAL POSITIONING SYSTEM

A system that uses 24 military satellites orbiting the earth to pinpoint the offender's exact location intermittently or at all times.

EXCLUSION ZONES

Exact locations the offender is prohibited from being in or near.

INCLUSION ZONES

Exact locations, such as employment, school, or an appointment, where the offender is required to be at a certain time.

BOX 9.1   **TECHNOLOGY IN CORRECTIONS**

USING TRANSDERMAL METHODS TO MEASURE BLOOD-ALCOHOL CONTENT

Only about 10 percent of all offenders who were using or abusing alcohol at the time of their offense are actually ordered to abstain from alcohol while on probation or parole. For the client who is ordered not to drink alcohol, a company in Colorado developed a system they call "SCRAM" (Secure Continuous Remote Alcohol Monitoring). SCRAM combines electronic monitoring with the use of transdermal technology to measure the "offender's blood alcohol level by measuring the ethanol migrating through the surface of the skin" (p. 43). The measurements can occur randomly or continuously, and like an offender's location at a home-based electronic monitoring system, the ethanol readings can be communicated via a smart modem (900 MHz radio frequency) to a central monitoring station. Tests at the University of Colorado show that the SCRAM units are as valid as breath analyzer readings, but there was no information on the unit's validity compared with blood test and/or urinalysis. The use of transdermal technology is designed to work in addition to substance abuse treatment and other probation and parole conditions.

Source: Phillips, Kirby. 2001. Reducing Alcohol-Related Crime Electronically. *Federal Probation* 65(2): 42–44.

Another avenue that is currently being pursued is the use of a video camera hooked up to a computer that is plugged into the Internet. Offenders under this system would be required to step in front of the camera when beeped or called. The video camera allows for interaction (for example, a weekly meeting) between a probation officer and the offender. With the technological advances made in computers and satellites, the potential for offender tracking is limitless (see Box 9.1 for how electronic monitoring is combined with transdermal methods to measure alcohol levels).

Frequency of Use

There are over 150,000 offenders nationwide on some form of electronic monitoring system, most of them on probation, parole, or pretrial detention (see Table 9.2). Only about 1,200 offenders were being monitored via GPS monitoring in 16 states (Greek 2002). In the federal system, convicted EM offenders were monitored an average of four months and no longer than six months, whereas pretrial detainees were monitored from 17 days to 242 days (Gowen 2000). Unlike prerelease and convicted offenders who have an ending date on their sentence, pretrial detainees do not know how long they will be on EM, as the duration of pretrial supervision is dependent on the speed of the courts in case processing time. Offenders supervised in state EM programs wore an EM transmitter for an average of 12 to 18 weeks (Camp, Camp, and May 2003).

Each home-based EM transmitter and receiver system costs about $50,000 just for the equipment. Operating costs are additional, and offenders share the operating costs by paying a monthly fee, which is $10 per day for home-based EM supervision and $16 per day for GPS monitoring.

The cost-effectiveness of electronic monitoring has had mixed reviews. The federal system released figures showing that home confinement programs saved between $38 million and $70 million in fiscal year 1996 alone. The amount saved

TABLE 9.2 *How Electronic Monitoring is Used*

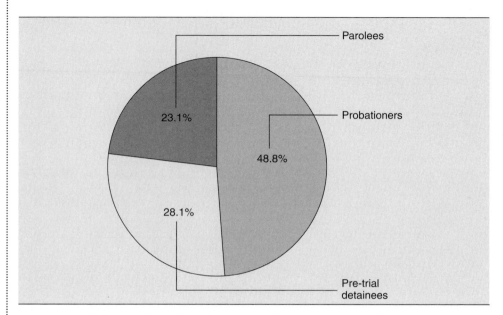

Source: American Probation and Parole Association. Accessed: http://www.appa-net.org/publications&resources/pubs/electronic_monitoring.pdf.

depended on what security level of facility the 13,000 detainees and offenders on home confinement would have been housed in (Altman and Murray 1997). A study in one Pennsylvania county reported a cost savings of $74,722 for 1992–1993 as a result of having EM for offenders who would have been sentenced to the county jail for one of the following crimes: driving under the influence of alcohol, retail theft, bad checks, simple assault, and second-degree burglary (Courtright, Berg, and Mutchnick 1997). Some argue that diversions of this kind would have happened anyway even without EM. With the additional staff that need to be hired, and the increased revocation rates and subsequent return to an already crowded jail, the additional daily cost of $4 to $24 per offender is a substantial cost increase, suggesting that EM is not cost effective (Fay 1995).

Attitudes toward EM

Electronic monitoring has had its share of critics, from those who are concerned that the widespread use of electronic monitoring has resulted in net widening (Fay 1995) to ethical concerns that private companies are profiting from electronic monitoring equipment for correctional supervision technology (Lilly 2006; Nellis 2006). Research has also examined attitudes of EM participants and of general citizenry.

ATTITUDES OF EM PARTICIPANTS.   EM participants tend to be offenders who are financially able to pay the required daily fees. Thus, EM participants either have this money in savings due to good financial management practices or accrued wealth through family, or have a job that pays well. One study examined 49 participants who had spent a short time in jail first before going out to EM, so participants were able to compare the two sanctions (Payne and Gainey 2004). EM was preferred over jail in every case, and offenders on EM reported that they experienced limitations on doing things spontaneously, they still felt a loss of control over their freedom, they felt

BOX 9.2 TECHNOLOGY IN CORRECTIONS

DOES REAL-TIME MONITORING OF COMPUTER USAGE WHILE ON COMMUNITY SUPERVISION INFRINGE UPON RIGHT TO PRIVACY?

The right to privacy is considered a fundamental right in the Fourth Amendment, particularly when applied to a person's home. When a person is under correctional supervision in the community, the right to privacy is limited by the need for probation and parole officers to search through personal effects like personal property, vehicles, and computers if these items are related to the crime (for example, monitoring the computer of a person convicted of fraud or identity theft).

A federal prisoner who anticipated leaving prison on supervised release in three years challenged a probation condition that allowed officers to use real-time monitoring to track the probationer's computer use. The defendant claimed that real-time monitoring was an unnecessary invasion of privacy, and that probation officers could periodically conduct checks during scheduled home visits. The defendant argued that the alternative could accomplish the same goal without being so invasive. The federal court recognized that the defendant would not begin supervised release for another three years, and with technology changing so fast, it is hard to anticipate the level of technological capabilities three years in the future. Furthermore, as technology changes, so does our definition of privacy. Thus, the court held that the remote monitoring condition was "unripe" for review. In other words, the case was brought before the court prematurely and the court was not yet ready to make a decision on whether real-time monitoring was invasive.

Source: *United States v. Balon*, 384 F.3d 38 (2d Cir. 2004).

shame from this sanction, and some experienced family problems from constantly being at home. EM was viewed as less controlling than jail and as a second chance sanction, allowing offenders to remain productive in the community (Payne and Gainey 2004).

Offenders have raised legal and constitutional issues regarding electronic monitoring, but the courts have consistently rejected them. Box 9.2 illustrates a federal court case opinion to a real-time monitoring claim of violation of the offender's right to privacy. Equal protection and due process arguments have also been raised without success. EM has passed constitutional muster and has become an often-used alternative to imprisonment, primarily because it is cost effective.

CITIZEN ATTITUDES.   A mail survey of over 500 New York citizens determined that 54 percent approved the use of electronic monitoring after an offender has served time in jail or prison, but only 31 percent approved EM in lieu of incarceration (Brown and Elrod 1995). Over half of respondents endorsed EM to reduce the cost of incarceration, particularly for the following offenses: driving under the influence of alcohol, property damage and/or theft under $1,000, and technical probation violations. EM was also supported by the public for use with pretrial detainees who cannot afford bail and who are unlikely to commit crimes while released. Citizens were less likely to endorse electronic monitoring for violent crimes involving injury (13 percent), selling illegal drugs (15 percent), or using drugs (30 percent), and for probationers who violated because of a new felony crime (7 percent). Although 89 percent of the general public surveyed thought it appropriate to have a device that informed authorities where the offender was at all times, three-fourths of the sample thought it was inappropriate for authorities to see or hear offenders in their own homes (Brown and Elrod 1995).

Empirical Evaluations of Home-Based Electronic Monitoring

Empirical evaluations tend to support the notion that EM technology makes a difference in how offenders act *while under supervision* when compared with similar offenders on traditional probation or parole. Florida offenders (*n* = 75,661 total) who were placed under one of two types of electronic monitoring (home-based and GPS monitoring) were separated into groups by type of sentence (for example, EM as a probation violation sanction, EM as a post-prison sentence, or a direct sentence to EM) and measured while under supervision. Offenders on EM were more likely to complete the terms of supervision and less likely to commit technical violations and new crimes than those in a comparison group. In addition, home-based EM was as effective as GPS in significantly reducing the likelihood of technical violation, committing new crimes, and absconding while under supervision. This means that EM has yielded positive short-term results.

LONG-TERM EFFECTS.   There is some support that EM widens the net of penal control for some drug offenders, but not for violent and property offenders (Padgett, Bales, and Blomberg 2006). Padgett and her colleagues suggest that EM is effective for monitoring serious offenders, but the long-term recidivism rates after supervision has ended remain unclear at this point. One study of the long-term effects (measured by recidivism after the supervision ended) found that EM generally had similar rates as those of offenders who served their full sentence in jail or prison. When federal offenders on EM were compared with federal offenders in a halfway house, rearrest rates were similar while on supervision. Within one year of release from supervision, EM participants were less likely than halfway house clients to be rearrested. Although drug use between the two groups of program participants was similar, EM offenders maintained more continuous employment than halfway house residents (Klein-Saffran 1992).

COMPLETION RATES.   EM program completion rates in other studies are quite impressive—97 percent completed the EM period of their probation successfully, and 80 percent completed the entire term of their probation (Lilly et al. 1992). Completion rates for convicted nonviolent federal offenders was higher (89 percent) than for pretrial detainees and community supervision violators (77 percent and 75 percent, respectively). The four reasons pretrial drug offenders and supervision violators were most likely to fail were because of unauthorized leave of the area (return later), flight/absconding (whereabouts unknown), arrest for a new crime, and tampering with EM equipment (Gowen 2000). It is recommended that EM sentences be ideally limited to no longer than 180 days, as success rates decreased after this time (Roy 1994).

GENDER DIFFERENCES.   It seems that family conditions play a significant role in the outcome of EM sentences. Men who lived with a significant other while on EM reported receiving positive family support and help with dependent children, but women offenders reported that significant others were a source of stress and conflict to their success on EM. The women offenders perceived little support from their partner in assisting them with the child care role. The lack of freedom to leave home because of EM affected women's primary caretaker role for dependent children (Maidment 2002).

Another study found that offender experiences with EM overall were not significantly different by race, sex, or age. Women were more likely than men to see EM as shameful, whereas offenders who were older or African American viewed EM as more restrictive to their daily lives than did offenders who were younger or Caucasian (Payne and Gainey 2002). With offenders spending much more time at home, it is clear that some situations improve whereas other situations worsen. Success of electronic monitoring depends on identifying the type of individual or home situation that creates the most ideal environment.

DAY REPORTING CENTERS

Day reporting centers (DRCs) are a type of nonresidential program typically used for defendants on pretrial release, for convicted offenders on probation or parole, or as an increased sanction for probation or parole violators. Day reporting centers are like a "one-stop shop" with all the resources and educational programs in one place, along with extended hours to accommodate offenders who work days and evenings.

DRCs have been popular in England and Wales since the 1970s and began to appear in the United States in 1985. DRCs developed using the "day centre" idea from the British, combined with inspiration from juvenile day treatment centers already established in the United States (Parent 1995, p. 125). Connecticut and Massachusetts were the first states to adopt day reporting centers with the goal of reducing jail or prison crowding and providing a closer level of supervision than traditional probation or parole. DRCs are frequently used to reduce pretrial confinement. This idea has caught on throughout the United States in a short period of time. In 1990, there were only 13 DRCs, but five years later the number swelled to 114 DRCs (Parent et al. 1995).

According to a nationwide study of 54 DRCs, these programs are used for a wide variety of clients:

- 87 percent of the DRCs admit probationers
- 73 percent allow probation and parole violators
- 42 percent enroll parolees from prison
- 37 percent of DRCs admit defendants on pretrial release

DAY REPORTING CENTERS

Nonresidential programs typically used for defendants on pretrial release, for convicted offenders on probation or parole, or as an increased sanction for probation or parole violators. Services are provided in one central location, and offenders must check in daily.

© David Harry Stewart/Getty Images

The day reporting center combines education and vocational training with family and individual counseling in a highly structured program setting. Individual Treatment and Supervision Plans (ITSPs) are created for each participant. Probation officers provide on-site and community supervision.

- 25 percent let in individuals who need to be released early from jail
- 20 percent supervise offenders on furlough or administrative release from prison
- 6 percent of DRCs accept prisoners on work release (Parent et al. 1995, p. 18)

Some DRCs, such as the one in Maricopa County, Arizona, will reject applicants for one or more of the following reasons: injured their victim, used a weapon, sex offenders, history of violence, escape risk, pending charges/warrant/hold, prosecutorial objection, nonverifiable residence, and offender refusal to participate. On the other hand, a DRC in Harris County, Texas, is specifically designed to accept sex offenders, stalkers, boot camp graduates, mentally ill offenders, developmentally disabled offenders, probation/parole violators, and graduates of prison-based therapeutic communities (Parent et al. 1995).

Five of the larger DRCs can handle more than 300 offenders at one time, but most DRCs have a capacity for an average of 85 offenders. The largest DRC in the country is located in Houston, Texas, and processes up to 2,000 offenders per day (Parent et al. 1995).

Purposes of DRCs

Although goals vary from program to program, the three primary purposes of DRCs are as follows:

- Saving space in jail and prison
- Providing a close level of community supervision
- Providing offenders with access to services and treatment programs (Diggs and Pieper 1994, pp. 9–12)

For example, three DRCs operating in Boston, Springfield, and Worcester, Massachusetts, are used for offenders who would otherwise be incarcerated. These DRCs serve the county jails and admit offenders who are within three months of discharging their jail sentence. These offenders are let out of jail and live at home. They must report every day to the day center, get tested randomly for drugs at least twice per week, and be in touch with program staff by phone at least twice per day. The offenders must either be employed full time, be going to school full time, or a combination of both (Larivee 1995).

Because some probationers do not take the conditions of their probation seriously, other DRCs serve to provide enforcement or "muscle" for probationers and parolees without sending them to jail or prison. Box 9.3 tells the story of a typical experience at a day reporting center.

The theory behind DRCs is that offenders will stay out of trouble when they are occupied, especially with activities that will improve their chances for a more normal life—for example, by obtaining a GED or finding a job. Connecticut uses DRCs because they offer cost savings, less bureaucracy, and accountability, and they provide more services to the state using fewer government employees (Coleman, Felten-Green, and Oliver 1998).

Treatment-Oriented versus Supervision-Oriented DRCs

Some DRCs are more "treatment oriented" and others are more "supervision oriented" (Anderson 1998, p. 56). Treatment-oriented DRCs provide a wide range of services such as social services representatives, drug abuse education, psychological counseling, life skills training, and classes in job-seeking skills. Treatment-oriented DRCs

BOX 9.3 COMMUNITY CORRECTIONS UP CLOSE •

A TYPICAL DAY REPORTING EXPERIENCE

John, 28 years old and unemployed, is arrested for possession of cocaine. He is sentenced to probation, but during that time he misses several meetings with his probation officer and tests positive for drug use. Rather than punishing John for this probation violation by sending him to the state prison, which is already 10 percent over capacity, the judge assigns him to a nearby DRC. The DRC, which the state judicial department began operating two years ago, accepts John because, based on his history and offense, he is of small risk to the community and is in need of drug abuse treatment and other services. Furthermore, by keeping John under community supervision, the judge avoids adding to the already high prison population.

John begins the first phase of the three-phase program in June. For the first three weeks, he must report to the DRC five times each week, where he twice is tested for drug use. The program is open from 8 A.M. to 6 P.M. Monday through Friday and from 9 A.M. to 1 P.M. on Saturdays. When he is not at the center, John must remain at home except to do errands that he has already planned on a weekly itinerary, on record at the DRC. Program staff telephone John several times during the day to monitor his whereabouts and ensure that he is abiding by his 8 P.M. curfew. Once a week, staff also make an unannounced visit to his home. John also begins to attend drug abuse education classes, GED classes, job skills training, and group counseling sessions, conducted on-site by program staff. In addition, twice a week he goes to a drug abuse outpatient clinic, referred by the DRC.

In the middle of his second week, John misses a counseling session and a GED class. Instead of moving to the second, more lenient, phase at the end of the third week, John must remain under the more intensive form of supervision for an additional week. Informed that another violation might land him in the state correctional facility, he subsequently commits no other violations. By the end of June, he is ready to begin the second phase, during which he must continue with his drug abuse treatment and classes but report to the DRC only twice a week. In addition, he joins many of the other 90 offenders in performing several cleanup and construction projects around the city.

After three months without violating any regulations, John begins the third and final phase of the program, during which he reports to the DRC only once a week. With assistance from a job placement agency that offers its services at the DRC, he finds employment with the state parks system. By the end of November, he has been released from the DRC. The cost to the state of his placement in the DRC has been half of what it likely would have been had he been incarcerated, and John seems on his way to making a more productive contribution to society.

Source: Dale Parent et al. 1995. *Day Reporting Centers* (vol. 1). Washington, DC: U.S. Department of Justice, National Institute of Justice, p. 23.

(or day treatment programs) are viable options for offenders who are physically disabled or developmentally disabled (Mawhorr 1997). DRCs require unemployed offenders to come to the center during daytime business hours to focus on literacy, GED classes, and finding a job. Employed offenders are required to attend treatment programs at night or on weekends, as well as check in with the DRC and provide the center with a 24-hour itinerary of their schedule. "The itineraries state when clients are to leave home, their destinations, how they will travel (walk, drive, take the bus, or get a ride), when they are to arrive, and when they are to return home" (Anderson 1998, p. 63). Itineraries are important for two reasons. First, clients learn (some for the first time) how to plan their days in advance. Second, the DRCs can monitor where the clients are when random phone calls are placed via a computer.

Supervision-oriented DRCs ensure that clients are abiding by their terms of probation. The DRC staff monitor the offender by random phone calls to the offender at home. DRCs are authorized to give out Antabuse, a prescription medication prescribed for alcoholics that prevents the use of alcohol. Urine screenings and alco-sensor tests ensure that clients have not been using drugs. Many DRCs have a mixture of both supervision and treatment orientations.

Many day centers operate on a levels system, where the initial level involves the most intense contact. Offenders can proceed to less frequent contacts the longer they remain in good standing in the program. Another characteristic of DRCs is that many clients are also on 24-hour electronic monitoring. As the clients remain longer in the program, DRCs may be able to give clients more freedom by removing the electronic monitoring device while they still remain on supervision (McDevitt and Miliano 1992).

In many ways, DRCs are nonresidential versions of halfway houses because the two programs provide very similar services, except DRC offenders live at home (Bahn and Davis 1998). Like most halfway houses, most DRCs are private facilities that contract out to state and local entities; exceptions include a few in Massachusetts and the one in Houston (Parent 1995). Furthermore, contact between program staff and offenders in DRCs is similar to or better than that with intensive supervision probation. ISP programs have more field visits (where the officer goes to the home or job site to visit the offender), but DRCs have more phone and office visits because the offender comes to the center (Parent 1995).

Sentences to DRCs range from 40 days to 12 months, with an average of six months' duration (Parent 1995). The average daily cost per offender is $35. This would make the DRC more costly than traditional probation or parole, and even more expensive than ISP. However, DRCs cost less than residential treatment or incarceration in jail or prison (Parent et al. 1995). Most DRC programs exist in states that do not have ISP as a sentencing option (Parent 1995). Much of the treatment program costs are absorbed by the DRC itself or by another agency (see Table 9.3). In one out of every four DRCs, offenders pay for their own drug treatment. Other DRCs have cost-sharing programs for their services, which helps keep program costs down.

TABLE 9.3   *Sources of Payment for Services at DRCs*

	PERCENTAGE OF DRCs IN WHICH:		
Service	DRC Pays	Another Agency Pays	Offender Pays (fees)
Job-seeking skills (N = 53)	74%	17%	4%
Drug abuse education (N = 52)	73	23	12
Group counseling (N = 51)	73	20	8
Job placement services (N = 50)	58	30	8
Education (N = 49)	53	43	10
Drug treatment (N = 48)	50	46	25
Life skills training (N = 49)	74	12	2
Individual counseling (N = 47)	72	19	13
Transitional housing (N = 32)	28	72	6
Recreation and leisure (N = 31)	77	10	16

Note: DRCs may have more than one payment source.

Source: Dale Parent, Jim Byrne, Vered Tsafaty, Laura Valade, and Julie Esselman, *Day Reporting Centers,* vol. 1 (Washington, DC: U.S. Department of Justice, National Institute of Justice, 1995).

Evaluations of DRCs

Evaluations of day reporting centers measure effectiveness using completion rates, rearrest rates, and predictions of program failure.

COMPLETION RATES.   DRC clients who failed in the program were "administratively terminated" and returned to custody (McDevitt and Miliano 1992, p. 161). Termination rates for the 54 DRCs surveyed averaged 50 percent within four to six months, and ranged from 14 percent to 86 percent. Termination rates were higher for service-oriented programs than for supervision-oriented DRCs. Failure rates were also higher for programs longer than six months in duration.

High failure rates resulted because of the level of supervision intensity and the type of offender admitted to the program. Whereas work release programs accepted lower risk offenders, DRCs tended to accept probation and parole violators and other types of higher-risk clients (Parent 1995).

Evaluations of European DRCs are roughly the same as those for U.S. DRCs. In one British study of more than 600 offenders in 38 DRC programs, 63 percent of offenders were reconvicted of a new crime within two years of being sentenced to a DRC (Mair, and Nee 1992). George Mair (1995) commented about this finding:

> On the face of it, this may look high, but the offenders targeted by centers represent a very high risk group in terms of probability of reconviction. Probation centers [DRCs] may be condemning themselves to what appears to be a high reconviction rate by successfully diverting offenders from custody, and this must be taken into consideration when interpreting the overall reconviction rate. (p. 137)

RATE OF REARREST.   John J. Larivee (1995) reported that the DRCs in Massachusetts have had about 3 percent of participants abscond or commit a new crime. Whereas Massachusetts DRCs recruit offenders from jail, North Carolina DRC offenders are on probation. In a 12-month follow-up evaluation of 15 DRC programs in North Carolina, Amy Craddock notes that the typical client has a history of prior convictions, suffers with a substance abuse problem, and is on probation for a nonviolent offense. The goals of this DRC are to reduce recidivism, reduce probation revocations, reduce substance abuse relapse, and provide a cost savings (Craddock 2000). Craddock examined 419 DRC clients on probation with 440 similarly situated probationers (the comparison group). Both groups had similar offense types and prior records. Day center participants were significantly more likely than the comparison group to be unemployed and less likely to have graduated from high school. Furthermore, a higher percentage of females and minorities were participating in the DRC program than in other types of probation. Craddock found that 20.1 percent of DRC participants were rearrested within one year compared with 24.5 percent of the probation group. However, more DRC clients committed technical violations (25.2 percent) than did the other probationers (14.2 percent).

This research also differentiates DRC program completers from noncompleters, something the Mair and Nee study did not do. The rate of rearrest for DRC participants who completed the program was only 13 percent versus noncompleters at 25.4 percent. Those who did not complete the program were also rearrested in a shorter amount of time than the DRC graduates and regular probationers. Only 11.2 percent of DRC offenders who completed the program accrued technical violations, whereas 34.2 percent of clients who did not complete the program accumulated violations that ultimately led to their removal from the program. The overall findings thus seem to indicate that not only was the DRC program successful at reducing the number of offenders who were rearrested, but also that DRC participants who completed the program were significantly more likely to have fewer rearrests and fewer technical violations than regular probationers (Craddock 2000).

The Illinois Criminal Justice Authority tracked a treatment group of pretrial detainees who had participated in a DRC for 70 or more days and compared it with a group that had been eligible for the DRC but had participated for 10 days or less, but did not drop out of the program. Members of these two groups were tracked for three years in terms of their rearrest and reincarceration rates. The treatment group was not only rearrested and reincarcerated at significantly lower rates than the control group, but the treatment group remained free for an average of 122 days longer than the control group (Martin, Lurigio, and Olson 2003).

PREDICTORS OF DRC FAILURE. The Illinois Criminal Justice Authority was also interested in factors that predicted who would be rearrested and who would remain crime free. The researchers found that previous criminal history (more prior arrests), being of a young age, and spending less time in the DRC program were the most significant predictors of rearrest following release from the DRC. Recommendations included lengthening the time in the DRC (Martin, Lurigio, and Olson 2003).

A study of completers versus noncompleters in the Vigo County, Indiana, DRC found similar results to the Illinois study in terms of age and criminal history. They also found that being married and living with anyone else except a boyfriend/girlfriend significantly predicted whether a person would finish the program (Roy and Grimes 2002). So it seems that some of the same factors predicting program completers also predicted likelihood of rearrest and reincarceration. However, the Indiana researchers found that offenders who were placed in the DRC for longer than 120 days were twice as likely to not complete the program as those who had 120 days or less in the DRC (Roy and Grimes 2002). An evaluation of a Utah DRC reported that the positive programmatic effects began to decrease as the duration of services extended beyond 120 days. So it seems that the threshold for an ideal period of time to derive the maximum benefit is a duration of no longer than 120 days.

In sum, there is no one "right way" to operate a DRC. Each day center has different goals and different kinds of clients. The key is to specifically define the goals of the DRC program (for example, reduce institutional crowding) and then measure whether the program is achieving those goals. Dale Parent (1995), who has been actively involved in DRC research and evaluation, concludes:

> If policy makers want DRCs to reduce prison and jail crowding, they should use day reporting as an early release mechanism and should let corrections officials [or bail officers rather than sentencing judges] select inmates for DRC placement. Among inmates released early, DRCs should be used for those who pose the greatest risk to the public or who have the most serious problems that are likely to impair their adjustment. To reduce total costs, officials should use less structured and less expensive forms of supervision for low-risk, low-need inmates who are granted early release. Future research should focus on DRC's costs and impacts on offenders' adjustments. (pp. 127–128)

TOP THINGS YOU SHOULD KNOW

- ISP programs, if they operate with close supervision and little treatment intervention, will not produce cost savings and will not significantly decrease the number of prison beds.

- Technical violation rates are high with closer supervision, and, as a result, probation and parole enhancement ISP programs may increase the number of jail and prison commitments.
- Potential for ISP programs lies in offering significantly higher treatment intervention strategies in concert with intensive supervision to decrease the number of revocations and the number of new crimes committed while on supervision.
- House arrest by itself provides cost savings but does not deter criminal misconduct. The level of monitoring is minimal unless house arrest is combined with electronic monitoring.
- Technological advances made in the area of electronic monitoring include the use of computers and satellites to monitor offenders in the community. No matter what type of electronic monitoring system is currently used, all offenders must minimally wear an ankle-monitoring device, and they cannot tamper or remove the device without sounding an alarm to a central control station.
- Day reporting centers typically accept convicted offenders or pretrial detainees who require a higher level of supervision than clients under electronic monitoring or house arrest. Day reporting centers also provide all the services in one place and are the most costly type of nonresidential intermediate sanction, but DRCs still cost less than jail or prison.
- All forms of nonresidential programs are more effective when goals are clarified and target offender populations are more accurately defined to best meet offender needs without unduly compromising public safety.

DISCUSSION QUESTIONS

1 How does intensive supervision probation differ from regular probation?
2 Discuss the relationship between ISP caseload size and recidivism.
3 What are the advantages and disadvantages of house arrest?
4 How does electronic monitoring support house arrest? What ethical and social criticisms are associated with EM?
5 How do electronic monitoring devices work? What are some of the technical problems associated with them?
6 How are day reporting centers different from ISP?
7 Do day reporting centers accomplish their objectives?
8 Which of the intermediate sanctions discussed in this chapter are probation or parole enhancements, and which sanctions are true alternatives to prison?
9 Why should intermediate sanction programs have clear goals and objectives?

 WEBSITES

American Correctional Association List of Community Corrections Publications

http://www.aca.org/publications/home.asp

Intermediate Sanctions in Florida

http://www.fcc.state.fl.us/fcc/reports/intermed

The Electronic Monitoring Program of Multnomah County

http://www.co.multnomah.or.us/dcj/insidedcj111505.shtml# electronicmonitoring

Evaluation of Maricopa County (Arizona) Day Reporting Center

http://www.nhtsa.dot.gov/people/injury/alcohol/repeatoffenders/ eval_dayreport.html

Atlanta, Georgia, Day Reporting Center

http://www.dcor.state.ga.us/Divisions/Corrections/ProbationSupervision/ DayReporting.html

Summary of the Salt Lake City, Utah, Day Reporting Center

http://www.justice.utah.gov/Research/Adult/Adult%20Day% 20Reporting%20Center%20Eval.pdf

The Juvenile Electronic Monitoring Program of Multnomah County

http://www.co.multnomah.or.us/dcj/jcjcommdetention.html

Site Visit to One Community-Based Correctional Program

Visit one community-based correctional program and use this visit to conduct your own case study. Your visit may be done individually or with a small group. You will likely need to clear the visit ahead of time with your instructor, or your instructor may suggest a facility with which he or she has some connections. If this is a group exercise, perhaps members can be assigned to each focus on a small section of the paper or presentation. There are four sections, and questions are presented so that each member can ask a few questions during the site visit. Write a paper or make a presentation to include one or more of the following areas:

Section 1: Program Description

What are the goals of this program?
What tools or techniques are used to meet these goals?
What is the capacity (how many clients can be treated at one time)?
How many contact hours/treatment hours are a part of this program?

Section 2: Clients

Who are the clients being served?
What does the typical client look like (gender, age, education, and so on)
What are the client's perspectives of the treatment program?

Section 3: Staff

What is the client to staff ratio?
What are the staff backgrounds and qualifications?
What are the perspectives of the staff about working there (or about program effectiveness)?

Section 4: Evaluation

How many clients finish the program (and how many drop out or do not complete it)?
What are the reasons for not completing the program?
What is the daily (or yearly) cost per client served?
Have any clients been tracked after they leave the program? What were the results?

Introduction

Restorative Justice Principles

Forms of Restorative Justice
Effectiveness of Restorative
  Justice Methods

Restitution

Restitution in History
Losses Eligible for Compensation
Problems Associated with
  Restitution
Effectiveness of Restitution

Community Service

History of Community Service
Purpose of Community Service
Prevalence of Community Service
Effectiveness of Community
  Service

Fines

Prevalence of Fines
Revoking Probation for Fine
  Nonpayment
Forfeitures
Day Fines
Evaluation of Day Fines

Fees and Costs

Top Things You Should Know

10

Economic and Restorative Justice Reparations

Courtesy Columbia River Correctional Institution

What You Will Learn in This Chapter

- *How restorative principles and practices differ from traditional criminal justice practices*
- *The forms that restorative justice takes, including victim–offender mediation, victim impact classes, family group conferencing, and circle sentencing*
- *How economic/monetary sanctions are used in both restorative and traditional criminal justice systems to include restitution, community service, fines, and forfeiture*

KEY TERMS

Community justice
Restorative justice
Restitution
Community service
Fine
Victim compensation fund
Forfeiture
Day fines
Fees

INTRODUCTION

When an offender is punished for a crime, the public may feel short-term satisfaction or the victim may find some closure, but many may be left wondering how the punishment will actually affect the offender's future thinking or behavior. In a traditional criminal justice system, the state acts on behalf of victims to punish the offender. It should be no surprise that even following sentencing victims may still feel angry, unsupported, more socially isolated, and more distrustful of a system that was designed to punish on their behalf. Many come to realize that government-legitimized retribution achieves a form of justice or revenge but does not necessarily heal. Traditional criminal justice strategies and the "get tough" movement may not be as effective as we once thought in dealing with the harm caused, the resulting social isolation, and the destruction of community trust that results when crimes are committed. Separating predatory and violent offenders from the general public is necessary, but incarceration is not the magic bullet for most offenders. Incarcerating more people for longer periods of time does not necessarily make our communities safer.

The concept of **community justice** is a philosophy of using the community to control and reduce crime and to rebuild community relationships through community policing, community courts, and restorative justice. Although some authors use the terms "community justice" and "restorative justice" interchangeably, community justice is actually a broader concept that describes a philosophy overriding the whole criminal justice system (police, courts, and corrections), whereas restorative justice deals only with the sentencing and corrections component (APPA n.d.).

In Chapter 1, we introduced the concept of **restorative justice** as a sentencing philosophy and practice that emphasized the offender taking responsibility to repair the harm done to the victim and the surrounding community. Balanced and restorative justice (BARJ) has been formally written into many juvenile codes to encourage the use of restorative justice methods with nonviolent juvenile delinquents. Restorative justice is more victim centered than traditional methods, involving the victim and the community throughout the whole justice process (Karp 1998; Van Ness and Strong 1997; Wright 1996). We also introduced the concept of "reinventing probation" in Chapter 6. Recall that probation practices are moving toward neighborhood-based offender supervision, which fits well within the framework of restorative justice (Rhine 2002). Let's begin by discussing restorative justice principles and comparing them with traditional criminal justice sentencing practices.

RESTORATIVE JUSTICE PRINCIPLES

Restorative justice is community based and combines mainstream American criminal justice with indigenous justice practiced by Native Americans long before

COMMUNITY JUSTICE

A philosophy of using the community to control and reduce crime through community policing, community courts, restorative justice, and broken-windows probation.

RESTORATIVE JUSTICE

A sentencing philosophy and practice that emphasizes the offender taking responsibility to repair the harm done to the victim and to the surrounding community.

TABLE 10.1　*Roots of Restorative Justice*

MAINSTREAM AMERICAN JUSTICE	INDIGENOUS NATIVE AMERICAN JUSTICE
Imported from Anglo-American models	Indigenous, shared views of the community and victims*
Written codified laws, rules, procedures*	Unwritten/oral customs, traditions, practices
Law is applied*	Law is a way of life
Justice is administered*	Justice is part of the life process*
Offender is focal point; privilege against self-incrimination	Victim is focal point*; offender is obligated to verbalize accountability
Adversarial (fact-finding) process; victim and offender have no contact	Communal*; victim and offender are involved in the whole process and decide action jointly
Conflict settled in court	Conflict settled through mediation and repairing relationships*
Public defender or lawyer representation*	Extended family member representation
Retributive	Restorative or holistic; connects everyone involved*
Incarceration, so criminal can pay debt to society	Community service, restitution*
Criminals are bad and responsible for their actions; they deserve to be punished	Criminal acts are a part of natural human error, which requires correctional intervention on behalf of the community*
Church and state are separated	Spiritual realm is cohesive with justice*

Note: * Applies to restorative justice

European settlers colonized North America (see Table 10.1). In contrast to mainstream criminal justice, which focuses on the punishment of the offender, restorative justice focuses on the victim, the offender, and the community throughout the whole process.

Restorative justice can be used for community-based sanctions or for prisoner reentry. Community-based sanctions are discussed in this chapter, and prisoner reentry is discussed in Chapter 12. Restorative justice uses the theory of reintegrative shaming as opposed to disintegrative stigmatization (Braithwaite 1989) to emphasize offender responsibility to repair the injustice and wrong the offender has caused the victim.

Rather than focusing on deficits, restorative justice attempts to strengthen community life by drawing on the participation of the victim, the victim's social support network, the offender, the offender's social support network, and the community (Umbreit 1999). Thus, community-based corrections programs are necessary and important to guide the restorative justice process.

Forms of Restorative Justice

A variety of forms are used in restorative justice, including victim–offender mediation, reparation boards, family group conferencing, and circle sentencing. All forms of restorative justice take place postconviction in the sentencing phase and have the following commonalities:

1. One or more sessions are held in the community, with the first goal to provide the victim (and/or the victim's social support networks) with the opportunity to communicate how the crime affected them physically, emotionally, financially, and socially.
2. The second goal is to develop a reparative plan that is accepted by both the victim and the offender in which the offender will repair the harm caused.
3. Victim participation is voluntary, and conditions of each meeting are defined on the victim's terms.

4. The parties rely on community partners and volunteers, such as Mothers Against Drunk Driving, Parents of Murdered Children, battered women's shelters, mediators, community prosecutors, school-based officers, and various faith-based organizations.
5. Offenders must accept full responsibility for their criminal behavior.
6. All forms are community-based sanctions, as a condition of either probation or diversion.

VICTIM–OFFENDER MEDIATION. Victim–offender mediation (VOM) has existed since the early 1980s in the United States, and there are approximately 320 programs in the United States and Canada, and more than 1,300 programs in 18 countries around the world (Bazemore and Umbreit 2001; Umbreit, Coates, and Vos 2001). This type of mediation is different from the mediation found traditionally in civil courts because in VOM there is no dispute about liability. Rather, the mediator is present in the same room with the offender and the victim. The three parties, in one or more sessions, reach a mutually desirable agreement to repair the harm.

In a review of 38 evaluation studies of VOM, between 40 and 60 percent of victims refused to participate because they didn't want to take the time for a perceived trivial offense, they feared meeting the offender, or they desired traditional punishment for the offender (Umbreit, Coates, and Vos 2001). Victims of juvenile crimes who participated in VOM were significantly more satisfied (79 percent) with the case outcome than a comparison group of victims who experienced traditional case processing methods (57 percent), according to a study in four states (Umbreit and Coates 1993).

The primary reasons victims chose to participate were to seek restitution/repayment, to oversee punishment, and to share their grief with the offender. The quality of the mediator and the face-to-face format were key variables in the victims' satisfaction. Other positive findings included that restitution payments were higher with VOM participants, victims reported being less fearful of being revictimized, and "[VOM] is at least as viable an option for recidivism reduction as traditional approaches. And in a good number of instances, youth going through mediation programs are actually faring better" (Umbreit, Coates, and Vos 2001, p. 32). One negative outcome from these evaluation studies was that some VOM programs resulted in net widening.

REPARATION BOARDS. Otherwise known as youth panels or community diversion boards, panels consisting of members from the community have existed as a part of the juvenile justice system since the 1920s (Bazemore and Umbreit 2001). Community reparation boards function as mediators between the court and the offender and may or may not involve the victim. The board does not decide guilt or innocence; rather, it meets postconviction with the offender and the victim separately (or together if the victim wishes) to discuss and clarify how the offender will repair the harm and to identify strategies for reducing future offending (Karp and Clear 2002). Each board has a chair who manages the session, and sanctions are decided by the board rather than by the judge. Local volunteers and members of faith-based organizations agree to mentor or assist in the supervision of the offender's reparation through a volunteer reparations board. Board members typically receive some training prior to serving, and the vast majority of board members serve voluntarily. The board reports back to the court monthly or quarterly on the offender's progress, or lack thereof. Should the offender fail to comply with the sanctions, the board makes a recommendation to the court (Bazemore and Umbreit

2001). Of all forms of restorative justice, this method seems to have more community than victim participation.

FAMILY GROUP CONFERENCING. The family group conferencing model uses school resource officers or police officers to organize and facilitate family meetings at school or at a community resource center. Individuals selected for voluntary participation include the families of both the offender and the victim. Family group conferencing more actively involves parents of adjudicated delinquents and assists in ensuring offender compliance (Bazemore and Umbreit 2001).

One study of family group conferencing for juvenile delinquents adjudicated for violent and nonviolent offenses discovered that many nonviolent cases were not selected. For example, shoplifting and theft were not selected because victims (retail stores) refused to participate, and "runaway cases were also avoided . . . because they often involve complicated family issues and not the resolution of a specific wrongdoing" (Walker 2002, p. 39). Like every other form of restorative justice, family group conferencing also required that juveniles take responsibility for their actions. In Walker's (2002) study, 15.6 percent of the youths selected for the conference denied criminal involvement and were excluded for that reason. For the youths who participated in the conference, most sanctions consisted of a "symbolic" apology, community service, offender counseling, or some combination of the three. Walker's findings included a measure of recidivism, which did not significantly differ overall between juveniles who participated and juveniles who did not. When juveniles were divided by their adjudication offense (violent versus nonviolent), those who participated in the conferences for nonviolent offenses were less likely to be adjudicated for a violent offense compared to a matched juvenile group that did not participate in the conferences.

CIRCLE SENTENCING. Circle sentencing is based most closely on tribal justice and the use of reintegrative shaming by more parties than the victim or a single mediator. A circle group consists of the offender, the victim, family, friends, and coworkers of both the offender and the victim, social service personnel, juvenile justice personnel, and interested community members who all gather simultaneously in a circle. A "talking piece" such as a stick or feather is used to systematize who has the floor to speak. Of all four forms of restorative justice, circle sentencing involves the largest number of participants and therefore the most organization. It may be the most effective form for repeat offenders, or where offending behavior intersects with dysfunctional relationships, but it should be used sparingly with offenders convicted of minor crimes (Bazemore and Umbreit 2001). An example of a circle sentencing session is described in Box 10.1.

Effectiveness of Restorative Justice Methods

Measures of restorative justice can include victim satisfaction with the outcome/process, payment of restitution, cost savings, and recidivism rate. Restorative justice is most effective for property crimes, particularly those committed by juveniles or first-time adult felony offenders, because the victim can be compensated for property losses. In traditional criminal justice, the victim is rarely compensated. When given a choice between compensation and incarceration, 75 percent of respondents to a study conducted in Minnesota indicated that they would rather be compensated for a property crime than demand that the offender be incarcerated (Umbreit 1999). At this time, however, restorative justice as the only community-based sanction is less likely to be endorsed for violent crimes.

BOX 10.1 COMMUNITY CORRECTIONS UP CLOSE •

A CIRCLE SENTENCING SESSION IN CANADA

"The victim was a middle-aged man whose parked car had been badly damaged when the offender, a 16-year-old, crashed into it while joyriding in another vehicle. The offender had also damaged a police vehicle.

"In the circle, the victim talked about the emotional shock of seeing what had happened to his car and his costs to repair it (he was uninsured). Then, an elder leader of the First Nations community where the circle sentencing session was being held (and an uncle of the offender) expressed his disappointment and anger with the boy. The elder observed that this incident, along with several prior offenses by the boy, had brought shame to his family. . . .

"After the elder finished, a feather (the 'talking piece') was passed to the next person in the circle, a young man who spoke about the contributions the offender made to the community, the kindness he had shown toward elders, and his willingness to help others with home repairs. . . . The Royal Canadian Mounted Police officer whose vehicle had also been damaged, then took the feather and spoke on the offender's behalf. The officer proposed to the judge that in lieu of statutorily required jail time for the offense, the offender be allowed to meet with him on a regular basis for counseling and community service.

"After asking the victim and the prosecutor if either had any objections, the judge accepted this proposal. The judge also ordered restitution to the victim and asked the young adult who had spoken on the offender's behalf to serve as a mentor for the offender. After a prayer in which the entire group held hands, the circle disbanded and everyone retreated to the kitchen area of the community center for refreshments."

Source: As quoted in Gordon Bazemore and Mark Umbreit. 2001. A Comparison of Four Restorative Conferencing Models. Juvenile Justice Bulletin (February). Washington, DC: U.S. Department of Justice, Office of Juvenile Justice and Delinquency Programs, p. 7.

Restorative justice can entail some problems. In particular, it involves community members. Any time the community plays a role, it introduces the unpredictability of public opinion, which can vary widely. Community members may be undereducated about the nature of the crime and may even incorrectly believe the victim is to blame. The offender may take advantage of this by shifting the blame to the victim or minimizing the harmful behavior. The involvement of family and friends of both the victim and offender (particularly when the victim and offender know each other) can be difficult if the family seems more supportive or even approves of the offender's behavior (Daly and Stubbs 2006).

Finally, some victims' groups are opposed to restorative justice initiatives because some find them still centered around offenders, and others find then offensive because reintegrative shaming is used over retribution and stigmatization. Some victims are not able to communicate or be an advocate on their own. This may exert too much pressure on some victims. "The greatest challenge victims pose to restorative justice is indifference. Restorative processes depend, case by case, on victims' active participation, in a role more emotionally demanding than that of a complaining witness in a conventional criminal prosecution—which is itself a role avoided by many, perhaps most victims" (Smith 2001, p. 5).

Restorative justice sanctions are primarily economic in nature (paying back losses) and labor intensive (bettering the community). Economic sanctions such as restitution, community service, and fines are used in both restorative and traditional justice systems and will be discussed next.

©Jacqueline Ramseyer Orrell

Two staff members of a restorative justice program attempt to give youths a second chance following a first-time nonviolent offense.

RESTITUTION

Court-ordered payment by the offender to the victim to cover tangible losses that occurred during or following the crime.

RESTITUTION

As the costs to crime victims continue to rise, it is estimated that victims suffer tangible losses of $105 billion dollars every year. Part of that loss is reimbursed by the very people who caused the harm in the first place. **Restitution** is defined as court-ordered payment by the offender to the victim (or the victim's family) to cover tangible losses that occurred during or following the crime. Figure 10.1 depicts two different beneficiaries (the community and the victim) and two different forms of payment (money and working without pay to provide services). The money or services offered by the offender help rehabilitate the victim financially. Restitution is also designed to be an act of atonement for the criminal (see Box 10.2 for how restitution can be used in restorative justice).

Restitution in History

Restitution has a long history. The Old Testament specified fivefold restitution for stealing and then killing an ox and fourfold restitution for stealing and killing a sheep. Double restitution was mandated for stealing (Exodus 21). Leviticus commanded that

FIGURE 10.1   *Typology of Restorative Justice Sanctions*

		RECIPIENT	
		Victim	Community
FORM OF PAYMENT	Monetary	Monetary Restitution	Fine or Day Fine
	Service	Personal Service Restitution	Community Service

Source: Burt Galaway. 1992. Restitution as Innovation or Unfilled Promise? In *Towards a Critical Victimology*, edited by Ezzat A. Fattah. New York: St. Martin's Press, p. 350.

BOX 10.2 USING RESTITUTION IN RESTORATIVE JUSTICE

Restitution can be used as a correctional tool in restorative justice, particularly during victim–offender mediation sessions. Five purposes of restitution include:

1. Restitution provides a less severe and more humane sanction for the offender.
2. Restitution aids the rehabilitation of the offender, and it integrates the punitive and rehabilitative purposes of the criminal law. Because the rationale incorporates the notion that punishment is related to the extent of damages done, it is perceived as just by offenders and allows them a sense of accomplishment as they complete the requirements. Restitution also provides offenders with a socially appropriate, concrete way of expressing their guilt and atoning for their offenses.
3. Restitution benefits the criminal justice system by providing an easily administered sanction that reduces demands on the system.
4. Restitution may reduce the need for vengeance in the administration of criminal law because offenders are perceived as responsible people taking active steps to make amends for their wrongdoing.
5. Restitution provides redress for crime victims.

Source: Burt Galaway. 1992. Restitution as Innovation or Unfilled Promise? In *Towards a Critical Victimology*, edited by Ezzat A. Fattah. New York: St. Martin's Press, pp. 347–371.

restitution plus an additional fifth be made by robbers (Leviticus 6). The Code of Hammurabi, developed between 1792 and 1750 B.C., mandated thirtyfold restitution if the victim was a "god" or a "palace," and tenfold restitution if the victim was a "villein" (a low-status laborer).

British philosopher Jeremy Bentham (1748–1833) prescribed restitution as an essential means of making the punishment fit the crime. In the mid-1800s, Quaker prison reformer Elizabeth Fry viewed repaying the victim as a step toward offender rehabilitation. The authority of courts to grant restitution originates from federal statutes. From 1925 to 1982, restitution could only be imposed as a condition of probation, and it was strictly discretionary. One of the earliest proponents of restitution was Stephen Schafer, who in the 1960s argued that restitution must be an integral part of the criminal justice system to elevate the victim's importance. Schafer believed that the criminal justice system had become too centered on the offender and the state's interests, and the role of the crime victim seemed to have become lost in the process. As the victim rights movement gained momentum, the Federal Victim Witness Protection Act (VWPA) of 1982 helped by broadening the use of restitution to the offense of conviction. In the 1990s, Congress passed a series of three acts to increase the offenses for which restitution could be collected:

1992	Mandatory provision for courts to impose restitution for back child support
1994	Violence against Women Act passed to mandate restitution in cases of sexual abuse, sexual exploitation of children, domestic violence, and telemarketing fraud
1996	Mandatory Victims Restitution Act passed to require that restitution be imposed for violent crimes and Title 18 property offenses, and as a sentencing option in juvenile delinquency cases (Office for Victims of Crime 2002).

More recently, states are moving toward greater use of restitution through notifying the victim of the right to request restitution, and ensuring that the courts order the restitution.

Losses Eligible for Compensation

States have broadened the types of losses eligible for compensation as well as the parties eligible to receive restitution. For example, restitution is available for the purpose of lost income as a result of physical injury or time in court, medical expenses, transportation to and from the courthouse, necessary child care during litigation, expenses involving the investigation and prosecution of the case, counseling sessions, sexual assault exams, human immunodeficiency virus (HIV) testing, occupational and rehabilitative therapy, moving expenses, case-related travel and meal expenses, and burial expenses. Restitution may be ordered for psychological counseling in cases in which the victim suffered physical injury (*United States v. Laney* 1999). Restitution is limited to the replacement value of direct or actual losses as a result of the crime and cannot be ordered for losses defined as indirect or consequential, such as victims' attorney fees.

Eligible parties may include the victim or the victim's family (in cases of homicide). Eligible organizations that may receive restitution include those that provided medical care, shelter, or counseling to the victim. Many states authorize the collection of interest on the unpaid restitution amount, varying from between 6 percent and 10 percent per year (Office for the Victims of Crime 2002).

Victims typically apply for restitution through the prosecutor's office. To receive restitution, the victim must press charges and agree to testify if necessary. Restitution is declared as a victim right in 19 state constitutions (AK, AZ, CA, CT, ID, IL, LA, MI, MO, MT, NM, NC, OK, OR, RI, SC, TN, TX, and WI), even when the offender has been incarcerated. Despite the mandatory policy, victims are more likely to get reimbursed if the offender is sentenced to a community sanction so that he or she can work to pay the victim back. In other states where restitution is defined as offender rehabilitation, restitution is forfeited if the offender goes to prison.

Problems Associated with Restitution

Restitution remains underutilized in both misdemeanor and felony cases. Nationally, courts order restitution in only 14 percent of felony convictions, with the highest rate for property offenses (26 percent of the time), and only 13 percent of all violent offenses (Durose and Langan 2004). Restitution is more often required for probationers than for people who are sentenced to prison. About one-third of probationers are required to pay restitution, with the average restitution ordered at $3,368 (Cohen 1995). Even though restitution may not often be ordered even when it becomes mandatory, a Pennsylvania study of 170,260 restitution-eligible cases determined that restitution was ordered for the appropriate offenders and that

> the odds of receiving an order of restitution were significantly greater for property than person crimes, for offenders with no or low prior records, for female offenders, and for White offenders. (Ruback, Ruth, and Shaffer 2005, p. 332)

One barrier to obtaining restitution is the victim's lack of participation in the justice process and lack of education that restitution is available. Many victims fail to request restitution or have not retained documentation showing their losses. Three other problems associated with restitution are indigence of the defendant, determining the restitution amount, and collecting restitution.

INDIGENT OFFENDERS. If the defendant is indigent and cannot pay, courts generally cannot cite the defendant for contempt or send the defendant to prison. However, indigence at the time of sentencing does not entitle the offender to immunity from restitution; it is more dependent on the offender's future ability to pay (*United States v. Bachsian* 1993). If the defendant is able to pay but refuses, then incarceration is valid. In the federal system, if an incarcerated federal prisoner has restitution to pay and has the ability to pay, parole release can be contingent upon the prisoner first paying off the entire restitution amount while incarcerated (U.S. Parole Commission 2003). There are other standards in some state jurisdictions. For example, an Indiana court ruled that incarcerating a probationer for failure to pay depends solely on the type of probationary sentence. If restitution is ordered as a *suspended* probationary sentence, the defendant could be imprisoned for being unable to pay. If restitution is ordered as part of an *executed* probationary sentence, the defendant cannot be imprisoned for failure to pay (*Wooden v. State*, 2001).

Declaring bankruptcy no longer excuses offenders from paying restitution. A federal statute declared that restitution orders are not dischargeable in Chapter 13 bankruptcies (11 U.S.C.A., sec 1328(a)(3)). A Texas Criminal Appeals court extended this same line of reasoning to Chapter 7 bankruptcy cases (*Cabla v. State* 1999).

DETERMINING THE RESTITUTION AMOUNT. In restorative justice cases, restitution amounts are determined at the victim–offender mediation session. In traditional criminal or civil cases, the court sets restitution amounts according to harm caused to the victim and the defendant's ability to pay based on full disclosure of assets and liabilities. Probation officers who complete presentence investigation (PSI) reports can suggest a restitution amount to the judge. To accurately determine a restitution amount, probation officers consider:

- Whether restitution is discretionary or mandatory (usually defined by offense of conviction)
- The victims of the offense of conviction
- The harms to the victim that are directly caused by the offense of conviction
- The harms and costs that qualify for restitution
- The effect of a plea agreement on the restitution amount (Goodwin 2001)

The offender's financial resources, existing financial obligations, and ability to pay are considered, as well as whether or not the victim was insured or was partially at fault. The defendant usually has the opportunity prior to sentencing to challenge the victim's claims or the amount of restitution recommended in the PSI.

Because it is often difficult to accurately establish a fair restitution amount, the government has the burden to prove, based on preponderance of the evidence, that the victim did suffer the harm for which the victim is requesting restitution from the offender (Goodwin 2001). The amount of restitution must be based on expenses the victim incurred by the time of sentencing and can be based only on the offense for which the offender was actually convicted.

COLLECTING RESTITUTION. Collecting restitution is the responsibility of probation officers, day reporting centers, and restitution centers. The entity responsible for collecting restitution acts as both a finance officer and a collection agent by determining the weekly or monthly installment payment schedule and making sure that the victim receives the money. Offenders who get too far behind on payments, or who are able to pay but refuse to do so, might be reassigned to a formal collection agency.

How successful are agencies in collecting restitution? A Bureau of Justice Statistics study reported that 60 percent of felony offenders had paid restitution in full by the time they completed their sentence (Langan and Cunniff 1992). Other studies indicate that collection rates vary between one-third and half of offenders (Ruback and Bergstrom 2006).

INCREASING RESTITUTION COLLECTION RATES. Victim–offender mediation sessions in cases using restorative justice may show some promise of increasing the number of offenders who succeed in making all of their restitution payments. Youthful offenders who participated in victim–offender mediation sessions were significantly more likely to complete restitution payments (81 percent) than a similar group of youth offenders who did not participate in VOM (57 percent completion) (Umbreit and Coates 1993).

One Illinois study determined that probationers who received a notification letter were significantly more likely to pay restitution than probationers who did not receive such a letter or who were not employed (Lurigio and Davis 1990). The letter instructed offenders on how to make a restitution payment and how much was owed, and warned them of the consequences for failing to make payments. This seems to suggest that minimal effort needs to be taken by probation officers to increase the likelihood that restitution, or a portion thereof, will be collected from offenders.

Effectiveness of Restitution

Adult probation cases in Pennsylvania indicated that probationers who made their restitution payments were also less likely to be rearrested compared to probationers who did not comply. The researchers suggest that this is not an indicator of the effectiveness of restitution per se, but they found that people who were already integrated in the community were more likely to comply with restitution (Outlaw and Ruback 1999).

A second study assessed recidivism rates using a predefined group of prison inmates who owed restitution on their case. Out of this group, inmates were selected randomly to be released to the Minnesota Restitution Center to take part in paying the restitution. The control group remained in prison and did not pay the restitution. The study found that there was "no difference in the likelihood of return to prison between the two groups. The restitution group, however, was somewhat more likely to have been returned to prison for technical parole violations, whereas the control group was more likely to have been returned to prison for a new offence" (Galaway 1992, p. 357). The same offenders in these two groups were tracked for 16 months after their release. Members of the restitution group had fewer convictions and were employed for more of the time than members of the control group. So it seems that inmates who owe restitution can effectively pay restitution through a restitution center. Similar results have been found with experimental studies of youths in restitution and comparison groups (Schneider 1986).

VICTIM AND PUBLIC VIEWS TOWARD RESTITUTION. Victim–offender reconciliation projects (VORP) require that the victim agree to meet with the offender, and restitution is made a large part of the incentive for victim participation. In a two-year study of VORP with juvenile property offenders in Minnesota, 55 percent of victims agreed to meet with the offender. Out of the VORP sessions, 95 percent of the meetings resulted in mutual agreement, with a 93 percent completion rate (Galaway 1992, p. 354).

In another study, victims and juvenile offenders were asked their perceptions on the "fairness" of restitution as a punishment for juvenile offenders. A vast majority of both offenders and victims reported that paying restitution was fair, and many preferred restitution to other punishments (Novack, Galaway, and Hudson 1980, pp. 63–69). The general public is also supportive of restitution as a community sanction, especially when informed of the cost of incarceration versus community corrections punishments (Galaway 1992).

COMMUNITY SERVICE

Community service has been called "the most underused intermediate sanction in the United States" (Tonry 1998, p. 89). **Community service** is defined as unpaid service to the public to compensate society for harm done by the offender. Community service is typically ordered by the judge as a part of probation, and the place of work is chosen by either the judge or the supervising officer. Community service might consist of working for a tax-supported or nonprofit agency such as a hospital, public park, or library, or for a poverty or public works program. The most frequent type of community service work is picking up roadside litter, doing landscape maintenance, removing graffiti, or painting buildings. Some work assignments have trucks or vans that transport work crews to the site where they are supervised for the day, but most assignments require the offender to take the initiative and report to complete the service order.

History of Community Service

Community service first began in the United States as an organized program in 1966 in Alameda County, California. This initiative was created as a substitute for paying fines for low-income female traffic offenders. The women worked without pay in lieu of their fine and avoided jail for fine nonpayment. Because of the positive attention this program received, hundreds of community service programs were established in the 1970s, especially for juveniles and nonviolent adults. In the United States, community service developed as an alternative to fines or as an additional condition of probation (Tonry 1999a).

THE ENGLISH MODEL.   Between 40 and 240 hours of community service suffices in England and Wales as an acceptable alternative to prison. Special community service officers administer the sanction. The English model became popular in other areas of Europe, such as Scotland and the Netherlands. The United States did not follow the English model, believing instead that community service was not punitive enough to substitute for prison. It is not uncommon to see U.S. judges order between 100 and 1,000 hours of community service in addition to other probation conditions (Tonry 1999a). This difference in American perceptions of community service demonstrates that, in comparison with most other countries in the world, community corrections sanctions are more punitive (and are not just reflected in long prison sentences).

Purpose of Community Service

Like monetary restitution, community service is both punitive and rehabilitative. It is punitive in that the offender's time and freedom are partially restricted until the work is completed. It is rehabilitative in the sense that it allows offenders to do something constructive, to increase their self-esteem, to reduce their isolation from society, and to benefit society through their efforts. In comparison with restitution, community service requires neither that there be an identifiable victim nor that the victim be cooperative in the prosecution process.

Furthermore, community service provides an alternative sanction for poor offenders who are unable to afford significant monetary sanctions or for those whose financial resources are so great that monetary restitution has no punitive or rehabilitative effect (del Carmen et al. 1989). Community service is a good example of a restorative justice program, and it can also be used to divert offenders from having a formal conviction on their record.

Prevalence of Community Service

Community service was reportedly used in at least 34 states as a sentencing alternative. In a study of 79,000 felons, Langan and Cunniff (1992) reported that 14 percent of felons had a special condition requiring community service, whereas another study five years later estimated that number to be just 6 percent of all felons (DiMascio 1997).

This nationwide estimate appears to differ widely by region. For example, community service is used in Texas as a condition of probation in 76 percent of cases, most commonly with drug and property offenders. Although community service is used as a jail alternative, it is rarely or never used as a sole sanction (Caputo 2005). The number of hours of community service varies depending on the nature and seriousness of the offense. For example, Texas provides for the following community service hours for probation (Texas Code of Criminal Procedure, Art. 42.12 Sec. 22(a)(1)):

PUNISHMENT RANGE	MAXIMUM HOURS	MINIMUM HOURS
First-degree felony	1,000	320
Second-degree felony	800	240
Third-degree felony	600	160
State jail felony	400	120
Class A misdemeanor	200	80
Class B misdemeanor	100	24

Community service orders ranged from 20 to 600 hours, with the average number of hours at 230 for felons and 60 for misdemeanants. In most jurisdictions, the offender's employment status must be considered in determining the community service schedule, in that employed offenders must be able to work and retain gainful employment, so they are limited to 16 hours of community service per week. Unemployed offenders can perform up to 32 community service hours per week (Caputo 2005). Offenders in some jurisdictions may be able to "work off" fines by performing community service in lieu of the fine or, with judicial permission, in lieu of incarceration. In Texas, eight hours of community service is equivalent to one day of jail confinement regardless of the offense committed (Caputo 2005).

Effectiveness of Community Service

Community service has always had wide public support, but scant attention has been paid to research evaluating the effectiveness of community service. Community service had positive effects on federal offenders in Georgia and for members of the general public (see Box 10.3). Many nonprofit organizations, such as churches, homeless

BOX 10.3 COMMUNITY CORRECTIONS UP CLOSE •

COMMUNITY SERVICE OF FEDERAL OFFENDERS

Carl worked as a mail carrier for the U.S. Post Office. He repeatedly threw away all third-class mail in a dumpster because he deemed it a nuisance to his customers. When his crime was detected, he was fired and prosecuted for a misdemeanor. He was ordered to pay restitution and to perform 300 hours of community service. The presentence investigation indicated that Carl was one quarter short of obtaining a B.A. degree in mathematics, and he was a nonviolent misdemeant. The community service probation officer assigned Carl to work a seven-hour shift once per week at an elementary school for 42 weeks. He was initially assigned to playground and lunchroom duties, but his knowledge and leadership qualities were so impressive that he became assigned as a math tutor for three boys in the third grade. Because part of the boys' learning problem was due to lack of

parental discipline, Carl met with the parents of the boys to discuss the problem. The boys improved their math grades and overall classroom performance. At the end of his community service, Carl was offered a job as a teacher's aide. Although he turned down the offer, Carl felt he had touched the lives of a few kids and had received much more in return. Because of the success of Carl's placement, the courts have expanded community service to four other schools.

Carl's case is one example of the many federal offenders who must complete community service. In a 10-year period in the Northern District of Georgia, offenders worked 300,000 hours and finished projects valued at over $3 million. The success of community service programs depends on good agency relationships between the probation department and outside community agencies. Success also

depends on the placement skills and monitoring from probation officers. The officers must be attuned to whether the court intends the community service to be punitive or rehabilitative. The placement also must match the skills and risk level of the offender.

Richard Maher, a supervising U.S. probation officer of the Northern District of Georgia, reports that over a three-year period, 5 percent of probationers who are sentenced to community service later accept paid jobs with their placement or through contacts established while doing community service work. Community service saves money, provides workers for nonprofit agencies, and provides opportunities for offenders.

Source: Richard J. Maher. 1994. Community Service: A Good Idea That Works. *Federal Probation* 58(2): 20–23; and Richard J. Maher. 1997. Community Service: A Way for Offenders to Make Amends. *Federal Probation* 61(1): 26–28.

shelters, libraries, and the U.S. Forest Service, have benefited from the labor provided by offenders.

Agencies report that the completion rates vary from 50 percent to a high of 85 percent, depending on how community service is enforced (Anderson 1998). One of the main reasons offenders do not complete community service orders is the lack of enforcement on completing the hours before the probation sentence is served. Rarely are probationers extended on probation because they fail to complete community service hours. The second main reason for not completing the hours is if the judge revokes probation for a new arrest or technical violation and the offender is resentenced or transferred (Caputo 2005).

As the search continues for less costly and more effective methods of dealing with offenders, community service has the potential to be a growing trend in U.S. corrections. One difficult problem with evaluating and expanding community service programs is that most do not have clear goals and objectives. In expanding their use, the following must be delineated:

- Is the purpose of community service to reduce recidivism, to divert offenders, or both?
- Should community service be used instead of or in addition to other sanctions?
- Should community service be expanded for prison-bound offenders?
- How is the value of community service work calculated compared to days in jail or fine amounts?

There are no easy answers to these questions. The potential for greater use of community service through offender labor as an alternative to jail or prison is limitless if developed without further increasing community risk.

FINES

FINE

A fixed monetary sanction defined by statute and imposed by a judge, depending on the seriousness of the crime.

VICTIM COMPENSATION FUND

A state fund that dispenses compensation to victims of violent crimes and paid for by offenders who are convicted.

A **fine** is defined as a monetary sanction imposed by the judge, with the amount depending on the severity of the offense. There are three types of fines that we will discuss: fixed fines, forfeitures, and day fines.

The first type is a fixed monetary amount that is referred to in the field and in this text as a "fine." Ninety percent of fines go to victim/witness assistance programs or a general **victim compensation fund,** which is a state fund that dispenses compensation to victims of violent crimes for losses not covered by restitution (Ruback and Bergstrom 2006). A fine is viewed as a punishment, with the failure to pay grounds for revocation or issuance of a warrant.

A fine can be imposed as a sole penalty, as in the case of traffic offenses, or accompanied by probation, an intermediate sanction, or incarceration. Fines have been used in European criminal justice systems as a primary sanction. For example, in Germany, more than 80 percent of all crimes committed by adults are punished by a fine as the only penalty. However, fines in the United States have generally been underused and their collection not well enforced.

Prevalence of Fines

Fines are used in only 25 percent of all state felony cases and in 13 percent of federal cases (Durose and Langan 2004). When fines are used, they are in addition to a probation sentence. In the federal system, fines are used as a stand-alone or sole means of punishment in nearly one-third of misdemeanor offenses, but less than 1 percent

Fines can be used as a punishment for offenses ranging from traffic violations to felony crimes. Fines for serious offenses are typically accompanied by probation or incarceration. Fines tend to be underused because their collection is not well enforced.

© Leanne Fiftal Alarid

of federal felony cases (United States Department of Justice 2005a). Fines are routinely imposed as the primary sanction for organizational or corporate defendants in cases of corporate or white-collar crime. Organizational fines range from thousands of dollars into the millions. One study found that when a fine was imposed in individual-level felony cases, the most common fine was $500, but fines ranged from $28 to as much as $10,000, with an average of $1,000 (Vigorita 2002).

Fines are assessed for offenders who are eligible for a community sentence and have the ability to pay. State-level judges rarely have information on the defendant's ability to pay, so eligibility rests largely on offense severity and prior criminal record. Employed offenders are more likely to be assessed fines than unemployed offenders. Judges who are reluctant to use fines point out that offenders tend to be poor and may have no means other than additional criminal activity to obtain the funds to pay their fines. Fixed fines may overly burden a poor person but be less consequential to an affluent offender. When the financial penalty is too high, however, offenders are significantly more likely to revoke their probation (Ruback and Bergstrom 2006).

Revoking Probation for Fine Nonpayment

Fine collection rates vary, ranging from 14 percent (Parent 1990) to nearly two-thirds of probationers satisfying their financial obligations in full (Allen and Treger 1994). One legal issue is the actions that may be taken as a result of nonpayment. A defendant can avoid paying a fine, in part or in full, if the defendant can show that he or she is unable to pay. In *Bearden v. Georgia* (1983), the U.S. Supreme Court held that probation cannot be revoked solely because of an offender's inability to pay a fine or restitution. The Court said that revocation based on indigence violates the equal protection clause of the Fourteenth Amendment. The Court distinguished, however, between indigence (inability) and unwillingness (refusal) to pay. Unwillingness to pay court-ordered restitution or fines despite a probationer's ability to do so may result in revocation. Statutes in most states and the federal system provide for allowing a flexible payment schedule if the defendant is unable to pay the entire fine immediately, modifying the sentence to reduce the fine, and in some cases forgoing the fine and imposing an alternative sanction. The federal system mandates that federal prisoners shall not be released on parole or mandatory release until the fine is paid in full (U.S. Parole Commission 2003). Since many fines go unpaid in the state system, the American Bar Association (1994) recommended that state legislatures designate a public official to collect the fines and authorize that official either to file a court order holding the ex-offender in criminal contempt of court or to file a civil lawsuit against the offender for the remaining fine balance.

Forfeitures

A **forfeiture** is a "government seizure of property because it is illegal contraband, was illegally obtained, was acquired with resources that were illegally obtained, or was used in connection with an illegal activity. Forfeiture can be either criminal or civil" (Ruback and Bergstrom 2006, p. 257). Whereas criminal forfeiture occurs after a conviction, civil forfeiture can occur when proof by preponderance of the evidence is met. Preponderance of the evidence is a lower standard of proof. The purpose of a forfeiture is to make certain that offenders cannot keep illegal property and make a profit, and to discourage criminals from using houses and businesses to conduct criminal transactions. Unlike a traditional fixed fine, the Supreme Court does not consider forfeiture to be a punishment. However, a forfeiture is limited in that it must not be "grossly disproportionate to the gravity of the defendant's offense [or else] the

FORFEITURE

A government seizure of property that was illegally obtained, was acquired with resources that were illegally obtained, or was used in connection with an illegal activity.

forfeiture would violate the excessive fines clause" of the Eighth Amendment (Ruback and Bergstrom 2006, p. 257). The authors estimate that 40,000 forfeitures occur every year, 80 percent of which are civil and the remaining 20 percent of which are from criminal cases.

Day Fines

Using fixed fines in criminal sentencing presents difficulties due to offenders' socioeconomic differences. For this reason, a pilot program began in Staten Island, New York, to use fines in a different way, based on a system used in many European countries. **Day fines,** otherwise known as structured fines, are court fines figured as multiples of the offender's daily income. For example, a school custodian and a stockbroker, both convicted of the same offense, with the same criminal history and identical risk factors, would pay different amounts because they earn different amounts of money. The stockbroker, who makes an annual income of $100,000 per year, would pay more than the custodian, who makes $25,000 per year. Based on a day fine, the stockbroker would be fined, say, $10,000 and the custodian would pay $2,500. Here is how the system works. The two offenders would be fined the same multiple or percentage of income, which would be determined by their crime and prior history. In this way, day fines would provide the same degree of financial hardship to each offender. Using the previous example, in a tariff or conventional fine situation, the stockbroker and the custodian may have received fines of the same amount. Thus, day fines overcome many of the shortcomings associated with fixed fines.

Evaluation of Day Fines

Day fines were first evaluated in Staten Island, New York, and Milwaukee, Wisconsin (McDonald, Greene, and Worzella 1992). In Staten Island, day fines were used only for misdemeanor cases, and fines were limited to a maximum of $1,000. Lawyers and judges alike were in full acceptance of this system. The study found that in comparison with fines assessed and collected before the study began, the average fine amount increased, as did the proportion of fines collected. Seventy percent of those assessed day fines paid in full, 13 percent were resentenced to community service or to a jail sentence averaging 11 days, and 14 percent of offenders absconded. As a result of this study, the New York legislature examined the possibility of removing the cap of $1,000 (which reflected the old tariff system) to make it possible to bring in more revenue under the day fine system (up to 18 percent more revenue). The researchers found that a workable day fine system could be developed for regular use in courts (p. 25).

The Milwaukee project involved the impact of day fines on noncriminal violations. There were two groups (an experimental and a control group), and simultaneous comparisons could be made between regular fines and day fines. The results were somewhat disappointing as 59 percent of the day fine group and 61 percent of the conventional fine group failed to pay in full. However, of those who paid in full, 37 percent were from the day fine group and 25 percent from the conventional group. Using day fines did seem to benefit the collection of fines from the poorest offenders. Offenders with monthly incomes less than $197 were more likely to pay a day fine (33 percent) than a regular fine (14 percent). Day fines do not seem to deter future criminal conduct any more than a conventional fine. Within nine months after sentencing, the evaluators found no significant difference in recidivism between the experimental group (day fines) and the control group (tariff fines). Furthermore, the county treasury received less in total collections overall, which resulted in resistance to further use of day fines, and the project was abandoned (pp. 6–7).

As a result of the earlier studies, other pilot project sites were selected for evaluation in Connecticut, Iowa, Oregon, and Phoenix. Day fines in Phoenix were used as a substitute for probation for low-risk offenders who were not in need of formal supervision. Potential candidates of the Financial Assessment Related to Employability (FARE) program are identified by probation officers during the completion of the presentence investigation report. FARE offenders are supervised by a special FARE probation officer, whose primary job is fine collections. FARE was considered a success because a high rate of probationers paid their fines, saving probation officer time (Turner and Petersilia 1996a). Despite these encouraging results, day fines have not caught on in the United States as an alternative sanction.

FEES AND COSTS

A fee is differentiated from a fine, in that a **fee** is a court-imposed reimbursement that the offender pays for the administration of the criminal justice system. Fees are also known as "costs" in other regions of the country, but the terms have the same meaning and we will use "fees" in this text. Examples of fees (see Box 10.4) include $250 for DNA testing, prosecution/court costs of $200, and corrections supervision fees of $40 per month—each of which may be itemized and may depend on the type of offense and type of sentence (Ruback and Bergstrom 2006). Electronic monitoring and global positioning system technology incur additional monthly fees. Probation fees were ordered in 55 percent of all Illinois cases, and probationers paid nearly three-fourths of the ordered amounts. Offenders in rural areas were more likely to be assessed fees than

FEE

A monetary amount imposed by the court to assist in administering the criminal justice system by the offender's repayment of debt accrued by the investigation, prosecution, and supervision of the case.

BOX 10.4   WHAT EXPENSES ARE DEFENDANTS REQUIRED TO PAY AS FEES?   •

Fees are the government's attempt to recover from individual offenders the expenses that were incurred in the investigation and prosecution of the defendant's case. Fee payment ranges greatly by jurisdiction from one state-mandated fee to up to 36 various county-based costs, not including what is mandated by the state (Ruback and Bergstrom 2006). One thing is clear: acquitted defendants do not pay fees. The lower courts are divided, however, on the legal costs for convicted offenders. Although some jurisdictions have fixed

court costs, others are variable depending on ability to pay.

Examples of fees, as they apply to the case, include court clerk, crime lab, fingerprint card, bail administration, DUI testing, drug testing, psychological evaluation, drug treatment evaluation, victim impact panel, highway safety class, electronic monitoring, and community service fees. The U.S. Supreme Court authorized repayment of legal fees for attorney's fees as a probation condition (*Fuller v. Oregon* 1974), appointed defense counsel for defendants who were later found

not to be indigent (*United States v. Angulo* 1988), and offender repayment of defense witness fees (*United States v. Dougherty* 1987). The high court has remained silent on the requirement of most other types of fees and court costs. To muddy the waters a bit more, most trial courts do not have any authority over parole conditions, so court costs are often assessed for probationers but not for parolees, unless the parole board is statutorily authorized to require repayment (some are, but most are not).

offenders in urban areas perhaps because officials have the time to enforce their collection or perhaps because these jurisdictions rely more heavily on reimbursement if they have a lower available tax base from which to draw (Ruback and Bergstrom 2006)

A fee is not considered punitive and is therefore subject to different legal standards for nonpayment than a fine. Courts have held that it is unacceptable to require an indigent defendant to pay court costs. In addition, the Seventh Circuit Court of Appeals held that the federal district court was not authorized to order a defendant to pay fines to private charities because fines are paid to the government, not to private parties (*United States v. Wolff* 1996).

Regardless of the type of monetary sanction, effective collection techniques are important for restitution, fines, fees, and forfeitures. The federal government recommended that there be:

- A short time period for payment (three months), which increases the likelihood of full payment
- A convenient location to make payments (police stations, probation departments, night deposit boxes outside the court, payment by mail, and so on)
- A wide variety of payment methods (credit cards, debit cards, cash, personal checks, money orders)
- Discounts for early payment
- Surcharges for late payment
- Overdue payment reminder notices in the mail or by telephone
- Consequences for nonpayment (Bureau of Justice Assistance 1996, pp. 29–33)

TOP THINGS YOU SHOULD KNOW

- Community justice is a philosophy of using the community to control and reduce crime through community policing, community courts, and neighborhood-based probation.
- Once a crime has been committed, restorative justice emphasizes the offender taking responsibility to repair the harm done to the victim and to the surrounding community.
- Restorative justice is more victim centered than traditional methods, involving the victim and the community throughout the whole justice process.
- Restorative justice programs rely heavily on community partners and volunteers to carry out mediation, reparation boards, face-to-face meetings with the victim, and victim impact classes. Present patterns in the use of restitution still vary widely although observers predict greater emphasis on restitution in the future, particularly in conjunction with other sentences.
- Community service also holds some promise, but at present it is not well enforced.
- The use of fixed fines is still perceived as either too lenient or problematic for impoverished offenders sinking deeper into poverty.
- Forfeitures and day fines are two other types of fines.
- Although asset forfeitures have greatly increased, day fines did not catch on as an approved community sanction.
- Collection rates of the various economic sanctions remains a huge unresolved issue at present.

DISCUSSION QUESTIONS

1. How is restorative justice different from traditional justice approaches?
2. Using the restorative justice approach, what would you require as a sentence for a 17-year-old offender who forcefully broke a window to get into a house and stole property valued at $1,000 when the occupants were at work?
3. How is community service used as a correctional tool?
4. How do monetary restitution and community service differ? How are they alike?
5. Does restitution provide for integration of both offender and victim in the criminal justice system?
6. How can restitution be used in the juvenile justice system?
7. Is it fair to require that probationers pay court costs, but not parolees? Why or why not?
8. How specific do statutes need to be in itemizing required expenses?
9. Why is it that the collection of fines is treated differently from the collection of fees? Should they be treated the same if they are not paid in full?
10. How does a day fine overcome the problems associated with fixed fines? Why has the day fine idea *not* caught on in American criminal justice?

 WEBSITES

Rethinking Crime and Punishment

  http://www.rethinking.org.uk/press/march03speechCSR.htm

National Center for Victims of Crime

  http://www.ncvc.org/ncvc/main.aspx

Restorative Justice

  http://www.restorativejustice.org

The Center for Restorative Justice and Peacekeeping, University of Minnesota

  http://rjp.umn.edu

The Centre for Restorative Justice, Simon Fraser University, Canada

  http://www.sfu.ca/crj

Fresno Pacific University's Center for Peacemaking and Conflict Studies
Website Links Dealing with Restorative Justice

  http://fresno.edu/pacs/

The Purpose of Economic Sanctions

  http://www.econlib.org/library/Enc/Sanctions.html

Community Service and Restitution Programs in Alberta, Canada

  http://www.solgen.gov.ab.ca/corrections/alternative_measures.aspx?id=2733

CHAPTER 10

CASE STUDY EXERCISE

Restorative Justice

In the following scenarios, conditions of the offender's supervision will provide for a form of restorative justice. For each of the following cases, discuss one or more community service and/or restorative justice referrals or conditions that would aid the offender in complying with the community sentence.

CASE A

An 18-year-old male with no prior record has been convicted of a "hate" crime. He, with two juveniles, burned a cross in the yard of a church and painted derogatory racial messages on the front door of the church. Most of the church congregation is African American; the offender is white and reports affiliation with a white suprema-cist organization. The offender states he began his involvement with the organization only recently and became involved in the offense as a part of his initiation into the organization.

CASE B

A 40-year-old woman is convicted of a drug trafficking offense. She has little prior legitimate employment history and has prior convictions for other offenses involving sales of illegal drugs. Despite her lack of legitimate earnings, this offender has acquired many assets. Most of the assets have been forfeited as the prosecutor has proven they were purchased with funds obtained in illegal activities. The offender denies illegal drug usage. She states she was involved in the sale of illegal drugs for the money. She shows no remorse for her crime and has no understanding of the harm her criminal conduct has on society. In fact, she quickly states she believes her sale of illegal drugs is a "victimless" crime.

CASE C

A college professor has been granted diversion after an arrest for driving under the influence. He states he was taking a prescription medication and had three drinks at a colleague's home before driving home. The driver realized his judgment was impaired while he was driving and pulled to the shoulder of the road. Law enforce-ment observed him driving erratically and nearly driving in the ditch before bringing his vehicle to a stop on the shoulder of the road. They questioned him, and he admit-ted he had been drinking alcoholic beverages.

IV

Prisoner Reentry

About 95 percent of all prisoners will be released from prison someday, and most of them will reenter society on either mandatory supervision or discretionary parole release. In this text, as in most other texts, *parole* is a broad term that includes both discretionary and mandatory release. Reentry is a very broad term that means both the process of preparing oneself for release from prison, as well as the release into the community itself while remaining under community supervision. Parole supervision, mandatory supervision, and unconditional release are three methods by which prisoners reenter the community, and they will be the subject of the next three chapters.

Unconditional release is when prisoners reenter society without any supervision because they have served 100 percent of their sentence behind bars. Mandatory supervision has replaced discretionary parole in many states as a result of a change in sentencing philosophy and a decrease in prison rehabilitation programs. As in the case of probation, the number of parolees has outstripped funding for reentry and supervised release programs, which has led to higher caseloads and less supervision.

The structure of the discretionary paroling process—including the composition and selection of the parole board, caseloads, training, authority of field staff, and procedures used for the parole grant or revocation—varies considerably from jurisdiction to jurisdiction. The same is true for the use of parole. Some states continue to parole many adult prisoners, whereas legislative action in other states has abolished all discretionary parole release. Variations in the structure and use of the parole process, as well as the accompanying variations in sentencing structures from one jurisdiction to another, account in good part for the lack of agreement about the legal status of parole across the country.

The next three chapters focus on different methods of release from prison. The history and philosophy of reentry began as discretionary parole, and have over time been substituted and even replaced by mandatory release. This history is the subject of Chapter 11. Chapter 12 pays particular attention to issues involved in the preparation for prisoner reentry. Chapter 13 examines parole conditions and legal aspects of community supervision as well as what happens when these conditions are not met. It also reviews the effectiveness of parole.

Introduction

The Origins of Parole
Manuel Montesinos
Georg Michael Obermaier
Alexander Maconochie
Sir Walter Crofton and the Irish
  System

**Development of Parole in the
United States**
Reward for Good Conduct
Postrelease Supervision
Zebulon R. Brockway and the
  Indeterminate Sentence
Reducing the Cost of
  Incarceration

**The Medical Model:
1930–1960**
Changing Public Opinion

A Philosophical Change
Origins of Modern Determinate
  Sentencing
The Justice Model

**Changing of the Guard: From
Discretionary Parole to
Mandatory Release**

Parole Today
Characteristics of Parolees
Functions of Parole

Top Things You Should Know

11

The History of Parole: From Its Origin to the Present

What You Will Learn in This Chapter

- *How transportation and ticket-of-leave influenced the development of parole*
- *How parole was inspired by the work of Alexander Maconochie at the penal colony of Norfolk Island*
- *How parole was subsequently implemented by Walter Crofton in Ireland and by Zebulon R. Brockway in New York's Elmira Reformatory*
- *The history of parole into the modern era, including the criticisms that nearly led to its demise*
- *The role discretionary parole and mandatory supervised release play in reentry today*

INTRODUCTION

About 600,000 state and federal prisoners reenter the community every year—120,000 of them (20 percent) are **unconditional releases,** receiving no supervision whatsoever after they leave prison because they have served their full sentence behind bars. In prison language, this is known as "maxing out" or "killing your number." The remaining 480,000 prisoners who reenter the community do so under a period of supervised release. With a total of 765,500 parolees already on supervision currently across the country, most parolees released this year will be off supervision completely by next year, with the rest of the offenders off parole within two years (Petersilia 2000a). **Parole** is the conditional release of a convicted offender from a correctional institution, under the continued custody of the state, to serve the remainder of his or her sentence in the community under supervision. Parole is a broad concept that in this text refers to release both according to mandatory laws or by a parole board.

Individuals on **mandatory release** (otherwise known as "postrelease supervision" or "supervised release") enter the community automatically at the expiration of their maximum term minus credited time off for good behavior. Mandatory release is decided not by a parole board but by legislative statute or good-time laws.

In contrast to mandatory release, individuals released on **discretionary release** enter the community because members of a parole board have decided that the prisoners have earned the privilege of being released from prison while still remaining under supervision of an indeterminate sentence. (Chapter 12 focuses on the methods by which parole boards decide who should be released.) Parolees on both mandatory release and discretionary release are supervised by a parole officer and adhere to similar conditions. If these conditions are not followed, either type of parolee (mandatory or discretionary) can be returned to prison for the remainder of the sentence. Figure 11.1 shows the types of release and how their numbers have changed over the years. You can see that mandatory release has increased, whereas prisoners leaving prison on discretionary release has decreased.

THE ORIGINS OF PAROLE

The English word *parole* is derived from the French **parole d'honneur,** meaning "word of honor." The French seem to prefer the term *conditional liberation* to the one borrowed from their language. In 1791, during the French Revolution, the Comte de

KEY TERMS

Unconditional release

Parole

Mandatory release

Discretionary release

Parole d'honneur

Alexander Maconochie

Transportation

Ticket-of-leave

Marks system

Norfolk Island

Sir Walter Crofton

The Irish system

Indeterminate sentence

Zebulon R. Brockway

Medical model

Just deserts

Justice model

Determinate sentence

Presumptive sentence

Medical parole

UNCONDITIONAL RELEASE

A type of release from prison without correctional supervision because the full sentence has been served behind bars. Also known as "maxing out" or "killing your number."

PAROLE

Release of a convicted offender from a penal or correctional institution, under the continual custody of the state, to serve the remainder of his or her sentence in the community under supervision, either by discretionary or mandatory release stipulations.

MANDATORY RELEASE

Conditional release to the community under a determinate sentence, that is automatic at the expiration of the minimum term of sentence minus any credited time off for good behavior.

DISCRETIONARY RELEASE

Conditional release because members of a parole board have decided that the prisoner has earned the privilege while still remaining under supervision of an indeterminate sentence.

PAROLE D'HONNEUR

French for "word of honor," from which the English word *parole* is derived.

FIGURE 11.1 *Releases from State Prison, by Method of Release, 1980–2003*

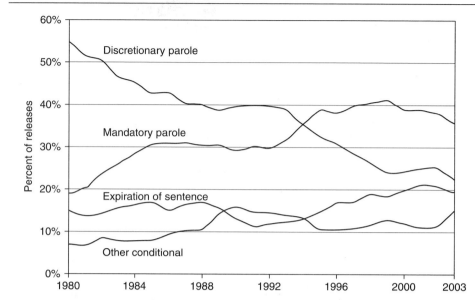

Note: Data are from the National Prisoners Statistics (*NPS*-1) series.

Source: Lauren E. Glaze and Seri Palla. 2005. *Probation and Parole in the United States, 2004*. Washington, DC: U.S. Department of Justice.

Mirabeau (Honore-Gabriel Rigueti) anticipated modern penal theories when he published a report based on the idea of reformation, which emphasized the principles of labor, segregation, rewards under a mark system, conditional liberation, and aid on discharge. Another Frenchman, Bonneville de Marsangy, public prosecutor of Versailles, published a book in 1847 in which he discussed conditional liberation, police supervision of discharged convicts, aid upon discharge, and rehabilitation. This book was distributed by the government to the members of both chambers of Parliament (Wines 1919).

Parole as a practice originated almost simultaneously with three European prison administrators: a Spaniard, Manuel Montesinos; a German, Georg Michael Obermaier; and an Englishman, Alexander Maconochie.

Manuel Montesinos

In 1835 Col. Manuel Montesinos was appointed governor of the prison at Valencia, Spain, which held about 1,500 convicts. He organized the institution using military-type discipline, and he encouraged prisoner vocational training and education. The novelty of his plan was that there were practically no officers to watch the prisoners, who nevertheless made few, if any, attempts to escape. Each prisoner could earn a one-third reduction in the term of his sentence by good behavior and positive accomplishments. The number of prisoner recommitments while Montesinos was governor was significantly reduced. Despite all his efforts, the law that allowed this program was subsequently repealed, and Montesinos ultimately resigned. Montesinos drew the following conclusions from his experiment:

> Self-respect is one of the most powerful sentiments of the human mind, since it is the most personal; and he who will not condescend, in some degree, according to circumstances, to flattery of it, will never attain his object by any amount of chastisement; the

effect of ill treatment being to irritate rather than to correct, and thus turn from reform instead of attracting to it. The moral object of penal establishments should not be so much to inflict punishment as to correct, to receive men idle and ill-intentioned and return them to society, if possible, honest and industrious citizens. (as quoted in Wines 1919, p. 194)

Georg Michael Obermaier

When Georg Michael Obermaier became governor of a prison in Munich, Germany, in 1842, he found approximately 700 rebellious prisoners being kept in order by more than 100 soldiers (Wines 1919). In a short time he gained the men's confidence, removed their chains, discharged nearly all of their guards, and appointed one of them superintendent of each of the industrial shops. His success in reforming prisoners was so great that reportedly only 10 percent of prisoners relapsed into crime after their discharge. He was aided by two favorable circumstances: Many of the men had no fixed term of imprisonment, and discharged inmates were supervised by prison aid societies.

Alexander Maconochie

Chief credit for developing early parole systems, however, goes to **Alexander Maconochie,** who was in charge of the English penal colony on Norfolk Island.

TRANSPORTATION OF ENGLISH PRISONERS TO AMERICA.   The **transportation** of English criminals to the American colonies evolved from a 1597 law that provided for the banishment of dangerous criminals. The government transported convicted felons to the American colonies as a partial solution to the poor economic conditions and widespread unemployment in England. The king approved the proposal to grant

Courtesy Michael Maconochie, London

Alexander Maconochie served as superintendent of the penal colony on Norfolk Island, where he and his family lived with 2,000 incorrigible convicts. Maconochie was best known for his early "marks system" and as a champion of prisoner rights and privileges to encourage good behavior. Although he was successful at transforming the lives of many convicts, his humane treatment of prisoners was politically unfavorable, and he was subsequently replaced.

ALEXANDER MACONOCHIE

A British naval captain who served as governor of the penal colony on Norfolk Island, who instituted a system of early release that was the forerunner of modern parole. Maconochie is known as the "father of parole."

TRANSPORTATION

The forced exile of convicted criminals. England transported convicted criminals to the American colonies until the Revolutionary War and afterward to Australia.

reprieves and stays of execution—pardons—to convicted felons who could physically be employed in the colonies.

Until 1717 the government had paid a fee to contractors for each prisoner transported. Under a new procedure adopted that year, the contractor was given "property in service," and the government took no interest in the welfare or behavior of the offender unless he or she violated the conditions of the pardon by returning to England before the sentence expired. Upon arrival in the colonies, the "services" of the prisoner were sold to the highest bidder, and thereafter the prisoner was an indentured servant.

TRANSPORTATION OF ENGLISH PRISONERS TO AUSTRALIA. The Revolutionary War brought an end to the practice of transporting criminals to America, but the transportation law was not repealed. Detention facilities in England became overcrowded, resulting in a more liberal granting of pardons. During a serious crime wave, the English public demanded enforcement of the transportation law, and Australia was designated as a convict settlement, with the first shipload arriving there in January 1788. Transportation to Australia differed from transportation to the American colonies in that the government incurred all expenses of transportation and maintenance, and the prisoners remained under government control instead of being indentured. The governor of New South Wales granted conditional pardons—setting deserving convicts free and giving them grants of land, and even assigning newly arrived convict laborers to them. In 1811 a policy was adopted that required prisoners to serve specific periods of time before becoming eligible to receive **ticket-of-leave** (for example, a seven-year sentence became eligible for the ticket-of-leave after four years, and those serving life sentences after eight years). However, there were no provisions for supervision of "ticket-of-leave men."

MARKS SYSTEM. In 1837 Alexander Maconochie, a retired British naval captain and professor of geography, proposed to the House of Commons a system whereby the duration of the sentence would be determined not by time but by the prisoner's industry and good conduct. He proposed a **marks system** by which "marks" or credits would be credited daily to prisoners in accordance with their behavior and the amount of labor they performed. As prisoners demonstrated evidence of good behavior and a good work ethic, their freedom and privileges gradually increased. Marks were deducted for negative behavior. Maconochie's system allowed prisoners to move from strict imprisonment, to labor in work gangs, through conditional release around the island, and finally to complete restoration of liberty (Morris 2002).

NORFOLK ISLAND. Maconochie was given the opportunity to test his mark system in 1840 when he was appointed superintendent of the notorious penal colony on **Norfolk Island,** 1,000 miles off the eastern coast of Australia. Norfolk Island was known to have 2,000 of the most incorrigible convicts; they had been sent there from other prisons in Britain and Ireland because they had committed crimes of violence while incarcerated (a "supermax" of the 1800s). Within a span of four years, Maconochie's system and humane treatment of the prisoners transformed their horrific lives into a peaceful orderly existence. Maconochie discontinued flogging and chain gangs and introduced adequate food, health care, disciplinary hearings, and reading material (Morris 2002).

Despite Maconochie's successes, many influential colonists in Australia who believed that convicts should be kept in irons and flogged saw Maconochie's treatment of prisoners as radical and lobbied the governor for Maconochie's dismissal. The governor was torn between his hope that Maconochie's experiment would succeed and his fear of the political power of the colonists who opposed the project.

TICKET-OF-LEAVE

A license or permit given to a convict as a reward for good conduct, which allowed him to go at large and work for himself before his sentence expired, subject to certain restrictions and revocable upon subsequent misconduct. A forerunner of parole.

MARKS SYSTEM

A theory of human motivation organized by Maconochie that granted credits for good behavior and hard work, or took away marks for negative behavior. Convicts used the credits or marks to purchase either goods or time (reduction in sentence).

NORFOLK ISLAND

The notorious British supermax penal colony 1,000 miles off the coast of Australia that housed the most incorrigible prisoners.

Maconochie was dismissed in 1844, and his experiment came to an abrupt end. As free settlers in Australia increased in number, they protested the use of the country as a dumping ground for prisoners. In 1867 transportation of prisoners from England to Australia was terminated (Morris 2002).

The years following saw an outbreak of crime and prison riots in England, which were attributed to poor prison administration and the lack of supervision of the ticket-of-leave men. The British public thus came to regard the ticket-of-leave system as a menace to public safety. A royal commission was appointed to investigate both areas, and the report resulted in policemen being given responsibility for supervising released prisoners. Later, a number of prisoner aid societies, supported in part by the government, were established.

Sir Walter Crofton and the Irish System

Sir Walter Crofton, who had studied Maconochie's innovations on Norfolk Island, became the administrator of the Irish prison system in 1854. Crofton adopted the use of the marks system inside prison. Under Crofton's administration, the **Irish system** became renowned for its three levels: strict imprisonment, indeterminate sentence, and ticket-of-leave. Each prisoner's classification was determined by the marks he or she had earned for good conduct and achievement in industry and education, a concept borrowed from Maconochie's experience on Norfolk Island.

The ticket-of-leave system was different from the one in England. The general written conditions of the Irish ticket-of-leave were supplemented with instructions designed for closer supervision and control and thus resembled the conditions of parole in the United States today. Ticket-of-leave men and women residing in rural areas were under police supervision, but a civilian employee called the inspector of released prisoners supervised those living in Dublin. The inspector had the responsibility of securing employment for the ticket-of-leave person, visiting his or her residence, and verifying employment. The Irish system of ticket-of-leave had the confidence and support of the public and of convicted criminals.

DEVELOPMENT OF PAROLE IN THE UNITED STATES

In the United States, parole was first tried in New York at Elmira Reformatory in 1876. Federal parole began in June 1910 because of legislation that established the first three federal penitentiaries. In 1930, a formalized federal parole board was created under the U.S. attorney general's office. In 1950, because of a larger prison population in the federal system, the parole board expanded and was placed under the Justice Department.

Four concepts justified the development of parole in the United States: (1) reduction in the length of incarceration as a reward for good conduct, (2) supervision of the parolee, (3) imposition of the indeterminate sentence, and (4) reduction in the rising cost of incarceration.

Reward for Good Conduct

Release as a result of a reduction in the time of imprisonment was always accompanied by a written agreement by which the prisoner would abide by the conditions specified by those authorizing the release. The agreement stipulated that any violation of the conditions would result in a return to the institution. The first legal recognition of shortening the term of imprisonment as a reward for good conduct in the United States was the 1817 good-time law in New York.

Postrelease Supervision

Volunteers and prison society members originally supervised those released from prison. The Philadelphia Society for Alleviating the Miseries of Public Prisons recognized the importance of caring for released prisoners as early as 1822. In 1851 the society appointed two agents to assist prisoners discharged from the Philadelphia County Prison and the penitentiary. The first public employees paid to assist released prisoners were appointed by the state of Massachusetts in 1845.

Zebulon R. Brockway and the Indeterminate Sentence

INDETERMINATE SENTENCE

A broad sentence in which the duration is not fixed by the court but is determined by a parole board after the prisoner has become rehabilitated. Release is discretionary.

ZEBULON R. BROCKWAY

The American prison reformer who introduced modern correctional methods, including parole, to the Elmira Reformatory in New York in 1876.

By 1865 American penal reformers were well aware of the reforms achieved by the conditional release programs of the Irish system. As a result, an **indeterminate sentence** law was adopted in 1876 in New York with the help of prison superintendent **Zebulon R. Brockway.** The system established at Elmira included grading inmates on their conduct and achievement, compulsory education, and careful selection for parole. Volunteer citizens, known as guardians, supervised the parolees. A condition of parole was that parolees report to the guardian the first day of each month. Written reports became required and were submitted to the institution after being signed by the parolee's employer and guardian. By 1944, every U.S. jurisdiction had adopted some form of parole release and indeterminate sentencing.

Reducing the Cost of Incarceration

Howard Abadinsky (1978) maintained that the idea of parole was initiated in the United States primarily for economic reasons. For about one century between the 1840s and 1940s, American prisons were self-supported entirely by convict labor. Many southern penitentiaries turned a huge profit from convict labor by leasing out their convicts to private companies. The private companies benefited because they paid the prison less than they otherwise would have had to pay nonincarcerated workers for hard labor such as building railroads, making goods to sell on the open market, and growing crops. The prisons pocketed the money, given that the prisoners did not get paid. Most prisoners worked long hours "under the gun" in remote prison camps miles away from the main prison unit (Walker 1988).

Private companies liked the idea of using convict labor so much that it began to affect the employment rate of "free world" people (those who were not prisoners). Organized labor unions outside of prison began to apply pressure to limit private companies' use of convict labor. Legislation was finally passed to limit convict labor only to goods that could be sold to other government entities. Because of this legislation, prisoners in remote prison camps had to be relocated to a prison unit where they could be behind bars and work within the walls. More prisons had to be constructed to make space for these incoming prisoners. The profits decreased, and for the first time, taxpayers began to bear some of the cost of incarceration (Walker 1988). It was at this point that the idea of parole became more popular. Nearly every state had some form of discretionary release from prison by 1944—shortly after legislation was passed that limited convict labor to behind the walls.

THE MEDICAL MODEL: 1930–1960

Parole was seen as a major adjunct to the rehabilitation philosophy that dominated American corrections from the 1930s through the 1960s. This rehabilitative ideal, called the **medical model,** assumed that criminal behavior had its roots in environmental and psychosocial aspects of the offender's life and that these behaviors could be corrected. This meant that every offender would be dealt with on an individual basis to determine the causes of his or her criminal behavior.

Under the old punitive model of corrections, the question was "What did he do?" The medical model was more concerned with why criminals commit crime and what can be done to improve the convict's situation. According to the medical model, if prison staff could diagnose and treat "badness," then the lawbreaker should be released when "cured." The mechanisms for accomplishing this were the indeterminate sentence and parole. The release decision was thus shared between the court, which sets a minimum and a maximum period of incarceration, and the correctional system. The parole board's responsibility was to determine the optimal release time at which the inmate is most ready to reenter the community as a responsible citizen.

The medical model assumed that correctional specialists had the ability to diagnose an offender's problems and develop a means of curing those problems. Because one cannot know at the time of diagnosis how long it will take to effect a cure, the indeterminate sentence makes it possible, in theory at least, to confine an offender as long as is necessary and to follow up that confinement with community supervision.

> **MEDICAL MODEL**
>
> The concept that, given proper care and treatment, criminals can be cured into productive, law-abiding citizens. This approach suggests that people commit crimes because of influences beyond their control, such as poverty, injustice, and racism.

Changing Public Opinion

Although parole has generally drawn support from many sources and has a history of consensual acceptance, it has been subject to vigorous criticism and reexamination. After World War I, various parole boards came under attack by critics who claimed that parole was not fulfilling its promise. Antiparole groups believed that parole release failed to produce the desired lasting changes in offenders' behavior and attitudes. This was a severe criticism at a time of increasing acceptance of the rehabilitative ideal with its emphasis on treatment and cure in criminal corrections. Other critics of the system pointed out that release was granted after only a cursory review of the inmates' records and that prison authorities had no criteria by which to measure rehabilitation as a basis for release decisions.

These criticisms led to two major changes in parole administration and organization. First, more emphasis was placed on postrelease supervision, and the number of parole conditions was increased. Second, a shift occurred in parole authority from prison personnel to parole boards with independent authority and statewide jurisdiction.

The years between World War II and 1970 saw the advent and development of classification systems, vocational training, academic training, group and individual therapy, conjugal visitation in some prisons, work release, and numerous other reforms. By 1967 (at the height of the reform era), a nationwide Harris poll found that 77 percent of the population believed that prisons should be mainly corrective, whereas only 11 percent believed they should be mainly punitive (Harris Poll 1967). The belief that criminals could be changed if they were given the opportunity and if sufficient skills, funds, and personnel were available was the central philosophy of the rehabilitative model of corrections. Parole was once again considered a viable and necessary aspect of the American system of corrections.

A PHILOSOPHICAL CHANGE

In the 1970s, individualism, rehabilitation, sentence indeterminacy, and parole all seemed to fall from grace and appeared to be on their way out. A national commission stated, "One of the movements we are currently witnessing in the criminal justice field is the trend toward the establishment of determinate or 'fixed' sentencing of criminal offenders" (National Advisory Commission on Criminal Justice Standards and Goals 1973).

The correctional system's failure to reduce the steadily increasing crime rate and its inability to reduce recidivism, rehabilitate offenders, or make predictive judgments about offenders' future behavior brought about public disillusionment, disappointment, and resentment. Concern also arose that wide and unfair disparities existed in sentencing based on the offender's race, socioeconomic status, and place of conviction (Petersilia 2000b). The pendulum began to swing, and by the late 1970s it seemed to have moved 180 degrees from the rehabilitative ideal to the "just deserts" approach to criminal correction.

In contrast to the rehabilitative ideal, the **just deserts** or **justice model** changes the focus of the system from the offender to the offense. Liberals and conservatives alike embraced determinate sentencing and the abolition of parole, but for different reasons (Cullen and Gilbert 1982). The Vietnam War, the Kent State shootings, and the Attica prison uprising convinced many liberals that the state could not be trusted to administer rehabilitation in a just and humane manner. For conservatives, contemporary research by Robert Martinson (1974) found that few correctional treatment programs were successful in reducing recidivism or drug and alcohol addiction, or in fostering personality and attitude change or community adjustment. Martinson concluded that "with few and isolated exceptions, the rehabilitative efforts which have been reported so far have had no appreciable effect on recidivism" (p. 25). For liberals, the indeterminate sentence was too vague and without due process protections to limit discretion. The just deserts approach was perceived as stressing fair punishment. For conservatives, the indeterminate sentence, parole, and treatment programs were too "soft" on crime. They viewed determinate sentencing and the just deserts approach as consistent with their political and social agenda—a return to the "hard line" and a punishment-oriented correctional system.

The general aim of those favoring determinate sentencing was to abolish, or at least to tightly control, discretion. This included the discretion of judges in sentencing and of parole boards in releasing prisoners. Determinate sentencing was the reformers' answer to this problem. The proposals of the mid-1970s called for clear, certain, uniform penalties for all crimes, either through legislative action or the promulgation of guidelines to which prosecutors, judges, and parole boards would be required to adhere (Cullen and Gilbert 1982).

Origins of Modern Determinate Sentencing

Where did all this talk of the **determinate sentence** begin? John Irwin, a college professor and former prisoner, contends that inmates themselves, particularly inmates in California prisons in the 1960s, were advocates of determinate sentences (Irwin 1974). The situation in California prisons prompted the formation of a working group of the American Friends Service Committee, which produced the book *Struggle for Justice* in 1971. In it the group denounced the very existence of U.S. prisons as well as the rehabilitative model of corrections, declaring coercion of prisoners for any purpose to be immoral. Although *Struggle for Justice* said that all prisons should be shut down, it recognized that such a proposal was unrealistic. The book argued that the

---

JUST DESERTS

The concept that the goal of corrections should be to punish offenders because they deserve to be punished and that punishment should be commensurate with the seriousness of the offense.

JUSTICE MODEL

The correctional practice based on the concept of just deserts and even-handed punishment. The justice model calls for fairness in criminal sentencing, in that all people convicted of a similar offense will receive a like sentence. This model of corrections relies on determinate sentencing and abolition of parole.

DETERMINATE SENTENCE

A narrow-range sentence for a fixed period of time, in which release is specified by statute. Also known as a presumptive, fixed, or mandatory sentence. Release is mandatory.

least that should be done was to repeal all indeterminate sentencing laws and design a system in which offenders convicted of similar crimes served roughly equal terms in prison.

The Justice Model

David Greenberg, one of the primary authors of *Struggle for Justice,* was also a member of a group called the Committee for the Study of Incarceration. Together with Andrew von Hirsch, the committee's executive director, Greenberg persuaded the committee that the most important subject to study was not the conditions of incarceration but the haphazard and irrational manner in which some offenders ended up in prison, and the equally chaotic system of release. The committee's final report was published in 1976 under the title *Doing Justice: The Choice of Punishments* (von Hirsch 1976). The report said that large numbers of widely disparate crimes were often punished with the same indeterminate term, with the setting of a release date left to parole boards, which judged particular offenders' potential rehabilitation and dangerousness.

Doing Justice pointed out that the goal of sentencing should be to punish offenders, that it is proper to punish the criminal because he or she "deserves" to be punished, and that each punishment should be commensurate with the gravity of the last offense or series of offenses. The committee recommended the adoption of a **presumptive sentence** for each crime or category of crimes, with the presumptive sentences graded according to the severity of the crime. The severity of the crime would be graded on two scales: the harm done by the offense and the offender's culpability. The judgment of the degree of culpability would be based partly on the offender's prior record. Having proposed punishment as the main goal of sentencing, the committee then ruled out prison as the punishment for all but the most serious offenses, those in which bodily harm is threatened or done to the victim. The committee proposed alternatives such as periodic imprisonment, increased use of fines, and other lesser sanctions.

At about the same time *Doing Justice* was making the academic rounds, another determinate sentencing model emerged. David Fogel (1979), author of *". . . We Are the Living Proof . . .": The Justice Model for Corrections,* is considered by many to be the "father of determinate sentencing." As early as 1970 he had actively urged a narrowing of sentencing and parole discretion and had been among the most influential determinate sentencing advocates in drafting legislation in various states.

One of the main goals of Fogel's sentencing reforms was to humanize the internal operation of correctional institutions by extending much more freedom to inmates and "unhooking" their release date from their progress or participation in programs. He advocated abolishing parole boards and establishing "flat-time" sentencing—a single sentence for each class of felonies that could be altered slightly for aggravating or mitigating circumstances.

In 1977, Norval Morris, a respected and outspoken scholar, questioned the ability of parole or the parole board to do any of the following:

- Find the optimum moment for release
- Provide an incentive for rehabilitation
- Facilitate prison control and discipline
- Share sentencing responsibility to maximize deterrence while reducing the time served
- Control the size of the prison population
- Rectify unjust disparity in sentencing (Rhine, Smith, and Jackson 1991, p. 25)

PRESUMPTIVE SENTENCE

A statutorily determined sentence offenders will presumably receive if convicted. Offenders convicted in a jurisdiction with presumptive sentences will be assessed this sentence unless mitigating or aggravating circumstances are found to exist.

CHANGING OF THE GUARD: FROM DISCRETIONARY PAROLE TO MANDATORY RELEASE

About 88 percent of prisoners were released via a parole board in 1977. Because of the trend toward determinate sentencing and the criticisms of disparity in decision making, some state correctional departments began to abolish the policy of discretionary release. From this point forward, "parole" was now split into "discretionary release" and "mandatory release." By 1990, 12 states had placed severe restrictions on discretionary release or eliminated it completely. Now only 24 to 39 percent of prisoners are released via discretionary release, whereas mandatory release numbers have increased (Petersilia 2003). As of 2001, 15 states and the federal system had replaced discretionary release with mandatory release by abolishing parole boards for all offenses, and another five states had abolished discretionary release for violent offenses (Hughes, Wilson, and Beck 2001).

Under discretionary release, offenders reentered society when correctional authorities and board members believed they were ready or they had improved their lives enough to earn the privilege to be released. This meant that offenders had to show they had a reentry plan and knew how they were going to stay out of trouble. Under mandatory release, offenders are released no matter how many disciplinary reports they have had or how they acted while incarcerated. Thus, many offenders under mandatory release are ill-prepared for the transition and may not have the right kind of social support when they go home (Petersilia 2003). "In the long run, no one is more dangerous than a criminal who has no incentive to straighten himself out while in prison and who returns to society without a structured and a supervised release plan" (p. 18).

First-time offenders on mandatory release serve less time on average in prison than do first timers with discretionary release. A nationwide examination concurred that this was the case for all types of offenders, except for public-order offenders (of both genders and all races) and African American offenders who were incarcerated for property and drug crimes (Hughes, Wilson, and Beck 2001). Repeat offenders convicted of two or more felonies are serving longer sentences now than repeat offenders were in 1990 (Hughes, Wilson, and Beck 2001). Table 11.1 provides more specific numbers of prisoners entering parole via a discretionary or mandatory sentence in each state and in the federal system.

In response to public pressure, the legislature of "truth-in-sentencing" states limited the releasing power of the parole board in some jurisdictions by requiring that prisoners serve a flat minimum or some proportion of the maximum sentence before becoming eligible for parole. Other jurisdictions that retained discretionary release have established guidelines to reduce and structure release decision making. A small number of states have not only abolished parole but also have no postrelease supervision for prisoners returning to the community.

Both the American Probation and Parole Association and the Association of Paroling Authorities favor retaining parole boards as an important correctional institution tool. Some of the arguments in favor of discretionary release include:

- Parole boards can impose prisoner participation in treatment programs as incentives for release; with automatic release, there are no incentives for prisoners to better themselves while behind bars.
- Parole boards have improved their techniques for more objective and open decision making through parole guidelines.
- Victims can attend parole board hearings to convince the board not to release their offender, but victims have no say in mandatory or automatic release situations.

TABLE 11.1   *Adults Entering Parole by Type of Sentence*

Region and Jurisdiction	NUMBER OF ADULTS ENTERING PAROLE				
	Total	Discretionary[a]	Mandatory[b]	Reinstatement[c]	Other, Unknown, or Not Reported
U.S. total	434,209	176,040	229,887	21,427	6,855
Federal	24,895	24,471	424	0	0
State	409,314	151,569	229,463	21,427	6,855
Northeast	72,626	60,549	6,596	4,824	657
Connecticut	1,449	1,449	0	0	0
Maine	2	0	0	2	0
Massachusetts	3,718	3,507	0	211	0
New Hampshire	565	0	565	0	0
New Jersey[d]	16,281	11,749	...	4,532	0
New York	25,096	18,408	6,031	0	657
Pennsylvania[d]	24,726	24,726	...	...	0
Rhode Island	532	453	...	79	0
Vermont	257	257	0	0	0
Midwest	69,798	28,675	37,009	1,542	2,572
Illinois	23,773	30	22,632	236	875
Indiana	4,681	24	3,896	141	620
Iowa	2,608	2,598	0	10	0
Kansas	4,982	4,534	198	110	140
Michigan	10,503	9,193	564	746	0
Minnesota	3,011	0	2,764	0	247
Missouri[d]	5,034	3,894	1,140	:	0
Nebraska	710	710	0	...	0
North Dakota	338	338	0	0	0
Ohio	9,275	4,765	3,601	296	613
South Dakota	825	340	482	3	0
Wisconsin	4,058	2,249	1,732	0	77
South	99,334	51,537	44,588	727	2,482
Alabama[d]	2,423	2,423	0	:	0
Arkansas[d]	5,415	3,554	1,629	:	0
Delaware	:	:	:	:	0
District of Columbia[d]	1,553	836	247	286	184
Florida	4,315	4,200	0	115	0
Georgia	10,360	10,360	...	...	0
Kentucky	2,938	2,876	...	62	
Louisiana	13,533	889	10,320	26	2,298
Maryland	8,459	2,952	5,507	0	0
Mississippi	1,094	1,088	...	6	0
North Carolina	6,923	3,873	3,050	0	0
Oklahoma	317	317	...	...	0
South Carolina	939	939	0	0	0
Tennessee	3,086	3,086	:	:	0
Texas[d]	32,189	12,138	20,051	0	0
Virginia	5,115	1,331	3,784	0	0
West Virginia	675	675	0	0	0

(continued)

TABLE 11.1 *(Contd.)*

Region and Jurisdiction	NUMBER OF ADULTS ENTERING PAROLE				
	Total	Discretionary[a]	Mandatory[b]	Reinstatement[c]	Other, Unknown, or Not Reported
West	167,556	10,808	141,270	14,334	1,144
Alaska[d]	313	229	229	13	0
Arizona[b]	6,207	553	5,148	261	245
California	140,724	144	127,174	13,406	0
Colorado	4,421	3,011	1,161	:	249
Hawaii	791	783	0	8	0
Idaho	832	832	...	:	0
Montana	:	:	:	:	0
Nevada[d]	2,606	2,384	:	222	0
New Mexico	1,671	...	1,671	:	0
Oregon	7,010	321	5,887	424	378
Utah	2,686	2,686	0	0	0
Washington[d]	23	23	...	...	0
Wyoming[d]	272	:	:	:	272

[a] Discretionary parole entries are people entering because of a parole board decision.

[b] Mandatory parole entries are people whose releases from prison were not decided by a parole board. Includes those entering because of determinate sentencing statutes, good-time provisions, or emergency releases.

[c] Reinstatement entries are people returned to parole after serving time in a prison because of a parole violation.

[d] Some or all detailed data are estimated for entries

Source: *Correctional Populations in the U.S. 2004*. Washington, DC: U.S. Department of Justice.

- Release from prison is a right under automatic supervision, not a privilege under discretionary parole.
- Release decisions are made by computer under automatic release, not by a human parole board that can keep prisoners in prison if it feels the offenders remain a danger to society.
- Prisoners on postrelease supervision generated by automatic release can still commit crimes. For example, the brutal killing of Polly Klaas in California in 1993 by Richard Allen Davis, who had been on mandatory parole release, led the way to the initiation of California's "three strikes" law.
- Abolishing discretionary release does not mean that prisoners will serve their full sentence; it does not prevent prisoners from getting out, and it does not necessarily increase public safety (Burke 1995).

To learn more about the politics behind abolishing parole in Virginia, read the case study at the end of this chapter.

PAROLE TODAY

"While abolishing parole [discretionary release] may make good politics, it contributes to bad correctional practices—and ultimately, less public safety. . . . The public doesn't understand the tremendous power that is lost when parole is abandoned" (Petersilia

2000a, p. 32). Parole is far from completely disappearing from the correctional scene. Growth in the sheer number of releases is expected when prisoners complete the minimum terms of their sentences.

In fact, after abolishing parole boards, some states were forced to reintroduce discretionary release to control for institutional crowding. Table 11.2 lists by state the current discretionary capability of the parole board to release prisoners. "Full" discretion means that the parole board has discretion to release all inmates, although in most states prisoners must still serve a minimum percent of their sentence. "Limited" discretion means the parole board has discretion to release only certain kinds of offenders and parole release is completely denied to recidivists or offenders convicted of violent crimes. States that have no discretionary release anymore for anyone still honor the few cases that were committed in the past under the old law. These states are labeled "old cases." This table also classifies the current sentencing philosophies

TABLE 11.2 *Release Authority of Parole Boards*

State	Discretion to Release	Indeterminate or Determinate	Comments: Who Is Eligible for Discretionary Release?
Alabama	Full	I	
Alaska	Full	I, D	
Arizona	Old cases	D	Offenses prior to 1994
Arkansas	Old cases	D	Offenses prior to 1994
California	Limited	I, D	Lifers only with concurrence of governor
Colorado	Full	I, D	
Connecticut	Full	I, D	Violent offenders have face-to-face hearings
Delaware	Old cases	D	Offenses prior to 6/30/90
Florida	Old cases	D	Capital murder/sexual batt. prior to 10/1/94
Georgia	Limited	I, D	All nonviolent offenders
Hawaii	Full	I, D	Violent off. must meet mandatory minimum
Idaho	Full	I, D	Violent off. must meet mandatory minimum
Illinois	Limited	D	Juveniles only
Indiana	None	D	
Iowa	Full	I	
Kansas	Old cases	D	Offenses prior to 7/1/93
Kentucky	Full	I, D	Violent off. must meet mandatory minimum
Louisiana	Limited	I, D	All nonviolent offenders
Maine	None	D	
Maryland	Limited	I, D	All offenders eligible except lifers
Massachusetts	Full	I	
Michigan	Full	D	All must meet minimum time first
Minnesota	Limited	I, D	Strictly controlled Hearing/Release Unit
Mississippi	Old cases	D	Offenses prior to 7/1/95
Missouri	Full	I, D	Violent must meet minimum first
Montana	Full	D	All must meet minimum time first
Nebraska	Full	D	All must meet minimum time first
Nevada	Full	I	
New Hampshire	Full	I	
New Jersey	Full	I	
New Mexico	Old cases	D	Offenses prior to 1979
New York	Full	I, D	All must meet minimum time first
North Carolina	Old cases	D	Offenses prior to 1994
North Dakota	Full	I, D	Violent must meet minimum first

(continued)

TABLE 11.2 *(Contd.)*

State	Discretion to Release	Indeterminate or Determinate	Comments: Who Is Eligible for Discretionary Release?
Ohio	Old cases	D	Offenses prior to 7/1/96
Oklahoma	Limited	D	Governor has releasing authority
Oregon	Old cases	D	Offenses prior to 11/1/89
Pennsylvania	Full	I	With sentences of 2 years or more
Rhode Island	Full	D	All must meet minimum time first
South Carolina	Limited	I, D	Sentences must be below 20 years
South Dakota	Old cases	D	Offenses prior to 7/1/96
Tennessee	Limited	I, D	Nonviolent offenders eligible only
Texas	Full	I, D	
Utah	Full	I	
Vermont	Full	I	
Virginia	Old cases	D	Offense prior to 1995
Washington	Limited	I, D	
West Virginia	Full	D	All must meet minimum time first
Wisconsin	Old cases	D	Offenses prior to 2000
Wyoming	Full	D	All must meet minimum time first

Full = Parole board has discretion to release all inmates (though some must still serve a minimum percent of their sentence)

Limited = Parole board has discretion to release only certain kinds of offenders, whereas parole release is denied to others

Old cases = No parole discretionary release exists on current cases—only on the few cases left that were committed in the past that were under the "old law"

Indeterminate/Determinate sentence = The philosophy of sentencing practiced currently (if both are listed, determinate sentencing is usually assigned to violent or repeat offenders)

Adapted from the Association of Paroling Authorities International. Accessed: http://www.apaintl.org/pub-paroleboard-survey2004.html.

for each state as "indeterminate," "determinate," or a mix of both depending on the type of offense.

Characteristics of Parolees

More than 765,300 people were on parole by the beginning of 2005, representing 347 people on parole per 100,000 people in the general population (Glaze and Palla 2005). The northeast region of the United States had the most parolees and the Midwest had the fewest per 100,000 residents (see Table 11.3).

Parolees typically served between one and two years of time on supervision, with 38 percent on parole for a drug offense, 26 percent for a property offense, and 24 percent for a crime of violence. Over half (53 percent) are on mandatory release, whereas 40.5 percent are on some form of discretionary parole. Most parolees were men, but since 2000, 12 percent of offenders on parole have been women (see Table 11.4). Despite released offenders' having served more time and a greater portion of their sentence before release, parole success rates have remained unchanged, with less than half of all parolees able to successfully complete their parole term (Glaze and Palla 2005).

TABLE 11.3   *Adults on Parole, 2004*

Region and Jurisdiction	Parole Population Dec. 31, 2004	Percent Change in Parole Population during 2004	Number on Parole on Dec. 31, 2004, per 100,000 Adult Residents
United States, total	**765,355**	**2.7%**	**347**
Federal	89,821	3.8	41
State	675,534	2.6	307
Northeast	**154,819**	**1.5**	**371**
Connecticut	2,552	8.9	96
Maine	32	0	3
Massachusetts	3,854	7.1	78
New Hampshire[a]	1,212	1.1	122
New Jersey	14,180	7.0	217
New York	54,524	−2.4	372
Pennsylvania	77,175	—	806
Rhode Island	368	1.4	44
Vermont	922	15.8	190
Midwest	**127,840**	**4.2**	**258**
Illinois	34,277	−2.1	362
Indiana	7,499	6.8	162
Iowa[b]	3,317	11.5	146
Kansas[b]	4,525	9.2	221
Michigan	20,924	3.4	276
Minnesota	3,872	7.7	100
Missouri[a]	17,400	9.9	398
Nebraska	805	24.2	61
North Dakota	239	6.2	48
Ohio	18,882	2.5	218
South Dakota	2,217	14.0	382
Wisconsin	13,883	9.9	330
South	**231,994**	**3.1**	**305**
Alabama[a]	7,745	11.4	225
Arkansas	14,844	12.6	715
Delaware	539	1.9	85
District of Columbia[a]	5,318	9.4	1,198
Florida	4,888	−4.1	36
Georgia	23,344	10.3	359
Kentucky[b]	8,006	3.4	253
Louisiana	24,387	2.7	728
Maryland	14,351	4.4	345
Mississippi	1,979	9.0	92
North Carolina	2,882	7.7	45
Oklahoma[a]	4,329	7.0	163
South Carolina	3,292	1.5	104
Tennessee	8,410	5.7	186
Texas[a]	102,072	−0.2	629
Virginia[a]	4,392	−9.1	78
West Virginia	1,216	6.4	85
West	**160,881**	**1.6**	**324**
Alaska[b]	951	2.6	204
Arizona	5,671	5.7	135
California[b]	110,261	−0.1	419
Colorado	7,383	12.6	216

(continued)

TABLE 11.3   *(Contd.)*

Region and Jurisdiction	Parole Population Dec. 31, 2004	Percent Change in Parole Population during 2004	Number on Parole on Dec. 31, 2004, per 100,000 Adult Residents
Hawaii	2,296	2.5	238
Idaho	2,370	1.8	232
Montanab	810	−0.6	113
Nevada	3,610	−12.5	209
New Mexico	2,676	14.9	190
Oregon	20,858	7.2	761
Utah	3,312	2.6	201
Washingtona	120	14.3	3
Wyoming	563	−2.6	145

a All data were estimated. bExcludes parolees in one of the following categories: absconder, out of state, or inactive.

Source: Lauren E. Glaze and Seri Palla. 2005. *Probation and Parole in the United States, 2004*. Washington, DC: U.S. Department of Justice, Bureau of Justice Statistics, p. 5.

Functions of Parole

The function of parole is arguably different now than it was in the past. Parole used to serve as a gradual transition from prison to the community to aid in reintegration and reduce recidivism by helping ex-offenders remain gainfully employed so they could support themselves. Williams, McShane, and Dolny (2000a) observe that the function of parole has changed:

TABLE 11.4   *Characteristics of Adults on Parole, 1995, 2000, and 2004*

	1995	2000	2004		1995	2000	2004
Gender				**Type of Offense**			
Male	90%	88%	88%	Violent	*	*	24
Female	10	12	12	Property	*	*	26
Race				Drug	*	*	38
White	34	38	40	Other	*	*	12
Black	45	40	41				
Hispanic	21	21	18	**Adults Entering Parole**			
American Indian/				Discretionary parole	50	37	31
Alaska Native	1	1	1	Mandatory parole	45	54	52
Asian/Pacific Islandera	**	**	1	Reinstatement	4	6	8
Status of Supervision				Other	2	2	9
Active	78	83	85	**Adults Leaving Parole**			
Inactive	11	4	3	Successful completion	45	43	46
Absconded	6	7	7	Returned to incarceration	41	42	39
Supervised out of state	4	5	4	With new sentence	12	11	12
Other	**	1	1	Other	29	31	27
Sentence Length				Absconderb	*	9	10
Less than one year	6	3	5	Other unsuccessfulb	*	2	2
One year or more	94	97	95	Death			1
				Other	10	2	2

Note: For every characteristic there were people of unknown status or type. *Not available. **Less than 0.5 percent.
a Includes Native Hawaiians. b In 1995 absconder and other unsuccessful were reported among "other."

Source: Lauren E. Glaze and Seri Palla. 2005. *Probation and Parole in the United States, 2004*. Washington, DC: U.S. Department of Justice, Bureau of Justice Statistics.

One of the functions of parole is to provide a release valve for crowded prisons so that prison conditions do not become unconstitutional.

[P]arole is tasked primarily with protecting the public from released offenders. This goal is accomplished in three general objectives: (1) by enforcing restrictions and controls on parolees in the community, (2) by providing services that help parolees integrate into a noncriminal lifestyle, and (3) by increasing the public's level of confidence in the effectiveness and responsiveness of parole services through the first two activities (that is, in part a reduction in fear of crime). (pp. 45–59)

Some would argue that parole has essentially changed from being a reintegrative component of higher tolerance to merely enforcing the law with low tolerance for mistakes. This focus may be one reason why revocation rates remain so high.

PRISON POPULATION CONTROL.   Parole boards have also functioned as the "back doorkeeper" of America's prisons, often serving as the operators of safety valves to relieve crowded institutions (Bottomley 1990). Some states have given legislative authority and direction to their parole boards to control prison populations. Others have done so through informal agreements among the governor, the director of corrections, and the parole board. Boards in states such as Georgia, Michigan, and Texas became actively involved in prison population management out of necessity. Prison populations in those states had risen to levels that threatened the correctional authorities' ability to maintain control of their institutions (Rhine, Smith, and Jackson 1991, pp. 97–98). Federal court orders established "caps" on the prison populations in Michigan and Texas. Through a variety of formal and informal methods, parole boards in each of these jurisdictions have been utilized in efforts to reduce and maintain the prison population, with varying degrees of success.

Most authorities agree that in the long term, it is not feasible to control prison populations only by parole board action. Using parole for population control has had detrimental effects on postrelease supervision because of escalating caseload sizes. Jurisdictions have increased and expanded community correctional facilities—such as halfway houses, work release centers, house arrest, electronic monitoring, and intensive supervision—to monitor the offenders who are granted release. Furthermore, in some states the continuing escalation in prison populations has had another, albeit unanticipated, effect on the ability of parole officers to revoke parole for anything other than serious criminal violations. In several states parole officers have experienced difficulty in revoking parolees for technical violations of the conditions of supervision, even when indications exist of deteriorating behavior on the part of the parolee (this issue is discussed more in Chapter 13).

MEDICAL PAROLE.   Parole can be a back-end release strategy for prisoners who pose minimal security risk and who would be better served in the community. Prisoners who would likely be eligible for this category are those with terminal illnesses, particularly those with full-blown AIDS or cancer.

Medical parole, or compassionate release, is the conditional release from prison to the community of prisoners with a terminal illness who do not pose an undue risk to public safety if released. Sixty-five percent of state and federal prison systems and 44 percent of city/county jails have a medical parole policy, but few states utilize this option (Hammett, Harmon, and Maruschak 1999). In 1996, 12 prison systems permitted compassionate release for 143 offenders, and 15 jails granted early release for an additional 171, bringing the total number to just over 300 prisoners released early nationwide in a single year for medical purposes (Hammett, Harmon, and Maruschak 1999). Box 11.1 presents detailed information and research about medical parole in Maryland. Large-scale evaluations of medical parole have not been conducted, so its effect on public safety and how parolees receive treatment services in the community remain unknown.

Should other mechanisms be developed in place of parole? If so, what alternatives to parole are available? Some people answer this question by saying that more prison time should replace parole. The problem with this answer is that bed space does not exist for everyone sentenced to prison to serve their full sentence. Furthermore, most

BOX 11.1   COMMUNITY CORRECTIONS UP CLOSE   •

THE MARYLAND MEDICAL PAROLE PROGRAM

Every state has its own procedures for determining candidacy for medical parole and establishes for itself which parties (doctors, judges, parole boards, wardens, and governors) partake in the decision-making process. In Maryland's medical parole program, inmates were initially nominated by prison nurses and doctors who worked with terminally ill prisoners with a documented diagnosis and full medical evaluation. Once the inmates were medically eligible, the warden and a case management team performed a security evaluation of the level of risk that the inmate might pose in the community. If the inmate posed a

minimal risk, then an aftercare plan would be put together by a social worker. Kendig, Boyle, and Swetz (1996) found that inmates were candidates for this program if

They "no longer jeopardized public safety if released" and at least one of the following three conditions existed:

1. A verifiable terminal medical condition
2. A medical condition that incapacitated the individual so that imprisonment was not required to ensure public safety
3. A medical condition that could be more

appropriately treated in a community treatment facility instead of a prison (p. 22)

The researchers described the next level of scrutiny that these nominated cases undergo after they pass the inspection of prison unit employees:

These evaluations were reviewed by the DOC [Department of Corrections] medical director, the director of social work, and the assistant commissioner for inmate health care, who then recommended for or against medical parole to the commissioner of correction. Upon review of the

prisoners are not emerging from prison with the skills and knowledge that will keep them out of prison for very long. Jeremy Travis (2000), former director of the National Institute of Justice, states:

> The overarching goal of reentry, in my view, is to have returned to our midst an individual who has discharged his legal obligation to society by serving his sentence and has demonstrated an ability to live by society's rules. . . . [We should be] asking a different question "How should we manage the reentry of large numbers of people who have been imprisoned for a long time?" (pp. 2–3)

Government and sentencing commissions have gone back and forth between recommending the extension of parole and indeterminacy of sentencing and the outright abolition of these practices. The optimal solution is not yet at hand. History teaches that all too often the unanticipated and unintended consequences of reform have aggravated rather than mitigated the problems they sought to solve. Prudence in reform efforts is advisable, and such lessons as can be learned from past efforts should be carefully evaluated.

TOP THINGS YOU SHOULD KNOW

- Parole has its origins in the work of penal reformers in Germany, Spain, and France, and on Norfolk Island in the early decades of the nineteenth century.
- Walter Crofton of Ireland and U.S. prison reformer Zebulon R. Brockway studied Maconochie's work on Norfolk Island and implemented his ideas.

relevant assessments and recommendations, the commissioner of correction either ruled against medical parole or forwarded his recommendation for medical parole to the Maryland Parole Commission. . . . Inmates with life sentences or parole-restricted sentences . . . were referred by the Maryland Parole Commission with a recommendation for parole to the governor for gubernatorial approval or denial. (Kendig, Boyle, and Swetz 1996, p. 22)

The researchers reviewed all 230 cases that were submitted for medical parole from 1991 to 1994. Of those cases, 144 (62 percent) were approved for parole, but only 120 were released (some prisoners died prior to being approved or released). A follow-up of the 120 released inmates at the end of 1994 revealed that 60 inmates were still on parole in the community, 54 inmates died, two inmates had successfully completed their sentences (and were not on parole), and four inmates had failed parole and returned to prison. Three of the four inmates who had returned to prison committed technical violations (for example, verbally threatening staff, using illegal drugs, or moving to a new address without notifying the parole officer). One inmate violated parole by committing an armed robbery. After serving 12 months in prison for the robbery, this inmate was released and died two months later. The researchers concluded that "early release for inmates with terminal illnesses can be accomplished expeditiously and with minimal impact on public safety" (p. 25).

Source: Newton Kendig, Barbara Boyle, and Anthony Swetz. 1996. The Maryland Division of Correction Medical-Parole Program: A Four-Year Experience, 1991 to 1994. *AIDS & Public Policy Journal* 11(1): 21–27.

- Steadily increasing crime rates, the perceived failure of rehabilitation programs, and the perception that parole boards were incapable of making predictive judgments about offenders' future behavior caused the medical rehabilitation model and indeterminate sentencing philosophies of the 1930s to be replaced by the justice model and determinate sentencing in the 1970s.
- Parole is now split into "discretionary release" and "mandatory release." Under discretionary release, which has decreased, offenders reenter society when correctional authorities believe they are ready or they have improved their lives enough to earn the privilege to be released. Under mandatory release, which has steadily increased, offenders are released regardless of disciplinary reports or their behavior while incarcerated. Thus, many offenders under mandatory release are ill prepared for the transition.
- Twenty percent of all people released from prison do not receive postprison supervision.
- Parole is focused on enforcement of conditions and public safety, and secondarily on reintegration and treatment services. Although parole is still a way to control prison crowding, medical parole is hardly used at all.

DISCUSSION QUESTIONS

1 Discuss the founders of parole and their contributions.

2 What was the English ticket-of-leave, and how did that compare with the marks system?

3 Why did England transport convicts to America and Australia? What was the connection between transportation and parole?

4 What was the significance of Alexander Maconochie's style of prison administration on the behavior of the convicts?

5 Why was Maconochie dismissed from Norfolk Island despite his success?

6 How did parole develop in the United States? Be sure to include discussions of the Irish system and the indeterminate sentence in your explanation.

7 Why did the medical model fall out of favor? What factors were associated with this phenomenon?

8 What is the justice model of corrections? What factors were associated with its emergence in the 1970s?

9 What happened to parole under the justice model? Why?

10 What role does parole play in the twenty-first century?

11 What are the pros and cons of abolishing parole?

12 How do you feel about the use of medical parole?

 WEBSITES

U.S. Parole Commission

http://www.usdoj.gov/uspc/parole.htm

U.S. Department of Justice Parole Statistics

http://www.ojp.usdoj.gov/bjs/pandp.htm

History of Parole in Alabama

http://www.pardons.state.al.us

History of Parole in Delaware

http://www.state.de.us/parole/default.shtml

History of Parole in New York

http://parole.state.ny.us/introhistory.html

History of Parole in Texas

http://tdcj.state.tx.us/parole/parole-history.htm

History of Parole in Utah

http://bop.utah.gov/history.html

History of Parole in Canada

http://www.npb-cnlc.gc.ca/infocntr/parolec/phistore.htm

The Politics of Abolishing Discretionary Parole

Part of this chapter inferred that abolishing parole in some states was due in part to the changing political climate. The case study below is perhaps an example of how politics ultimately influenced the decision in Virginia. Read the following case study and answer or discuss the following questions:

1. Did the Virginia commission act effectively to abolish parole?
2. What were some problems with how the commission went about abolishing parole?
3. Was the parole board operating in a manner that had public safety interests in mind?
4. Will abolishing parole reduce public confidence in the criminal justice system?
5. What other impacts will this decision have on sentencing and on the prison system?

George Allen, a Virginia governor, established a Commission on the Abolition of Parole and Sentencing Reform. The very name of the commission indicated how completely the initiative had committed itself to a "solution"—abolishing parole—before the commission had even begun its work of assessing how sentencing could be reformed in the commonwealth. The governor apparently had two goals in mind: He wanted to send a clear message to the citizens of Virginia that he was committed to fighting crime, and he wanted to take decisive, visible action that would underline his commitment. A major part of the strategy for demonstrating his commitment was the abolition of parole.

The legislature complied with the recommendations of the commission and abolished parole for offenders and also proposed[1] other changes, which included:

- Dramatic increases in time to be served in prison by violent offenders, from a minimum of 100 percent to as much as 700 percent over average time served during the last several years
- Maintaining current time served for nonviolent offenders, although it was suggested that time might be served in lower-cost work camps
- Implementation of "truth in sentencing" through the requirement that all offenders serve 85 percent of sentences imposed
- Replacing existing "good-time" provisions with "earned sentence credits" in order to provide for the 15 percent reduction in sentences

[1]Governor's Commission on Parole Abolition and Sentencing Reform, *Final Report* (Richmond: Commonwealth of Virginia, August 1994), p. 9.

The commission further recommended that incapacitation is more important a goal than rehabilitation, when it decided on:

- Longer times in prison for violent offenders than nonviolent offenders
- An expanded array of alternatives to incarceration for "appropriate offenders"
- Transitional policies for offenders approaching release
- Sentence reduction credits as a necessary and appropriate way to "control inmate behavior"
- Special "release provisions" and "special executive clemency rules" because long sentences may cause some inmates to remain incarcerated "past the point at which . . . they have ceased to pose a threat to the community . . . [and] the interests of the law-abiding citizenry may not be served by continued incarceration of such inmates"
- A program for the gradual "step-down of inmates" whose release from incarceration is imminent
- Postrelease supervision.

The major difference between these suggested changes (above) and a system of parole is that the responsibility for these decisions is not clearly assigned to identifiable, accountable decision makers.

Much has been lost in the process of this crusade to abolish parole. First, much of the truth about how the system was really operating has been lost. In its zeal to stress the need for change, the commission report vastly overstates some of the real problems with sentencing in Virginia and is simply inaccurate about a number of issues. It strongly implies that virtually all of the problems of crime and criminal justice in Virginia are a result of parole. The commission report concludes that

As long as there is the hidden hand of parole sweeping aside the solemn judgments of judges and juries, neither criminals nor law-abiding citizens will respect the criminal justice system in Virginia.[2]

The report also posits a frightening scenario in order to justify drastic and costly action. It speaks of an impending "criminal reign of terror" and exhorts Virginians not to "stand idly by in the face of this deadly threat to our safety and the well-being of our families." A recent Virginia Commission on Prison and Jail Overcrowding paints a somewhat different picture. Referencing FBI data, this commission's report indicates that "the violent crime rate experienced in Virginia is lower than most of the surrounding states and lower than the national average. When compared to national indices, Virginia is a low crime state. . . . Virginia ranks 42nd in the nation in Index Crimes."[3]

What the governor's commission did not include is the fact that sentences in Virginia are already longer than in most states, and that the time offenders actually serve in Virginia is also longer than in most states. What this means is that criminals in Virginia serve longer behind bars, and that, once released, they are supervised and subject to return to prison for vastly longer periods of time than the national average.[4] Somewhat ironically, the commission's report speaks of the "softness of our punishment scheme" in Virginia. It uses this misleading assessment of Virginia's existing punishment scheme as justification for dismantling parole—an element of Virginia's criminal justice system that has assured longer periods of incarceration for violent, dangerous offenders.

[2]Ibid., p. 32.

[3]Commission on Prison and Jail Overcrowding, *Final Report* (Richmond: Commonwealth of Virginia, December 11, 1989), p. 15.

[4]Ibid.

With respect to parole itself, the commission sent a clear message that it felt the Virginia Parole Board operated in secret, releasing offenders in such a way as to circumvent the intent of the sentencing court, and with complete disregard for the safety of the community or for appropriate punishment. The only explanation for this conclusion drawn by the commission is that they had no knowledge of parole in Virginia. Interestingly, not one member of the Parole Board was allowed to serve on the commission.

Did the Virginia Parole Board operate like a "hidden hand . . . sweeping aside the solemn judgment of judges and juries?" If we are to believe this statement to be true, then we must believe that all of the judges in Virginia are completely ignorant of the law and its mandate regarding eligibility for parole review. In fact, the commission's report itself lists, quite simply, when offenders are eligible for parole review. It is quite clear, then, that any responsible judge in Virginia knew when eligibility for parole occurred. Judges could thus fashion sentences to assure periods of incarceration appropriate to their assessment of deserved punishment and appropriate incapacitation. The commission's report paints a picture of judges in Virginia able only to fashion sentences with "haphazard results" in an "atmosphere of confusion" as they "attempt" to "achieve roughly the amount of incarceration the court deems appropriate." In the rush to abolish parole, the governor's commission implies great incompetence on the bench in Virginia.

Of course, the law established only "eligibility" for parole review. Offenders are not released automatically when they reach eligibility, but rather begin the rigorous review process during which the Parole Board revisits such issues as community safety and victims' concerns. They must determine whether offenders have indeed "earned" the privilege of release. Did the Parole Board operate in secret, "deceiving" citizens as the commission's report alleges? Again the record is quite clear. The Virginia Parole Board, like many of its sister agencies across the country, had stepped up to its responsibility to be open and clear with the public, with courts, with victims, and with offenders in its release policies. It had published a detailed set of guidelines, which stated clearly the concerns that would guide its decisions. Those guidelines were the result of a five-year, exhaustive effort to clearly define the role of parole in the system, and that involved an advisory panel drawn from the criminal justice system and the community. One of several key goals of these guidelines, in the words of the Virginia Parole Board, was "to make the parole process accessible and understandable."[5]

Three major concerns were built into these guidelines: community safety, appropriate punishment time in prison, and performance while in prison. These are precisely the concerns that are raised again and again in the commission's report. Can this offender function safely in the community? Having served to the time of "eligibility" as defined by the sentence imposed by the judge, has this offender served "enough" time in light of the seriousness of his or her crime and any aggravating or mitigating circumstances? Even if the time served is "enough" in light of the crime, can this offender function safely in the community, or is more time needed for drug treatment, counseling, or for incapacitation? What does the prisoner's performance in the institution tell us about readiness for release? How can the offender demonstrate that he has earned release? The Virginia Parole Board fashioned a system to gather answers to these questions in an organized and methodical manner, building on the efficiencies of an automated data system that was among the most effective in the nation. It also conducted the research to build and use a sound risk-assessment system that resulted in significant reductions in the rate of problems with offenders after release.

[5]Virginia Parole Board's Response to item 7143 of the Appropriations Act of 1990: Parole Guidelines, October 1990, transmittal letter to Secretary of Public Safety, p. 2.

In addition, the five members of the board spent much of their time in personal interviews with victims of crime, their families, members of the community, and other interested parties, eliciting their views and concerns about specific cases. Provisions existed for crime victims to provide input in writing, if they preferred, or to have a family member speak for them. Or, if they so desired, victims could allow their statements made at the time of sentencing to stand, and not continue their involvement in the process. In short, the Virginia Parole Board invested enormous time and effort into humanizing the process and making sure that victims and communities had a voice in decisions affecting the transition of offenders from prison back into the community. Ironically, the commission report also charges parole with worsening and compounding the agony of victims of crime.

In effect, serious charges were made by the Governor's Commission on the Abolition of Parole and Sentencing Reform, including: the Virginia Parole Board was secretive; it operated behind closed doors; it circumvented the explicit will of sentencing judges; it contributed to sentencing disparities; and it deceived the citizens of Virginia. There is ample public record to discount these charges out of hand. But for those in Virginia who believed the charges, the quotient of faith and credibility in our system of justice has likely been reduced.

Source: Peggy B. Burke. 1995. *Abolishing Parole: Why the Emperor Has No Clothes*. Lexington, KY: American Probation and Parole Association; and California, MO: Association of Paroling Authorities, International. Used with Permission from the APPA.

Introduction

Issues in Reentry
The Prisoner's Family
The Victim's Role in Reentry
Reentry and the Community
Community-Based Reentry
  Initiatives
Types of Reentry

Eligibility for Parole
Time Sheets and Eligibility Dates
Prerelease Preparation within the
  Institution

The Parole Board
Term and Qualifications of the
  Parole Board

The Parole Hearing
Number of Parole Board Members
Recommendations and Attendees
Victim Participation in Parole
  Hearings

**Models of Parole Release
Decisions**
The Surveillance Model
The Procedural Justice Model
The Risk Prediction Model

**Due Process during
Discretionary Parole Hearings**
Menechino v. Oswald
*Greenholtz v. Inmates of the
  Nebraska Penal and Correctional
  Complex*
State-Created Liberty Interest
Extending the Time Intervals
  between Parole Hearings

**Prisoners' Perceptions of Parole
Selection**

Top Things You Should Know

12

Preparing for Prisoner Reentry: Discretionary Parole and Mandatory Release

© Raymond Alarid, Jr.

What You Will Learn in This Chapter

- *Most prisoners will one day be released, so it is good public policy to make preparations for the reentry process while they are incarcerated.*
- *Reentry affects the prisoner, the victim, the community, and the prisoner's family.*
- *Upon release, most prisoners are supervised on some form of mandatory supervision or discretionary parole.*
- *The discretionary parole selection process relies on objective measures of potential risk.*
- *Special attention is paid to the question of due process in parole selection, with an emphasis on appellate court decisions.*

INTRODUCTION

More than 95 percent of incarcerated prisoners will eventually return to their communities. Given that about 600,000 offenders are released *every year,* that is a substantial number of people who are making a major life transition, most of whom will do so without having a concrete plan of employment, savings, and living arrangements. Not only will prisoners lack a release plan, many will not have the resources to sustain themselves while finding a job and may spiral downward into a life of depression and drug use. Parolees may find acceptance by their own family or community a difficult challenge. All of these factors may contribute to many offenders returning to criminal behavior. Prisoner **reentry** is any activity or program dedicated to preparing and integrating parolees into the community as law-abiding citizens using a collaborative approach with parole officers, treatment providers, and the community.

Reentry into the community is a vulnerable time that affects the prisoner, his or her family, his or her employer, the victim, and the surrounding community. Box 12.1 examines what it would be like to get out of prison so you can better understand some of the needs and challenges former prisoners face when coming back to the larger community.

ISSUES IN REENTRY

Successful reentry includes prerelease planning, community referrals, and quick access to benefit programs and continuity of care so there is no gap between the care received at the institution and in the new community situation (Hammett, Roberts, and Kennedy 2001). As Box 12.1 illustrates, a number of challenges stand between the offender and successful reentry. First, recently released offenders are indigent but still may need medications for medical or psychological conditions. They may not be eligible for certain benefits, and the prerelease institution may need to assist them in applying for various programs, which may take a few months for approval. Second, there is a difference between giving offenders a list of referrals and actually making appointments for them. Some offenders lack the initiative or the education to find a specific service provider that is right for their situation, and they will be more likely to follow through if they are expected to appear for a prescheduled appointment. Third, parolees and other recently released offenders have other survival needs to meet, such as finding and maintaining stable employment, finding suitable housing, and staying clean of illegal drugs. Their health care or mental health may be overlooked in light of all the other responsibilities that need their attention (Hammett, Roberts, and Kennedy 2001). In addition to the problems

KEY TERMS

Reentry
Reentry courts
Parole board
Minimum eligibility date
Maximum eligibility date
Good time
Parole eligibility date
Prerelease facility
Prerelease plan
Full board review
Victim impact statement
Salient Factor Score
Liberty interest

REENTRY

The process of preparing and integrating parolees into the community as law-abiding citizens using a collaborative approach with parole officers and treatment providers.

BOX 12.1   COMMUNITY CORRECTIONS UP CLOSE   ●

WHAT MIGHT IT BE LIKE TO TRANSITION FROM PRISON TO THE COMMUNITY?

Imagine that you've just gotten out of prison after spending three years of your life locked up in the same routine and boring life you've grown accustomed to. Now that you're out, you want to celebrate, get back with your old friends, and try to catch up on the time you lost. After all, there's a lot of catching up to do. The people and situations you remember seem different, however. You get back to your neighborhood and realize that the people who were doing well have moved on and all you see now in your neighborhood are the people who are not doing so well. They'll be glad to lend you a couple of bucks or get you drunk so you can celebrate. But those were the people and situations that helped you get yourself into this mess to begin with. What now? You burned your bridges

with your brothers, who won't talk to you. Your mother will let you stay with her only until you can get on your feet again, but you don't know how long her support will last. You have a daughter who has been living with her grandmother (your mom). Your daughter is now 5 years old and doesn't even know you. You desperately want to connect with her but don't feel confident you have the skills to make the first move. You also feel guilty for not being able to pay your mom for raising your daughter and are afraid you'll never be able to pay her back. You feel this huge sense of urgency, but at the time same time, fear and depression set in and you wonder if leaving prison early was a mistake.

Like most people who relocate to a new state, offenders

need to obtain identification cards, change their address, find housing, and find a job. If relocation isn't stressful enough on its own, think of the additional challenges of finding a job with only a high school education or GED, having to explain a transient (or nonexistent) employment record, and the additional stigma of admitting your felony record. Other challenges include overcoming a drug or alcohol addiction, managing stress and anger, and avoiding situations that may contribute to the beginnings of bad habits. Most offenders who do not make the transition will fall short within the first six to nine months after they leave prison. The reentry process therefore starts while prisoners are incarcerated and attempts to bridge this crucial phase.

already mentioned, women parolees also reported the need for education and employment services, protection from abusive relationships in the community (their abuser continuing to stalk or hurt them), and child advocacy and family reunification (Richie 2001). Even after being incarcerated for as little as two months, women experienced shifts in family structure like separation, divorce, and where dependent children lived (Arditti and Few 2006).

The Prisoner's Family

The prisoner's family has suffered during the period of incarceration with the stigma of having a loved one behind bars. As the years go by, prisoners tend to receive less financial support and fewer face-to-face visits and letters. Even when prisoners are released to the community, only about 25 percent actually have someone there to meet them at the prison or to pick them up at the bus station to take them home (Seiter and Kadela 2003). If the prisoner was supporting dependents prior to arrest, years of financial and emotional neglect will have changed this relationship. A significant number of prisoners' children may be being raised by extended family members such as grandparents, aunts, or sisters. More than 1.5 million children under age 18 have at least one parent who is currently incarcerated. Reentry means that these ties must be reestablished or mended.

An example of a New York reentry program using a family case management technique is PARTNER, which stands for Parolees and Relatives toward Newly Enhanced Relationships. A team consists of a family case manager from La Bodega, a New York parole officer, the offender, and the offender's family. The case manager visits the offender's family and conducts a needs assessment prior to the offender's release. PARTNER is a model program for how communities and government agencies can work together to enhance prisoner reentry (Lehman et al. 2002).

The Victim's Role in Reentry

Most offenders know their victim as an intimate or an acquaintance. Under the philosophy of restorative justice (discussed in Chapter 10), the offender has a responsibility for repairing the harm done to both the victim and the community. Therefore, the victim's participation in the prerelease process assists in establishing special conditions at reentry. For example, some victims become active in victim impact panels or victim mediation sessions (Herman and Wasserman 2001). The parole board will be more receptive to the victim if the victim is present at the hearing. Furthermore, the community (for example, potential employers, landlords, and neighbors) will be more receptive to the offender's reentry if community members know the victim supports the reentry efforts (Lehman et al. 2002).

Even though the victim may not want to see the offender released early by the parole board, discretionary parole is viewed as safer for the victim than merely releasing offenders to the community without supervision because they have "maxed out" their sentence (Herman and Wasserman 2001).

Reentry and the Community

We know that the locations where parolees reside are *not* evenly spread within the community. Certain areas of the city receive a disproportionately larger number of parolees, and these areas have a high amount of unemployment, open drug use, and community instability and disorganization. As more and more prisoners return to the same communities, the community becomes less cohesive and more unstable, with the potential to become more criminogenic (Seiter and Kadela 2003). Some experts believe that reentry can encompass restorative justice and civic community service using a model of civic engagement if the community is willing to accept offenders returning to their communities (Bazemore and Stinchcomb 2004). Other experts say that reentry encompasses more than community acceptance:

> The reentry philosophy is based on the belief that police, courts, institutions, and community corrections all have a role in creating significant, long-term rehabilitative change for offenders. This philosophy assumes that criminal justice agencies cannot create long-lasting change for offenders without the inclusion of the family, community-based service providers, and the faith community. (Wilkinson, Rhine, and Henderson-Hurley 2005, p. 160)

This means that reentry is based on more than just criminal justice, but it must overlap with workforce development, family/social policy, and health policy to be truly successful. This is why the federal government began various community-based reentry initiatives with funding from the Department of Justice, the Department of Labor, and the Department of Health and Human Services.

Community-Based Reentry Initiatives

In 2001, the federal government allocated $100 million to the U.S. Department of Justice to support the reentry of criminal offenders, particularly with respect to housing, job placement, mentoring services, and some faith-based initiatives. In 2004, that number tripled when Congress allocated an unprecedented amount of more than $300 million over a three-year period (Wilkinson and Rhine 2005). However, when we consider what that means, that is equivalent to $50 million per state each year for a three-year period, translating to spending about $100 per parolee per year (Lattimore 2006). Some states have opted to use the funds on parolees who have committed violent crimes so they can use more resources on a smaller number of people. Out of these funds stemmed reentry partnerships with faith-based organizations and grassroots community groups in neighborhoods that receive a disproportionate number of prisoners returning to the streets (Robinson and Travis 2000). Reentry partnerships do not necessarily involve more resources—they merely involve using existing resources in a smarter and more holistic way by collaborating with other agencies in criminal justice and the larger community. Let's examine reentry courts as an example.

REENTRY COURTS.   **Reentry courts** are a collaborative, team-based program that occurs after prison with the aim of improving the link between parole supervision and treatment providers. Reentry court programs initially identify and begin to work with offenders prior to release. After release, the offender has structured court appointments with the reentry team, which coordinates job training, housing, substance abuse treatment, and transportation. Reentry courts are similar to drug courts (discussed in Chapter 2) in that they use judges, court hearings, and graduated sanctions and incentives to reward positive behavior and predictably punish negative behavior. They operate on contracts that keep offenders law abiding for fear of returning to prison (Robinson and Travis 2000). At least nine states have implemented reentry courts programs, two of which we discuss below.

A Colorado reentry court has the goal of reintegrating parolees under mandatory release who have a dual diagnosis of mental illness and a substance abuse problem. The parolee initially meets with an administrative law judge within 14 days of leaving prison. The judge, together with the offender, the parole officer, and the mental health treatment provider, establishes monthly goals, and this group meets every month for one year to revisit the reentry goals (Robinson and Travis 2000).

Another reentry court in East Harlem targeted nonviolent felons who had at least two convictions. The program had three phases, which one-third of participants had successfully completed; the other two-thirds were in an earlier stage of the program. Initial evaluations of 45 participants found that 22 percent were convicted of committing a new crime while under a one-year supervision of the reentry court. The 45 participants were compared with a matched group of 90 parolees who did not attend reentry court, and the two groups had similar recidivism rates (Farole 2003). Whereas these sample sizes are too small to make any general statements about reentry courts, researchers may need to better understand factors that involve success after prison. Preliminary analyses of a reentry preparation program called Project Greenlight compared participants with a matched group of parolees and found that Greenlight participants performed no better than regular parolees (Wilson and Davis 2006). As more is learned about why ex-convicts return to prison, the increased attention paid to the idea that prisoners need substantial assistance with reentry has certainly been a step in the right direction.

Types of Reentry

Both determinate and indeterminate sentencing policies allow the reentry of felony offenders from prison. In general, determinate sentencing has automatic or mandatory release, which has become more common. A parole officer usually supervises release in this manner, but in some states there are release options without any community supervision following prison. For example, states that release inmates without community supervision include Nevada (45 percent of its releasees), Ohio (37 percent), Washington (35 percent), and Georgia (30 percent). There are many other states with similar numbers (Austin 2001). Automatic release with supervision does not involve a parole board but is decided solely by how much time has been served according to a time sheet (this is discussed in the next section).

On the other hand, a distinguishing characteristic of indeterminate sentencing is discretionary release by a **parole board.** Adult parole services are administered either by a state correctional agency or by an independent or autonomous board. Some juvenile parole services remain under the auspices of institutional staff, but they are increasingly becoming more like the adult system. Parole boards have four basic functions:

1. To decide when individual prisoners should be released
2. To determine any special conditions of parole supervision
3. To successfully discharge the parolee when the conditions have been met
4. To determine whether parole privileges should be revoked should the conditions be violated

Some parole boards have additional functions, such as granting furloughs, reviewing pardons and executive clemency decisions made by the governor, restoring civil rights to ex-offenders, and granting reprieves in death sentence cases. Each state establishes the extent of its own parole board's authority.

Once an offender is released on parole, parole officers enforce the conditions set by the parole board by supervising the parolee in the community. Offenders released in states without parole boards are still supervised by parole officers.

ELIGIBILITY FOR PAROLE

© Ericka Watson/The Childress Index

PAROLE BOARD

An administrative body empowered to decide whether inmates shall be conditionally released from prison before the completion of their sentence, to revoke parole, and to discharge from parole those who have satisfactorily completed their terms.

Project RIO is a program that exists within the Texas Department of Criminal Justice to reduce recidivism through preparing prisoners and parolees for gainful employment upon release. Project RIO stands for "Re-Integration of Offenders," which remains one of the purposes of parole.

The first step in the reentry process is that an offender must be eligible for parole consideration. Those permanently ineligible for release include offenders on death row, offenders serving life *without* parole, and some habitual offenders sentenced under statutes such as "three strikes and you're out."

Time Sheets and Eligibility Dates

For the rest of the inmates (those with mandatory or discretionary releases), a computer keeps track of all good time earned and the number of days served to determine minimum and maximum eligibility dates. The **minimum eligibility date** is the shortest amount of time defined by statute, minus good time earned, that must be served before the offender can go before the parole board. In some states, such as Nebraska, parole boards are required to see offenders once per year even if the minimum eligibility date has not yet been met (Proctor 1999). The **maximum eligibility date** is the longest amount of time that can be served before the inmate must, by law, be released (where the offender has "maxed out" his or her sentence).

Good time (or "gain time") was originally introduced as an incentive by prison authorities for institutional good conduct. Good time reduces the period of sentence an inmate must serve before parole eligibility. Now, good time is automatically granted (in states that have it) unless the inmate commits a disciplinary infraction. That is, good time is lost for misbehavior in prison, not awarded for good behavior. Good-time credits vary greatly from state to state, ranging from five days per month to as much as 45 days per month. In recent years large amounts of good time have been awarded (for example, 120 days for every month served) by correctional authorities who are forced to temporarily increase the good time to reduce prison overcrowding and avoid a lawsuit. When jail and prison crowding subsides, good time is decreased to the usual amount.

Typically, the case manager at each prison institution submits good time earned (or in some cases submits good time lost for misbehavior) to the parole board or the division within the department of corrections that prepares status or time sheets. Offenders receive an updated time sheet every six months to one year so they know when to expect their first parole hearing.

Prisoners generally become eligible for release at the completion of their minimum sentence. The manner in which a **parole eligibility date** is established varies from state to state. Mandatory minimum states require that between 50 and 85 percent of the entire sentence be served before the prisoner first becomes eligible. Other discretionary parole states require an inmate to have served one-third of the imposed sentence to be eligible for consideration for early parole. However, most statutes allow further reductions in the eligibility date through credit for time served in jail before sentencing and good-time credits. Federal law provides mandatory parole when an offender has served two-thirds of a term of five years or longer unless the offender has serious disciplinary infractions in prison or there is a high probability of recidivism (U.S. Parole Commission 2006).

Some states credit good time to the inmate upon arrival in prison and calculate the eligibility date by subtracting credited good time from the maximum sentence. An inmate who is serving a 15-year sentence and receiving standard good time of 20 days per month (50 days' credit on his or her sentence for each 30 days served) would thus be eligible for parole consideration after 40 months.

As the first parole eligibility date approaches, institutional case managers (also called institutional parole officers in some states) prepare an individualized prerelease plan for the parole board. Leanne Alarid, one of this book's coauthors, prepared prerelease plans and attended monthly parole board hearings with offenders on her

MINIMUM ELIGIBILITY DATE

The shortest amount of time defined by statute, minus good time earned, that must be served before the offender can go before the parole board.

MAXIMUM ELIGIBILITY DATE

The longest amount of time that can be served before the inmate must be released by law.

GOOD TIME

Sentence reduction of a specified number of days each month for good conduct.

PAROLE ELIGIBILITY DATE

The point in a prisoner's sentence at which he or she becomes eligible to be considered for parole. If the offender is denied parole, a new parole eligibility date is scheduled in the future.

caseload who were scheduled to see the board. The next section discusses preparation for discretionary parole release by assembling a prerelease plan.

Prerelease Preparation within the Institution

Some prisoners are fortunate enough to be transferred to a prerelease program within the system in preparation for their release. A **prerelease facility** is a minimum-security program that houses inmates who have earned this privilege through good institutional conduct and are within two years of their release date. Prerelease facilities in Georgia, Missouri, Ohio, Pennsylvania, Texas, and Washington provide increased opportunities for job readiness, education, housing assistance, and furloughs. In Washington, between 30 and 40 percent of all prisoners experienced some time at the prerelease center, which is considered quite high compared with most other states surveyed (Austin 2001). Halfway houses are also seen as prerelease facilities prior to either mandatory or discretionary release.

Another way that institutions prepare for an inmate's release is through the **prerelease plan.** A prerelease plan is typically used by discretionary parole boards (and not used much for mandatory or automatic releases). A prerelease plan includes a summary of institutional conduct and program participation, as well as plans for housing and employment upon release. Some states have hearing officers who interview the prisoners and report directly to the parole board with their recommendation. Other states submit written reports along with the case file. Having some form of prerelease plan prepared in advance of a scheduled parole hearing has three main advantages:

1. A prerelease plan increases an offender's chances of parole because it solidifies living arrangements and work opportunities.
2. A prerelease plan saves time during the parole board hearing.
3. Ties to the community will likely increase an offender's success on parole and make it less likely that the offender will return to crime.

An institutional case manager meets with the prisoner in an interview to document exactly where the inmate will be living, and the names of who he or she will live with. A different (local) field parole officer will check out the address and interview household members to ensure that the address is a valid and acceptable place for the offender to live. Positive family relations increase the likelihood of parole (Silverstein 1997). Offenders are discouraged from paroling to "themselves," which means living and supporting oneself without any assistance. Because most offenders, at the time of release from prison, do not have the money required for rent and utility deposits, the vast majority must parole to an existing household of a friend or relative. In an effort to assist offenders in community reintegration, paroling some offenders to a halfway house or community residential center is helpful. Halfway houses can provide a graduated sanction that provides less supervision than prison but provides more than regular parole. This is ideal for offenders who are nearing the end of their sentences (so release is inevitable) but who pose a risk to public safety.

The institutional case manager documents the amount of money the prisoner has in savings and any job leads or specific employment plans the prisoner has. According to Petersilia (2000b), most prisoners leave prison without any savings and with few solid job prospects. The case manager then summarizes any programs the offender has attended or completed (for example, general equivalency diploma courses) while in prison and lists all disciplinary infractions (write-ups) the prisoner received during the entire period of incarceration.

PRERELEASE FACILITY

A minimum-security prison that houses inmates who have earned this privilege through good institutional conduct and who are nearing their release date.

PRERELEASE PLAN

A case management summary of institutional conduct and program participation, as well as plans for housing and employment upon release, that is submitted to the parole board in cases of discretionary parole or to the parole officer in cases of automatic release.

Essentially, the case manager brings together official data (for example, current conviction, current age, amount of time served for the current conviction, number of prior prison incarcerations, number and type of prior convictions) and data about the offender's education level, employment history, and substance abuse history. All of the information is scored in a systematic way, and the report is provided to the parole board for the parole hearing. The report is prepared according to predefined state parole guidelines, and the parole board uses it much like a probation officer's presentence investigation report is used by a judge at the time of sentencing. Time is saved during the parole board hearing because the parole board does not have to search through offender files (many of which are fairly thick) to find the factors that measure the risk level that the offender will pose when released.

The rest of this chapter focuses solely on discretionary parole release and does not apply to prisoners who are considered mandatory or automatic releases, particularly those who do not go before a parole board.

THE PAROLE BOARD

Parole board release discretion varies, with most parole boards having some limits on their discretion (see Table 12.1). Although many states still retain some full-time salaried employees (such as the chair), more boards have some combination of full- and part-time employees. Terms of service are by appointment and average five years nationwide.

TABLE 12.1 *Parole Board Characteristics by State*

State	Discretion Type	Appointed Term (in years)	Number of Full-Time	Number of Part-Time
Alabama	Full	6	7	0
Alaska	Full	5	0	5
Arizona	Very limited	5	5	0
Arkansas	Very limited	7	6	1
California	Very limited	3	17	0
Colorado	Full	3	7	0
Connecticut	Full	4	1	12
Delaware	Very limited	4	1	4
Florida	Very limited	a	15	0
Georgia	Limited	7	5	0
Hawaii	Full	4	1	2
Idaho	Full	3	0	5
Illinois	Very limited	b	6	15
Indiana	Abolished	NA	NA	NA
Iowa	Full	4	2	3
Kansas	Very limited	4	3	0
Kentucky	Full	4	7	2
Louisiana	Full	NR	NR	NR
Maine	Abolished	NA	NA	NA
Maryland	Full	6	10	0
Massachusetts	Full	5	7	0
Michigan	Full	4	10	0
Minnesota	Abolished	NA	NA	NA
Mississippi	Very limited	NR	NR	NR
Missouri	Limited	6	7	0
Montana	Full	4	0	7

(continued)

TABLE 12.1   *(Contd.)*

State	Discretion Type	Appointed Term (in years)	Number of Full-Time	Number of Part-Time
Nebraska	Full	6	5	0
Nevada	Full	4	7	0
New Hampshire	Full	NR	NR	NR
New Jersey	Full	6	15	3
New Mexico	Very limited	6	0	9
New York	Limited	6	19	0
North Carolina	Very limited	4	3	0
North Dakota	Limited	3	0	6
Ohio	Very limited	NA	9	0
Oklahoma	Very limited	4	0	5
Oregon	Very limited	4	3	0
Pennsylvania	Full	6	9	0
Rhode Island	Full	3	1	6
South Carolina	Limited	6	0	7
South Dakota	Very limited	4	0	9
Tennessee	Limited	6	7	0
Texas	Full	6	7	0
Utah	Full	NR	NR	NR
Vermont	Full	NA	5	0
Virginia	Very limited	NR	NR	NR
Washington	Very limited	5	1	2
West Virginia	Full	6	5	0
Wisconsin	Very limited	NA	7	0
Wyoming	Full	6	0	7

Full = Full releasing discretion for all offenders with minor statutory limits

Limited = Releasing discretion for all offenders, except for violent or repeat felony offenders

Very limited = None or very little releasing discretion for current cases; Releasing discretion only for old cases (such as prisoners sentenced prior to 1996 or 1989)

NR = Agency not reporting/information not available

NA = Not applicable

[a] = 5 members serve 1 year, 5 for 2 years, and 5 for 3 years; All can be reappointed for 6 years

[b] = full time serve 10 years; part-time serve 3 years

Source: Association of Paroling Authorities International. 2004. *Parole Board Survey 2004.* APAI: Association of Paroling Authorities International and National Institute of Corrections. Accessed: http://www.apaintl.org/pub-parole-boardsurvey2004.html.

Parole boards range from three to 19 members, with an average of seven board members. Given that many states are large and require extensive travel, boards may be divided in half, with (for example) three members responsible for the western half of the state and the other three responsible for the eastern half. In cases like these, the release decisions require the vote of two out of three board members to grant or revoke parole for that region. Crimes of a violent or sexual nature may require a **full board review,** or the requirement that all members of the parole board review the case. If this is the case, all board members meet with the chair at a central office for a few days out of every month. A violent or sex offender is paroled if the full board decides by a majority or quorum vote that the offender should be released (Silverstein 1997). In Colorado, a quorum is defined as four of seven members who recommend release (West-Smith, Pogrebin, and Poole 2000).

FULL BOARD REVIEW

The statutory requirement that all members of the parole board review and vote on the early release from prison of individuals who have committed felony crimes, usually of a violent or sexual nature. Some states require this type of review on every discretionary release.

Term and Qualifications of the Parole Board

In states that retain parole boards, the governor usually appoints members for an average of five years (ranging from one year to life appointments, depending on the statute). Parole board members must possess integrity, intelligence, and good judgment to command respect and public confidence. Board members should have sufficiently broad academic training and experience to be qualified for professional practice in fields such as criminology, education, psychology, law, social work, and sociology. Each member must have the capacity and the desire to learn and understand legal processes, the dynamics of human behavior, and cultural conditions contributing to crime. Ideally, parole board members have previous professional experience that has given them intimate knowledge of the human experience—situations and problems confronting offenders.

THE PAROLE HEARING

As we discussed in the preceding section, a parole hearing or review is granted when the prisoner is eligible. Eligibility is determined by when the minimum sentence has been served by statute or the board has rescheduled a hearing from a previous denial.

Number of Parole Board Members

Face-to-face parole board hearings take place at the prison in which the eligible prisoner is located. File-review parole hearings have no face-to-face contact with the prisoner, and the board makes a decision based on the file kept at the prison. A hearing consists of two or three board members (or "hearing examiners") who represent the entire board. Some states may even send only one board member to conduct hearings for nonviolent offenders (West-Smith, Pogrebin, and Poole 2000). In a face-to-face hearing, one hearing examiner thoroughly reviews the file and leads with the most questions. If other members are present, they review the file less thoroughly and ask

A parole board asks questions to determine a prisoner's readiness for early community release.

supplemental questions from a different angle or ask follow-up questions to the leading parole board member's questions (Silverstein 1997). At least two signatures are required to parole a person convicted of a nonviolent crime (West-Smith, Pogrebin, and Poole 2000).

The parole board makes a decision on each case out of three possible options: grant parole, deny parole, or defer to a later date. A decision to grant parole results in conditional release before the expiration of the maximum term of imprisonment. A denial results in continued imprisonment. A deferral means that the parole board has delayed their decision (to grant or deny) until a later time, somewhere between six months and a year (Proctor 1999). In the federal system, a denial of parole on a sentence less than seven years in length allows the offender to go before the board again in 18 months. A sentence longer than seven years delays the next parole board hearing for another two years (U.S. Parole Commission 2006).

For indeterminate sentences, the parole release decision is often more important than the court's sentence in determining how long the prisoner spends incarcerated. Parole decisions aim to maximize both public safety and offender rehabilitation (Petersilia 2003).

Recommendations and Attendees

Parole hearings are held inside designated state prisons and are recorded. The federal Parole Commission and some states conduct parole release hearings using videoconference technology (see Box 12.2), which has greatly reduced the need to travel. The parole board members have access to the entire offender case file with the summary report completed by the institutional case manager. As previously mentioned, some

---

BOX 12.2   TECHNOLOGY IN CORRECTIONS

FEDERAL PAROLE DECISIONS USING VIDEOCONFERENCE

The Parole Commission used to travel to more than 60 facilities all over the United States to conduct parole release and revocation hearings face to face. Prisoners facing parole release hearings saw the Commission in a prerelease facility. Prisoners facing revocation hearings (to be discussed in Chapter 13) traveled by airplane from a local jail to a central transfer facility in Oklahoma or the detention center in Philadelphia within a 90-day period. Following their revocation hearing, they would again travel to wherever the

Commission felt was best to place them.

Now, using videoconferencing, Parole Commission members can remain in Maryland and both the prisoner and the Commission can see and interact with each other, from any federal facility in the United States. The technology was initially tried with parole release hearings. The Commission found that the "video and audio transmissions are clear and the hearings are seldom interrupted by technical difficulties . . . [and] the prisoner's ability to effectively participate in the hearing has not

been diminished" (U.S. Department of Justice 2005b, p.19262). Videoconferencing saves travel time and money for the Commission members as well as travel time, money, and risk involved in transferring prisoners. Videoconferencing has had such great success with parole release hearings that in 2005 the practice was extended to revocation hearings.

U.S. Department of Justice. 2005b. 28 CFR Part 2: Paroling, Recommitting, and Supervising Federal Prisoners: Prisoners Serving Sentences under the U.S and D.C. Codes. *Federal Register* 70(70), April 13, 2005, p. 19262.

---

hearing examiners scrutinize the case file only without interviewing the offender, whereas other parole boards have access to both the case file and the offender in person. In the federal system, the sentencing judge, the assistant U.S. attorney, and the defense attorney may all make written recommendations to the parole board. Federal prisoners may later request a copy of their parole hearing recording under the Freedom of Information Act (U.S. Parole Commission 2006).

Each state varies as to who can attend the hearing. Most states do not permit legal representation or the offender's family at parole hearings, but they will allow relatives or others associated with the offender to write letters or submit any other pertinent information for use at the hearing. The federal system allows each offender to have one "representative" to make a statement on the offender's behalf (U.S. Parole Commission 2006). Victims are allowed to either attend or to submit impact statements.

Victim Participation in Parole Hearings

The victim rights movement that began nearly 30 years ago paved the way for victims to get the chance to become more active in parole board hearings. Most parole boards provide victims with information about the parole process, and 70 percent of states allow victims to attend the parole hearing (Petersilia 2000a). Only 17 states mention in their state statutes that the parole board is to consider victim impact statements (if available) in the parole release decision. A **victim impact statement** mentions how the crime has taken a toll physically, emotionally, financially, or psychologically on the victim and the victim's family. Many victim impact statements cite how the victim continues to experience psychological, physical, or financial difficulties as a direct result of the actions of the offender (Bernat, Parsonage, and Helfgott 1994). An impact statement can be written or oral, but guidelines are less clear as to when the victim is to be notified and whether the offender has the right to read or respond to these statements. States such as Alabama specify that impact statements should be confidential because of the concern that prisoners may attempt to further harm their victim(s) for opposing the offender's release (Bernat, Parsonage, and Helfgott 1994). Other states are more proactive, such as Arizona and Oklahoma, because they allow victims to veto (refuse) a parole release decision if the victim requested notification of the hearing but was not given a chance to contribute his or her opinion (Bernat, Parsonage, and Helfgott 1994).

The effects of victim participation on parole hearings are noteworthy. One study in Pennsylvania found that victim testimony through impact statements was the most significant variable associated with parole refusal decisions. Parole was refused in 43 percent of cases in which victim impact statements were present, but only 7 percent of cases were denied when victim statements were absent (Bernat, Parsonage, and Helfgott 1994).

A similar study conducted in Alabama examined all parole records for one year for violent offenses in which injury to the victim occurred ($N = 763$). Cases were screened at first based on such factors as offense seriousness, prior criminal history, time served on current conviction, prison disciplinary record, and participation in treatment programs. Once the cases were screened on those factors, victims were notified only in the cases that had a likelihood of parole ($N = 316$). During the parole decision-making process of the screened cases, victims who made a statement in person at the hearing had a greater negative impact on the parole board's decision than victims who sent in a letter (Smith, Watkins, and Morgan 1997). Further analysis of this same data set revealed that the greater the amount of victim input and participation, the more likely that parole would be denied. Victim participation was a stronger predictor of parole decision-making behavior than other variables such as offender or offense characteristics (Morgan and Smith 2005).

VICTIM IMPACT STATEMENT

A written account by the victim(s) as to how the crime has taken a toll physically, emotionally, financially, or psychologically on the victim and the victim's family. Victim impact statements are considered by many states at time of sentencing and at parole board hearings.

MODELS OF PAROLE RELEASE DECISIONS

Statutes have typically directed parole boards to base their decisions on one or more of these criteria:

- The probability of recidivism
- The welfare of society
- The conduct of the offender while in the correctional institution
- The sufficiency of the parole plan

Three models guiding parole decision making have existed over time: (1) the surveillance model, (2) the procedural justice model, and (3) the risk prediction model.

The Surveillance Model

Early parole decisions were based not on formally articulated criteria or policies but on subjective intuition of individual decision makers. Parole decision making encompassed a surveillance perspective, which was defined as an attempt to control "the dangerous classes." The surveillance approach was based on the theory that informal social controls, including positive family relations, coworkers, and friends, would help the offender by providing structure and enforcement of the rules (Foucault 1977). Rothman (1980) reported that parole boards considered primarily the seriousness of the crime in determining whether to release an inmate on parole. However, no consensus was reached on what constituted a serious crime. Instead, "each member made his own decisions. The judgments were personal and therefore not subject to debate or reconsideration" (Rothman 1980, p. 173). The courts, to the extent that they were willing to review the parole decision at all, agreed with the contentions of paroling authorities that to impose even minimal due process constraints on the decision process would interfere with the fulfillment of their duty to engage in diagnosis and prognosis.

The Procedural Justice Model

In the 1970s, given the concerns about discrepant decision making, there was a movement toward the use of objective guidelines in the release decision. Parole decisions were made more visible and parole authorities were accountable for their decisions through the use of explicit parole selection policies. Known as the procedural justice or due process model, this perspective advocated fairness and emphasized legal factors. Parole guidelines were established to make parole selection decisions more rational and consistent.

The Risk Prediction Model

The risk prediction model was a "natural outgrowth of the procedural justice perspective" in that parole release decisions focused on community protection rather than due process and any potential progress the offender made while incarcerated (Silverstein 1997, p. 24). Researchers found that parole decisions could be predicted by using offense seriousness and the risk of recidivism, defined by prior criminal history. The **Salient Factor Score** (SFS) was developed to provide explicit guidelines for release decisions based on a determination of the potential risk of parole violation. The SFS measures six offender characteristics based on age and prior institutional commitments and assigns a score to each. Note in Figure 12.1 that the first offender characteristic considered in the Salient Factor Score calculation is prior convictions or adjudications. This offender characteristic has a score range of 0 to 3. Offenders

SALIENT FACTOR SCORE

The parole guidelines developed and used by the U.S. Parole Commission for making parole release decisions. Served as the model for parole guidelines developed in many other jurisdictions.

FIGURE 12.1   *Salient Factor Score (SFS/98)*

Item A. Prior Convictions/Adjudications (Adult or Juvenile)
None	= 3
One	= 2
Two or three	= 1
Four or more	= 0

Item B. Prior Commitment(s) of More Than 30 Days (Adult or Juvenile)
None	= 2
One or two	= 1
Three or more	= 0

Item C. Age at Current Offense/Prior Commitments

26 years or more
3 or fewer prior commitments	= 3
4 prior commitments	= 2
5 or more commitments	= 1

22–25 years
3 or fewer prior commitments	= 2
4 prior commitments	= 1
5 or more prior commitments	= 0

20–21 years
3 or fewer prior commitments	= 1
4 prior commitments	= 0
19 years or less (any number of prior commitments)	= 0

Item D. Recent Commitment-Free Period (Three Years)

No prior commitment of more than 30 days (adult or juvenile) or released to the community from last such commitment at least three years prior to the commencement of the current offense = 1
Otherwise = 0

Item E. Probation/Parole/Confinement/Escape Status Violator This Time

Neither on probation, parole, confinement, or escape status at the time of the current offense; nor committed as a probation, parole, confinement, or escape status violator this time = 1
Otherwise = 0

Item F. Older Offenders

If the offender was 41 years of age or more at the commencement of the current offense (and the total score from Items A–E above is 9 or less) = 1
Otherwise = 0

TOTAL SCORE (Sum of Items A through F)

Source: United States Parole Commission. 2003. *Rules and Procedures Manual,* Revised August, 15, 2003, p. 58. Accessed: http://www.usdoj.gov/uspc/rules_procedures/rulesmanual.htm.

with no prior convictions are assigned a score of 3; one prior conviction results in a score of 2; two to three prior convictions gives a score of 1; and four or more gives a score of 0. Each offender characteristic is scored in a similar manner, and the sum of the six items yields the predictive score. The higher the score (maximum of 10), the less likely is the probability of recidivism (Hoffman 1994). Although no prediction device is 100 percent accurate, the SFS has been able to acceptably predict different probabilities of recidivism according to a small number of known variables.

Decision makers then use guidelines to determine the customary time to be served for a range of offenses based on the severity of the offense (see Figure 12.2). Severity is based on eight categories, ranging from the least to the most severe. For example, an adult offender whose SFS/98 score was 5 and whose offense severity was rated in Category Two would be expected to serve 12 to 16 months before being paroled.

FIGURE 12.2 *Guidelines for Decision Making: Customary Total Time to be Served before Release*

Offense Characteristics: Offense Severity (Some Crimes Eliminated or Summarized)	Offender Characteristics (from Salient Factor Score in Figure 12.1)			
	Very Good (10–8)	Good (7–6)	Fair (5–4)	Poor (3–0)
Category One *Low:* possession of a small amount of marijuana; simple theft under $1,000	≤ 4 months	8 months	8–12 months	12–16 months
Category Two *Low/Moderate:* income tax evasion less than $10,000; immigration law violations; embezzlement, fraud, forgery under $1,000	≤ 6 months	10 months	12–16 months	16–22 months
Category Three *Moderate:* bribery; possession of 50 lb. or less of marijuana, with intent to sell; illegal firearms; income tax evasion $10,000 to $50,000; nonviolent property offenses $1,000 to $19,999; auto theft, not for resale	10 months	12–16 months	18–24 months	24–32 months
Category Four *High:* counterfeiting; marijuana possession with intent to sell, 50 to 1,999 lb.; auto theft, for resale; nonviolent property offenses, $20,000 to $100,000	12–18 months	20–26 months	26–34 months	34–44 months
Category Five *Very High:* robbery; breaking and entering bank or post office; extortion; marijuana possession with intent to sell, over 2,000 lb.; hard drugs possession with intent to sell, not more than $100,000; nonviolent property offenses over $100,000 but not exceeding $500,000	24–36 months	36–48 months	48–60 months	60–72 months
Category Six *Greatest I:* explosive detonation; multiple robbery; aggravated felony (weapon fired—no serious injury); hard drugs, over $100,000; forcible rape	40–52 months	52–64 months	64–78 months	78–100 months
Category Seven *Greatest II:* aircraft hijacking; espionage; kidnapping; homicide	52–80 months	64–92 months	78–110 months	100–148 months
Category Eight (parole extremely unlikely) Contract murders, murder of law enforcement officer, murder by torture, felony murder	100+ months	120+ months	150+ months	180+ months

Source: United States Parole Commission. 2003. *Rules and Procedures Manual,* Revised August, 15, 2003, p. 28. Accessed: http://www.usdoj.gov/uspc/rules_procedures/rulesmanual.htm.

Following the lead of the federal system, many states adopted guidelines for use in release decision making. Some states adopted a matrix guideline system similar to the SFS, whereas others adopted different types of guidelines that consider factors such as criminal history, whether the current crime involved deviant sexual activity, and the offender's history of violence. Regardless of the form that parole release guidelines take, they structure the exercise of discretion. Some parole boards with full discretion are free to deviate from their guidelines, but they must give reasons for doing so in case of appeal.

Researchers have attempted more recently to fine-tune parole risk prediction instruments according to gender. Because female parolees have lower recidivism rates than male parolees, a group of researchers examined various models to determine which factors most accurately predicted success and failure rates on parole for female parolees (McShane, Williams, and Dolny 2002). The researchers found that for women, age at first arrest, age at release, release status (new release or parole violator), and number of prior arrests most accurately predicted parole failure (McShane, Williams, and Dolny 2002).

DUE PROCESS DURING DISCRETIONARY PAROLE HEARINGS

One of the most striking aspects of the traditional parole release process has been the virtual inability to challenge parole decisions (Palacios 1994). In recent years courts have provided some procedural protections and articulated criteria for reviewing the conditions that parole boards have set on parolees' conduct and for revoking parole and returning parolees to prison. This has to do with the courts' view that parole is a privilege and there is no expectation of due process.

Menechino v. Oswald

In *Menechino v. Oswald* (1971), a prisoner argued that the New York State Board of Parole's denial of parole was illegal because he had not received the right to counsel, the right to cross-examine witnesses, the right to produce favorable witnesses, and the specification of the grounds upon which the denial decision was based. The court ruled that due process was not an issue in parole because parole was a privilege and not a right.

Greenholtz v. Inmates of the Nebraska Penal and Correctional Complex

In 1979 the U.S. Supreme Court directly addressed the issue of due process in parole release decision making. In *Greenholtz v. Inmates of the Nebraska Penal and Correctional Complex* (1979), the inmates of a Nebraska prison brought a class action alleging they had been unconstitutionally denied parole by the Nebraska Board of Parole. The inmates also contested three other procedures: (1) the state's hearing process, (2) the board's practice of informing inmates when it denies parole, and (3) the procedure of informing inmates in advance of the month their parole hearing will be held. After the lower federal courts held in favor of the inmates, the U.S. Supreme Court reversed the decision of the court of appeals. The Court emphasized that parole boards have broad discretion in their decision making, even if it is at times imperfect:

> The Nebraska procedure affords an opportunity to be heard, and when parole is denied it informs the inmate in what respect he falls short of qualifying for parole; this

affords the process that is due under these circumstances. The Constitution does not require more. (p. 16)

The Court concluded that parole release and parole revocation "are quite different" because "there is a . . . difference between losing what one has and not getting what one wants" (*Greenholtz v. Inmates of the Nebraska Penal and Correctional Complex* 1979, pp. 9–10). Although the *Greenholtz* case did not extend due process as far as desired by the plaintiffs, it did establish that some due process protections were available in the parole-granting process. In summary, *Greenholtz* required reasonable notice of a parole hearing date (one month before the hearing is reasonable); an initial hearing wherein the prisoner is allowed to present the case; and, if parole is denied, written reasons must be given for denial.

Even if the parole board changes its mind about its decision, no due process rights are necessary provided the prisoner has not actually been released from the institution (*Jago v. Van Curen* 1981).

State-Created Liberty Interest

Following the *Greenholtz* case, many state courts examined state parole statutes in cases brought forth by inmates to determine whether the mandatory wording of some statutes created a constitutionally protected **liberty interest.** The courts decided that prison inmates did not have a protected liberty interest in parole unless the state creates that interest via mandatory wording in the state statute.

For example, in 1987, in *Board of Pardons v. Allen,* the U.S. Supreme Court held that the state of Montana had created a protected liberty interest in its parole statute. The statute read:

> Subject to the following restrictions, the board shall release on parole . . . any person confined in the Montana state prison or the women's correction center . . . when in its opinion there is reasonable probability that the prisoner can be released without detriment to the prisoner or to the community.

The mandatory wording in the statute is "shall," and this word creates a liberty interest that triggers due process protections. If the mandatory wording were amended to discretionary language (such as "may"), no liberty interest would be at stake and thus no additional due process would be required beyond that of *Greenholtz.*

LIBERTY INTEREST

Any interest recognized or protected by the due process clauses of state or federal constitutions.

Extending the Time Intervals between Parole Hearings

As parole releases have become more scrutinized, the parole board has also tightened its own guidelines, which includes offering prisoners fewer opportunities for a parole hearing. One way is through lengthening the interval of time between parole hearings, so that if a prisoner was denied parole, he or she would have to wait longer to see the board again. In Georgia, the parole board increased the interval for prisoners serving "life" sentences from three years to eight years and applied the rule retroactively to prisoners who were already incarcerated under an old set of parole guidelines. Prisoner Jones challenged this, saying that applying it retroactively violated the ex post facto clause of the U.S. Constitution. The U.S. Supreme Court disagreed saying that the extended time interval did not violate the ex post facto clause. The increased interval to the next parole hearing did not affect the length of the sentence; it only affected *where* that time was to be served, particularly with lifers who had a slim chance of being released (*Garner v. Jones* 2000).

PRISONERS' PERCEPTIONS OF PAROLE SELECTION

The parole process has been criticized as being secretive and arbitrary and failing to provide prisoners with a clear indication of what they need to do to obtain early release. This may be because parole board hearings are truly deliberative processes, and parole board members themselves do not know the outcome of the hearing in at least 80 percent of the cases (Silverstein 1997). More often, however, prisoners feel they may have prepared themselves as much as possible for what they think will earn them release, only to be denied based on "inadequate time served" even though they have met their minimum parole eligibility date (West-Smith, Pogrebin, and Poole 2000). The renewed interest in reentry has increased the importance of the release plan and the transition from prison to the community.

Mika'il A. Muhammad (1996) interviewed 263 prisoners from the Eastern New York Correctional Facility and found that 60 percent of inmates favored a form of contract parole, "wherein the inmate negotiates with parole and correctional personnel at the beginning of the sentence a plan to address specific needs that, if met, would facilitate parole readiness and insure release on a specified date" (p. 146). Contract parole is not used at this time, but reducing uncertainty about the parole process would likely decrease prisoner stress.

Although a history of violence is important to consider, any system that reduces the importance of positive institutional behavior runs the risk of creating a nightmare for prison administrators who are supervising prisoners with "nothing to lose" and increases reentry problems in the future. Gauging what factors to consider is no easy task. Some suggest that career criminals know how to do time; that is, they can manipulate the parole board by avoiding institutional violations and participating in rehabilitation programs that look good on their record when they are reviewed for parole. Good behavior while in prison does not always predict law-abiding behavior in the community.

Although the parole board determines release and/or sets parole conditions, the day-to-day supervision of parole is left to field parole officers who work either for the parole board or for another government agency independent of the parole board, such as the parole division of a department of corrections. Parole supervision is the subject of the next chapter.

TOP THINGS YOU SHOULD KNOW

- Reentry programs include those that take place in the prison setting, as well as community-based programs that follow up the transition process.
- Reentry initiatives include reentry courts and collaborations between parole agencies and grassroots community organizations or other criminal justice agencies.
- Issues in reentry affect not only the parolee but the offender's family, the victim, and the community.
- A parolee faces issues related to finding stable employment, finding suitable housing, and reestablishing contact with his or her family. Being that most releasees are also on supervision, they face the pressure of being mindful of who they associate with and checking in with the parole officer.
- There are three types of release from prison—those without any supervision, those under a short period of mandatory supervision by a parole officer, and those under discretionary parole release.

- Parole boards have the power to decide whether to release prisoners who are doing sentences with the eligibility for discretionary parole.
- Parole boards determine when revocation of parole and return to prison are necessary.
- Because discretionary parole is defined as a privilege rather than a right, the courts have allowed very minimal, if any, due process.

DISCUSSION QUESTIONS

1 What issues do prisoners face in preparing for their reentry into the community?

2 What are the major functions of a parole board?

3 What are the primary qualifications of a good parole board member? Why are these qualities important?

4 Why are good public relations necessary to parole's effectiveness?

5 How is parole eligibility typically determined?

6 What is good time, and what is its relationship to eligibility for parole consideration?

7 If you were a victim of a violent crime, would you take the time to write an impact statement or attend the parole board hearing? Why or why not?

8 How does prisoner reentry potentially affect the victim and/or the victim's family?

9 What issues exist with respect to prisoner reentry and the impact on the community?

10 How did the ruling in *Menechino v. Oswald* affect parole decision making?

11 If you were a parole board member, what factors would you consider in attempting to arrive at a fair and just decision? Why?

12 If you were a prisoner, what method of release from prison would you prefer, discretionary or mandatory/automatic? Why?

13 In light of the composition of the present Supreme Court, what do you think will be the result of future decisions on parole issues?

 ## WEBSITES

The Reentry Policy Council—a private/public partnership that is federally funded

http://www.reentrypolicy.org

Transition from Prison to Community Initiative

http://www.nicic.org/pubs/2002/017520.pdf#search=%22Transition%20From%20Prison%20to%20Community%20Initiative%22

Reentry Trends in the U.S.

http://www.ojp.usdoj.gov/bjs/reentry/releases.htm

RAND Study: Public Health Challenges of Prisoner Reentry

http://www.rand.org/publications/RB/RB6013

Open Society Institute—Baltimore: Various Policy Papers on Prisoner Reentry

http://www.soros.org/baltimore/policypapers.htm

Overview of Prisoner Reentry in Pennsylvania

http://www.cor.state.pa.us/

U.S. Parole Commission

http://www.usdoj.gov/uspc/parole.htm

Missouri Office of Victim Services: Parole Hearings

http://www.doc.missouri.gov/victims/victimparolehearings.htm

Oregon Victims' Rights at Parole Board Hearings

http://www.ncvc.org/policy/issues/parole/tables/or.html

Ohio Parole Board

http://www.drc.state.oh.us/web/parboard.htm

Tennessee Board of Parole

http://www2.state.tn.us/bopp/home.htm

Texas Parole Release Guidelines

http://www.tdcj.state.tx.us/bpp/new_parole_guidelines/new_parole_guidelines.html

Parole Board, United Kingdom

http://www.paroleboard.gov.uk

Preparing for Prisoner Reentry

Various systems are used to make release decisions for incarcerated offenders. In states where sentences are indeterminate, a paroling authority often must make the decision to release the offender and decide when that release should occur. Sentencing laws may determine when an offender is eligible for release, but the offender is not granted a release until the parole authority approves the release.

In the following cases, the paroling authority must consider the offender cases and make a determination to release or not to release the offender to the community. Factors considered often involve probability of recidivism, victim impact, community impact, conduct of the offender in the institution, and release plan offered. Consider these cases and determine if the offender's release has merit.

CASE A

Joseph is serving a 10-to-25-year sentence for two counts of armed robbery. He has served the mandatory minimum of five years and is being considered for release for the first time; by statute he can be held in custody for 13 years before he reaches a mandatory release date. Joseph served a previous sentence for burglary and successfully completed the release period before he committed the current crimes. The victims in both robberies were elderly gas station attendants, and very small amounts of money were obtained from the robberies. The victims remain fearful of the offender, and both indicate that their lives were significantly affected by the experience. Neither victim ever returned to work out of fear of similar future events. While incarcerated, Joseph has completed substance abuse treatment for his cocaine dependence, and the treatment summary calls for his attendance in facility Cocaine Anonymous meetings. He attends the meetings about half of the time they are offered. He has also completed an anger management program, has been assigned to several inmate jobs, and has had no rule violations while incarcerated. Joseph would like to have gone to a work release facility, but due to a waiting list he was not able enter this program prior to being considered for release. His community plan is to return to the same community where the crimes were committed, live with his elderly aunt, seek work as a construction laborer, and attend community substance abuse aftercare. He would be under the supervision of a parole officer upon his release, if granted.

CASE B

Fred is a 39-year-old individual serving 14 years for possession with intent to sell a controlled substance. This is his second prison term, having served a six-year sentence for sale of heroin in the 1990s. He was paroled on the first offense after four years and successfully completed parole supervision. However, he was arrested on the current charge within two months of being released from parole supervision. Law enforcement officials reported that he had been under surveillance for several months before the arrest and was suspected of dealing drugs during most of the period of his parole supervision. While under supervision, he reported regularly to his parole officer and worked steadily at a job in a warehouse owned by his brother-in-law. There were no known law violations during the period of supervision. Fred's institutional adjustment has been excellent. He attended drug counseling and is a member of the prison Narcotics Anonymous group. He attained his GED certificate and reports that he wants to attend community college when released. He will work for his brother-in-law again when released and live with his sister and her husband until he can afford to rent an apartment. The sheriff in the county to which he would be released has protested his parole release, stating that Fred is a manipulative and devious individual who maintains a façade of cooperation and honest living while continuing to sell drugs. Fred has served five years of his current 14-year sentence. Institutional counselors recommend his release at this time.

CASE C

Marie is a 55-year-old female who has served 30 years of a 20-years-to-life sentence for murder. She was convicted of killing her two young children (ages 2 and 4 years). She reported that her live-in boyfriend would not agree to stay with her as long as she had children. She chose to kill the children to maintain the relationship. She has maintained a near-perfect prison record and is considered by authorities to be a model inmate. She reports great remorse for her actions. The prison chaplain has counseled her for many years and states that she has been "born again" and forgiven for her crimes and sins. Marie works as a chaplain's assistant in the institution and is well thought of by both inmates and prison officials alike. If paroled, she will work for the Prison Ministries in her hometown and will be provided with a place to stay by her employers.

13

Parole Conditions and Revocation

Introduction

Prisoner Perspectives on Getting Out
California Study
Iowa Study

The Field Parole Officer
The Officer's Perspective

Conditions of Parole
Legal Issues in Parole Conditions
Limited Parolee Rights

Violating Parole
Warrants and Citations
Due Process Rights under "Preparole"

Characteristics of Parole Violators
Parole Revocation Rate
Reasons for Revocation
Why Have Revocation Rates Increased?
Attitudes on Revocation

Parole Absconders
Why Do Parolees Leave?
Locating and Apprehending Fugitives
Predicting Absconding Behavior

Parole Effectiveness
Recidivism Studies
Predicting Parole Outcomes

Top Things You Should Know

© Bob Daemmrich

What You Will Learn in This Chapter

- *Parole conditions imposed by parole boards are subject to the same limitations as probation conditions.*
- *The main goal of parole is societal protection, accomplished by enforcing parolee restrictions and providing services that assist in community reintegration.*
- *There are certain reasons why people violate parole and/or abscond from community supervision, as well as ways to decrease this behavior.*
- *There are certain variables that consistently predict recidivism following release from prison.*
- *The parolees who violate on parole will typically do so in the first six months after release.*

INTRODUCTION

The factors and conditions that lead to prisoner reentry were discussed in Chapter 12. In this chapter, we discuss what it is like to be on parole. Parole is a form of community supervision of offenders. Therefore, as with probation, supervision conditions are an integral part of parole. **Parole conditions** imposed determine the amount of freedom versus restrictions a parolee has.

PAROLE CONDITIONS

The rules under which a paroling authority releases an offender to community supervision.

The main goal of parole is societal protection, which is accomplished by enforcing parolee restrictions and providing services that assist in community reintegration while at the same time maintaining public confidence in parole (Williams, McShane, and Dolny 2000a). Whatever may be the primary goal behind parole release, conditions imposed play a big role in achievement and often determine whether the parolee succeeds or fails.

The length of time spent on parole averages about two years nationwide, although the amount of time is longer for violent offenders and shorter for property and drug offenders (Camp, Camp, and May 2003). The length of supervision largely depends on the laws of the state of conviction. For example, parole is limited to six months in Oregon and one year in Indiana, regardless of the type of crime. Most states allow parolees to be discharged before the full term of their sentence. Federal offenders under mandatory release are automatically discharged 180 days prior to their maximum expiration date. Offenders who remain in prison with less than 180 days left on their entire sentence are released without any community supervision whatsoever (U.S. Parole Commission 2006).

As with probation, parole revocation occurs if the parolee violates the conditions of parole. Parolees are automatically returned to jail or prison to serve the remainder of their sentence. Revocation is also important to society because the parolee will once again be under the care and custody of the state, and with that comes the high cost of keeping an offender incarcerated. Much is at stake for both the parolee and the state in parole revocation.

PRISONER PERSPECTIVES ON GETTING OUT

Few studies have examined the prisoner's perspective while on parole. Most researchers conduct studies about inmate life experiences inside prison, primarily because institutional prisoners make captive audiences. An exception to this is research conducted with prisoners recently released from prison. Craig Hemmens supervised a research team that interviewed 775 former inmates as they were waiting for the bus within a few minutes to a few hours of release from prison. Hemmens (1998) found that as prisoners age, their apprehension about reentry decreased. Less reentry apprehension also applied to prisoners who served sentences of three years or less compared with those who served sentences longer than three years. Because this study was cross-sectional, none of the prisoners were tracked to see if they succeeded. Prisoners generally have good intentions and plan on staying out of prison. Many prisoners do attempt to live a legitimate life by finding employment after release, but prisoners experience a great deal of stress and disdain during the transition period (Glaser 1969; Irwin 1970).

One such individual is Robert Grooms (1982), who wrote about the perils of release from prison and why, despite all the advantages he had over most other convicts upon release, he did not make it. When he was released, Grooms had problems finding a job, found he had nothing in common with old friends, and was uncomfortable around "square-johns" (pp. 541–545). He wrote:

> I had another problem common among recently released prisoners. I wanted to make up all at once for lost time. I wanted the things that others my age had worked years to achieve, and I wanted them right away. (p. 543)

Grooms could not "sit still" and he did not want to be alone, so he began to hang around places and people where he felt comfortable. He found himself talking to ex-convicts in taverns, and they talked about what they all had in common: crime, the prison experience, and violence. Grooms concluded by saying:

> When he is released, a prisoner is in a real sense cast out into a totally alien society. Overnight he is expected to discard months and years of self-survival tactics, to change his values, to readjust to situations and circumstances that he had long forgotten, and to accept responsibility. More important, he has to overcome, in a society that rejects him, his lack of self-worth; he has to become accepted where he is not wanted. Is it any wonder that so many newly released prisoners feel out of their natural environment, that many first-time, petty offenders leave prison and find someone weak to prey on, or that the recidivism rate is so high. (p. 545)

California Study

A classic study of parolee perspectives was completed in California. A collaborative team of researchers, students, and ex-convicts was assembled to interview 60 parolees about their experiences as they first left prison (Erickson et al. 1973).

The researchers found that the reentry process was a negative experience for about half of all parolees, as most of them had experienced failure on parole many times before. While on parole, offenders felt pressure to obtain a job, money, food, clothes, and a place to stay. Many parolees relied more on friends and other ex-convicts for these basic needs than they did on their own family. For example, Lloyd Nieman, age 36 with an eighth-grade education and convicted of forgery, was in the process of enrolling at a state college while on parole. Nieman explained:

> The first few days I was out were about the roughest days of this entire period. I've only been out a short time—five weeks—but the first three days were a hassle. . . . [N]o money, no transportation, no job, and no place to live. Now these things have a way of working themselves out in time, but you have to contact the right people, and sometimes it's hard to find the right people. . . . I was lucky that I had two friends here, too,

that could help me. Nick [an ex-con] gave me a place to stay, because I was out of money within four days. They [the prison] give you $60, and out of that you got to buy your own clothes. (pp. 16–17)

Shortly after his interview, Nieman absconded, leaving the state and never returning. A warrant was issued for his arrest. After one year, Nieman could not be located.

Many parolees were socially detached and many admitted to being lonely. For example, Anthony Mendez, age 46, spent the last 16 years in prison for possession of narcotics and had been out on parole for three months when interviewed. Mendez's experience is a bit different from Nieman's. Mendez had more financial assistance from his family in Los Angeles, but he was paroled to an area of San Diego where he did not know anyone. Mendez explains his experience:

I was just kinda lost when I got out. If you've been in a while, so many things are new and different. . . . I've always gotten a lot of help [from family], so I think I've just been lucky; but I know there's a lot of other guys that didn't get the help I got. . . . I really couldn't talk to anybody, which is hard. . . . For the majority of fellows in the joint, they're so starved emotionally and so closed in, so shut off from any warmth, any friendship, that it takes a long time when you get out to break out of these bonds and be a normal person out here where you can talk to people. . . . I think that when a guy first gets out, it's a very important thing that that man go to work, if for no other reason than that eight hours is going to be occupied . . . and its not going to let him dwell on how much he's missed and how much he's missing again. (Erickson et al. 1973, pp. 27–29)

One year after Mendez was interviewed, he was still on parole but had lost his job.

Through the interviews, parolees made suggestions ranging from increasing rehabilitation and vocational programs inside prison to increasing community resources on release. The lack of reentry resources has been a continual problem for parolees nationwide. For example, one parolee stated:

It just doesn't seem fair to give the convict such a little money and tell him to make it. What regular citizen today can set out in the world, with less than a high school education, no job, $50, and no close ties or other resources, and make it? That is what we are asking the parolee to do, and we will not let him forget that he is an outsider. (Erickson et al. 1973, p. 98)

One of the most innovative suggestions made in some of the interviews was that everyone released from prison be assigned a mentor in his or her area. The mentor would be a successful ex-convict who has remained out of the system, and he or she would be available to deal with emotional and social problems the parolee faces. Even though this research was conducted 30 years ago, the needs and problems of parolees remain the same today.

Iowa Study

Richards and Jones (1997) conducted a study of the transition from prison to a correctional halfway house, and then to parole. They interviewed 30 men who were just released from prison and were sentenced to a halfway house as a form of graduated release. The researchers found that the men had not been prepared for release from prison to an environment that required them to pay rent, look for employment, sustain a job, and pay for food. One prisoner explained the pressures of getting behind in rent upon his arrival at the halfway house:

You leave the penitentiary on a Tuesday, you come here [to the halfway house], and you're broke for the whole week or two till they send your money from the penitentiary.

What kind of shit is that? Ya know, I mean a man come home from the penitentiary they don't even give you gate money. They give you $5 [and] bus fare. . . . I owe for [bed] sheets, owe for bus tokens, I owe for my rent. You're automatically 2 weeks behind in rent, see what I'm saying. . . . I didn't ask to come here and be put in the hole by your all program. Ya all know that when I come here it would take a while for me to find a job. (pp. 13–14)

One of the issues that likely affects the success rate at the halfway house is financial pressures, which includes not only daily living expenses but also setting aside money for paying court costs, fees, victim restitution, and back child support that accumulated while the prisoner was behind bars. In sum, then, the intent of parolee interview research is to determine parolee needs from the prisons' point of view so that intervention programs can be designed to help address problems that ultimately lead many to fail or to sabotage themselves while on parole.

THE FIELD PAROLE OFFICER

A field parole officer enforces the conditions of parole that are mandated by the parole board. Parole officers ordinarily manage caseloads of between 60 and 75 prisoners, although others have smaller, more specialized caseloads (numbering 25 to 50) of prisoners who need more intensive supervision. "Regular" supervision typically means about two 15-minute face-to-face contacts per month, with an annual cost of about $2,200 per parolee (Petersilia 2000b).

Parole officers are expected to perform five main functions:

1. Carry out and enforce the conditions of parole through supervision and monitoring by means of home visits, employment checks, and meeting with the parolee at the office.
2. Refer parolees to drug and alcohol treatment, anger management programs, parenting classes, and other community-based services according to their individual needs.
3. Conduct investigations; write reports; and evaluate, interpret, and report serious violations to the paroling authority.
4. Provide crime victims with information on the offender's living and working arrangements, parole conditions, and restitution payment schedule, if applicable.
5. Share applicable information with law enforcement personnel and take into custody parolees who violate their conditions.

To perform these functions, a parole officer must possess certain basic qualifications and specialized knowledge. The minimum qualifications should be a working knowledge of the principles of human behavior, knowledge of the laws of the jurisdiction in which he or she will work and of the powers and limitations of the position, and familiarity with the operation of related law enforcement agencies in the particular jurisdiction.

The Officer's Perspective

Lynch (1998) conducted an ethnographic study of California parole officers to examine how officers managed job pressures of maintaining a specific number of contacts, having their parolees take drug tests, and filing reports within a specific time period.

Lynch found that parole officers came from a variety of backgrounds, but their "role identity" was similar in that they viewed parole more as an art than as a science. In other words, parole officers perceived that "keeping a pulse on their caseload"—knowing what their parolees were doing—through face-to-face interactions and monitoring was more important than the increased paperwork that resulted from using the computerized tracking records.

> The agents generally strove toward a very traditional law enforcement role, where they did not need to assess danger or risk or criminal activity by anything more than their own developed intuition and personal investigative skills. (Lynch 1998, p. 855)

A survey of Missouri parole officers' perceptions on the importance of their job in assisting prisoners with successful community reentry revealed that "close monitoring of behavior, assessing and referring parolees to community agencies based on their needs, helping parolees maintain employment, and holding offenders accountable for their behavior" were identified as the most important tasks (Seiter 2002, p. 53). When asked to ascertain the most important features of successful reentry programs, steady employment was mentioned by parole officers as the key element. The next three were that the parolee remain drug free, have positive family and peer social support systems, and have plenty of structure in daily activities. The last two were related to consistent officer monitoring and the officers' holding offenders accountable for their successes and failures. The five programs parole officers thought best assisted with parolee reentry were identified as job skills/vocational rehabilitation, substance abuse treatment, halfway houses, work release, and employment assistance (Seiter 2002).

CONDITIONS OF PAROLE

As in the case of probation, parole conditions may be classified into standard conditions which are mandatory for all parolees in a jurisdiction, and special conditions which are tailored to fit the needs of an offender and therefore vary between offenders. Table 13.1 shows an example of parole conditions for the state of Oklahoma, which is fairly representative of conditions in other states. The average number of standard conditions for a parolee was fifteen (Rhine, Smith, and Jackson 1991). This raises the question as to whether all of these conditions are realistic expectations for parolees. Is the system of conditions so rigid and strict that the parolee is destined to fail? The courts will generally uphold reasonable conditions but will strike down illegal conditions or those considered unreasonable because they are impossible to meet. As in probation, appellate courts generally allow parole boards great discretion in imposing conditions of parole (Holt 1998).

Legal Issues in Parole Conditions

Recent court cases have raised interesting legal issues involving parole conditions. For example, the Tenth Circuit Court of Appeals upheld a condition that paroled Colorado sex offenders must provide blood and saliva samples to create a DNA (deoxyribonucleic acid) bank for easy identification should the parolee commit a similar offense (*Boling v. Romer* 1996). The condition was challenged as violating parolees' right against unreasonable searches and seizures. The court held that this requirement was reasonable because of the significance of DNA evidence in solving sex offenses, the minimal intrusion on the inmate's right to privacy, and the inmate's diminished constitutional rights.

TABLE 13.1 *Rules and Conditions of Oklahoma Parole*

1. I will report to my parole officer and my employer immediately upon arrival at my destination.
2. I will obey all city, state and federal laws. I agree to immediately report any new arrests to my parole officer.
3. I agree not to leave the State of Oklahoma without prior written permission by my officer and not leave the county without permission of my officer or his/her district office.
4. I agree to report as directed by my officer in person and in writing on the forms provided by my officer. I agree to allow the officer to visit at home, work or other convenient places.
5. I agree to immediately report in person, in writing or by telephone any changes in residence, employment or marital status.
6. I agree not to use or possess drugs other than those legally prescribed by a physician. I agree not to use alcohol nor go onto the premises where alcoholic beverages are served.
7. I agree not to lie or misrepresent the truth to any member of the Pardon and Parole Board, any employee of the Department of Corrections or any official of the government.
8. I agree not to associate with persons on parole or probation or persons with criminal records, communicate with inmates of any penal institution, except members of the immediate family, unless my parole officer gives permission because of work or other good reason.
9. I agree to pay parole fees of $40 per month, payable in cashier's check or money order to the Department of Corrections Restitution and Accounting.
10. I will comply with all lawful directives issued by my supervising officer or any member of the Department of Corrections.
11. I understand that at any time or place, I am subject to search. In addition, my vehicle and any property under my control are subject to search.
12. I agree to submit to urinalysis or any other substance abuse testing procedures as required by my parole officer.
13. I agree to pay, during the term of my parole, all fines and court costs imposed by the court at the time of my conviction.
14. I understand that Oklahoma State Statute 21 § 1283(d) prohibits anyone under the supervision of the Oklahoma Department of Corrections to own or possess a firearm. I agree not to own, possess or travel in a vehicle with a firearm or explosives.
15. Sex offenders will abide by special sex offender rules.
16. I understand that violations may result in the imposition of sanctions including but not limited to:

Financial Planning	Reintegration Training	Electronic Monitoring	Day Reporting
Mental Health Counseling	Intensive Supervision	Community Service	Temporary Placement in
Attend AA	Attend N/A	Victim Impact Panel	a community correctional
Attend MRT	Curfew	Weekend Incarceration	facility or jail for up
GED Courses	Intensive Parole	Nighttime Incarceration	to 30 days' supervision

17. I agree to follow the **special condition(s)** listed below:

I have read these conditions and understand that I must obey them until the term of my parole expires. I understand that failure to comply with these rules and conditions may result in the imposition of intermediate sanctions or revocation of my parole. I also understand that a finding of guilt, or plea of guilty or nolo contendere will be evidence that I failed to obey the law. I will be arrested and sent back to prison to serve the remainder of my sentence plus any new sentences.

_____
WITNESS SIGNATURE AND DATE

_____
PAROLEE'S SIGNATURE AND DATE

_____
NUMBER

Accessed May 1, 2006: http://www.ppb.state.ok.us/Docket/Rules%20of%20Parole/Rules%20and%20Conditions.rtf

Similar cases have been decided in two other federal circuit courts of appeal (*Jones v. Murray* 1992; *Rise v. Oregon* 1995). Plaintiffs argued that they were unconstitutionally required to incriminate themselves with such samples; that they were being singled out as sex offenders, thus violating their right to equal protection; and that it denied them liberty interest under the Fourteenth Amendment. The courts held the tests constitutional, saying that parole is discretionary and may be conditioned on a requirement that is itself legal.

Legal issues have also been raised concerning requirements that offenders who are on parole for sex offenses register in communities where they reside, even if the registration law was passed after the offense was committed. Some states require registration and notification in the community of the presence of sex offenders on parole even after they have completed their sentence (see Chapter 15). The validity of those statutes has been upheld, but higher courts have not yet decided whether these laws should apply to sex offenders convicted before the laws were passed.

The Seventh Circuit Court of Appeals has upheld submission to a penile plethysmograph as a parole condition for a Michigan inmate who was convicted in federal court of kidnapping and allegedly molesting a 6-year-old boy before attempting to drown him (*Walrath v. Getty* 1995). The offender in this case objected to the condition, saying that it was fundamentally unfair and therefore denied him due process. His parole was revoked. On appeal, the Seventh Circuit ruled that "the Commission may impose or modify other conditions of parole so long as they are reasonably related to the nature of the circumstances of the offense and the history and characteristics of the parolee."

Limited Parolee Rights

An offender on parole does not lose all constitutional rights. However, as with probationers, the rights enjoyed are **diminished,** meaning that they are not as highly protected by the courts as similar rights enjoyed by nonoffenders.

FIRST AMENDMENT RIGHTS.   Even **preferred rights** such as First Amendment rights can be limited if an offender is on parole or probation. For example, a defendant was convicted for obstructing a federal court order arising from the defendant's antiabortion activities. The court imposed as a condition of supervision that the defendant was prohibited from "harassing, intimidating, or picketing in front of any gynecological or abortion family planning services center" (*United States v. Turner* 1995). The defendant challenged that condition, claiming it violated her rights under the First Amendment. On appeal, the Federal Court of Appeals for the Tenth Circuit held the condition valid, saying "conditions which restrict freedom of speech and association are valid if they are reasonably necessary to accomplish the essential needs of the State and public order."

FOURTH AMENDMENT RIGHTS.   As a condition of parole, parolees must allow parole officers to search their car or place of residence without a search warrant. This condition has been upheld for parole revocation hearings but not for a new criminal prosecution. A parolee's "consent" to warrantless searches by state parole agents, based on reasonable suspicion that the parolee had committed a parole violation as specified in the conditions of release, was proper under both the Fourth Amendment and the applicable provision of the Pennsylvania constitution (*Commonwealth v. Williams* 1997).

The **exclusionary rule** was initially used to exclude any evidence obtained or seized illegally by the police in violation of the Fourth Amendment. In the case of parolees, *Pennsylvania Board of Probation and Parole v. Scott* (1998) and probationers *(State v. Pizel* 1999), the court ruled that the exclusionary rule does not apply to parole or probation revocation hearings. The court ruled in the direction it did in part because parole officers do not need a warrant to conduct a legal search, and the burden of proof is lower in parole revocation hearings than it is in criminal court prosecutions. A different standard must be met for searches conducted for individuals under parole supervision compared with individuals not under community supervision (Hemmens, Bennett, and del Carmen 1998). Parolees and probationers have less expectation of privacy than individuals not under a correctional sentence.

DIMINISHED CONSTITUTIONAL RIGHTS

Constitutional rights enjoyed by an offender on parole that are not as highly protected by the courts as the rights of nonoffenders.

PREFERRED RIGHTS

Rights more highly protected than other constitutional rights.

EXCLUSIONARY RULE

A rule of evidence that enforces the Fourth Amendment, the purpose of which is to deter police misconduct.

VIOLATING PAROLE

Most of the discussion in Chapter 7 on probation revocations also applies to parole revocations and won't be repeated here. Instead, we will present a short legal issues section, highlighting any *differences* between parole and probation revocations. We will then focus on why people violate parole and/or abscond from community supervision and how this behavior can be decreased.

The parole violation process is depicted in Figure 13.1 as a series of decision points. This process begins with the field parole officer, who must discover the violation and, after investigation, can decide to arrest the parolee, keep the parolee under supervision, or issue a citation to appear at a revocation hearing. When an arrest warrant is issued, the parolee is detained in the county jail until a preliminary hearing. When a citation is issued, the parolee remains in the community until a revocation hearing. The decision of whether or not to revoke parole resides with the parole board (recall that the judge revoked probation, so this is one major difference).

Warrants and Citations

The time it takes to revoke parole varies from one jurisdiction to another. The federal system requires that revocation hearings be held within 90 days from the time the offender is taken into custody (U.S. Parole Commission 2006). In a nationwide study of the parole revocation process, Burke (1997) found that the time from violation detection by the officer to disposition by the parole board or the court ranged from 44 to 64 days.

A parole officer conducts a home visit to one of his parolees.

FIGURE 13.1   *The Parole Revocation Process*

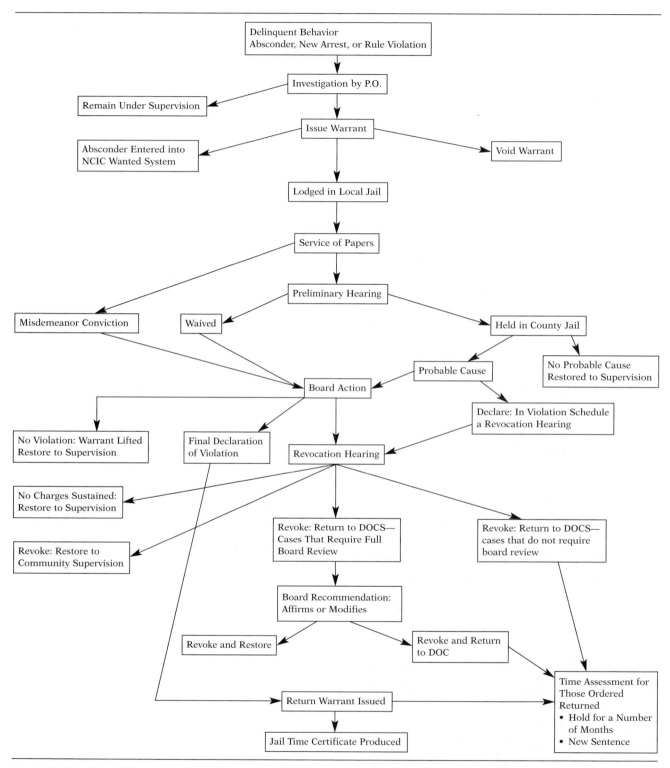

Source: Adapted with permission from New York State Division of Parole, Office of Policy Analysis and Information (1993). "Overview of the Parole Revocation Process in New York," in *Reclaiming Offender Accountability: Intermediate Sanctions for Probation and Parole Violators,* edited by Edward E. Rhine. (Laurel, MD: American Correctional Association, p. 41.)

Most violators (82 percent) were brought in by warrants, and the remaining answered summons or citations to appear. More jurisdictions are using citations in place of automatic warrants for most probation and parole violators waiting for revocation hearings unless the violation was violent or indications exist that the offender may abscond from the area. This allows the offender to continue working and supporting dependents while at the same time preparing for a possible entrance or return to jail or prison. Another distinct advantage is that citations save jail space.

Although most states have a two-stage hearing parole revocation process (as for probationers), the two-stage process is not required in parole revocations. Therefore, some states merge these two proceedings into one, with a conviction for a new offense while on parole as enough evidence to revoke parole (U.S. Parole Commission 2006).

Due Process Rights under "Preparole"

One difference between parole and probation is the use of a "preparole " status to ease crowding in higher custody level prisons. For example, Oklahoma established a "preparole" release program that allowed prisoners conditional release after serving just 15 percent of their sentence, and then to become eligible for regular parole after one-third of the sentence had elapsed. Preparole program participants and regular parolees were released subject to similar conditions.

Prisoner Harper was released on preparole; after five months the governor denied Harper's parole, and he was ordered back to prison without any type of hearing. The Court held that Oklahoma's preparole release program was similar to parole, and therefore inmates released on preparole were entitled to the due process rights given in *Morrissey*. In essence, the Court said that any state program for relieving prison congestion that has parole features is considered parole, regardless of what the program is called (*Young v. Harper* 1997).

CHARACTERISTICS OF PAROLE VIOLATORS

Of the parole violators who returned to state prison (most with a new sentence), more than 95 percent were men, over half were African American, and most were young or middle-aged (between 25 and 39 years of age). The most serious offense was a violent crime in 34 percent of cases, a property crime for 33 percent of violators, a drug crime in 23 percent of cases, and a public-order crime in 13 percent of cases (see Table 13.2).

Parole Revocation Rate

Most rearrests of parolees occur in the first six months after release from prison, and within three years two-thirds of all parolees have been rearrested. The rate of parole failure, or revocation rate, has increased. According to Figure 13.2, parole violators constituted *40 percent of all state prison admissions* who returned to prison with a new sentence—a number that has more than doubled since 1980 and tripled over the last 50 years (Petersilia 2000b).

Parolees who were convicted of property, drug, and public-order crimes were less likely to violate their parole than offenders who went to prison for violent crimes, weapons, or immigration offenses.

TABLE 13.2 *Characteristics of Parole Violators in State Prison*

Characteristic	All 50 States	California	New York	Texas
Gender				
Male	95.3%	92.9%	96.7%	94.6%
Female	4.7	7.1	3.3	5.4
Race/Hispanic origin				
White non-Hispanic	27.5	30.8	11.1	23.1
Black non-Hispanic	51.8	33.4	54.2	50.3
Hispanic	18.3	31.9	33.1	26.0
Other	2.4	3.9	1.6	0.6
Age at prison release				
17 or younger	0.1	0.2	0.0	0.0
18–24	9.4	8.8	8.6	6.1
25–29	20.8	19.8	19.8	19.1
30–34	24.1	25.5	26.0	23.3
35–39	20.3	22.9	20.3	21.1
40–44	13.9	12.8	13.3	15.5
45–54	9.3	8.0	10.2	12.3
55 or older	2.0	2.0	1.8	2.5
Most serious offense*				
Violent	33.7	24.4	40.9	33.3
Property	30.1	25.3	15.6	36.8
Drug	23.1	27.1	33.6	21.3
Public order	12.9	22.9	9.4	8.6
Number of prior incarcerations				
1	42.3	28.9	52.9	44.1
2	14.0	12.6	12.6	14.1
3 to 5	26.3	27.1	26.7	28.4
6 or more	17.3	30.7	7.8	13.5

*Excludes other/unspecified offenses.

Source: Timothy A. Hughes, Doris James Wilson, and Allen J. Beck. 2001. *Trends in State Parole, 1990–2000.* Washington, DC: U.S. Department of Justice, Bureau of Justice Statistics, p. 14.

Reasons for Revocation

Table 13.3 provides various reasons state parolees who were sent back to state prison were revoked nationwide and compares nationwide rates with California, New York, and Texas. Across the United States, approximately 70 percent of parolees in state prison were arrested or convicted of a new offense, 22 percent absconded, and nearly 34 percent were returned for technical violations that included using drugs, failure to report for drug testing/treatment, possession of a firearm, and failure to maintain employment. Of course, it is important to note that Table 13.3 represents parolees who were sent back to prison. As mentioned previously, most revoked parolees do not go to prison; rather, they remain in the community with more restrictions or remain in the county jail for the rest of their original sentence.

Most federal parolees failed on parole for a technical violation:

• 60 percent returned to prison following a technical violation

FIGURE 13.2 *Percent of State Prisoners Who Enter Prison Because of Parole or Probation Revocation, 1930–2005*

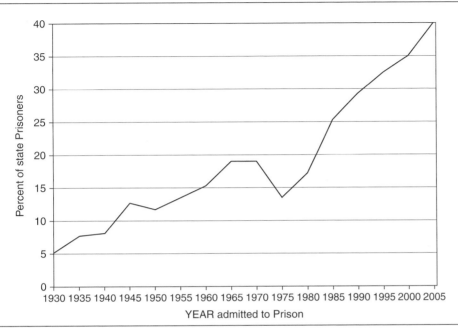

Sources: Robyn L. Cohen. 1995. *Probation and Parole Violators in State Prison, 1991.* NCJ 149076. Washington, DC: U.S. Department of Justice, Bureau of Justice Statistics; Joan Petersilia. 2000b. When Prisoners Return to the Community: Political, Economic, and Social Consequences. In *Sentencing and Corrections: Issues for the 21st Century* [paper 9 from the Executive Sessions on Sentencing and Corrections]. Washington DC: U.S. Department of Justice (November).

- 30 percent committed a new crime
- 10 percent returned for "other violations" (Sabol et al. 2000 p. 1).

Why Have Revocation Rates Increased?

With the increase in rates of violations in recent years, research has been undertaken to discover the underlying causes of parole and probation revocations. One reason involves the shift in the way offenders are monitored, changing from a treatment perspective to one of control. With more emphasis placed on control and punishment, the threshold level is lowered for what behavior is tolerated before a revocation occurs. Second, an increase in the average number of offenders that each parole officer has to supervise may actually mean that offenders receive less face-to-face contact. Officers spend less quality time with offenders and more time on rule enforcement and paperwork. A third reason is that parolees and probationers alike have more parole conditions, and thus more ways to violate. An increased number of conditions means that offenders have more pressure to perform and to try to meet all those conditions. Finally, with the advances made in drug testing technology, more drug use is now detected. In addition, with the increased use of electronic monitoring in parole and probation, more hardened offenders tend to be placed in the community to avoid institutional overcrowding (Parent et al. 1994).

TABLE 13.3 *Reasons for Revocation among Parole Violators in State Prison*

Reason for Revocation	All 50 States	California	New York	Texas
Arrest/conviction for new offense	69.9%	60.3%	87.1%	78.8%
Drug-related violations	16.1	23.1	11.4	10.7
Positive test for drug use	7.9	12.2	5.6	4.3
Possession of drug(s)	6.6	8.9	5.6	5.6
Failure to report for drug testing	2.3	4.6	1.3	1.3
Failure to report for alcohol or drug treatment	1.7	1.1	1.9	1.2
Absconders	22.3	26.6	18.4	19.7
Failure to report/absconded	18.6	24.7	17.2	17.2
Left jurisdiction without permission	5.6	3.9	2.5	4
Other reasons	17.8	20.7	10.6	13.8
Failure to report for counseling	2.4	1.2	2	1.9
Failure to maintain employment	1.2	0.7	0.6	0.9
Failure to meet financial obligations	2.3	0.2	0	2.7
Maintained contact with known offenders	1.2	1.6	0.4	0.8
Possession of gun(s)	3.5	3.8	1.9	2.3

Excludes 37,440 parole violators who reported that their parole had not been revoked. Detail adds to more than 100% because some inmates have had more than one violation of parole.

Source: Timothy A. Hughes, Doris James Wilson, and Allen J. Beck. 2001. *Trends in State Parole, 1990–2000.* Washington, DC: U.S. Department of Justice, Bureau of Justice Statistics, p. 14.

An increase in revocation rates puts pressure on a number of other components in the criminal justice system. For example, parole and probation officers must devote more of their time to revocation paperwork and less time to supervising other offenders on their caseload who are functioning satisfactorily. Furthermore, while probation and parole revocators are awaiting hearings, revocation drains court resources, parole board resources, and county jail bed space (Parent et al. 1994).

Attitudes on Revocation

The frequency of parole revocation has generated controversy. Too many parole revocations lead to prison congestion, and too few revocations lead to public apprehension about safety from convicted offenders. The implication is that parole officials are reluctant to revoke if it means adding prisoners to an already overcrowded prison system. A balance must be achieved between reintegrating offenders into society and public protection.

The public tends to view the rate of parole violation as indicative of parole success or failure. Criminal justice practitioners, in contrast, recognize that what may appear to be good parole statistical results can, in light of the quality and extent of supervision, indicate just the opposite. In truth, violation rates do not accurately measure the success or failure of parole (Parent et al. 1994).

PAROLE ABSCONDERS

One of the more serious, and surprisingly frequent, types of technical violations resulting in parole failure is absconding. An **absconder** is defined as an offender under community supervision who, without prior permission, escapes or flees the jurisdiction he or she is required to stay within. Different sources estimate that between 11 and 27 percent of all parolees abscond from supervision (Schwaner 1997; Williams, McShane, and Dolny 2000b). In some jurisdictions that list absconding from supervision as a criminal offense, a parole absconder can be charged with a new crime. For most parolees, leaving the area without notifying the parole officer is a technical violation.

Why Do Parolees Leave?

Parolees who abscond do so ultimately to avoid having their parole revoked and possibly being sent back to prison. "Absconders rarely intend to run immediately, but a continuous perception of having one's opportunities stifled creates feelings of despair and ultimately . . . a long-established pattern of running from supervision" (Schwaner, McGaughey, and Tewksbury 1998, p. 48). Many parolees are uncertain about what their parole officer will do once he or she discovers a violation, and that uncertainty translates into fear. This fear leads parolees to do anything to avoid a revocation hearing. Parole absconders fall into two main categories: benign and a possible threat to community safety.

TYPE I ABSCONDERS: BENIGN.   The first and most common category is absconders who have committed technical violations and do not understand the system well enough to predict what the outcome of their actions will be. The uncertainty and fear get the better of them, and in a highly emotional state the offender drops all responsibilities and pressures that have been building up and leaves them without thinking about the more serious consequences of escape. Ironically, the violations that led up to their escape are usually less serious than the escape label that will affect them for the remainder of their sentence and for any future convictions. For this type of person, reasons for absconding range from drug use to financial difficulties to leaving the state to visit a dying relative. Parent substantiates the benign type of absconder by noting that "typical absconders are low-risk property offenders who remained in the community after they absconded. . . . [M]ost were not arrested for new crimes while on absconder status" (Parent 1993, p. 10).

TYPE II ABSCONDERS: MENACE TO SOCIETY.   The second category of absconders includes individuals who understand the system too well. These individuals constitute a very small percentage of all absconders, and they will have committed one or more new crimes (some of which are serious) while on community supervision. They know with certainty that they will return to prison anyway. If the recent criminal behavior is serious enough, they know that they may never get out of prison again, so they take the chance of living out of prison until they are caught. This type of absconder is more likely than the first type to come to the attention of law enforcement officers and to be extradited (returned) to the original state of conviction. Type II absconders are the ones most likely to return to prison, as well as the ones prone to threaten community safety. Because absconders' whereabouts are not known for what could be an extended period of time, the true extent of absconder criminal activity, and whether they threaten public safety or whether they threaten the credibility of community supervision, is also largely unknown (Parent et al. 1994).

Locating and Apprehending Fugitives

Most states take a passive approach to locating and apprehending fugitives. When a parolee (or probationer) absconds from supervision, a warrant is filed with local, state, or national crime information systems. The parole officer will first contact the offender's family, friends, and employer to check the offender's whereabouts and ask them to call the parole office or police if they find out any information or see the offender again. Many absconders are caught from a routine check for a traffic violation, and some are arrested because they commit a new crime. Ironically, many absconders never leave the state and could later be located through searching public utility records or other applicable databases (Parent et al. 1994).

Type II absconders are pursued through more aggressive tactics because they may pose a threat to community safety. Parent and his colleagues found that states that aggressively pursue an absconder use one of three methods:

1. Their own fugitive apprehension unit
2. Receiving assistance from the Federal Bureau of Investigation (FBI)
3. Contracting out with a private apprehension unit

Six states had enhanced fugitive units that operated in certain counties or statewide (Arizona, California, Massachusetts, Minnesota, Oklahoma, and Utah). One of these fugitive units, the Special Operations Unit in Massachusetts, is highlighted in Box 13.1.

Most states do not have their own fugitive units and must seek assistance from the FBI or a private contractor. When the FBI is used, the U.S. attorney's office is made aware of the situation and agrees to extradite the absconder back to the original state of conviction from wherever the offender is captured. The state requesting the extradition must pay the extradition costs, which are about $4,000 per fugitive.

BOX 13.1 COMMUNITY CORRECTIONS UP CLOSE •

THE MASSACHUSETTS PAROLE BOARD SPECIAL OPERATIONS UNIT

The Special Operations Unit reports directly to the executive director of the Parole Board. The purposes of this unit are to

- Reduce the backlog of outstanding absconder warrants
- Emphasize the detection and apprehension of absconders
- Increase the credibility of detection and apprehension efforts within the system.

The fugitive unit—within the Special Operations Unit—has two apprehension officers and two other staff who specialize in data entry, warrant information, and responding to information from other states.

The officers in this unit respond to requests from supervising officers in all areas of the state to assist in locating and apprehending absconders. The unit also cooperated with local and state law enforcement in the execution of "sweeps" to apprehend violators. The officers apprehend over 200 absconders annually and decrease the backlog of absconder warrants. Officials think that the board's commitment to cracking down on absconders has prompted better

cooperation from other system officials. Today, judges are reportedly more likely to detain people with outstanding parole warrants long enough for the Parole Board to take custody of them. Having this unit has not changed the absconding behavior of parolees. In fact, the number of new absconder warrants increased. But staff feel the unit has been a major improvement in system efficiency.

Source: Dale G. Parent et al. 1994. *Responding to Probation and Parole Violations.* Washington, DC: U.S. Department of Justice, pp. 29–30.

The fugitive is usually accompanied by two federal officers and is transported (from long distances) by aircraft to designated airports used by the U.S. Marshall's office. At that point, the fugitive is transported by car to the home state of conviction (Parent et al. 1994).

A final option for states that wish to apprehend certain absconders would be to hire a private contractor. For a heftier price, one individual or an assembled team will actively attempt to locate and transport the absconder back to the original state of conviction to answer charges.

Predicting Absconding Behavior

The argument can be made that if absconding behavior can be predicted, then it can be prevented—or at least decreased. Shawn Schwaner (1997) compared a sample of absconders (11 percent) with nonabsconders (89 percent) in Ohio using two different data sets. Using bivariate analyses, he found that the following variables were most predictive of absconding behavior:

- Juvenile and adult felony convictions
- Arrests within five years of the current crime
- Previous adult incarcerations
- Previous probation or parole revocations

Furthermore, high-risk parole absconders were more likely to be apprehended than low-risk absconders (Schwaner 1997).

Williams, McShane, and Dolny (2000b) collected data on 863 California parolees who absconded during their first time on parole, representing 21.3 percent of their entire sample of about 4,052 parolees. This included 186 parolees (4.6 percent of the sample) who absconded two or more times in one year. The researchers found no gender differences in the absconding rate. However, individuals of Hispanic origin were less likely than people of other race or ethnic groups to abscond. Using multivariate statistical techniques, the researchers ascertained that the following seven variables contributed significantly to predicting absconding behavior (in order of highest to lowest importance):

1. Unstable living arrangements
2. Frequent unemployment
3. Previous parole violations
4. Low stakes
5. Larger number of prior arrests
6. Single marital status
7. Previous felonies

Unstable living arrangements contributed 29 percent to the explanation, making it the most powerful predictor. The bottom four variables, collectively, contributed only half as much (14 percent) to the model. Another drawback, which the researchers themselves point out, is that about 27 percent of nonabsconders also fit the absconder profile (a false positive), and thus separating absconders from nonabsconders is difficult. More work needs to be done to improve predicting absconder behavior.

To prevent absconding, parole officers must understand factors and situations leading up to an offender's decision to leave. Then, parole officers should "keep a pulse" on each person on their caseload, noting changes in behavior, to determine if a revocation pattern is occurring. Preventing absconding behavior will be more effective for the first, more benign, type of absconders. The second, more serious, type is more difficult to predict. Until more resources can be devoted to studying absconders, this behavior seems to be a casualty of community supervision.

Some jurisdictions have experimented with different methods of returning absconders to community supervision with some changes in the parole conditions. The District of Columbia's "Find and Fix" program is one such example. In Minneapolis, Minnesota, absconders were offered a brief period of amnesty. Absconders could voluntarily turn themselves in and not be reimprisoned. These programs have reported significant success (Parent et al. 1994).

PAROLE EFFECTIVENESS

Parole has been widely criticized as a "revolving door" to prison that reduces the impact of criminal sentences and threatens public safety. Critics claim that studies have failed to provide any assurance that paroled inmates will not continue their criminal activities while under supervision. Some public concerns are valid. For example, one study found that California parole officers "lost track of about one-fifth of the parolees they were assigned to in 1999" (Petersilia 2000b, p. 3). However, many parolees do complete their term of supervision successfully, and in fact, national parole success rates have remained the same since 1990 (Hughes, Wilson, and Beck 2001).

A study of nearly 300,000 prisoners released in 1994 in 15 different states found that 67.5 percent were rearrested for a new offense and over half were returned to prison within three years (Langan and Levin 2002). These facts, however, do not fully answer the question: Is parole effective? Completion of parole without revocation may represent parole officers' failure to adequately supervise offenders. On the one hand, violations, particularly technical violations, might not come to the attention of an officer who cannot or refuses to supervise closely. On the other hand, closer supervision would probably reveal a larger number of technical violations, which could be reflected in higher recidivism statistics. Yet many of the particular offenders may not be considered failures.

To illustrate this point, consider the following examples. Which parolees are successful, and which are not?

1. Richard has not been arrested for any offense during the term of his supervision but was cited several times for technical violations, such as failure to report, failure to maintain employment, and excessive use of alcohol.
2. Vincent has no known technical violations but was arrested on two occasions for failure to pay court-ordered child support. A review of the records indicates that he got very far behind while incarcerated but has been paying regularly since being placed under supervision. He has not been able to "catch up" the delinquent balance, however, and his ex-wife regularly files charges of delinquent child support against him.
3. Josephine has no known technical violations but was arrested for driving under the influence of alcohol two months after being placed under supervision. She agreed to enter an alcohol treatment program, and there have been no further reported violations. Her alcohol treatment counselor reports that her progress is favorable.
4. David has no new crimes and no technical violations. However, he has a bad attitude and refuses to cooperate with the parole officer beyond the bare minimum required by his parole agreement.
5. Jean successfully completes five years of supervision with no arrests or technical violations. One year before she is scheduled to be terminated from supervision, she is arrested for a new offense. This is the first time in her adult life that she has gone more than six months without being arrested.

6. Jeffrey is not arrested for any new offenses, and there are no reported technical violations. However, the supervising officer has been advised repeatedly by law enforcement authorities that Jeffrey is heavily involved in narcotics trafficking.
7. Raymond was released from prison a year ago. He is working regularly and has no reported violations. One evening when returning from a movie with his wife he is involved in a minor traffic accident. In the aftermath he and the other driver exchange blows, and both are arrested. He is charged with simple assault and fined $200.

Which of these parolees is successful? The question cannot be answered by arrest and conviction statistics only. A strict accounting might conclude that David and Jeffrey (offenders 4 and 6) are successful. A subjective analysis might suggest that the same offenders are failures. When examining recidivism studies, pay attention to three factors:

1. How recidivism is defined (by rearrest, conviction, parole revocation, return to prison, or other form of returning to criminal behavior)
2. The duration of time that the subjects were studied (the longer the period of time subjects were followed—for example, up to three years—the better)
3. The size of the sample studied (a larger sample, or one that samples from more than one area of the country, is more generalizable)

Recidivism Studies

Some recidivism studies are fraught with methodological problems that limit how well they can be generalized. Others, which have more methodologically sound research methods, have reported mixed findings on the impact that certain factors have on parole success. Some of these factors include:

- Race and ethnicity
- Involvement in prison education programs
- Length of time served in prison
- Behavior while incarcerated
- Current conviction type
- Parolee age

Some studies show that these factors are significant in predicting parole outcome, and other studies show no differences. For example, one study found an inverse relationship between time served in prison and parole success. Don Gottfredson and colleagues (1997) found that the less time offenders served in prison, the greater the likelihood of parole success.

Regarding type of crime, studies have consistently found that murderers have a significantly higher parole success rate (Vito, Wilson, and Latessa 1991). One study by Langan and Levin (2002) measured the rate of rearrest for state-level offenders for three years following release. With the exception of robbery, property offenders (burglars, larcenists, and other thieves) had higher rates of rearrest than offenders convicted of violent crimes. In a different study of offenders returning to the federal system between 1986 and 1997, offenders convicted of violent crimes (for example, robbery) were more likely to return to federal prison within three years than any other offender type. About 32 percent of violent offenders returned to prison as opposed to only 13 percent of drug offenders (Sabol et al. 2000).

Some of these differences stem from the different patterns of offending behavior that criminals exhibit. Some criminals begin their "criminal career" at an earlier age, accrue more arrests, and sustain criminal behavior for a long time before decelerating the rate of offending. These criminals are termed "repeat" or "habitual" offenders. Other criminals, such as murderers, do not have criminal careers per se, but they commit a serious offense, for which they get caught and serve time. These criminals are much less likely to recidivate.

Related to this idea of criminal careers and offending patterns is the relationship between age and recidivism. Research that examines this relationship has found that younger parolees, especially those under the age of 25, are more likely to recidivate than older parolees (Joo, Eckland-Olson, and Kelly 1995). One recent study of California parolees determined that gang membership should also be taken into consideration when examining different age groups. In this study, Williams and his colleagues found that younger parolees who were not gang members had rates of reoffending that were similar to those of older parolees:

> In sum, our analyses lead us to believe that the youngest parolees, as a group, are not the worst of the parolee population. There is some evidence that they may be slightly worse than the average in parolee failure, violent and serious reoffending, dangerousness, and consumption of intervention resources. But when gang membership is controlled, much of that trend is called into question. On the other hand, they are not among the best of the parolee population either. (Williams et al. 2000)

Predicting Parole Outcomes

The three variables that have shown more consistent findings in predicting parole outcome are gender, number of prior arrests, and supervision versus no supervision.

GENDER DIFFERENCES.   In general, studies have shown that male parolees return to prison at higher rates than female parolees (16 percent compared with 12 percent, respectively; Sabol et al. 2000). Another research study found that female parolees are more compliant with parole conditions than are male parolees (Acoca and Austin 1996).

NUMBER OF PRIOR ARRESTS.   An inverse relationship exists between prior criminal history and parole outcome. Specifically, the lower the number of previous arrests, the greater the likelihood of parole success (Hughes, Wilson, and Beck 2001; Solomon 2006).

SUPERVISION VERSUS NO SUPERVISION.   A small number of studies have been conducted comparing parolees on supervision with prisoners released unconditionally, which means they are released without any supervision whatsoever. These studies show mixed results. Two studies (Sabol et al. 2000; Sacks and Logan 1980) measured recidivism defined as a new conviction for any crime (felony or misdemeanor), and found that recidivism rates were lower for those on supervision. By the end of three years, 85 percent of the unconditional group without supervision recidivated, whereas 77 percent of parolees returned to crime (Sacks and Logan 1980). The difference was more pronounced between the two groups after just the first year, indicating that parole supervision slows down the recidivism rate and may assist some offenders in maintaining law-abiding lives. A second study of federal offenders supports this finding (Sabol et al. 2000). Of the offenders who recidivated in the federal system, offenders released on some form of community supervision were in the community for an average of 17 months before returning to prison for a new crime. Offenders released without any supervision stayed out for just over 13 months before returning to prison for a new crime (Sabol et al. 2000).

A third study by the Urban Institute measured recidivism by rearrest over a two-year period, and used Bureau of Justice Statistics data on a sample of 30,624 prisoners released from 15 states (Solomon 2006). Although the data did not factor in state-level differences in supervision, the sample was divided into three groups: unconditional (no supervision), mandatory supervised release, and discretionary parole release. The unconditional releasees served the most time behind bars and more of them had previously been arrested for violent offenses than either of the other two groups, suggesting that the unconditional releasees were significantly more disconnected from community ties than supervised parolees. Despite this difference, mandatory supervised release and unconditional releases recidivated at the same rate—61 percent and 62 percent, respectively, over the two-year period. A slightly lower rate—54 percent—of those released on discretionary parole by a parole board recidivated. Even when technical violators were removed from the data, those committing new crimes did not change on the three types of supervision because most rearrests were for new crimes rather than technical violations. Although technical violators are taken into custody, official statistics do not record them as "arrests." Parole supervision did benefit women and offenders with few prior convictions who were significantly less likely to recidivate while being supervised than if they were not supervised at all. In interpreting the overall recidivism findings among the three groups, Solomon (2006, pp. 31–32) says:

> Clearly there is a value judgment being made here, in characterizing a four percentage point difference as "relatively small," differing "only slightly." . . . Because parole boards take into account factors such as a prisoner's attitude and motivation level, institutional conduct, preparedness for release and connections to the community . . . I would expect this group to be substantially, rather than marginally, less likely to recidivate. The suggestion here is that lower rearrest rates may be largely due to who is selected for discretionary release rather than discretionary supervision itself, which is not systematically different than mandatory supervision across states.

Hughes and colleagues (2001) also used data from the Bureau of Justice Statistics and compared those on mandatory release with those who were released by a parole board (unconditional releases were not part of the sample). These data, however, spanned over a 10-year period, while the previous study by the Urban Institute was cross-sectional from releases over one year. The rates of success on discretionary parole varied between 50 and 56 percent, whereas mandatory parolees were successful only 24 to 33 percent of the time between 1990 and 1999. They concluded, "In every year between 1990 and 1999, state prisoners released by a parole board had higher success rates than those released through mandatory parole" (p. 11).

In sum, parole practices and types of supervision vary widely, and no one type of supervision (or lack of supervision) has consistently been shown to be more effective than another. The future of parole supervision involves the expanded use of risk and need assessment instruments to predict who will succeed (see Box 13.2). Community supervision, whether it is probation or parole, is more successful with people who have less severe criminal pasts; or another way of interpreting this could be that people with a more distinctive criminal history are more likely to be revoked for the same behavior because of their past. Regardless of the type of supervision, treatment interventions and reentry assistance increase success.

BOX 13.2   TECHNOLOGY IN CORRECTIONS

USING COMPUTERIZED RISK/NEEDS ASSESSMENTS TO PREDICT PAROLE SUCCESS

The future of postrelease supervision involves attempting to predict the future behavior of offenders being considered for parole, as well as examining patterns of behavior that may reliably indicate when a parolee may become too much of a public safety risk to allow him or her to remain in the community. Prediction research into the causes of recidivism and subsequent revocation could be invaluable in equipping the parole officer with the tools necessary for supervision. Recall our detailed discussion of risk and needs assessment instruments in Chapter 6 when we discussed classification. It is interesting to note that the very same variables that initially classify offenders also can predict postrelease behavior on parole and may lead us to a deeper understanding of why some offenders succeed and some do not.

Most parole assessment instruments have both static and dynamic variables. Whereas static characteristics do not change, dynamic parolee characteristics are variable. Examples of static parolee characteristics are prior convictions, age at first arrest, absconding history, and prior revocations. Dynamic factors might be treatment needs, employment status, financial situation, and relationships with family and friends.

California has modified how its officers use risk assessments for day-to-day parole management. A computer database is used to adjust parole agent workload by current classification categories, degree of supervision required, expenditures, or treatment program needs. Field parole officers could use laptop computers to "dial in to intranets and automatically recalculate parolee risk scores." Ultimately, the parole classification system would be linked with other automated parole information, such as program cost for specific types of parolees, and program success rates.

Frank P. Williams III, Marilyn D. McShane, and H. Michael Dolny. 2000a. Developing a Parole Classification Instrument for Use as a Management Tool. *Corrections Management Quarterly* 4(4): 45–59.

TOP THINGS YOU SHOULD KNOW

- Parole boards enjoy a high level of discretion when imposing parole conditions. The extent of authority and the limitations are similar to those for probation.
- Parole revocation is the formal termination of a parolee's conditional freedom, usually (but not always) resulting in a reinstatement of imprisonment.
- *Morrissey v. Brewer*, the leading case on parole revocation, held that prior to revocation parolees must be given five basic rights. However, parolees do not have a constitutional right to counsel at a revocation hearing; this right is given on a case-by-case basis.
- Parolees do not have a constitutional right to appeal a revocation, but about half of the states, by law or agency policy, allow parolees this chance.
- Parole violators constituted 40 percent of all people who returned to prison with a new sentence.
- The increase in the revocation rate is due to a shift in the way offenders are monitored; greater emphasis is placed on control and punishment, and less time is spent on treatment and reentry concerns (due to a higher caseload per officer).
- Fear and uncertainty about community supervision leads probationers and parolees who lack community ties and relationships to abscond or escape from the area.

- Computer modeling and risk prediction assessments can be used to predict parole release as well as how to respond to parole violators, making parole less of an art and more of a science.

DISCUSSION QUESTIONS

1 What problems do parolees have when they are released from prison? What ideas do you have that might assist parolees in their reintegration to society?

2 Is submission to a penile plethysmograph valid as a parole condition? Support your answer.

3 Discuss what this statement means: "Parolees have diminished constitutional rights." Does that statement apply to preferred rights?

4 Imagine that you are a parole officer supervising the seven parolees described in the chapter. In two or three sentences, evaluate each case as a success or as a failure.

5 Why do some parolees abscond?

6 What can be done to decrease parole absconding rates?

7 Is supervised release an effective sanction? For whom?

8 If you were considering a violent offender convicted of robbery, and you had to choose between early release with supervision versus leaving him behind bars his entire sentence with no supervision upon release, which would you choose and why?

 WEBSITES

U.S. Parole Commission Rules and Procedures Manual

http://www.usdoj.gov/uspc/rules_procedures/rulesmanual.htm

Connecticut Juvenile Parole Revocation Hearing Policy

http://www.state.ct.us/DCF/Policy/Hear22/22-9-2.htm

Georgia Parole Conditions

http://www.pap.state.ga.us/parole_conditions.htm

Iowa Code for Parole Revocations

http://www.legis.state.ia.us/IACODE/2003/908/

Missouri Department of Corrections Code of State Regulations
Parole guidelines, conditions on parole, and parole revocation procedures

http://www.sos.mo.gov/adrules/csr/current/14csr/14c80-3.pdf

Matthews v. NY State Division of Parole (2001) court case on revocations

http://www.law.cornell.edu/ny/ctap/comments/i01_0001.htm

CHAPTER 13

CASE STUDY EXERCISE
Parole Conditions and Revocation

As indicated in this chapter, the courts have granted a great deal of leeway to paroling authorities in setting parole standard conditions and special conditions for offenders. Court rulings seem to center around whether the condition is reasonable, acknowledgment that parolees have diminished rights, and whether the condition is related to the convicted criminal behavior.

Conditions pertaining to sex offenders have received added attention in recent years. In some jurisdictions standard conditions for sex offenders include some or all of the following:

- No contact with any minor child (including offender's minor children) if victim of sexual crime was a minor, or no contact with minors at all even if the victim(s) were adult age
- Contact with minor children approved only if parole officer approves another supervising adult to be present at the time of the contact
- No possession of sexually explicit material—written, audio, or visual
- If the offense involved the use of the Internet or a computer, cannot have a personal computer and cannot work where access to Internet is allowed, or in some jurisdictions no computer access at all, even if offense did not involve computer usage
- Notification to neighbors and employers of their sexual offense history and supervision status
- Mandatory participation in sexual offender treatment or aftercare programs
- Mandatory routine polygraph exams as a part of treatment or supervision
- If offense involved filming or pictures of victims, no camera or video equipment access allowed
- Cannot work in any employment that would allow access to children or victim-aged groups; cannot be self-employed
- Cannot live within a certain distance of schools, playgrounds, public parks, or other places where minors congregate

Using the case examples below, what conditions (if any) should be imposed on the offenders if paroled? What are some of the challenges of parole supervision that these cases present?

CASE A

Steven is serving a 5- to 15-year sentence for Sexual Assault of a Minor. He has served seven and one-half years of his sentence, which is five years beyond the minimum time to be served. Because he has three prior convictions for similar offenses he does not have to be released until he has served 10 years of his sentence. Steven spent time in prison for two of the three prior offenses against minors. Each time he was released he successfully completed the release period of parole supervision. All of his victims have been his grandchildren; family members are strongly opposed to his release and feel he will commit similar acts upon release. Steven has completed a sexual offender treatment program during this incarceration; he always refused to participate in treatment during prior incarcerations. The prognosis by the treatment counselor is guarded, but indicates Steven has worked hard on learning his offending triggers and knows what to avoid if released. He has not had any rule violations while incarcerated and has been employed in a private prison industry. He proposes a release to a community where none of his family reside and does not want to have contact with his family. He has been accepted into a halfway house program and plans on attending community-based sexual offender aftercare groups. If released, he would be under the supervision of a parole officer.

CASE B

Gloria is being considered for parole after serving three years on her nine-year sentence for Lewd Sexual Conduct and Sexual Contact with a Minor. She was 27 years old at the time of the offense, and her victim was 16. Currently, Gloria is 30 years old and her victim is now 19 years of age and enrolled as a full-time college student in another state. This is Gloria's first felony offense, and she has no history of previous behavior on community supervision. Gloria agreed to complete a sex offender treatment program during her incarceration, but claimed during her counseling sessions that she and her victim loved each other and everything was consensual. Gloria still reports feelings for him, but the victim's family wishes to have no contact with Gloria. However, at this time, no one knows how the victim feels about the relationship because his most recent contact information was unavailable when the field officer performed her investigations. The field officer did find out that Gloria's former employer would not accept her back in her former occupation as a nurse despite Gloria's statements that they would. Gloria is a registered nurse who wishes to parole back to her former neighborhood and has one male child, aged 13, who has been staying with Gloria's mother over the last three years. If released, Gloria would be under the supervision of a parole officer.

V

Special Issues in Community Corrections

In recent years we have witnessed an increase both in the number of juvenile offenders and in the seriousness of the offenses they commit. Nationally, approximately 1.7 million delinquency cases occur every year, and millions of additional cases of status offenders and dependent and neglected children come to the attention of the juvenile justice system as well. Chapter 14 discusses in detail legal issues and community corrections programs to deal with juvenile delinquents.

Every adult convicted of a felony suffers additional disabilities that are not directly imposed by the court. That is, even after a person has completed serving his or her sentence for a felony crime, civil disabilities (varying by state) may disallow that person from voting in a public election, holding a public office, being employed in certain occupations, owning a firearm, or being able to parent his or her own children. Chapter 15 examines these disabilities and investigates the mechanisms by which convicted offenders may be able to restore some or all of these civil rights.

Introduction

Background and History
Mens Rea and Juveniles
Parens Patriae and Its Decline

Juvenile Justice and Adult Justice Systems Compared
Differences
Reality

Juvenile Courts
Created in the U.S.A.
Jurisdiction of Juvenile Courts
Differences from Adult Courts
Transfer from Juvenile Courts to
  Adult Courts

An Overview of the Juvenile Justice Process
Procedure before Adjudication
The Intake Stage
The Adjudication Stage
The Disposition Stage
Blended Sentences
Release from an Institution

***In re Gault:* The Most Important Juvenile Justice Case**

Juvenile Probation
Origin
Conditions of Probation
Supervision
Juvenile Probation Officers
Intensive Supervision Probation
School-Based Probation
Fare v. Michael C.: An Important
  Case in Juvenile Probation
  Supervision
The Probation Record of Juveniles

Juvenile Parole (or Aftercare)
Background
Similarities with Probation
Differences from Probation
Parole Boards
Responsibilities of Juvenile Parole
  Officers
Evaluating Juvenile Parole
  Programs

Revocation of Juvenile Probation or Parole
No Standards for Revocation
Result of Revocation

14

Juvenile Justice, Probation, and Parole

© Bob Daemmrich/Stock, Boston Inc.

What You Will Learn in This Chapter

- The background and history of the juvenile justice system.
- What parens patriae means and how it influences the way we deal with juvenile offenders.
- The similarities and differences between the juvenile and adult justice systems.
- How a juvenile offender is processed through the system.
- The various forms of juvenile probation.
- The basics of juvenile parole (aftercare).

KEY TERMS

Parens patriae

Juvenile delinquency

Conduct in need of supervision (CINS)

Transfer of jurisdiction

Concurrent jurisdiction

Statutory exclusion

Judicial waiver

Intake

Adjudication

Disposition

Intensive supervision probation

School-based probation

INTRODUCTION

Juvenile crime is a recurring problem in the United States. The increase in violent juvenile crime from the 1980s to the early 1990s alarmed the nation. The House Judiciary Committee of the U.S. Congress reported that "between 1965 and 1992, the number of 12-year-olds arrested for violent crimes increased 211 percent; the number of 13- and 14-year-olds rose 301 percent; and the number of 15-year-olds rose 297 percent" ("Putting a Sterner Face on Juvenile Justice" 1997). Despite gloomy predictions, however, the number of serious juvenile crimes decreased in succeeding years. The number of victimizations by violent crime for every 1,000 teenagers dropped from about 130 victimizations in 1993 to about 60 in 2003 (Juvenile Victimization and Offending 1993–2003, 2004).

Although the rate of violent juvenile crime began to decline in the early 1990s and continues to decline, state and local governments continue to seek legislative solutions to a problem that still alarms and mobilizes the nation. The main concern is what ought to be done to juveniles who violate laws, particularly those who commit serious and violent crimes. Answers do not come easily, partially because society wrestles with differing philosophical approaches to juvenile offending. On the one hand, the benevolent parens patriae doctrine seeks to do what is best for the juvenile; on the other hand, the theory of just deserts advocates punishing offenders based on the seriousness of the act committed and not on the personal circumstances of the offender.

Public attitude on juvenile crime sways from punitiveness to rehabilitation and back again. The pendulum will continue to swing from one side (vengeance) to the other (mercy) as long as juvenile crime exists. The public currently looks favorably at the "balanced approach and restorative justice" as the latest promising panacea in juvenile justice. The effectiveness of this approach, however, is yet to be established, and so the search continues for a lasting solution to the problem of juvenile crime.

BACKGROUND AND HISTORY

Mens Rea and Juveniles

Criminal liability is based on the concept of mens rea, which is the Latin term for "a guilty mind" (Black's Law Dictionary 1991, p. 680). Without intent, an act is generally not considered criminal. A guilty mind implies that the actor knows what he or she is doing; therefore, the act is punishable because the actor intended for the injury to occur. Children below a certain age, however, are presumed by law to be unaware of the full consequences of what they do. Absent *mens rea,* they should not and cannot be punished like adults.

During the latter part of the eighteenth century children younger than 7 years old were deemed incapable of *mens rea* and exempt from criminal liability. Those above 7 years of age could be prosecuted and sentenced to prison or given the death penalty if found guilty (Snyder and Sickmund 1995, p. 70). No state in the United States at present punishes juveniles so severely at such a young age, but the minimum age for juveniles to come under the jurisdiction of juvenile courts varies from state to state.

Parens Patriae and Its Decline

Juvenile justice is heavily influenced by ***parens patriae,*** a Latin term for the doctrine that "the state is parent" and therefore serves as guardian of people under legal disability, such as juveniles. *Parens patriae* led to the family model of processing juveniles, which treats juveniles like members of one's family. The main concern of juvenile courts is to ensure that legal proceedings are presided over by judges who act as wise parents and have the best interest of the child in mind. Constitutional safeguards are not a priority (children are not entitled to constitutional rights at home when under the care of parents) and used to be minimal or nonexistent. Instead, personal attention, love, and care are to be provided.

Over the years pure *parens patriae* gradually declined, paving the way for due process. Juveniles now have essentially the same rights as adults, at least during adjudication proceedings and in cases involving serious offenses. The case of *In re Gault* (1967) signaled the erosion of *parens patriae.* In that case the U.S. Supreme Court said that "neither the Fourteenth Amendment nor the Bill of Rights is for adults alone." Since then the Court has decided other cases giving rights to juveniles, but juvenile and adult proceedings still differ in the amount and type of legal rights given to offenders.

JUVENILE JUSTICE AND ADULT JUSTICE SYSTEMS COMPARED

Juvenile justice and adult justice are basically similar. Both represent efforts by the state to preserve public order and at the same time protect the basic constitutional rights of offenders. Despite *parens patriae,* the government is the offended party in juvenile cases and is represented by the prosecutor. In both juvenile and adult proceedings the offender provides his or her own lawyer, except when indigent. When an offender is found to have committed the offense charged, the punishment in both proceedings includes deprivation of liberty by the state, through the use of either jails, prisons, or state institutions.

Differences

Despite similarities, differences exist, as summarized here (del Carmen, Parker, and Reddington 1998, p. 9):

Adult Proceedings	**Juvenile Proceedings**
1. Arrested	1. Taken into custody by police
2. Charged	2. Prosecutor petitions court
3. Accused of crime under the penal code	3. Violation comes under the juvenile code or family code

4. Trial
5. Formal, public trial

6. Judge is neutral
7. Found guilty of a criminal offense by an impartial judge or jury
8. Disposition
9. Committed to a state facility

10. Judge or jury determines length of incarceration
11. Serves sentence for definite term, subject to parole law

12. Purpose is mainly punishment
13. Released on parole, if eligible
14. A criminal case
15. Adults can be given the death penalty

4. Adjudication
5. Usually a private, informal hearing
6. Judge acts as wise parent
7. Found to have engaged in delinquent conduct
8. Sentenced if found guilty
9. Sent to jail or prison for juveniles
10. Youth detention authorities determine when to release
11. Committed for an indeterminate amount of time, but usually released upon reaching age of majority
12. Purpose is rehabilitation
13. Released on aftercare
14. A civil or quasi-civil case
15. Juvenile can no longer be given the death penalty (*Roper v. Simmons* 2005)

Reality

In reality, the above differences are more terminological than substantive and are therefore more symbolic than real. They have minimal impact on the process because the procedures are similar regardless of the term used. For example, adults who are arrested and juveniles who are taken into custody are deprived of liberty and are under the control of the justice system. Neither is there much difference between the adult suspect being charged and the prosecutor petitioning the court for the juvenile to be adjudicated because both processes lead to hearings. Sentencing and disposition both subject the offender to lawfully prescribed sanctions, including incarceration. Whether an adult is on parole or a juvenile is in aftercare, the degree of supervision and the results in case of violation are similar. Nonetheless, society shuns the use of adult criminal law terms in juvenile proceedings and refuses to brand juveniles as criminals in hopes that rehabilitation is better served by not labeling them as such.

The main difference between juvenile and adult justice, however, is the severity of the punishment imposed. For instance, juveniles spend limited time in institutions because they are released upon reaching a maximum age specified by state law. In contrast, adult criminals can be made to spend life in prison, a sanction that cannot be administered to juveniles unless they are tried as adults through a waiver or certification process. And whereas adults can be given the death penalty, juveniles under 18 years of age who commit a crime, however brutal or heinous, cannot be given a death sentence.

JUVENILE COURTS

Created in the U.S.A.

Juvenile courts are an American creation. The first U.S. juvenile court was established in Chicago in 1899 with the enactment of the Illinois Juvenile Court Act. The court was anchored on the belief that a child's behavior was the product of poor family background and surroundings. It operated informally, was civil in nature, and was geared toward rehabilitation (del Carmen and Trulson 2006, p. 222).

Initially there were those who believed that juvenile courts were created so the public could "go easy" on young criminals (Butts and Harrell 2003, p. 3) This is likely an oversimplification. Indeed, although "some reformers were motivated by a desire to save growing numbers of poor and homeless children from the streets of America's cities, [others were] mainly interested in removing the legal obstacles that prevented criminal courts from dealing effectively with young hoodlums" (Butts and Harrell 2003, p. 4). Another observer says that "the 1899 Illinois Juvenile Court Act was, in part, yet another response to the growing incidence of jury nullification, concern about the dominance of sectarian industrial schools in Chicago filling with immigrants, and reform-based opposition to confining youth with adults" (Shepherd 1999, p. 16). Whatever the motivation, the idea of a separate court for juvenile offenders caught on and spread quickly. By 1925, 46 states, three territories, and the District of Columbia had juvenile courts (Shepherd 1999, p. 16). Juvenile courts have evolved since they were first established more than a century ago, but they are still the core of juvenile justice processing in the United States. As one source notes,

> Today's juvenile courts process well over 2 million cases a year. Estimates are that 61 percent of the cases are delinquency proceedings, which center on criminal actions committed by juveniles that would also be considered criminal if committed by adults. Another 19 percent are cases generated as a result of children being victims of abuse. Of the remainder, 16 percent are for status offenses, which are offenses that would not be illegal if committed by an adult. . . ." (Roberts 2004, p. 249)

Juvenile court judges play a central role in the administration of juvenile justice because of *parens patriae*. Under this concept, the judge is expected to play the role of a wise parent instead of an impartial arbiter, as judges are expected to do in criminal proceedings. In the words of one observer:

> In addition to the traditional judicial capacity, the juvenile court judge has the authority to affect case processing long before and after a formal adjudication hearing. In many jurisdictions, the juvenile court judge is the direct administrator of the juvenile probation department and/or court staff. When operating in this capacity, the juvenile court judge can assure coordination of services between the court and the probation department and may also take on the burden of fiscal management. (Kurlychek, Torbet, and Bozynski 1999, p. 2)

Jurisdiction of Juvenile Courts

The types of cases that go to juvenile courts are defined by state law. Jurisdiction (meaning the authority to try cases) of juvenile courts therefore varies from state to state. Such jurisdiction is usually based on two variables: the *age* of the offender and the *act* committed.

BASED ON AGE.   In juvenile cases, there is a youngest age and an oldest age, as determined by state law. Wide variations exist among states—from a youngest age of 6 years (when a juvenile court can assume jurisdiction) to an oldest age of 24 (when a juvenile is released). Most states, however, have a youngest age of 10 years and an oldest age of 17 years (see Figure 14.1) for juvenile court jurisdiction. Juveniles younger than the youngest age who commit criminal acts are usually processed informally by the police or placed in the care of state social welfare services. Offenders above the oldest age are processed as adult criminals. The youngest and oldest ages apply to the time the act was committed, not when the offender was caught or tried in court. Despite these ages, some states provide that the juvenile can be kept in a juvenile institution or supervised until he or she reaches an older age (such as 18, 21, or 24), particularly in juvenile delinquency cases when state authorities see the need for continued supervision.

FIGURE 14.1 *Minimum and Maximum Ages for Juvenile Delinquency*

Youngest age for original juvenile court jurisdiction in delinquency matters:

Age	State
6	North Carolina
7	Maryland, Massachusetts, New York
8	Arizona
10	Arkansas, Colorado, Kansas Louisiana, Minnesota, Mississippi, Pennsylvania, South Dakota, Texas, Vermont, Wisconsin

Oldest age for original juvenile court jurisdiction in delinquency matters:

Age	State
15	Connecticut, New York, North Carolina.
16	Georgia, Illinois, Louisiana, Massachusetts, Michigan, Missouri, New Hampshire, South Carolina, Texas, Wisconsin
17	Alabama, Alaska, Arizona, Arkansas, California, Colorado, Delaware, District of Columbia, Florida, Hawaii, Idaho, Indiana, Iowa, Kansas, Kentucky, Maine, Maryland, Minnesota, Mississippi, Montana, Nebraska, Nevada, New Jersey, New Mexico, North Dakota, Ohio, Oklahoma, Oregon, Pennsylvania, Rhode Island, South Dakota, Tennessee, Utah, Vermont, Virginia, Washington, West Virginia, Wyoming

Oldest age for which the juvenile court may retain jurisdiction in delinquency matters:

Age	State
18	Alaska, Iowa, Kentucky, Nebraska, Oklahoma, Tennessee
19	Mississippi, North Dakota
20	Alabama, Arizona, Arkansas, Connecticut, Delaware, District of Columbia, Georgia, Idaho, Illinois, Indiana, Louisiana, Maine, Maryland, Massachusetts, Michigan, Minnesota, Missouri, Nevada, New Hampshire, New Mexico, New York, North Carolina, Ohio, Pennsylvania, Rhode Island, South Carolina, South Dakota, Texas, Utah, Vermont, Virginia, Washington, West Virginia, Wyoming
21	Florida
22	Kansas
24	California, Montana, Oregon, Wisconsin
*	Colorado, Hawaii, New Jersey

* Until full term of disposition

Source: Howard N. Snyder and Melissa Sickmund. 2006. *Juvenile Offenders and Victims.* Washington, DC: U.S. Department of Justice, Office of Juvenile Justice and Delinquency Prevention, p. 103.

BASED ON ACTS COMMITTED.   Juvenile acts that trigger court intervention are of two types: **juvenile delinquency** and **conduct in need of supervision (CINS).** Each state, by law, determines what acts come under each category. In general, juvenile delinquents are those who commit acts that are punishable under the state's penal code. Examples are murder, robbery, burglary, and any act considered criminal in that state. In 2002, juvenile courts in the United States handled an estimated 1.6 million juvenile delinquency cases (Snyder and Sickmund 2006). Most of these cases (82 percent) were referred by law enforcement agencies to the court. In contrast, CINS (also known in some jurisdictions as CHINS [children in need of supervision], MINS [minors in need of supervision], or JINS [juveniles in need of supervision]) are juveniles who commit acts that would not be punishable if committed by adults. These are usually status offenses (meaning they are punished because of their status, in this case, their age) and include such categories as truancy, ungovernibility, running away from home, tobacco use, inhalant abuse, curfew violation, and underage drinking (Snyder and Sickmund 2006).

Law enforcement agencies refer few CINS cases to court. In 2002, only 55 percent of cases in juvenile courts were referred to them by law enforcement agencies. The rest reached the courts through reports from social services agencies, victims, probation officers, schools, or parents. One source notes: "In many jurisdictions, agencies other than juvenile courts are responsible for handling status offense cases. In come communities, for example, family crisis units, county attorneys, and social services agencies have assumed this responsibility" (Snyder and Sickmund 2006, p. 191).

Sanctions imposed for juvenile delinquents are often more severe than those for conduct in need of supervision. Juvenile delinquents can be confined in a state institution, whereas conduct in need of supervision merely results in probation or referral to juvenile programs in the community. Nothing prevents a state, however, from imposing severe penalties even on juveniles who commit lesser offenses, as long as the penalty is not greatly disproportionately to the offense.

Differences from Adult Courts

Despite the growing similarity between juvenile and adult criminal proceedings, some differences persist, the most notable being the role played by the juvenile court judge. First, a juvenile court judge takes a more active part in the proceedings. He or she is expected to act as a wise parent rather than as an impartial arbiter, which is the judge's role in adult criminal cases. The juvenile court judge may initiate the questioning of the alleged offender, cross-examine witnesses, bring up a juvenile's background, or actively admonish or counsel an offender. A second difference is in the imposition of the death penalty as an ultimate sanction. In *Thompson v. Oklahoma* (1988), the U.S. Supreme Court held it is unconstitutional to sentence a juvenile to death if he or she was 15 years of age or younger at the time of the commission of the act, regardless of its nature. A year later, in *Stanford v. Kentucky* (1989), the Court held that it is constitutional for a state to impose the death penalty on a juvenile who was at least 16 years old at the time the crime was committed. Together the *Thompson* and *Stanford* cases held that juveniles could not constitutionally be given the death penalty if the crime was committed at 15 years of age, but the death penalty could be administered if the crime was committed when the juvenile was 16 or 17 years old. In 2005, however, the Court said in *Roper v. Simmons* (543 U.S. __ [2005]) that it is unconstitutional to execute juveniles who committed their crime before the age of 18. So whereas adult offenders can be given the death penalty, offenders under 18 years of age cannot be given a death sentence regardless of the seriousness or nature of the crime.

Transfer from Juvenile Courts to Adult Courts

All states have provisions for the **transfer of jurisdiction** from juvenile courts to adult courts. Once transferred, the juvenile ceases being a juvenile and virtually becomes an adult for all purposes including the trial proceedings and the imposition of a penalty. Transfer (some states use the term "waiver" or "certification") provisions may be classified into three general categories, according to the National Report Series Bulletin (Sickmund 2003):

- Judicial Waiver. "[T]he juvenile court judge has the authority to waive juvenile court jurisdiction and transfer the case to criminal court." This process is known in some states as certification, remand, or bind over for criminal prosecution. In 1997, judicial waiver was used in 46 states and the District of Columbia.
- Concurrent Jurisdiction. "[O]riginal jurisdiction for certain cases is shared by both criminal and juvenile courts, and the prosecutor has discretion to file such cases in either court." This process is also known in some states as prosecutorial waiver, prosecutor discretion, or direct file. In 1997, **concurrent jurisdiction** was used in 14 states and the District of Columbia.
- Statutory Exclusion. "[S]tate statute excludes certain juvenile offenders from juvenile court jurisdiction." **Statutory exclusion** is also known in some states as legislative exclusion.

Transfer provisions, which are generally more punitive, have gained more popularity as the public's response to the problem of violent juvenile crime. Adult sanctions are imposed if a juvenile is tried in adult court; hence, much is at stake for the juvenile and the public. Of the three categories, **judicial waiver** is the most commonly used, but the two other approaches are also available in some states. Although judicial waivers are widely available, only a small portion of juvenile cases go through this procedure. One study reports that, in 1997, waivers to criminal court represented "less than 1 percent (approximately 8,400 cases) of the formally processed delinquency

TRANSFER OF JURISDICTION

The transfer of a juvenile from juvenile court to adult court for trial.

CONCURRENT JURISDICTION

Original jurisdiction for certain juvenile cases is shared by both criminal and juvenile courts, and the prosecutor has discretion to file such cases in either court.

STATUTORY EXCLUSION

The automatic exclusion of certain juvenile offenders from juvenile court jurisdiction by state statute, requiring the case to be filed directly with the adult criminal court.

JUDICIAL WAIVER

Transferring a juvenile case from a juvenile court to an adult court.

© Tonya Paul/Oroville Mercury Register

A youth suspected of a violent gang-related crime is arrested and may be tried as an adult.

caseload" (Puzzanchera 2000, p. 1). Wide variation exists among states on judicial waivers, with some states making waivers mandatory and others considering it discretionary. Twenty-two states and the District of Columbia have at least one provision for transferring juveniles to the criminal court for which no minimum age is specified (OJJDP Statistical Briefing Book, n.d.).

AN OVERVIEW OF THE JUVENILE JUSTICE PROCESS

Although the juvenile justice process (see Figure 14.2) is similar to the adult justice process, differences do exist. Different terms are used, juvenile proceedings are deemed civil or quasi-civil (some consider it semicriminal, others call it administrative), and the discretion given to a juvenile court judge is more extensive than that given to criminal court judges.

FIGURE 14.2   *Juvenile Justice and Criminal Justice Systems Compared*

JUVENILE JUSTICE SYSTEM	COMMON GROUND	CRIMINAL JUSTICE SYSTEM
Intake-Prosecution		
• In many instances, juvenile court intake, not the prosecutor, decides what cases to file. • The decision to file a petition for court action is based on both social and legal factors. • A significant portion of cases are diverted from formal case processing. • Intake or the prosecutor diverts cases from formal processing to services operated by the juvenile court, prosecutor's office, or outside agencies.	• Probable cause must be established. • The prosecutor acts on behalf of the state.	• Plea bargaining is common. • The prosecution decision is based largely on legal facts. • Prosecution is valuable in building history for subsequent offenses. • Prosecution exercises discretion to withhold charges or divert offenders out of the criminal justice system.
Detention-Jail/Lockup		
• Juveniles may be detained for their own protection or the community's protection. • Juveniles may not be confined with adults unless there is "sight and sound separation."	• Accused offenders may be held in custody to ensure their appearance in court. • Detention alternatives of home or electronic detention are used.	• Accused individuals have the right to apply for bond/bail release.
Adjudication-Conviction		
• Juvenile court proceedings are "quasi-civil" (not criminal) and may be confidential. • If guilt is established, the youth is adjudicated delinquent regardless of offense. • Right to jury trial is not afforded in all states.	• Standard of "proof beyond a reasonable doubt" is required. • Rights to be represented by an attorney, to confront witnesses, and to remain silent are afforded. • Appeals to a higher court are allowed. • Experimentation with specialized courts (for example, drug courts, gun courts) is underway.	• Defendants have a constitutional right to a jury trial. • Guilt must be established on individual offenses charged for conviction. • All proceedings are open.

(continued)

Procedure before Adjudication

The juvenile justice process starts in various ways and casts a wider net than that of adult justice. Juvenile behavior that sets the process in motion may come to the attention of the government through oral or written reports from diverse sources such as the general public, probation officers, victims, parents, neighbors, school authorities, or the police. The Office of Juvenile Justice and Delinquency Prevention reports that in 1998, 84 percent of all delinquency cases referred to juvenile court were referred by law enforcement agencies and that the remaining 16 percent were made by parents, victims, schools, probation officers, and others (Sickmund 2003, p. 2).

Contact with the police can lead to a variety of actions, such as taking the juvenile into custody for possible prosecution, taking the juvenile into protective custody, referring the juvenile to pertinent agencies, or releasing the juvenile. One source notes that "most state statutes explicitly direct police officers to release to a parent or refer to court those juveniles who are taken into custody" (Juvenile Probation Officer Initiative Working Group 1993, p. 32). In practice, police officer decisions can include such informal procedures as outright release, warning, referral to community agency for services, referral to a "citizen hearing board," or referral to court intake.

FIGURE 14.2 *(Contd.)*

JUVENILE JUSTICE SYSTEM	COMMON GROUND	CRIMINAL JUSTICE SYSTEM
Disposition-Sentencing		
• Disposition decisions are based on individual and social factors, offense severity, and youth's offense history. • Dispositional philosophy includes a significant rehabilitation component. • Many dispositional alternatives are operated by the juvenile court. • Dispositions cover a wide range of community-based and residential services. • Disposition orders may be directed to people other than the offender (for example, parents). • Disposition may be indeterminate, based on progress demonstrated by the youth.	• Decisions are influenced by current offense, offending history, and social factors. • Decisions hold offenders accountable. • Decisions may give consideration to victims (for example, restitution and "no contact" orders). • Decisions may not be cruel or unusual.	• Sentencing decisions are bound primarily by the severity of the current offense and by the offender's criminal history. • Sentencing philosophy is based largely on proportionality and punishment. • Sentence is often determinate, based on offense.
Aftercare-Parole		
• Function combines surveillance and reintegration activities (for example, family, school, work).	• The behavior of individuals released from correctional settings is monitored. • Violation of conditions can result in reincarceration.	• Function is primarily surveillance and reporting to monitor illicit behavior.

Source: Howard N. Snyder and Melissa Sickmund. 1999. *Juvenile Offenders and Victims; 1999 National Report*. Washington, DC: Office of Juvenile Justice and Delinquency Prevention (September), pp. 95–96.

Juvenile cases are handled formally or informally. Formal handling means that the case goes through a formal charge, a hearing, and a disposition. Informal processing means that the case is handled outside the regular procedures so that the juvenile can be diverted from the system. The number of cases handled informally has increased over the years. In 2003, about half of all cases referred to juvenile court intake were reportedly handled informally, and most of the informally processed cases were dismissed. Many of these cases were dismissed after the juvenile agreed to specific conditions for a specified time period. These conditions are documented in a written agreement known as a consent decree. It includes such conditions as victim restitution, school attendance, drug counseling, curfew, and other provisions similar to those imposed in regular probation (Sickmund 2003, p. 2).

The Intake Stage

A juvenile taken into custody by the police usually goes through the **intake** process, considered by some to be "one of the most crucial case processing points in the juvenile justice system" (Juvenile Probation Officer Initiative Working Group 1993, p. 32). *Intake* is a term unique to juvenile justice, but its meaning varies from one state to another. In general it refers to a process whereby a juvenile is screened to determine if the case should proceed further into the juvenile justice system or whether other alternatives are better suited for the juvenile. A probation officer or other individuals designated by the court or the prosecutor usually handle the intake. Arnold Binder, Gilbert Geis, and Dickson D. Bruce (1997, p. 260) summarize the functions of the intake process as follows:

- Determine whether the circumstances of the case bring it within the jurisdiction of the juvenile court.
- Determine whether the evidence is sufficient to warrant a court hearing.
- Decide whether the case is serious enough to require a court hearing.
- Arrange for a process of informal supervision if that alternative seems desirable.

Intake may also involve detention screening, presentence investigation, crisis intervention, or other procedures mandated by the court. It does what state law or court policy intends for the process to accomplish. A juvenile may be detained by the police, but only for a limited time. The laws in all 50 states now dictate that a detention hearing must be held within a few days (generally within 24 hours) after a juvenile is taken into custody (Snyder and Sickmund 2006, p. 168). Federal law provides that juveniles be separated from adult offenders by "sight and sound." This assures that juveniles are detained in facilities separate from those used for adults. The U.S. Supreme Court has held that preventive detention of juveniles (where a juvenile is detained because of the likelihood that he or she will commit other offenses) is constitutional, although subject to limitations (*Schall v. Martin* 1984).

If the intake officer decides to refer the case to court, the prosecutor petitions the court for the juvenile to be adjudicated. A summons is issued directing the juvenile to appear before the court at a specified time and place for an initial appearance on the petition. An arraignment is then held, and the juvenile is given the opportunity to admit or deny the allegations.

The Adjudication Stage

Adjudication is the equivalent of a trial in adult criminal cases. However, it is less formal, and the judge takes a more active part in the hearing—including asking

INTAKE

The process whereby a juvenile is screened to determine whether the case should proceed further in the juvenile justice system or whether other alternatives are better suited for the juvenile.

ADJUDICATION

Juvenile justice equivalent of a trial in adult criminal cases.

FIGURE 14.3 *What Are the Stages of Delinquency Case Processing in the Juvenile Justice System?*

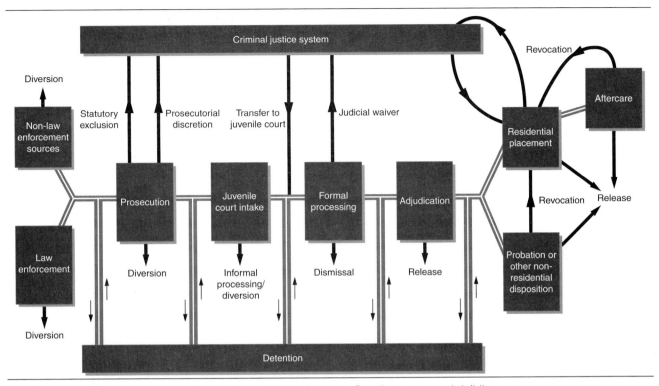

Note: This chart gives a simplified view of caseflow through the juvenile justice system. Procedures vary among jurisdictions.

Source: Howard N. Snyder and Sickmund, Melissa. 2006. *Juvenile Offenders and Victims: 2006 National Report.* Washington, DC: U.S. Department of Justice, Office of Justice Programs, Office of Juvenile Justice and Delinquency Prevention, p. 105.

questions of juveniles, their parents or guardians, and witnesses. Juvenile courts were designed to be different from adult courts (see Figure 14.3). Originally no lawyers were allowed, formal rules of evidence were waived, and the juvenile enjoyed no legal or constitutional protections. This led critics to label them "kangaroo courts." That has changed considerably. Now the features of the original juvenile courts are barely recognizable. In the words of Peter Greenwood (1985): "The informality is largely gone. Juveniles sit with their lawyers like adult defendants. Juvenile hearings or trials proceed along the same lines as criminal trials. The rules of evidence and rights of the parties are about the same, except that juveniles still do not have the right to a jury trial or to bail." (p. 1)

The Disposition Stage

If a juvenile is found to have engaged in the conduct alleged in the petition, the disposition stage follows. **Disposition** is the equivalent of sentencing in adult cases, but the juvenile court judge wields greater discretion than do judges in adult criminal trials. Because most states consider rehabilitation an integral part of juvenile corrections, the judge typically has a wide choice of available dispositions ranging from a mild reprimand to confinement in a state institution. Institutionalization (also known as residential commitment) is usually the most severe disposition in juvenile cases and is imposed primarily in juvenile delinquency cases. In 1998, most adjudicated delinquency cases resulted in residential placement or formal probation. Of these cases, "26 percent were sent by the court to resident placement, such as a training

DISPOSITION

Juvenile justice equivalent of sentencing in adult cases.

school, treatment center, boot camp, drug treatment, or private placement facility or group home," but in 58 percent of adjudicated delinquency cases, probation was the most severe punishment given (Sickmund 2003, p. 22).

CINS (usually status offenders) are typically placed on probation as the maximum sanction. If probation is revoked, however, the juvenile may then be classified as a delinquent because of a violation of a court order and may be sent to a state institution.

Blended Sentences

The trend in many states toward a more punitive treatment of juveniles has led to the passage of blended sentencing laws. These laws authorize courts to impose juvenile or adult punishment on young offenders, thus creating a "middle ground" between traditional juvenile and adult sanctions. Blended sentences give judges the power to choose from a wider assortment of punishments and impose one that best fits the offense committed. It also narrows the gap between juvenile and adult punishments. As of the end of legislative sessions for 2004, 15 states had blended sentencing laws that authorized juvenile courts to impose criminal sentences on certain juvenile offenders (Snyder and Sickmund 2006).

Release from an Institution

Once a juvenile is confined in a state institution, release is left to the discretion of institutional officials. Many states provide for aftercare (the equivalent of parole) for juveniles who are fit for release before serving the maximum amount of time set by state law. If released on aftercare, the juvenile is supervised, but supervision usually ceases after the juvenile reaches the age of majority—generally 18. If the provisions of aftercare are breached, the juvenile is sent back to a state juvenile institution (after a hearing at which the breach is established) instead of to a state prison.

IN RE GAULT: THE MOST IMPORTANT JUVENILE JUSTICE CASE

The leading case in juvenile justice is *In re Gault* (1967). In that case a 15-year-old boy and a friend were taken into custody in Arizona as a result of a complaint that they had made lewd telephone calls. Gault's parents were not informed that he was in custody, and they were not shown the complaint that was filed against their son. The complainant never appeared at any hearing, and no written record was made of the hearing that was held. Gault was committed to a state institution as a delinquent until he reached the age of majority—a total of six years from the date of the hearing. The maximum punishment for the offense, had it been committed by an adult, was a fine of from $5 to $60 or imprisonment for a maximum of two months. Gault appealed the conviction, saying he was denied his rights during the hearing. The U.S. Supreme Court agreed.

Gault holds that juveniles must be given four basic due process rights in adjudication proceedings that can result in confinement in an institution where their freedom would be curtailed. These rights are:

- Reasonable notice of the charges
- Counsel, appointed by the state if the juvenile is indigent
- The ability to confront and cross-examine witnesses
- The privilege against self-incrimination

In re Gault is significant because it was the first case decided by the U.S. Supreme Court that gave juveniles due process rights, thus initiating the decline of the pure *parens patriae* approach. *Parens patriae* is still alive in juvenile justice, but its purity has been sapped by a gradual process of "adultification" through judicial intervention (see Figure 14.4).

FIGURE 14.4 *Major United States Supreme Court Decisions in Juvenile Justice*

Cases Giving Constitutional Rights to Juveniles

Kent v. United States (383 U.S. 541 [1966]): Juveniles must be given due process rights when transferred from juvenile to adult court. These rights are

> A hearing
> Representation by counsel at such hearing
> Access to records considered by the juvenile court
> A statement of the reasons in support of the waiver order

In re Gault (387 U.S. 1 [1967]): Juveniles must be given four due process rights in adjudication proceedings that can result in confinement in an institution where their freedom would be curtailed. These rights are

> Reasonable notice of the charges
> Counsel, appointed by the state if the juvenile is indigent
> The ability to confront and cross-examine witnesses
> The privilege against self-incrimination

In re Winship (397 U.S. 358 [1970]): Proof beyond a reasonable doubt, not simply a preponderance of the evidence, is required in juvenile adjudication hearings in cases where the act would have been a crime if committed by an adult.

Breed v. Jones (421 U.S. 517 [1975]): Juveniles are entitled to the constitutional right against double jeopardy in juvenile proceedings.

Cases That Do Not Give Constitutional Rights to Juveniles

McKeiver v. Pennsylvania (403 U.s. 528 [1971]): Juveniles have no constitutional right to trial by jury even in juvenile delinquency cases where the juvenile faces a possible incarceration.

Davis v. Alaska (415 U.S. 308 [1974]): Despite confidentiality laws, the fact that a juvenile is on probation may be brought out by the opposing lawyer in the cross-examination of a juvenile witness.

Smith v. Daily Mail Publishing Co. (443 U.S. 97 [1979]): A state law making it a crime to publish the name of a juvenile charged with a crime is unconstitutional because it violates the First Amendment right to freedom of the press.

Schall v. Martin (467 U.S. 253 [1984]): Preventive detention of juveniles is constitutional.

Fare v. Michael C. (442 U.S. 707 [1985]): A request by a juvenile to see his probation officer is not equivalent to asking for a lawyer. Moreover, there is no probation officer–client privilege, meaning that any information a juvenile gives to a probation officer may be divulged in court even if the information was given by the juvenile in confidence.

New Jersey v. T.L.O (469 U.S. 325 [1985]): Public school officials need reasonable grounds to search students; they do not need a warrant or probable cause.

Death Penalty Cases

Eddings v. Oklahoma (455 U.S. 104 [1983]): Mitigating circumstances, including age and social history, must be considered in juvenile capital cases.

Thompson v. Oklahoma (487 U.S. 815 [1988]): It is unconstitutional to sentence a juvenile to death if he or she was 15 years of age or younger at the time of the commission of the offense.

Stanford v. Kentucky (492 U.S. 361 [1989]): It is constitutional for a state to impose the death penalty on a juvenile who was 16 years old or older at the time the crime was committed.

Roper v. Simmons (2005): The death penalty is unconstitutional if imposed on juveniles under 18 years of age when the crime was committed.

JUVENILE PROBATION

As it is with adults, probation is the disposition most often used by judges when formally adjudicating juvenile delinquency cases. Juvenile probation can be formal or informal. Formal probation takes place through court action after an adjudication hearing where the juvenile is found to have committed a delinquent act. Informal probation occurs when a juvenile, with prior consent from him or his parents, agrees to be placed on probation even prior to adjudication. If the juvenile adheres to the conditions imposed, the charges are dropped and nothing appears in the juvenile's record. In 2002 more than 385,400 juveniles were placed on formal probation, more than double those placed on formal probation in 1985 (Snyder and Sickmund 2006, p. 174).

Origin

The origin of juvenile probation is traced to John Augustus, the Boston shoemaker who in 1847 persuaded judges in Massachusetts to place wayward youth under his care. As one source notes, he "came up with a less high-handed and ultimately much more influential method of keeping children out of jail in that he simply asked the court to release the juveniles to his supervision so he could help them" (Griffin and Torbet 2002, pp. 6–7).

Augustus assured the judge that if those he had chosen were released, he "would note their general conduct, see that they were sent to school or supplied with some honest employment" (p. 6). From time to time, he would "make an impartial report to the court, whenever they should desire it" (p. 6). And if their good behavior continued long enough—"I wished ample time to test the promises of these youth to behave well in the future," (pp. 6–7) Augustus later explained—they would be let off with small fines that Augustus himself sometimes paid. John Augustus later extended this approach to adult offenders. When he died in 1859, he had bailed out more than 1,800 people, had a liability totaling $243,234, and was destitute (Griffin and Torbet 2002, p. 7). But he had made a major impact on how juvenile justice deals with wayward youth, and his legacy survives to this day (see Figure 14.5).

FIGURE 14.5   *John Augustus: Founder of Juvenile Probation*

"In 1847, I bailed nineteen boys, from seven to fifteen years of age, and in bailing them it was understood, and agreed by the court, that their cases should be continued from term to term for several months, as a season of probation; thus each month at the calling of the docket, I would appear in court, make my report, and thus the cases would pass on for five or six months. At the expiration of this term, twelve of the boys were brought into court at one time, and the scene formed a striking and highly pleasing contrast with their appearance when first arraigned. The judge expressed much pleasure as well as surprise, at their appearance, and remarked that the object of law has been accomplished. The sequel thus far shows that not one of this number has proved false to the promises of reform they made while on probation."

Source: John Augustus. 1852. *A Report of the Labors of John Augustus, for the Last Ten Years, and in Aid of the Unfortunate.* As cited in Patrick Griffin and Patricia Torbet. (Eds.). 2002. *Desktop Guide to Good Juvenile Probation Practice.* Washington, DC: Office of Juvenile Justice and Delinquency Prevention, p. 6.

Conditions of Probation

JUDGES HAVE MUCH DISCRETION. Juvenile court judges have considerable discretion when imposing probation conditions because very few states specify the conditions that should be imposed. Instead, setting conditions is left to the sound discretion of the juvenile court, usually upon recommendation of the probation officer, and acting as a wise parent. Typically conditions include provisions designed to control as well as rehabilitate the juvenile (Sickmund 2003, p. 23). These dual goals make the imposition of conditions more challenging for the court but, at the same time, assure wide discretion in that just about any condition of probation can be justified as rehabilitative and contributing to behavior control.

TYPES OF CONDITIONS. Juvenile probation conditions are usually of two types: mandatory or discretionary. Both may be specified by law or left to the discretion of the juvenile court judge or to the releasing authority in the case of aftercare. Only a few states impose mandatory conditions, and where imposed, they vary from one jurisdiction to another. Mandatory conditions usually include the following rules (Juvenile Probation Officer Initiative Working Group 1993, p. 16):

- Probationers may not commit a new local, state, or federal delinquent act.
- Probationers must report as directed to their probation officers.
- Probationers must obey all court orders.
- Discretionary conditions also vary from one jurisdiction to another. As an example, the New Jersey Juvenile Statutes list the following discretionary conditions:
  - Pay a fine.
  - Pay restitution.
  - Perform community service.
  - Participate in a work program.
  - Participate in programs emphasizing self-reliance.
  - Participate in a program of academic or vocational education or counseling.
  - Be placed in a suitable residential or nonresidential program for the treatment of alcoholic or narcotic abuse.
  - Be placed in a nonresidential program operated by a public or private agency, providing intensive services to juveniles for specified hours.
  - Be placed in any private group home with which the Department of Correction has entered into a purchase of service contract.

Supervision

Supervision is the essence of juvenile probation and its most effective tool for rehabilitation. The *Desktop Guide* (Juvenile Probation Officer Initiative Working Group 1993) states that "the common thread that runs through all approaches to supervision is utility; that is, that juvenile justice intervention must be designed to guide and correct the naturally changing behavior patterns of youth" (p. 79). It adds that "unlike adult probation, juvenile supervision views a young offender as a developing person, as one who has not yet achieved a firm commitment to a particular set of values, goals, behavior patterns, or lifestyle. As such, juvenile justice supervision is in the hopeful position of influencing that development and thereby reducing criminal behavior" (p. 79).

Juvenile Probation Officers

Probation officers supervise juveniles on probation. They have a difficult job, which is made more challenging by changing philosophies, innovative programs, and an

Schooner's is a public fast-food restaurant operated solely by staff and residents from Excell Center, a residential treatment center for at-risk boys. The program is designed to train youths to seek and retain employment.

increasingly high-risk clientele. Probation officers are usually appointed and also terminated by the juvenile court judge. The following provision from the state of Indiana typifies the legal provisions in many jurisdictions:

> The judge of the juvenile court shall appoint a chief probation officer, and may appoint other probation officers, and an appropriate number of other employees to assist the probation department. The salaries of the probation officers and other juvenile court employees shall be fixed by the judge and paid by the county, subject to the approval of the county council. In addition to their annual salary, probation officers shall be reimbursed for any necessary travel expenses incurred in the performance of their duties in accord with the law governing state officers and employees. (Indiana Juvenile Code, Title 31)

The job of a juvenile probation officer is often more demanding than that of an adult probation officer. As the *Desktop Guide* observes: "The probation officer is expected to fulfill many different roles, often 'taking up the slack' after judges, attorneys, social agencies, parents, and so on have met what they see as their own clearly defined responsibilities in the case and have expressed an unwillingness to extend themselves beyond these limits" (Juvenile Probation Officer Initiative Working Group 1993, pp. 119–120).

In many cases, the juvenile probation officer is the last hope of rehabilitation for the juvenile, and is expected, among other things, to be a cop, a prosecutor, a confessor, a rat, a teacher, a friend, a problem solver, a crisis manager, a hand holder, a community resource specialist, and others (p. 120). Another writer notes that although the duties of juvenile probation officers are many, they mainly fall under three general categories: intake screening and assessment, presentence investigations, and supervision (Corbett 2000, pp. 22–30).

It is recommended that probation departments "consider the converging interests of the juvenile offender, the victim, and the community at large in developing individualized case plans for probation supervision" (Juvenile Probation Officer Initiative Working Group 1993). To reconcile conflicting goals (such as rehabilitation versus punishment, treatment versus control, and public safety versus youth development), the *Desktop Publication* states that probation "must endeavor to not only protect the public and hold the juvenile offender accountable, it must also attempt to meet his needs" (p. 79). Thus the ideal form of juvenile probation supervision aims more at rehabilitation than merely meting out punishment. Standards proposed by several organizations recommend that a needs assessment be conducted and a service plan be developed before a juvenile is placed on probation (p. 44). These standards further suggest that the probation officer, in conjunction with the juvenile and the family, assess needs in the following areas: medical problems, proximity of the program to the youth, the capacity of the youth to benefit from the program, and the availability of placements. In addition, the standards place strong emphasis on the "availability of supplemental services to facilitate the youth's participation in a community-based program" (p. 53).

Intensive Supervision Probation

Intensive supervision probation (ISP) is a type of supervision used in both juvenile and adult probation. It is defined as a program of intensive surveillance of and contact with an offender and is aimed at reducing criminal conduct by limiting opportunities to engage in it. Strategies vary from one state to another, but one scholar identifies the following common features in intensive supervision for juveniles:

- A greater reliance is placed on unannounced spot checks. These may occur in a variety of settings including home, school, known hangouts, and job sites.
- Considerable attention is directed at increasing the number and kinds of collateral contacts made by staff, including family members, friends, staff from other agencies, and concerned residents in the community.
- Greater use is made of curfew, including both more rigid enforcement and lowering the hour at which curfew goes into effect.
- Surveillance is expanded to ensure seven-day-a-week, 24-hour-a-day coverage. (Juvenile Probation Officer Initiative Working Group 1993, p. 87)

Contrary to popular belief, intensive probation is usually not designed to deal with violent juvenile offenders. The majority of juveniles placed on intensive supervision are "serious and/or chronic offenders who would otherwise be committed to a correctional facility but who, through an objective system of diagnosis and classification, have been identified as amenable to community placement" (p. 65).

School-Based Probation

A comparatively new but increasingly popular concept in juvenile probation supervision is **school-based probation.** Griffin and Torbet (2002) indicate that "in recent years, juvenile probation officers in jurisdictions across the country have been moving out of traditional district offices, into middle, junior high, and high school buildings—and supervising their caseloads right in the schools" (p. 92). They list the benefits of school-based probation as follows:

- *More contact.* More direct contact with probationers—in some cases daily contact—can lead to better relationships and more awareness of school, home, and peer problems.
- *Better monitoring.* Closer monitoring of juvenile offenders and better observation of their behavior and interactions can lead to more effective and immediate responses to problems.
- *Focus on school success.* Juveniles with school-based probation officers may have more incentive to attend regularly, try hard, and refrain from misconduct, increasing their overall chances of succeeding as students.

A study of school-based probation in the State of Pennsylvania (see Figure 14.6) found that "school-based probation officers, school administrators, and students on school-based probation strongly believed that the program was effective in boosting attendance and academic performance and reducing misbehavior in school" (Griffin and Torbet 2002, p. 92).

Fare v. Michael C.: An Important Case in Juvenile Probation Supervision

The only case ever to be decided by the U.S. Supreme Court on juvenile probation supervision is *Fare v. Michael C.* (1985). This important California case helps define the relationship between a probation officer and a probationer during probation supervision.

Michael C., a juvenile, was taken into police custody because he was suspected of having committed a murder. He was advised of his *Miranda v. Arizona* (1966) rights (anything he said could be used against him, and he could have a lawyer). When asked if he wanted to waive his right to have an attorney present during questioning, he responded by asking for his probation officer. He was informed by the police that the probation officer would be contacted later but that he could talk to the police if he wanted.

FIGURE 14.6   *School-Based Probation Agreements*

School-Based Probation Agreements

School-based probation program arrangements and procedures should be formalized via a written agreement between the juvenile court/probation department and the participating school district. At a minimum, such an agreement should contain the following:

- A statement of the philosophy, goals, and objectives of school-based probation
- A clear definition of the role of the probation officer within the school environment
- A clear definition of the role of the school district administration and staff in supporting the probation officer
- A list of probation officer responsibilities, including participation in any student assistance or pupil services team involving a probationer
- If probation officers are permitted to carry firearms, the procedure for carrying and storing that firearm while on school property
- A list of the school district's responsibilities, including the provision of a telephone line and office space affording privacy within the school for the probation officer
- Procedures ensuring probation officers' access to probationers' student records, including attendance, discipline, grading, and progress reports
- Provisions for meetings between probation department administrators and school administrators to discuss ongoing program issues

---

Source: Pennsylvania Juvenile Court Judges' Commission. 2002. Standards Governing School-Based Probation Services. As cited in Patrick Griffin and Patricia Torbet. (Eds.). *Desktop Guide to Good Juvenile Probation Practice.* Washington, DC: Office of Juvenile Justice and Delinquency Prevention, p. 93.

Michael C. agreed to talk and during questioning made statements and drew sketches that incriminated himself. When charged with murder in juvenile court, Michael C. moved to suppress the incriminating evidence, alleging it was obtained in violation of his *Miranda* rights. He said that his request to see his probation officer was, in effect, equivalent to asking for a lawyer. However, the evidence was admitted at trial, and Michael C. was convicted.

On appeal, the U.S. Supreme Court affirmed the conviction, holding that the request by a juvenile probationer during police questioning to see his or her probation officer, after having received the *Miranda* warnings, is not equivalent to asking for a lawyer and is not considered an assertion of the right to remain silent. Evidence voluntarily given by the juvenile probationer after asking to see his probation officer is therefore admissible in court in a subsequent criminal trial.

The *Michael C.* case is significant because the Supreme Court laid out two principles that help define the supervisory role of a juvenile probation officer. First, the Court stated that communications of the accused with the probation officer are not shielded by lawyer–client privilege. This means that information given by a probationer to the probation officer may be disclosed in court, unlike the information given to a lawyer by a client—which cannot be revealed to anyone unless the right to confidentiality is waived by both the client and the lawyer. Said the Court:

> A probation officer is not in the same posture [as a lawyer] with regard to either the accused or the system of justice as a whole. Often he is not trained in the law, and so is not in a position to advise the accused as to his legal rights. Neither is he a trained advocate, skilled in the representation of the interests of his client before police and courts. He does not assume the power to act on behalf of his client by virtue of his status as advisor, nor are the communications of the accused to the probation officer shielded by the lawyer–client privilege.

Fare v. Michael C. shows that despite *parens patriae*—a doctrine based on a parent–child relationship—confidentiality of communication between the probation officer and a probationer does not exist. Confidentiality of juvenile records exists in most jurisdictions, but it stems from state law or agency policy prohibiting disclosure.

Second, the *Fare v. Michael C.* case is also significant because the Court in that case emphasized that a probation officer's loyalty and obligation is to the state, despite any obligation owed to the probationer. The Court said:

> Moreover, the probation officer is the employee of the State which seeks to prosecute the alleged offender. He is a peace officer, and as such is allied, to a greater or lesser extent, with his fellow peace officers. He owes an obligation to the State notwithstanding the obligation he may also owe the juvenile under his supervision. In most cases, the probation officer is duty bound to report wrongdoing by the juvenile when it comes to his attention, even if by communication from the juvenile himself.

This statement defines where a probation officer's loyalty lies. Professionalism requires that the officer's loyalty must be with the state and not with the probationer, regardless of the sympathy the officer might have for the juvenile.

The Probation Record of Juveniles

One traditional characteristic of juvenile proceedings is confidentiality. Although the criminal and probation records of adults are public and can be accessed by just about anybody, juvenile records are either confidential or can be disclosed only to certain individuals. A member of the public does not have access to the probation record of a juvenile. The exception is if such records are made public by state law. Probation records contain such data as the offense for which a juvenile is on probation, the length of probation, and probation conditions. But whereas probation records are generally closed to the public, the fact that a juvenile is on probation is a matter of public record. Court personnel can disclose the fact that a juvenile is on probation, but not much more beyond that (such as the offense committed, the conditions and length of probation, and the treatment programs prescribed) because the details of juvenile probation are shielded from public scrutiny.

The confidentiality of juvenile records, however, is not a constitutional right and may be lifted by state law or agency policy. Over the years, confidentiality has gradually diminished. One publication notes that "juvenile codes in 42 states allow names (and sometimes pictures and court records) of juveniles involved in delinquency proceedings to be released to the media." In 16 states, juvenile court records or proceedings (including probation records) are now public. In 27 states, the identity of the juvenile in delinquency cases may be released, but only in cases involving certain crimes and/or repeat offenders. In 11 states, media access to juvenile courts is allowed, but with a court order (Snyder and Sickmund 1999, p. 101). The general rule, however, still is that in the absence of state law or agency policy allowing disclosure, juvenile records are confidential.

JUVENILE PAROLE (OR AFTERCARE)

Background

One difference in terminology between adult and juvenile justice is that some jurisdictions use the term *aftercare* instead of parole for juveniles. Many jurisdictions, however, still use the term *parole*. One source characterizes juvenile aftercare thus: "Juvenile aftercare is not a new idea. Its foundations date to the 18th century, when youth were released to "masters" for additional training. Today youth are released to their families or guardians and monitored by the court. . . . Thus aftercare today is concerned with creating a smooth transition from institution to community, identifying community support systems and resources for youth, assisting in the development of positive peer interaction, and monitoring youth's progress" (Gordon in McShane and Williams 2003, pp. 5–6).

The discussion in this chapter deals with juvenile probation because there are more juveniles on probation than there are on parole or aftercare. Most of the literature and studies on juvenile community corrections focus on probation, not parole. Many topics discussed in this chapter on probation (such as conditions of probation and supervision) also apply to parole. In some jurisdictions, juvenile probation and parole are administered by the same agency and officers supervise juvenile probationers and parolees. The conditions of probation and parole are the same in many jurisdictions, the most common being not committing violations of the law, getting gainful employment, curfew, electronic monitoring, drug testing, reporting regularly, and allowing home visits.

Similarities with Probation

One publication (del Carmen and Trulson 2006, p. 303) notes the similarities and differences between probation and parole:

- Both are community-based corrections programs, meaning that the offender is in the community instead of in jail, prison, or an institution.

- The offender has been found to have engaged in a prohibited conduct or convicted.
- Both are privileges, not a constitutional right. They are acts of grace, meaning that an offender can be denied probation or parole, at the option of the judge or parole board, in lieu of incarceration or continued incarceration.
- The juvenile is supervised.
- If prescribed conditions are violated, the juvenile is sent to jail, prison, or an institution to serve out the sentence if on probation or the unserved term if on parole.

Differences from Probation

Probation	Parole
1. Offender has not been to jail or prison for the offense ("halfway in")	1. Offender has been to prison for the offense ("halfway out")
2. Granted by a judge or jury and is therefore an act of the judicial department	2. Granted by the parole board or detention authorities and is therefore an act of the executive department
3. Usually supervised by probation officers, who are state or local employees	3. Usually supervised by parole officers, who are state employees

Parole Boards

As of 2004, five states had a separate juvenile parole board (California, Colorado, New Jersey, South Carolina, and Utah) whose memberships vary from five to nine members. Some members serve full time, others serve part time; most are appointed by the governor, others are elected; some are paid, others are unpaid. (Frendle 2004, p. 2).

Responsibilities of Juvenile Parole Officers

One state lists the characteristic duties and responsibilities of juvenile parole officers as follows: (State of New Hampshire, Human Resources)

- Conducts predispositional and other investigations as directed by the court or Juvenile Parole Board concerning juvenile delinquents and/or children in need of services
- Prepares written reports and recommendations for the court or Juvenile Parole Board, including reporting alleged violations of conditional release and juvenile parole
- Supervises juveniles on conditional release or juvenile parole in order to ensure compliance with the terms of conditional release or parole, or other conditions set forth by the court or Juvenile Parole Board
- Takes into custody juveniles who violate conditional release or juvenile parole, and prepares case information for prosecution before the court or Juvenile Parole Board
- Coordinates with court officials, law enforcement agencies, community-based agencies, state agencies, family members, and the public to assist the court in making dispositional determinations in matters of juvenile delinquency and children in need of services

- Provides family-centered intervention to families and caretakers to help maintain the family unit
- Coordinates suitable out-of-home care to meet a specific need of the juvenile and family, including facilitating transportation
- Manages cases to ensure case plan is carried out and court and administrative reviews under state and federal laws are completed in a timely manner

Another state lists the duties and responsibilities of juvenile parole officers as similar to those of probation officers, which are as follows: correctional case planning, case management, community resource development, report writing, and other miscellaneous duties (State of Oregon, Department of Administrative Services, Juvenile Parole and Probation Officer). It then adds that the job requires basic knowledge of:

- Legal codes, regulations, and court procedures
- Procedures for arrest, investigations, and rights of juveniles
- Resources available to diagnose and treat maladjusted adolescents and young adults
- Techniques and methods used in individual and group counseling
- Techniques and methods of investigation and evidence presentation
- Methods of report writing

Evaluating Juvenile Parole Programs

One source notes that "in general, the use of juvenile aftercare has been unsuccessful," attributing the lack of success to the following: "(1) a lack of communication between institutional staff and aftercare staff during the transitional period, (2) the inability to identify appropriate service providers for youth, (3) large caseload sizes for aftercare workers, and (4) selection of inappropriate youth for aftercare" (Gordon in McShane and Williams 2003, p. 4). Another study that evaluated the success of some aftercare programs concludes that "the overall picture is mixed," but observes that "the implementation of juvenile aftercare programming is still in its infancy." ("Reintegration, Supervised Release, and Intensive Aftercare," OJJDP 1991, p. 1). This source used an intensive study of reintegrated confinement and intensive aftercare programs, using five recent juvenile initiatives funded by the government. These are such diverse programs as the Philadelphia Intensive Probation Aftercare Program, Juvenile Aftercare in Maryland Drug Treatment Program, the Schulman Intensive Aftercare Project, the Michigan Nokomis Challenge Program, and the OJJDP Intensive Aftercare Program. The study then suggests reform measures, including a recommendation that aftercare programs "must be preceded by parallel services in the corrections facility and must include careful preparation for the aftercare to follow," and that these programs be funded and staffed at levels that would enable it to provide enhanced service delivery (p. 2).

REVOCATION OF JUVENILE PROBATION OR PAROLE

Violation of probation or parole conditions leads to revocation. In juvenile probation, revocation proceedings take place before the judge; in parole cases, revocation cases are handled by the parole board or agency. As in adult probation or parole, revocation is largely discretionary with the juvenile court or parole board. The only exception is when revocation is mandated by law for certain serious violations.

Revocation of juvenile probation or parole is usually initiated by the juvenile officer or agency. In many jurisdictions the motion to revoke probation is filed in court by the prosecutor or with the parole board by the parole officer. Prosecutors are usually not involved in parole revocation; instead designated parole officers perform that responsibility because hearings are conducted with the parole board and are not judicial in nature. A warrant is then issued for the juvenile's arrest. In most states the warrant is served by law enforcement officers. Some states authorize juvenile probation or parole officers to make an arrest and conduct searches and seizures. Once arrested, the juvenile is held in custody in a juvenile facility pending a revocation hearing.

No Standards for Revocation

The judge or parole board has a lot of discretion to revoke or not to revoke juvenile probation, and these decisions are usually final and unappealable. The justification for no appeal is that the judge or board knows what is best for the juvenile and therefore should not be second-guessed by an appellate court that has not even seen the juvenile. The judge or board has options ranging from keeping the juvenile out in the community without any change of conditions whatsoever, imposing more severe conditions or changing treatment, or revoking probation and sending the juvenile to an institution. Judges or boards usually rely on the recommendations of the probation or parole officer to determine the proper action to be taken. The *Desktop Guide* says that the probation officer's recommendation "should not, and need not, be all or nothing," urging instead that the officer "should recommend just what is needed to produce the juvenile's compliance with his probation and no more" (Juvenile Probation Officer Initiative Working Group 1993, p. 19). The implication is that revocation should be used as a last resort and not as a first option. The *Desktop Guide* then adds that ordering the juvenile to perform community work or adding curfew restriction as a condition may suffice to convince the juvenile that the effects of violation are serious. Restraint, not quick revocation, is recommended.

Result of Revocation

Revocation sends the probationer or parolee to an institution for juveniles. Probation revocation is similar to a finding of juvenile delinquency in that the juvenile may now be given the same sanctions as a juvenile delinquent, which include being deprived of freedom and confinement in a juvenile institution. Unlike adult probationers who must serve the jail or prison term originally imposed (subject to parole law), juveniles are kept in state institutions only until they reach the age of majority (adulthood). The release of a juvenile on parole prior to reaching the age of majority is determined by the juvenile authorities who run the state institution, not by the judge. In some cases, certain types of juveniles are kept beyond the age of majority by special laws that mandate harsher sanctions. For example, some states allow detention of parole violators or other serious offenders in state institutions until they are 24 years old.

TOP THINGS YOU SHOULD KNOW

- Juvenile justice in the United States is heavily influenced by *parens patriae* and the concept of diminished *mens rea*.
- Juvenile courts are an American creation and have jurisdiction based on age and acts committed. Minimum and maximum ages for juveniles vary from state to state.

- Juvenile delinquency refers to acts that if committed by adults are punishable under the state's penal code; conduct in need of supervision comprises acts committed by juveniles that if committed by adults would not be punishable at all.
- Juveniles may be transferred for trial from a juvenile court to an adult court. Once transferred to an adult court, the juvenile ceases to be a juvenile and is tried and punished like an adult.
- The most important juvenile law case ever decided by the United States Supreme Court is *In re Gault* (1967), which holds that a juvenile is entitled to due process if charged with an offense that can result in being sent to a juvenile institution.
- After a juvenile is taken into custody, the processing sequence for juveniles consists of: intake, adjudication, disposition, institutionalization (for certain offenses), and then release from an institution.
- Probation is the disposition judges use most often in delinquency cases.
- Supervision is the essence of juvenile probation and parole (aftercare) and its most effective tool for rehabilitation.
- Probation officers are usually appointed and dismissed by the judge; parole officers are appointed by and under the supervision of the parole board.
- If conditions are violated, probation or parole is revoked and the juvenile is sent to an institution.
- No conclusive data or study establishes that juvenile probation or parole is more effective than other approaches to corrections.

DISCUSSION QUESTIONS

1 How does *parens patriae* influence the way we process juveniles offenders?

2 Give some terminology differences between juvenile justice and adult justice.

3 What is the main difference between juvenile delinquency and conduct in need of supervision (CINS)?

4 What are transfer provisions? Give the characteristics of the three transfer categories.

5 Discuss what happens in the following stages: intake, adjudication, and disposition.

6 What is blended sentencing? Discuss its variations.

7 *In re Gault* is the most important case ever decided by the U.S. Supreme Court in juvenile law. What does it say and why is it important?

8 Discuss the contributions of John Augustus to juvenile probation.

9 Give examples of probation or parole conditions usually imposed on a juvenile.

10 What is school-based probation and what are its characteristics?

11 What did the Court say in the case of *Fare v. Michael C.*? Why is that case important for probation officers?

12 Other than *In re Gault* and *Fare v. Michael C.*, what other juvenile justice cases have been decided by the U.S. Supreme Court, and what did these cases say?

 **WEBSITES**

American Bar Association Juvenile Justice Center

http://www.abanet.org/dch/committee.cfm?com=CR200000

Juvenile Justice Clearinghouse

http://www.fsu.edu/~crimdo/jjclearinghouse

National Council on Crime and Delinquency

http://www.nccd-crc.org

National Youth Gang Center

http://www.iir.com/nygc

A Bibliography of Gangs

http://www-lib.usc.edu/~anthonya/gang.htm

Kansas Juvenile Intensive Supervision Probation

http://courts.jocogov.org/cc_jisp.htm

Listing of State Juvenile Corrections

http://www.cor.state.mt.us/Resources/YouthServices.asp

South Dakota Juvenile Aftercare

http://www.state.sd.us/corrections/juvenile_aftercare.htm

Texas Youth Commission

http://www.tyc.state.tx.us/

Juvenile Justice, Probation, and Aftercare

You are a juvenile probation officer who is attempting to decide what to do with each of the court referrals before you, so that you can make recommendations to the judge. Should the case be dismissed? Should the case be diverted to another program (for example, to teen court)?

Should the case be adjudicated? If so, should the case be adjudicated within the juvenile justice system, or should the case be waived to adult court?

CASE A

Brian is a 13-year-old male who has come to the attention of the court for the offense of vandalism. He and a friend "tagged" a school building with graffiti and broke several windows in the school gymnasium. The school principal estimated the total damage and cleanup costs to be approximately $1,300. Brian resides with both natural parents and two younger siblings. The family income is $65,000 annually. Brian admits the offense but refuses to identify his co-offender to authorities. The family has agreed to pay complete restitution. Brian has no prior juvenile record although he has been disciplined several times in school in the past year for minor violations of school rules. His grades, which were formerly As and Bs, have fallen off to Cs and Ds.

CASE B

Quint is a 17-year-old male who has been referred to the court for aggravated robbery. Quint is accused of robbing a convenience store and assaulting the clerk. Quint is a high school dropout with a lengthy history of arrests including robbery, burglary, car theft, and larceny. He was adjudicated delinquent for burglary 10 months before the current offense and placed on probation. His probation officer reports that he has been uncooperative and hostile toward supervision. He lives off and on with his mother and three younger siblings. His mother reports that she has little control over his behavior and that he spends many nights away from home. She suspects that he is using drugs.

CASE C

Carlos is a 15-year-old male who was referred to the court for truancy. Carlos has missed 34 school days in the past 90 days. He is failing in all his classes. His parents report that they send him to school every day but he never stays. Even when they take him to the front door of the school, he leaves immediately after they do. Carlos is of average intelligence and relates well to his peers. He has no other involvement with illegal activity, and until this past school year he did well in school and attended regularly. His parents have no explanation for the change in his behavior.

CASE D

Cathy is a 14-year-old female who has been referred to the court for running away. Cathy's parents report that she is a chronic runaway, having left home on more than 10 occasions since age 12. She is in the seventh grade. She has been "left back" twice and is thus two grade levels behind her peers. Cathy was diagnosed with attention deficit disorder at age 7. She is currently taking Ritalin under a physician's supervision. Her parents have attempted to get help for Cathy on many occasions, but nothing seems to be effective. She has been referred once for shoplifting, three times for truancy, and three times previously for running away.

15

Collateral Consequences of Conviction, Pardon, and Restoration of Rights

Introduction
Civil and Political Rights Defined
Background of Civil Disabilities

Civil Disabilities Today
Differences by State
Other Differences

Civil and Political Rights Affected by Conviction
Loss of Right to Vote
Loss of Right to Serve on a Jury
Loss of Credibility As a Witness
Loss of Right to Hold Public Office
Loss of Employment-Related Rights
Loss of Right to Own or Possess a Firearm
Loss of Welfare Benefits
Loss of Parental Rights

Problems with Civil Disability Laws

Other Effects of Conviction
Sex Offender Registration Laws
Sex Offender Notification Laws
Involuntary Commitment of Sexual Predators
Social Stigmatization

Pardon
Definition and Purpose
The Power to Pardon
Kinds of Pardon
Procedure for Obtaining a Pardon
Legal Effects of a Pardon
Effects of a Pardon on Occupational Licensing

Restoration of Rights
Restoration upon Application
Automatic Restoration
Restoring the Right to Vote

Restoring Good Moral Character

Expungement of Criminal Records

Sealing of Criminal Records

© Tony Freeman/PhotoEdit

Have you been convicted of a crime in the past ten years other than misdemeanors and summary offenses?

Yes ☐   No ☐

If yes, explain circumstances and disposition of matter below.

What You Will Learn in This Chapter

- *Civil and political rights differ, but both may be lost as a result of conviction.*
- *Civil disabilities vary from one state to another.*
- *Many rights are lost as a result of conviction. Among them are the right to vote, serve on a jury, hold public office, own or possess a firearm, and collect welfare benefits. Public and private employment can also be affected.*
- *States have passed sex offender registration and notification laws and provide for the involuntary commitment of sexual predators.*
- *Pardon is available for offenders, but its legal effect varies from one jurisdiction to another.*
- *Lost rights can be restored, some automatically, others only upon application by the offender.*
- *Loss of good moral character can have a lasting effect on a convicted offender.*
- *Expungement and sealing of criminal records can be done in many states, but procedure and legal effect vary.*

KEY TERMS

Civil rights

Political rights

Outlawry

Attainder

Good moral character

Moral turpitude

Public offices

Surety bond

Pardon

Conditional pardon

Rehabilitation certificate

Automatic restoration of rights

Certificate of discharge

Expungement

Sealing of records

INTRODUCTION

Conviction of a crime carries direct and collateral (indirect) consequences. Direct consequences are penalties such as a fine, probation, and commitment to jail or prison. Collateral consequences are disqualifications or deprivations that are civil in nature and of which the offender may be unaware and not immediately affected. This chapter discusses collateral consequences and how the rights lost might be restored.

The distinctions between the direct and collateral consequences of conviction may be summarized as follows:

Direct Consequences	**Collateral Consequences**
Criminal penalties, as specified in the state or federal penal code	Civil consequences, as specified in various state or federal laws or by administrative agencies, local agencies, or private employers
Includes fines, probation, jail, or prison	Includes loss of right to vote, disqualification for jury service, loss of good moral character, and so on
Lasts only during the time specified in the sentence	Can last after probation, jail or prison time, or for a lifetime
Time served cannot be restored	The right or benefit lost can be restored by legislation, court decision, or agency decision

Collateral consequences may include the following:

- Loss of right to serve on a jury
- Loss of credibility as a witness
- Public office restrictions
- Employment-related restrictions
- Loss of capacity to be bonded
- Loss of right to own or possess a firearm

- Denial of welfare benefits
- Loss of parental rights
- Grounds for divorce
- Barred from serving in the armed forces
- Dishonorable discharge from the armed forces
- Required registration with local law enforcement
- Cannot serve as union officer
- Loss of pension rights
- Cannot serve as a notary public
- Denial of federal financial aid for higher education (felony drug offenders)
- Denial of Social Security, Medicare, and/or Medicaid payments to prisoners while incarcerated

As discussed later in this chapter, rights lost may be restored in various ways. Some rights, however, are more difficult to restore than others and are often lost forever because the offender is unaware of restoration procedures.

Civil and Political Rights Defined

Black's Law Dictionary defines **civil rights** as "personal, natural rights guaranteed and protected by the Constitution" (*Black's Law Dictionary* 1991, p. 168). Examples are freedom of speech, freedom of the press, freedom from discrimination, and freedom of assembly. **Political rights** are "rights of citizens established or recognized by constitutions which give them the power to participate directly or indirectly in the establishment or administration of government" (*Black's Law Dictionary* 1991, p. 803.). Civil rights are broader in scope and include political rights, which are also guaranteed by the Constitution. The two categories of rights vary, however, in that civil rights are broader and usually enjoyed by all people within the geographical boundary of a country. On the other hand, the exercise of political rights is limited to citizens of a state. Thus, anybody in the United States (citizens, aliens, legal residents, or illegal residents) enjoys freedom of speech, association, or assembly, but only U.S. citizens enjoy the right to vote or hold public office.

Background of Civil Disabilities

Civil disabilities as a consequence of crime go way back to ancient Greece (Damaska 1968). The Greeks called the disability *infamy,* a word that found its way into Anglo-American criminal law in the term *infamous crimes*. Infamous crimes carried severe penalties as well as the additional sanctions of outlawry and attainder. **Outlawry** considered a person outside the protection of the law and, in effect, established an open season on the offender, who could then be hunted down and killed by any citizen. This person (considered "an outlaw") lost all civil rights and forfeited all property to the Crown through **attainder,** which is defined in common law as "that extinction of civil rights and capacities which took place whenever a person who had committed treason or felony received sentence of death for his crime" (*Black's Law Dictionary* 1991, p. 85). The justification for both outlawry and attainder was that the offender had declared war on society by committing an infamous crime and therefore the community had the right to retaliation and retribution against the offender. Outlawry as a form of punishment is forbidden in the United States, and Article l of the U.S. Constitution forbids "bills of attainder."

Many collateral consequences flow from the assumption that a convicted offender lacks **"good moral character"** and therefore lacks the requirement to vote,

CIVIL RIGHTS

"Personal, natural rights guaranteed and protected by the Constitution."

POLITICAL RIGHTS

"Rights of citizens established or recognized by constitutions which give them the power to participate directly or indirectly in the establishment or administration of government."

OUTLAWRY

A situation where a person is considered outside the protection of the law and, in effect, established an open season on the offender, who could then be hunted down and killed by any citizen.

ATTAINDER

"That extinction of civil rights and capacities which took place whenever a person who had committed treason or felony received a sentence of death for his crime."

GOOD MORAL CHARACTER

A requirement that qualifies a person to vote, to be a credible witness, to obtain and retain many occupational licenses, to hold a public office, or to be a member of certain professions.

to be a credible witness, to obtain and retain many occupational licenses, to hold a public office, or to be a member of certain professions. A criminal act involving "moral turpitude" is defined as "the act of baseness, vileness, or the depravity in private and social duties which man owes to his fellow man, or to society in general, contrary to accepted and customary rule of right and duty between man and man" (*Black's Law Dictionary* 1991, p. 698). In some cases, state laws provide for loss of good moral character only if the criminal act involves moral turpitude. Most states, however, provide for loss of good moral character if a person is convicted of any criminal act, or at least of a felony.

CIVIL DISABILITIES TODAY

Buckler and Travis (2003) list four main justifications for collateral consequence statutes:

- Practical reasons, such as divorce and historical civil death statutes
- Financial punishment (employment restrictions, denial of welfare, pension, or financial aid)
- Maintain perception of confidence in government (public office, voting, juror restrictions)
- Public safety and to protect the public/children from harm (firearms restriction, sex offender registration, loss of parental rights)

Differences by State

States differ in the way civil rights are removed or restricted. Some statutes deprive the criminal of all or almost all civil rights while he or she is serving a prison sentence (Buckler and Travis 2003). In some cases, conviction results in the loss of rights only within a particular state; in other cases the loss extends to other states if the offender relocates (Kuzma 1998). What happens if the laws of the state where the offender was convicted differ from those of the state where the offender relocates? To illustrate, some states define a felony as an offense punishable by incarceration of one year or more; other states designate a crime as a felony or a misdemeanor without regard to amount of time served. For example, assume that Jeff was convicted of misdemeanor theft and served the maximum sentence of 18 months in a county jail. The conviction state designates this theft a misdemeanor, but Jeff moved across state lines into another state that defines any criminal act that carries a sentence of more than 12 months a felony, which carries civil disabilities. Does Jeff lose his civil rights? The answer is usually determined by the laws of the state where the crime was committed; therefore Jeff in this case does not lose his civil rights. However, there are states that provide for such loss even if the crime was committed elsewhere. In this case, Jeff loses his civil liberties while he is in that state.

Another issue involves military offenses. Because military crimes are not classified as either felonies or misdemeanors, and some military crimes do not constitute a crime under civilian law, do people convicted of a military crime lose their rights as civilians? Susan Kuzma (1998), of the Office of the United States Pardon Attorney, discusses both the relocation issue and the resolution of military crimes, saying: "Some states' laws permit resolution of such interpretational problems by providing that the disability applies only when the conduct would constitute a felony under the law of the state imposing the disability (the state of residence)" (p. 72).

Other Differences

Other differences exist. For example, some rights can be lost through judicial or administrative discretion. A judge may decide in a particular case that the offender loses a certain civil right. This is valid as long as the loss is related to the offense committed. For example, a judge might deny welfare benefits to a person convicted of a conspiracy to defraud the government. The loss may also be caused by an administrative decision of governmental agencies. Licensing agencies may decide to deny a license to an individual who commits an offense, provided that such denial is related to the offense committed. To illustrate, an agency that licenses bartenders might deny a license to an applicant who has been convicted of DWI even if state laws do not provide for such denial. Moreover, private employers are not bound by the provisions of the Bill of Rights and may deny offenders certain rights to which they are otherwise entitled if employed by public agencies. Private employers may refuse to hire an individual who applies for work if he or she refuses to disclose an arrest record.

In some states, a conviction must be followed by incarceration for a specified period before rights are lost. The right is not lost if conviction is followed by probation or if the sentence to probation is not considered a conviction, as in the case of deferred adjudication or informal probation. Some rights are permanently lost and cannot be restored; others are automatically restored upon completion of the sentence or may be restored by action of the executive or a court. To determine the status of a particular convicted offender's rights, one must examine the statutory provisions, judicial decisions, administrative rulings and practices, and actions of individuals in both the state of conviction and the state in which a particular right is sought to be enforced (Office of the Pardon Attorney 1996). Because of variations, the extent of civil disabilities in a state, or even within a local jurisdiction, is difficult to ascertain.

Collateral consequences may amount to a complete denial of a right, or may merely impose restrictions and conditions on its exercise. In some jurisdictions, the right to vote and the right to hold public office are denied for life unless restored by a pardon or a certificate. A conviction generally does not completely disqualify the offender from serving as a witness, but if the witness's prior criminal record becomes public it can result in diminished credibility.

CIVIL AND POLITICAL RIGHTS AFFECTED BY CONVICTION

As previously noted, many privileges and rights are restricted or removed following conviction of a crime. This section discusses the eight most commonly restricted rights, which are:

- Loss of right to vote
- Loss of right to serve on a jury
- Loss of credibility as a witness
- Loss of right to hold public office
- Limitations of employment-related rights
- Loss of the right to own and possess a firearm
- Denial of welfare benefits
- Loss of parental rights

Loss of Right to Vote

The current state of voting disenfranchisement is summarized in a publication titled "Felony Disenfranchisement Laws in the United States" (p. 1), published by the Sentencing Project, as follows:

- "48 states and the District of Columbia prohibit inmates from voting while incarcerated for a felony offense.
- "only two states—Maine and Vermont—permit inmates to vote.
- "36 states prohibit felons from voting while they are on parole and 31 of these states exclude felony probationers as well.
- "Three states deny the right to vote to all ex-offenders who have completed their sentences.
- "Each state has developed its own process of restoring voting rights to ex-offenders but most of these restoration processes are so cumbersome that few ex-offenders are able to take advantage of them."

The same publication summarizes the impact of felony disenfranchisement with these figures (p. 1):

- "An estimated 5.3 million Americans, or one in 41 adults, have currently or permanently lost their voting rights as a result of felony conviction.
- "1.4 million African American men, or 13 percent of black men, are disenfranchised, a rate seven times the national average.
- "An estimated 676,730 women are currently ineligible to vote as a result of felony conviction.
- "More than 2 million white Americans (Hispanic and non-Hispanic) are disenfranchised.
- "In six states that deny the vote to ex-offenders, one in four black men is permanently disenfranchised.
- "Given current rates of incarceration, three in 10 of the next generation of black men can expect to be disenfranchised at some point in their lifetime. In states that disenfranchise ex-offenders, as many as 40 percent of black men may permanently lose their right to vote.
- "2.1 million disenfranchised people are ex-offenders who have completed their sentences.
- "The state of Florida had an estimated 960,000 ex-felons who were unable to vote in the 2004 presidential election."

The right to vote in the United States for federal, state, or local offices is generally governed by state law (see Table 15.1). Limiting the right to vote is widely practiced, as the above summary shows, the assumption being that the votes of offenders (those who are currently serving or have served their sentences) somehow dilutes the purity of the voting process and therefore the denial of that right of citizenship is justifiable. The United States Supreme Court, in *Richardson v. Ramirez* (1974), held it is constitutional for a state to deprive ex-felons of the right to vote, thus giving states a lot of authority to disenfranchise offenders, if they so desire. Although setting voting requirements is left up to individual states, there are limits. For example, the U.S. Supreme Court struck down an Alabama constitutional provision that barred from voting people convicted of crimes involving **moral turpitude**—or offensive behavior, because this type of behavior is difficult to determine and therefore violates due process (*Hunter v. Underwood* 1985). Some state courts have recently decided cases involving the voting rights of convicted felons. In 1998, a New Hampshire state

MORAL TURPITUDE

"The act of baseness, vileness, or the depravity in private and social duties which man owes to his fellow man, or to society in general, contrary to accepted and customary rule of right and duty between man and man."

TABLE 15.1 *Voting Restrictions*

STATES HAVE ABSOLUTE POWER TO DECIDE WHETHER SOMEONE WITH A CRIMINAL RECORD CAN VOTE					
No Restrictions	Cannot Vote While Incarcerated	Cannot Vote While Incarcerated or on Parole	Cannot Vote Until Completion of Sentence	Lifetime Bar That Can Be Lifted	Lifetime Bar
Maine	Hawaii	Alaska	Arizona	Alabama	Delaware
Vermont	Indiana	California	Arkansas	Iowa	Kentucky
	Illinois	Colorado	Florida	Nebraska	Maryland
	Massachusetts	Connecticut	Georgia	Nevada	Mississippi
	Michigan	New York	Idaho	Virginia	Tennessee
	Montana	Wisconsin	Kansas	Washington	
	New Hampshire		Louisiana	Wyoming	
	North Dakota		Minnesota		
	Ohio		Missouri		
	Oregon		New Jersey		
	South Dakota		New Mexico		
	Utah		North Carolina		
			Oklahoma		
			Pennsylvania		
			Rhode Island		
			South Carolina		
			Texas		
			West Virginia		

Source: Legal Action Center. 2004. After Prison: Roadblocks to Reentry: A Report on State Legal Barriers Facing People with Criminal Records, p.14. Accessed: http://www.lac.org/roadblocks.html.

court prohibited the disenfranchisement of inmates, but that the ruling was later reversed by the State Supreme Court and so the disenfranchisement continues (*Fischer v. Governor* 2000). In Pennsylvania, the state Supreme Court "affirmed a lower court decision in 2000, overturning a disenfranchisement clause passed as part of the Pennsylvania Voting Rights Act of 1995 (*Mixon v. Commonwealth of Pennsylvania* 2001). Other state courts are in the process of addressing legal issues related to felons' disenfranchisement (Uggen and Manza 2004, p. 71).

Loss of Right to Serve on a Jury

The exclusion of convicted people from jury service has its origin in common law. The federal rule is that citizens are not competent to serve on a federal grand or petit (trial) jury if they have been convicted of a crime punishable by imprisonment for more than one year and if that person's civil rights have not been restored (28 U.S.C. sec. 1865). Felons are deprived of the right to serve on a jury except in four states (Alaska, Illinois, Maine, and Missouri). Eight states offer no restoration mechanisms for this right. Eleven states and the District of Columbia permit felons to serve on juries after they complete their sentences. Others suspend the right only until the offender is released from incarceration, or through the passage of time (Buckler and Travis 2003). In 22 states, the right to serve on a jury may be restored through a pardon or expungement (Office of the Pardon Attorney 1996).

Loss of Credibility as a Witness

Absolute disqualification to be a witness in court applies to people convicted of perjury (telling a lie under oath) or subornation of perjury (inducing another person to take a false oath). The justification for absolute disqualification for those convicted of perjury is that a person who has been convicted of a crime cannot be trusted to give truthful testimony. The usual situation, however, is that a person who has been convicted of a crime other than perjury or subordination of perjury is permitted to testify, but the fact of the conviction may be used to discredit a witness's testimony, the court or jury being allowed to take the conviction into account. The witness can be asked if he or she has been convicted of a felony or other crime and must answer truthfully. Opposing counsel may then argue, and usually does, that because the witness is a convicted offender the testimony should not be believed. Whether a witness who is an ex-offender is entitled to full credibility or no credibility at all is up to the judge or jury.

Loss of the Right to Hold Public Office

Elective positions in federal, state, and municipal governments as well as some appointive positions are generally regarded as **public offices.** A public office does not have to carry any compensation; examples are positions on a school board or a municipal council. Federal statutes and the U.S. Constitution contain provisions that exclude certain offenders from holding certain positions in the government of the United States. Congress may bar ex-felons from holding any nonconstitutional public office for offenses that include falsifying, destroying, or removing public records or documents; receiving compensation in matters affecting the government; rebellion; and treason (Office of the Pardon Attorney 1996, p. 7). Conviction for treason disqualifies the defendant from holding "any office under the United States."

A total of 40 jurisdictions limit or restrict felons from holding public office. Twelve states restrict the right to hold public office after a felony conviction unless the convicted person receives a pardon. Fifteen states return the right to hold public office after discharge from probation, parole, or prison. Four states restrict this right to felons until a mandatory period of time has elapsed following the completion of their sentence, ranging from three to 15 years. Nine states permanently restrict this right and do not allow any means of restoration (Buckler and Travis 2003).

Employment-Related Rights

Among the issues related to employment of former convicts are restrictions on various occupational licenses, loss of good moral character, limitations in public and private employment, and the restriction on an individual's capacity to be bonded. These limitations apply in various ways and are characterized by wide variations from one state to another.

PUBLIC EMPLOYMENT.   Paid employment with some type of governmental agency (federal, state, or local) constitutes public employment. It differs from public office in that public employment usually refers to anybody whose pay or salary comes from the public coffers, whereas public office refers to somebody who is working for the government, with or without pay, but is involved in policy making. Thus, a janitor in the office of a police chief is a public employee, but not a public officer because he or she does not have policy-making responsibilities. On the other hand, a police chief is both a public officer and a public employee.

Most state statutes permit public employment for people convicted of a felony. Some statutes allow employment after completion of a sentence. A felony conviction may not be the sole grounds for denial of public employment unless the offense bears a direct relationship to the position sought. In addition, a small number of states apply a direct relationship test and consider other factors such as rehabilitation, the time lapse since offense, the offender's age at the time of conviction, and the nature and seriousness of the offense. No statutory restrictions are placed on public employment of convicted people in the District of Columbia, Maine, Utah, or Vermont (Burton, Cullen, and Travis 1987).

PRIVATE EMPLOYMENT.   A job applicant with a criminal record faces almost insurmountable barriers to private employment. One study in four major cities found that 60 percent of all employers surveyed were reluctant to hire anyone with a criminal record (Holzer 1996). Furthermore, job applicants with a felony conviction are not protected from discrimination if they are hired by private employers. For example, Kansas allows employers to exclude an applicant if the conviction is reasonably related to trustworthiness, safety, or well-being of employees or customers (Kan. Stat. Ann Section 22-4710(f)). On the other hand, Hawaii allows employers to consider convictions only after a conditional offer of employment has been made (Haw. Rev. Stat., Section 378-2.5). Some business and trade organizations and private employers provide jobs to convicted offenders. The Solution to Employment Problems (STEP) program of the National Association of Manufacturers is one such effort. In this program, employers provide equipment and instructors to train offenders while they are in prison and then guarantee them jobs upon their release. In the absence of laws specifically prohibiting it, private employers may discriminate on the basis of prior conviction, claiming risk and lack of good moral character as justifications.

RIGHT TO AN OCCUPATIONAL LICENSE.   Federal, state, and local governments throughout the United States restrict entry into more than 800 occupations and professions through licensing requirements (see Table 15.2). The number of occupations that require licenses has doubled in the last 30 years. According to one writer, as of 2005, "thirty-three states have general laws that prohibit a refusal to hire and/or issue a professional or occupational license to a person 'solely' because of their criminal record, or otherwise limit consideration of a conviction in connection with employment or licensing" (Love 2005, p. 10).

Most states prohibit employers from denying ex-convicts a job or occupational licensing unless the conviction is related to the occupation. For example, an offender who has served time for robbery may be denied a license to be a bank teller, but not to be a land surveyor. Restrictions also vary due to local licensing regulations. For some occupations, such as attorneys, any felony conviction is cause for suspension or revocation of an existing certification, or may disqualify an applicant from obtaining a license. Other occupations require that a license may be issued only to "people of good moral character," which could exclude convicted individuals. The exact provisions of licensing statutes vary from state to state, from occupation to occupation, and even within occupations. The criminal record that disqualifies may be a felony conviction, a misdemeanor conviction, or only certain types of crimes. The lack of uniformity in the laws and practices of the various states and localities makes it difficult for people with criminal records to determine where they might be allowed to apply their training and skills, whether they acquired them in or out of prison. The ironic part is that ex-offenders are expected to remain out of prison and in legitimate jobs, but then they are limited in the kinds of jobs they can obtain.

TABLE 15.2   *Examples of Occupations That Require a License*

Accountant/CPA	Acupuncturist	Aircraft Dispatcher/Mechanic/Pilot
Alarm Systems	Alcohol Server	Appraiser, Real Estate
Architect	Asbestos Removal	Athletic Trainer
Attorney/Lawyer	Auctioneer	Audiologist
Banking	Barber/Hairdresser	Boiler Operator
Building Codes	Bus Driver, School	Charter Boat Operator
Child Care Provider	Chiropractor	Collection Agency Operator
Commercial Fisher	Commercial Vehicle Operator	Concert Promoter
Contractor	Cosmetologist	Counselor/Therapist
Customs Broker	Dentist/Dental Hygienist	Dietician/Nutritionist
Electrician	Electrology	Emergency Medical Technician
Engineer	Explosives Handler	Forester
Freon Technician	Funeral Director/Services	Geologist
Hearing Aid Dealer	Home Inspector	Insurance Occupations
Investment Broker/Dealer	Land Surveyor	Law Examiner
Locksmith	Long-Term Health Care	Massage
Medical Examiner	Midwife	Mortician
Naturopath	Nursing (LPN, RN, Aide)	Occupational Therapist
Optician	Optometrist	Osteopath
Painter	Paramedic	Pastoral Counselor
Pesticide Applicator	Pharmacist/Technician	Physical Therapy
Physician/Surgeon	Plumber	Podiatrist
Psychologist	Real Estate	Refrigeration
Residential Builder	Respiratory Care	Sanitarian Examiner
Security Guard	Social Worker	Speech-Language Pathologist
Tattooing	Taxidermist	Teacher
Therapeutic Recreation	Veterinarian	Water Systems Operator

Sources: Illinois Department of Professional Regulation (http://www.dpr.state.il.us/); North Carolina
Secretary of State Occupational Boards (http://www.secretary.state.nc.us/blio/occboards.asp); South
Carolina Department of Labor, Licensing, and Regulation (http://www.llr.state.sc.us/pol.asp);
Washington State Department of Licensing (http://www.dol.wa.gov).

LOSS OF CAPACITY TO BE BONDED. Jobs in which employees handle money or merchandise may require the employee to be bonded. For example, banks, warehouses, truck-driving companies, collection agencies, bookkeepers, ticket takers, and vendors may require a bond before the employee will be allowed to work. A bond protects the employer or the company from losses caused by dishonest employees. The bonded employee is known as the principal. He or she signs and pays the fee to obtain a simple bond. A surety bond is signed by the principal and by one or more third parties, known as sureties, who promise to pay money in the event that the assured, the party in whose favor the bond is written, suffers damage because the principal failed to perform as agreed. The decision to write or deny a bond rests with the insurance company, which carefully investigates all people who request bonds and refuses to bond people it considers poor risks. A person with a felony criminal record is considered a poor risk.

The U.S. Department of Labor, through the Employment and Training Administration, offers fidelity bonding coverage for job applicants. The coverage is available to people who cannot obtain suitable employment because they have police, credit, or other records that preclude their being covered by the usual commercial bonds. Ex-offenders are eligible for the bonds if they are qualified and suitable for the job and are not commercially bondable under ordinary circumstances.

The applicant applies for the bond through a state employment office. The bond becomes effective when the applicant begins work and the manager of the local employment service office or other authorized representative of the state agency has certified the bond (U.S. Department of Labor 1990). Unfortunately, few ex-offenders take advantage of this program and instead refrain from applying for jobs that require bonding. Both employers and prospective employees seem to lack information about the bonding that is available through state employment agencies.

LOSS OF GOOD MORAL CHARACTER.   The most serious obstacle to an offender's obtaining a license for an occupation are the many licensing statutes requiring that the licensee possess good moral character. It is usually assumed that a person who has been convicted of a criminal offense is not of good moral character. The obstacles created by the provisions and assumptions about good moral character are all the more serious because a convicted person has a difficult time proving or restoring his or her good moral character. Moreover, almost all procedures for restoring civil rights never erase a conviction or adjudication of delinquency and therefore "good moral character" is seldom, if ever, restored. As a practical matter, licenses are refused or revoked according to the various meanings that licensing agencies place on such terms. In general, however, a licensing agency regards a conviction as conclusive evidence of bad character, and the courts seldom overrule such decisions (*Peterson v. State Liquor Authority* 1973).

Loss of Right to Own or Possess a Firearm

For some individuals, the right to own a firearm continues to be the most restrictive of all civil disabilities lost by conviction. Federal law prohibits convicted felons from possessing, shipping, transporting, or receiving any firearms or ammunition (18 U.S.C., sec. 921(a)(20)). It also prohibits the possession of guns by anybody convicted in any court of domestic violence, which is a misdemeanor crime (18 U.S.C. sec. 922(g)(9)). (According to Buckler and Travis [2003], 37 states restrict both firearm possession and ownership for people convicted of a felony crime, and seven additional states restrict just the possession of all firearms. Twenty-one states allow firearms restrictions to be restored [12 through passage of time from completion of sentence and nine through restoration of rights proceedings]. Seven states have no such firearms restrictions whatsoever [Massachusetts, Missouri, New York, Ohio, Pennsylvania, Tennessee, and Vermont].)

The issue of the loss of the right to own a firearm has been litigated in a number of cases. In *Beecham v. United States* (1994), the U.S. Supreme Court held that "federal felons remain subject to the federal firearms disability until their civil rights are restored through a federal, not a state, procedure." This means "federal felons who have had their civil rights restored by state law or procedure nonetheless are still prohibited by federal law from possessing firearms." In a later case, the U.S. Supreme Court addressed the issue of "whether a state offender is still subject to the federal firearm disability if his civic rights have been restored, but state law continues to restrict his firearms privileges to some degree." The Court held that "although state law allowed him to possess rifles and shotguns, the federal firearms law nonetheless prohibited his possession of those guns." In effect, the Court said that federal law prevails over state law in case of conflict concerning firearms regulation (Federal Statutes Imposing Collateral Consequences Upon Conviction [2000], pp. 17–18). Various state courts have also decided cases involving loss of firearms privileges both under state and federal laws.

Loss of Welfare Benefits

Withholding welfare benefits is the most recent form of collateral consequence for convicted drug offenders. When the government overhauled the welfare system with its Welfare Reform Act, the former Aid to Families with Dependent Children (AFDC) was replaced with a program called "Temporary Assistance for Needy Families." The federal Welfare Reform Act denied food stamps and benefits to anyone convicted of possession or sale of controlled substances. Buckler and Travis (2003) report that "of the 42 states that deny eligibility for welfare benefits, 22 states deny benefits entirely, 10 states partially deny welfare benefits, and 10 states have enacted statutes stipulating that the denial of welfare benefits is contingent upon drug treatment" (p. 444).

Loss of Parental Rights

About one and a half million children under age 18 had at least one parent serving time in prison. Of the 48 states that allow parental rights to be terminated for felony offenders, 18 states may terminate a parent's rights for long-term prison confinement, "which deprives the child of a normal home life or produces negative effects on the parent-child relationship" (Buckler and Travis 2003, p. 442). Most states (37) will terminate parental rights for a serious felony conviction against one or more children in the household, which includes murder/manslaughter or felonious assault/battery. In Indiana, if it can be shown to the court that a continuation of the parent-child relationship will pose a threat to the child's well-being, any conviction will result in the termination of parental rights (Buckler and Travis 2003).

PROBLEMS WITH CIVIL DISABILITY LAWS

Civil disability laws create a number of problems for offenders, which are summarized by Margaret Colgate Love as follows: "In almost every U.S. jurisdiction, offenders seeking to put their criminal past behind them are frustrated by a legal system that is complex and unclear and entirely inadequate to the task. Categorical disqualifications are generally overbroad, and discretionary decision-making is often unfair and unreliable" (Love 2005, p. 92). Some of the main research findings in the same publication are:

- "In every U.S. jurisdiction, the legal system erects formidable barriers to the reintegration of criminal offenders into a free society.
- "These legal barriers are always difficult and often impossible to overcome . . . .
- "While every jurisdiction provides at least one way that convicted persons can avoid or mitigate the collateral consequences of conviction, the actual mechanisms for relief are generally inaccessible and unreliable, and are frequently not well understood even by those responsible for administering them" (Love 2005, pp. 4–5)

The constitutionality of civil disability laws has been challenged on the ground that they violate the provisions on due process and equal protection, and constitute cruel and unusual punishment. Challengers allege that these laws serve none of the objectives of modern correctional theory and impede offenders' rehabilitation, both within the correctional institution and in the community. Recommendations to remedy these conditions include the following:

- Elimination of unnecessary restrictions, such as those on voting
- Reasonable application of necessary restrictions

- Greater participation by the sentencing court in determining the civil disabilities to be imposed on the individual defendant
- Automatic restoration of rights and privileges five years after the convict's release into the community, provided the offender has lived a crime-free life during that time

OTHER EFFECTS OF CONVICTION

Sex Offender Registration Laws

All 50 states and the District of Columbia require that sex offenders, both on and off supervision, register with the local authorities, usually within one month following release or completion of their sentence. Sex offender registration statutes (otherwise known as Megan's Law) were enacted to protect children and improve the competence of the police to investigate sex crimes. These laws were passed for public safety and crime control. Registration with the local police is required and many states make the information a matter of public record, available through the electronic and printed media. This has a great impact on sex offenders and ex-offenders in terms of finding a place to live, privacy loss, and obtaining employment. The effects can be serious and devastating.

Public information and required registration of convicted sex offenders have made it more difficult for former offenders to return to their communities.

As of 2004, there were nearly 387,000 sex offenders registered throughout the United States . Washington was the first state to actively require registration of all sex offenders in 1990. California actually enacted the first registration statute in 1947, but it wasn't used much and didn't catch the nation's attention quite like Washington's statute did (Tewksbury 2002). Other states, such as New Jersey, developed three tiers of risk, with each tier having its own set of notification procedures. Sex offenders are believed to pose different levels of risk to the community depending on the nature and prevalence of their crimes as well as their choice of victim. Of the 32 states that have notification statutes, 21 permit or require proactive dissemination (knocking on doors, flyers, and so on) and the other 11 permit information dissemination only in response to individuals first contacting their local police department (Finn 1997). As of 2001, in 30 jurisdictions public websites contained searchable information on sex offenders. Six states were developing websites at the time, and eight states had a website with only general information on sex offender laws for public viewing (Adams 2002).

Most states require sex offenders to register annually for 10 years, whereas others require registration throughout the offender's lifetime. Information typically requested includes name, address, date of birth, Social Security number, vehicle registration, place of employment, fingerprints, and a recent photo. Thirty-two states also collect blood or DNA samples as a part of the registration or separate from registration requirements (Adams 2002).

The U.S. Supreme Court has decided two cases on the issue of sex offender registration. In one case, the Court said that the public posting of a sex offender registry does not violate the due process clause of the Fourteenth Amendment (*Connecticut Department of Public Safety et al. v. Doe* 2003). In this case, Connecticut law provided that sex offenders must register with the Connecticut Department of Public Safety upon their release into the community. The personal information needed includes name, address, photograph, and DNA samples, and notification of any change in residence. Connecticut law requires sex offenders to register for 10 years, but those convicted of sexually violent offenses must register for life. The offender in this case alleged that this law was unfair because he was no longer "currently sexually dangerous" and therefore it violated his due process rights. The Court disagreed, saying that the defendant had to register because he was a sexual offender, not because he continued to be dangerous. The Court said that the law was constitutional even if no prior opportunity is given to prove that the defendant is not dangerous.

In another case, also decided in 2003, the Court said that a sex offender registration and notification law that is not punitive does not violate the ex post facto clause of the Constitution (*Smith v. Doe* 2003). In this case, the Alaska Sex Offender Registration Act required a registration system and a notification system that were both retroactive, meaning they applied to offenders who were convicted even before the law was passed. Defendants challenged its constitutionality, saying its retroactive application violated the ex post facto clause (the clause that prohibits punishment without prior trial) of the Constitution. The Court upheld the Alaska law, saying that the Alaska Offender Act regulates rather than punishes; therefore its retroactive application does not violate the ex post facto clause. The Court reasoned that what Alaska wanted to do with the statute was to "regulate" instead of "punish" conduct. Since the law was primarily regulatory instead of punitive, the ex post facto clause does not apply.

Sex Offender Notification Laws

Notification statutes are a supplement to registration statutes and have been around for more than a decade. Notification is required in at least 32 states (see Table 15.3). One publication characterizes registration laws as "statutes that either make information

TABLE 15.3   Principal Features of Seven Sex Offender Notification Statutes

State	Year Statute Went into Effect	How Long Offenders Remain Subject to Notification	Notification Mandatory or Discretionary	Notification Proactive or Only in Response to Request	Sex Offenses Covered by Statute	Implementing Agency	Immunity Explicitly Provided to Implementers	Who May be Notified	Retroactivity	Information That May be Disseminated
Alaska	1994	*for life:* 2 or more convictions *15 years:* 1 conviction	mandatory by administrative regulation	upon request	all offenses	State Dept. of Public Safety	provided	anyone	retroactive	limited by statute
Connecticut	1996	10 years after end of probation or parole	discretionary	proactive	selected offenses	probation	not provided	anyone	not retroactive	unrestricted
Louisiana	1992	10 years after release	mandatory	proactive	all offenses	offenders-supervised by probation	provided	limited by statute	retroactive to June 1992	limited by statute
New Jersey	1994	indefinitely, but may petition for relief 15 years after release	mandatory	proactive	selected offenses	prosecutor and police	provided	people likely to encounter the offender	retroactive	not specified
Oregon	1993, 1995	for life; may petition for waiver after 10 years	varies[1]	proactive and upon request	selected offenses	probation and police	not provided	anyone	retroactive	unrestricted
Tennessee	1995	10 years minimum; then may petition for relief	discretionary	proactive	all offenses	Tennessee Bureau of Investigation	provided	not specified	retroactive	"relevant" information
Washington	1990	for life, 15 years, or 10 years depending on seriousness of offense	discretionary	proactive and upon request	all offenses	police	provided	not specified	retroactive	not specified

[1] Mandatory if under supervision; discretionary if not.

Source: Peter Finn. 1997. *Sex Offender Community Notification.* Washington, DC: U.S. Department of Justice (February), p. 4.

about sex offenders available on request to individuals and organizations or authorize or require probation and parole departments, law enforcement agencies, or prosecutor offices to disseminate information about released offenders to the community at large" (Finn 1997, p. 1). The publication adds that notification statutes "reflect the perception that registration alone is inadequate to protect the public against released sex offenders and that better notification provides the public with a better means of protecting itself (Finn 1997, p. 1). The provisions of notification statutes are complex and diverse. In some states, notification is required, others simply authorize it, and in others notice is given only if it is specifically requested. The responsibility of notifying the community about the presence of ex-offenders rests with police departments, probation and parole officers, or the prosecutor's office, or whichever agency is designated by law. In at least one state, the law gives the responsibility of notification to sexual offenders themselves (Finn 1997, p. 1).

One study examined whether community notification of sex offenders reduced recidivism and whether the program aided law enforcement in offender apprehension. The study used a treatment and a matched control group, and found that after 54 months there was no statistically significant difference between the two groups on the rate of arrest. However, the offenders who participated in the notification program were arrested more quickly than members of the control group (Finn 1997).

Zevitz and Farkas (2000) investigated the impact of community notification on the workloads of Wisconsin probation and parole officers who supervise sex offenders. Because Wisconsin is a state that has authorized proactive information dissemination, the researchers found much effort went into dealing with the community itself. Overall results indicated that sex offender supervision takes an extraordinary amount of training, time, and resources to find suitable housing, conduct home and employment visits, and monitor sex offenders to the rising community expectations. Another study (Tewksbury 2002) examined information from the Kentucky State Police Sex Offender Registry website and found insufficient information on a significant number of listed sex offenders. For example, half of all the listings had no photographs, and many either had no address or the address on file did not exist or was not a residential address. Tewksbury concluded that a sex offender registry such as this, with inaccurate or incomplete information, could not possibly provide any public safety benefit. To address this problem, the Department of Justice began a national sex offender registry to allow the public "real-time" access nationwide (see Figure 15.1).

Involuntary Commitment of Sexual Predators

Convicted sex offenders are also subject to possible involuntary civil confinement following incarceration. The sex offender may be subject to involuntary civil confinement if the following requirements are present: he or she poses a continuous and dangerous threat to public safety, that threat is related to a lack of control over behavior, and the offender has a severe mental illness or disorder that requires treatment. Since involuntary commitment is a civil statute, the commitment decision does not constitute double jeopardy (*Seling v. Young* 2001). The attorney general's office for each state screens the cases, but the lack of written guidelines affords authorities wide discretion as to whom should be committed.

The commitment process is private and confidential. However, Mansnerus (2003) was allowed to attend six hearings with special permission. She reports,

> The hearings are roughly modeled on commitments for the mentally ill, but with a key difference. In a regular civil commitment, the focus is on the patient's current state of mind; crimes committed long ago are usually not considered relevant. In the hearings at

FIGURE 15.1 *Example of a Notification*

SEX OFFENDER NOTIFICATION

The Thurston County Sheriff's Office is releasing the following information pursuant to RCW 4.24.550 which authorizes law enforcement agencies to inform the public when the release of information will enhance public safety and protection.

The individual who appears on this notification has been convicted of a sex offense that requires registration with the Sheriff's Office. Further, his previous criminal history places him in a classification level which reflects the potential to reoffend.

This individual has served the sentence imposed on him by the courts and has advised this office that he will be living in the location below. This notification is not intended to increase fear, rather, it is our belief that an informed public is a safer public.

NAME:

AGE:

RACE: White

SEX: Male

HEIGHT: 5-07

WEIGHT: 160

HAIR: Brown
EYES:

RESIDENCE:

VEHICLES:

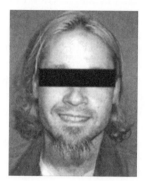

SYNOPSIS: In 1981 pled guilty in Clark County Superior Court to indecent Liberties. This resulted from his sexual contact with an 8-year-old girl who was known to him. In 1988 again pled guilty to Indecent Liberties for multiple sexual contacts with a different 8-year-old girl, also known to him. In 1995 he pled guilty to Luring a Child for inviting another 8-year-old girl into his apartment. This girl was a stranger to him. After his release form custody, moved to Thurston County. He is under the supervision of the Washington State Department of Corrections and is not allowed unsupervised contact with juveniles.

For additional information, call Detective Jack Furey at 786-5 or Detective Roland Weiss at 786-5.

Source: Peter Finn, "Sex Offender Community Notification", National Institute of Justice, Research in Action, February 1997, p.10.

Kearney, however, criminal records are considered critical evidence of the patient's thoughts, behaviors and possibility of committing future crimes . . . almost any information about him is admissible . . . like hearsay evidence, evaluations written years ago by the police or psychiatrists, statements to therapists and the patient's own writings. (p. 2)

In *Kansas v. Hendricks* (1997), the Supreme Court decided that a Kansas statute that permits the potentially indefinite commitment of sexually violent predators is constitutional. The Kansas Sexually Violent Predator Act authorizes the civil commitment of people who are likely to engage in predatory acts of sexual violence due to a mental or personality disorder. Defendant Hendricks had an extensive history of sexually molesting children and was scheduled for release from prison. But the state filed a petition to commit him under this act. The Court said that the Kansas law did not violate the prohibition against double jeopardy. However, five years later, in *Kansas v. Crane* (2002), the Supreme Court held that the civil commitment of a dangerous sex offender is not permitted without proof of serious difficulty in controlling behavior. It added, however, that total inability to control behavior is not required.

Rather, the state must show that an offender has difficulty controlling that behavior and that the lack of control is related to the serious mental illness. Taken together, the *Hendricks* and *Crane* cases say that the civil commitment of dangerous sex offenders is constitutional, but the state must prove prior to a civil commitment that the offender is unable to control his behavior (del Carmen, Ritter, and Witt 2005, p. 321).

Social Stigmatization

Social stigmatization is understudied in scholarly circles, but is perhaps the most frequently occurring collateral consequence of conviction. Its effects are unquantifiable and informal. The status degradation that follows a person with a conviction extends beyond the offender's discharge from the correctional process. This is particularly true when the person is committed to a state or federal correctional institution after conviction. One study found, through a mail survey of 281 respondents, that an inverse relationship existed between the degree of ex-convict stigmatization and the degree to which the respondents thought prisons were effective. In other words, as belief in the effectiveness of prisons decreased, the level of stigmatization of ex-felons increased (Bobys 1992). Occasionally, ex-offenders are preferred by employers because convicts are perceived to be dedicated and appreciative (Conte 2000). In other cases, former convicts may be appointed or gain high-profile positions that receive media attention (*Kentucky Post* staff writer, August 15, 2003). In the great majority of cases, however, social stigmatization leads to difficulties in obtaining or keeping a job.

Whether the removal of continuing civil disabilities would change community attitudes toward the offender remains an open question. On the one hand, rehabilitated ex-offenders have a right to start their lives over with the tools that they have been given through treatment efforts. Conversely, however, the public has a right to know of the previous criminal record to protect itself against the recidivist offender. Kuzma (1998) points out the importance of achieving some kind of balance within competing perspectives:

> [Restrictions] . . . require careful consideration and reflection about whether the rigidity and severity of such an approach is justified by identifiable societal gains in protecting the community. . . . It's a tough issue for society as a whole to resolve. When has an offender paid his debt to society? The price for crime can't be too cheap, lest no one follow the law. Yet, do we achieve another bad result by making it impossible to stop paying for having committed a crime? (p. 72)

PARDON

Definition and Purpose

Pardon is defined as "an act of grace, proceeding from the power entrusted with the execution of the laws, which exempts the individual on whom it is bestowed from the punishment the law inflicts for a crime which he has committed" (*Black's Law Dictionary* 1991, p. 768). Operating as a distinct subsystem of the criminal justice process, a **pardon** is an act of forgiveness, or mercy. One author notes: "Pardon is assigned a central role in overcoming the legal barriers to reintegration of criminal offenders in almost every U.S. jurisdiction, and in most jurisdictions it is the only mechanism by which adult felony offenders can avoid or mitigate collateral penalties and disabilities" (Love 2005, p. 7). But despite its importance to a well-balanced system of justice, pardon has received little scholarly attention. This lack of study has led to misunderstandings about its nature and function.

SURETY BOND

A type of bond signed by the principal and by one or more parties, known as sureties, who promise to pay money in the event that the party in whose favor the bond is written suffers damage because the principal failed to perform as agreed.

PARDON

"An act of grace, proceeding from the power entrusted with the execution of the laws, which exempts the individual on whom it is bestowed from the punishment the law inflicts for a crime which he has committed."

Courts differ on the issue of a pardon's legal effect. Some jurisdictions hold that a pardon wipes out the crime as though it never happened; thus the offender is a "new person." Other jurisdictions hold that for some purposes a pardon does not wipe out the fact of a conviction. Under this view, the recipient of a pardon is regarded not as a "new person" but as a convicted criminal. This happens, for example, when the pardoned criminal takes the stand as a witness in a trial. His or her testimony may be impeached and credibility is diminished because of the previous conviction even though a pardon has been granted. Again, states differ on how the results of a pardon are viewed.

The Power to Pardon

Historically, the power to pardon belonged to the king or sovereign. Because a crime was considered to be an offense against the king, he was deemed to have the power to forgive it. In early American law, the power to pardon was given to the legislature. When it was granted to the executive, it was severely restricted. By the time the U.S. Constitution was written, the older rule was again followed. The president was given the power of pardon in all federal cases except that of impeachment (*In re Bocchiaro* 1943). The Office of the Pardon Attorney in the Department of Justice receives applications from all over the country, and the Pardon Attorney is responsible for making recommendations to the president.

In most states today the power to pardon state felony cases belongs to the governor, acting alone or in conjunction with some official or board of pardons. When granted to the governor, the power may be either restricted or unrestricted. In some states the governor's power to pardon does not extend to treason and impeachment. In these states, those guilty of these acts or proceedings may be pardoned by the legislature. The power to pardon usually does not extend to violations of municipal ordinances; it extends only to offenses against the state because the power to pardon belongs to a state official. In some states, pardon can be given at any time after the person is charged or indicted, but in other states pardon can be granted only after conviction. Other states forbid pardon until the minimum sentence or a certain length of sentence has been served or until a specific number of years of successful parole have been completed. Where state law so provides, both absolute and conditional pardons may be given.

Kinds of Pardon

Pardons are either absolute (full) or conditional. An absolute pardon freely and unconditionally absolves an individual from the legal consequences of his or her conviction. Absolute pardon does not require that the prisoner or offender accept or reject it since no conditions whatsoever are attached (*Biddle v. Perovich* 1927). An absolute pardon, once delivered, cannot be revoked, and it restores citizenship rights. By contrast, a **conditional pardon** does not take effect until certain conditions are met or until after the occurrence of a specified event. For example, a public officer who commits an offense while in office and is convicted may be pardoned if he or she shows remorse, apologizes to the public, and resigns from public office. A conditional pardon generally does not restore the full civil rights of the offender unless express language to that effect is stated in its proclamation. This type of pardon may be revoked for violation of the conditions imposed. A prisoner may prefer to serve out his or her sentence rather than accept the conditions attached to the pardon, which the offender may deem burdensome or onerous. Some courts restrict the right of the governor to revoke a conditional pardon by prohibiting revocation without a determination that the person pardoned has violated the conditions.

CONDITIONAL PARDON

A type of pardon that does not take effect until certain conditions are met or until after the occurrence of a specified event.

Procedure for Obtaining a Pardon

The procedure for obtaining a pardon is fixed by statute or by regulations of the pardoning authority. Generally the convicted person must apply for a pardon, and time must elapse after release from confinement or discharge on parole before the offender may apply. When the offender applies, he or she is required to notify certain people, typically the prosecuting attorney, the sheriff, and the court of conviction. Posting (meaning the publication of a public notice) may be required. There may be limitations on repeated applications for pardon, such as a minimum time interval between applications. In most cases the pardoning authority conducts an investigation. A public hearing on the application may be held in some states.

Legal Effects of a Pardon

An absolute pardon restores most, but not all, civil rights that were lost upon conviction. For federal offenses, one publication notes that "a presidential pardon restores civil rights lost as a result of a federal conviction, including the rights to vote, to serve on a jury, and to hold public office, and generally relieves other disabilities that attach solely by reason of the commission or conviction of the pardoned offense" (*Federal Statutes Imposing Collateral Consequences Upon Conviction* 2000, p. 13). For federal offenders, the Supreme Court has held that only federal law can nullify the effect of a federal conviction through pardon, expungement, or restoration of civil rights (*Beecham v. United States* 1994).

There are two points of view on the issue of whether a pardon wipes out guilt. The classic view, which represents the minority position today, was expressed by the U.S. Supreme Court over a century ago when it said:

> A pardon reaches both the punishment prescribed for the offense and the guilt of the offender; and when the pardon is full, it releases the punishment and blots out the existence of the guilt, so that in the eyes of the law the offender is as innocent as if he had never committed the offense. (*Ex parte Garland* 1867)

The opposite and majority view states that a pardon is an implied expression of guilt and that the conviction is not obliterated (*Burdick v. United States* 1915). Each state determines which view it upholds. State law, a court decision, or the state pardoning authority defines the procedures and determines the effects of a pardon for state felony convictions. These determinations are binding only in that state. For example, a pardon given in one state may be used to increase the punishment of a subsequent offense in that state (*State v. Walker* 1983), but not in other states. An absolute pardon usually restores eligibility for public office, but will not restore a person to any public office he or she held at the time of conviction. By contrast, a conditional pardon usually does not restore rights or remove disqualifications for office (*Ex parte Lefors* 1957). Generally, a conviction for which a witness has been conditionally pardoned can nonetheless be used for witness impeachment in some courts.

Effects of a Pardon on Occupational Licensing

A pardon does not automatically restore an occupational license that has been revoked as a result of a criminal conviction. Although loss of a professional license is a penalty, some court decisions hold that the proceedings to revoke a license are not penal in nature (*Marlo v. State Board of Medical Examiners* 1952; *Murrill v. State Board of Accountancy* 1950). A professional license that is lost through conviction is usually not restored by a pardon because licenses are issued by licensing authorities or boards that have their own power and are independent from the pardoning authority. In California, the law provides that a pardon shall:

> operate to restore to the convicted person all the rights, privileges, and franchises of which he has been deprived in consequence of said conviction. . . . [N]othing in this article shall affect any of the provisions of the Medical Practices Act, or the power or authority conferred by law on the Board of Medical Examiners therein, or the power or authority conferred by law upon any board which permits any person or persons to apply his or their art or profession on the person of another. (Cal. Penal Code, sec. 4853)

RESTORATION OF RIGHTS

Restoration of rights may be done in two ways: by application or by automatic restoration. Most states provide for automatic restoration because it is easier to administer and is less discriminatory toward certain types of offenders.

Restoration upon Application

Some states, by statute, provide procedures the offender can initiate to remove the disabilities that follow a conviction. Typically, a certificate is furnished upon completion of the proceedings that specifies the rights that are restored. An ex-offender must possess one of these certificates to apply for a job or a license barred by virtue of a criminal conviction. These certificates and the order of the court usually restore the ex-offender to such political rights as the right to vote and provide him or her with a document that establishes good conduct since release from custody. Nonetheless, they are not binding and do not prevent a prospective employer or a licensing agency from taking the conviction into account in deciding whether to give the offender a job or a license.

Six states (Arizona, California, Illinois, Nevada, New Jersey, and New York) offer **rehabilitation certificates** that allow former offenders to obtain a license or work in certain occupations that have barred felons upon conviction. Other states have some form of administrative pardon system that offers a similar form of relief to enter occupations and obtain licensing (Alabama, Connecticut, Georgia, Nebraska, and South Carolina).

Automatic Restoration

The Office of the United States Pardon Attorney has published a state-by-state survey titled *Civil Disabilities of Convicted Felons*. The study reported that 33 states have laws for **automatic restoration of rights** upon completion of sentence. The remaining states require some affirmative action on the part of the offender (Office of the Pardon Attorney 1996).

A New Hampshire statute, which provides automatic restoration by virtue of a **certificate of discharge,** reads, in part,

> the order, certificate, or other instrument of discharge, given to a person sentenced for a felony upon his discharge after completion of service of his sentence or after service under probation or parole, shall state that the defendant's rights to vote and to hold any future public office of which he was deprived by this chapter are thereby restored and that he suffers no other disability by virtue of his conviction and sentence except as otherwise provided by this chapter. (N.H. Rev. Stat. Ann., sec. 607-A:5)

REHABILITATION CERTIFICATE

A certificate that allows former offenders to obtain a license or work in certain occupations that have barred felons upon conviction.

AUTOMATIC RESTORATION OF RIGHTS

Rights lost upon conviction are automatically restored after the sentence is completed.

CERTIFICATE OF DISCHARGE

A certificate given to a person discharged upon complete of sentence and which restores the rights the person lost upon conviction.

The laws of the other states that grant automatic restoration of rights are basically similar, but the provisions differ somewhat. The Illinois Unified Code of Corrections, for example, contains this language:

> On completion of sentence of imprisonment or on a petition of a person not sentenced to imprisonment, all license rights and privileges granted under the authority of this State which have been revoked or suspended because of conviction of an offense shall be restored unless the authority having jurisdiction of such license rights finds after investigation and hearing that restoration is not in the public interest. (Illinois Unified Code of Corrections, sec. 1005-5-5(d))

Most courts consider the effect of automatic restoration of rights as equivalent to a pardon. A certificate of good conduct and/or an automatic restoration of rights retains the conviction. Thus, the conviction remains on record as a prior conviction for purposes of increasing a future sentence if the offender is ever convicted again of another offense. The ex-offender is not restored to eligibility to receive an occupational or professional license and still must report the conviction on job application forms.

Restoring the Right to Vote

In a recent study, Margaret Colgate Love notes the following about the restoration of the right to vote in the various states (see Table 15.4):

- "In 48 states and the District of Columbia, some or all felony offenders lose the right to vote upon conviction, but in all but a handful of states most offenders regain the vote upon completion of sentence.
- "A total of 39 States, the District of Columbia and the territories, either do not suspend the right to vote at all upon conviction, or restore it automatically to all felony offenders upon the satisfaction of some objective criterion (for example, release from prison, discharge from sentence, or expiration of sentence plus an additional specified term of years).
- "Eleven states make restoration of the right to vote discretionary for at least some offenders who have completed their court-imposed sentences, but only four states permanently disenfranchise all felony offenders." (Margaret Colgate Love, "Relief from Collateral Consequences of a Criminal Conviction: A State-by-State Resource Guide," The Sentencing Project: Executive Summary, pp. 1–3. http://www.sentencingproject.org/rights-restoration.cfm.)

RESTORING GOOD MORAL CHARACTER

None of the methods and procedures for removing or reducing the collateral consequences of a criminal conviction discussed in this chapter restores good moral character to the ex-offender. Licensing statutes almost universally require that the holders of a professional or occupational license be of good character, and many private employers of nonlicensed workers impose the same requirement. This effectively closes the door for many convicted people in job markets that require a license. The lack of a generally accepted standard is one of the problems with determining good moral character. The Supreme Court in *Konigsberg v. State Bar* (1957) noted that

> the term [good moral character] by itself is unusually ambiguous. It can be defined in an almost unlimited number of ways, for any definition will necessarily reflect the attitudes, experiences, and prejudices of the definer. Such a vague qualification, which is easily adapted to fit personal views and predilections, can be a dangerous instrument for arbitrary and discriminatory denial of the right to practice law.

TABLE 15.4   Discretionary Restoration of the Vote after a Felony Conviction

State	Right to Vote Not Lost	Right to Vote Lost Only If Incarcerated	Right to Vote Lost upon Conviction, Restored upon Completion of Sentence	Right to Vote Lost upon Conviction, Restored after Additional Waiting Period	Right to Vote Lost upon Conviction, Restoration Discretionary
Alabama	X (offenses not involving moral turpitude)				X (felony offenses involving moral turpitude must obtain executive restoration of rights or pardon)
Arizona			X (first offenders only)		X (recidivists must obtain pardon or judicial restoration)
Delaware				X (five years, except for certain serious offenses)	X (pardon required for certain serious offenses)
Florida					X (executive restoration of rights or pardon)
Kentucky					X (pardon)
Maryland			X (first offenders only)	X (three years for recidivists)	X (pardon required if two or more violent felonies)
Mississippi	X (offenses not specified in constitution)				X (for all constitutionally specified offenses, pardon or legislative restoration)
Nevada			X (first offenders only)		X (pardon or judicial restoration)
Tennessee					X (pardon or judicial restoration)
Virginia					X (executive restoration of rights or pardon)
Wyoming				X (five years for first-time nonviolent offenders)	X (executive restoration of rights or pardon for violent offenders and recidivists)

Source: Margaret Colgate Love, Relief from the Collateral Consequences of a Criminal Conviction, July 2005 (Accessed: http://www.sentencingproject.org/rights_restoration/table8.html)

Yet the rule remains as it was when announced by the Supreme Court in 1898:

> [The state] may require both qualifications of learning and of good character, and if it deems that one who has violated the criminal laws of the state is not possessed of sufficient good character, it can deny to such a one a right to practice medicine, and further, it may make the record of a conviction conclusive evidence of the fact of the violation of the criminal law and of the absence of the requisite good character (*Hawker v. New York* 1898).

This rule has been generally followed in subsequent legislation and court decisions (*De Veau v. Braisted* 1960). When good moral character is required for occupational licensing, courts or enforcement agencies can disqualify an applicant based on differing perceptions of what that term means; thus the term becomes subjective. Conviction of any offense may be good enough for disqualification in some courts or agencies, but other jurisdictions require conviction of only certain types of serious offenses for good moral character to be lost.

EXPUNGEMENT OF CRIMINAL RECORDS

The word *expunge* means to "erase." Thus the purpose of **expungement** statutes is to allow the record of a crime to be erased as if it never happened, including the fact of having been arrested. It differs from a pardon in that whereas a pardon is given after conviction, expungement is granted only when the person has not yet been convicted of a crime. Although laws in states vary, any type of record related to a crime can be expunged (see Figure 15.2). This includes records in police departments, courts, or correctional facilities where the person has been detained or imprisoned. As of 2004, there were 21 states with procedures for expungement of a felony offender (Legal Action Center 2004, p. 6). However, even if the record is expunged, the publication notes that "the information still can be accessible to government agencies and the public." The same publication makes the following observations about expungement and sealing in the various states (p. 15):

- "Most states never expunge or seal conviction records, but do allow arrest records to be sealed or expunged when the arrest did not lead to a conviction.
- "Thirty-three states do not permit the expungement or sealing of any conviction records.
- "Seventeen states allow some conviction records to be expunged or sealed, such as first-time offenses.
- "Forty states allow people to seal or expunge records of some or all arrests that did not lead to conviction.
- "Thirty states allow you to deny the existence of a sealed or expunged arrest record when it did not lead to a conviction, if asked on employment applications or similar forms."

However, the same publication adds that access to criminal records is easy on the Internet, and further notes that:

- "Twenty-eight states allow Internet access to criminal records or post records on the Internet.
- "Fourteen of these states make all conviction records available on the Internet.
- "Six make available on the Internet records of people who are incarcerated and those on probation or parole.
- "Eight post on the Internet only records of people currently incarcerated."

EXPUNGEMENT

A procedure that allows the record of a crime to be erased as if the crime never happened, including the fact of having been arrested.

FIGURE 15.2   *Conditions of Expungement–State of Oregon*

1. YOU MAY NOT HAVE BEEN CONVICTED OF ANY OTHER CRIME WITHIN THE PAST 10 YEARS. IF YOU SIGN THE AFFIDAVIT AND HAVE BEEN CONVICTED OF A CRIME, IT WILL BE CONSIDERED FALSE SWEARING WHICH WILL RESULT IN A CRIMINAL PROCEEDING;
2. Must be over three (3) years from the date of CONVICTION;
3. Class C Felony or less;
4. Only one CONVICTION every ten (10) years can be EXPUNGED;
5. All arrests that resulted in our TAKING NO ACTION MUST WAIT ONE (1) YEAR FROM THE DATE OF ARREST;
6. Dismissed cases do not have to wait to apply for Expungement;
7. TRAFFIC CASES CANNOT BE EXPUNGED;
8. A CASHIERS CHECK in the amount of **$80.00** made payable to the OREGON STATE POLICE must accompany the papers that are delivered to the District Attorney's Office;
9. THERE IS NO CHARGE FOR DISMISSED OR NO ACTION CASES;
10. You CANNOT be on any form of probation for the CONVICTION that you are applying for Expungement

Source: Term for Benton County, Oregon.

The typical expungement statute requires that action be initiated by the offender after he or she meets certain qualifications. In Ohio, after a period of three years for non-violent first-time felonies, and after one year for misdemeanors, offenders pay a fee of $50 to be considered for expungement. If the judge agrees to expunge the records, at least 13 agencies must be notified, which makes it quite difficult to actually clear a person completely. Such expunged records include complaints, arrests, warrants, institutional commitments, photographs, fingerprints, judicial docket records, and presentence reports. In addition, the records are sealed rather than destroyed, and state law still permits sealed records to be viewed by some employers, such as agencies that work with children or the elderly (Horn 2000).

Only certain types of offenses can be expunged a certain number of years after the sentence has been served successfully. In New Jersey, a person may apply to expunge an "indictable offense" 10 years later, a "disorderly people" offense or a juvenile adjudication five years later, a municipal ordinance two years later, and a possession of a controlled substance charge as a juvenile one year after the sentence is completely served. Types of offenses that cannot be expunged include murder, manslaughter, kidnapping, sexual assault, crimes against children, arson, perjury, robbery, motor vehicle offenses, sale or distribution of large quantities of drugs, and occupational crimes committed by people holding public office. Even after records are expunged, certain occupations, such as law enforcement, the judicial branch, and corrections agencies, require applicants to report in detail information about any expunged arrests and/or convictions (Stewart Law Firm 2000).

SEALING OF RECORDS

A procedure whereby "a person's criminal record is sealed so that it can no longer be examined except by order of the court or by designated officials."

SEALING OF CRIMINAL RECORDS

Sealing of records is a practice in some states whereby a person's criminal record is sealed so that it can no longer be examined except by order of the court or by designated officials (*Black's Law Dictionary* 1991, p. 938). It differs from expungement in that in expungement the record is erased, whereas in sealing it is closed. Sealing of records usually applies to juvenile proceedings, but is also available in some states in adult cases. The process must be initiated by the offender. Sealed records restricts public access to everyone (including the person who wants the records sealed), and the person is not obligated to disclose any information to any employer, governmental agency, or any official. Legally, the applicant who has his or her records sealed can say no such records exist. Note that sealed records are retained and not physically destroyed. The only way sealed records can be examined is if the original applicant or a prosecutor files a court order and that order is granted by the court to unseal the record if public interest outweighs the original justification to seal.

In some states with sealing statutes (an example is Colorado), criminal records may be sealed only for crimes where a person was not charged, the case was dismissed, or the defendant was acquitted. The applicant must establish that the applicant's desire to seal the records outweighs the right of the public to have access to that information. Sealing may include the following records: fingerprint cards, arrest records, photos, the indictment, the prosecutorial information, competency hearing, a disposition, pretrial custody, correctional institution records while in custody, and any probation or parole records. No information involving a conviction may be sealed (Colorado Revised Statutes 1998, sec. 24-72-308).

Although expungement and sealing are available procedures, their use is infrequent. As one writer notes: "[A]s more and more people have a criminal record, relief from the collateral consequences of conviction has never seemed more elusive in most of the states and for federal offenders. It would seem that if rehabilitation of criminal offenders is a desirable social goal, it would be helpful to begin serious discussion of the growing contrary pressures that seem to consign all persons with a criminal record to the margins of society, and to a permanent outcast status in the eyes of the law" (Love 2005, p. 12).

TOP THINGS YOU SHOULD KNOW

- Collateral consequences, which are in the form of civil disabilities, can deprive a person of civil and political rights and may make finding or holding a job difficult.
- The types of civil disabilities for conviction vary from one state to another and are governed by federal and state laws.
- Some of the civil and political rights that are lost after conviction are the right to vote, serve on a jury, hold public office, own and possess a firearm, receive welfare benefits, and exercise parental rights.
- Private and public employers may discriminate against offenders unless such is prohibited by law.
- All 50 states and the District of Columbia have sex offender registration laws; most states also have sex offender notification laws.
- In some states, sexual predators may be civilly committed.
- Pardon is an act of grace and is available for offenders, but it is hard to obtain.
- The effects of a pardon vary from one state to another. In some states it erases guilt; in others it does not.
- Rights lost may be restored through various ways.
- Criminal records may be expunged or sealed, but their use is infrequent.

DISCUSSION QUESTIONS

1. Distinguish between civil and political rights.
2. Compare and contrast the concepts of outlawry and attainder.
3. If you were an employer, would you hire a former felon who has stayed out of trouble for five years? Support your answer.
4. Identify and discuss the variations in the type and extent of loss of civil rights of offenders.
5. "Former felons have the same rights and credibility as other witnesses in civil and criminal trials." Is that statement true or false? Explain your answer.
6. In your opinion, what are the arguments for and against sex offender registration laws?
7. Should the residents be notified about the presence of a sex offender in a neighborhood? Discuss this issue from the perspective of the residents and then from the perspective of the offender.
8. Assume you are an offender and are given a choice between an absolute pardon and a conditional pardon. Which would you prefer and why?
9. Are you in favor of restoring some, all, or none of the rights of ex-offenders discussed in this chapter? If you were a state legislator or a judge, which rights, if any, would you want restored and why?
10. Should an ex-felon be allowed to own or possess a firearm? Argue both sides of this issue.
11. Assume you are an ex-offender and are given a choice between expungement and sealing. Which would you choose and why?
12. Should ex-felons be given the right to vote? Explain why or why not.

 WEBSITES

The Sentencing Project Discussion on Felony Disenfranchisement

> *http://www.sentencingproject.org/pubs_05.cfm*

Civil Disabilities of a Federal Felony Conviction

> *http://www.alanellis.com/cm/publications/federal-felony-convicton.asp*

Felony Disenfranchisement

> *http://millercenter.virginia.edu/programs/natl_commissions/*
> *commission_final_report/task_force_report/hansen_chap8_disfranchisement.pdf*

Department of Justice National Sex Offender Public Registry

> *http://www.nsopr.gov*

State Sex Offender Registry Websites (Federal Bureau of Investigation)

> *http://www.fbi.gov/hq/cid/cac/states.htm*

Code Amber Sex Offender Registries by State

> *http://codeamber.org/sor.html*

Resources from the Office of the Pardon Attorney

> *http://www.usdoj.gov/pardon/readingroom.htm*

Pardon and Clemency in the United States

http://en.wikipedia.org/wiki/Pardon

Resources from the Office of the Pardon Attorney

http://www.usdoj.gov/pardon/readingroom.htm

Alaska Board of Parole Clemency Handbook of Definitions

http://www.correct.state.ak.us/corrections/Parole/handbook.pdf

Legally Speaking: Be Careful What You Ask for When Advocating Enforcement
Article by Karen L. MacNutt, published in *Gun Week,* a magazine advocating the right
to bear arms

http://www.tyksnews.com/Depts/2nd_Amend/legally_speaking.htm

Office of the Pardon Attorney
Presidential pardons, 1945–2001

*http://www.nytimes.com/images/2001/01/29/national/010129_nat_
PARDONch.html*

The Pardon Resource Center
Twelve steps to a federal pardon

http://www.silicon-valley.com/pardonme/index.html

Automatic Restoration of Rights in Texas

http://www.sentencingproject.org/pdfs/rights-restoraton/Texas.pdf

CHAPTER **15**

CASE STUDY

This chapter presents controversial issues on the loss of rights as a result of conviction for a crime. States differ on what specific rights are lost upon conviction, the duration or the loss, and whether the rights lost should automatically be restored after the sentence is served or whether the right is restored only upon application by the ex-offender. There are no authoritative national answers to these hypothetical case studies because laws, court decisions, agency rules, and practices in the private sector vary. The aim of these case studies is to make the reader think about what he or she would do if given the final decision on what the law, court, agency chief, or private employer should say or would do in these cases. Each decision must be justified based on the reader's personal opinion instead of on what established law or practice says. In sum, disregard the law in these cases and simply give your well-considered opinion.

1. THE RIGHT TO VOTE: Assume that Citizen A, the head of a prominent investing firm in your community for many years, was charged, tried, and convicted of defrauding investors in his company. Prior to that, A was an active citizen in civic and humanitarian activities as well as in political circles. He was a member of the Rotary Club and was president of that organization for five years. He is sentenced to 10 years in prison. Assuming your state has no law governing this issue: (a) Should Citizen A be allowed to vote while he is in prison? (b) If your answer is no, should he be allowed to vote after he gets out of prison and is back in the community? and (c) if Citizen A were an ordinary member of the community, without any previous involvement or influence, would your answer be different?

2. THE RIGHT TO HOLD PUBLIC OFFICE: B, a current prominent member of your city council is charged, tried, and convicted of sexually harassing her male secretary while she was in office. She was convicted because she threatened to fire her male secretary if he did not engage in intimate relations with her. The secretary refused and was fired. Assume that kind of conduct by B is criminal in your state. B was placed on probation for two years, which she successfully served. She now wants to run for the same office, saying she has "learned her lesson," is now married, and promises to be on her best behavior if elected. You are in her district and voted for her in previous elections. Questions: (a) Should she be allowed to hold public office again? and (b) Will you vote for her again?

3. THE RIGHT TO PUBLIC EMPLOYMENT: C served time in city jail for one year because he was convicted of beating up his wife, which resulted in her confinement in a hospital for two days. He is now divorced from his wife and is jobless. He has served time in jail with good behavior and is applying for a job as a janitor at the community college where you are a student. Questions: (a) Are you in favor of hiring him for the job or not? (b) Assume that C in fact is a former professor in the community college and, after having served time for the same crime, is now reapplying for the same job as professor. Do you think he should be rehired as professor? and (c) Assume C is a professor and was convicted of reckless homicide of a student because he recklessly drove one evening on campus while drunk. Would your answer be the same or different?

4. THE RIGHT TO AN OCCUPATIONAL LICENSE: D, a medical doctor in the community where you reside, was convicted of shooting one of his neighbors after they had a big fight. The fight ensued because D had an affair with his neighbor's wife, which the neighbor later discovered. D was placed on probation for five years on a plea bargain after pleading to the charge. Assume you are a legislator and are asked the following questions by reporters: (a) Should D be allowed to practice medicine while he is on probation? and (b) Should D be denied an occupational license if he violates the terms of his probation and serves time in prison for two years for the offense?

5. THE WISDOM OF A PRIVATE EMPLOYER: You are the owner of a big grocery store in town and run a successful business. One day an applicant comes to you and applies for any job he could get in your store. He says he did not finish high school and did drugs. He further tells you that he was confined in a state institution for juveniles when he was 16 years old because he took part in a robbery with other members of a gang. He is now 20 years old, is no longer a member of a gang, uses drugs occasionally, and is in a rehabilitation program for drug users. As sole owner of the store, you have the final decision to hire or not to hire. What will you do and why?

6. THE RIGHT TO OWN A FIREARM: Citizen E is an avid hunter and a member of the local gun club. He has all kinds of firearms in his house, which he uses to hunt. One night, he had a serious quarrel with one of his neighbors. In a fit of great anger, he went inside the house, pulled out one of his guns, and shot and seriously injured the neighbor. This was his first offense ever involving a firearm. He was tried, convicted, and sentenced to serve 12 years in a state prison. While in prison he was a model prisoner, and he was released on parole after eight years. Assume that both state and federal laws provide for C to be deprived of his right to own a firearm. Do you agree with these laws? Suppose C was convicted instead of shooting a burglar who broke into his home and was sentenced to serve time in jail for three months. Would your answer be the same? Suppose C was convicted of a misdemeanor using his firearm to threaten his wife and was given probation for that offense? Should he be allowed to keep his firearms?

7. PROVISIONS FOR SEX OFFENDER REGISTRATION AND NOTIFICATION: F, an immigrant carpenter who had a wife and three young children, was charged with and pleaded guilty to molesting the child of a rich couple for whom he worked occasionally. He did not want to plead guilty and claimed innocence all throughout the proceedings. But he pleaded guilty after spending almost a year in jail because he could not afford to post bail and could not support his family any longer while he was in jail (this is known in law as an Alford plea, a plea where a defendant pleads guilty for practical reasons even though he or she continues to maintain innocence). Assume that the state where F works provides for sex offender registration and notification. Should there be exceptions in those laws for offenders like F? Does it make any difference to your answer if you truly believe F is innocent?

8. THE RIGHT TO A PARDON: G, one of your former classmates, was convicted of rape while he was under the influence of drugs based mainly on the testimony of three witnesses who claimed to have been at the same fraternity party when the crime was committed. G is currently serving a 10-year sentence in a state prison. New DNA evidence now shows that G did not commit the offense and that somebody else at the party did it, as proved by the DNA test results.

The same three witnesses, however, say that they stand by their court testimony and that for them nothing has changed. Should G be pardoned as soon as possible by the governor (who is the only person authorized in the state to grant a pardon)? If the pardon is given, should it restore G's good moral character and all other rights he may have lost as a result of conviction?

9. THE DECISION TO EXPUNGE OR SEAL: J, a juvenile who was 15 years old when he committed a burglary, served time in a juvenile state institution. He had a string of offenses before that, including robbery and sale of drugs. He is now 18 years old and wants his juvenile records expunged and sealed. Assume you are the juvenile court judge before whom J's request is made. Assume further that your state law gives you, the judge, the discretion to expunge and seal juvenile records. Will you grant J's request? Does it make sense for you to grant J's motion to seal his record, but not grant expungement? Or vice versa? Will your decision be the same or different if J's only offense was that burglary and he had an exemplary record while in the juvenile state institution?

Glossary

absconder An offender under community supervision who, without prior permission, escapes or flees the jurisdiction he or she is required to stay within.

absolute immunity Protection from legal action or liability unless workers engage in discretion that is intentionally and maliciously wrong.

adjudication Juvenile justice equivalent of a trial in adult criminal cases.

Alexander Maconochie A British naval captain who served as governor of the penal colony on Norfolk Island, who instituted a system of early release that was the forerunner of modern parole. Maconochie is known as the "father of parole."

amercement A monetary penalty imposed arbitrarily at the discretion of the court for an offense.

attainder At common law, the extinction of civil rights and capacities that occurred when a person received a sentence of death or outlawry for treason or another felony. The person's estate was forfeited to the Crown.

automatic restoration of rights Reinstatement of some or all civil rights upon completion of sentence. The extent of restoration varies by state and by offense type.

bail Monetary payment deposited with the court to ensure the defendant's return for the next court date in exchange for the defendant's release.

boot camp A form of shock incarceration that involves a military-style regimen designed to instill discipline in young offenders.

brokerage of services Supervision that involves identifying the needs of probationers or parolees and referring them to an appropriate community agency.

caseload The number of individuals or cases for which one probation or parole officer is responsible.

casework A community supervision philosophy that allowed the officer to create therapeutic relationships with clients through counseling and directly assisting in behavior modification to assist them in living productively in the community.

certificate of discharge Official written document signifying that an offender has completed his or her sentence.

civil disenfranchisement The loss of the right to vote for felony offenders.

civil rights Rights that belong to a person by virtue of citizenship.

classification A procedure consisting of assessing the risks posed by the offender, identifying the supervision issues, and selecting the appropriate supervision strategy.

clear conditions Conditions that are sufficiently explicit so as to inform a reasonable person of the conduct that is required or prohibited.

clemency An act of mercy by a governor or the president to erase consequences of a criminal act, accusation, or conviction.

collateral consequences Disabilities that follow a conviction that are not directly imposed by a sentencing court—such as loss of the right to vote, serve on a jury, practice certain occupations, or own a firearm.

collateral contact Verification of the probationer or parolee's situation and whereabouts by means of the officer speaking with a third party who knows the offender personally (such as a family member, friend, or employer).

community corrections A nonincarcerative sanction in which offenders serve all or a portion of their sentence in the community.

Community Corrections Act A statewide mechanism through which funds are granted to local units of government to plan, develop, and deliver correctional sanctions and services. The overall purpose of this mechanism is to provide local sentencing options in lieu of imprisonment in state institutions.

community justice A philosophy of using the community to control and reduce crime through community policing, community courts, restorative justice, and broken-windows probation.

community resource management team (CRMT) model A supervision model in which probation or parole officers develop skills and linkages with community agencies in one or two areas only. Supervision under this model is a team effort, with each officer utilizing his or her skills and linkages to assist the offender.

community service Unpaid labor to the public to compensate society for harm done by the offense of conviction.

commutation Shortening sentence length or changing a punishment to one that is less severe, as from a death sentence to life in prison without parole.

completion rates Individuals who are favorably discharged from drug court as a percentage of the total number admitted and not still enrolled.

concurrent jurisdiction Original jurisdiction for certain juvenile cases is shared by both criminal and juvenile courts, and the prosecutor has discretion to file such cases in either court.

conditional pardon A pardon that becomes operative when the grantee has performed some specific act(s) or that becomes void when some specific act(s) transpires.

conduct in need of supervision (CINS) Acts committed by juveniles that would not have been punishable if committed by adults; status offenses.

conviction A judgment of the court, based on a defendant's plea of guilty or nolo contendere, or on the verdict of a judge or jury, that the defendant is guilty of the offense(s) with which he or she has been charged.

day fines Fines that are calculated by multiplying a percentage of the offender's daily wage by the number of predefined punishment units (the number of punishment units depend on the seriousness of the crime).

day reporting centers Nonresidential programs typically used for defendants on pretrial release, for convicted offenders on probation or parole, or as an increased sanction for probation or parole violators. Services are provided in one central location, and offenders must check in daily.

delegated release authority Statutory authority that allows pretrial services officers to release the defendant before the initial court appearance in front of the judge.

determinate sentencing A sentencing philosophy that focuses on certainty and severity for the crime committed and specifies by statute an exact amount of time or narrow sentencing range of time to be served in prison or in the community. Amount of time served depends on the legislative statutes or the sentencing guidelines, which mandate how much time is to be served before the offender is eligible (if at all) for mandatory release. Also known as a presumptive, fixed, or mandatory sentence.

diminished constitutional rights Constitutional rights enjoyed by an offender on parole that are not as highly protected by the courts as the rights of nonoffenders.

disclosure The right of a defendant to read and refute information in the presentence investigation report prior to sentencing.

discretionary release Conditional release because members of a parole board have decided that the prisoner has earned the privilege while still remaining under supervision of an indeterminate sentence.

disposition Juvenile justice equivalent of sentencing in adult cases.

diversion An alternative program to traditional criminal sentencing or juvenile justice adjudication that provides first-time offenders with a chance or addresses unique treatment needs, with the successful completion resulting in the dismissal of the current charges.

drug courts A diversion program for drug addicts in which the judge, prosecutor, and probation officer play a proactive role and monitor the progress of clients through weekly visits to the courtroom, using a process of graduated sanctions.

due process Laws must be applied in a fair and equal manner. Fundamental fairness.

dynamic factors Correlates of the likelihood of recidivism that can be changed through treatment and rehabilitation (drug and alcohol abuse, anger management, quality of family relationships, and so forth).

early termination Termination of probation at any time during the probation period or after some time has been served.

electronic monitoring A correctional technology used as a tool in intensive supervision probation, parole, day reporting, or home confinement, using a radio frequency or satellite technology to track offender whereabouts using a transmitter and receiver.

exclusion zones Exact locations the offender is prohibited from being in or near.

exclusionary rule A rule of evidence that enforces the Fourth Amendment's prohibition against unreasonable search and seizure, whereby illegal police searches are not admissible in a court of law. The purpose is to deter police misconduct.

expungement An erasure. Process by which the record of a criminal conviction (or juvenile adjudication) is destroyed or sealed after expiration of time.

failure to appear A situation in which a defendant does not attend a scheduled court hearing.

fee A monetary amount imposed by the court to assist in administering the criminal justice system by the offender's repayment of debt accrued by the investigation, prosecution, and supervision of the case.

field contact An officer's personal visit to an offender's home or place of employment for the purpose of monitoring progress under supervision.

filing A procedure under which an indictment was "laid on file," or held in abeyance, without either dismissal or final judgment in cases in which justice did not require an immediate sentence.

final revocation hearing A due process hearing that must be conducted before probation or parole can be revoked.

fine A fixed monetary sanction defined by statute and imposed by a judge, depending on the seriousness of the crime.

forfeiture A government seizure of property that was illegally obtained, was acquired with resources that were illegally obtained, or was used in connection with an illegal activity.

full board review The statutory requirement that all members of the parole board review and vote on the early release from prison of individuals who have committed felony crimes, usually of a violent or sexual nature. Some states require this type of review on every discretionary release.

full pardon A pardon without any attached conditions.

global positioning system A system that uses 24 military satellites orbiting the earth to pinpoint the offender's exact location intermittently or at all times.

good moral character The totality of virtues that form the basis of one's reputation in the community.

good time Sentence reduction of a specified number of days each month for good conduct.

halfway house The oldest and most common type of community residential facility for probationers or parolees who require a more structured setting than would be available if living independently.

hearsay evidence Information offered as a truthful assertion that does not come from the personal knowledge of the person giving the information but from knowledge that person received from a third party.

home-based electronic monitoring An intermittent or continuous radio frequency signal transmitted through a land line telephone into a receiver that determines whether the offender is or is not at home.

house arrest A community-based sanction in which offenders serve their sentence at home. Offenders have curfews and may not leave their home except for employment and correctional treatment purposes. Also called home detention or home confinement.

inclusion zones Exact locations, such as employment, school, or an appointment, where the offender is required to be at a certain time.

indeterminate sentence A sentencing philosophy that focuses on treatment and incorporates a broad sentencing range or undetermined amount of time served in prison or in the community where discretionary release is determined by a parole board based on the offender's rehabilitation or readiness to function prosocially.

in-service training Periodic continuing education training for seasoned officers.

institutional corrections An incarcerative sanction in which offenders serve their sentence away from the community in a jail or prison institution.

intake The process whereby a juvenile is screened to determine if the case should proceed further in the juvenile justice system or whether other alternatives are better suited for the juvenile.

intensive supervision probation A form of probation that stresses intensive monitoring, close supervision, and offender control.

intermediate sanctions A spectrum of community supervision strategies that vary greatly in terms of their supervision level and treatment capacity, ranging from probation to partial custody.

intermediate sanctions A range of punishments that fall between probation and prison.

interstate compact An agreement signed by all states and U.S. territories that allows for the supervision of parolees and probationers across state lines.

Interstate Compact for Adult Offender Supervision A formalized decree granting authority to a commission to create and enforce rules for member states for the supervision of offenders in other states.

the Irish system Developed in Ireland by Sir Walter Crofton, the Irish system involved graduated levels of institutional control leading up to release under conditions similar to modern parole. The American penitentiaries were partially based on the Irish system.

John Augustus A Boston bootmaker who was the founder of probation in the United States.

just deserts The concept that the goal of corrections should be to punish offenders because they deserve to be punished and that punishment should be commensurate with the seriousness of the offense.

justice model The correctional practice based on the concept of just deserts and even-handed punishment. The justice model calls for fairness in criminal sentencing, in that all people convicted of a similar offense will receive a like sentence. This model of corrections relies on determinate sentencing and abolition of parole.

juvenile delinquency Acts committed by juveniles that are punishable as crimes under a state's penal code.

law violations Violations of probation or parole conditions that involve the commission of a crime.

liberty interest Any interest recognized or protected by the due process clauses of state or federal constitutions.

mandatory release Conditional release to the community under a determinate sentence that is automatic at the expiration of the minimum term of sentence minus any credited time off for good behavior.

marks system A theory of human motivation organized by Maconochie that granted credits for good behavior and hard work, or took away marks for negative behavior. Convicts used the credits or marks to purchase either goods or time (reduction in sentence).

maximum eligibility date The longest amount of time that can be served before the inmate must be released by law.

medical model The concept that, given proper care and treatment, criminals can be cured into productive, law-abiding citizens. This approach suggests that people commit crimes because of influences beyond their control, such as poverty, injustice, and racism.

medical parole The conditional release from prison to the community of a prisoner with a terminal illness who does not pose an undue risk to public safety.

mental health courts A diversion program for mentally ill defendants in which the judge, prosecutor, and probation officer play a proactive role and monitor the progress of clients through weekly visits to the courtroom.

minimum eligibility date The shortest amount of time defined by statute, minus good time earned, that must be served before the offender can go before the parole board.

moral turpitude   An act of vileness, or socially offensive behavior, that is contrary to the public's accepted moral standards.

motion to quash   An oral or written request that the court repeal, nullify, or overturn a decision, usually made during or after the trial.

negligence   The failure of an officer to do what a reasonably prudent person would have done in like or similar circumstances.

neighborhood-based supervision   A supervision strategy that emphasizes public safety, accountability, partnerships with other community agencies, and beat supervision.

net widening   Using an intermediate sanction as a stiffer punishment for offenders who would have ordinarily been sentenced to probation or other lesser sanctions.

Norfolk Island   The notorious British supermax penal colony 1,000 miles off the coast of Australia that housed the most incorrigible prisoners.

offender-based presentence report   A presentence investigation report that seeks to understand the offender and the circumstances of the offense and to evaluate the offender's potential as a law-abiding, productive citizen.

offense-based presentence report   A presentence investigation report that focuses primarily on the offense committed, the offender's culpability, and prior criminal history.

outlawry   In old Anglo-Saxon law, the process by which a criminal was declared an outlaw and placed outside the protection and aid of the law.

pardon   An executive act of clemency that serves to mitigate or set aside punishment for a crime.

parens patriae   Latin term meaning that the government acts as a "substitute parent" and allows the courts to intervene in cases in which it is in the child's best interest that a guardian be appointed for children who, through no fault of their own, have been neglected and/or are dependent.

parole   Release of a convicted offender from a penal or correctional institution, under the continual custody of the state, to serve the remainder of his or her sentence in the community under supervision, either by discretionary or mandatory release stipulations.

parole board   An administrative body empowered to decide whether inmates shall be conditionally released from prison before the completion of their sentence, to revoke parole, and to discharge from parole those who have satisfactorily completed their terms.

parole conditions   The rules under which a paroling authority releases an offender to community supervision.

parole d'honneur   French for "word of honor," from which the English word parole is derived.

parole eligibility date   The point in a prisoner's sentence at which he or she becomes eligible to be considered for parole. If the offender is denied parole, a new parole eligibility date is scheduled in the future.

Peace Officer State Training   Specialized and standardized training that officers are required to complete before they may carry a firearm on the job.

penile plethysmograph   A device that measures erectile responses in male sex offenders to determine level of sexual arousal to various types of stimuli. This device is used for assessment and treatment purposes.

political rights   Rights related to the establishment, support, or management of government.

postsentence report   A report written by a probation officer after the defendant has pled guilty and been sentenced in order to aid probation and parole officers in supervision, classification, and program plans.

preferred rights   Rights more highly protected than other constitutional rights.

preliminary hearing   An inquiry conducted to determine if there is probable cause to believe that the offender committed a probation or parole violation.

preponderance of evidence   A level of proof used in a probation revocation administrative hearing, in which the judge decides based on which side presents more convincing evidence and its probable truth or accuracy, and not necessarily on the amount of evidence.

prerelease facility   A minimum-security prison that houses inmates who have earned this privilege through good institutional conduct and who are nearing their release date.

prerelease plan   A case management summary of institutional conduct and program participation, as well as plans for housing and employment upon release, that is submitted to the parole board in cases of discretionary parole or to the parole officer in cases of automatic release.

prerelease program   A minimum-security community-based or institutional setting for offenders who have spent time in prison and are nearing release. The focus of these programs includes transitioning, securing a job, and reestablishing family connections.

presentence investigation   An investigation undertaken by a probation officer for the purpose of gathering and analyzing information to complete a report for the court.

presentence investigation (PSI) report   A report submitted to the court before sentencing describing the nature of the offense, offender characteristics, criminal history, loss to the victim, and sentencing recommendations.

preservice training   Fundamental knowledge and/or skills for a newly hired officer in preparation for working independently.

presumptive sentence   A statutorily determined sentence offenders will presumably receive if convicted. Offenders convicted in a jurisdiction with presumptive sentences will be assessed this sentence unless mitigating or aggravating circumstances are found to exist.

presumptive sentencing grids A narrow range of sentencing guidelines that judges are obligated to use. Any deviations must be provided in writing and may also be subject to appellate court review.

pretrial release A defendant's release in the community following arrest as an alternative to detention while the defendant prepares for the next scheduled court appearance.

pretrial supervision Court-ordered correctional supervision of a defendant who has not yet been convicted whereby the defendant participates in activities such as reporting, house arrest, and electronic monitoring to ensure appearance at the next court date.

prisoner reentry Any activity or program conducted to prepare ex-convicts to return safely to the community and to live as law-abiding citizens.

private probation An agency that is owned and operated by a private business or nonprofit organization, and contracts with the state, local, or federal government to supervise clients.

probation The community supervision of a convicted offender in lieu of incarceration under conditions imposed by the court for a specified period during which the court retains authority to modify the conditions or to resentence the offender if he or she violates the conditions.

public employment Paid employment at any level of government.

public office Uncompensated, elected or appointed government position.

qualified immunity Protection from liability in decisions or actions that are "objectively reasonable."

real-time access The ability to track locations of the offender as they occur (as opposed to obtaining the data up to 24 hours later).

reasonable conditions Probation conditions that the offender can reasonably comply with.

receiving state Under the interstate compact, the state that undertakes the supervision.

recidivism The repetition of or return to criminal behavior, variously defined in one of three ways: rearrest, reconviction, or reincarceration.

recognizance Originally a device of preventive justice that obliged people suspected of future misbehavior to stipulate with and give full assurance to the court and the public that the apprehended offense would not occur. Recognizance was later used with convicted or arraigned offenders with conditions of release set.

reentry The process of preparing and integrating parolees into the community as law-abiding citizens using a collaborative approach with parole officers and treatment providers.

reentry courts A collaborative, team-based program that aims to improve the link between parole supervision and treatment providers to help recent parolees become stabilized.

relapse When an offender with a substance abuse problem returns to using alcohol or drugs.

remote location monitoring Verifying an offender's physical location by phone caller identification, use of a pager, and voice pattern verification.

reprieve Postponing or interrupting a sentence (for example, a prison term or an execution).

residential community corrections facilities A sanction in the community in which the convicted offender lives at the facility and must be employed, but he or she can leave the facility for a limited purpose and duration if preapproved. Examples include halfway houses, prerelease centers, restitution centers, drug treatment facilities, and work release centers.

restitution Court-ordered payment by the offender to the victim to cover tangible losses that occurred during or following the crime.

restitution center A type of residential community facility specifically targeted for property or first-time offenders who owe victim restitution or community service.

restorative justice A sentencing philosophy and practice that emphasizes the offender taking responsibility to repair the harm done to the victim and to the surrounding community.

retention rates The combined total of the successful completers and those actively enrolled compared to the total number admitted to drug court.

revocation The process of hearings that result when the probationer is noncompliant with the current level of probation. Results of a revocation are either modifying probation conditions to a more intensive supervision level, or the complete elimination of probation and sentence to a residential community facility, jail, or prison.

risk assessment A procedure that provides a measure of the offender's propensity to further criminal activity and indicates the level of officer intervention that will be required.

role ambiguity The discretion that exists in the role of the probation and parole officer to treat clients fairly and consistently and according to individual circumstances.

role conflict The two functions of a probation and parole officer, that of enforcing the rules and laws, and providing support and reintegration, that are sometimes contradictory and difficult to reconcile.

Salient Factor Score The parole guidelines developed and used by the U.S. Parole Commission for making parole release decisions. Served as the model for parole guidelines developed in many other jurisdictions.

school-based probation A type of probation where probation officers move out of traditional district offices into middle, junior high, and high school buildings and supervise their caseloads right in the schools.

sealing of records   The legal concealment of a person's criminal (or juvenile) record such that it cannot be opened except by order of the court.

security for good behavior   A recognizance or bond given the court by a defendant before or after conviction conditioned on his or her being "on good behavior" or keeping the peace for a prescribed period.

sending state   Under the interstate compact, the state of conviction.

sentencing   The postconviction stage, in which the defendant is brought before the court for formal judgment pronounced by a judge.

sentencing commission   A governing body that monitors the use of the sentencing guidelines and departures from the recommended sentences.

shock incarceration   A brief period of incarceration followed by a term of supervised probation. Also called shock probation, shock parole, intermittent imprisonment, or split sentence.

Sir Walter Crofton   An Irish prison reformer who established an early system of parole based on Alexander Maconochie's experiments with the mark system.

social stigmatization   Loss of social status and respect by members of the community as a result of having a conviction; a form of shaming.

special conditions   Conditions tailored to fit the needs of an offender.

standard conditions   Conditions imposed on all offenders in all jurisdictions.

standard of proof   The level of proof, measured by the strength of the evidence, needed to render a decision in a court proceeding.

static factors   Correlates of the likelihood of recidivism that (once they occur) cannot be changed (age at first arrest, number of convictions, and so forth).

statutory exclusion   The automatic exclusion of certain juvenile offenders from juvenile court jurisdiction by state statute, requiring the case to be filed directly with the adult criminal court.

supervision   The oversight that a probation or parole officer exercises over those in his or her custody.

surety   An individual who agrees to become responsible for the debt of a defendant or who answers for the performance of the defendant should the defendant fail to attend the next court appearance.

surety bond   A certificate signed by the principal and a third party, promising to pay in the event the assured suffers damages or losses because the employee fails to perform as agreed.

suspended sentence   An order of the court after a verdict, finding, or plea of guilty that suspends or postpones the imposition or execution of sentence during a period of good behavior.

technical violations   Multiple violations that breach one or more noncriminal conditions of probation.

therapeutic community   A type of residential community facility specifically targeted for drug offenders, offenders who are alcoholics, and/or drug addicts who are amenable to treatment.

ticket-of-leave   A license or permit given to a convict as a reward for good conduct, which allowed him to go at large and work for himself before his sentence expired, subject to certain restrictions and revocable upon subsequent misconduct. A forerunner of parole.

transfer of jurisdiction   The transfer of a juvenile from juvenile court to adult court for trial.

transportation   The forced exile of convicted criminals. England transported convicted criminals to the American colonies until the Revolutionary War and afterward to Australia.

unconditional release   A type of release from prison without correctional supervision because the full sentence has been served behind bars. Also known as "maxing out" or "killing your number."

victim compensation fund   A state fund that dispenses compensation to victims of violent crime and paid for by offenders who are convicted.

victim impact statement   A written account by the victim(s) as to how the crime has taken a toll physically, emotionally, financially, or psychologically on the victim and the victim's family. Victim impact statements are considered by many states at time of sentencing and at parole board hearings.

voluntary sentencing guidelines   A narrow range of strategies or suggested determinate sentences based on offense seriousness and prior criminal history that the judge may or may not choose to accept.

widening the net   When an individual who should have received probation is sentenced to a harsher intermediate sanction only because that sanction is available, not because the offender requires more intensive supervision.

work ethic camp   A 120-day alternative to prison that teaches job skills and decision making using a cognitive-behavioral approach, followed by intensive supervision probation.

work release   A program in which offenders who reside in a facility (a community facility, jail, or prison) are released into the community only to work or attend education classes or both.

Zebulon R. Brockway   The American prison reformer who introduced modern correctional methods, including parole, to the Elmira Reformatory in New York in 1876.

References

Abadinsky, Howard. 1978. Parole history: An economic perspective. *Offender Rehabilitation* 2(3): 275–278.

Acoca, Leslie, and James Austin. 1996. *The crisis: The woman offender sentencing study and alternative sentencing recommendations project: Women in prison.* Washington, DC: National Council on Crime and Delinquency.

Adams, Devon B. 2002. *Summary of state sex offender registries, 2001.* Washington, DC: U.S. Department of Justice, Bureau of Justice Statistics.

Administrative Office of the U.S. Courts. 1995. *The presentence investigation report for defendants sentenced under the Sentencing Reform Act of 1984* [Publication 107]. Washington, DC: Administrative Office of the U.S. Courts.

—. 2006. Gang member supervision growing part of job for probation officers. *The Third Branch* 38(2): 1–3. Accessed June 2, 2006: http://www.uscourts.gov/ttb/02-06/gangsupervision/index.html.

Alarid, Leanne F., and Paul Cromwell. 2006. *In her own words: Women offenders' views on crime and victimization.* Los Angeles, CA: Roxbury.

Alaska Judicial Council. 1998. Probation revocation and ethnicity. *Alaska Justice Forum* 15(3). Accessed May 2, 2006: http://www.justice.uaa.alaska.edu/forum/15/3fall1998/c_prob.html.

Albonetti, Celesta A., and John R. Hepburn. 1997. Probation revocation: A proportional hazards model of the conditioning effects of social disadvantage. *Social Problems* 441: 124–137.

Allen, Frederick G., and Harvey Treger. 1994. Fines and restitution orders: Probationers' perceptions. *Federal Probation* 58(2): 34–40.

Altman, Robert N., and Robert E. Murray. 1997. Home confinement: A '90s approach to community supervision. *Federal Probation* 61(1): 30–32.

Altschuler, David M. 1999. Trends and issues in the adultification of juvenile justice. In *Research to results: Effective community corrections,* edited by Patricia M. Harris. Lanham, MD: American Correctional Association, pp. 233–271.

American Bar Association. 1994. *Standards for criminal justice, sentencing,* 3rd ed. Sec. 18-3.16f.

American Friends Service Committee. 1971. *Struggle for justice.* New York: Hill and Wang.

American Probation and Parole Association. n.d. APPA position statement: Community justice. Accessed August 1, 2000: http://www. appa-net.org/about%20appa/communityjustice_1.htm.

—. 1994. APPA position statement: Weapons. Accessed: http://www.appa-net.org/about%20appa/weapons.htm.

—. 2006. *APPA adult and juvenile probation and parole national firearm survey 2005–2006.* Lexington, KY: APPA. Accessed October 1, 2006: http://www.appa-net.org/information%20clearing%20house/survey.htm.

Anderson, David C. 1998. *Sensible justice: Alternatives to prison.* New York: New Press.

Anderson, James F., Laronstine Dyson, and Jerald Burns. 1999. *Boot camps: An intermediate sanction.* Lanham, NY: University Press of America.

Andrews, D. A., James Bonta, and J. Stephen Wormith. 2006. The recent past and near future of risk and/or need assessment. *Crime and Delinquency* 52(1): 7–27.

Arditti, Joyce A., and April L. Few. 2006. Mothers' reentry into family life following incarceration. *Criminal Justice Policy Review* 17(1): 103–123.

Associated Press. 2006. The truth is out with second autopsy: Boy's boot-camp death now said to be result of beating. *The Kansas City Star,* March 17, A7.

Association of Paroling Authorities International. 2004. *Parole Board Survey 2004.* APAI: Association of Paroling Authorities International and National Institute of Corrections. Accessed September 1, 2006: http://www.apaintl.org/pub-paroleboardsurvey2004.html

Augustus, John. 1939. *First probation officer.* New York: National Probation Association.

—. 1972. *A report of the labors of John Augustus, for the last ten years, in aid of the unfortunate.* Montclair, NJ: Patterson Smith. (Originally published 1852)

Austin, James. 2001. Prisoner reentry: Current trends, practices, and issues. *Crime and Delinquency* 47(3): 314–334.

Bahn, Charles, and James R. Davis. 1998. Day reporting centers as an alternative to incarceration. *Journal of Offender Rehabilitation* 27: 139–150.

Barthwell, Andrea G., Peter Bokos, J. Bailey, Miriam Nisenbaum, Julien Devereux, and Edward C. Senay. 1995. Interventions/Wilmer: A continuum of care for substance abusers in the criminal justice system. *Journal of Psychoactive Drugs* 27(1): 39–47.

Barton, William, and Cheryl Justice. 2000. The John P. Craine House: A community residential program for female offenders and their children. Paper presented at the annual meeting of the American Society of Criminology, San Francisco, California, November 14–17.

Bayens, Gerald, Michael Manske, and John Ortiz Smylka. 1998. The attitudes of criminal justice workgroups toward intensive supervised probation. *American Journal of Criminal Justice* 22(2): 189–206.

Bazemore, Gordon, and Jeanne Stinchcomb. 2004. A civic engagement model of reentry: Involving community through service and restorative justice. *Federal Probation* 68(2): 14–24.

Bazemore, Gordon, and Mark Umbreit. 2001. A comparison of four restorative conferencing models. *Juvenile Justice Bulletin* (February). Washington, DC: U.S. Department of Justice, Office of Juvenile Justice and Delinquency Programs.

Beck, Allen J. 2000. *Prisoners in 1999*. Washington, DC: U.S. Department of Justice, Bureau of Justice Statistics (August).

Bernat, Frances P., William Parsonage, and Jacqueline Helfgott. 1994. Victim impact laws and the parole process in the United States: Balancing victim and inmate rights and interests. *International Review of Victimology* 3(1/2): 121–133.

Beto, Dan Richard. 2000. Reinventing probation: A history of the national movement and the Texas initiative. *Criminal Justice Mandate* 8(1): 9–13.

Binder, Arnold, Gilbert Geis, and Dickson D. Bruce. 1997. *Juvenile delinquency*, 2nd ed. Cincinnati, OH: Anderson.

Black's Law Dictionary. 1991. Abridged 6th ed. St. Paul, MN: West.

Bloom, Barbara, and Anne McDiarmid. 2000. Gender-responsive supervision and programming for women offenders in the community. In *Topics in community corrections annual issue 2000: Responding to women in the community*. Longmont, CO: LIS, Inc. and National Institute of Corrections.

Bobys, Richard. 1992. Perceived effectiveness of prisons and mental hospitals and its influence on stigmatization. *Free Inquiry in Creative Sociology* 20(1): 87–89.

Bonczar, Thomas P., and Lauren E. Glaze. 1999. *Probation and parole in the United States, 1998*. Washington, DC: U.S. Department of Justice, Bureau of Justice Statistics.

Bonta, James, S. Wallace-Capretta, and J. Rooney. 2000. A quasi-experimental evaluation of an intensive rehabilitation supervision program. *Criminal Justice and Behavior* 29(June): 312–329.

Bosco, Robert J. 1998. Connecticut probation's partnership with the private sector. In *Topics in community corrections: Annual issue 1998: Privatizing community supervision*. Longmont, CO: National Institute of Corrections, U.S. Department of Justice, pp. 8–12.

Bottcher, Jean, and Michael E. Ezell. 2005. Examining the effectiveness of boot camps: A randomized experiment with a long-term follow-up. *Journal of Research in Crime and Delinquency* 42(3): 309–332.

Bottomley, Keith. 1990. Parole in transition: A comparative study of origins, developments, and prospects for the 1990s. In *Crime and justice: A review of research*, vol. 12, edited by Michael Tonry and Norval Morris. Chicago: University of Chicago Press.

Bourque, Blair B., Mei Han, and Sarah M. Hill. 1996. *A National Survey of Aftercare Provisions for Boot Camp Graduates*. NCJ 157664. Washington, DC: National Institute of Justice.

Braithwaite, John. 1989. *Crime, shame, and reintegration*. Cambridge, NY: Cambridge University Press.

Brame, Robert, and Doris Layton MacKenzie. 1996. Shock incarceration and positive adjustment during community supervision: A multisite evaluation. In *Correctional boot camps: A tough intermediate sanction*, edited by Doris L. MacKenzie and Eugene E. Hebert. Washington, DC: U.S. Department of Justice.

Brown, J. 1997. Drug diversion courts: Are they needed and will they succeed in breaking the cycle of drug-related crime? *New England Journal on Criminal and Civil Confinement* 23(1): 63–99.

Brown, Michael P., and Preston Elrod. 1995. Electronic house arrest: An examination of citizen attitudes. *Crime and Delinquency* 41(3): 332–346.

Buckler, Kevin G., and Lawrence F. Travis. 2003. Reanalyzing the prevalence and social context of collateral consequence statutes. *Journal of Criminal Justice* 31: 435–453.

Bureau of Justice Assistance. 1996. *How to use structured fines day fines as an intermediate sanction*. Washington, DC: U.S. Department of Justice, Bureau of Justice Assistance.

—. 1998. *Critical elements in the planning, development, and implementation of successful correctional options*. Washington, DC: U.S. Department of Justice, Bureau of Justice Assistance.

Burke, Peggy B. 1995. *Abolishing parole: Why the emperor has no clothes*. Lexington, KY: American Probation and Parole Association, and California, MO: Association of Paroling Authorities, International.

—. 1997. *Policy-driven responses to probation and parole violations*. Washington, DC: U.S. Department of Justice, National Institute of Corrections (March).

Burton, Velmer S., Francis T. Cullen, and Lawrence F. Travis III. 1987. The collateral consequences of a felony conviction: A national study of state statutes. *Federal Probation* (September): 52.

Burton, Velmer S., James Marquart, Steven J. Cuvelier, Leanne Fiftal Alarid, and Robert J. Hunter. 1993. A study of attitudinal change among boot camp participants. *Federal Probation* 57(3): 46–52.

Butts, Jeffrey A., and Adele V. Harrell. 2003. Delinquents or criminals: Policy options for young offenders. Accessed May 1, 2006: http://www.urban.org/.

Byrne, James M., and Faye S. Taxman. 1994. Crime control policy and community corrections practice. *Evaluation and Program Planning* 17: 227–233.

Camp, Camille Graham, and George M. Camp. 1999. *The corrections yearbook: 1999*. Middletown, CT: Criminal Justice Institute.

Camp, Camille Graham, George M. Camp, and Bob May. 2003. *The 2002 corrections yearbook: Adult corrections*. Middletown, CT: Criminal Justice Institute, Inc.

Caputo, Gail A. 2005. Community service in Texas: Results of a probation survey. *Corrections Compendium* 30(2): 8–9, 35–37.

Carey, S., and Michael Figgin. 2004. A detailed cost analysis in a mature drug court setting. *Journal of Contemporary Criminal Justice* 20(3): 315–334.

Carter, Madeline M. (Ed.). 2001. *Responding to parole and probation violations: A handbook to guide local policy development.* Prepared for the National Institute of Corrections, U.S, Department of Justice (Washington, DC).

Carter, Madeline M., and Ann Ley. 2001. Making it work: Developing tools to carry out the policy. In *Responding to parole and probation violations: A handbook to guide local policy development,* edited by Madeline M. Carter. Washington, DC: National Institute of Corrections, U.S, Department of Justice.

Clark, Cherrie L., David W. Aziz, and Doris L. MacKenzie. 1994. *Shock incarceration in New York: Focus on treatment.* Washington, DC: National Institute of Justice (August).

Clark, John, and D. Alan Henry. 2003. *Pre-trial services programming at the start of the 21st century: A survey of pretrial services programs.* Washington, DC: Bureau of Justice Assistance (July).

Clark, Michael D. 2005. Motivational interviewing for probation staff: Increasing the readiness to change. *Federal Probation* 69(2): 22–28.

Clear, Todd, R., and Ronald Corbett. 1997. Community corrections of place. Accessed September 1, 1999: http://www.corrections.com/njaca/Fact_Sheets/Fact_sheets_start.htm.

Cohen, Neil P. 2005. *The law of probation and parole,* 2nd ed. St. Paul, MN: West Group (supplement 2005).

Cohen, Robyn L. 1995. *Probation and parole violators in state prison, 1991.* Washington, DC: U.S. Department of Justice, Bureau of Justice Statistics.

Cohen, Thomas H., and Brian A. Reaves. 2006. *Felony defendants in large urban counties, 2002.* Washington, DC: U.S. Department of Justice.

Coleman, Patrick, Jeffrey Felten-Green, and Geroma Oliver. 1998. *Connecticut's alternative sanctions program: $619 million saved in estimated capital and operating costs.* Washington, DC: Bureau of Justice Assistance Practitioner Perspectives (October).

Conte, Andrew. 2000. Ex-cons filling employer demands. *Cincinnati Post,* May 15. Accessed April 29, 2004: http://www.cincypost.com/news/2000/con/051500.html.

Cooprider, Keith W., Rosemarie Gray, and John Dunne. 2003. Pretrial services in Lake County, Illinois: Patterns of change over time, 1986–2000. *Federal Probation* 67(3): 33–41.

Corbett, Ronald P. Jr. 2000. Juvenile probation on the eve of the next millennium. *Perspectives* (Fall): 22–30.

Courtright, Kevin E., Bruce L. Berg, and Robert J. Mutchnick. 1997. The cost effectiveness of using house arrest with electronic monitoring for drunk drivers. *Federal Probation* 61(3): 19–22.

Craddock, Amy. 2000. Quasi-experimental examination of outcomes of community corrections programs established under North Carolina's structured sentencing law. Paper presented at the annual meeting of the American Society of Criminology, San Francisco, November.

Crank, John. 1996. The construction of meaning during training for probation and parole. *Justice Quarterly* 13(2): 265–290.

Cullen, Francis T., John E. Eck, and Christopher T. Lowenkamp. 2002. Environmental corrections: A new paradigm for effective probation and parole supervision. *Federal Probation* 66(2): 28–37.

Cullen, Francis T., and Karen E. Gilbert. 1982. *Reaffirming rehabilitation.* Cincinnati, OH: Anderson.

Cushman, Robert, and Dale Sechrest. 1992. Variations in the administration of probation supervision. *Federal Probation* 56(3): 19–29.

Czuchry, Michael, Tiffiny L. Sia, and Donald F. Dansereau. 2006. Improving early engagement and treatment readiness of probationers. *The Prison Journal* 86(1): 56–74.

Daly, Kathleen, and Julie Stubbs. 2006. Feminist engagement with restorative justice. *Theoretical Criminology* 10(1): 9–28.

D'Angelo, L. 2002. Management note—Women and addiction: Challenges for drug court practitioners. *The Justice System Journal* 23(3): 385–400.

Damaska, R. 1968. Adverse legal consequences of conviction and their removal: A comparative study. *Journal of Criminal Law, Criminology, & Police Science* 59: 347.

Dannerbeck, A., Paul Sundet, and Kathy Lloyd. 2002. Drug courts: Gender differences and their implications for treatment strategies. *Corrections Compendium* 27(12): 1–9.

del Carmen, Rolando V. 2003. *Criminal procedure: Law and practice,* 6th ed. Belmont, CA: Wadsworth.

del Carmen, Rolando, Maldine Beth Barnhill, Gene Bonham, Lance Hignite, and Todd Jermstad. 2001. *Civil liabilities and other legal issues for probation/parole officers and supervisors,* 3rd ed., National Institute of Corrections, U.S. Department of Justice.

del Carmen, Rolando V., Mary Parker, and Francis P. Reddington. 1998. *Briefs of leading cases in juvenile justice.* Cincinnati, OH: Anderson.

del Carmen, Rolando, Sue E. Ritter, and Betsy A. Witt. 2005. *Briefs of leading cases in corrections,* 4th ed. Cincinnati, OH: Anderson.

del Carmen, Rolando V., and Chad R. Trulson. 2006. *Juvenile justice: The system, process, and law.* Belmont, CA: Thomson/Wadsworth.

del Carmen, Rolando, Betsy Witt, Thomas Caywood, and S. Layland. 1989. *Probation law and practice in Texas.* Huntsville, TX: Sam Houston State University, Criminal Justice Center.

Deschenes, Elizabeth Piper, Susan Turner, and Joan Petersilia. 1995. A dual experiment in intensive community supervision: Minnesota's prison diversion and enhanced supervised release programs. *The Prison Journal* 75(3): 330–356.

Desktop guide to good juvenile probation practice. 1993. Washington, DC: National Center for Juvenile Justice, Office of Juvenile Justice and Delinquency Prevention [Juvenile Probation Officer Initiative Working Group].

Diggs, David, and Stephen Pieper. 1994. Using day reporting centers as an alternative to jail. *Federal Probation* 58: 9–12.

DiMascio, William M. 1997. *Seeking justice: Crime and punishment in America*. New York: Edna McConnell Clark Foundation.

Domurad, F. 1999. So you want to develop your own risk assessment instrument. In *topics in community corrections: NIC annual report 1999: Classification and Risk Assessment*. Longmont, CO: National Institute of Corrections.

Donnelly, P. G., and B. Forschner. 1984. Client success or failure in a halfway house. *Federal Probation* 48: 38–44.

—. 1987. Predictors of success in a co-correctional halfway house: A discriminant analysis. *Journal of Crime and Justice* 10: 1–22.

Duffee, David E. 1984. Models of probation supervision. In *Probation, and justice: Reconsideration of mission*, edited by Patrick D. McAnany, Doug Thomson, and David Fogel. Cambridge, MA: Oelgeschlager, Gunn, and Hain, pp. 175–201.

Durose, M. R., & Langan, Patrick A. 2004. *Felony sentences in state courts, 2002* (NCJ 206916). Washington, DC: Bureau of Justice Statistics.

Eagleton Institute of Politics, Center for Public Interest. 2002. Prisoner reentry: The state of public opinion. Rutgers, NJ: New Jersey Institute for Social Justice. Accessed July 2004: http://www.njisj.org/reports/eagleton_report.html.

Eisenberg, Michael, and Tony Fabelo. 1996. Evaluation of the Texas correctional substance abuse treatment initiative: The impact of policy research. *Crime & Delinquency* 42(2): 296–308.

Ely, John F. 1996. Inside-out: Halfway house staff management of punishment and empathy on the ambiguous boundary between prison and the outside [Unpublished Ph.D. dissertation]. University of California-Santa Barbara.

English, Kim K., and M. J. Mande. 1991. Empirical support for intervention strategies in community corrections. *Journal of Contemporary Criminal Justice* 7: 95–106.

English, Kim, Suzanne Pullen, L. Jones, and M. Kruth. 1996. *Managing adult sex offenders: A containment approach*. Lexington, KY: American Probation and Parole Association.

Erickson, Rosemary J., Wayman Crow, Louis A. Zurcher, and Archie V. Connett. 1973. *Paroled but not free*. New York: Behavioral Publications.

Evjen, Victor H. 1975. The federal probation system: The struggle to achieve it and its first 25 years. *Federal Probation* 39(2): 3–15.

Farkas, Steve. 1993. Pennsylvanians prefer alternatives to prison. *Overcrowded Times* 4(2): 1, 13–15.

Farole, Donald. 2003. The Harlem parole reentry court evaluation: Implementation and preliminary impact. New York: Center for Court Innovation. Accessed July 20, 2006: http://www.courtinnovation.org/_uploads/documents/harl emreentryeval.pdf.

Farrall, Stephen. 2003. J'accuse: Probation evaluation-research epistemologies, part one: The critique. *Criminal Justice* 32: 161–179.

Fay, Stephen J. 1995. Electronically monitored justice: A consideration of recent evidence as to its effectiveness. *Anglo-American Law Review* 24(4): 397–425.

Federal Statutes Imposing Collateral Consequences upon Conviction. 2000. Accessed September 1, 2006: http://www.sentencingproject.org/pubs_05.cfm.

Festervan, Earlene. 2003. *Women probationers: Supervision and success*. Lanham, MD: American Correctional Association.

Finn, Peter. 1997. *Sex offender community notification*. Washington DC: National Institute of Justice.

Fischer, Brenda. 2003. "Doing good with a vengeance": A critical assessment of the practices, effects and implications of drug treatment courts in North America. *Criminal Justice* 3(3): 227–248.

Fogel, David. 1979. *. . . We are the living proof . . . The justice model for corrections*, 2nd ed. Cincinnati, OH: Anderson.

Forst, Brian. 1995. Prosecution and sentencing. In *Crime*, edited by James Q. Wilson and Joan Petersilia. San Francisco, CA: Institute for Contemporary Studies, pp. 363–386.

Foucault, Michel. 1977. *Discipline and punish*. New York: Pantheon Books.

Frendle, Julie Wesley. 2004. *An overview of juvenile parole boards in the United States*. Prepared for the New Mexico Sentencing Commission.

Friel, Charles, and Joseph B. Vaughn. 1986. A consumer's guide to electronic monitoring. *Federal Probation* 50(3): 3–14.

Galaway, Burt. 1992. Restitution as innovation or unfilled promise? In *Towards a critical victimology*, edited by Ezzat A. Fattah. New York: St. Martin's Press, pp. 347–371.

Galloway, Alyson L., and Laurie A. Drapela. 2006. Are effective drug courts an urban phenomenon? *International Journal of Offender Therapy and Comparative Criminology* 50(3): 280–293.

Geerken, Michael R., and Hennessey D. Hayes. 1993. Probation and parole: Public risk and the future of incarceration alternatives. *Criminology* 31(4): 549–564.

Gemignani, Robert. 1983. Rethinking probation. *Change* 5(4): 2–3.

Gendreau, Paul. 1998. Keynote speech: What works in community corrections: Promising approaches in reducing criminal behavior. In *Successful community sanctions and services for special offenders*, edited by B. J. Auerbach and T. C. Castellano. Lanham, MD: American Correctional Association, pp. 59–74.

General Accounting Office: Harris, D. C., Charles Michael Johnson, Barry J. Seltser, Douglas M. Sloane, David P. Alexander, Stuart M. Kaufman, Pamela V. Williams, Thelma Jones, George H. Quinn, Katherine M. Wheeler, Jena Sinkfield, Jan B. Montgomery, and Ann H. Finley. 1997. *Drug courts: Overview of growth, characteristics, and results*. Washington, DC: United States General Accounting Office.

Glaser, Daniel. 1969. *The effectiveness of prison and parole systems*. Indianapolis, IN: Bobbs-Merrill.

—. 1995. *Preparing convicts for law-abiding lives: The pioneering penology of Richard A. McGee*. Albany, NY: State University of New York Press.

Glaze, Lauren E., and Seri Palla. 2005. *Probation and parole in the United States, 2004*. Washington, DC: Bureau of Justice Statistics, U.S. Department of Justice.

Goldapple, Gary C., and Dianne Montgomery. 1993. Evaluating a behaviorally based intervention to improve client retention in therapeutic community treatment for drug dependency. *Research on Social Work Practice* 31: 21–39.

Goldkamp, John S., and Michael D. White. 1998. *Restoring accountability in pretrial release: The Philadelphia pretrial release supervision experiments* [NCJ 189164]. Washington, DC: U.S. Department of Justice.

Goodwin, Catharine M. 2001. Looking at the law: Update on selected restitution issues. *Federal Probation* 65(1): 54–62.

Gordon, Jill. 2003. Aftercare. In *Encyclopedia of Juvenile Justice*, edited by McShane, Marilyn D. and Frank P. Williams III. Thousand Oaks, CA: Sage.

Gottfredson, Denise C., and M. Lyn Exum. 2002. The Baltimore city drug treatment court: One-year results from a randomized study. *Journal of Research in Crime and Delinquency* 39(3): 337–356.

Gottfredson, Denise C., Stacy S. Najaka, and Brook Kearley. 2003. Effectiveness of drug treatment courts: Evidence from a randomized trial. *Criminology & Public Policy* 2(2): 171–196.

Gottfredson, Don, Michael Gottfredson, and James Garofalo. 1997. Time served in prison and parolee outcomes among parolee risk categories. *Journal of Criminal Justice* 5: 1–12.

Gowen, Darren. 2000. Overview of the federal home confinement 1988–1996. *Federal Probation* 64(2): 11–18.

—. 2001. Remote location monitoring—A supervision strategy to enhance risk control. *Federal Probation* 65(2): 38–41.

Gray, M. Kevin, Monique Fields, and Sheila Royo Maxwell. 2001. Examining probation violations: Who, what and when. *Crime and Delinquency* 47(4): 537–557.

Greek, Cecil E. 2002. The cutting edge: Tracking probationers in space and time: The convergence of GIS and GPS systems. *Federal Probation* 66(1): 51–53.

Greenwood, Peter. 1985. *Juvenile offenders* [National Institute of Justice, Crime File Study Guide]. Washington, DC: National Institute of Justice.

Griffin, Patrick, and Patricia Torbet (Eds.). 2002. *Desktop guide to good juvenile probation practice*. Washington, DC: National Center for Juvenile Justice.

Grooms, Robert M. 1982. Recidivist. *Crime and Delinquency* 28: 541–545.

Hammett, Theodore M., Patricia Harmon, and Laura M. Maruschak. 1999. *1996-1997 update: HIV/AIDS, STDs, and TB in correctional facilities*. Washington, DC: National Institute of Justice, Bureau of Justice Statistics, and Centers for Disease Control and Prevention.

Hammett, Theodore M., Cheryl Roberts, and Sofia Kennedy. 2001. Health-related issues in prisoner reentry. *Crime and Delinquency* 47(3): 390–409.

Hansen, Christopher. 2001. The cutting edge: A survey of technological innovation: Where have all the probation officers gone? *Federal Probation* 65(1): 51–53.

Harlow, Robert E., John M. Darley, and Paul H. Robinson. 1995. The severity of intermediate sanctions: A psychophysical scaling approach for obtaining community perceptions. *Journal of Quantitative Criminology* 11(1): 71–95.

Harries, Keith. 2003. Using geographic analysis in probation and parole. *National Institute of Justice Journal* 249: 32–33.

Harris, M. Kay. 1996. Key differences among community corrections acts in the United States: An overview. *The Prison Journal* 76(2): 192–238.

Harris Poll. 1967. *Los Angeles Times*, August 14.

Hartmann, David J., Paul C. Friday, and Kevin I. Minor. 1994. Residential probation: A seven year follow-up study of halfway house discharges. *Journal of Criminal Justice* 22(6): 503–515.

Hemmens, Craig. 1998. Life in the joint and beyond: An examination of inmate attitudes and perceptions of prison, parole, and self at the time of release [Unpublished Ph.D. dissertation]. Sam Houston State University.

Hemmens, Craig, Kathryn Bennett, and Rolando del Carmen. 1998. The exclusionary rule does not apply to parole revocation hearings: An analysis of *Pennsylvania Board of Probation and Parole v. Scott*. *Criminal Law Bulletin* 35(4): 388–409.

Hensley, Denise Bray. 1995. One boy's life. *Houston Chronicle* (September 17).

Herman, Susan, and Cressida Wasserman. 2001. A role for victims in offender reentry. *Crime and Delinquency* 47(3): 428–445.

Hindman, Jan, and James M. Peters. 2001. Polygraph testing leads to better understanding adult and juvenile sex offenders. *Federal Probation* 65(3): 8–15.

Hoffman, Peter B. 1994. Twenty years of operational use of a risk prediction instrument: The United States Parole Commission's Salient Factor Score. *Journal of Criminal Justice* 22(6): 477–494.

—. Holgate, Alina M., and Ian J. Clegg. 1991. The path to probation officer burnout: New dogs, old tricks. *Journal of Criminal Justice* 19: 325–337.

Holsinger, Alex M., Christopher T. Lowenkamp, and Edward J. Latessa. 2003. Ethnicity, gender, and the level of service inventory-revised. *Journal of Criminal Justice* 31: 309–320.

Holsinger, Alex M., Arthur J. Lurigio, and Edward J. Latessa. 2001. Up to speed: Practitioners' guide to understanding the basis of assessing offender risk. *Federal Probation* 65(1): 46–50.

Holt, Norman. 1998. The current state of parole in America. In *Community corrections: Probation, parole, and intermediate sanctions*, edited by Joan Petersilia. New York: Oxford University Press, p. 36.

Holzer, Harry J. 1996. *What employers want: Job prospects for less-educated workers*. New York: Sage.

Horn, Dan. 2000. Offenders find records hard to erase. *Cincinnati Enquirer*, December 18.

Hughes, Timothy A., Doris James Wilson, and Allen J. Beck. 2001. *Trends in state parole, 1990–2000*. Washington, DC: U.S. Department of Justice, Bureau of Justice Statistics.

International Community Corrections Association. Accessed January 15, 2001: http://www.iccaweb.org/icca_info/icca_info.html.

Irwin, John. 1970. *The felon*. Englewood Cliffs, NJ: Prentice-Hall.

Israel, Michael. 2003. *Washington report* [108th Congress, Number 15 September 15]. Greenbelt, MD: Academy of Criminal Justice Sciences. Accessed April 15, 2004: http://www.acjs.org.

Jenuwine, Michael J., Ronald Simmons, and Edward Swies. 2003. Community supervision of sex offenders—Integrating probation and clinical treatment. *Federal Probation* 67(3): 20–27.

Johnson, Richard. 2001. Intensive probation for domestic violence offenders. *Federal Probation* 65(3): 36–39.

Joo, Hee-Jong, Sheldon Ekland-Olson, and William Kelly. 1995. Recidivism among paroled property offenders released during a period of prison reform. *Criminology* 33(3): 389–410.

Jones, Mark. 1995. Predictors of success and failure on intensive probation supervision. *American Journal of Criminal Justice* 19: 239–254.

Jones, Mark, and Darrell L. Ross. 1997. Electronic house arrest and boot camp in North Carolina. *Criminal Justice Policy Review* 8(4): 383–403.

Juvenile Victimization and Offending, 1993–2003. 2004. Accessed September 1, 2006: http://www.ojp.usdog.gov.bjs.

Juvenile Probation Officer Initiative Working Group. 1993. *Desktop guide to good juvenile probation practice*. Washington, DC: National Center for Juvenile Justice, Office of Juvenile Justice and Delinquency Prevention.

Karp, David R. 1998. *Community justice: An emerging field*. Lanham, MD: Rowman and Littlefield.

Karp, David R., and Todd R. Clear. 2002. *What is community justice?* Thousand Oaks, CA: Pine Forge Press.

Karuppannan, Jaishankar. 2005. Mapping and corrections: Management of offenders with geographic information systems. *Corrections Compendium* 30(1): 7–9, 31–33.

Keller, Oliver J., and Benedict S. Alper. 1970. *Halfway houses: Community-centered correction and treatment*. Lexington, MA: D.C. Heath.

Kelly, Brian J. 2001. Supervising the cyber-criminal. *Federal Probation* 65(2): 8–10.

Kelly, Phaedra Athena O'Hara. 1999. The ideology of shame: An analysis of first amendment and eighth amendment challenges to scarlet-letter probation conditions. *North Carolina Law Review* 77(2): 783–864.

Kendig, Newton, Barbara Boyle, and Anthony Swetz. 1996. The Maryland Division of Correction medical-parole program: A four-year experience, 1991 to 1994. *AIDS & Public Policy Journal* 11(1): 21–27.

Kentucky Post staff writer. 2003. Ph.D. in crime: Professor at Northern is a former convict. *Kentucky Post*, August 15. Accessed April 30, 2004: http://www.kypost.com/2003/08/15/rich081503.html.

Kilgour, D., and S. Meade. 2004. Look what boot camps done for me: Teaching and learning at Lakeview Academy. *Journal of Correctional Education* 55: 170–185.

Kittrie, Nicholas N., Elyce H. Zenoff, and Vincent A. Eng. 2002. *Sentencing, sanctions, and corrections: Federal and state law, policy, and practice*, 2nd ed. New York: Foundation Press.

Klein-Saffran, Jody. 1992. *Electronic monitoring versus halfway houses: A study of federal offenders* [Unpublished Ph.D. Dissertation]. University of Maryland.

Klockars, Carl B. Jr. 1972. A theory of probation supervision. *Journal of Criminal Law, Criminology and Police Science* 63(4): 550–557.

Krauth, Barbara, and Larry Linke. 1999. *State organizational structures for delivering adult probation services*. Longmont, CO: LIS, Inc. for the National Institute of Corrections.

Kurlychek, Megan, Patricia Torbet, and Melanie Bozynski. 1999. Focus on accountability: Best practices for juvenile court and probation. *JAIBTG Bulletin* (August): 2.

Kuzma, Susan M. 1998. Civil disabilities of convicted felons. *Corrections Today* (August): 68–72.

Langan, Patrick. 1994. Between prison and probation: Intermediate sanctions. *Science:* 791–793.

Langan, Patrick A., and Mark Cunniff. 1992. *Recidivism of felons on probation, 1986–1989*. Washington, DC: U.S. Department of Justice, Bureau of Justice Statistics (February).

Langan, Patrick A., and David J. Levin. 2002. *Recidivism of prisoners released in 1994*. Washington, DC: U.S. Department of Justice, Bureau of Justice Statistics (June).

Larivee, John J. 1995. Day reporting in Massachusetts. In *Intermediate sanctions in overcrowded times*, edited by Michael Tonry and Kate Hamilton. Boston, MA: Northeastern University Press.

Latessa, Edward J., and Alexander Holsinger. 1998. The importance of evaluating correctional programs: Assessing outcome and quality. *Corrections Management Quarterly* 2(4): 22–29.

Latessa, Edward J., and Lawrence Travis. 1991. Halfway house or probation: A comparison of alternative dispositions. *Journal of Crime and Delinquency* 14(1): 53–75.

—. 1992. Residential community correctional programs. In *Smart sentencing: The emergence of intermediate sanctions*, edited by J. M Byrne, A. J. Lurigio, and J. Petersilia. Newbury Park, CA: Sage.

Latessa, Edward, Lawrence Travis, and Alexander Holsinger. 1997. Evaluation of Ohio's community corrections act programs and community based correctional facilities [Unpublished agency report]. University of Cincinnati, Division of Criminal Justice.

Lattimore, Pamela K. 2006. Reentry, reintegration, rehabilitation, recidivism, and redemption. *The Criminologist* 31(3): 1–6.

Legal Action Center. 2004. After prison: Roadblocks to reentry: A report on state legal barriers facing people with criminal records. Accessed September 1, 2006: http://www.lac.org/roadblocks.html.

Lehman, Joseph, Trudy Gregorie Beatty, Dennis Maloney, Susan Russell, Anne Seymour, and Carol Shapiro. 2002. *The three r's of reentry*. Washington, DC: Justice Solutions.

Lehnerer, Melodye. 1992. Becoming involved: Field research at a halfway house for ex-offenders [Unpublished Ph.D. dissertation]. York University.

Leznoff, JoAnne. 1998. Privatization of community supervision as a public safety issue. In *Topics in community corrections: Annual issue 1998: Privatizing community supervision*. Longmont, CO: National Institute of Corrections, U.S. Department of Justice, pp. 19–24.

Lilly, J. Robert. 2006. Issues behind empirical EM reports. *Criminology & Public Policy* 5(1): 93–102.

Lilly, J. Robert, Richard A, Ball, G. David Curry, and Richard Smith. 1992. The Pride, Inc., program: An evaluation of 5 years of electronic monitoring. *Federal Probation* (December): 42–47.

Lindner, Charles, and Margaret R. Savarese. 1984a. The evolution of probation: Early salaries, qualifications, and hiring practices. *Federal Probation* 48(1): 3–10.

—. 1984b. The evolution of probation: The historical contributions of the volunteer. *Federal Probation* 48(2): 3–10.

—. 1984c. The evolution of probation: University settlement and the beginning of statutory probation in New York City. *Federal Probation* 48(3): 3–12.

—. 1984d. The evolution of probation: University settlement and its pioneering role in probation work. *Federal Probation* 48(4): 3–13.

Linke, Larry, and Barbara Krauth. 2000. *Perspectives from the field on the interstate compact on juveniles: Findings from a national survey* [NIC-016491]. Longmont, CO: National Institute of Corrections.

Lipton, Douglas, Robert Martinson, and J. Wilks. 1975. *The effectiveness of correctional treatment*. New York: Praeger.

Listwan, Shelley Johnson, Jody L. Sundt, Alexander M. Holsinger, and Edward J. Latessa, 2003. The effect of drug court programming on recidivism: The Cincinnati experience. *Crime and Delinquency* 49(3): 389–411.

Locke, Hubert G. 1998. Closing comments. In *Successful community sanctions and services for special offenders*, edited by B. J. Auerbach and T. C. Castellano. Lanham, MD: American Correctional Association, pp. 253–259.

Logan, Janette. 1992. HIV/AIDS-core competencies for practice: A framework for the education and training of social workers. *Social Work Education* 11(3): 22–35.

Love, Margaret Colgate. 2005. Relief from the collateral consequences of a criminal conviction: A state by state resource guide. The Sentencing Project. Accessed September 1, 2006: http://www.sentencingproject.org/rights-restoration.cfm.

Lowenkamp, Christopher T., Alexander M. Holsinger, and Edward J. Latessa. 2001. Risk/need assessment, offender classification, and the role of childhood abuse. *Criminal Justice and Behavior* 28(5): 543–563.

Lowenkamp, Christopher T., and Edward J. Latessa. 2005. Increasing the effectiveness of correctional programming through the risk principle: Identifying offenders for residential placement. *Criminology & Public Policy* 4(2): 263–290.

Lowenkamp, Christopher T., Edward J. Latessa, and Alexander M. Holsinger. 2006. The risk principle in action: What have we learned from 13,676 offenders and 97 correctional programs? *Crime and Delinquency* 52(1): 77–93.

Lubitz, Robin L., and Thomas W. Ross. 2001. Sentencing guidelines: Reflections on the future. In *Sentencing and corrections: Issues for the 21st century* (No. 10, June). Washington, DC: U.S. Department of Justice.

Lurigio, Arthur. 1987. The perception and attitudes of judges and attorneys toward intensive probation supervision. *Federal Probation* 51: 16–24.

Lurigio, Arthur J., and Robert C. Davis. 1990. Does a threatening letter increase compliance with restitution orders? A field experiment. *Crime & Delinquency* 364: 537–548.

Lutjen, Karen. 1996. Culpability and sentencing under mandatory minimums and the federal sentencing guidelines: The punishment no longer fits the criminal. *Notre Dame Journal of Law, Ethics, and Public Policy* 10(1): 389–466.

Lutze, Faith E., and David C. Brody. 1999. Mental abuse as cruel and unusual punishment: Do boot camp prisons violate the eighth amendment? *Crime and Delinquency* 45(2): 242–255.

Lutze, Faith E., R. Peggy Smith, and Nicholas P. Lovrich. 2004. A practitioner-initiated research partnership: An evaluation of neighborhood based supervision in Spokane, Washington. An unpublished manuscript.

Lynch, Mona. 1998. Waste managers? The new penology, crime fighting, and parole agent identity. *Law and Society Review* 32(4): 839–869.

Mack, Julian W. 1909. The juvenile court. *Harvard Law Review* 23: 102.

MacKenzie, Doris L. 2000. Evidence-based corrections: Identifying what works. *Crime and Delinquency* 46(4): 457–472.

MacKenzie, Doris L., Robert Brame, D. McDowall, and Claire Souryal. 1995. Boot camp prisons and recidivism in eight states. *Criminology* 33(3): 327–357.

MacKenzie, Doris L., Angela R. Gover, Gaylene Styve Armstrong, and Ojmarrh Mitchell. 2001. A national study comparing the environments of boot camps with traditional facilities for juvenile offenders. *National Institute of Justice Research in Brief*. Washington, DC: U.S. Department of Justice.

MacKenzie, Doris, L., and Eugene E. Hebert (Eds.). 1996. *Correctional boot camps: A tough intermediate sanction*. Washington, DC: U.S. Department of Justice.

MacKenzie, Doris L., and Claire Souryal. 1995. Inmates' attitude change during incarceration: A comparison of boot camp with traditional prison. *Justice Quarterly* 12(2): 325–354.

MacKenzie, Doris L., David B. Wilson, and Gaylene S. Armstrong. 2001. The impact of boot camps and traditional institutions on juvenile residents: Perceptions, adjustment, and change. *Journal of Research in Crime and Delinquency* 38(3): 279–313.

Maher, Richard J. 1994. Community service: A good idea that works. *Federal Probation* 58(2): 20–23.

—. 1997. Community service: A way for offenders to make amends. *Federal Probation* 61(1): 26–28

Maidment, MaDonna R. 2002. Toward a woman-centered approach to community-based corrections: A gendered analysis of electronic monitoring in eastern Canada. *Women and Criminal Justice* 13(4): 47–68.

Mair, George. 1995. Day centers in England and Wales. In *Intermediate sanctions in overcrowded times,* edited by Michael Tonry and Kate Hamilton. Boston, MA: Northeastern University Press.

Mair, George, and Claire Nee. 1992. Day centre reconviction rates. *British Journal of Criminology* 32: 329–339.

Maloney, Dennis, Gordon Bazemore, and Joe Hudson. 2001. The end of probation and the beginning of community corrections. *Perspectives* 25(3): 22–30.

Mansnerus, Laura. 2003. Questions rise over imprisoning sex offenders past their terms. *New York Times,* November 17: 1–6. Accessed November 18, 2003: http://www.nytimes.com.

Martin, Christine, Arthur J. Lurigio, and David E. Olson. 2003. An examination of rearrests and reincarcerations among discharged day reporting center clients. *Federal Probation* 67(1): 24–30.

Martinson, Robert. 1974. What works? Questions and answers about prison reform. *Public Interest* 35(Spring): 22–35.

Maxfield, Michael G., and Terry L. Baumer. 1990. Home detention with electronic monitoring: Comparing pretrial and postconviction programs. *Crime and Delinquency* 36(4): 521–536.

Mawhorr, Tina L. 1997. Disabled offenders and work release: An exploratory examination. *Criminal Justice Review* 22(1): 34–48.

Mayzer, Roni, and M. Kevin Gray. 2000. Probation absconders. Paper presented at the annual American Society of Criminology meeting, San Francisco, California, November 15–18.

McDevitt, Jack, and Robyn Miliano. 1992. Day reporting centers: An innovative concept in intermediate sanctions. In *Smart sentencing: The emergence of intermediate sanctions,* edited by James M. Byrne, Arthur J. Lurigio, and Joan Petersilia. Newbury Park, CA: Sage.

McDonald, Douglas, Judith Greene, and Charles Worzella. 1992. *Day fines in American courts: The Staten Island and Milwaukee experiments.* Washington, DC: U.S. Department of Justice, National Institute of Justice.

McKay, Brian. 2002. The state of sex offender probation supervision in Texas. *Federal Probation* 66(1): 16–20.

McManus, Patrick D., and Lynn Z. Barclay. 1994. *Community Corrections Act: Technical assistance manual.* College Park, MD: American Correctional Association.

McShane, Marilyn, Frank P. Williams, and H. Michael Dolny. 2002. Do standard risk prediction instruments apply to female parolees? *Women and Criminal Justice* 13(2/3): 163.

Michigan Judicial Institute. 2003. Case review and probation revocation in designated case and automatic waiver proceedings. In *Juvenile justice benchbook* (Revised edition), pp. 457–467.

Milligan, Jessie. 2001. Blood, sweat, and fears. *Fort Worth Star Telegram Sunday Magazine,* March 18, 2001.

Minor, Kevin I., James B. Wells, and Crissy Sims. 2003. Recidivism among federal probationers-predicting sentence violations. *Federal Probation* 67(1): 31–36.

Moczydlowski, K. 1980. Predictors of success in a correctional halfway house for youthful and adult offenders. *Corrective and Social Psychiatry and Journal of Behavior Technology, Methods, and Therapy* 26: 59–72.

Moreland, John. History and prophecy: John Augustus and his successors. An unpublished paper presented at the 35th Annual Conference of the National Probation Association, Boston, Massachusetts, May 29, 1941.

Morgan, Kathryn D. 1994. Factors associated with probation outcome. *Journal of Criminal Justice* 22: 341–353.

—. 1995. Variables associated with successful probation outcome. *Journal of Offender Rehabilitation* 22(3/4): 141–153.

Morgan, Kathryn, and Brent L. Smith. 2005. Victims, punishment, and parole: The effect of victim participation on parole hearings. *Criminology & Public Policy* 4(2): 333–360.

Morris, Norval. 2002. *Maconochie's gentlemen: The story of Norfolk Island and the roots of modern prison reform.* New York: Oxford University Press.

Morris, Norval, and Michael Tonry. 1990. *Between prison and probation: Intermediate punishments in a rational sentencing system.* New York: Oxford University Press.

Moscicki, Ronald W. 1996. If you don't take responsibility, you take orders. In *Juvenile and adult boot camps,* edited by American Correctional Association. Lanham, MD: American Correctional Association.

Muhammad, Mika'il A. 1996. Prisoners' perspectives on strategies for release. *Journal of Offender Rehabilitation* 23: 131–152.

Mumola, Christopher J. 2000. *Incarcerated parents and their children.* Washington, DC: U.S. Department of Justice, Bureau of Justice Statistics.

Mumola, Christopher J., with Thomas P. Bonczar. 1998. *Substance abuse and treatment of adults on probation, 1995.* Washington, DC: U.S. Department of Justice, Bureau of Justice Statistics.

National Advisory Commission on Criminal Justice Standards and Goals. 1973. *Report on corrections.* Washington, DC: U.S. Department of Justice.

National Institute of Corrections and the Council of State Governments. 2002. *Interstate compact for adult offender supervision: State officials guide.* Longmont, CO: National Institute of Corrections, U.S. Department of Justice (July).

National Institute of Justice. 1994. *Program Focus Shock Incarceration in New York.* Washington, DC: U.S. Department of Justice, National Institute of Justice (August).

Nellis, Mike. 2006. Surveillance, rehabilitation, and electronic monitoring: Getting the issues clear. *Criminology & Public Policy* 5(1): 103–108.

Newville, Lanny L. 2001. Cyber crime and the courts: Investigating and supervising the information age offender. *Federal Probation* 65(2): 11–17.

New York State Division of Parole, Office of Policy Analysis and Information. 1993. Overview of the Parole Revocation Process in New York. In *Reclaiming offender accountability: Intermediate sanctions for probation and parole violators,* edited by Edward E. Rhine. Laurel, MD: American Correctional Association.

Nielsen, Amie L., Frank R. Scarpitti, and James Inciardi. 1996. Integrating the therapeutic community and work release for drug-involved offenders: The CREST program. *Journal of Substance Abuse Treatment* 13(4): 349–358.

Nieto, Marcus. 1996. *The changing role of probation in California's criminal justice system.* Sacramento, CA: California Research Bureau.

Norman, Michael D., and Robert C. Wadman. 2000. Probation department sentencing recommendations in two Utah counties. *Federal Probation* 64(2): 47–51.

North Carolina Sentencing and Policy Advisory Commission. 1994. *Structured sentencing for felonies-training and reference manual.* Raleigh, NC: Author.

Novack, S., B. Galaway, and J. Hudson. 1980. Victim offender perceptions of the fairness of restitution and community service sanctions. In *Victims, offenders, and alternative sanctions,* edited by J. Hudson and B. Galaway. Lexington, MA: D. C. Heath/Lexington Books, pp. 63–69.

OJJDP. 1999. Reintegration, Supervised Release, and Intensive Aftercare. Juvenile Justice Bulletin. Accessed April 15, 2004: http:// ojjdp.ncjrs.org/jjbulletin/9907_3/ contents. html.

Office for the Victims of Crime. 2002. *Victims' rights and services.* Washington, DC: U.S. Department of Justice, Office for Victims of Crime.

Office of the Pardon Attorney. 1996. *Civil disabilities of convicted offenders.* Washington, DC: U.S. Department of Justice.

Ogden, Thomas G., and Cary Horrocks. 2001. Pagers, digital, audio, and kiosk: Officer assistants. *Federal Probation* 65(2): 35–37.

Olson, David E., Brendan Dooley, and Candice M. Kane. 2004. The relationship between gang membership and inmate recidivism. *Illinois Criminal Justice Information Authority Research Bulletin* 2(12): 1–12.

Ostrom, Brian J., Matthew Kleiman, Fred Cheesman, Randall M. Hansen, and Neal B. Kauder. 2002. *Offender risk assessment in Virginia.* Williamsburg, VA: National Center for State Courts.

Outlaw, M.C., and R. Barry Ruback. 1999. Predictors and outcomes of victim restitution orders. *Justice Quarterly* 16: 847–869.

Padgett, Kathy G., William D. Bales, and Thomas G. Blomberg. 2006. Under surveillance: An empirical test of the effectiveness and consequences of electronic monitoring. *Criminology & Public Policy* 5(1): 61–92.

Palacios, Victoria J. 1994. Go and sin no more: Rationality and release decisions by parole boards. *South Carolina Law Review* 45: 613.

Palmer, Ted. 1992. *The re-emergence of correctional intervention.* Newbury Park, CA: Sage.

—. 1994. *A profile of correctional effectiveness and new direction for research.* Albany, NY: State University of New York Press.

Palumbo, Dennis, Mary Clifford, and Joann K. Snyder-Joy. 1992. From net-widening to intermediate sanctions: The transformation of alternatives to incarceration from benevolence to malevolence. In *Smart sentencing: The emergence of intermediate sanctions,* edited by James M. Byrne, Arthur J. Lurigio, and Joan Petersilia. Newbury Park, CA: Sage.

Panzarella, Robert. 2002. Theory and practice of probation on bail in the report of John Augustus. *Federal Probation* 66(3): 38–42.

Paparozzi, Mario A. and Paul Gendreau. 2005. An intensive supervision program that worked: Service delivery, professional orientation, and organizational supportiveness. *The Prison Journal* 85(4): 445–466.

Parent, Dale. 1990. *Day reporting centers for criminal offenders: A descriptive analysis of existing programs.* Washington, DC: U.S. Department of Justice.

—. 1993. Structuring policies to address sanctions for absconders and violators. In *Reclaiming offender accountability: Intermediate sanctions for probation and parole violators,* edited by Edward E. Rhine. Laurel, MD: American Correctional Association.

—. 1995. Day reporting centers. In *Intermediate sanctions in overcrowded times,* edited by Michael Tonry and Kate Hamilton. Boston, MA: Northeastern University Press.

—. 1996. Boot camps and prison crowding. In *Correctional boot camps: A tough intermediate sanction,* edited by Doris L. MacKenzie and Eugene E. Hebert. Washington, DC: U.S. Department of Justice.

—. 2003. *Correctional boot camps: Lessons from a decade of research.* Washington, DC: National Institute of Justice.

Parent, Dale, Jim Byrne, Vered Tsafaty, Laua Valade, and Julie Esselman. 1995. *Day reporting centers,* vol. 1. Washington, DC: U.S. Department of Justice, National Institute of Justice.

Parent, Dale, Terence Dunworth, Douglas McDonald, and William Rhodes. 1997. *Key legislative issues in criminal justice: The impact of sentencing guidelines.* Washington, DC: U.S. Department of Justice, National Institute of Justice (November).

Parent, Dale G., Dan Wentworth, Peggy Burke, and Becky Ney. 1994. *Responding to probation and parole violations* Washington, DC: U.S. Department of Justice.

Parisi, Nicolette. 1981. A taste of the bars. *Journal of Criminal Law and Criminology* 72: 1109–1123.

Parsonage, William H., and W. Conway Bushey. 1989. The victimization of probation and parole workers in the line of duty: An exploratory study. *Criminal Justice Policy Review* 2(4): 26–45.

Payne, Brian K., and Randy R. Gainey. 2002. The influence of demographic factors on the experience of house arrest. *Federal Probation* 66(3): 64–70.

—. 2004. The electronic monitoring of offenders released from jail or prison: Safety, control, and comparisons to the incarceration experience. *The Prison Journal* 84(4): 413–435.

Petersilia, Joan. 1987. *Expanding options for criminal sentencing.* Santa Monica, CA: RAND (November).

—. 1995. A crime control rationale for reinvesting in community corrections. *The Prison Journal* 75(4): 479–496.

—. 1998a. Probation in the United States, part 1. *Perspectives* 22(Spring): 30–41.

—. 1998b. *Community corrections: Probation, parole, and intermediate sanctions.* New York: Oxford University Press.

—. 2000a. Parole and prisoner reentry in the United States, part 1. *Perspectives* 24(Summer): 32–46.

—. 2000b. When prisoners return to the community: Political, economic, and social consequences. In *Sentencing and corrections: Issues for the 21st century* [paper 9 from the Executive Sessions on Sentencing and Corrections]. Washington DC: U.S. Department of Justice (November).

—. 2002. *Reforming probation and parole in the 21st century.* Lanham, MD: American Correctional Association.

—. 2003. *When prisoners come home.* New York: Oxford University Press.

—. 1993a. *Evaluating intensive supervised probation/parole: Results of a nationwide experiment* [NCJ 141637]. Washington, DC: U.S. Department of Justice, National Institute of Justice.

—. 1993b. Intensive probation and parole. In *Crime and justice: A review of research,* vol. 17, edited by Michael Tonry. Chicago: University of Chicago Press.

Petersilia, Joan, Susan Turner, James Kahan, and J. Peterson. 1985. *Granting felons probation: Public risks and alternatives.* Santa Monica, CA: RAND.

Phillips, Kirby. 2001. Reducing Alcohol-Related Crime Electronically. *Federal Probation* 65(2): 42–44.

Pollock, Jocelyn. 1999. *Criminal women.* Cincinnati, OH: Anderson.

Prendergast, Michael, Jean Wellisch, and Mamie Mee Wong. 1996. Residential treatment for women parolees following prison-based drug treatment: Treatment experiences, needs and service, outcomes. *The Prison Journal* 76(3): 253–274.

President's Commission on Law Enforcement and Administration of Justice. 1967. *The challenge of crime in a free society.* Washington, DC: U.S. Government Printing Office.

Proctor, Jon L. 1999. The new parole: An analysis of parole board decision making as a function of eligibility. *Journal of Crime and Justice* 22(2): 193–217.

Purkiss, Marcus, Misty Kiefer, Craig Hemmens, and Velmer S. Burton. 2003. Probation officer functions—A statutory analysis. *Federal Probation* 67(1): 12–23.

Putting a sterner face on juvenile justice. 1997. *Christian Science Monitor,* May 9.

Puzzanchera, Charles M. 2000. Delinquency cases waived to criminal court: 1988–1997. OJJDP Fact Sheet (February).

Quinn, Frederick. 2002. *The courthouse at Indian Creek.* Santa Ana, CA: Seven Locks Press.

Rainey, James. 2002. Probation cadets see job from behind bars. *Los Angeles Times,* February 8, p. A3.

Ransom, George, and Mary Ellen Mastorilli. 1993. The Massachusetts boot camp: Inmate anecdotes. *The Prison Journal* 73(3/4): 307–318.

Reddington, Frances P., and Betsy Wright Kreisel. 2000. Training juvenile probation officers: National trends and practice. *Federal Probation* 64(2): 28–32.

—. 2003. Basic fundamental skills training for juvenile probation officers: Results of a nationwide survey of curriculum content. *Federal Probation* 67(1): 41–45.

Reichel, Philip, and Billie Sudbrack. 1994. Differences among eligibles: Who gets an ISP sentence? *Federal Probation* 58(4): 51–58.

Reinventing Probation Council [Manhattan Institute]. 1999. Broken windows probation: The next step in fighting crime. *Civic Report* 7 (August).

Reske, Henry J. 1996. Scarlet letter sentences. *ABA Journal* 82: 16–17.

Rhine, Edward E. 2002. Why "what works" matters under the "broken windows" model of supervision. *Federal Probation* 66(2): 38–42.

Rhine, Edward E., William R. Smith, and Ronald W. Jackson. 1991. *Paroling authorities: Recent history and current practice.* Laurel, MD: American Correctional Association.

Richards, Stephen C., and Richard S. Jones. 1997. Perpetual incarceration machine: Structural impediments to post-prison success. *Journal of Contemporary Criminal Justice* 13(1): 4–22.

Richie, Beth E. 2001. Challenges incarcerated women face as they return to their communities: Findings from life history interviews. *Crime and Delinquency* 47(3): 368–389.

Roberts, Albert. 2004. *Juvenile Justice Sourcebook: Past, Present, and Future.* Oxford: Oxford University Press.

Robinson, Laurie, and Jeremy Travis. 2000. Managing prisoner reentry for public safety. *Federal Sentencing Reporter* 12(5) (March/April).

Roman, John, Wendy Townsend, and Avinash Singh Bhati. 2003. *Recidivism rates for drug court graduates: Nationally based estimates* [NCJ 201229]. Washington, DC: U.S. Department of Justice.

Rothman, David J. 1980. *Conscience and convenience: The asylum and its alternatives in progressive America*. Boston, MA: Little, Brown.

Rotman, Edgardo. 1995. The failure of reform. In *The Oxford history of the prison*, edited by Norval Morris and David Rothman. New York: Oxford University Press, pp. 71–197.

Roy, Sudipto. 1994. Adult offenders in an electronic home detention program: Factors related to failure. *Journal of Offender Monitoring* 7: 17–21.

—. 1997. Five years of electronic monitoring of adults and juveniles in Lake County, Indiana: A comparative study on factors related to failure. *Journal of Crime and Justice* 20: 141–60.

Roy, Sudipto, and Jennifer N. Grimes. 2002. Adult offenders in a day reporting center—A preliminary study. *Federal Probation* 66(1): 44–50.

Ruback, R. Barry, and Mark H. Bergstrom. 2006. Economic sanctions in criminal justice: Purposes, effects, and implications. *Criminal Justice and Behavior* 33(2): 242–273.

Ruback, R. Barry, Gretchen R. Ruth, and Jennifer N. Shaffer. 2005. Assessing the impact of statutory change: A statewide multilevel analysis of restitution orders in Pennsylvania. *Crime and Delinquency* 51(3): 318–342.

Ruby, Charles. 1984. Defusing the hostile ex-offender: Rational behavior training. *Emotional First Aid: A Journal of Crisis Intervention* 1(1): 17–22.

Ruddell, Rick, Brian Roy, and Sita Diehl. 2004. Diverting offenders with mental illness from jail: A tale of two states. *Corrections Compendium* 29(5): 1–5, 38–42.

Sabol, William J., William P. Adams, Barbara Parthasarathy, and Y. Yuan. 2000. Offenders returning to federal prison, 1986–1997 [Special report]. Washington, DC: U.S. Department of Justice, Bureau of Justice Statistics (September).

Sacks, Howard R., and Charles H. Logan. 1980. *Parole: Crime prevention or crime postponement?* Storrs, CT: University of Connecticut School of Law Press.

Samenow, Stanton E. 1984. *Inside the criminal mind*. New York: Times Books.

Sandhu, Harjit S., Richard A. Dodder, and Minu Mathur. 1993. House arrest: Success and failure rates in residential and nonresidential community-based programs. *Journal of Offender Rehabilitation* 19(1/2): 131–44.

Scharr, Timothy M. 2001. Interactive video training for firearms safety. *Federal Probation* 65(2): 45–51.

Schloss, Christine S., and Leanne F. Alarid. 2007. Standards in the privatization of probation services: A statutory analysis. *Criminal Justice Review* (forthcoming).

Schneider, Anne. 1986. Restitution and recidivism rates of juvenile offenders: Four experimental studies. *Criminology* 24(3): 533–552.

Schwaner, Shawn. 1997. They can run, but can they hide? A profile of parole violators at large. *Journal of Crime and Justice* 20(2): 19–32.

Schwaner, Shawn L., Deanna McGaughey, and Richard Tewksbury. 1998. Situational constraints and absconding behavior: Toward a typology of parole fugitives. *Journal of Offender Rehabilitation* 27(1/2): 37–55.

Scott, Jim. 1997. Deconsolidation: Design for the future stolen from the past. *Journal of the Texas Probation Association* 9(1): 1.

Seiter, Richard P. 2002. Prisoner reentry and the role of parole officers. *Federal Probation* 66(3): 50–54.

Seiter, Richard P., and Karen R. Kadela. 2003. Prisoner reentry: What works, what does not, and what is promising. *Crime and Delinquency* 49(3): 360–388.

Sentencing Accountability Commission and the Statistical Analysis Center. 2005. First Year Assessment of the 2003 Probation Reform Law's Impact on the Administration of Justice in Delaware (Senate Bill 50 & 150). Report prepared January 15, 2005. Accessed May 10, 2006: http://www.state.de.us/budget/sac/publications/sb50.pdf.

Sentencing Project. 1998. *Felony Disenfranchisement Laws in the United States*. Accessed June 15, 2001: http://www.hrw.org/reports98/vote/usvot98o.htm.

Shelden, Randall G. 1999. Detention diversion advocacy: An evaluation [OJJDP Juvenile Justice Bulletin]. Washington, DC: Office of Juvenile Justice and Delinquency Prevention.

Shepherd, Robert E. Jr. 1999. The juvenile court at 100 years: A look back. In *Juvenile justice: An evolving juvenile court, 100th anniversary of the juvenile court, 1899–1999*. Washington, DC: National Center for Juvenile Justice, Office of Juvenile Justice and Delinquency Prevention.

Sickmund, Melissa. 2003. *Juveniles in court* [National Report Series Bulletin,]. Washington, DC: Office of Juvenile Justice and Delinquency Prevention.

Siedschlaw, Kurt D., and Beth A. Wiersma. 2005. Costs and outcomes of a work ethic camp: How do they compare to a traditional prison facility? *Corrections Compendium* 30(6): 1–5, 28–30.

Silverstein, Martin. 1997. Doing justice: National parole board decision making [Unpublished Ph.D. dissertation]. Arizona State University, Tempe.

Sims, Barbara, and Mark Jones. 1997. Predicting success or failure on probation: Factors associated with felony probation outcomes. *Crime and Delinquency* 43: 314–327.

Skeem, Jennifer L., Paula Emke-Francis, and Jennifer Eno Louden. 2006. Probation, mental health, and mandated treatment. *Criminal Justice and Behavior* 33(2): 158–184.

Slate, Risdon N. 2003. From the jailhouse to Capitol Hill: Impacting mental health court legislation and defining what constitutes a mental health court. *Crime and Delinquency* 49(1): 6–29.

Slate, Risdon N., Richard Feldman, Erik Roskes, and Migdalia Baerga. 2004. Training federal probation officers as mental health specialists. *Federal Probation* 68(3): 9–15.

Slate, Risdon N., W. Wesley Johnson, and Terry L. Wells. 2000. Up to speed: Probation officer stress: Is there an organizational solution? *Federal Probation* 64(1): 56–59.

Slate, Risdon N., Erik Roskes, Richard Feldman, and Migdalia Baerga. 2003. Doing justice for mental illness and society: Federal probation and pretrial service officers as mental health specialists. *Federal Probation* 67(3): 13–19.

Sluder, Richard, Robert Shearer, and Dennis Potts. 1991. Probation officers' role perceptions and attitudes toward firearms. *Federal Probation* 55: 3–11.

Small, Shawn E., and Sam Torres. 2001. Arming probation officers: Enhancing public confidence and officer safety. *Federal Probation* 65(3): 24–28.

Smith, Brent L., Erin Watkins, and Kathryn Morgan. 1997. The effect of victim participation on parole decisions: Results from a southeastern state. *Criminal Justice Policy Review* 8(1): 57–74.

Smith, Michael E. 2001. What future for "public safety" and "restorative justice" in community corrections? *Sentencing and corrections: Issues for the 21st century* (No. 11, June). Washington, DC: U.S. Department of Justice.

Smith, Michael E., and Walter J. Dickey. 1999. Reforming sentencing and corrections for just punishment and public safety. *Sentencing and corrections: Issues for the 21st century* (No. 4). Washington, DC: U.S. Department of Justice.

Snyder, Howard, and Melissa Sickmund. 1995. *Juvenile offenders and victims: A national report.* Washington, DC: National Center for Juvenile Justice, Office of Juvenile Justice and Delinquency Prevention (August).

—. 1999. *Juvenile offenders and victims: 1999 national report.* Washington, DC: National Center for Juvenile Justice (September).

—. 2006. *Juvenile offenders and victims: 2006 national report.* Washington, DC: Department of Justice, Office of Justice Programs, Office of Juvenile Justice and Delinquency Prevention

Solomon, Amy L. 2006. Does parole supervision work? Research findings and policy opportunities. *Perspectives* (Spring): 26–37. Accessed September 1, 2006: http://www.urban.org/uploadedpdf/1000908_parole_supervision.pdf.

Stageberg, Paul, and Bonnie Wilson. 2005. *Recidivism among Iowa probationers.* Iowa Division of Criminal and Juvenile Justice Planning. Accessed May 10, 2006: http://www.state.ia.us/government/dhr/cjjp/images/pdf/recidivism%20among%20Iowa%20probationers.pdf#.

State of New Hampshire, Human Resources. 2006. Accessed September 1, 2006: http://nh.gov/hr/classpec_j/5462.htm.

State of Oregon, Department of Administrative Services, Juvenile Parole and Probation Officer. Accessed September 1, 2006: http://www.hr.das.state.or.us/hrsd/class/6634.HTM.

Steiner, Benjamin. 2004. Treatment retention: A theory of post-release supervision for the substance-abusing offender. *Federal Probation* 68(3): 24–29.

Stewart Law Firm. 2000. Expungement under the New Jersey Code of Criminal Justice. Accessed March 19, 2001: http://home.pro-usa.net/rstewart/lexpunge.htm.

Stinchcomb, Jeanne B., and Daryl Hippensteel. 2001. Presentence investigation reports: A relevant justice

model tool or a medical model relic? *Criminal Justice Policy Review* 12(2): 164–177.

Storm, John P. 1997. What United States probation officers do. *Federal Probation* 61(1): 13–18.

Stowe, Michael L. 1994. Professional orientation of probation officers: Ideology and personality [Unpublished Ph.D. dissertation]. University of Pittsburgh.

Taxman, Faye. 2002. Supervision—Exploring the dimensions of effectiveness. *Federal Probation* 66(2): 14–27.

Taxman, Faye S., and Jeffrey A. Bouffard. 2003. Drug treatment in the community—A case study of system integration issues. *Federal Probation* 67(2): 4–14.

Tewksbury, Richard. 2002. Validity and utility of the Kentucky sex offender registry. *Federal Probation* 66(1): 21–26.

Tonry, Michael. 1997. *Intermediate sanctions in sentencing guidelines.* Washington, DC: U.S. Department of Justice, National Institute of Justice (May).

—. 1998. Evaluating intermediate sanction programs. In *Community corrections: Probation, parole and intermediate sanctions,* edited by Joan Petersilia. New York: Oxford University Press.

—. 1999a. Parochialism in U.S. sentencing policy. *Crime and Delinquency* 45(1): 48–65.

—. 1999b. Reconsidering indeterminate and structured sentencing. *Sentencing and corrections: Issues for the 21st century.* Washington, DC: U.S. Department of Justice.

—. Travis, Jeremy. 2000. But they all come back: Rethinking prisoner reentry, *Sentencing and corrections: Issues for the 21st century.* Washington, DC: U.S. Department of Justice.

Turner, Michael G., Francis T. Cullen, Jody L. Sundt, and Brandon K. Applegate. 1997. Public tolerance for community-based sanctions. *The Prison Journal* 77(1): 6–26.

Turner, Susan, and Joan Petersilia. 1996a. *Day fines in four jurisdictions.* Santa Monica, CA: RAND.

—. 1996b. Work release in Washington: Effects on recidivism and correctional costs. *The Prison Journal* 76(2): 138–164.

Twill, Sarah E., Larry Nackerud, Edwin Risler, Jeffrey Bernat, and David Taylor. 1998. Changes in measured loneliness, control, and social support among parolees in a halfway house. *Journal of Offender Rehabilitation* 27(3/4): 77–92.

—. 2004. Disenfranchisement and the civil reintegration of convicted felons. Accessed May 15, 2006: http://72.14.203.104/search?=cache:1aXjPKfm_MJ:www.soc.umn.edu/~uggen?Uggen_.

Ulrich, Thomas E. 2002. Pretrial diversion in the federal court system. *Federal Probation* 66(3): 30–37.

Umbreit, Mark S. 1999. Restorative justice: What works. In *Research to results: Effective community corrections,* edited by Patricia M. Harris. Lanham, MD: American Correctional Association.

Umbreit, Mark S., and Robert B. Coates. 1993. Cross-site analysis of victim–offender mediation in four states. *Crime and Delinquency* 39: 565–585.

Umbreit, Mark S., Robert B. Coates, and Betty Vos. 2001. The impact of victim–offender mediation: Two decades of research. *Federal Probation* 65(3): 29–35.

U.S. Department of Justice. 1974. *Attorney general's survey of release procedures.* New York: Arno.

—. 2005a. *Compendium of federal justice statistics, 2003.* Washington, DC: U.S. Department of Justice.

—. 2005b. 28 CFR Part 2: Paroling, recommitting, and supervising federal prisoners: Prisoners serving sentences under the U.S and D.C. codes. *Federal Register* 70(70), April 13, 2005: 19262.

—. 2006. *Sourcebook of criminal justice statistics 2005.* Washington, DC: U.S. Department of Justice. Accessed: http://www.albany.edu/sourcebook.

U.S. Department of Justice, Bureau of Justice Statistics. 1995. *Correctional Populations in the United States 1994.* Washington, DC: U.S. Department of Justice.

U.S. Department of Labor. 1990. *Guidebook for operation of the federal bonding program.* Washington, DC: U.S. Government Printing Office (November).

—. 2006. *Occupational outlook handbook, 2006–07 edition.* Probation officers and correctional treatment specialists, Bureau of Labor Statistics. Accessed April 10, 2006: http://www.bls.gov/oco/ocos265.htm.

U.S. Parole Commission. 2003. *Rules and procedures manual, revised August 15, 2003.* Washington, DC: U.S. Parole Commission. Accessed September 1, 2006: http://www.usdoj.gov/uspc/rules_ procedures/rulesmanual.htm.

—. 2006. Answering your questions. Accessed June 1, 2006: http://www.usdoj.gov/uspc/questionstxt.htm.

U.S. Sentencing Commission. 2002a. *2001 Sourcebook of federal sentencing statistics.* Washington, DC: U.S. Sentencing Commission.

U.S. Sentencing Commission. 2002b. *Federal Sentencing Guidelines* Chapter 3603, 1–10:1001–1002. Accessed September 1, 2006: http://www.ussc.gov/2002guid/ TABCON02.htm

Van Ness, Daniel, and Karen Strong. 1997. *Restoring justice.* Cincinnati, OH: Anderson.

Vigorita, Michael S. 2002. Fining practices in felony courts: An analysis of offender, offense, and systemic factors. *Corrections Compendium* 27(11): 1–5, 26.

Vito, Gennaro, and Harry Allen. 1981. Shock probation in Ohio: A comparison of outcomes. *International Journal of Offender Therapy and Comparative Criminology* 25: 70–76.

Vito, Gennaro, D.G. Wilson, and Edward J. Latessa. 1991. Comparison of the dead: Attributes and outcomes of Furman-commuted death row inmates in Kentucky and Ohio. In *The Death Penalty in America: Current Research,* edited by Robert M. Bohm. Cincinnati, OH: Anderson, pp. 101–111.

Vollum, Scott, and Chris Hale. 2002. Electronic monitoring: A research review. *Corrections Compendium* 27(7): 1–4, 23–27.

von Hirsch, Andrew. 1976. *Doing justice: The choice of punishments.* New York: Hill and Wang.

von Zielbauer, Paul. 2003. Court treatment system is found to help drug offenders stay clean. *New York Times,* November 9. Health section. Accessed at: www.nytimes. com.

Walker, Donald R. 1988. *Penology for profit.* College Station, TX: Texas A&M University Press.

Walker, Lorenn. 2002. Conferencing: A new approach for juvenile justice in Honolulu. *Federal Probation* 661: 38–43.

Walsh, C. L., and S. H. Beck. 1990. Predictors of recidivism among halfway house residents. *American Journal of Criminal Justice* 15(1): 137–156.

Warren, Jennifer. 2006. Plan puts female inmates in centers by their families. *Los Angeles Times,* February 11, 2006. Accessed June 1, 2006: http://www.latimes.com/news/ local/la-me-women11feb11,0,6116670.story?track= tothtml.

Wells, Terry L. 1997. Halfway house counselors: An empirical assessment of job orientation [Unpublished Ph.D. dissertation]. Sam Houston State University.

Wells, Terry, Sharla Colbert, and Risdon N. Slate. 2006. Gender matters: Differences in state probation officer stress. *Journal of Contemporary Criminal Justice* 22(1): 63–79.

West-Smith, Mary, Mark R. Pogrebin, and Eric D. Poole. 2000. Denial of parole: An inmate perspective. *Federal Probation* 64(2): 3–10.

Whitehead, John T. 1985. Job burnout in probation and parole: Its extent and intervention implications. *Criminal Justice and Behavior* 12(1): 91–110.

—. Wicharaya, Tamask. 1995. *Simple theory, hard reality: The impact of sentencing reforms on courts, prisons, and crime.* New York: State University of New York Press.

Wilkinson, Reginald A., and Edward E. Rhine. 2005. The international association of reentry: Mission and future. *Journal of Correctional Education* 56(2): 139–145.

Wilkinson, Reginald A., Edward E. Rhine, and Martha Henderson-Hurley. 2005. Reentry in Ohio corrections: A catalyst for change. *Journal of Correctional Education* 56(2): 158–172.

Williams, Frank P. III, Marilyn D. McShane, and H. Michael Dolny. 2000a. Developing a parole classification instrument for use as a management tool. *Corrections Management Quarterly* 4(4): 45–59.

—. 2000b. Predicting parole absconders. *The Prison Journal* 80(1): 24–38.

Williams, Frank P. III, Marilyn D. McShane, Lorraine Samuels, and H. Michael Dolny. 2000. The youngest adult parolees: Do they have different parole experiences? Paper presented at the annual meeting of the American Society of Criminology, San Francisco, California, November 14–17.

Wilson, James A., and Robert C. Davis. 2006. Good intentions meet hard realities: An evaluation of the Project Greenlight reentry program. *Criminology & Public Policy* 5(2): 303–338.

Wines, Fredrick H. 1919. *Punishment and reformation: A study of the penitentiary system.* New York: T.Y. Crowell.

Wolf, Thomas J. 1997. What United States pretrial services officers do. *Federal Probation* 61(1): 19–24.

Wright, Martin. 1996. *Justice for victims and offenders: A restorative response to crime,* 2nd ed. Winchester, England: Waterside Press.

Zevitz, Richard, and Mary Ann Farkas. 2000. The impact of sex-offender community notification on probation/parole in Wisconsin. *International Journal of Offender Therapy and Comparative Criminology* 44(1): 8–21.

Codes

California Interstate Compact on Juveniles, Cal. Welf. and Inst. Code, secs. 1300–1308 (West).

California Penal Code, sec. 1203, 4853 (West).

Colorado Revised Statutes 1998, sec. 24–72–308.

Community Corrections Act, Oregon Revised Statutes 423.505 (Oregon Laws 1995).

Federal Rules of Criminal Procedure, Art. 3564.

Federal Criminal Code and Rules, 2004. Belmont, CA: West.

Illinois Unified Code of Corrections, sec. 1005–5–5(d).

Indiana Juvenile Code Title 31, Article 6, Chapter 9, Section 31–6–9–4(a).

McKune v. Lile 536 U.S. 24 2002, 224 F. 3d. 1175.

Model Penal Code, sec. 7.07 (5); sec. 301.2.

N.H. Rev. Stat. Ann. sec. 607–A:5.

New York Penal Law, sec. 65.00–1 (McKinney).

Texas Code of Criminal Procedure, Article 42.12, Sec. 7, Sec. 11(1), Sec. 20, Sec. 22(a)(1). (Vernon).

Ill. Unified Code of Corrections sec. 1005–6–5(2).

United States Codes, Title 10, U.S.C., sec. 504; Title 11, U.S.C.A., sec. 1328 (a)(3); Title 18 U.S.C. sec. 921 (a)(20); sec. 922g1; sec. 3561; sec. 3563(a)(2); sec. 3563 (b)(11); sec. 3583 (e)(3); sec. 3606; sec. 5037 (c)(1); sec. 5037 (c)(2); Title 28 U.S.C. sec. 235(a)(1)(B)(ii)(IV); sec. 1865 (b)(5); Title 29 U.S.C., sec. 405.

U.S. Constitution, Article 1.

Wis. Stat. Ann. sec. 57.078.

Court Cases

Ballenger v. State, 436 S.E.2d 793 (Ga. App. 1993).

Bearden v. Georgia, 461 U.S. 660 (1983).

Beecham v. United States, 511 U.S. 368 (1994).

Belk v. Purkett, 15 F.3d 803 (8th Cir. 1994).

Benton v. State, 2003 WL 22220501, Ala. Crim. App. (2003)

Best v. State, 264 A.D.2d 404, 694 N.Y.S.2d 689 (2d Dep't 1999).

Biddle v. Perovich, 274 U.S. 480, 47 S. Ct. 664, 71 L. Ed. 1161 (1927).

Board of Pardons v. Allen, 482 U.S. 369 (1987).

Boling v. Romer, 101 F.3d 1336 (10th Cir. 1996).

Breed v. Jones, 421 U.S. 517 (1975).

Bruggeman v. State, 681 So.2d. 822 (1996).

Burdick v. United States, 236 U.S. 79, 59 L. Ed. 476 (1915).

Cabell v. Chavez-Salido (1982) 454 U.S. 432

Cabla v. State, 6 S.W.3d 543 (Tex. Crim. App.1999).Caron v. United States, 524 U.S. 308 (1998).

Commonwealth v. Chase, in Thacher's Criminal Cases, 267 (1831), recorded in vol. 11 of the Records of the Old Municipal Court of Boston, 199.

Commonwealth of Massachusetts v. Talbot, 444 Mass. 586, 830 N.E.2d 177 (2005).

Commonwealth v. Williams, 1997 Pa. LEXIS 786 (1997).

Connecticut Department of Public Safety et. al. v. Doe, 538 U.S. 1 (2003).

Davis v. Alaska, 415 U.S. 308 (1974).

De Veau v. Braisted, 363 U.S. 144, 80 S. Ct. 1146, 4 L. Ed. 2d 1109 (1960).

Eddings v. Oklahoma, 455 U.S. 104 (1983).

Ex parte Garland, 71 U.S. 333, 18 L. Ed. 366 (1867).

Ex parte Lefors, 303 S.W.2d 394 (Tex. Crim. App. 1957).

Ex parte United States, 242 U.S. 27, 37 S. Ct. 72, 61 L. Ed. 129 (1916).

Fare v. Michael C., 442 U.S. 707 (1985).

Fields v. State, 2002 WL 126972, Ala. Crim. App. (2002)

Fischer v. Governor, 145 N.H. 28 (2000).

Fuller v. Oregon, 417 U.S. 40 (1974).

Gagnon v. Scarpelli, 411 U.S. 778 (1973).

Garner v. Jones, 529 U.S. 244 (2000)

Goldschmitt v. State, 490 So.2d 123 (Fla. Dist. Ct. App. 1986).

Greenholtz v. Inmates of the Nebraska Penal and Correctional Complex, 442 U.S. 1, 99 S. Ct. 2100, 2107, 60 L. Ed. 2d 668 (1979).

Griffin v. Wisconsin, 483 U.S. 868 (1987).

Hampton v. State, 786 A.2d 375 (R.I. 2001).

Hawker v. New York, 170 U.S. 189, 18 S. Ct. 573, 42 L. Ed. 1002 (1898).

Hawkins v. Freeman, 166 F.3d 267 (1999).

Herrington v. State, 534 S.W.2d. 311 (Tex. Crim. App. 1976).

Higdon v. United States, 627 F.2d 893 (9th Cir. 1980).

Hunter v. Underwood, 471 U.S. 222 (1985).

In re Bocchiaro, 49 F. Supp. 37 (W.D.N.Y. 1943).

In re Gault, 387 U.S. 1 (1967).

In re Winship, 397 U.S. 358 (1970).

Jago v. Van Curen, 454 U.S. 14 (1981).

Jones v. Murray, 962 F.2d 302 (4th Cir. 1992).

Jones v. State, 916 S.W.2d 766 (Ark. App. 1996).

Kansas v. Crane, 534 U.S. 407 (2002).

Kansas v. Hendricks, 521 U.S. 346 (1997).

Kent v. United States, 383 U.S. 541 (1966).

King v. Simpson, 189 F.3d 283 (2d Cir. 1999).

Konigsberg v. State Bar, 353 U.S. 252, 77 S. Ct. 722, 1 L. Ed. 2d 810 (1957).

Lay v. Louisiana Parole Board, 741 So.2d 80 (La. Ct. App. 1st Cir. 1999).

Marlo v. State Board of Medical Examiners, 112 Cal. App. 2d 276, 246 P.2d 69 (1952).
Matter of J.B.S., 696 S.W.2d 223 (Tex. App. 1985).
McKeiver v. Pennsylvania, 403 U.S. 528 (1971).
McKune Warden v. Lile, U.S. (2002).
Mempa v. Rhay, 389 U.S. 128, 88 S. Ct. 254, 19 L. Ed. 2d 336 (1967).
Menechino v. Oswald, 430 F.2d 403, 407 (2d Cir. 1970), cert. denied, 400 U.S. 1023, 91 S. Ct. 588, 27 L. Ed. 2d 635 (1971).
Meyer v. State, 596 P.2d. 1270 (Okla. Crim. App. 1979).
Miller v. District of Columbia, 294 A.2d 365 (D.C. App. 1972).
Miranda v. Arizona, 384 U.S. 436 (1966).
Mixon v. Pennsylvania, 783 A.2d (2000).
Moore v. United States, 571 F.2d 179 (3rd Cir. 1978).
Morrissey v. Brewer, 408 U.S. 471 (1972).
Murrill v. State Board of Accountancy, 97 Cal. App. 2d 709, 218 P.2d 569 (1950).

Newsom v. State, 2004 WL 943861, Miss. Ct. App. (2004).
New Jersey v. T.L.O., 469 U.S. 325 (1985).

Pennsylvania Board of Probation and Parole v. Scott, 524 U.S. 357 (1998).
People v. Colabello, 948 P.2d 77 (Colo. App. 1997).
People v. Heckler, 16 Cal. Rptr. 2d 681, 13 C. A. 4th 1049 (1993).
People v. Letterlough, 655 N.E. 2d 146 (N.Y. 1995).
People v. Meyer, 176 Ill. 2d 372, 680 N.E. 315 (1997).
People v. Price, 24 Ill. App. 2d. 364 (1960).
People v. Ramos, 48 CrL 1057 (Ill.S.Ct.) (1990).
People v. Sweeden, 116 Cal. App. 2d. 891 (1953).
Perry v. State, 778 So. 2d 1072 (Fla. Dist. Ct. App. 5th Dist. 2001)
Peterson v. State Liquor Authority, 42 A.D. 2d 195, 345 N.Y.S. 2d 780 (1973).

Reyes v. Tate, 91 Ohio St. 3d 84, 742 N.E.2d 132 (2001).
Richardson v. New York State Executive Department, 602 N.Y.S.2d 443 (1993).
Richardson v. Ramirez, 418 U.S. 24, 94 S. Ct. 2655, 41 L. Ed. 2d 551 (1974).
Rise v. Oregon, 59 F3d 1556 (9th Cir. 1995).
Rodriguez v. State, 378 So.2d 7 (Fla. Dist. Ct. App. 1979).

Scarpa v. United States Board of Parole, 477 F.2d 278, 281 (5th Cir. 1972), vacated as moot; 414 U.S. 809, 94 S. Ct. 79, 38 L. Ed. 2d 44 (1973).
Schall v. Martin, 104 S. Ct. 2403 (1984).
Seling v. Young, 531 U.S. 250 (2001).

Smith v. Daily Mail Publishing Co., 443 U.S. 97 (1979).
Smith v. Doe, 538 U.S. 84 (2003).
Soliz v. State, 171 Tex. Crim. 376 (1961).
Spaulding v. Nielsen, 599 F.2d 728 (5th Cir. 1979).
Stanford v. Kentucky, 109 S.Ct. 2969 (1989).
State v. Bourrie, 190 Or. App. 572, 80 P.3d 505 (2003).
State v. Graham, 30 P.3d 310 (Kan 2001).
State v. Gropper, 888 P.2d 12211 (Wash. App. 1995).
State v. Pizel, 987 P.2d 1288 (Utah Ct. App. 1999).
State v. Varnado, 384 So. 440 (L.A. 1980).
State v. Walker, 432 So.2d 1057 (La. Ct. App. 1983).
Summers v. State, 817 So. 2d 950 (Fla Dist. Ct. App. 2d Dist. 2002).

Thompson v. Oklahoma, 487 U.S. 815 (1988).

United States v. Allen, 13 F.3d 105 U.S. (4th Cir. December 1993).
United States v. Angulo, 864 F.2d 504 (7th Cir. 1988).
United States v. Bachsian, 4 F.3d 288 (1993).
United States v. Balon, 384 F.3d 38 (2d Cir. 2004).
United States v. Booker, 125 S. Ct. 738, 160 LED 2d 621 (U.S. 2005).
United States v. Caron, 941 F. Supp. 238 (D. Mass. 1996); 77 F.3d 1 (1st Cir, en banc, 1996); 524 U.S. 308 (1998).
United States v. Dougherty, 810 F.2d 763 (8th Cir. 1987).
United States v. Fowler, U.S. (11th Cir. 1999).
United States v. Gordon, 4 F.3d 1567 U.S. (10th Cir. September 1993).
United States v. Knights, 534 U.S. 112 (2001).
United States v. Laney, 189 F.3d 954 (9th Cir. 1999).
United States v. Lasky, 592 F.2d 5670 (9th Cir. 1979).
United States v. Lockhart, 58 F.3d 86 (4th Cir. June 1995).
United States v. McCormick, 54 F.3d 214 U.S. (5th Cir. 1995).
United States v. Pettus, 303 F.3d 480 (2d Cir. 2002).
United States v. Porotsky, 105 F.2d 69 U.S. (2nd Cir. 1997).
United States v. Rivera, 96 F.3rd 41 (2nd cir. September 1996).
United States v. RLC, 503 U.S. 291 (1992).
United States v. Thurlow, 44 F.3d 46 U.S. (1st Cir. 1995).
United States v. Trevino, 89 F.3d 187, U.S. (4th Cir. July 1996).
United States v. Turner, 44 F.3d 900 (10th Cir. 1995).
United States v. Washington, 11 F.3d 1510 U.S. (10th Cir. November 1993).
United States v. Wolff, 90 F.3d 191 (7th Cir. 1996).

Walrath v. Getty, 71 F.3d 679 (7th Cir. 1995).
Warner v. Orange County Department of Probation, 870 F. Supp. 69 (S.D.N.Y. 1994).
Williams v. New York, 337 U.S. 241 (1949).
Williams v. Oklahoma, 358 U.S. 576 (1959).

Young v. Harper, 520 U.S. 143 (1997).

Table of Cases

B

Ballenger v. State 1993, 46
Bearden v. Georgia 1983, 225
Beecham v. United States 1994, 346
Belk v. Purkett 1994, 150
Benton v. State 2003, 149
Board of Pardons v. Allen 1987, 275
Boling v. Romer 1996, 286
Breed v. Jones 1975, 321

C

Cabell v. Chavez-Salido 1982, 95
Commonwealth of Massachusetts v.
    Talbot 2005, 58
Commonwealth v. Chase 1830, 78
Connecticut Department of Public Safety
    et al. v. Doe 2003, 349

D

Davis v. Alaska 1974, 321

E

Eddings v. Oklahoma 1983, 321
Ex parte Garland 1867, 355
Ex parte United States 242 U.S. 27,
    1916, 79

F

Fare v. Michael C. 1985, 321,
    326–327
Fischer v. Governor 2000, 341–342

G

Gagnon v. Scarpelli 1973,
    148–149
Garner v. Jones 2000, 275
Goldschmitt v. State 1986, 46

Greenholtz v. Inmates of the Nebraska
    Penal and Correctional Complex
    1979, 274–275
Griffin v. Wisconsin 1987, 46–47

H

Hawker v. New York 1898, 359
Hunter v. Underwood 1985, 341

I

In re Gault 1967, 310, 320–321
In re Winship 1970, 321

K

Kansas v. Crane 2002, 352–353
Kansas v. Hendricks 1997, 352–353
Kent v. United States 1966, 321
Killits case, 1916, 78–79
King v. Simpson 1999, 105
Konigsberg v. State Bar 1957, 357

M

McKeiver v. Pennsylvania 1971, 321
McKune Warden v. Lile 2002, 47–48
Mempa v. Rhay 1967, 149
Menechino v. Oswald 1971, 274
Miranda v. Arizona 1966, 58
Mixon v. Commonwealth of
    Pennsylvania 2001, 342
Morrissey v. Brewer 1972, 148–149

N

New Jersey v. T.L.O. 1985, 321

P

Pennsylvania Board of Probation and
    Parole v. Scott 1998, 288

People v. Colabello 1997, 150
People v. Heckler 1993, 46–47
People v. Letterlough 1995, 47
People v. Meyer 1997, 47
People v. Ramos 1990, 192

R

Richardson v. Ramirez 1974, 341
Roper v. Simmons 2005, 314, 321

S

Schall v. Martin 1984, 321
Smith v. Daily Mail Publishing Co.
    1979, 321
Smith v. Doe 2003, 349
Stanford v. Kentucky 1989,
    314, 321
State of Missouri v. Anthony
    Williams, 52
State v. Pizel 1999, 288

T

Thompson v. Oklahoma 1988, 314
Thompson v. Oklahoma 1988, 321

U

United States v. Balon 2004, 199
United States v. Booker 2005, 148
United States v. Trevino 1996, 56
United States v. Turner 1995, 288

W

Walrath v. Getty 1995, 288
Wooden v. State 2001, 219

Y

Young v. Harper 1997, 291

Name Index

A

Abadinsky, Howard, 238
Adams, William P., 300–301
Alarid, Leanne, 106, 167–168, 264–265
Albonetti, Celesta A., 152
Allen, George, 254
Applegate, Brandon K., 7
Augustus, John, 79–82, 322

B

Bales, William D., 200
Barton, William H., 183
Bayens, Gerald, 189
Bazemore, Gordon, 214
Beck, Allen J., 292, 294, 301
Beck, S. H., 168
Bentham, Jeremy, 217
Bergstrom, Mark H., 225–226
Bernat, Jeffrey, 166
Binder, Arnold, 318
Blomberg, Thomas G., 200
Bloom, Barbara, 129
Bobys, Richard, 353
Bouffard, Jeffrey A., 33
Boyle, Barbara, 250–251
Bozynski, Melanie, 312
Brockway, Zebulon R., 238
Brody, David C., 176
Bruce, Dickson D., 318
Buckler, Kevin G., 339, 346–347
Burke, Peggy, 144–146, 289, 295–296
Burnham, L. P., 83
Burton, Velmer S., 90
Bushey, W. Conway, 104
Butts, Jeffrey A., 312
Byrne, Jim, 203–204

C

Camp, Camille Graham, 99, 125
Camp, George M., 99, 125
Carter, Madeline M., 143

Chase, Jerusha, 78
Clark, John, 25–27
Clear, Todd, R., 6
Coates, Robert B., 213
Cohen, Robyn L., 292
Cohen, Thomas H., 24–25
Connett, Archie V., 283–284
Cook, Rufus R., 83
Coolidge, Calvin, 82
Corbett, Ronald P. Jr., 6, 325
Craddock, Amy, 205
Crofton, Sir Walter, 237
Crow, Wayman, 283–284
Cullen, Francis T., 7
Cuniff, Mark, 152, 222

D

del Carmen, Rolando V., 328–329
Deschenes, Elizabeth Piper, 190
DiMascio, William M., 9, 14, 222
Dodder, Richard A., 192
Dolny, H. Michael, 248–249, 297, 300, 302
Domurad, F., 122–123
Dooley, Brendan, 126
Duffee, David E., 94

E

Eisenberg, Michael, 181
Ely, John F., 168
Eng, Vincent A., 55–56
Erickson, Rosemary J., 283–284
Esselman, Julie, 203–204

F

Fabelo, Tony, 181
Farkas, Mary Ann, 351
Fields, Monique, 144
Finn, Peter, 350–351
Flower, Lucy L., 83
Fogel, David, 241

Friel, Charles, 195
Fry, Elizabeth, 217

G

Galaway, Burt, 216–217, 220, 221
Galileo, 191
Garofalo, James, 299
Geerken, Michael R., 153
Geis, Gilbert, 318
Gendreau, Paul, 14–15, 190
Gibson, Mel, 41
Glaze, Lauren E., 113–114, 234, 247–248
Goldkamp, John S., 26–27
Gordon, Jill, 328, 330
Gottfredson, Don, 299
Gottfredson, Michael, 299
Gowen, Darren, 195–196
Gray, M. Kevin, 144
Greek, Cecil E., 196
Greenberg, David, 241
Greene, Judith, 226
Greenwood, Peter, 319
Griffin, Patrick, 322, 325–326
Grooms, Robert, 283

H

Hansen, Christopher, 55
Harrell, Adele V., 312
Harries, Keith, 115
Harris, Daniel C., 30, 33
Harris, M. Kay, 93–94
Hayes, Hennessey D., 153
Hemmens, Craig, 90, 283
Henderson-Hurley, Martha, 261
Henry, D. Alan, 25–27
Hensley, Denise Bray, 174–175
Hepburn, John R., 152
Holsinger, Alex M., 121
Horrocks, Cary, 125
Hudson, J., 221
Hughes, Timothy A., 292, 294, 301

I

Irwin, John, 240

J

Johnson, R., 190
Jones, Mark, 189
Jones, Richard S., 284–285
Justice, Cheryl, 183

K

Kane, Candice M., 126
Karuppannan, Jaishankar, 115
Kelly, Brian J., 54
Kelly, Phaedra Athena O'Hara, 16
Kendig, Newton, 250–251
Kennedy, Anthony, 6
Kennedy, Robert F., 165
Kiefer, Misty, 90
Kittrie, Nicholas N., 55–56
Klockars, Carl B. Jr., 94
Kreisel, Betsy Wright, 99–100
Kurlychek, Megan, 312
Kuzma, Susan, 339, 353

L

Langan, Patrick A., 152, 222, 299
Larivee, John J., 205
Latessa, Edward J., 121, 168
Lehnerer, Melodye, 167–168
Levin, David J., 299
Limbaugh, Rush, 140
Lindner, Charles, 82–84
Lipton, Douglas, 17
Locke, Hubert G., 17
Logan, Charles A., 300–301
Love, Jack, 194
Love, Margaret Colgate, 339, 347, 353,
    357, 361
Lurigio, Arthur J., 121, 189
Lutze, Faith E., 176
Lynch, Mona, 285–286

M

Mack, Julian W., 84
Maconochie, Alexander, 235–237
Maher, Richard J., 223
Mair, George, 205
Manske, Michael, 189
Mansnerus, Laura, 351–352
Marsangy, Bonneville de, 234
Martinson, Robert, 17, 240
Mastorilli, Mary Ellen, 173, 176
Mathur, Minu, 192
Maxwell, Sheila Royo, 144
May, Bob, 99
McDiarmid, Anne, 129

McDonald, Douglas, 226
McGaughey, Deanna, 295
McKay, Brian, 126
McShane, Marilyn D., 248–249, 297,
    300, 302
Mendez, Anthony, 284
Mirabeau, Comte de, (Honore-Gabriel
    Rigueti), 233–234
Montesinos, Manuel, 234–235
Moore, Joel R., 83
Moreland, John, 82
Morgan, Kathryn D., 151
Morris, Norval, 161, 190, 241
Moscicki, Ronald, 170
Muhammad, Mika'il A., 276

N

Nackerud, Larry, 166
Nee, Claire, 205
Ney, Becky, 295–296
Nieman, Lloyd, 283–284
Norman, Michael D., 55–56
Novack, S., 221

O

Obermaier, Georg Michael, 235
Ogden, Thomas G., 125
Olson, David E., 126
Outlaw, M.C., 220

P

Padgett, Kathy G., 200
Palla, Seri, 113–114, 234, 247–248
Paparozzi, Mario A., 190
Parent, Dale, 177, 203–204, 206
Parent, Dale G., 295–296
Parisi, Nicolette, 170
Parsonage, William H., 104
Parthasarathy, Barbara, 300–301
Petersilia, Joan, 18–19, 117, 124, 190,
    192, 242, 244, 265, 293, 298
Phillips, Kirby, 197
Prendergast, Michael, 181
Purkiss, Marcus, 90
Puzzanchera, Charles M., 315–316

R

Ransom, George, 173, 176
Reaves, Brian A., 24–25
Reddington, Frances P., 99–100
Reichel, Philip, 189
Rhine, Edward E., 261
Richards, Stephen C., 284–285
Risler, Edwin, 166
Roberts, Albert, 312
Rothman, David J., 271

Ruback, R. Barry, 218, 220, 225–226
Russell, Richard V., 119–120
Ruth, Gretchen R., 218

S

Sabol, William J., 300–301
Sacks, Howard R., 300–301
Samuels, Lorraine, 300
Sandhu, Harjit S., 192
Savarese, Margaret R., 82–84
Schafer, Stephen, 217
Scharr, Timothy M., 102–103
Schloss, Christine S., 106
Schwaner, Shawn, 295, 297
Schwarzenegger, Arnold, 165
Schwitzgebel, Robert, 194
Scott, Jim, 93
Shaffer, Jennifer N., 218
Shelden, Randall G., 29
Shepherd, Robert E. Jr., 312
Sickmund, Melissa, 313–317, 319–320,
    328
Smylka, John Ortiz, 189
Snyder, Howard N., 313–314, 316–317,
    319, 328
Solomon, Amy L., 301
Spear, John Murray, 82
Steiner, Benjamin, 129, 190
Storm, John P., 54–56
Sudbrack, Billie, 189
Sundt, Jody L., 7
Swetz, Anthony, 250–251

T

Taxman, Faye S., 33
Taylor, David, 166
Tewksbury, Richard, 295, 351
Thacher, Peter Oxenbridge, 78
Tonry, Michael, 18, 161, 190, 221
Torbet, Patricia, 312, 322, 325–326
Travis, Jeremy, 251
Travis, Lawrence, 168
Travis, Lawrence F., 339, 346–347
Trulson, Chad R., 328–329
Tsafaty, Vered, 203–204
Turner, Michael G., 7
Turner, Susan, 190
Twill, Sarah E., 166

U

Umbreit, Mark, 214
Umbreit, Mark S., 213

V

Valade, Laura, 203–204
Vaughn, Joseph B., 195

von Hirsch, Andrew, 241
Vos, Betty, 213

W

Wadman, Robert C., 55–56
Walker, Lorenn, 214
Walsh, C. L., 168
Wellisch, Jean, 181
Wentworth, Dan, 295–296
White, Michael D., 26–27

Wicharaya, Tamask, 41
Wilkinson, Reginald A., 261
Wilks, Judith, 17
Williams, Frank P., III, 248–249, 297, 300, 302
Wilson, Doris James, 292, 294, 301
Wines, Fredrick H., 234–235
Wong, Mamie Mee, 181
Worzella, Charles, 226

Y

Yuan, Y., 300–301

Z

Zenoff, Elyce H., 55–56
Zevitz, Richard, 351
Zurcher, Louis A., 283–284

Subject Index

A

absolute immunity, 105
absolute pardons, 354
actuarial risk assessment, 121
addicts. *See* drug abuse; drug courts
adjudication, juvenile, 50, 68–69, 316, 318–319
Administrative Office of United States Courts, 83, 127, 139
administrators, parole and probation, 100
adult preservice training of probation officers, 98
adult probation systems, 90–92, 97
    characteristics of persons in, 110, 113–114
    and firearms policies, 101–102
aftercare. *See* juvenile justice, juvenile parole
AfterShock, 171
age
    and juvenile court jurisdiction, 312–313
    parole violator, 292
agents of change, probation officers as, 85
Alaska Sex Offender Registration Act, 349
alcohol
    testing, 118
    use during probation, 45, 112, 197
alcoholics
    and early probation movement, 80–81
    supervising, 128–129
    therapeutic communities for, 178–181
Alcoholics Anonymous (A.A.), 46
amercement, 77

America, transportation of British convicts to, 235–236
American Bar Association, 99, 225
American Correctional Association, 98, 100
American Friends Service Committee, 240–241
American Probation and Parole Association (APPA), 11, 101–102, 125, 198
ankle devices, electronic monitoring, 195
Antabuse, 129, 204
APPA (American Probation and Parole Association), 11, 101–102, 125, 198
appointment system, for probation officers, 96–97
apprehension of fugitives, 297
arrests by probation officers, 147
asset-building supervision, 117
Association of Paroling Authorities International, 245–246, 266–267
attainder, 338
attitudinal change, 173, 176, 177
attorneys, 58–59, 149, 326–327
Australia, transportation of British convicts to, 236

B

bail bond offices, 23
bail decision, 12
banked probation, 124
bankruptcies and restitution, 219
base offense levels, 68
behavioral change
    basic principles of, 104
    levels systems in halfway houses and, 166–167
    in probation boot camps, 173, 176, 177

and purposes of probation, 10–11
    through rehabilitation, 14–15
    through supervision process, 117
benign absconders, 295
Biblical restitution, 216–217
Black's Law Dictionary, 338–339, 353
blood-alcohol content, 197
bonded employees, 345–346
boot camps, 9, 169–177
    correctional, 170–171
    criticisms of, 176
    evaluations of, 176–177
    future of, 177
    offender perspectives, 173–176
    prison boot camps, 171–172
    probation boot camps, 172–173
British criminal law, 77, 221, 235–237
Brockway, Zebulon R., 238
broken windows probation. *See* neighborhood-based supervision
brokerage of services era (1970... 1980), 85–86
budgets, correctional, 8–9
bumper stickers, shaming, 46
Bureau of Justice Statistics, 4, 220

C

California
    citizenship of probation officers, 95
    Penal Code on pardons, 356
    probation statute, 85
    risk assessment, 302
Career Criminal Provision, 68
careers, criminal, 300
Carlie's law, 141
case classification instruments, 122–123
case files and management, O-Track, 163
caseflow through juvenile justice system, 319
caseloads
    specialized, 34, 126–131

caseloads *(continued)*
    supervising mentally ill offenders, 127–128
    supervising offenders who have abused drugs and alcohol, 128–129
    supervising sex offenders, 130–131
    standards, 126
case managers
    halfway house, 167–168
    institutional, 264–266
case plan, developing, 124
cases, old, 245–246
casework era (1900–1970), 85
cash bonds, 25
categories, offense, 273
certificates of discharge, 356
chief probation officers, 96–97
child offenders. *See* juvenile justice
children, women offenders living with, 182–184
children in need of supervision (CHINS), 314
Children's Aid Society, 83
child safety zones, 130
child savers, 83
child support, probationer, 113
CHINS (children in need of supervision), 314
CINS (conduct in need of supervision), 314
circle sentencing, 214–215
citizenship of probation officers, 95
civil and political rights
    affected by conviction, 340–347
        employment-related rights, 343–346
        loss of credibility as a witness, 343
        loss of parental rights, 347
        loss of right to own or possess a firearm, 346
        loss of right to serve on a jury, 342
        loss of right to vote, 341–342
        loss of the right to hold public office, 343
        loss of welfare benefits, 347
    defined, 338
    holding public office, 364
    juvenile, 310
    obtaining occupational licenses, 365
    owning firearms, 365
    pardoning, 365–366
    privacy, 199
    restoration of, 356–357
        automatic restoration, 356–357
        restoration upon application, 356
        restoring right to vote, 357

voting, 358, 364
civil disabilities, 307, 339–340
    background of, 338–339
    differences by state, 339
    problems with laws addressing, 347–348
civil service probation officers, 97
classification as first step in supervision, 118–126
    actuarial risk assessment, 121
    caseload and workload standards, 126
    developing the case plan, 124
    identifying treatment needs, 121–124
    levels of supervision, 124–126
clear conditions, 45
Client Management Classification (CMC), 121
CMC (Client Management Classification), 121
Code of Hammurabi, 217
collateral bonds, 25
collateral contact, 124
Colorado reentry courts, 262
commission, interstate, 132
Commission on Prison and Jail Overcrowding, Virginia, 255
Commission on the Abolition of Parole and Sentencing Reform, Virginia, 254–257
Committee for the Study of Incarceration, 241
community, and prisoner reentry, 261
community agencies and probation, 85–86
community-based therapeutic communities, 180–181
community controllees in Florida, 191
community corrections acts, 93–94
Community Corrections Centers. *See* halfway houses
community diversion boards, 213–214
community diversion centers, 178
community justice, 211. *See also* neighborhood-based supervision
community reintegration, 15
community resource management team (CRMT), 86
community safety, 6–7, 150, 295
community service, 8, 221–224
    effectiveness of, 222–224
    history of, 221
    prevalence of, 222
    purpose of, 221–222
    See also restitution centers
community treatment centers (CTC), 192–193

compact administrators, 132
companies, use of convict labor by private, 238
COMPAS (Correctional Offender Management Profiles for Alternative Sentences), 121
compassionate release, 250–251
Compendium of Federal Justice Statistics, 142, 153
compensation for crime. *See* restorative justice
completion rates
    community service, 223
    in day reporting centers, 205–206
    drug court, 31–32
    electronic monitoring, 200
    therapeutic community, 180
Comprehensive Crime Control Act, 83
concurrent jurisdiction, 315
conditional pardons, 354
conditional release, 25, 233–234
conditions, probation, 110–113, 323
Conditions of Federal Probation, 111–113
conduct in need of supervision (CINS), 314
confidentiality
    in juvenile proceedings, 327–328
    of presentence investigation reports, 57
Connecticut
    private probation in, 106
    sex offender registration in, 349
consent decrees, 318
conservative politics, 17
constitutionality
    of citizenship requirement for probation officers, 95
    of sex offender registration, 349
    of supervision conditions, 45–48
    See also rights
contact requirements, supervision class, 124–125
continuing education training, probation and parole staff, 99–100
contract parole, 276
controlled substances. *See* drug abuse
conviction
    civil and political rights affected by, 340–347
        employment-related rights, 343–346
        loss of credibility as a witness, 343
        loss of parental rights, 347
        loss of right to own or possess a firearm, 346
        loss of right to serve on a jury, 342
        loss of right to vote, 341–342

loss of the right to hold public office, 343
loss of welfare benefits, 347
effects of, 348–353
  involuntary commitment of sexual predators, 351–353
  sex offender notification laws, 349–351
  sex offender registration laws, 348–349
  social stigmatization, 353
convict labor, 238
correctional boot camps, 170–171
Correctional Offender Management Profiles for Alternative Sentences (COMPAS), 121
correctional treatment, 14–15
Corrections Program Assessment Inventory (CPAI), 14–15
costs, 227–228
  of day reporting centers, 204
  of electronic monitoring systems, 196–198
  of incarceration, reducing, 238
  of intensive supervision probation, 190
  of probation boot camps, 177
  of probation vs. imprisonment, 139–140
Council of State Governments, 132
county-based probation systems, 85
courts
  drug courts, 29–31, 128, 178–179
    evaluating, 32–33
    gender and drug court treatment strategies, 31–32
  Illinois Supreme Court, 47
  mental health courts, 34
  New York Court of Appeals, 47
  probation violation decision guidelines, 143
  reentry, 262
  and revocation, 141, 146
  See also Federal Court of Appeals; U.S. Supreme Court
CPAI (Corrections Program Assessment Inventory), 14–15
CREST program, 182
crimes
  classes of, 43
  and house arrest, 192
  infamous, 338
  military crimes, 339
  new, by probationers, 143–144
  presentence reports focused on, 50–51
  severity of, 5, 241, 272–273

understanding of by parole officers, 53–54
  See also victims
criminal history, 50, 68–70, 300–301
criminal justice agencies, 163
criminal procedure, 77
criminal records
  expungement of, 359–360
  sealing of, 360–361
criminals, transportation of, 235–237
CRMT (community resource management team), 86
Crofton, Walter, 237
crowding in prisons, 4–5, 177, 190, 249–250
cruel and unusual punishment, 16, 176
CTC (community treatment centers), 192–193
custody options, PSI reports, 72
cybercriminals, 54

D

Dallas, Texas therapeutic community, 181
databases, offender tracking, 163
day fines, 226–227
day reporting centers, 201–206
  evaluations of, 205–206
  purposes of, 202
  treatment-oriented vs. supervision-oriented, 202–204
death penalty for juveniles, 314, 321
deferred adjudication probation, 140
deferred parole, 269
deferred prosecution, 30
deficit-focused supervision, 117
Delancey Street facility, 179
Delaware's Probation Reform Law, 152
delayed revocation, 150–151
delegated release authority, 24
deoxyribonucleic acid (DNA) banks, 286–287
Department of Corrections
  New York State, 172
  Utah, 163
deportation of probationers, 113
deposit bonds, 25
detention centers, probation, 146
detention of juveniles, 316, 318
determinate sentencing, 5–6, 42, 50
diminished constitutional rights, 288
direct consequences of crime, 337
disabilities, civil, 307
discretion
  abolishment of through determinate sentencing, 240

of judges in juvenile system, 323
and loss of rights as collateral consequence, 340
overview, 9
parole board, 245–246
and probation officer stress, 104–105
discretionary parole, 231, 233–234, 242–244, 301
discretionary probation conditions, 110–113
discretionary revocation, 141
discrimination, 344
diseases, and parole, 250–251
disenfranchisement, 341–342
dispositions, 317, 319–320
diversion, 28–35
  candidates for, 28
  criticisms of diversion programs, 35
  drug courts, 29–31
  evaluating drug courts, 32–33
  gender and drug court treatment strategies, 31–32
  mental health courts, 34
DNA (deoxyribonucleic acid) banks, 286–287
DOJ (U.S. Department of Justice), 4, 142, 153, 262, 269
domestic violence
  and intensive supervision probation, 190
  probation conditions concerning, 111
  as result of house arrests, 192
drug abuse
  education programs regarding, 127
  offender, in PSI reports, 71
  parole violations related to, 294
  probation conditions concerning, 111–112
  revocation of offenders with history of, 152
  supervising drugs abusers, 128–129
  testing for proof of, 118
  therapeutic community treatment, 178–181
  treatment for, 8
drug courts, 29–31, 128, 178–179
  evaluating, 32–33
  gender and drug court treatment strategies, 31–32
Drug Punishment Program, Florida, 180
due process, 56–57, 148, 271, 310, 320–321
dynamic parolee characteristics, 302
dynamic recidivism factors, 121

E

Eastern District of Missouri firearms policy, 102
East Harlem reentry court, 262
economic and restorative justice reparations, 210–229
  community service, 221–224
    effectiveness of, 222–224
    history of, 221
    prevalence of, 222
    purpose of, 221–222
  fees and costs, 227–228
  fines, 224–227
    day fines, 226–227
    forfeitures, 225–226
    prevalence of, 224–225
    revoking probation for fine nonpayment, 225
  overview, 211
  restitution, 216–221
    effectiveness, 220–221
    in history, 216–218
    losses eligible for compensation, 218
    problems associated, 218–220
  restorative justice, 211–216
    effectiveness of, 214–216
    forms of, 212–214
education
  of offenders, 71
  of probation officers, 98
effectiveness of community-based corrections, 17–19
  measuring, 18–19
  outcome measures for evaluation, 19
  what works, 17–18
Eighth Amendment rights, 16, 176
electronic monitoring, 9, 193–201
  attitudes toward, 198–199
  frequency of use, 197–198
  global positioning systems, 196–197
  history of, 194
  home-based, empirical evaluations of, 200–201
  problems of early programs, 194–195
  remote location monitoring, 195–196
Elmira Reformatory, 238
emotional health, offender, in PSI reports, 71
empathy training, 100
employment
  after reentry, 259–260
  offender, in work release, 181–182
  private, 344, 365
  public, 343–344, 364

record of offenders in PSI reports, 71–72
  services, 117–118
Employment and Training Administration, 345–346
employment-related rights, 343–346
English criminal law, 77, 221, 235–237
ethanol, 197
evidence
  corrections based on, 17
  hearsay, 57–58, 150
  illegally obtained, 58, 288
  level required, 149–150
  preponderance of, 149
Excell Center, 324
exclusionary rule, 58, 288
exclusion zones, 196
executive branch administration of probation, 92–93
expiration of probation, 150–151
explicit conditions, probation, 111
ex post facto clause of U.S. Constitution, 349
expungement of criminal records, 366
extradition of fugitives, 296–297

F

face-to-face parole hearings, 268–270
failure to appear (FTA), 25
failure to pay
  restitution, 219
  and revocation of probation, 150
families of prisoners, 260–261
family data, PSI reports, 50–51, 70
family group conferencing, 214
FARE (Financial Assessment Related to Employability) program, 227
FATS (Firearms Training System), 97, 102–103
FBI (Federal Bureau of Investigations), 296–297
FBP (Federal Bureau of Prisons), 83
Federal Bail Reform Act, 22–23
Federal benefits, denial of, 73
Federal Bureau of Investigations (FBI), 296–297
Federal Bureau of Prisons (FBP), 83
Federal Court of Appeals
  alcohol use during probation, 45
  Seventh Circuit, 228, 288
  Tenth Circuit, 58, 286, 288
Federal Criminal Code and Rules 2004, 146, 151
federal funding
  for halfway houses, 165
  for reentry, 262

federal justice system
  community service, 223
  fees, 227–228
  pardons, 354
  parole, 243, 247, 269–273
  pretrial release decisions, 23, 25
  probation, 111–113, 127, 142
  probation officers, 96–97, 102, 119–120
federal probation, development of, 82–83
federal sentencing guidelines, 5–6, 42
Federal Sentencing Reform Act, 79
Federal Victim Witness Protection Act (VWPA) of 1982, 217
fees, 150, 227–228
felony cases, 49, 111
felony sentencing grid, North Carolina, 43
female offenders
  and diversion, 28
  and drug courts, 31–32, 34
  and electronic monitoring, 200
  growth in numbers of, 3
  and halfway houses, 165
  living with their children, 182–184
  and parole, 248, 300
  and prediction of recidivism, 274
  and reentry, 260
  and substance abuse treatment approaches, 129
  therapeutic communities for, 181
female probation officers, 83–84
fidelity bonding coverage, 345–346
field contacts, 125
Fifth Amendment, 47–48, 147
file-review parole hearings, 268–270
filing, 77
final revocation hearings, 148
Financial Assessment Related to Employability (FARE) program, 227
financial information, defendant's, in PSI reports, 51, 72
fines, 8, 51, 72, 150, 224–227
  day fines, 226–227
  forfeitures, 225–226
  prevalence of, 224–225
  revoking probation for fine nonpayment, 225
firearms, 105, 365
  loss of right to own, 346
  policies for probation and parole, 101–102
Firearms Training System (FATS), 97, 102–103

First Amendment rights, 45–46, 288
first-time offenders, 28, 169–170, 178
fixed fines, 224–226
fixed sentencing. *See* determinate
   sentencing
Florida
   Drug Punishment Program, 180
   house arrest in, 191
   telecommuting by presentence offi-
      cers in, 55
follow-up actions, FTA, 26–27
formal handling of juvenile cases, 318
formal juvenile probation, 322
foster homes, 83
Fourth Amendment rights, 46–47, 58,
   199, 288
freedom of religion, 46
FTA (failure to appear), 25
fugitive probationers, 145
full board reviews, 267
full cash bonds, 25
full discretion, 245–246
fundamental skills training, 98–100
funding
   correctional, 8–9
   for drug courts, 32

G

gain time, 264
gang members, 127, 300
"Gang Member Supervision Growing
   Part of Job for Probation
   Officers," 127
GAO (U.S. General Accounting Office),
   30, 32–33
gender
   and electronic monitoring, 200
   of parolees, 248
   and parole outcomes, 300
   of parole violators, 292
   probationer, 110, 113
   and substance abuse treatment
      approaches, 129
   See also female offenders; male
      offenders
geographic information systems (GIS),
   115
Georgia
   community diversion centers, 178
   community service in, 223
   intervals between parole hearings in,
      275
   probation detention centers in, 146
GIS (geographic information systems),
   115

global positioning systems (GPS),
   130–131, 196–197
goals, correctional, 13–16
   community reintegration, 15
   protection of public, 13–14
   public shaming as punishment, 16
   rehabilitation, 14–15
   restorative or community justice,
      15–16
good abearance, 77
good conduct, reward for, 237–238
good moral character, 338–339, 346
governor's power to pardon, 354
GPS (global positioning systems),
   130–131, 196–197
graduated release from prison, 166
Greenlight, Project, 262
gross negligence, 105
guilt
   admissions of in revocation hearings,
      149
   determination of in historical Britain,
      77
   of minors, 309–310

H

habitual offenders, 5, 300–301
halfway houses, 9, 162–169, 265,
   284–285
   history of U.S., 164–166
   program components, 166–167
   worker perspectives and role orienta-
      tion, 167–168
   See also residential community
      corrections facilities
Hammurabi's Code, 217
Harris Poll 1967, 239
hearings, right to, 148–149
hearsay evidence, 57–58, 150
home-based electronic monitoring,
   195
home visits, parole officer, 53
house arrest, 9, 191–193
   criticisms of, 191–192
   effectiveness of, 192–193
   purposes of, 191
House Judiciary Committee, U.S.
   Congress, 309
humiliation, 46–47, 180

I

illegally-obtained evidence, 58, 288
Illinois
   Criminal Justice Authority, 206
   Department of Professional
      Regulation, 345

Juvenile Court Act, 83, 311–312
Supreme Court, 47
tolled terms of probation, 151
Unified Code of Corrections and
   restoration of rights, 357
illnesses, terminal, and parole, 250–251
incarceration
   vs. compensation, 16
   cost of vs. probation, 139–140
   growth in rates of, 3–5
   as occasional necessity, 11–12
   overview, 13
   as result of revocation of parole, 146
   See also boot camps; jails; prisons
inclusion zones, 196
indeterminate sentencing, 3–5, 49, 239,
   245–246
Indiana
   John P. Craine House, 183–184
   Juvenile Code, 324
   restitution by indigent offenders, 219
   results of day reporting centers in,
      206
indigenous Native American justice,
   211–212, 214
indigent offenders and restitution, 219
infamous crimes, 338
informal handling of juvenile cases, 318
informal juvenile probation, 322
informal social controls, 118
infractions, probation conditions for, 111
in-service training of probation/parole
   staff, 99, 100
institutional case managers,
   264–266
institutional corrections. *See*
   incarceration
institutionalization, juvenile, 331
intake, 316, 318
intensive supervision probation (ISP),
   8, 188–191, 325
   attitudes toward, 189
   caseloads, 189
   evaluations of, 189–191
intent, 309–310
interactive video training, firearms
   safety, 102–103
Interagency Linkages, O-Track, 163
intermediate sanctions, 7, 12, 18, 159,
   161
intermittent incarceration. *See* boot
   camps
International Association of Residential
   and Community Alternatives, 165
International Halfway House
   Association, 165

interstate compacts on probation, 131
new interstate compact for adult offender supervision, 132
revocation and interstate compact, 132
interviews
bond, 24
for PSIs, 54
introductory training, probation/parole staff, 99
investigations, presentence, 49
Irish prison system, 237
iSecureTrac, 130–131
ISP. *See* intensive supervision probation
itineraries for day reporting centers

J

jails
boot camps in, 171
cost of vs. probation, 139–140
growth in population of, 3–4
and juvenile system, 316
overview, 9, 22
See also prisons
JINS (juveniles in need of supervision), 314
job stress, probation officers, 102–105
decreasing, 104–105
sources of, 103–104
John P. Craine House, 183–184
judges
discretion of in juvenile system, 323, 331
in drug courts, 29–30
juvenile court, 314
presentence investigation reports, 48
and revocation of probation, 141, 148
sentence recommendations by parole officers, 55–56
and sentencing guidelines, 5
judicial branch probation departments, 91–93
judicial waivers, 315–316
juries, 147–148, 342
jurisdiction, concurrent, 315
just deserts model, 240
justice, Native American, 211–212, 214
justice model, 240, 241
justice model of supervision (1980–1995), 86–87
Juvenile Code, Indiana, 324
Juvenile Court Act, Illinois, 311–312
juvenile delinquency, 312–314, 331
juvenile justice, 308–333
background and history, 309–310

compared to adult justice systems, 310–311
and diversion, 28–29
and interstate compacts, 131
juvenile courts, 311–316
differences from adult courts, 314
jurisdiction of, 312–314
transfer to adult courts, 315–316
juvenile parole (aftercare), 328–330
background, 328
differences from probation, 329
evaluating juvenile parole programs, 330
parole boards, 329
responsibilities of juvenile parole officers, 329–330
similarities with probation, 328–329
overview of, 307, 309, 316–320
adjudication stage, 318–319
blended sentences, 320
disposition stage, 319–320
intake stage, 318
procedure before adjudication, 317–318
release from institutions, 320
probation, 83–84, 322–328
conditions of, 323
Fare v. Michael C., 326–327
and firearms policies, 101–102
intensive supervision probation (ISP), 325
juvenile probation officers, 323–325
organizational structure of, 90–92
origin, 322
probation record of juveniles, 327–328
revocation of, 141–143, 150
school-based probation, 325–326
supervision, 323
probation officers, 97, 327, 331
In re Gault case, 320–321
and restorative justice, 213–214
revocation of juvenile probation or parole, 330–331
toughening of, 6
Juvenile Probation Officer Initiative Working Group, 317–318, 323–325, 331
juveniles in need of supervision (JINS), 314

K

Kansas Sexually Violent Predator Act, 352

Kentucky State Police Sex Offender Registry, 351
kiosk machines, 125

L

labor, convict, 238
law enforcement, information exchange with, 127
law enforcers, probation officers as, 94, 146
lawyers, 58–59, 149, 326–327
Legal Action Center, 342, 359
legal protection, probation and parole officer, 104–105
Level of Service Inventory-Revised (LSI-R) risk assessment tool, 121, 124
levels of supervision, 124–126
levels systems
in day reporting centers, 203–204
in halfway houses, 166–167
liability for negligence, peace officer, 105
licenses, occupational, 344–345, 365
limitations of special conditions, 45
limited discretion, 245–246
local-level probation systems, 91–94
lockup, juvenile, 316
LSI-R (Level of Service Inventory-Revised) risk assessment tool, 121, 124

M

Maconochie, Alexander, 235–237
Maine Criminal Code, 147
male offenders
and drug court treatment strategies, 31–32
and electronic monitoring, 200
and halfway houses, 165
and parole, 248, 300
and substance abuse treatment approaches, 129
mandatory minimum sentencing laws, 5–6
mandatory probation conditions, 110–111, 323
mandatory release, 5–6, 233–234, 242–244, 301
mandatory restitution laws, 217–218
mandatory revocation, 141–143
mandatory sentencing. *See* determinate sentencing
mandatory supervision, 231
Mandatory Victims Restitution Act of 1996, 217
Manhattan Bail Project, 22

marks system, 236–237
Maryland, medical parole in, 250–251
Massachusetts
    day reporting centers in, 202
    defendant's right to lawyer during
        PSI interview, 58
    precursors to probation in, 77–78
    probation movement in, 80–82
    Special Operations Unit, 296
maximum ages for juvenile delinquency,
    312–313
maximum eligibility dates, 264
maximum supervision, 124–126
medical model (1930... 1960), 239
medical parole, 250–251
medium supervision, 124–126
men. See male offenders
mens rea and juveniles, 309–310
mental health courts, 34
mental health of offenders in PSI
    reports, 71
mentally ill defendants, 25, 28
mentally ill offenders, supervising,
    127–128
mentoring, 127, 284
merit system, for probation
    officers, 97
Methadone, 129
Michigan, mandatory revocation in,
    141–143
military crimes, 339
Milwaukee, Wisconsin, day
    fines, 226
minimum ages for juvenile delinquency,
    312–313
minimum eligibility dates, 264
minimum security facilities, 265
minimum sentencing laws, mandatory,
    5–6
minimum supervision, 124–126
Minnesota Restitution Center (MRC),
    178, 220
Minnesota Sentencing
    Commission, 44
minors in need of supervision (MINS),
    314
Miranda warnings, 326–327
misdemeanors, 48, 111
Missouri
    Eastern District firearms
        policy, 102
    private probation in, 106
modern determinate sentencing, origins
    of, 240–241
monetary sanctions. See fines
Montana, liberty interests in, 275

Montesinos, Manuel, 234–235
moral turpitude, 339, 341
motions to quash, 77
motivational interviewing, 117
MRC (Minnesota Restitution Center),
    178, 220
Multnomah County, Oregon drug
    court, 32

N

Naltrexone, 129
National Advisory Commission on
    Criminal Justice Standards and
    Goals, 85, 240
National Association of Manufacturers,
    344
National Association of Pretrial
    Services, 24
National Institute of Corrections (NIC),
    132
National Institute of Justice, 172
National Probation Act, 82
National Report Series Bulletin, 315
Native American justice, 211–212, 214
NBS. See neighborhood-based proba-
    tion supervision
Nebraska Board of Parole, 274–275
needs assessment, 302
negligence, 105
neighborhood-based probation supervi-
    sion (NBS), 110–118
    developing prosocial behaviors,
        117–118
    surveillance function in supervision,
        116–117
net widening, 18, 35, 161, 176, 189–190
New Hampshire
    automatic restoration of rights, 356
    juvenile parole officers, 329–330
New Jersey, expungement of criminal
    records in, 360
New York
    Board of Parole, 274
    Children's Aid Society, 83
    Court of Appeals, 47
    day fines, 226
    Elmira Reformatory, 238
    parole revocation process in, 290
    probation law in, 84–85
    qualified immunity for parole
        officers, 105
    reentry courts, 262
NIC (National Institute of Corrections),
    132
noncompliance, 26–28, 128, 139,
    143–144

nonresidential community corrections,
    159
nonresidential intermediate sanctions,
    187–208
    day reporting centers, 201–206
        evaluations of, 205–206
        purposes of, 202
        treatment-oriented vs.
            supervision-oriented, 202–204
    electronic monitoring, 193–201
        attitudes toward, 198–199
        frequency of use, 197–198
        global positioning systems, 196–197
        history of, 194
        home-based, empirical evaluations
            of, 200–201
        problems of early programs,
            194–195
        remote location monitoring,
            195–196
    house arrest, 191–193
        criticisms of, 191–192
        effectiveness of, 192–193
        purposes of, 191
    intensive supervision probation
        (ISP), 188–191
        attitudes toward, 189
        caseloads, 189
        evaluations of, 189–191
        overview, 188
        See also residential intermediate
            sanctions
nonresidential phase, halfway house
    programs, 167
Norfolk Island penal colony, 236–237
North Carolina
    day reporting centers in, 205
    Secretary of State Occupational
        Boards, 345
    structured presumptive sentencing
        zone, 42–43
notification laws, sex offender,
    352, 365
notification letters, restitution, 220

O

Obermaier, Georg Michael, 235
obstruction of justice, 67
occupational licenses, 344–345, 365
occupational licensing, effects of par-
    don on, 355–356
offender-based presentence reports,
    49–50
offender characteristics, presentence
    reports, 70–72
offender management systems, 163

offense-based presentence reports, 50–51
offense level computation, 68
offenses, types of, 114
Office of Juvenile Justice and Delinquency Prevention, 317
Office of the United States Pardon Attorney, 356
officers, parole, 263
officers, probation. *See* probation officers
Ohio
    Community Corrections Act, 94
    expungement of criminal records in, 360
    sentence recommendations by parole officers, 55
    shock incarceration program in, 169
OJJDP, 330
Oklahoma
    parole conditions in, 287
    preparole in, 291
old cases, 245–246
Old Testament and restitution, 216–217
Oregon
    juvenile parole officers, 330
    Multnomah County drug court, 32
orientation training of probation officers, 98–100
O-Track, 163
outlawry, 338

P

pagers, 125, 195
paperwork, 103–104
pardon, 353–356, 365–366
    definition and purpose, 353–354
    effects on occupational licensing, 355–356
    kinds of, 354
    legal effects, 355
    power to, 354
    procedure for obtaining, 355
parens patriae, 84, 310, 312, 321, 327
parental rights, loss of, 347
parents, substitute, 84. *See also parens patriae*
parole, 281–303
    characteristics of parolees, 246–248
    conditions of, 286–288
        legal issues in parole conditions, 286–288
        limited parolee rights, 288
    effectiveness of, 298–302
        predicting parole outcomes, 300–302
        recidivism studies, 299–300
    eligibility for, 263–266

prerelease preparation within institution, 265–266
time sheets and eligibility dates, 264–265
federal, 82–83
field parole officers, 285–286
functions of, 248–251
funding for, 8–9
history of, 232–252
    development in U.S., 237–238
    from discretionary parole to mandatory release, 242–244
    medical model (1930... 1960), 239
    origins of parole, 233–237
    overview, 233
    philosophical change, 240–241
juvenile, 328–330
    background, 328
    differences from probation, 329
    evaluating juvenile parole programs, 330
    parole boards, 329
    responsibilities of juvenile parole officers, 329–330
    similarities with probation, 328–329
in juvenile system, 317
models of parole release decisions, 271–274
    procedural justice model, 271
    risk prediction model, 271–274
    surveillance model, 271
number of adults on, 3–5
overview, 231, 282
See also supervision in probation and parole
parole absconders, 295–298
    locating and apprehending fugitives, 296–297
    predicting absconding behavior, 297–298
parole board, 266–268
parole hearings, 268–270, 274–278
    extending time intervals between, 275
    Greenholtz v. Inmates of the Nebraska Penal and Correctional Complex, 274–275
    Menechino v. Oswald, 274
    number of parole board members, 268–269
    recommendations and attendees, 269–270
    state-created liberty interest, 275
    victim participation in, 270
prisoner perspectives on getting out, 282–285

California study, 283–284
Iowa study, 284–285
prisoners' perceptions of parole selection, 276
purpose of, 13
staff introductory and in-service training, 99
violating, 289–291
    characteristics of parole violators, 291–294
    due process rights under preparole, 291
    warrants and citations, 289–291
Parole Act, 82
Parole and Probation Compact Administrators' Association (PPCAA), 132
Parole Board, O-Track, 163
parole boards
    increasing limits on discretion of, 242
    in juvenile system, 329, 330–331
    overview, 3–5, 263
    and prison population management, 249
    release authority of, 245–246
    in Virginia, 256–257
parole d'honneur, 233
parolees, probationers compared with, 153
Parolees and Relatives toward Newly Enhanced Relationships (PARTNER), 261
parole officers, 263
PARTNER (Parolees and Relatives toward Newly Enhanced Relationships), 261
payments
    day reporting center services, 204
    lack of and probation revocation, 150
    restitution, 216, 219
peace officers, 90, 95, 105, 146
Peace Officer State Training (POST), 98
penile plethysmographs, 130, 288
Pennsylvania
    Children's Aid Society, 83
    historical prison system, 164
    Juvenile Court Judges' Commission, 326
    sentencing guidelines, 44
    structured presumptive sentencing zone, 42
perjury, 343
permanent residents as probation officers, 95

personal data, PSI reports, 70
Philadelphia Society for Alleviating the Miseries of Public Prisons, 238
philanthropists, 81–82
physical condition of offenders, PSI reports, 71
placing out juvenile delinquents, 83
police
    in juvenile system, 317
    as probation officers, 84
    surveillance of probationers, 117
political rights. *See* civil and political rights
polydrug addicts, therapeutic communities for, 178–181
polygraph tests, 130
portable receivers for remote monitoring, 196
POST (Peace Officer State Training), 98
postadjudication proceedings, 29–30
postrelease supervision, 238. *See also* mandatory release
postsentence reports, 49
PPCAA (Parole and Probation Compact Administrators' Association), 132
prediction instruments, recidivism, 271–272, 274
predispositional reports, 48
preferred rights, 288
preliminary revocation hearings, 147, 148
preponderance of evidence, 149
prerelease preparation within institution, 265–266
prerelease programs, 13
presentence investigation (PSI) report, 48–56, 124
    contents of, 49–52
    evaluative summary, 54–55
    example of, 64–74
    initial interview, 53–54
    investigation and verification, 54
    legal issues, 56–59
        disclosure of PSI report, 56–57
        hearsay in PSI report, 57–58
        inaccuracies in PSI report, 57
        Miranda warnings and PSI interview, 58
        right to lawyer during PSI interview, 58–59
        whether exclusionary rule applies, 58
    See also sentencing
    preparing, 52–53
    purposes of, 48–49
    sentence recommendation, 55–56
presentence investigations, 49

President's Commission on Crime and Administration of Justice, 165
President's Commission on Law Enforcement and Administration of Justice (1967), 15
presumptive sentencing, 42–43, 241
pretrial, 12
pretrial detainees, 193
pretrial services, 22–28
    failure to appear, 26–28
    release decision, 22–25
    supervision, 26
Pretrial Services Programming at the Start of the 21st Century: A Survey of Pretrial Services Programs, 25–27
prison boot camps, 171–172
prisoner reentry, 13, 231, 251, 258–277
    and community, 261–262
    eligibility for parole, 263–266
        prerelease preparation within institution, 265–266
        time sheets and eligibility dates, 264–265
    models of parole release decisions, 271–274
        procedural justice model, 271
        risk prediction model, 271–274
        surveillance model, 271
    overview, 259
    parole board, 266–268
    parole hearings, 268–270, 274–278
        extending time intervals between, 275
        Greenholtz v. Inmates of the Nebraska Penal and Correctional Complex, 274–275
        Menechino v. Oswald, 274
        number of parole board members, 268–269
        recommendations and attendees, 269–270
        state-created liberty interest, 275
        victim participation in, 270
    prisoner's family, 260–261
    prisoners' perceptions of parole selection, 276
    types of, 263
    victim's role in reentry, 261
    See also parole
prisons
    cost of vs. probation, 139–140. *See also* jails
    crowding, 4–5, 177, 190, 249–250
    and development of halfway houses, 164

funding for, 8–9
graduated release, 166
growth in population of, 3–5
overview, 9
public opinion of, 7
reentry of parole violators, 292–293
therapeutic communities based in, 180–181
privacy, right to, 199
private apprehension units, 297
private companies, use of convict labor by, 238
private employment, 344, 365
private halfway houses, 165
private probation, 106
probable cause, 117, 148–149
probation, 138–157
    abstinence from alcohol during, 45
    boot camps, 171
    effectiveness of, 151–153
        probationers compared with parolees, 153
        probation recidivism rates, 151–152
        who is more likely to succeed or fail, 152–153
    funding for, 8–9
    history of, 76–88
        changing concepts of supervision, 85–87
        early probation, 79–85
        overview, 77
        precursors to American probation, 77–78
        suspended sentence, 78–79
    juvenile justice, 322–328
        conditions of, 323
        Fare v. Michael C., 326–327
        intensive supervision probation (ISP), 325
        juvenile probation officers, 323–325
        origin, 322
        probation record of juveniles, 327–328
        school-based probation, 325–326
        supervision, 323
    modifying conditions, 140–141
    number of adults on, 3–5
    overview, 8, 139–140
    purposes of, 10–12
    revocation, 145–147
        decision to revoke, 141–143
        power to arrest probationers, 146
        rights of probationers and parolees, 147–151

probation (continued)
    and time on probation or parole, 146–147
    revoking for fine nonpayment, 225
    violations against, 143–145
        law violations, 143–144
        probation absconders, 145
        technical violations, 144
    See also supervision in probation and parole
probation boot camps, 172–173
probation detention centers, 146
probation officers, 89–108
    adult preservice training, 98
    education and experience, 98
    firearms policies for probation and parole, 101–102
    in-service training, 100
    job stress, 102–105
        decreasing, 104–105
        sources of, 103–104
    juvenile, 323–325, 327
    juvenile preservice and orientation training, 98–100
    and organization of probation services, 90–94
        community corrections acts, 93–94
        state vs. executive branch administration, 92–93
    overview, 82, 90
    private probation, 106
    probation violation decision guidelines, 143
    requirements for hiring, 106
    salary, 100–101
    selection and appointment of, 95–97
        appointment system, 96–97
        combined system, 97
        merit system, 97
    as social workers in casework era, 85
    as specialists in CRMT model, 86
    work styles, 94–95
    See also presentence investigation (PSI) report
Probation Reform Law, Delaware, 152
procedural justice model, 271
Prohibition Amendment, 82
Project Greenlight, 262
Project RIO, 263
proof
    level required, 149–150
    standards of, 144
property bonds, 25
property crimes, 16
prosecution
    deferred, 30

juvenile vs. adult, 316
prosecutors, 12, 55–56
prosocial behaviors, developing, 117–118
Pro Tech Monitoring Inc., 130–131
protected liberty interests, 275
protection of public, 13–14
PSI. *See* presentence investigation (PSI) report
public, protection of, 13–14
public defenders, 55–56
public employment, 343–344, 364
public office, 343, 364
public perceptions of community corrections, 7
public safety, 6–7, 150, 295
public shaming, 16, 45–47
punishment
    in halfway houses, 168
    in justice model, 240–241
    probation as, 11, 86–87
    public shaming as, 16

Q

qualified immunity, 105

R

race
    and drug court participation, 34
    of parolees, 248, 292
    of probationers, 110, 113
random assignment to drug courts, 33
rational behavior training, 100
RCCFs. *See* residential community corrections facilities (RCCFs)
reactionary politics, 17
release on recognizance (ROR), 25
real-time access, 196
real-time monitoring, 199
rearrest
    of day reporting center participants, 205–206
    of drug court participants, 33–34
    of parolees, 294, 299
reasonable conditions, 45
reasonable suspicion, 117, 288
receiving states, 131
recidivism
    after electronic monitoring, 200
    and community-based sanctions, 17
    in day reporting centers, 205–206
    of drug court participants, 33–34
    in halfway houses, 168
    in John P. Craine House, 183–184
    of parolees, 300–301

predictions of, 271–272, 274
    in prison boot camps, 172
    probation boot camps, 173, 176–177
    and restitution, 220
    and risk assessment, 29, 121
    in therapeutic communities, 181
recipients of restitution payments, 216
Reclaiming Offender Accountability: Intermediate Sanctions for Probation and Parole Violators, 290
recognizance, 78–79
recycling, boot camp, 174–175
"Reducing Alcohol-Related Crime Electronically," 197
reentry. *See* prisoner reentry
reentry, prisoner. *See* prisoner reentry
reentry courts, 262
reentry decision, 13
registration of sex offenders, 288, 365
registry of probationers, 111
rehabilitation, 14–15
    in medical model, 239
    and PSI reports, 46–49
    through community service, 221–222
    through probation, 85–87, 90
rehabilitation certificates, 356
reinstatement of parole, 243–244
reintegration with community, 15
relapses in drug abuse treatment programs, 30, 181
release
    compassionate, 250–251
    decision to revoke, 22–25
    discretionary, 233–234
    graduated, from prison, 166
    mandatory, 5–6, 233–234, 301
    unconditional, 231, 233–234
reliable hearsay evidence, 150
religious element of Alcoholics Anonymous, 46
remote location monitoring, 195–196
reparation boards, 213–214
reparations for crime. *See* restorative justice
repeat offenders, 5, 300–301
residences, probationer, 111
residential community corrections facilities (RCCFs), 162, 177–184
    evaluations of, 168–169
    restitution centers, 178
    therapeutic communities, 178–181
    women offenders living with their children, 182–184
    work release and work ethic camps, 181–182
    See also halfway houses

residential community treatment centers (CTC), 192–193
residential intermediate sanctions, 160–186
  boot camps
    correctional, 170–171
    criticisms of, 176
    evaluations of, 176–177
    future of, 177
    offender perspectives, 173–176
    prison boot camps, 171–172
    probation boot camps, 172–173
  halfway houses, 162–169
    history of U.S., 164–166
    program components, 166–167
    worker perspectives and role orientation, 167–168
  overview, 161
  residential community corrections facilities (RCCFs), 162, 177–184
  evaluations of, 168–169
  restitution centers, 178
  therapeutic communities, 178–181
  women offenders living with their children, 182–184
  work release and work ethic camps, 181–182
  shock incarceration, 169–177
  See also nonresidential intermediate sanctions
residential prerelease programs, 9, 13
residents, permanent, as probation officers, 95
responsibility, acceptance of, 67–68
restitution, 8, 51, 111, 150, 216–221
  effectiveness, 220–221
  in history, 216–218
  losses eligible for compensation, 218
  problems associated, 218–220
restitution centers, 178
restoration of rights, 356–357
  automatic restoration, 356–357
  restoration upon application, 356
  restoring right to vote, 357
restorative justice, 159, 189, 261
restorative justice reparations. See economic and restorative justice reparations
restorative or community justice, 15–16
revocation, 145–147
  attitudes on, 294
  decision to revoke, 141–143
  and interstate compact, 132
  of parole, 249–250
  parole revocation rate, 291–292
  power to arrest probationers, 146

of probation, 139
  reasons for, 292–293
  rights of probationers and payrolees, 147–151
  and time on probation or parole, 146–147
  warrants, 105
  why revocation rates have increased, 293–294
rewards for good probationer behavior, 140–141
Rhode Island probation system, 85
rights. See civil and political rights
risk assessment
  and determination of diversion eligibility, 29
  and least restrictive option, 24
  for prediction of parole success, 302
risk levels
  and electronic monitoring devices, 195
  and medical parole, 250–251
  and success of RCCFs, 169
risk prediction model, 271–274
role ambiguity, 104
role conflict
  of halfway house staff, 168
  of probation officers, 94, 104
ROR (release on recognizance), 25
rules violation during probation, 144

S

Sacramento Intelligence Unit (SIU), 127
Safe Streets Act, 165
safety
  community, 6–7, 150, 295
  probation and parole officer, 102–103
salary, probation officers, 100–101
Salient Factor Score (SFS), 271–273
sanctions. See intermediate sanctions; probation
Satellite Monitoring and Remote Tracking (SMART®) System Technology, 130–131, 196
scarlet-letter sanctions, 16, 45–47
school-based probation, 325–326
Schooner's restaurant, 324
SCRAM (Secure Continuous Remote Alcohol Monitoring), 197
sealed records, 366
searches, 46–47, 58, 117, 288
Secure Continuous Remote Alcohol Monitoring (SCRAM), 197
security for good behavior, 77
seizures and searches, 46–47, 58
self-defense training, 102–103

self-incrimination, 47–48, 147, 327
sentences, suspended, 140
sentencing
  change in laws, 3–6
  commissions, 44
  community sentence, factors affecting granting of, 40–41
  conditions of community corrections, 44–48
    constitutional supervision conditions, 45–48
    special conditions, 44–45
    standard conditions, 44
  decisions about, 12
  determinate, 5–6, 42, 50
  guidelines, 41–43, 49, 55–56, 72
  and inaccurate PSIs, 57
  indeterminate, 3–5, 49, 239, 245–246
  in juvenile courts, 317
  presumptive, 241
  to probation, 110
  in PSI reports, 51, 72–74
  See also presentence investigation (PSI) report
Sentencing Project, 341
Seventh Circuit Court of Appeals, 228, 288
severity of crimes, 5, 241, 272–273
sex offenders, 46–48, 286–288, 304–305, 352, 365
  involuntary commitment of sexual predators, 351–353
  notification laws, 349–351
  registration laws, 348–349
SFS (Salient Factor Score), 271–273
shaming, 45–47, 180
shock incarceration. See boot camps
show cause hearings, 148–149
sickness and parole, 250–251
SIPP (superintensive probation program), 173
SIU (Sacramento Intelligence Unit), 127
SMART® (Satellite Monitoring and Remote Tracking) System Technology, 130–131, 196
social agencies and probation, 85–86
social controls, informal, 118
social histories, 48
social stigmatization, as effect of conviction, 353
social workers, probation officers as, 85
Solution to Employment Problems (STEP) program, 344
South Carolina Department of Labor, Licensing, and Regulation, 345
specialists, probation officers as, 86

specialized caseloads, 34, 126–131
supervising mentally ill offenders, 127–128
supervising offenders who have abused drugs and alcohol, 128–129
supervising sex offenders, 130–131
Special Operations Unit, Massachusetts, 296
special probation conditions, 110–113
split sentence. *See* boot camps
standard conditions
parole, 286
probation, 110–111
standardization of private probation, 106
standards of proof, 144, 149
state administration of probation, 92–93
Staten Island, New York, day fines, 226
states
firearms policies for probation and parole officers, 101
pardons, 354
parole systems, 243–248, 266–267
pretrial release decisions, 23
prisons, 292–294
probation systems, 84–85, 90–94, 99, 106
right to vote of persons with criminal records, 342
sentencing guidelines, 5
static parolee characteristics, 302
static recidivism factors, 121
status offenses, 312, 314
statutory exclusion, 315
statutory provisions, sentencing, in PSI reports, 72–73
STEP (Solution to Employment Problems) program, 344
strength-based supervision, 117
structured fines, 226
structured presumptive sentencing zones, 42–43
substance abuse. *See* drug courts
substitute parents, 84. *See also parens patriae*
superintensive probation program (SIPP), 173
supervised release, 72, 153. *See also* mandatory release
supervising sex offenders, 130–131
supervision, justice model of (1980... 1995), 86–87
supervision in probation and parole, 109–134

classification as first step in supervision, 118–126
actuarial risk assessment, 121
caseload and workload standards, 126
developing case plan, 124
identifying treatment needs, 121–124
levels of supervision, 124–126
interstate compacts on probation, 131
new interstate compact for adult offender supervision, 132
revocation and interstate compact, 132
neighborhood-based probation supervision, 110–118
developing prosocial behaviors, 117–118
surveillance function in supervision, 116–117
overview, 110
specialized caseloads, 126–131
supervising mentally ill offenders, 127–128
supervising offenders who have abused drugs and alcohol, 128–129
supervising sex offenders, 130–131
supervision-oriented day reporting centers, 202–204
Supreme Court. *See* U.S. Supreme Court
sureties, 78
surety bonds, 25, 345
surveillance function in supervision, 116–117
surveillance model, 271
suspects. *See* pretrial
suspended sentence, 78–79
kinds of, 78
power to suspend sentence, 78–79
suspended sentences, 140
suspicion, reasonable, 117
synthetic officers, probation officers as, 94

T

TCs (therapeutic communities), 178–181, 182
technical violations, 144, 152, 295
telecommuting, presentence officer, 55
Temporary Asylum for Discharged Female Prisoners, 165
Tenth Circuit Court of Appeals, 58, 286, 288
terminal illnesses and parole, 250–251

termination of probation, 142
Texas
Code of Criminal Procedure, 148
community service in, 222
probation boot camps, 172–173
probation system in, 93
therapeutic communities in, 181
therapeutic agents, probation officers as, 85, 94, 146
therapeutic communities (TCs), 178–181, 182
three strikes laws, 5
tickets-of-leave, 236–237
time-servers, probation officers as, 94
time sheets, and parole eligibility dates, 264–265
tolled terms of probation, 151
track points, GPS, 130–131
training of probation officers
adult preservice training, 98
in-service training, 100
juvenile preservice and orientation training, 98–100
transdermal methods and electronic monitoring, 197
transportation of convicts, 235–237
treatment
correctional, 14–15
goals of halfway house, 167–168
identifying needs, 121–124
interventions. *See* drug courts
probation as
treatment-oriented day reporting centers, 202–204
treatment retention model, 129
tribal justice, 211–212, 214
truth in sentencing laws, 5, 242

U

unconditional release, 231, 233–234, 300–301
United States. *See* U.S.
University Settlement, 82
unsecured bonds, 25
Urban Institute, 301
U.S. citizenship of probation officers, 95
U.S. Code, Title 18, Part II, Chapter 227, Subchapter B, Sec. 3563, 111–113
U.S. Congress, 309
U.S. Department of Justice (DOJ), 4, 142, 153, 262, 269
U.S. Department of Labor, 100, 345–346
U.S. General Accounting Office (GAO), 30, 32–33

U.S. Parole Commission, 269,
271–273
U.S. Sentencing Commission, 42, 96
U.S. Supreme Court
citizenship of probation officers, 95
constitutional conditions, 46–48
conviction and right to own or possess firearms, 346
disclosure of PSI reports, 56
fees, 227
involuntary commitment of sexual
predators, 352–353
juvenile rights, 310, 320–321
loss of voting rights, 341
nonpayment of fines and probation
revocation, 225
parole hearings and due process,
274–275
restoration of good moral character,
357, 359
revocation of probation, 148
role of juvenile probation officers,
326–327
sex offender registration, 349
Utah
sentence recommendations by parole
officers, 55
use of O-Track in, 163

V

VeriTracks, 130–131, 196
Vermont probation statute, 85

victim–offender mediation (VOM), 213,
220
victim–offender reconciliation projects
(VORP), 220
victims, 10, 15–16, 257
See also restorative justice
compensation funds, 224
impact statements, 51–52, 270
role in prisoner reentry, 261
video cameras for electronic monitoring, 197
videoconference technology, 269
video training for firearms safety,
102–103
violations of probation, 141, 143–145,
152, 153
law violations, 143–144
probation absconders, 145
technical violations, 144
Violence against Women Act of 1994, 217
violent offenders, violations of probation by, 153
Virginia, discretionary parole in,
254–257
vocational skills, offender, in PSI
reports, 71
voice verification, 195
Volstead Act, 82
volunteer probation officers,
80–82
VOM (victim–offender mediation),
213, 220

VORP (victim–offender reconciliation
projects), 220
voting rights, 358, 364
loss of, 341–342
restoring, 357
VWPA (Federal Victim Witness
Protection Act) of 1982, 217

W

waivers of juveniles to adult courts,
315–316
warrantless searches, 288
warrants, arrest, 146
Washington State Department of
Licensing, 345
Washington Total Abstinence Society,
80
welfare benefits, loss of, 347
willful negligence, 105
Wisconsin
day fines in, 226
sex offender notification, 351
witnesses, loss of credibility, 343
women. *See* female offenders
work release and work ethic camps,
181–182
wrist devices, electronic monitoring,
194–195

Y

youth panels, 213–214

Photo Credits